GARDEN PLANTS
for SCOTLAND

Kenneth N.E. Cox & Raoul Curtis-Machin

GARDEN PLANTS
for SCOTLAND

Foreword by Jim McColl

F

FRANCES LINCOLN LIMITED
PUBLISHERS

Quarto is the authority on a wide range of topics.

Quarto educates, entertains and enriches the lives of our readers—enthusiasts and lovers of hands-on living.

www.quartoknows.com

TO JANE AND GYLL

First published in 2008 by
Frances Lincoln Ltd, an imprint of The Quarto Group
The Old Brewery, 6 Blundell Street,
London, N7 9BH
www.QuartoKnows.com

A catalogue record for this book is available from the
British Library.

ISBN 978-0-7112-3668-4

Printed and bound in China

8 9

PAGE 1 *Lavandula angustifolia* hedge at
Carestown Steading

PAGES 2–3 Woodland garden at Glendoick, Perth

CONTENTS

LISTS OF PLANTS TO USE IN PARTICULAR SITUATIONS AND FOR PROBLEM CORNERS:

FOREWORD

Those of us who are involved in writing and giving advice on matters horticultural can be caught out by one extremely popular and useful modern method of communication, emails, especially when they are read out on live radio. They give no indication of location, unless the sender has an appreciation that a sense of place might be important. Experienced gardeners will know that there is a vast difference between trying to garden halfway up a Grampian and doing so on the shores of the Solway. Similarly, gardening almost anywhere in the 'central belt', most of which was one great bog, is extremely difficult compared with gardening in the Land of Goshen, otherwise known as East Lothian, sometimes referred to as 'The Garden of Scotland'.

The location of a garden will dictate aspect, topography, soil type and climate. All these must be viewed as a package, which will have a bearing on what can be grown successfully. It could be said that plants are rather parochial, but like children, many are a great deal more resilient that we might suspect. That resilience is going to be sorely tested in years to come if we are to be subjected to the climate change predicted by pundits. Scientists have already decreed that the growing season has extended by four weeks. (Though how can that be calculated, I wonder, on temperature alone? The day/night balance hasn't altered one iota and that is also implicated in the length of the growing season.)

In recent times, there have been other changes affecting our horticultural world. Firstly, society itself has become ever more mobile. In the early eighties, when the North Sea oil boom was raging, Aberdeen was seething with oil company personnel flying in from oil installations around the world, many bringing their families with them. To their credit, the oil companies helped to integrate these families into the lifestyle, society, climatic conditions, etc. by having family days at a local hotel and offering advice on a wide range of local issues. My late Beechgrove Garden colleague George Barron and I conducted several sessions with these folks, describing our growing seasons and the limitations with which we had to work. We answered many questions, explaining for example (once we had overcome the language barrier!) why people couldn't plant a few banana trees in the yard and why their pumpkin seeds would need to be started off indoors. In other words, the limitations of that package I mentioned earlier were explained in full. My regular advice to people who have moved to a new area is rather obvious: take a walk round the village/town, have a look over a few garden gates, visit the local park, talk to local gardeners.

My next point relates to a very changed marketplace. Newcomers to an area at one time could rely on the local nurseryman to give sound advice about the kinds of plants that would thrive in the district. The chances are that nowadays, with some notable exceptions, there isn't such an establishment. The expansion of the supermarket multiple is now well established in horticulture and as these outlets gain a dominant share of the market, we must recognise that eventually this will limit choice. Because of their powerful bargaining position, they can offer goods at prices which independent retailers find difficult to match. As a result, the choice will be limited to what they choose to offer. In part, the message is: try to support the independents to retain your options .The horticultural retail industry is now dominated by garden supermarkets with all that implies – central buying being the problem. Although it may be disappointing that your Dunlop cheese, bought in the supermarket, has come from Holland or Tuscany, the flavour will be the same. You can't be so certain that the same will apply to plants from these areas. Don't get me wrong – there is no argument about quality: the problems concern hardiness and seasonality. One wonders if buyers are sufficiently well versed in these matters when some subjects appear as part of 'collections' that would score a low H2 on the hardiness chart. Sound information and advice are essential if you are to make the right decisions and these are not always available or to be believed at the checkout desk. In this day and age of ultra-specialism, it is not their job to know.

In recent times there has been a trend to growing perennials, especially woody perennials in containers. I always advise that the container should be filled with a soil-based compost to help combat some of the problems that may arise. For example, the root system in a container sitting above ground is subject to many more stresses than when it colonises a piece of Mother Earth. I would pinpoint three as follows: excessively high summer temperatures; excessively low winter temperatures; and huge fluctuations in availability of water and nutrients.

All of the foregoing prefaces my contention that you must start from a position of knowing what you want to plant, especially when it is perennials you have in mind. If they are to perform well in your garden, and therefore 'earn their keep', you must choose plants that suit the location.

In Scotland, there is a dearth of relevant literature to aid aspiring gardeners in this regard. Investing in plants to create a garden is a significant commitment. Not only that: mistakes may be expensive in monetary terms and in time. That is why I commend this publication to you, and I have confidence in doing so. I have known and worked with the joint authors for a lot of years now and seen them develop into sound, well-respected and exciting practitioners in the skills of growing plants and in enthusing others through their writing and lecturing.

I also commend their decision to use the Scottish Gardenplant Award, a much needed initiative which I hope will be endorsed by grower and customer alike.

Jim McColl, Oldmeldrum, January 2008

INTRODUCTION
What grows well, where, how and why

Scotland is a fantastic place to garden: the maritime climate, ample rainfall and rarity of both severe droughts and really hot weather mean that huge numbers of plants from all over the globe are happy here. The climate is also the major factor in dictating which plants grow well and which ones struggle. Our latitude, topography, prevailing winds and surrounding oceans and seas all combine to give us the various doses of gales, rain, sun and gloom with which we are all familiar. For a small country, the climate variation from region to region is considerable; where you live in Scotland has a huge bearing on the weather you can expect and therefore the plants you can grow. The mountainous areas of Scotland are colder, cloudier, wetter and windier than the low-lying areas, and inland areas tend to be colder than coastal areas. Mountainside gardens can experience an average of fewer than 1,100 hours of annu-

al sunshine, compared to 1,400 hours in lower-lying or coastal areas. The annual rainfall of the western Highlands is an average of more than 3000mm (120in), whereas along much of the east coast, it is under 800mm (30in). The highest recorded wind speed of 170 miles per hour was at Cairngorm weather station, while the record low temperature of -27°C was recorded both at Braemar, Aberdeenshire, in 1982, and at Altnaharra, Highland, in 1995. In contrast, there are gardens on Arran, Islay, Mull and in Galloway which rarely get frosts at all, and where tender plants thrive outdoors all year round. You might expect Lerwick in Shetland to be one of the coldest places, but the moderating influence of the sea means that the lowest temperature recorded between 1961 and 1990 was a relatively mild -8°C. The average annual temperature is 7°C in Shetland, 9°C on the coasts of Ayrshire and Dumfries

Rest and Be Thankful pass, Argyll (RC-M)

and Galloway, 6.4°C at Braemar at 339m above sea level inland and 0.3°C on the summit of Ben Nevis. Snow tends to lie for more than fifty days a year in inland and high altitude regions, while coastal areas receive less than ten days of snow a year.

Grasses in hoar frost

The genesis of this book is quite simple. Virtually all the gardening books available are written for places other than Scotland. They are full of advice which might well apply in the south of England, or North America, but which is often inaccurate, misleading or just plain wrong for Scotland. To redress this, we wished to acknowledge and celebrate the variations in Scotland's climate and the resulting diversity of plants that the country's gardens can grow. Scotland is one of the best places in the world for gardening and there are more world-class gardens and plant collections here than in any other country of comparable size. We may moan about the climate, but the fact that it never gets really hot keeps a lot of mountain-origin plants such as alpines, meconopsis and rhododendrons very happy. But if you live in Scotland it is also easy to spend money on plants that simply will not tolerate the conditions you have. For some plants, your garden may be too cold, too wet, too windy or too dry, or the soil too acidic. The key is both to manipulate conditions through shelter and soil preparation, and to work with nature, choosing plants that are suited to your own individual conditions. There are thousands of great plants ideally suited for wherever you live, and we hope that this book will help Scots plan and plant more successful and more colourful gardens.

Scotland's climate: 'Aye, but that'll never grow here . . .'

Hardy: 'able to grow in the open air all year'
(*Concise Oxford English Dictionary*)

Plant hardiness is a complex business, partly a matter of the individual plant's innate toughness or tenderness, but also influenced greatly by where and when it is planted and how well established it is. It's tempting to decide which plants will grow in a garden purely by checking their minimum winter temperature rating (H1 for tender to H5

for the hardiest – see page 25), but it's not as simple as that. Many plants that are very cold hardy cannot tolerate a damp, poorly drained soil and/or heavy rainfall. Others may tolerate -20°C, but foliage can be burned by cold winds. Inevitably, some trial and error is necessary; only through experimenting with different plants will you get to know your own garden and be able to gauge what should grow well. Plants rarely do what gardeners want them to – they don't read the textbooks – and much of the real fun in gardening comes from successfully growing the most unlikely things, especially if you have been told it is not worth trying. For many gardeners, 'happy accidents' are amongst the biggest delights and unintended self-sown seedlings have thrilled some of the most famous gardeners through the years, from John Claudius Loudon to Gertrude Jekyll and Christopher Lloyd.

It is by cultivating the same space for years, and presiding over both successes and failures, that a gardener really gets to know the site – the way the sun moves around the garden, the way frost settles in one area more than any other; the differing drainage characteristics and the way the wind eddies more fiercely over one side than the other. That's the ideal, but it's easier said than done in the twenty-first century, as we move house, we move on, we are time poor, and we want a good garden with the least effort and in the shortest time. One solution is to seek out local wisdom. Almost all gardeners love to talk about their gardens: so look around and see what is doing well, and visit gardens – get hold of Scotland's Garden Scheme's 'Yellow Book' (*Gardens of Scotland*, published annually) of gardens open to the public or look at their website (www.gardensofscotland.org). You'll usually find the proud owners on hand, ready to share their secrets or even sell you their home-propagated plants. This accumulated knowledge is the real definition of 'green fingers'.

Treat this book as a general guide to what should do well in your area, but remember that there are no absolute rules. Whatever generalizations we make, there will be someone who can prove otherwise.

Coldness, wind exposure and drainage are the three main factors that affect plant hardiness, and we deal with these in more detail in the following pages. As everyone knows, the climate is changing. The wonderfully named SNIFFER (Scotland and Northern Ireland Forum for Environmental Research) has collated weather data from 1960 to 2004. Their findings are pretty conclusive. The average length of growing season (from last to first frosts) has increased in that period by an average of more than four weeks. The average temperature has risen by more than 1°C and the number of nights with air frosts have decreased by almost 25 per cent. Heavy rainstorms are deluging us with up to 20 per cent more precipitation in one go (bigger rainstorms, less often), and there is more rain in winter and less in summer. All these factors mean that the list of plants we could grow in 1960 is not the same list that we have today and according to Meteorological Office statistics, the pace of climate change is increasing. The changing habits of wildlife in our gardens illustrate this. Hummingbird hawk moths, for example, have been regular summer visitors to Scottish gardens for years, but they are now starting to winter here.

Logan: the tropical look of a mild west coast garden (RC-M)

The greatest single contributing factor to Scotland's climate is the Gulf Stream, a so-called 'oceanic conveyor belt', which brings warm air and rainfall from the Gulf of Mexico to north-west Europe. It is because of the Gulf Stream's warming effect that although Glasgow and Edinburgh lie at the same latitude (55 degrees) as Labrador in Canada and parts of southern Alaska, both are far colder than Scotland. Some scientists believe that the Gulf Stream will sink under the cold water of the melting ice caps – an effect of global warming – thus weakening its flow (it is already reported to be weakened by 20 per cent or more). Potentially in Scotland and northern Europe, the climate will in fact become far colder. There is little point in our adding to the speculation already taking place – suffice to say that we gardeners will just have to adapt to changing conditions as they arise.

The hardiness ratings used in this book (see page 25 for the table of ratings) are based on the Royal Horticultural Society's (RHS) Hardiness ratings. In the first publication of this book in 2008 we argued for the need for additional ratings and our suggestions have been incorporated into the updated RHS guidelines for gardeners. The old RHS system stated that an H4 rating was hardy throughout the British Isles. This was patently not the case for many areas of Scotland. The new ratings add H5, H6 and H7 to rate a plant's hardiness down to -20°C or below. This is more suitable for Scottish gardens and indeed many other inland UK sites. Our H5 rating in this book means that a plant is likely to be hardy throughout Scotland and equates to the top categories of the new RHS ratings. Our ratings are based on the advice of gardeners all over Scotland.

Temperature fluctuations, frosts, soils and drainage

There is still the perception that the north of the UK becomes an icy frozen wasteland in winter but, as the companies trying to sustain Scotland's skiing industry can attest, there are few cold winters any more, though spring 2006 was somewhat of a return to form. Wet, windy and miser-

Excellent frost drainage at Abriachan, Loch Ness (RC-M)

able it often is, but those sustained periods of freezing snowy weather that many of us recall from a few decades ago seem to have left us behind. So does that mean we can grow more tender plants than before? Well, yes and no. As we will attempt to make clear, there is much more to hardiness than minimum temperatures. Cold is traditionally perceived to be the biggest killer of plants, but in Scotland, we are convinced that poor drainage and wind are just as likely to be the cause of failure.

Cold damage does not simply depend on how cold it gets. Just as important is the timing and length of the cold spell and whether plants are in growth, coming into growth, slowing down or fully hardened off. Most plants come from countries with more clearly defined and consistent seasons – regular hot summers and cold winters, for example – but unfortunately, Scotland's seasons are more vague and fickle. Winter and spring are stop–start: one minute it's mild and moist and buds are opening, and the next it's sharp and frosty. Heavy snow can appear overnight, only to turn to slush twenty-four hours later. In general, plants like to rest in winter. Think of the alpine saxifrage, clinging to a ledge on the side of a mountain, happily asleep under a thick duvet of snow that appeared in November and won't leave until spring; all growth has stopped, and resources are conserved for the following year's efforts. No such luck for the garden saxifrage in Scotland, where the fluctuating temperatures trick the plant into thinking that it's spring, only for the cold to return again days later. Likewise plants found in Mediterranean regions, such as lavender, are able to withstand winter chills, but their native winters are usually drier than in Scotland: they don't get prolonged periods of damp cold.

The fungal diseases and dieback often seen on older lavender plants in Scotland are partly the result of the humidity of our winters and springs.

When the temperature drops below freezing, frozen water crystals are formed in the air (frost). Frost is heavier than air, so it sinks on to the land and then flows downhill. Frost will settle wherever its journey ends or is halted: in hollows, along rivers, at valley bottoms and, in a garden, at the lowest point against walls and fences. If you have an enclosed hillside garden, opening a gate or leaving a gap to let the frost out can make all the difference. Frost damage takes place when moisture in soft (growing or not hardened-off) plant tissue freezes, rupturing cells in leaves, stems and flowers. As soon as the plant thaws out, the damaged tissue turns to mush. Damage can be above ground or below. A heavy frost can penetrate the soil down to a hand's depth – enough to freeze the moisture in plant roots – and this can be fatal to many tender plants such as dahlia tubers.

Plants are 90 per cent water, and they are most vulnerable to frost either when the moist sap is rising and new-season growth has started, or when the plant is still growing at the tail end of a warm year. The amount of damage done depends on the timing of the frost in relation to the plant's growth cycle. Most woody shrubs produce new soft green stems during spring and summer, which harden up and become woody by autumn. That's the theory, at least, but it can be a risky business in Scottish gardens, where there is often insufficient summer heat for ripening. Frosts can occur as late as May or even early June, scything flowers

Frosted rhododendron flowers

and/or young growth, turning leaves and stem tips black, and in severe cases killing plants completely. Some plants may recover later in the season, with new shoots breaking from old wood or roots, but often there is nothing for it but to dig the remains out and start again.

At the other end of the season, plants need to stop growing and harden up. The dry summers and moist/wet autumns of recent years have encouraged many plants to start growing again in September, only for frosts in late September, October or even November to cause significant damage. Penstemons and salvias were killed in many parts of Scotland after a sudden cold snap in November 2005. Frost damage can be reduced or prevented by protective coverings such as fleece, and cloches are perfect for alpines and small bulbs. Bubble wrap or another insulating material might not look the prettiest addition to the

garden, but it might save the life of a cherished plant. Mature tree ferns (*Dicksonia antarctica*) can thrive in some cold corners of our country with their trunks tied up with bubble wrap in winter. The huge-leaved *Gunnera manicata* has a frost-sensitive crown, which can easily be protected by piling some of its old leaves on top. Such techniques can also help many young plants to get established: a mulch of compost or well-rotted organic matter will not only protect the crowns of plants such as *Stokesia*, *Delphinium*, *Imperata* and *Kniphofia* in winter but also provide nourishment during the following growing season. In the plant entries on pages 26 onwards we recommend where protection is appropriate.

A good precautionary measure for borderline-hardy plants is to take cuttings in summer and early autumn. This works well for plants such as penstemon, fuchsia and helianthemum, which can be killed off during a severe winter.

Frost pockets

The areas worst affected by regular frosts during the early part of the growing season are known as frost pockets. The valley bottom can be as much as 8°C colder at dawn (the coldest time) than land at 200m up the surrounding hillsides, where frost drains readily down the slopes. Inland river valleys are Scotland's severest frost pockets: the Tweed valley and its tributaries (one of the coldest areas of Scotland), the Forth/M8 corridor, Lanarkshire and the Clyde valley, the Earn valley, Strathmore, the Dee and Don valleys and the Spey valley are all examples of places where late frosts are relatively common. Those who garden in frost pockets might be advised to stick largely to H5 plants, and they may have to wait till late May/early June before putting out tender bedding. Those who garden on the slopes above a river may escape damage, as the frost is likely to drain away, while those who garden by the river itself are usually the worst affected. Those at higher altitudes may, of course, have other problems such as strong winds and more persistent snow to contend with.

What should you do if you garden in these areas to reduce the ill effects of frost and cold? Place your early

Using walls to create a favourable microclimate at Torosay, Mull

flowering and growing plants in the most favourable sites in the garden – against and beside west- and south-facing walls, for instance. Keep a roll of white spun polypropylene (horticultural fleece) handy for covering plants, and don't be tempted to plant out bedding and other tender plants until mid or late May unless you can cover them up. Young plants are particularly vulnerable to unseasonal or sudden frosts, as freezing sap may rupture the main stem and kill the plant; as the plant matures a woody trunk or stem is produced and the damage becomes more cosmetic, and new growth is usually produced below the damage. Repeated spring frosts on shrubs such as *Hydrangea macrophylla* are seldom fatal, but they can reduce flowering so that the shrubs don't earn their keep in your garden.

Microclimates

> *Micro-climate*: 'Local conditions of shade, exposure, wind, drainage and other factors that affect plant growth at any particular site. Gardeners take advantage of microclimates to grow plants that would otherwise not succeed in their general area.'
> (*Taylor's Dictionary for Gardeners*, 1997)

Microclimates, or variations in climate within an area, can occur because of various natural geographical influences such as water, shelter, slope or aspect, as well as man-made intervention. In cities and towns the local climate is influenced by what is known as the 'heat island effect': the cumulative heat escaping from buildings artificially raises the temperature, making it higher than the rural equivalent. Microclimates can also occur within gardens, even small ones, and they can be created and manipulated by changing the garden's structure and planting. A bed or border beside a house will be warmer than ones in the open or away from heated buildings. South-facing walls are consistently warmer than other walls because

they soak up the sun's warmth for the longest daytime period and then slowly reflect this heat back. Old stone and brick absorb and radiate more heat than other materials. White paints and renders will reflect heat and light too, which helps plants to ripen wood.

Walled gardens provide a particularly good opportunity to exploit differences in microclimate. Each aspect provides differing light and temperature, with north walls being the coldest where plants are the latest into growth, and showing the smallest temperature fluctuations. East-facing walls catch early morning sun, which can damage frozen leaves or flowers on shrubs such as camellias, while west-facing walls are warm but often catch the prevailing winds. Using the microclimates offered by walls has long been a feature of Scottish gardening. Traditionally, the earliest gardens in Scotland were either in monastic cloisters, as at Pluscarden Abbey, near Elgin, or built as walled enclosures around the house, as can still be seen today at Edzell Castle in Angus. Building a walled garden separately from the house became fashionable from the eighteenth century onwards. The high walls of many town gardens present opportunities for walled gardens in miniature, with walls facing different directions giving support and shelter to different plants.

Large bodies of water – both the sea and nearby rivers or lochs – have a warming influence in winter and a cooling effect in summer, because the temperature of the water does not drop or heat up as quickly as that of the land. The wide expanses of water in the river estuaries of the Forth, Tay, and Moray Firth have a benign influence on the winter climate. The influence of the Gulf Stream on Scotland's climate, mentioned above, allows gardeners in parts of the Western Isles and the west coast to grow all sorts of exotics, not normally hardy at such northerly latitudes.

Wind, shelter and shade

As many major Atlantic depressions pass close by or over Scotland, the frequency of strong winds and gales is higher than in other parts of the United Kingdom. The

Trees creating shelter in a typical Scottish woodland garden, Glendoick

windiest areas are the Western Isles, the north-west coast, and Orkney and Shetland, where there is an average of as many as thirty days of gales per year. Infrequent strong gusts do the most damage to buildings and trees, but for plants it is as much the constant buffeting in exposed sites that can cause failures. Wind physically rocks taller plants, particularly trees and shrubs, putting immense strain on the roots. It also desiccates (dries out) leaves and stems by causing a plant to lose more water through its foliage than it can take up through its roots. Winds are most damaging to newly planted stock, the roots of which have barely started to grow into the surrounding soil. Each time the wind rocks the plants, it tears the tiny and delicate new roots, requiring the plant to start all over again, with the consequence that young growth is stunted and the plant may die. Strong winds physically tear the more fragile leaves of some plants, and in coastal gardens winds are often laden with salt, which burns young foliage. The strongest winds in Scotland come from the south-west and west and the coldest from the east, particularly in spring. Concentrate your wind shelter on these two directions, but bear in

Shelter in a walled garden at Geilston, west Scotland

mind that severe damage to trees can often occur when winds come unexpectedly from the south, where the roots and branches have not built up sufficient resistance.

You can't stop the wind blowing, so the trick is to manipulate its flow. The first instinct is generally to put up a solid, physical barrier, such as a wall or fence. Most gardens in Orkney can be found inside high walls, which protect plants from the almost constant winds and salt-laden air. But walls and other solid barriers are not always the most effective way, especially in larger gardens. A solid barrier just diverts the wind, which strikes with even more force beyond the barrier at a distance of roughly three times its height. Damaging eddies and undercurrents can be created too, as the wind swirls around the barrier and strikes elsewhere. A permeable barrier, such as a hedge, baffle fencing or a shelterbelt of trees and shrubs, filters the wind rather than re-directing it; tests have shown that wind strength can be cut significantly (by 50 per cent or

Protection from salt spray with fuchsia hedging on Iona

more) after passing through a shelterbelt or hedge. The more space you have, the wider and more effective you can make the shelterbelt.

Many of the famous Scottish west-coast gardens such as Inverewe and Arduaine were only made possible through the thick tree and shrub shelterbelts that combat the ferocious North Atlantic winds. It took twenty to thirty years – as Gerald Loder patiently waited for the shelterbelt of oaks, pines, sycamores, rowans and birch to mature – for the extraordinary gardens at Colonsay House to become established. Exotic large-leaved tree ferns and blechnums, Antipodean prostrantheras and South African gladioli all thrive on this Hebridean isle, but they wouldn't stand a chance if they were exposed to the full force of the wind. Climb to the top of the ridge and you will find oak trees kept stunted at 1m tall, the howling winds clipping their growth. If our own native trees are kept to almost bonsai height, imagine what wind power would do to a tender young fleshy South African agapanthus, or a glossy-leaved camellia more used to the sheltered foothills of China. Trees in the teeth of the wind are often bent like an old lady struggling to keep hold of her umbrella. The coast road from Edinburgh to Gullane has a remarkable demonstration of perfectly wind-pruned trees, especially around Gosford House.

Not all of us have the luxury of space that a tree and shrub shelterbelt requires, but these principles can be adapted to the domestic garden scale. Woven polypropylene attached (with strong ties) to a fence makes an ideal temporary shelter, which allows plants to establish more quickly. Don't discount the infamous x *Cupressocyparis leylandii*, because in the right place it is one of the most effective shelterbelt hedges there is. In rural situations (where neighbours are a healthy distance away), it's a quick, reliable and easily established windbreak. In more suburban situations, it needs to be properly and regularly kept down to a manageable size. There are lots of slower conifers that make equally good but less rampant hedges (see page 123).

In smaller gardens where there isn't the space for shelterbelts, tough, wind-tolerant shrubs (for recommended

Carestown Steading, Aberdeenshire, courtyard provides excellent shelter

plants, see page 129) can be planted singly to act as a buttress for smaller plants. Mike Swift, horticultural consultant and former head gardener at Torosay Castle on Mull, used this method to enable him to grow such tender specimens as *Euphorbia mellifera* and *Echium pininana*, using tough shurbs such as *Olearia*, *Eleaegnus ebbingei*, *Griselinia littoralis* and *Phormium tenax* as buttress plants. In a small exposed cottage garden, you could plant a mixed border, using regularly spaced buttress shrubs, which would allow you to grow a wide range of plants in between. At Lea Gardens, on the Shetland Islands, Rosa Steppanova has created a beautiful garden in what must be one of the most challenging climates in Scotland. Using low walls for shelter and sourcing the most wind-tolerant shrubs from around the world, she has succeeded in sheltering her garden to such an extent that she can grow a huge range of plants, hitherto considered certain 'gonners' on the Shetland Islands. Her book *The Impossible Garden* (see Bibliography, page 234) recounts the garden's creation.

At Carestown Steading, on a hillside near Buckie, Aberdeenshire, in north-east Scotland, there are 2m-high tree ferns, 3m echiums, and apricots and figs fruiting outdoors. These exotics thrive in the middle of an old stone steading quadrangle, out of the wind, and almost frost free, because of the heat generated from the house. The gardens extend all around the steading, and a leylandii hedge keeps the wind at bay, allowing lavenders, cistus, *Magnolia grandiflora* and many other tender trees, shrubs and plants to grow. Heavy frosts rarely settle on their journey down to the valley bottom.

Most plant and gardening books, written by authors from more southerly latitudes, recommend that many shrubs, including rhododendrons and azaleas, are planted in shade or part shade to protect foliage from sunburn and to keep soil temperatures down; you will also find this advice on plant labels in many garden centres. In Scotland, this advice should, in the main, be ignored. Our northern latitude, mountains and hills, and the proximity of low-pressure movements from the Atlantic, make us a cloudier, cooler country with lower light intensity, so very few plants need protection/shelter from sun. Sunlight encourages compact growth, the formation of flower buds and the ripening of wood to withstand the winter. The ideal garden is one with plenty of wind shelter from the south-west and east but full light overhead for most of the planting area. Woodland gardens should be clearings in woodland, rather than plantings under trees, wherever possible. Plants in part day shade – with sun on the foliage and roots only in morning or afternoon – are often happiest of all.

Soils, drainage and rainfall

'Soils are the raw material of the gardener's art,' according to the late great gardener Geoff Hamilton. As well as the particles that make up the soil's structure, one teaspoon of soil contains millions of micro-organisms, all playing a small part of a large underground ecosystem. Experts categorize soils into several types:

Clay Most gardeners can recognize a clay soil: it feels lumpy and sticky when wet, is heavy to turn with a spade, dries rock hard and drains poorly because of the tiny particles, which stick together, leaving few airspaces. It holds lots of nutrients, however, and there are a good number of plants that grow well in clay soils. Unfortunately, lots of others just turn up their toes, as heavy clay soils often stay cold, wet and airless for long periods. Adding well-rotted organic matter, such as dung, leaf mould, peat and compost, will improve the structure, but in extreme cases, plant on top of it and not in it (see page 16).

Examples of plants for heavy and wet soils: *Gunnera*, *Astilbe* and *Hosta*

Sandy soil The opposite of clay: its larger, gritty particles form a light soil, which is easy to work. Sandy soils tend to drain too well, however, drying out very rapidly and holding on to few nutrients. Many coastal gardens have this type of soil and it can be improved by adding lots of well-rotted organic matter, manure and heavier topsoil.

Loam Often considered the perfect soil, between sandy and clay soils in particle size: easy to work, with good structure and drainage qualities, but retaining moisture and nutrients well. You can grow the widest range of plants in loam.

Peat Much of Scotland has very peaty, acidic soil, which is dark in colour and very fibrous in texture. Heather and other acid lovers (known as ericaceous plants) such as rhododendrons grow well in it. It soaks up huge amounts of water and can become too boggy for most plants, unless the drainage is improved. It is not rich in nutrients, but many acid-loving plants do not need large amounts of feed. Some plants dislike like very acid soil and you may need to add lime and grit to raise the pH (see below) and improve drainage.

Silt soils (found in river valleys) and **chalk soils** are rare in Scotland. Squeezing and breaking lumps of soil between your fingers will give you a good rough guide as to how open and free-draining your soil is. If the soil sticks together in tiny lumps in your fingers, it's likely to contain a high percentage of clay. If it falls apart and disappears between your fingers, it's very sandy. A loam is between the two. Spongy, dark-coloured soil is likely to be very peaty. Give the earth a good smell too, because poor-draining soils invariably give off a stale and musty smell, not unlike corked wine or sweaty gym shoes.

Gardening in containers in an Edinburgh New Town basement

Gardening in containers
Not everyone has soil to garden in; many urban gardeners have to do most of their growing in containers. We are often asked for a list of suitable plants for containers, and in theory at least you can grow almost anything. But there are several issues to bear in mind when making a choice.

Plants in containers need more looking after than plants in the ground: roots are more vulnerable to freezing, plants tend to be buffeted by wind, compost easily dries out or becomes over-wet and plants need more feeding than they would in the ground. In cold areas, growing plants such as camellias and magnolias in pots is risky, as their sensitive roots will feel the cold; but if you're determined you can insulate the containers in winter with fleece. Many plants need sharp drainage and hate sitting in wet conditions for any length of time – Mediterranean plants

like lavender are a prime example; for these it's best to ensure that the pot has adequate drainage holes, covered with crocks (broken bits of terracotta or stones) to keep the drainage clear. Perlite and/or coarse grit can be mixed into the compost to improve drainage, and in winter moving the pots up against the walls of the house, where they will remain drier, can help.

If you can't find anyone to water your containers when you are away on holiday, move them to a shady spot where they won't dry out. Try to shelter plants from strong winds, particularly in their soft young growth phase in spring. Once the roots have filled the container (and the top growth and/or flowers start getting a bit thin), you will need to consider repotting to a larger container size.

Acidity, alkalinity and fertility
The pH scale gives a measure of a soil's acidity or alkalinity, and runs between 0 (very acid) and 14 (very alkaline). A pH of 7 is neutral, and a reading between 5.7 and 6.7 or even 7 is ideal for growing a wide range of plants. Basic soil-test kits (available in most garden centres and DIY stores) should give a pH reading and an indicator of key nutrient levels, but they are not always very accurate. Scotland, for the most part, has soil and water on the acidic side, which is ideal for growing most plants. Many plants can be grown in both acidic and alkaline soil, but some are choosier than others. Acid-loving (ericaceous) plants such as rhododendrons and heathers cannot tolerate alkaline soil, while some plants such as dianthus and some saxifrages prefer alkaline soil. Scotland has nothing to compare with the alkaline chalk downs of the south of England, and although much of the country consists of limestone, most of it is covered with a layer of acid soil. In a few places, seams of limestone are found at or near the surface, which can create pockets of neutral or alkaline soil. We have reports of this in parts of Fife (St Michaels and St Andrews), Angus (around north-west

Peat blocks used to terrace a bank for acid-loving plants at Glendoick

Forfar), East Lothian (Haddington and Dunbar); and in a few places in the north-east, but even there, the alkaline soil is very localized, and most gardeners will have acid soil. Farmland is commonly limed artificially (to raise the pH), as many agricultural crops including vegetables do best in limed soil. New-build houses and new gardens built on farmland may therefore have soil with a higher pH than the average, but the lime generally washes out over four or five years. Building rubble and lime mortar can also create pockets of alkaline soil, and this can sometimes 'lie dormant' for many years, until the sudden yellowing of camellia or rhododendron leaves reveals its presence. Incorporating peat into the soil when you plant will bring the pH down to a more acidic level, which will probably be maintained as long as the local water is soft or acid, as most of Scotland's water is.

Most fertilizers contain the same three ingredients and do more or less the same job; you don't need to buy lots of different ones for different plants. Just take care to feed at the right time of year (usually spring and early summer) and do not overdose, as it can burn foliage and even kill plants. The three key nutrient elements are nitrogen (N) for plant growth, phosphorus (P) for root growth and potassium (K) for flowers and fruit. Some fertilizers, known as straights, contain only one of these: ammonium sulphate (nitrogen), superphosphate (phosphorus) and sulphate of potash (potassium). These should be used with care. Balanced fertilizers contain all three, and the relative quantities are given in the NPK ratio on the fertilizer packs: 8:4:4 contains a higher ratio of nitrogen, while in a ratio of 4:4:4 the amounts are even.

Many fertilizers also contain trace elements, such as iron, zinc, copper, manganese and molybdenum. These are only needed in tiny quantities, but are essential for different aspects of plant health. The soil is the engine room of the garden, and if you don't feed it, it will gradually grow nutrient-poor and less able to support a wide range of plants.

Fertilizers can be organic (manure, or other animal waste including bonemeal, dried blood, etc.) or inorganic (manufactured from rock or chemicals). There is no difference in the nutrients supplied, but organic fertilizers are claimed by some to work more in harmony with the soil's micro-organisms. Many organic feeds such as chicken manure and bonemeal have rather singular smells, due to their origins. Inorganic fertilizers, such as Growmore and Vitax Q4, are useful because they are formulated to supply a good general mixture that will benefit a broad range of plants. Slow-release fertilizers, such as Osmocote, which release feed slowly throughout the growing season, are particularly useful for containers, where there is a high demand for nutrients. Liquid feeds are ideal for containers, while granular ones are easier to apply in the garden.

Well-rotted organic matter is a 'magic' ingredient that acts as a feed and soil conditioner, both helping to maintain healthy nutrient levels and improving the soil's structure. If you have access to it, it is well worth adding organic matter to the soil whenever you plant. Worms and soil micro-organisms will break it down, converting it into a form that plant roots can use. It is important that the material is well rotted rather than fresh, because micro-organisms require a huge amount of energy to break down raw matter, and you can actually deplete the soil of vital elements – a process called de-nitrification – by adding raw matter such as sawdust or bark. Animal manures, leaf mould, household compost and composted bark are the most commonly available forms of organic matter. You can make your own excellent leaf mould by raking up autumn leaves and letting them compost for a year or more. Conifer needles are also good: at Glendoick, near Perth (the author Kenneth Cox's rhododendron and azalea nursery), leylandii prunings are run through a chipper and left to rot down for a year. Peat is useful for acidifying the soil, and holds water well; ericaceous compost is usually just a mixture of peat and fertilizer. Spent mushroom compost is a mixture of well-rotted horse manure, peat and chalk, and is a good conditioner, although it should be used with caution around acid-loving plants as it can be too alkaline. One of the best organic conditioners is seaweed: it is rich in trace elements and alginate compounds, which bind soil particles together. Pile it up and let the rain wash some of the salt off before using it.

Mulching with stones, Tillypronie rock garden, Aberdeenshire

Mulching, where a layer of organic matter or gravel is put down on the soil, offers several benefits. It reduces the need to weed (and makes it easier to pull the weeds out), and it helps retain moisture in lighter, drier soils. The underlying earth is also kept warmer in winter and cooler in hot summers, encouraging worms and micro-organisms. Mulching prevents mud from splashing on to foliage and capping after heavy rains, which creates an impervious layer that stops moisture getting down to roots. Mulches are not a complete wonder-drug, however, as they may harbour insect eggs and the spores of rusts and other fungal plant diseases, so if you have disease problems it might be worth removing and renewing the mulch seasonally. When mulching, be careful not to pile layer upon layer, as some plants such as rhododendrons resent having their roots buried too deep. Some plant crowns and surface-dwelling rhizomes such as those of iris should be kept clear of mulch, to avoid damp material sitting in direct stem contact and causing rots to set in.

Prairie planting style, using grasses and perennials, at Cambo, Fife

Rainfall

There is a huge variation in the rainfall between the east coast of Scotland and the west. Parts of the western Highlands receive an average of more than 3000mm (120in) a year, whereas the east coast often gets less than 800mm (30in). Our prevailing weather comes from the west, where clouds pile up over the Atlantic Ocean. They mostly drop their heavy loads of water over the first western mountains they hit, and the east coast receives whatever is left after they have crossed the rest of the country. This is called the rain shadow effect.

There are parts of Scotland where it seems to do nothing else but rain, and yet these same regions boast some marvellous gardens. The secret is good drainage. The gardens at Torosay Castle on Mull get an average of 2000mm of rain a year – most of which falls in the winter – so you might expect there to be huge numbers of plants rotting away every year. This is not the case, however, because Torosay's soil has been built up on top of a beach so that the heavy rains drain away immediately, never lingering long enough in the soil for the roots to suffer. Benmore in Argyll has a similar rainfall, and in this case the steeply sloping site prevents rainwater from building up around the plant roots. Problems occur in high-rainfall areas on a flat site, or one with a heavy clay soil, where water does not drain away and the roots sit in cold, damp conditions, starved of oxygen. We humans would get trenchfoot in these conditions, and unfortunately many of the plants we try to grow don't like it either. Digging drainage ditches and/or creating raised plantings is the best solution for these sites.

Drainage

'Consult the genius of the place in all; / That tells the waters or to rise, or fall . . .' Thus the eighteenth-century gardener-poet Alexander Pope summed up the importance of getting to know your own site before you start trying to change it. Test the drainage of different parts of a new garden by digging down a couple of spade depths, pouring a can of water into the hole and watching how long it takes to drain away. More than a minute, and there could be a drainage problem. Deep digging can break up any pan (solid compacted layer) that has formed, but often there is an underlying problem with the soil structure. Many new-build properties have gardens with poor drainage because the topsoil has been removed or become compacted through the repeated traffic of heavy machinery in wet weather. In our opinion, builders should be required to remedy this as a condition of gaining a completion certificate; then they might take more care.

Water flow is governed by gravity, so if you install a drainage system, it has to drain somewhere. You may be able to dig a soakaway, using gravel, but in a heavy clay soil, this may not work as your soakaway will turn into a pond. A more modest and realistic alternative is to raise the planting area. The display gardens at Glendoick Garden Centre near Perth are a useful demonstration of how raised beds and mounds have improved a heavy clay site to allow most plants to grow happily. Bed edges can be constructed using wood, log roll, stone, concrete, peat blocks, metal lawn edge, strong wire netting or anything else that comes to mind. Make up a mixture of your own soil, with peat, composted bark, imported topsoil, homemade compost, manure, grit, etc., and make sure that the water that drains out has somewhere to go. Bog garden, moat or pond are all possible uses for the damp/low-lying parts of the garden.

On much of the west coast, the peaty soil absorbs so much water that many plants simply rot away. Mound planting on top of the soil, rather than in it, works for many plants such as rhododendrons. Alternatively incorporate a percentage of sharp sand and gravel, so that the soil retains less water. What happens on the soil surface can also be important. Plants used to dry winters, or those with fleshy leaves such as lewisia, *Primula auricula* and some grasses, grow better with a layer of gravel to keep the leaves and resting buds out of contact with the cold wet winter soil. Scree or gravel gardens, where a whole area is covered with a gravel mulch, suit many plants, and with the addition of a few well-placed stones and boulders a wild mountainside look can be achieved, setting individual plants off beautifully. On a smaller scale, you may find you can grow a particular plant, such as dianthus, by using lime chippings, placing thin pieces of slate underneath the crown or growing it in between paving slabs.

Raised beds for plants that require sharp drainage at Cally Gardens

Throughout our countrywide travels in researching this book, we came across many examples of plants in locations that bucked the perceived wisdom on hardiness. We kept asking, 'How can that be doing so well there?' The key in almost every case was good drainage of both soil and frost, as at Abriachan, on Loch Ness, and Tillypronie, high up on an inland Aberdeenshire hillside: both are on steep south-facing slopes, with excellent frost drainage and no chance of waterlogging. Moreoever, in some ways, the more we researched, often the less we found we knew; we were forever being surprised by what grew where. In the end, for every statement that we make there will be someone who has proved the opposite is true. We fully expect this to be the case with our plant hardiness ratings, where we may judge a plant not to be hardy in Kelso or Braemar, and we hope to be sent pictures of thriving specimens to prove us wrong.

Selecting plants and planting them

Scotland's native flora is relatively impoverished compared with that of Continental Europe, because the 'island' of Britain broke away from Europe at a time when many plants had not had a chance to colonize. It is certainly possible to make a fine garden using only rowan, birch, pine, heather, gorse, broom, alpines, orchids and other native wild flowers (in the plant entries on page 26 onwards Scottish native plants are marked ✖), but most gardeners also like to grow exotics – that is, plants from other parts of the world. While it's reasonably likely that a plant originating from a similar climate and conditions will do well in a Scottish garden, that is not always the case. What does well in Scotland has largely become known through trial and error. Apart from the Glasgow rose trials (Tollcross Park), Which? trials at Greenbank, Glasgow, and the Scottish Crop Research Institute's work on fruit, there is very little formal testing of ornamental plants in Scotland. For this book, therefore, we have had to rely on the personal knowledge of many experienced fellow gardeners and nurserymen in different parts of the country. Similarly, to help ascertain the suitability of plants for Scotland, we developed the Scottish Gardenplant Award, voted for by many of Scotland's leading horticulturists, gardeners and nurserymen and women (see page 23).

Scottish grown versus imported plants: 'plant miles'

It might surprise you to know just how far away the plants in your local garden centre may have travelled. Garden centres usually do a fine job in presenting clean, healthy plants, but most of the big chains of garden centres no longer grow any plants themselves: they buy all of them in. Nursery stock is often imported from Germany, Holland and Italy as well as from the south of England. Sometimes plants pass through so many middlemen that garden centres may not even know the origins of what they sell. Should this be of concern? Maybe. Most of the plants sold are perfectly good; it would be churlish to claim otherwise. But 'food miles' are now a significant consideration for many customers and perhaps 'plant miles' should be just as important. Why should a plant that can easily be obtained from a Scottish grower be bought in from Europe in order to save a few pence? Think about the environmental impact of the transport involved in getting it to Scotland.

Another issue is the range of plants grown abroad, such as the conifers, camellias and euonymus offered as specimen plants by Italian nurseries, which are not always the ones that grow best in Scotland. Not surprisingly foreign nurseries grow what grows best in their climate, so beware of many of those tempting imported specimen plants: make sure that they are really suitable for your garden, especially if you live in a harsh climate.

Where and how a plant has been grown before going on sale plays an important role in its subsequent hardiness. Many garden centre plants are grown in large commercial nurseries, where they are often mollycoddled in comfortable heated greenhouses and tunnels, sheltered from wind, their roots happily feasting on perfect compost mixtures. Plants grown in tunnels often have their growth inappropriately advanced for the outside world, and if stock is brought north, this problem can be even more pronounced. In colder parts of Scotland new growth and flowering in the spring can be a month or more behind the south of England. Plants with advanced growth should be gradually hardened off – that is, placed outside in the spring daytime and then brought under cover (usually a greenhouse or cold frame) at night if frost is forecast, or if planted outside, then covered with fleece if nights are cold. Herbs are one type of plant which are commonly forced in tunnels and brought to Scotland far too early in the year to be planted out unprotected. We

Tempting displays at a garden centre

would not recommend planting them out until May at the earliest and June in coldest inland areas. The most vulnerable of all are most bedding plants, which are unable to withstand cold temperatures. They can be knocked back for months or killed when they are planted outdoors too early. That tempting osteospermum might look lovely flowering away on the sales bench, but in Scotland it is June before the weather warms up sufficiently to keep them going.

As a customer at a garden centre, how can you tell that a plant is from the Continent? Well, here's a wee secret: as their plants are sold to many different countries, Dutch, Italian and German stock tends to carry picture labels with few words other than the name and rows of rather unintelligible symbols. The plants on sale at your local nursery may not look as pretty as their Continental cousins, but if they have been outdoors in Scotland all winter, they will be adjusted to the seasons and therefore safer to buy and often quicker to establish.

The most ill-chosen selections of plants tend to be found in the shops of DIY chains, in those add-on garden centres out the back. From Land's End to John O'Groats, they sell the same plants at the same time of year, whether suitable for local conditions or not. A survey of one such store in Dundee revealed that over 30 per cent of the

stock on offer was unsuitable for eastern Scotland: palms, olives and oleanders were all being offered for planting outdoors, with little or no warning on the labels to indicate that customers should beware. None of the nursery stock was grown in Scotland. The same store was full of tender bedding plants for sale in late March, most of which would be dead within weeks because of late frosts. Such stores do little to help Scottish gardeners make informed choices: better ranging and customer guidance would help.

At the moment Scotland still has a vibrant sector of independent nurseries and garden centres which grow primarily for the Scottish market and therefore grow a range

Tree Shop, Argyll: a source of Scottish-grown trees

of plants chosen for our growing conditions. For example, Scottish azaleas ('Panda', 'Squirrel', etc.) bred at Glendoick have been trialled and tested specifically for Scotland. It therefore surely makes sense to buy Scottish-grown plants from local expert growers when you can.

Many of these growers are mentioned in this book in the plant entries, but it is worth mentioning a few of the many outstanding nurseries here: Cally Gardens and Elizabeth MacGregor's nurseries in Dumfries and Galloway; Binny Plants and Macplants, outside Edinburgh; Glendoick, near Perth; Abriachan, near Inverness; the Tree Shop, in Argyll; and Cardwell Nursery and Garden Centre, Gourock. Alpines are particularly well represented at numerous small nurseries from Edrom, near Berwick, to Ardfearn near Inverness. Shows such as Gardening Scotland, regional flower shows and the Scottish Rock Garden Club shows are a great opportunity to meet growers and ask their advice.

Many great garden plants don't make it to mass-market circulation and the garden centre shelves, not because they are particularly fussy or tender but because they may simply be unsuitable for large-scale commercial production. Some, for instance, are too slow growing to be economically viable for the big growers. The giant Himalayan lily (*Cardiocrinum giganteum*) is seldom

Embothrium coccineum

produced commercially – it takes seven years or more to reach flowering size from seed, making it seem expensive to buy – but it thrives in Scotland and represents remarkable value when you consider the years of nurturing involved in its production. It takes little extra effort to seek out such plants: enthusiastic independent nurserymen and garden centres will go the extra yard to offer something different.

Plant provenance

The hardiness of a plant species or variety can vary according to where the specimen has been raised, or where its wild origins are. For example, Abriachan Garden and Nursery on the side of Loch Ness offers a particularly tough strain of *Nerine bowdenii*, propagated from a specimen growing in a very cold garden in Strathglass, near Glen Affric, in the central Highlands. *Embothrium coccineum* is normally associated more with milder west-coast gardens; however, Rosa Steppanova, in her determination to grow this red-flowered beauty in Shetland, sourced a strain from one of the highest and coldest areas in its native Chile, and has achieved successful establishment. The determination of Shetlanders to re-establish tree cover has led them to the realization that only trees from similar latitudes (including southern Chile, Norway and Alaska) adapt well to Shetland's cool and windy conditions. Likewise in Orkney, seedlings from Orcadian rowans, birch and willows establish and grow much better than stock from further south. Over thousands of years, these strains have evolved and adapted to the conditions of the northern isles and equivalent climates.

Buying good plants and planting techniques

These days, most plants purchased are container grown, which makes them easier to transport and, in theory at least, they can be put in the ground at almost any time of year. As with everything else you purchase, there are a few things to look out for when buying plants. Left in the same container too long, a plant can become pot bound, the roots having grown in a spiral around the pot and turned inwards. In these circumstances, unless you can tease the roots carefully from their tangle, they may never grow outwards into the soil to find new nutrients, and the plant will languish or die. This tends to happen more with trees and shrubs, although it can occur with herbaceous perennials. If there are masses of roots coming out of the drainage holes or the plant is rooted to the ground, it is probably potbound. Containers should also be largely free of weeds, and the compost moist but not waterlogged. Most

shrubs should have several strong branches growing from the base. Trees often hang around for many months in garden centres, so look for signs that they have been looked after: the pot should be large enough for the plant and the foliage should be lush. Avoid specimens with branches that have rubbed against each other and bark that looks bruised or broken. Climbers are a nightmare for nurseries and garden centres, as they tend to grow into one another, creating an almighty tangle; and this gives you an indication of how long plants have been hanging around for. Some plants look as if they have been there for years. Ideally you want to buy plants which have not been on a garden centre bench for too long. Some well-known garden centres are vastly over-stocked – the plants are crowded too close together on the benches and not looked after. Even with half-price stickers plants may well not be bargains, so beware. There simply is no point in spending money on good plants and then not taking care to ensure they are planted and looked after properly.

In the plant entries we have tried to give individual planting tips where required. Here are some general rules. When planting, neither the compost in the plant pot nor the soil mix in the planting pit should be dry. Soak a plant before you plant it, then let the excess water drain out. Before planting, add plenty of organic matter to the soil, and break up the soil around the planting pit if it seems compacted. The roots should be encouraged to spread out into the surrounding soil as quickly as possible, so loosen the roots slightly when you have removed the pot, particularly if they are in a tight mass. If you are planting container-grown stock, the surface level of the compost in the pot should match the surface level of the soil. With grafted plants like roses, the graft (the swollen area on the lower stem) should sit just above the soil surface. Don't leave a garden full of new plants while you disappear for two weeks' summer holiday, without asking someone to water it. Newly planted stock needs regular watering, whereas established plants can better fend for themselves.

Evergreens are particularly susceptible to excessive moisture loss in their first year of planting, especially in windy, dry or frosty weather. Strong airflow around the top growth means the plant is continuously losing water through its leaves, while the roots are unable to suck up enough water to replace the deficit. The bigger the plant, the more water is lost in the first years of establishment.

While it is tempting to create an instant garden with large specimen plants, be aware that such plants need extra soil preparation and aftercare, especially staking and watering. It might also be worth considering that three small plants planted in a clump may well catch up and overtake one large specimen in a few years, as the smaller plants will establish more easily and therefore grow more vigorously. Really vigorous plants like leylandii are rarely worth planting as large specimens as their roots cannot hold them in strong winds and they blow over. Plants are stressed whenever they are moved: from pot to garden, or from tunnel to outdoors. You will have the best chance of success when you can minimize the shock of temperature changes, wind or extremes of drought or wet. Some plants are more sensitive than others: daphnes and embothriums are examples of plants which resent being moved, while it's difficult to imagine *Alchemilla mollis* being shocked by anything short of a nuclear bomb. While most gardeners buy and plant in spring, it is well worth considering plant-

Beware of starved, potbound plants in garden centres

ing in September and October too for establishing. When the soil is still warm but the summer sun is losing its strength, plants are not stressed and roots get a chance to grow into the new soil before winter. Bare-rooted plants (hedging, for example) are normally not available until November, but we would recommend preparing the soil beforehand. Some plants are better planted in late spring: ceanothus, lavender and cistus, for example, all of which come from a Mediterranean climate.

Pests and diseases

Although there are hundreds of pests and diseases that attack plants, the reality is that most of them are very rare: the list of common nasties is really fairly short. These are briefly discussed below. The list of chemicals available for amateurs to use to control pests and diseases diminishes year by year; sometimes they are withdrawn as they are not safe, but more often than not it is simply because the chemical companies do not find it economical to jump through the expensive hoops demanded by

law. The fact is, however, that more plants are killed by human endeavour – such as bad plant selection for the site, poor drainage or being left to dry out when newly planted or left exposed to wind damage – than by all the pests and diseases put together.

Among Scotland's most significant pests are deer and rabbits, which can cause devastation, particularly in hard winters and when there is heavy snow. They can bark trees and graze anything they can reach, sometimes down to the ground, often chewing and spitting out what they don't find palatable. Fencing, ferrets and/or shooting are the best options for control. The lists of deer- and rabbit-

Chemical controls can be useful for controlling pests

resistant plants above have been compiled from the experiences of many gardeners all over the UK, but is not infallible, and your local rabbit and deer populations weren't consulted and won't have read the rules.

Sap-sucking and root-eating insects do most damage in greenhouses and to potted plants. Red spider (tiny red mites on leaf undersides), scale (small white shell-like bugs) and aphids (including whitefly) all suck the sap of the plant, discolouring or puckering the leaves. There are insecticides and organic soaps to combat them, as well as various biological controls. Worst of all is the vine weevil grub (small, white and crescent-shaped, with a brown tip), which tends to hatch in pots and eats roots. The adults (slow-moving matt, dark-grey sinister beetle-like creatures) feed at night and notch leaves; each adult can lay hundreds of eggs and one grub can kill a plant. Unfortunately, often the first you know about a weevil infestation is when a plant collapses after being barked or having its roots eaten by larvae hidden under the soil. Certain chemicals used to control vine weevil – types of neonicotinoids – were with-

Plant health and threats to the landscape

There is now a real threat to our landscape from imported pests and diseases, some of which can enter through the plant trade. Ash dieback (*Chalara fraxinea*) is slowly spreading through our native ash populations, Phytophthora ramorum and Phytophthora kenoviae have killed whole valleys of larch and rhododendron and is now spreading into the native bilberry population. There are emerging threats such as the Emerald Ash Borer beetle and Asian Longhorn Beetle which are spreading across Europe towards our isles. These pests and diseases threaten not only our great gardens with their priceless exotic plant collections, but they also threaten our woodlands, forests and wider landscapes. Importing pests and diseases can be accidental, for example Dutch Elm Disease came from imported Canadian logs which contained a few beetles and larvae, but the consequences can be devastating. Our climate is becoming slowly milder, supporting new potential pest species which can enter the country on trees, shrubs, plants, food, packaging, and sometimes even just on the wind.

Woody plant material, woodchip fuel and wooden packaging crates are of major concern as potential carriers of pest and diseases. In the case of the outbreak of ash dieback in 2012, many trade nurseries had previously warned of the dangers of importing this disease from Europe but not enough was done to prevent it. Since this outbreak, the government (UK and Scotland) is taking tree and plant health very seriously and has introduced and strengthened a protection system which includes regular border inspections, movement bans on risk species such as those for ash and plane trees, a risk register to spot and assess the scale of new and emerging threats, and programs such as ObservaTree (www.observatree.org.uk) to educate the public about the risks and actions they can take. When you read this book there may be certain plants that are unavailable due to a specific pest or disease threat which has come to light since publication.

As gardeners we should try to be aware that the plants we buy are disease free and come from approved suppliers. These could be small independent nurseries which grow their own plants for sale, or approved suppliers who use the plant passporting system in the case of most garden centres. If buying over the internet or through magazine or newspaper offers, ask about what safeguards are in place to ensure that plants are clean. And no matter how tempting it is when we are on holiday, we should not squirrel away cuttings or any plant material to bring home because the threats can be microscopic.

drawn from use in 2014 following a disputed EU ban over concerns to bee health. It is possible that this pest will become more prevalent from 2015 onwards until a viable alternative treatment is developed. Current nematode biological controls are effective but they are temperature sensitive and don't work during cold winter conditions.

Fungal diseases attack most plants to some extent – they're nature's way of controlling alien species, which are not meant to be here – and often highly bred hybrids are worst affected. Mildews (downy and powdery), rusts and blackspot are common on a range of plants. You can either spray against them or let nature take its course, as they are rarely fatal. With most modern hybrid roses, you will need to spray regularly to keep them healthy, particularly in the west. Scab affects fruit trees and some shrubs such as pyracantha, and is worst in wet weather and high rainfall areas. To have clean fruit in most areas, you will need to spray against this preventatively (before signs of attack appear). You can't remove scabs from fruit, but you can still eat it (it just looks unappetizing). Cankers are often fatal fungal or bacterial diseases, which affect plums, apples, cherries, poplars and other trees, usually entering via pruning wounds or weather-damaged branches. The leaves on a branch or part of a tree suddenly turn crisp, and there are often signs of oozing or bleeding through the bark. There is not much you can do, apart from cutting the affected parts out and burning them. In the worst cases, you may lose the tree entirely. There is a lot more to say on pests and diseases, but this is primarily a plant book, and we want to devote more space to writing about plants rather than what can damage them. For more information, consult the books listed in the bibliography on page 234.

How we selected the plants in this book

The plant entries in this book include trees, shrubs, fruit, herbaceous perennials and bulbs. We have tried to include as many species and varieties as possible, but there are many plants that we have not had the space to cover. Some just hovered at the edge of inclusion, such as *Petasites* and *Echeveria*, and we are sorry that we could not include them all. Vegetables and annuals are not included; nor are those tender perennials such as dahlias, cannas, and gladioli that generally require lifting and storing for the winter. We haven't covered aquatics like water lilies either, although we have covered plants for pondsides and bogs.

With some plant species we have been able to cover most of or all the commonly available varieties. There are many others, such as roses, clematis, rhododendrons, peonies, irises and day lilies, with many species, and many thousands of hybrids, and we are only able to describe a

Plants not usually eaten by rabbits

This list has been compiled from reports from gardeners in various parts of the UK, but it cannot be totally relied upon – rabbits don't read lists, and plants some people find rabbit-proof are eaten with relish in other areas. Plants may be particularly vulnerable to damage when they are newly planted or with young growth emerging (novelty value?), or when the rabbits have little alternative choice of food (if ground is snow-covered or frozen). If protected for this critical period, they will be less likely to be attacked once the protection is removed. Rabbits prefer leaves and soft stems rather than flowers and woody stems. They seem to prefer feeding in open positions and often nibble plants at the edge of borders.

Shrubs
Aucuba japonica
Berberis thunbergii
Buddleia davidii,
   B. globosa
Buxus
Ceanothus
Cistus
Cornus alba
Cotoneaster dammeri
Daphne
Deutzia
Eleagnus
Euonymus
Gaultheria procumbens
Helianthemum
Hebe
Hedera
Hypericum
Hydrangea
Kalmia latifolia
Lonicera (climbing)
Mahonia aquifolium
Philadelphus
Phormium
Potentilla fructicosa
Rhododendron (larger
   leaved)
Ribes sanguineum
Rosa rugosa
Rosemary
Sambucus
Skimmia
Symphoricarpus albus
Syringa vulgaris
Viburnum
Vinca

Perennials and bulbs
Acanthus
Aconitum
Agapanthus
Agastache foeniculum
Alcea rosea
Alchemilla mollis
Anemone blanda
Anemone x hybrida, A.
   japonica, etc
   (Japanese
   anemones)
Anthemis
Aquilegia
Astilbe
Bergenia
Borago officinalis
Concollaria majalis
Cortaderia (pampas)
Corydalis lutea
Crocosmia
Cyclamen
Delphinium
Digitalis
Euphorbia
Geranium (some)
Geum
Grasses (most)
Helleborus
Hemerocallis
Herbs (most, including
   rosemary, lavender,
   etc.)
Inula
Iris
Kniphofia
Lupinus (lupin)
Lychnis chalcedonica
Malva moschata
Mint
Monarda
Narcissus (daffodil)
Nepeta
Onopordon nervosum
Ophiopogon
   planiscapus
Osteospermum
   (common species
   and hybrids)
Paeonia
Phormium tenax
Polygonatum
Potentilla (common
   species and hybrids)
Pulmonaria
Stachys
Symphytum

small fraction of what is available. Although we've had to be selective and stick to the most popular and widely available, we have covered most of the varieties grown by most of the major UK wholesalers and plant suppliers. We have also tried to include plants that have been bred in Scotland or have strong Scottish associations – Cocker's roses, Glendoick rhododendrons and the James Hutton Institue (formerly called the Scottish Crop Research Institute) soft fruit, for example. If there is a plant that you can't find in the book, it doesn't mean that it is not worth growing: we simply were not able to include everything. There are new plants coming on to the market all the time, and we were sometimes unable to give an authoritative opinion on a plant's character simply because it has not been around for long enough. If in doubt, go for the tried and tested and most reliable.

The Scottish Gardenplant Award

As we started the research for this book we realised that the Royal Horticultural Society's (RHS) Award of Garden Merit (AGM) was of limited use to Scottish gardeners, as it is too south-of-England orientated. Many AGM plants are not suitable for Scotland due to the climate. Our very varied and particular climate suits a huge variety of plants, but there are a great many that do well further south but struggle in Scotland, because of lack of heat, winter wet or other factors; conversely, many of the best performers in Scotland are not as happy further south – for example, many alpines, meconopsis, and Tropaeolum speciosum. Glendoick had already produced a popular leaflet called 'The 100 Best Plants for Eastern Scotland' and the notion of a 'Scottish Garden Plant Award' grew from this idea. The RHS Plant Finder contains 70,000 plant names. In the face of so many plants on offer, we thought it would

Deer-resistant plants

Scotland has far too many deer (one estimate places the numbers around 750,000) and for some gardeners they are a constant menace. To keep roe deer out requires an expensive deer fence not less than 1.5m and up to 2m high. Deer tend to cause most damage in cold winters with snow on the ground. Antler rubbing can also cause problems. The list below is far from infallible and hungry deer will eat almost anything. Small tree seedlings are inevitably browsed by deer which has meant that large swathes of the Highlands have little or no tree regeneration unless areas are fenced off.

Shrubs and trees

Amelanchier
Bamboos
Betula (mature)
Buddleja davidii
Buxus (box)
Choisya ternata
Clematis
Chaenomeles
Cornus alba and
C. sanguinea
    (dogwood)
Daphne
Eucalyptus
Forsythia
Hippophae
    rhamnoides
Hydrangea
Kerria japonica
Laurus nobilis (bay)
Lonicera species
    (honeysuckles)
Magnolia
Mahonia
Philadelphus
Phormium tenax
Potentilla fruticosa
Rhododendron larger
    hybrids
Rhus
Ribes (currants)
Rosa rugosa,
    R. spinosissima
Spiraea japonica
Viburnum (deciduous
    types)
Vinca major,
    V. minor
Weigela
Yucca

Perennials

Agapanthus
Aquilegia
Cistus
Cortaderia selloana
    (pampas grass)
Delphinium
Digitalis (foxglove)
Echinops species
    (globe thistles)
Euphorbia species
    (spurges)
Ferns
Grasses (most)
Helleborus
    (hellebores)
Kniphofia (red hot
    pokers)
Leucanthemum x
    superbum
Lupinus (lupins)
Monarda didyma
    (bergamot)
Narcissus (daffodils)
Nepeta x faassenii
    (catmint)
Nerine species
Romneya coulteri
    (Californian poppy)

be useful to point gardeners in the direction of the most reliable, tried-and-tested plants, which are the best of their type for Scottish gardens. We hope that the award will be used on plant labels in Scotland to help gardeners make the best selection of an often bewildering range of plants. The list of Scottish Gardenplant Award plants is also available on several websites including those of the Royal Caledonian Horticultural Society and Glendoick Gardens.

To consider which plants should receive the award, we assembled an impressive group of judges, representing a wide spectrum of Scottish horticultural expertise. Sometimes there was agreement, sometimes not. We now have a list of 500 plants that have been awarded the Scottish Gardenplant Award or SGA. You can be sure that plants listed here with the SGA symbol ♥ are a very good starting point for gardeners from one end of Scotland to the other.

Abbreviations

Hardiness ratings (see table on page 25)
H = hardiness

Note that the minimum temperature ratings given in the table apply only to plants that are perfectly hardened off.

H3 plants, for example, may well be badly damaged or even killed in autumn or spring by only moderately cold weather if growth is soft.

    H3–4 = ranging from H3 to H4
    H3/4 = borderline H3 or H4
    H(3)4–5 = most are H4–5, one or two or just one is H3
    H4(–5) = H4, possibly H5

Size, or 'how big will it grow?'
If two dimensions are given with an 'x' we are giving height (always first) and width. If there is a single figure, this is for height only. With trees we have tried to give two heights: what you can expect after 10 years and what the ultimate size (U:) might be after 25 years or more. Bear in mind with plant dimensions that in mild, wet and sheltered gardens plants will have a much faster growth rate than in cold, dry, inland or very windy gardens (where the wind will prune trees). And if you feed your plants they will grow much faster. Some perennials and grasses will spread, layer or seed themselves around; we have flagged the more invasive ones in the text.

HARDINESS RATINGS USED IN THIS BOOK				
H RATING	USDA RATING	MIN. TEMP F	MIN. TEMP C	AREAS OF SCOTLAND WHERE APPLICABLE
H5	6a	-10 to -5°F	-20.6 to -23.3 C	Hardy in all of Scotland, the toughest rated plants for the book. Extreme weather can still damage plants.
H4–5	6b	-5 to 0°F	-17.8 to -20.5°C	Hardy in almost all of Scotland: Borders, Highlands, inland river valleys and mountains. Some (cosmetic) damage in extreme winters, sudden cold snaps, late spring frosts.
H4	7a	0 to +5°F	-15.0 to -17.7°C	Hardy in most eastern gardens fairly near the coast, or on hillsides: Perth, S. Edinburgh, Dundee, Aberdeen, Inverness, etc. May not be reliably hardy in cold inland gardens.
H3	7b	+5 to +10°F	-12.3 to -14.9°C	Hardy in a sheltered site in most of coastal eastern and northern Scotland, N. Edinburgh, mildest parts of Forth and Tay and whole of south and west coasts. Damage may occur from early or late frosts. Plants may suffer from winter wet, or unripened wood, especially in far north.
H2	8a	+10 to +15°F	-9.5 to -12.2°C	Hardy outdoors in mildest parts of west coast and west coast islands, May well grow in colder areas with protection.
H1	9	Little frost		Greenhouse cultivation or with artificial winter protection except in mildest parts of western islands and Galloway.

Other abbreviations

⚑ Scottish native plant
☘ Irritant or toxic
☘☘ Extremely irritant or toxic if ingested
❀ Fragrant
❀❀ Very fragrant
♦ Disease resistant (roses, fruit trees)
♦♦ Very disease resistant
♛ Scottish Gardenplant Award

A note on plant names

Gardeners find it extremely annoying that plant names always seem to be changing, usually because of advances in botanical research. It is fair to admit there is a certain amount of taxonomic table tennis going on between rival camps in many of the more complex genera, so you sometimes don't know if new names will be accepted or not. In recent years

Pernettya has become *Gaultheria*, *Cimicifuga* becomes *Actea*, etc. We have used the latest nomenclature as it appears in the *RHS Plant Finder* through most of the book, but we have taken a pragmatic approach in some instances. With fruit, for example, we have not used the Latin names (*Malus*, *Pyrus*), as they are listed as apples and pears on plant labels. Other plants – astilbes for example – are listed by variety name, rather than the species/hybrid group, because that is how you will find them in garden centres and nurseries. Some plants are protected by plant breeder's rights (PBR) which allows a royalty to be paid to the breeder or discoverer. Most such plants rather confusingly have two names, a trade designation (the name they are sold under, which may differ from one country to another) and the clonal name, which is often a code or nonsense name, which appears in square brackets. An example is *Euphorbia* Excalibur ['Froeup']. The bit in brackets you can ignore.

SHRUBS AND CLIMBERS

⊠ Scottish native plant ᰚ Scottish Gardenplant Award
☠ irritant or toxic; ☠☠ extremely irritant or toxic if ingested
❀ fragrant; ❀❀ very fragrant
♦ disease resistant; ♦♦ very disease resistant

Abelia

H2–3 (2–3m x 1–1.5m) Popular shrubs for their masses of tiny pink and/or white flowers in late summer into autumn. Abelias are an excellent choice for coastal gardens, but they are not very hardy and can be badly damaged or killed in cold winters or early/late frosts in eastern and inland gardens. They may still be worth growing in cold gardens because they grow fast and flower well from a young age. Use the warmth and shelter of a south-facing wall if possible.

Abelia floribunda 'Edward Goucher'

A. floribunda H2 (3m) suitable for mildest gardens only, pendant cerise flowers in early summer. **'Edward Goucher'** *H3* lilac pink, long flowering season into autumn. *A. x grandiflora H3* (2–3m) ❀ semi-evergreen arching shrubs with glossy dark-green leaves and white, funnel-shaped, delicately scented flowers in mid- to late summer; **Confetti** ['Conti'] variegated foliage tinged pink, white fragrant flowers, **'Francis Mason'** leaves with golden-yellow margin, slightly fragrant white flowers, **'Gold Spot'** leaves yellow-green, flowers white, **Hopleys** ['Abghop'] pale-pink flowers, golden-variegated leaves turn pink in autumn.

Abutilon

H3 (3–5m x 1–2m) Although these upright deciduous shrubs with their mainly large disc-shaped flowers are

Abutilon vitifolium (RC-M)

Abutilon 'Kentish Belle'

more familiar as house and conservatory plants, those listed below are tough enough to grow outdoors in much of Scotland. They grow best in a warm sheltered site: a south-facing wall is probably best. Abutilons may be badly damaged in a cold winter but can be cut back and will usually grow away, though all tend to be fairly short lived.

'Kentish Belle' *H2–3* (2m+) pendent bells with a red calyx, yellow petals and purple stamens all summer long. *A. x suntense* (3–5m) violet-purple. *A. vitifolium* (5m) a Chilean species, white or pale purple-blue hollyhock-like flowers in mid-summer, vine-like leaves, very vigorous and often seeds itself.

Actinidia (kiwi fruit) (climber)

H3–4 These are deciduous, woody-stemmed twining climbers. The kiwi fruit *A. chinensis/deliciosa H3–4* (5–10m+) can be grown in Scotland but there is insufficient heat for it to fruit. It is too vigorous for a greenhouse, and you need both male and female plants to produce fruit. We had to get rid of it at Glendoick as it was so rampant, strangling other plants with its tentacles,

Actinidia kolmikta

but it is handsome if you have space – in a quarry, for instance. The non-fruiting *A. kolomikta H4* ᰚ is popular, and not quite so rampant, reaching 3–4m x 3–4m. Some of the heart-shaped leaves are pink or white, or splashed with pink or white. You might not notice the small fragrant white flowers. It is sometimes slow to establish, but vigorous once it gets going; probably best on a south- or west-facing wall and needs some support until the stems become woody.

Akebia see Trachelospermum, page 106

Amelanchier

H5 A useful and versatile fully hardy deciduous shrub or small tree with white flowers in spring and usually good autumn colour. The star-shaped white flowers are small but borne in dense clusters, often appearing

Amelanchier (autumn colour)

Amelanchier

Arctostaphylos uva-ursi

simultaneously with the attractive young bronzy leaves in April–May. In autumn, leaves turn gold or red, particularly in dry, cold weather. Amelanchiers can be grown either as a tree with a single trunk, reaching 3–10m in height, or with the leader pruned out to make a multi-stemmed shrub. They grow best in moist soil that does not dry out in summer.

A. alnifolia **'Obelisk'** (3–5m+) upright tidy habit. *A. canadensis* (to 7m) good in damp soil, but not all that ornamental. *A. x grandiflora* **'Ballerina'** a good choice for the small garden, reaching about 3m. *A. laevis* very similar with red young growth, flowering 1–2 weeks earlier, *A. lamarckii* (5–10m) ♥ probably the finest red and yellow autumn colour. Fruiting Amelanchier 'saskatoons' are also worth growing in Scotland: fruit like blueberries and spectacular autumn colour.

Arbutus (strawberry tree)

Arbutus unedo

H4 This is a small but useful genus of slow-growing evergreen shrubs or small trees with fine reddish-brown bark. They produce clusters of fragrant white bell- or urn-shaped flowers in late spring, similar to those of pieris (see page 82), followed by orange-red fruits in autumn.

'Marina' (4–6m) a hybrid with orange-red young growth, pink flowers and bright-red fruit. *A. menziesii* (5–10m x 2–3m) little known and little grown, but forms a fine, handsome tree with spectacular deep reddish-brown peeling bark; requires drought conditions in summer, so does better in east Scotland and should be planted under trees. *A unedo* (4–6m x 2m) ♥ commonly grown, with white flowers and red fruit appearing simultaneously in late autumn. In mild west-coast gardens can reach up to 10m in time. It is tolerant of neutral or limy soil. The Cruickshank Botanic

Garden in Aberdeen has a fine domed specimen, while University of Dundee Botanic Garden has thickets of it. It's likely to suffer damage in severe winters in cold inland gardens, especially young plants.

Arctostaphylos

H4–5 (25cm x 1.5m+) This is another member of the heath family, and mostly commonly seen in the evergreen spreading ground-cover forms, which are excellent in full sun in dry, gritty soil. White to pale-pink urn-shaped flowers in March–May are followed by red berries.

A. x media **'Wood's Red'** white-pink flowers, red fruits. *A. uva-ursi* dark leaves, white-pink flowers, red berries; includes the form **'Vancouver Jade'** with pink flowers.

Aucuba japonica

Aucuba japonica

H5 This is a tough and versatile evergreen shrub, with dark-green or variegated leaves. The insignificant flowers are followed by long-lasting large red berries on female forms, as long as there is a male form growing near by. Only forms of *A. japonica* are widely grown, mostly those with variegated leaves. Forming a dense bush, 1–1.5m x 1–1.5m in 5–10 years, it can reach 3m x 3m in time. Tolerant of sun or shade, wind and poor soil, and very pest and disease resistant, it is one of the toughest evergreen shrubs. Having said all that, the forms usually sold with blotches and splashes of yellow variegation all over the leaves are hideous, and look 'as if someone accidentally sprayed them with weedkiller' (KC).

'Crotonifolia' (female), **'Golden King** '(male), **'Variegata'** (male), **'Marmorata'** (female), **'Sulphurea Marginata'**, a form with yellow-edged leaves, which looks as if it has starvation and mineral deficiency. **'Rozannie'** is a self-fertile green-leaved form and by far the most tasteful.

Azara

H2–3 ❋ These small-leaved South American evergreen shrubs and small trees are suited for mild gardens not too far from the coast. The tiny, sweetly scented, strap-like yellow flowers in spring or summer are most attractive en

Azara microphylla

masse. In mildest west-coast gardens they can reach 6m+.

A. lanceolata H2 (2–4m x 1–2m) ❀ leaves to 6cm, lightly scented yellow flowers in April–May. ***A. microphylla H3*** (2–4m x 1–2m) ❀❀ very small leaves, tiny deliciously chocolate-vanilla scented pale yellow flowers in January–March, the form **'Variegata'** leaves edged pale yellow, less vigorous. ***A. serrata H2*** (2–4m x 2m+) ❀ large clusters of deep yellow vanilla-scented flowers in mid-summer.

Bamboos

Bamboos have seen a surge in popularity over the last few years and they are now widely available. They have long been common as shelter planting in many Scottish west-coast gardens such as Crarae in Argyll. Many bamboos have fine coloured stems, known as culms, and some have variegated leaves. The varieties listed below are hardy, but they can be damaged by wind in exposed positions, which causes burned leaf tips and a scruffy appearance. The mostly taller, clumping bamboos will reach 3–4m+ (more in milder gardens) and are easily controlled, whereas many of the lower-growing running bamboos can be invasive, although they are handy for covering large areas. Bamboos can be grown in containers, but in the larger-growing varieties, the leaves tend to turn brown unless kept moist and out of strong winds until well established. Bamboos flower occasionally, which usually results in the flowering culms dying. These canes can be harvested and used in the garden, and usually some young growth will sprout from the base. Many bamboos have had confusing name changes in the last few years, *Arundinaria* being split into numerous new genera (for example, *Arundinaria japonica* is now *Pseudosasa japonica*) and several varieties being sold under two or more names. There are hundreds of varieties; only the most commonly offered and reliable are listed below.

Clumping bamboos

Phyllostachys H4–5 (3–6m x 3–6m) These Chinese species are the hardiest and best of the larger bamboos for Scotland, but they need some wind shelter to establish well, and tend to look ragged in very exposed sites until the roots run into deep soil. They are slow-spreading and therefore relatively expensive to buy. Remove old canes (which are useful for staking) from time to time to encourage vigorous new ones. ***P. aurea H5*** (4–6m x 1.5m) striking yellow-brown culms. ***P. aureosulcata H5*** (5m x 2.5m) yellow-green culms, one of the hardiest of all bamboos, said to take -25°C, so a good choice for cold, inland gardens, along with the spectacular and equally hardy ***P. vivax f. aureocaulis H5*** (5–6m x 1.5m) pale green canes and a high foliage canopy. ***P. nigra H5*** (3–5m x 1.5m) green culms which age to a striking black colour – do not allow to dry out.

Fargesia These are tougher, faster growing and therefore cheaper to buy, though the culm colours are less striking. ***F. murieliae H5*** forming clumps 1–2+m wide, pale-green culms; there are several named selections: **'Bimbo'** (1m) the smallest selection, ideal for the front of a border or a container, **'Jumbo'** the largest form (3m+) with larger than normal leaves, **'Simba'** (to 1.5m) good for a small garden or container, with yellow-green culms. ***F. nitida H5*** (3–4m x 1–2m) unusual graceful leaves and green, purple-tinged culms. ***F. rufa H5*** (1–2m x 1m) said to be the hardiest, pink new growth and pale-green culms, suitable for hedging or containers.

Pleioblastus viridistriatus

Fargesia nitida

Phyllostachys aureosulcata

Phyllostachys vivax f. aureocaulis

Pleioblastus auricomus

Sasa veitchii 'Nana'

Running bamboos

Beware: the rampant ones can take over your garden.

Pleioblastus H4–5 These have running rhizomes and some varieties can be very invasive. You may be able to keep them under control with barriers of heavy-duty polythene in the soil, but they can even root through tarmac, so this is not a foolproof solution. *P. auricomus H4* (1.5m x 1.5m) seldom invasive, pale green with yellow stripes; in colder climates, cut down the culms to the ground in late winter. *P. chino H4* (2–3m) green leaves; *P.c.* f. *elegantissimus* (1.2m) attractive narrow white stripes on the leaves. *P. humilis H5* (1.5m x 2–4m) dark-green canes, tends to be very invasive. *P. pygmaeus H4–5* (30cm x 1m+) the smallest bamboo, tiny blue-green leaves, can be vigorous and invasive but easy to dig up, best hard pruned in late winter, good in containers. *P. variegatus H5* (1m x 2–3m) invasive with spiky blue-green, white-striped leaves, good for containers; 'Tsuboi' (2m x 2m) pale-green leaves, leaves suffused cream, very vigorous. *P. viridistriatus H5* (60cm–1m x 2m+) young growth striped bright yellow and green, later dark and light green, culms purple-green.

Pseudosasa japonica H4 (2–4m x 2–3m+) Vigorous, large leaves to 25cm long, green-brown culms, rampant; 'Tsutsumiana' a form with curious bulges on the stems. *Sasa palmata H5* (3m x 3m+) Green leaves with yellow midribs, rampant and hard to eradicate, one of the toughest, suitable for cold inland gardens; the form *nebulosa* large leaves, culms with whitish markings. *S. veitchii H5* (1.5m x indefinite spread) develops white leaf stripes in autumn, good winter-leaf retention; culms purple-tinged, invasive and good for stabilizing banks, as at Rouken Glen Park, south Glasgow.

Yushania anceps H2–3 (3–4m) A vigorous, spreading clump-former that behaves like a runner, only reliably hardy on the west coast, with an attractive arching habit and narrow leaves.

Berberis (barberry)

This is a really useful genus of colourful, tough and versatile plants, most of which are prickly or spiny, good for security and for discouraging people and animals from taking short cuts. There are good evergreen and deciduous varieties, many of them useful for hedging, ranging in height from 60cm to 3m or more. All have cup-shaped yellow-to-orange flowers in late spring. Most produce attractive reddish or black berries in autumn which usually persist until winter. Though most berberis grow best in full sun, some of the larger varieties make good woodland plants, and most are easy to please as long as soil is not too heavy or waterlogged. Height and spread are similar unless stated otherwise.

Deciduous berberis

H5 (unless stated otherwise) The most popular varieties are those with red-purple leaves, most of which turn a fiery orange-red in

Berberis x *ottawensis* 'Superba'

Berberis temolaica, B. thunbergii 'Aurea', *B.* x *ottawensis* 'Superba'

Berberis x *stenophylla*

autumn. Most are very tough. *B.* x *ottawensis* 'Superba' (to 1.5–2.5m) vigorous, upright habit with arching branches, red-purple leaves and hanging flowers. *B. thunbergii* (Japanese barberry) *H4* includes a wide range of bushy cultivars: 'Admiration' (60cm) new, purple-red leaves edged yellow, 'Atropurpurea Nana' (60cm) red-purple leaves, can be used as a low hedge, 'Aurea' slower but larger growing, yellow young growth fades to pale green, suffers occasional sunburn, 'Maria' said to be an improvement. 'Bagatelle' (30cm) very dwarf, red leaves, 'Golden Ring' (1–1.5m) upright habit, showy deep purple-red leaves marked gold around the edge, stronger colour in sun, 'Harlequin' (1m) leaves red with pink and white mottling, 'Helmund Pillar' (1.5m x 60cm) a narrow column, dark red-purple foliage, 'Pink Queen' (1.5m) red-purple leaves flecked with pink, grey and white, 'Red Pillar' erect to 1.5m, reddish purple, 'Rose Glow' (to 1.5m) ❦ young leaves purple with white and pink marbling. *B. wilsoniae H4* compact and spreading to 1m, semi-evergreen, with the narrow pointed leaves turning purple in autumn. One of finest, but rarely offered, is the striking grey-blue-leaved *B. temolaica H4–5* (2m), which is usually grafted and needs to have rootstock suckers removed.

Evergreen berberis

B. darwinii H4 (1.5–2m) ❦ a dense grower, often used for hedging, bright orange-yellow flowers and fine blue-black berries; 'Compacta' (1.5m) yellow flowers, black fruit. *B.* x *frikartii* 'Amstelveen' *H4* (50cm–1m x 1m) yellow flowers, glossy dark-green leaves with glaucous undersides. *B. linearifolia* 'Orange King' *H4* (1–1.5m) lance-shaped leaves, upright apricot flowers, bluish fruit. *B.* x *lologensis* 'Apricot Queen' *H4* (4m) arching branches, orange flowers, blue-black fruit. *B.* x *media* 'Parkjuweel' (80cm) semi-evergreen dark-green leaves, red in autumn; a sport of this, 'Red Jewel' has dark bronze-red young growth. *B.* x *stenophylla H4* (1.5m–2.5m) ❦ ❀ scented bright yellow flowers, blue-black fruit, on an arching, spreading plant,

Brachyglottis greyi

good for hedging and screening (plant 60cm apart); **'Irwinnii'** (1m) is a compact form. *B. verruculosa* (1.5m) compact, arching habit, dark-green leaves, yellow flowers, black fruit.

Brachyglottis (formerly *Senecio*)

H3(–4) These sun-loving New Zealand evergreen shrubs with yellow daisy-like flowers in mid-summer are planted in huge numbers, but beware: they are not reliably hardy in colder parts of Scotland. A large planting of them at the Beechgrove Garden, west of Aberdeen, was killed stone dead by a recent cold winter. They are ideal seaside plants as they are wind and drought/sandy soil tolerant, and they are some of the best evergreens for the Western Isles, Shetland and Orkney. The oval leaves are greyish above and white felted below, forming dense compact mounds up to 2m x 1.5m+. All can benefit from a haircut after flowering to keep them compact.

B. compacta H3 (1m) leaves edged silver. *B. greyi* usually sold as the form **'Sunshine'** *H3–(4)* (1m) silvery-white leaves on the upper and lower surface, the hardiest. Other varieties such as *B. repanda H2* have large handsome leaves but are less hardy and really only suitable for mild west-coast gardens.

Buddleja (syn. *Buddleia*) (butterfly bush)

There are over 100 species of this well-known plant, named after the Reverend Buddle, a seventeenth-century amateur botanist from Essex, and many of them make excellent garden plants. Most are vigorous deciduous shrubs with arching branches and mostly fragrant flowers in late summer. Many of them are attractive to insects, especially butterflies, and all enjoy well-drained soil in plenty of sun. They are best pruned after flowering, apart from *B. davidii* cultivars, which are usually left until winter.

B. davidii H5 ❀ By far the most popular species, a fast-growing vigorous shrub with dense panicles of purple, blue, red, pink or white flowers. Very tough and drought tolerant. The vigorous forms can reach 3–5m x 3–5m, though they are best hard pruned each spring. They are promiscuous seeders and can be a menace in wall crevices and gutters, and are often seen naturalized on railway embankments and canal sides. There are many named varieties (most are good). Some of the most widely grown include **'Black Knight'** (1.8m x 1.5m) ♛ deep violet-purple, one of the hardiest, **'Empire Blue'** (2.5m x 1.5m) ♛ smallish flowers of violet-blue with orange centres, **'Harlequin'** (3m x 4m) reddish

Buddleja alternifolia

Buddleja davidii 'Nanho Blue', 'Pink Delight' and 'White Bouquet'

Buddleja x *weyeriana* 'Sungold'

purple, leaves variegated but prone to reversion, **'Leela Kapila'** (1.2m x 1.2m) cerise-red, leaves golden, **'Pink Delight'** (2m x 2m) bright pink with orange centres, **'Royal Red'** (2m x 1.5m) ♛ deep purple-red, **'White Bouquet'** (1.5m x 1.5m) compact, white with a yellow eye, **'White Profusion'** (3m x 2m) ♛ white with orange centres. A range of slower and slightly lower-growing forms (derived from var. *nanhoensis*) have come on

to the market. **Nanho** series, **Buzz** series and **Pixie** series, various colour forms, all reaching 1.2–1.5m. *B. alternifolia H5* (2–3m x 2–3m) with intensely fragrant lilac flowers in late spring should be far more widely grown. The weeping habit and fine foliage make this a good specimen shrub, particularly in the form **'Argentea'** with silky, silvery leaves. Pruning annually after flowers go over encourages a good display the following year and a tidy habit. *B. globosa H4* (3–5m x 3–5m) ❀ from South America, very vigorous with ball-like honey-scented orange-yellow flowers in summer, but unfortunately it hangs on to its brown dead flowers. **'Lochinch'** *H4* (2.5m x 2m) ♛ greyish-leaved, fragrant violet-blue flowers with orange eyes. A hybrid of *B. globosa*, *B. x weyeriana H5* (3m x 2.5m) has some attractive fragrant yellow forms: **'Golden Glow'** and **'Sungold'** #, both golden yellow, **'Honeycomb'** two-toned yellow. **'Pink Pagoda'** [PBR] pink, attractive.

Many of the other garden-worthy species and varieties are more tender, best suited to mild and coastal gardens, against a warm wall. One of the best is **B. colvilei H2–3** (3–5m) relatively large pink or reddish flowers in June–July, considered a west-coast plant where it thrives, but also does well in a sheltered site at the Cruickshank Botanic Garden, Aberdeen, and the walled garden at Logie Estate, near Forres in Morayshire, with occasional winter dieback. It does not need regular pruning.

Buxus (box)

H5 These popular neat dense evergreen shrubs with neat shiny leaves and tiny yellow flowers have been grown in British gardens for hundreds of years, often used for formal hedges, parterres and topiary. It has to be said that Scottish weather is not always kind to box and it can suffer from snow breakage, fungal dieback (box blight), winter wet and wind burn, though most of the parterres we have

Buxus microphylla parterre, Carestown Steading

Buxus sempervirens 'Gold Tip'

examples in Scotland, at well over 2m x 2m in diameter, though they do need to be wired to prevent snow breakage. For hedging, plant 20–30cm apart.

Most garden box are forms of two species. **B. microphylla H5** (50–75cm x 60cm–1.5m) the form used for low parterre and border hedging, dark-green leaves turn bronze in winter. **B. sempervirens** (common box) **H5** (to 1m in 5 years) This British native can be used as a tree, reaching 9m if unpruned, and is also ideal for topiary and larger hedges; compact forms include **'Marginata'** (1.5m–2.5m) yellow-margined leaves, **'Elegantissima'** (to 1.5m) leaves with white margins, **'Gold Tip'** leaves often tipped yellow, **'Suffruticosa'** (1m) one of the slowest growing, said to be the most susceptible to blight.

seen lately seem to be doing OK. Box blight is said to be worse if water and snow are allowed to sit the flat top of the hedge, so cutting at an angle or leaving an apex should help. Box blight disfigures (brown or dead patches) or defoliates the plants, and can be controlled (but not eradicated) with fungicides such as *myclobutanil* and *penconazole*. Grow box in fertile, well-drained soil, in sun or part shade, in a sheltered spot. It does well in coastal gardens. Box should be trimmed to shape in summer, and cut back hard in spring if rejuvenation is required. The giant box balls at Balcarres in Fife are some of the most impressive

Callicarpa bodinieri

Callicarpa bodinieri

H4–5 (2–3m x 2.5m) The striking purple berries of this curious plant rarely fail to attract comment in autumn, and the commonly offered forms should be hardy in all but the very coldest gardens. It is deciduous; the unremarkable leaves turn yellow and fall, leaving the stark purple fruit clustered on the tips of the bare branches. You probably wouldn't notice the small purple flowers. Plant in well-drained soil in sun or part shade; best berrying will be after hot summers. No pruning is required, but it can be tidied up in late winter or early spring.

'Profusion' is the commonest clone, with bronze young growth. It is the best choice as it sets berries without a pollinator. Other varieties are best planted with another clone to obtain good fruit set.

Callistemon (bottle brush)

These distinctive sun-loving Australian evergreen shrubs have bottlebrush-

Callistemon rigidus (RC-M)

like spikes of flowers. They can be very showy and the leathery leaves are also attractive. They enjoy well-drained acid soil in full sun and are excellent in west-coast gardens and sheltered spots elsewhere. Logan, in Galloway, has a fine collection. The hardier species do well on the east coast and may even be worth trying in a sheltered site inland – on a south wall, for example. There is a fine specimen of *C. subulatus* at Hill of Tarvit, near Cupar in Fife.

C. citrinus H2 (2–4m x 2–3m) crimson, usually sold as the clone 'Splendens' with pinky-red young shoots. *C. linearis H2–3* (2–4m x 2–3m) red flowers in late summer and autumn, narrow leaves. *C. rigidus H3–4* (1–2m x 1–2m) said to be one of the toughest. Silky red bottle-brushes in summer. *C. salignus H3* (3–5m x 3–5m) green, pale yellow or white flowers and grey-green leaves. *C. subulatus H3–4* (1–1.5m x 1.5m) the hardiest species, bright red.

Calluna see Heathers, page 55

Camellia

H4(5) (2–3m x 2–3m) These large, stately evergreen shrubs, with glossy dark green leaves, produce sumptuous rose-like blooms in early spring. The flowers are single, double or semi-double, in shades of red, pink or white. The secret of success is to provide well-drained but moist acid soil and a sheltered, sunny site. Avoid an easterly aspect when planting, as early-morning sun can spoil the opening flowers. There are hundreds of named camellia varieties but only a small fraction of these are suitable for Scotland, because of the lack of summer heat. Many *C. japonica* and *C. sasanqua* hybrids require warmer summer night-time temperatures than Scotland can provide in order to flower. Most of Scotland's best performers are *C. x williamsii* hybrids, which set masses of flower buds every year and, unlike *C. japonica* cultivars, have the added bonus of not hanging on to old or frosted flowers, which can look like piles of sodden brown tissue paper. At Glendoick and elsewhere in eastern Scotland in 1981 almost all camellias were frozen to the ground; the *C. x williamsii* varieties recovered and grew away well. Overall, white-flowered camellias are the most problematic – apart from the small-flowered 'Cornish Snow', most will not flower well in Scotland. Some inland Scottish gardens are just too cold for camellias. They are also a challenge north of Aberdeen away from the coast, needing a sheltered south- or west-facing wall. Plants that have been under cover or indoors will have their growth advanced in spring and should not be planted out until danger of frost has passed. Pale- or yellowy-leaved shrubs indicate low soil acidity, poor drainage or starvation. A good feed with ericaceous fertilizer may do the trick. Many garden centres and DIY chains sell mostly unsuitable japonica camellias: don't be tempted by the flower buds, as these plants will have been grown in tunnels or in warm climates and may never flower again. Worst of all are unnamed camellias sold by colour, e.g. 'Camellia Pink': these are almost always a waste of money. The following are amongst the most reliable in Scotland.

C. x williamsii hybrids and varieties derived from them: *H4*, 2–3m x 2–3m unless stated otherwise: **'Anticipation'** ❦ large, glowing rose red, peony-flowered, compact habit and one of the hardiest, **'Black Lace' H3–4** ♦ stunning double dark red, **'Brigadoon' H4–5** large semi-double pink, one of the best for Scottish conditions with some of the hardiest buds and flowers, **'Debbie'** ❦ double deep pink, **'Donation'** ❦ one of the most floriferous, semi-double, rich pink, **'Freedom Bell'** smallish semi-double brilliant red over a long period on a neat erect plant, **'Golden Spangles' H2–3** pink, leaves with a splash of yellow, poor in Scotland, **'Inspiration' H4–5** semi-double bright pink, perhaps the hardiest of the *C. x williamsii* hybrids. **'Nicky Crisp' H4** semi-double lavender pink, compact. *C. x reticulata* **'Leonard Messel' H4–5** large semi-double pink, another of the toughest. *C. japonica* hybrids (the best of many trialled at Glendoick; many of the rest are best avoided): **'Adolphe Audusson'** semi-double red, **'Clarise Carleton'** semi-double crimson, **'Mercury'** large semi-double red, **'Sylva'** single scarlet. We like the white small-flowered **'Cornish Snow'**, which flowers right along the stems every year at Glendoick, but you will need to obtain it from a specialist nursery.

Camellia 'Anticipation'

Camellia 'Brigadoon'

Camellia 'Donation'

Camellia 'Freedom Bell'

Camellias

Carpenteria californica

Caryopteris x clandonensis
'Kew Blue'

Campsis see Trachelospermum, page 106

Carpenteria californica
(tree anemone)

H3 (2–3m) ❀ Dark-green shiny leaves show off the large fragrant white flowers, to 6cm across, with a mass of yellow stamens in the centre, which open in mid-summer. It is usually grown against a south- or west-facing wall, though it is not a climber. It is evergreen and only reliably hardy in gardens not far from the coast, although worth risking in sheltered sites inland. Pruning is only required to keep it compact and remove any winter-damaged shoots.

Caryopteris x clandonensis
(bluebeard)

H3–4 (1m x 1.5m) Clusters of tiny bright- to violet-blue flowers in late summer and fine aromatic silvery-green foliage make caryopteris excellent foils for brassier border plants. The aromatic leaves have white or grey undersides and some new selections have bright yellow leaves. They need full sun and an open well-drained soil – do not overfeed, or else you'll get few flowers and long floppy shoots. Although caryopteris are offered in garden centres throughout Scotland, most varieties are only reliably hardy in milder and coastal gardens, surviving inland only through mild winters or in a very sheltered site against a south-facing wall. Although woody shrubs, they behave like herbaceous plants, dying back sometimes to ground level in winter. Prune hard in early spring. Capsid bugs can cause problems. The following are selections of the hybrid *C. x clandonensis* (as are most forms offered), *H3–4* unless stated otherwise.

'Arthur Simmonds' *H4* the hardiest, bright purplish blue, 'Dark Night' dark purple-blue, 'First Choice' large cobalt-blue flowers, 'Heavenly Blue' erect, bright blue, 'Kew Blue' dark blue, Summer Sorbet ['Dyraisey'] bright blue, leaves margined yellow, 'Worcester Gold' lavender blue, leaves golden yellow.

Cassinia leptophylla subsp. fulvida
see Olearia, page 76

Cassiope see Heathers, page 55

Ceanothus (Californian lilac)

H3–4 Blue, blue, blue – there are few more arresting sights in summer than a wall covered with a ceanothus in full flower. There are dozens of varieties, both species and hybrids, in a wide range of shades; most are blue-purple, but some are pink or white. Most are vigorous and upright, with a few compact or spreading, and the majority are evergreen or semi-evergreen. The evergreen varieties flower in June–July, the deciduous ones a little later. As they come from California, Scotland is a bit of a culture shock for them, and they are best planted on a south- or west-facing wall in very well-drained soil. Most won't stand clay or waterlogging, though the deciduous ones are more tolerant of heavy soils. Good in coastal gardens, but a struggle in the far north because of lack of heat, ceanothus grow very fast once established, and any pruning of the evergreen ones should be a light annual trim, as they don't respond well to a hard prune into old wood. Evergreen ceanothus are best considered plants with a maximum lifespan of 10–12 years, to be replaced when they get sparse and woody. Unlike most shrubs, they are best planted in April–May, rather than autumn, so that they can establish their roots in warm and drier weather. In eastern and inland gardens, a really cold winter will kill most of them, as happened in 1981. With global warming causing milder winters, you may decide that the risk is worth taking as they grow so fast. Some of the new variegated forms have proved particularly tender (but they are no loss as we think them pretty horrible). Those listed below have roughly similar heights and spreads, and are late May/June–July-flowering evergreens unless stated otherwise.

C. arboreus 'Trewithen Blue' *H2–3* (4m+) very vigorous, vivid

Ceanothus 'Gloire de Versailles'

Ceanothus 'Zanzibar'

Ceanothus 'Puget Blue'

Ceanothus thyrsiflorus var. repens

Ceratostigma willmottianum at
St Andrews Botanic Garden

C. griffithii H2–3 (1m x 1.5m)
clusters of blue flowers,
evergreen, bristly purple-edged
leaves, for mild and western
gardens. *C. plumbaginoides H4*
(45cm x 20cm) small bright-blue
flowers. *C. willmottianum H4*
(1m x 1.5m) deciduous, masses
of bright-blue flowers; forms
include **Desert Skies**
['Palmgold'] yellow leaves which
contrast strongly with the dark-
blue flowers, **Forest Blue** ['Lice']
H3 compact, rich blue, with
good red autumn colour.

blue. **'Autumnal Blue' H3–4** (3m) lavender blue in June and
sometimes again in autumn. **'Burkwoodii' H3** (1.5–2m) lavender
blue late summer into autumn, large leaves, suitable for smaller
gardens. **'Cascade' H3** (3m) powder blue. **'Concha' H3(–4)** (2m)
indigo, more tolerant of shaping and heavier soils than most.
'Dark Star' H3 (2m x 3m) small dark leaves, cobalt blue,
spreading habit, a fine foliage plant. **'Gloire de Versailles' H4**
(2m) deciduous, powder blue, in late summer, habit rather untidy
and open, but it can be pruned and will break well. **'Italian Skies'
H3** (2m x 3m) one of our favourites, deep blue, with tiny leaves.
C. x pallidus **'Marie Simon' H3–4** (1–2m) pink in summer on
young red stems, low and compact with large deciduous leaves.
'Puget Blue' H3 (1.5m x 2m) cornflower blue. **'Southmead' H3**
(2m) rich blue, handsome leaves. **'Yankee Point' H3** (1.5m x 2m)
china blue, large leaves; a sport **'Silver Surprise' H3** is less
vigorous with creamy margined leaves. **'Zanzibar'** (syn. 'Pershore
Zanzibar') **H2–3** (1.2m) mid-blue flowers, yellow variegation, shy
flowering and not very tough, does best in a sheltered site.
Compact, bushy or shrubby ceanothus are mostly forms and
hybrids of the spreading *C. thyrsiflorus* var. *repens* **H4** (1m x
2.5m) lilac blue, a good border plant and ground-cover, hardier
than most of the taller forms, flowers in May–June; the following
are named selections: **'Blue Mound' H3** (1m x 1.5m) blue, later
than most of this type, **'Blue Sapphire' H3** (1m x 1.5m) green-
black leaves, violet-blue flower, rather sparse with age, **'Skylark'
H4** and **'Victoria' H4** (both 1.5m x 2m) bluish purple (probably
the same plant), best deadheaded after flowering.

Ceratostigma (hardy plumbago)

H2–4 This late-summer-to-autumn-flowering deciduous
subshrub is a rather over-rated plant, as it is not a
reliably good performer for much of the country,
requiring a warm site in well-drained soil in full sun.
The leaves of the hardier deciduous species turn reddish
in autumn. In the right place and in a mild autumn, it
provides lots of useful late colour: there are fine
examples of *C. willmottianum* at St Andrews Botanic
Garden in Fife, the Royal Botanic Garden Edinburgh
and Cruickshank Botanic Garden in Aberdeen.

Cercidiphyllum japonicum
(katsura tree)

H5 (3–5m x 1.5–3m in 10–20 years, ultimately 10–20m x
5–10m) ⚘ It's the autumn leaves of this large shrub or tree
that are its best feature. Not only do they turn shades of

Cercidiphyllum japonicum
(autumn colour)

yellow and coral but as they
turn colour, they give off an
irresistible aroma of burned
sugar. In ideal conditions,
this can form a very large
tree, up to 15m or more,
but it is more often grown
as a smaller multi-stemmed
tree with smooth rounded
leaves. There are a huge
number of fine specimens in
gardens all over Scotland;
we keep discovering more
and more: at Duntreath and
Geilston near Glasgow, The
Royal Botanic Garden
Edinburgh, Inchmarlo and
Kildrummy, Aberdeenshire
are just some examples. It is a tough plant once
established, but for the first few years it needs protecting
from winds and drying out; it definitely prefers fertile,
deep soil. The young growth can be frosted in cold inland
gardens, but damage is unlikely to be any more than
cosmetic. There are also less vigorous weeping forms
(var. *pendula*), which attain 3–5m.

Cercis

H2 If only Scotland were hotter, these wonderful slow-
growing small trees or large bushes could be more widely
grown. They need a warm and sheltered site to ripen their
wood and they tend to suffer from frosted growth, so they
seldom flower as well as they do further south.

Cercis canadensis 'Forest Pansy'

C. canadensis 'Forest Pansy' (2–4m x 2–4m) attractive heart-shaped reddish-purple leaves, rarely flowers. *C. siliquastrum* (Judas tree) (5m x 4m) pea-like, rosy-lilac flowers on bare branches in May, small dark-green, heart-shaped leaves; Dundee Botanic Garden has fine examples, including the rare white form.

Chaenomeles
(flowering quince, japonica)

H5 (1.5–2.5m x 1.5–4m) These are some of the best and toughest early-flowering shrubs for Scottish gardens: they deliver early spring colour even in the severest climates. The plentiful and long-lasting flowers come in shades of red, orange, pink and white, and open in late winter before the leaves. The apple-like autumn fruits can be made into jelly and are used in Chinese herbal medicine. Chaenomeles form upright, spiny, usually tidy shrubs, which are self-supporting but most commonly planted against a wall or fence, and they enjoy well-drained soil, in at least part sunshine. Any pruning should be done after flowering. They are subject to canker dieback (cut back any dead stems) but they are resistant to honey fungus.

There are dozens of named varieties. The best known and most widely available include: **'Crimson and Gold'** ❦ dark red with yellow anthers, **'Geisha Girl'** low growing, peach pink, **'Jet Trail'**, white, **'Knaphill Scarlet'** ❦ bright red, **'Moerloosei'** (syn. 'Apple Blossom') white flushed dark pink, **'Nicoline'** scarlet, **'Nivalis'** white, **'Orange Beauty'** bright orange, **'Pink Lady'** ❦ very early, dark pink, **'Winter Snow'**, white.

Chaenomeles 'Geisha Girl'

Chaenomeles 'Nivalis'

Chamaerops humilis see Palms, page 78

Choisya ternata
(Mexican orange blossom)

H3 ❄ This popular evergreen with fragrant white flowers and aromatic foliage is planted in huge numbers all over Scotland, but its Mexican origins betray its lack of hardiness in exposed cold and inland gardens, where it will need a sheltered site to survive a harsh winter. Forming compact, dense bushes with aromatic leaves and small, five-petalled, sweetly scented white flowers in May–June, it is often grown in containers as well as in mixed borders, where it needs well-drained soil in full sun. It can reach up to 2.5m, but probably only in mild west-coast gardens; 1.5m x 1.5m is more realistic for eastern and northern gardens. It is generally easy and undemanding but will soon look tatty in too much wind and the gold leaved ones can suffer sunburn, though frankly that's all too rare in Scotland.

Choisya ternata Sundance and Goldfingers

Choisya ternata

C. ternata ❦ dark-green leaves; there are now several selections and hybrids: **'Aztec Pearl'** pink-tinged flowers and distinctive narrow leaves, **Goldfinger** ['Limo'] a new golden narrow-leaved form, **Sundance** ['Lich'] ❦ bright-yellow young foliage produced all year round, but rarely flowers. **White Dazzler** ['Londaz'] narrow green leaves.

Cistus (rock rose)
and *Halimium* and x *Halimiocistus*
For other rock roses, see *Helianthemum*, page 60

H3–4 Considering the hot, dry, stony conditions that this group of plants enjoy in their native Mediterranean habitat, it is amazing how well they grow in Scotland. The saucer-shaped pink or white flowers last only one day but they are produced over several weeks in early summer. The foliage has a distinctive aroma which might remind you of your holidays. Cistus require well-drained soil in full sun and are good in raised beds, under the eaves of houses, in sandy, seaside gardens and in sun-baked containers. They prefer poor, open, well-drained soil; the best planting medium is garden soil with extra grit. They hate rich, peaty or heavy clay soils, and may not survive a cold wet winter. They also tend to be short lived and become rather ungainly as they get old and woody, but they grow fast and put on a good show even in their first year, so they are worth trying in most areas. Plant them from early summer to early autumn, not in winter. Rain can shatter the flowers, but new ones will open the following day. There are about 20 species and many hybrids and selections, mostly with an *H3* hardiness rating and growing to 60cm–1m x 60cm–1m unless stated otherwise.

C. x *aguilarii* **'Maculatus'** large white flowers with red and yellow centres, rich-green leaves. *C.* x *argenteus* **'Peggy Sammons'** free flowering, pale pink, grey-green leaves; *C.* x *a.* **'Silver Pink'** pink flowers with yellow stamens, but what is sold under this name is often 'Grayswood Pink'. *C.* x *dansereaui* (syn. *C. lusitanicus*) **'Decumbens'** *H3–4* white flowers with red central spots and a low, spreading habit. **'Grayswood Pink'** *H3–4* low and compact with small grey-green leaves and pale-pink flowers; one of the hardiest, so the best choice for colder gardens. *C.* x *florentinus* (1m x 1.5m) white flowers with yellow centre, grey-green leaves. *C.* x *hybridus* (syn. *C. corbariensis*) (1m x 1.5m) red buds that open to white flowers with yellow centres, and crinkled leaves; **Gold Prize** ['Wyecis'] golden-yellow leaves, white flowers, shy flowering. *C.* x *pulverulentus* **'Sunset'** magenta-pink. *C.* x *purpureus* dark-pink flowers with maroon spots.

Halimium H3 This is a closely related genus of similar hardiness which enjoy similar growing conditions. They make fine coastal plants, happiest in hot sunny gardens. The flowers are yellow or white, usually with a darker eye. *H. calycinum* (syn. *H. commutatum*) (60cm x 60cm) yellow flowers and an upright habit. *H. lasianthum* (1m x 1.5m) golden-yellow flowers, sometimes red centred, spreading bushy habit. *H.* **'Susan'** (50cm x 60cm) yellow with red purple centres. *H. ocymoides* (60cm x 1m) golden-yellow flowers with black-purple centres, the leaves silvery white.

x *Halimiocistus* Natural or man-made hybrids between the two genera above have made successful garden plants, usually a little hardier then the parent species. They form spreading mats and flower over long periods, making them ideal for border edges and rock gardens. **'Ingwersenii'** *H3–4* (50cm x 1.5m+) saucer-shaped white flowers, May–June. **x *H. sahucii* H4** (45cm) white flowers in mid-summer, lance-shaped leaves and a mounding or spreading habit, probably the hardiest of all. The flowers of **x *H. wintonensis* H3** (60cm x 75cm) are white with yellow stamens and a maroon band round the centre, and those of its sport **'Merrist Wood Cream'** *H3* creamy yellow with yellow centres, bordered by a red-purple band.

Clematis (climber)

Some of the most popular of all garden plants, and by far the best-selling climbers, the genus contains more than 200 species and hundreds of named hybrids. Most are deciduous, apart from a group of early-flowering evergreens, and most but not all the climbers can self-cling by tendrils to trellis and other framework. Though most commonly seen on walls, clematis are also excellent subjects for climbing through other shrubs and trees and on pergolas and arbours. The flowers consist of usually four to seven tepals surrounding a mass of stamens, often of a different colour. Clematis are fairly trouble-free plants. The main problems are weather damage from late frosts, and clematis wilt, where all or part of the young growth collapses. This particularly affects the large-flowered early-summer hybrids. Plants often recover from wilt, growing again from the base, but newly planted clematis are inclined to collapse and die. This fungal disease is best avoided by taking preventative measures: thorough soil preparation, ensuring good drainage and fertilizer, and planting deeply so that the top of the rootball is at least 10cm below the soil surface. While many books claim that clematis can be grown on north-facing walls, in Scotland they won't flower well if they don't get sun for at least part of the day. We are very grateful for advice for this section from the world's leading clematis breeder, Raymond Evison, from

Cistus x *corbariensis*

Cistus x *pulverulentus* 'Sunset'

Halimium calycinum

Halimium 'Susan'

Guernsey, who bred around half the cultivars covered below. We also recommend the excellent clematis website www.clematis.hull.ac.uk, which describes some 3,500 clematis varieties. To aid selection, we have divided the clematis into several groups.

Evergreen species and varieties

H3 These are now quite commonly offered in Scottish garden centres, but you need to be aware that they are some of the least hardy, so do best in coastal and milder gardens. The usually white or cream late-winter and early-spring flowers are often scented, and in the right conditions they are spectacular. No pruning is required. *C. armandii H3* (3–8m) ❀ vanilla or almond-scented white flowers; a fine form is **'Apple Blossom'** ❀ pink buds, opening to white, fragrant. *C. x cartmanii* **'Joe'** *H2–3* (1.5–2m) profuse small white flowers in spring, ferny foliage, raised by Henry and Margaret Taylor in Dundee. Similar are **Avalanche** ['Blaaval'] *H2–3* creamy white, requires a sheltered, warm site. **'Early Sensation'** *H3* small, pure white with green stamens. **Michiko** ['Evipo044'] white, very free flowering. **'Pixie'** (1m) ❀ scented, white, dwarf habit. *C. cirrhosa H3* (3–6m) ❀ citrus-scented cream bells, spotted red inside; *C.c.* **var.** *purpurascens* **'Freckles'** cream outside, heavily red-purple speckled inside, and **'Jingle Bells'** (4–5m) creamy white with yellow stamens.

Early-flowering deciduous

H5 The species and cultivars in this group are much tougher than their delicate and subtle flowers suggest, standing up to wind, salt spray, lack of summer heat and very low temperatures, so they can be grown all over Scotland as far north as Shetland. The flowers are bell shaped, blue, violet to pale pink and white, opening in spring, with the *C. alpina* group opening earlier (March–May) than the *C. macropetala* group (May–June). Both display attractive fluffy seed heads when flowers have passed. No pruning is required, but you can reduce the size (2–4m unless stated otherwise) after flowering if needed.

C. alpina H5 blue flowers with white centres; named selections and hybrids include **'Constance'** semi-double, deep purplish pink, **'Frances Rivis'** deep blue, with white-violet centres, **'Frankie'** mauve-blue with cream stamens, **'Jaqueline du Pré'** rosy mauve and white, **'Jan Lindmark'** mauve and pale purple, **'Markham's Pink'** pinky mauve to pink, **'Pamela Jackman'** deep blue with blue and cream anthers, **'Pauline'** semi-double pale blue, **'Pink Flamingo'** semi-double pink, **'Ruby'** purple-pink and cream, tinged red, not as good as 'Constance', **'Snowbird'** double white, tinged green, curved petals, **'White Swan'** large white and cream, compact, **'Willy'** early, pale pink, **'Stolwijk Gold'** said to be the first golden-leaved clematis – the leaves look a bit starved, so we are not sure it will catch on. **'Blue Eclipse'** (3m) a hybrid of *C. koreana* with fine purple and white flowers, vigorous. *C. macropetala H5* (2m) blue or violet-blue, hanging, appearing semi-double, with overlapping sepals; the form **'Maidwell Hall'** deep blue, often misnamed/confused with **'Lagoon'** which is very similar.

Montana

H4–5 These stunning spring beauties can easily turn into thugs if you don't have enough room for them. Equally, they are excellent for growing into trees and covering unsightly outbuildings: they are so vigorous that they could even be trained up the Forth Bridges to cheer up rail travellers and motorists. But don't be put off, because they won't grow beyond whatever tree, fence or trellis they are climbing, and they are a must for a spectacular

Clematis armandii 'Apple Blossom'

Clematis 'Early Sensation'

Clematis alpina, pink form

Clematis macropetala 'Jan Lindmark'

Clematis montana 'Warwickshire Rose', 'Freda' and var. *rubens*

Clematis montana 'Elizabeth'

Plants for exposed coastal gardens: wind and salt spray

In exposed coastal positions, plants may well need protection in first few years so that they can establish their roots. Use artificial windbreaks and stake plants well. It is often worth planting large numbers of cheap small plants, expecting to lose some of them. Large ones are harder to establish and of course more expensive.

Trees
Acer pseudoplatanus
Alnus
Betula pendula,
    B. lutea
Cupressus macrocarpa
Eucalyptus
Fraxinus excelsior
Nothofagus
Pinus mugo,
    P. muricata,
    P. nigra, P. radiata,
    P. sylvestris
Quercus ilex,
    Q. robur
Salix alba, S. caprea, S.
    hookeriana,
    S. pentandra

Sorbus aucuparia,
    S. aria

Shrubs
Arbutus unedo
Azaleas (deciduous)
Berberis (most
    varieties, but avoid
    yellow-leaved forms)
Brachyglottis (Senecio)
    'Sunshine'
Buddleja globosa,
    B. davidii
Cistus
Cordyline australis
Cytisus
Elaeagnus
Erica carnea

Escallonia
Fuchsia magellanica,
    'Versicolor', 'Mrs
    Popple'
Griselinia
Hebe
Hippophae rhamnoides
Hydrangea
    macrophylla/hortensia
Laurus nobilis
Lavandula 'Hidcote'
Leptospermum
    scoparium
Lupinus arboreus
Olearia haastii,
    O. macrodonta,
    O. solandri, O.
    traversii
Phormium
Pittosporum
Rosa rugosa,
    R. canina
Rosmarinus
Spartium junceum
Ulex
Viburnum tinus

Perennials
Agapanthus

Anchusa 'Loddon
    Royalist'
Armeria
Artemisia 'Lambrook
    Silver'
Centranthus
Crambe maritima
Dianthus
Eryngium
Euphorbia characias, E.
    wulfenii, E.
    myrsinites
Iberis
Limonium
Osteospermum
Primula veris
Pulsatilla
Romneya coulteri
Sedum
Viola odorata
Primula veris

Bulbs
Crocus
Galtonia
Narcissus
Nerine
Scilla
Zantedeschia

Plants for basement gardens below street level

Plants for basement gardens below street level Basements on the north side of buildings are the darkest and most difficult of sites. We observed all the following doing well in less than ideal conditions in Edinburgh basement gardens.

Shrubs and trees
Aucuba
Camellia williamsii
Clematis, including *C.*
    montana and *C.*
    orientalis
Cordyline
Dicksonia antarctica
    (tree ferns)
Fatsia japonica
Grasses

Hebe
Hedera
Ilex
Jasminium (clinging to
    banister railings)
Kerria japonica
Laurus noblis
Mahonia
Pieris
Skimmia
Trachycarpus fortunei

show in May and June, with four-petalled, flat-faced, often scented flowers in shades of pink and white, with yellow stamens. Typically 3–5m in height, they can reach 10m+, and the heavy framework or jungle of branches and foliage can cause a fence or trellis collapse. We find that the double-flowered varieties are less vigorous and more manageable. They are tough, but you can lose a year's flowers to a late frost. When you need to prune, do so immediately after flowering, as montanas flower on the previous season's wood, so if you hack them back in autumn or winter, you will chop the flower buds off. They are tolerant of some salt spray, so can be grown by the sea, and they do well as far north as Shetland.

C. montana is usually white flowered in the wild, but most garden selections are in shades of pink: **'Broughton Star'** double, two-toned pink, not too vigorous, **'Elizabeth'** ❀ pale pink, chocolate scented, **'Freda'** two-toned pink, less vigorous than most, so a good choice for the smaller garden, **'Giant Star'** very large pale-pink flowers, var. *grandiflora* large-flowered white, **'Marjorie'** semi-double creamy pink with pink stamens, **'Mayleen'** ❀ scented pinky mauve, **'Pink Perfection'** pale pink with cream stamens, var. *rubens* pale violet-pink, some scent, the hardiest, var. *rubens* **'Tetrarose'** deep pink, with a spicy scent, not all that vigorous, with bronze-green leaves, so a good smaller garden choice, var. *wilsonii* white, the latest to flower, in June–July, with narrow sepals giving the effect of a white cross, sweet scent, **'Warwickshire Rose'** rich pink with chocolate fragrance, bronzy foliage, recommended.

Early-summer Large-flowered
H4–5 This group, and the late-summer large-flowered group below, contains most of the spectacular single and double large-flowered hybrids. The main differences between the two groups are that the early-summer group (flowering late May–June/July) require little or no pruning and are the most susceptible to wilt (see above). There are now far too many named hybrids, many of which simply duplicate one another, and some of which are just a renaming of existing varieties. Most of the ones here are tried and tested, rather than brand new, and reach 2–3m unless stated otherwise.

Alabast ['Poulala'] large double cream with yellow anthers, producing single blooms later in the summer. **Arctic Queen** ['Evitwo'] double white. **'Barbara Jackman'** deep purple with a crimson stripe and white stamens. **'Bees' Jubilee'** mauve-pink with broad carmine stripes and maroon stamens. **Bourbon** ['Evipo018'] red with a yellow centre. **'Candy Stripe'** pale lilac pink with deep rose stripes. **'Daniel Deronda'** single violet-blue, with paler middle stripe and cream stamens. **'Doctor Ruppel'** bright pink with deeper centre stripe and golden stamens. **'Duchess of Edinburgh'** double white. **'Elsa Späth'** lavender with reddish-purple stamens. **Franziska Maria** ['Evipo008'] large double mauve with white stamens. **'General Sikorski'** mid-blue with yellow stamens, vigorous. **'Guernsey Cream'** cream with a pale-green stripe. **Guiding Promise** ['Evipo053'] purple, very free-flowering. **H.F.**

Clematis 'Alabast'

Clematis 'Bourbon' (patio)

Clematis 'Doctor Ruppel'

Clematis 'Guernsey Cream'

Clematis 'Josephine'

Clematis 'Nelly Moser'

Clematis 'Niobe'

Clematis 'Cezanne'

Young' pale blue. **Hyde Hall** ['Evipo009'] white with pink anthers. **Josephine** ['Evijohill'] early double flowers are greenish, later pink lilac. **Kingfisher** ['Evipo037'] intense mauve-blue. **'Lasurstern'** rich mauve-blue with yellow stamens, sometimes flowers again in late summer. **'Marie Boisselot'** huge white with a yellow centre. **'Miss Bateman'** white with reddish-brown stamens. **'Multi Blue'** double violet-blue. **'Nelly Moser'** mauve-pink, striped carmine, fading to near white with pink stripes, very popular and a good choice as it has some resistance to wilt. **'Niobe'** one of our favourites with very rich velvety red-purple flowers with a long flowering season. **Ooh La La** ['Eviop41'] pink with dark stripes, **Rebecca** ['Evipo16'] the reddest of all, stunning. **Rosemoor** ['Evipo002'] reddish purple. **'Sunset'** mauve-purple and red. **'The President'** deep purple with reddish-purple stamens, long flowering season. **Versailles** ['Evipo 025'] (1–2m) single violet with a darker bar and red stamens. **'Vyvyan Pennell'** blue, violet and purple, semi-double, not recommended, susceptible to wilt. **'Warszawska Nike'** (syn. 'Warsaw Nike') rich purple.

A range of early-summer (**H4–5**) Patio Clematis (The Boulevard™ Evison™ / Poulson® Collection) has recently been launched. They have a long flowering period and are suitable for containers or small spaces (1m tall). **Angelique** ['Evipo017'] pale lilac blue, **Cezanne** ['Evipo023'] (1m) sky blue, **Chantilly** ['Evipo021'] very pale pink with a darker stripe, **Parisienne** ['Evipo019'] mauve, **Picardy** ['Evipo024'] plum.

Late-summer Large-flowered
H4–5 These large-flowered varieties bloom in mid-summer to autumn; most are vigorous growers and easy to please, and usually resistant to wilt. Most will reach 2–4m or more in height and spread 1–3m. These clematis benefit from hard pruning in winter as it encourages vigorous growth and good flowers for the following year.

'Andromeda' cream with pink stripe. **'Blue Angel'** (syn. 'Blekitny Anoil') pale blue. **'Cardinal Wyszyński'** (syn. 'Kardynal W.') large crimson flowers with brown stamens. **Cassis** ['Evipo020'] striking semi-double mauve and plum red, semi-evergreen. **'Comtesse de Bouchaud'** a popular variety with pink flowers and yellow stamens. **Crystal Fountain** [syn.'Fairy Blue', 'Evipo38'] striking semi-double, subtle lilac blue. **'Ernest Markham'** large purple-red, stamens beige, somewhat shy flowering in Scotland. *C. florida H3* white with deeper stamens, borderline hardy in inland gardens and needing a sheltered site, usually sold in named selections: **'Alba Plena'** large-flowered white, **'Sieboldii'** (syn. *C.f.* var. *sieboldiana*) very attractive double cream with maroon stamens, not the most vigorous, **Viennetta** ['Evipo006'] (*H3–4?*) creamy white with mass of purple petalloid stamens, looks like a passion flower. **'Hagley Hybrid'** a dependable, disease-resistant and popular variety, pink with brown stamens, although can bleach in strong sun. **'John Huxtable'** white with yellow stamens. **'Huldine'** pure white with a purple stripe on reverse. **'Perle d'Azur'** pale violet with green stamens. **'Valge Daam'** large-flowered ghostly

Clematis 'Comtesse de Bouchaud'

Clematis florida 'Sieboldii'

Clematis 'Hagley Hybrid'

white, from Estonia. **'Ville de Lyon'** carmine-red in late summer, into October in some years, but inclined to be a little sparse.

Viticella/Jackmanii
H5 Closely related to and overlapping somewhat with the preceding group, though differing in having smaller flowers, these are first-class garden plants – perhaps the best of all clematis for Scotland. They are very easy to please, long and free flowering, disease free and weather resistant. They can reach 4–6m x 3m in size, but if you want to keep them manageable, just cut them back to near ground level each year. They are very easy to prune – just tidy them up sometime in winter or spring – and they won't even mind if you forget altogether. Although the flowers are smaller than those of the two large-flowered groups above, they more than make up for it in quantity. At Glendoick they do very well in the woodland garden, growing through rhododendrons and other shrubs, and giving late-summer colour, and they are also excellent growing through roses, fruit trees and even leylandii. These are not as widely available in garden centres as they should be, probably because they look dead in winter and early spring, and they tend to take a year or so to settle in before flowering well. Don't let them smother supporting plants too much, it is best to pull off some of the clematis every few years.

'Abundance' vivid pink-red, stamens creamy green. **'Alba Luxurians'** creamy white and green. **Avant-Garde** ['Evipo033'] red with mass of pink petalloid stamens, most unusual. **'Betty Corning'** ❀ scented, pale lavender-blue bells. **Bonanza** ['Evipo031'] mauve-blue. **Confetti** ['Evipo036'] nodding pink.

Clematis 'Etoile Violette' at Crathes

Clematis 'Madame Julia Correvon'

Clematis x durandii and
Philadelphus 'Belle Etoile'

Clematis recta

Clematis viticella
'Purpurea Plena Elegans'

Clematis texensis 'Princess Diana'

'Etoile Violette' large purple with cream stamens. **Galore** ['Evipo032'], purple with paler striping. **'Gipsy Queen'** bluish purple with dark reddish-purple stamens. **'Jackmanii'** deep purple, nodding flowers. **'Jackmanli Superba'** broader flowered, deep purple with green stamens. **'Kermesina'** deep wine-red with white basal spots (**'Rubra'** is almost identical). **'Madame Julia Correvon'** wine red with yellow stamens. **Palette** ['Evipo034'] purple fading to white. **'Polish Spirit'** deep purple-blue. **'Purpurea Plena Elegans'** double purple-red. **'Romantika'** dark purple, from Estonia. **'Rouge Cardinal'** purple red, over a long period till early autumn. **'Royal Velours'** reddish purple with reddish stamens. **Victor Hugo** ['Evipo007'] dark purple. *C. viticella* nodding deep-purple bells, usually sold in named forms listed in this section. **Wisley** ['Evipo001'] deep purple, similar to 'Jackmanii'.

Integrifolia, herbaceous and Texensis

This is a somewhat disparate group of plants, but they have in common their late-summer flowering and their non-self-clinging habit – as they lack tendrils, they need to be tied in to a framework as they grow, or left to scramble through other plants. The Integrifolia clematis are the toughest in this group, and without support will form clumps of about 1m x 1m, flowering in mid- to late summer. They have been bred from the species *C. integrifolia* , which has nodding mid-blue flowers.

'Alionushka' *H4* (2m) mauve-pink, tough. **'Arabella'** *H4* (2–3m) purple-blue, very long flowering period. *C. x durandii* and **Petit Faucon** ['Evisix'] *H3* (1.5m) striking deep long-lasting purple-blue nodding flowers; also similar is **Harlow Carr** ['Evipo004'] deep purple. *C. x eriostemon* (syn. *C. diversifolia*) **'Hendersonii'** *H4–5* (to 2m) late flowering, recurved, violet-blue. *C. heracleifolia* and *C. tubulosa* ('Wyvale') *H3* (70cm–1m x 1m) ❊ herbaceous varieties, striking, with clusters of small, scented, reflexed purple-

blue flowers in late summer, clump forming; need good drainage and will often not survive a cold or wet inland Scottish winter. *C. recta H3* (1–2m) ❊ non-climbing, small sweetly scented white flowers in late summer; **'Purpurea'** purple young growth – very fine at Kellie Castle, Fife. *C. texensis* **Group *H3*** (2–3m) striking, reflexed, deep-pink, orange-red or scarlet flowers of thick texture but rather tender in eastern and inland sites, needs shelter: **'Duchess of Albany'** pink, attractive fluted shape, Raymond Evison considers it the hardiest form, **'Princess Diana'** deep-pink fluted showstopper, **'Sir Trevor Lawrence'** reddish-purple.

Late-summer-flowering small-flowered/species
H4–5 (1–3m) Not only is this group of species useful for late-summer and autumn flowering, but also many of them have fine fluffy seed heads which last well into the winter.

Tangutica or Orientalis Group *H4–5* (3–4m) the only yellow hardy clematis, with small flowers like lanterns or bells, usually in shades of yellow, but they can be bronzy, deep purple or almost black. The taxonomy of this group is complex, and the same plants are sometimes attributed to *C. tangutica*, *C. orientalis* and *C. tibetana*. From a garden point of view, they are very similar and fill the same niche. **'Bill MacKenzie'** relatively large open yellow bells, over several weeks from July to early autumn. **Golden Tiara** ['Kugotia'] a new selection with yellow flowers and contrasting deep red stamens. **'Helios'** (1.2m) ❊ low growing with pale-yellow coconut-scented flowers, opening wide, suitable for a container. **'Lambton Park'** a large-flowered form of *C. tangutica*, yellow with some coconut fragrance, from early summer to autumn. *C. rehderiana H4* (3–5m+) ❊ cowslip-scented, single, bell-shaped, pale-yellow flowers in late summer to autumn. *C. x triternata* 'Rubromarginata' *H3–4* ❋ (4–6m) small star-like, sweetly marzipan-scented reddish-pink flowers with white centres, very long flowering, outstanding at Glendoick.

Clerodendron

H3–4 Clerodendrons have late-summer flowers and striking fruit clusters of vibrant blue seeds encased in a crimson shell. The leaves smell unpleasant when crushed.

Clematis 'Bill MacKenzie'

Clematis x triternata
'Rubromarginata'

There are only two deciduous species that are worth attempting to grow outdoors in Scotland; the rest are too tender. Keep an eye out for aphids, whitefly and red spider mite.

C. bungei H3–4 (1–2m x 1–2m) usually killed to the ground each winter, fragrant magenta-pink flowers in late summer–autumn, heart-shaped dark-green leaves, probably most suitable for mild and coastal gardens only, suckers freely and may become a nuisance; **'Pink Diamond'** (80cm x 1m) is a free-flowering low-growing form with leaves edged white. *C. trichotomum H3–4* (2.5m x 2.5m) fragrant white flowers, striking blue fruit in October–November although vulnerable to early frosts; there is a fine specimen at Falkland Palace, Fife; **var.** *fargesii* H4 (Glory Bower) (2.5m x 2.5m) bronze-purple young leaves, considered hardier.

Clerodendron bungei
'Pink Diamond'

Clethra

H3–5 A small genus of deciduous shrubs or small trees, related to the *Ericaceae* (heather and rhododendron family) and similarly enjoying acid, woodland conditions. The lily-of-the-valley-like flowers in late summer and autumn are attractive and some varieties also have spectacular bark.

Clethra alnifolia 'Pink Spice',
'Ruby Spice' and 'Hummingbird'

C. alnifolia H4 (2m x 2m) ❋ a North American suckering shrub with sweetly scented white or pink flowers in late summer, there are several named forms: 'Pink Spice' (pale pink), 'Ruby Spice' (deep pink) '16 Candles' and 'Hummingbird' (white). *C. barbinervis H4* (3m x 2m) ❋ spectacular peeling bark when mature, fragrant white flowers in late summer and autumn. *C. delavayi H3* (4m x 3m) ❋ an upright deciduous shrub with toothed and textured leaves, and racemes of fragrant white flowers in summer; a good woodland garden shrub to plant with rhododendrons.

Convolvulus cneorum

H3 (60cm x 70cm) this attractive plant is a spring staple in garden centres. It has evergreen softly hairy leaves and trumpet-shaped white flowers with a central pink stripe. It needs sharp drainage in a light dry soil, and struggles in a heavy wet one. Prune down to the ground after flowering to maintain a dense and bushy habit. Doubtfully hardy in colder inland gardens, where it may turn out to be an annual.

Convolvulus cneorum

Coprosma

H2–3 A group of tender Antipodean neat evergreen foliage plants, which are becoming more widely grown in mild west-coast gardens. The berries are colourful – both male and female plants are required for these to set – but the small greenish flowers are rarely noticed. They like full sun and a well-drained soil; they adapt to containers well and can be regularly trimmed to shape.

'Beatson's Gold' *H3* (1.5m x 1.5m) female, green leaves splashed yellow, red berries. **'Evening Glow'** *H2* (1m) green with yellow spots, turning orange in autumn. **'Fire Burst'** *H2* (1m) green and red leaves with orange margins. **'Karo Gold'** *H2* (60cm–1m) low growing, yellow leaves with a green margin. **'Kirkii Variegata'** *H3* (60cm x 1.5m) grey-green leaves with white margins on spreading shrub with red berries. **'Rainbow Surprise'** *H2* (1.5m x 1.5m) deep green with pale yellow-orange margins, turning orange in autumn. *C. repens* **'Pacific Night'** *H1–2* (1.5m x 1m) leaves very dark purple-bronze, very tender.

Coprosma 'Rainbow Surprise'

Cordyline (cabbage palm)

The common name 'cabbage palm' does not do justice to the exotic architectural form of these plants. The evergreen sword-like leaves in reddish-purple or green, sometimes variegated, grow vertically at first, gradually pointing outwards and then downwards to produce a porcupine effect of sharp points. Cordylines hail from New Zealand but are very at home in much of Scotland. On our travels we spotted mature cordylines in a surprising variety of towns and villages, from Logan and Castle Kennedy in the south-west all the way up the west coast to Sutherland. More surprising are the fine mature specimens in cold inland Angus towns such as Edzell, which have obviously survived for more than 20 years. Cordylines can easily be killed in cold winters inland, especially as young plants, generally by water inside the crown freezing. Tie leaves together for a few weeks in the coldest weather and/or wrap the trunk with sacking or straw; it may make the difference, but don't leave this on very long or else the crown or stem will rot though lack of air. Cordylines like well-drained soil in sun and can be grown especially well in containers. They can suffer from black leaf spot and rust, which leaves orange spots on the leaves: control both with fungicide.

C. australis H3–4 (2–2.5m, U: 5m) eventually forms a tree and can produce dense plumes of tiny white flowers, leaves green with a paler midrib; forms/hybrids include **'Albertii'** green with cream edges – may be the same as 'Torbay Dazzler', **'Coffee Cream'** bronzy purple with green midrib, **'Pink Champagne'** short stiff leaves variegated on the margins and flushed pink, **'Pink Stripe'** striped effect, pink with purple edges, **Purpurea Group** purple to bronze leaves, **'Red Star'** purple-red with lighter

midrib, **'Sparkler'** green with cream stripe, **'Sundance'** dark green, red at base with pink midrib, **'Torbay Dazzler'** bright green with white stripes and creamy yellow edges, **'Torbay Red'** plum red. *C. indivisa H2* less hardy with long green leaves forming a tree up to 6–10m high, suitable for mildest west-coast gardens only.

Cornus (dogwood)

A large genus of mostly deciduous shrubs grown either for their showy flowering bracts or for their coloured winter stems. The two groups are so different in appearance, effect and requirements that they are treated separately here.

Flowering dogwoods with showy bracts

These have clusters of tiny yellow flowers which are surrounded by often spectacular white, cream or pink bracts. The strawberry-like fruit add late-summer interest. The larger varieties make spectacular specimen shrubs or small trees for the woodland or sheltered garden. They like a well-drained soil in sun or part shade. There have been many new forms names in recent years, with ever larger flowers.

C. alternifolia 'Argentea' *H3* deciduous with handsome tiered branches and white variegation, small creamy flowers in June; needs heat for success. *C. canadensis* (creeping dogwood) *H5* (15cm x 30cm+) an easy and sometimes rather invasive ground-cover suitable for acid soil in sun or part shade, even in quite dry soils. *C. capitata H2–3* (5–10m+) a superb choice for west-coast gardens, as the sheets of creamy-white flowering bracts in summer can be breathtaking (there is a huge one at Torosay Castle, Mull); the hybrids (*C. capitata* x *C. kousa*) **'Norman Hadden'** and **'Porlock'** *H3–4* are hardier, bracts turn pink with age. *C. controversa H4* (table dogwood) (15m x 15m) attractive tiered branches with white flowers in early summer. Usually sold as the form **Variegata** (wedding cake tree) (1–3m, U: to 8m) leaves with white margins. A popular specimen plant, relatively expensive as it is grafted and slow growing when young. *C. florida* (6m) pink or white bracts; this does poorly in Scotland because of lack of heat, neither flowering or growing well, so is not recommended. *C. kousa H4–5* (/m x 5m) the best choice for eastern and more inland gardens, as it is the toughest species. The white bracts shade to pink as they age. The leaves can turn a showy red in autumn, but in Scotland they tend to not to colour well unless there is a dry cold autumn. The form **'Satomi'** has the pinkest bracts; *C.k.* var. *chinensis* has slightly larger leaves and a more open habit. The one member of this group without the white bracts is *C. mas H5* (3–5m x 3–5m) which produces a mass of frost-resistant yellow flowers in early spring. This should be much more widely grown as an alternative to *Hamamelis* (witch hazel – see page 55). There is also a variegated form. *C. nuttallii* (9m x 7m) has large white bracts, in May. Our experience is that this is harder to please and less long-lived than *C. kousa*. A fine hybrid between

Cordyline (cabbage tree)

Cordyline, red form

Cornus kousa at Knightshayes

Cornus kousa 'Satomi'

Cornus canadensis

Cornus alba 'Spaethii' and C. stolonifera (winter stems)

these two is **'Eddie's White Wonder'**. The white bracts are the most attractive.

Dogwoods mainly grown for their coloured stems

You might well not notice the tiny white flowers of this group of plants, which are mainly grown for their red, orange, yellow or bright green stems in winter. They will tolerate most soils, conditions and maintenance regimes – hence their frequent appearance in motorway, supermarket and municipal planting schemes. For best stem colour, cut back to near ground level from time to time, in early spring before the plants leaf up. If you have room, plant several forms with different-coloured stems. They show up well against a light or dark background, and are very effective beside water. There are also *Salix* (willow) species (see page 101) that can be used for similar effect.

C. alba H5 (2.5m x 2.5m unpruned) red winter stems, the toughest of this group, suitable for planting anywhere in Scotland, and tolerant of poor and wet soils; named forms include *C.a.* **'Aurea'** less vigorous than most, with golden leaves, **'Elegantissima'** leaves with white margins, **Ivory Halo** ['Bailhalo'] a compact version of 'Elegantissima' to 1.5m, **'Kesselringii'** reddish-purple stems and good autumn colour, **'Siberica'** bright-red stems, **'Siberica Variegata'** bright-red

stems, leaves with white margin, **'Spaethii'** green stems, not very vigorous, leaves margined yellow. *C. sanguinea H4* native to the UK, but mainly offered as the Dutch selection **'Midwinter Fire'** (syn. 'Winter Beauty') *H4* which has very showy orange-yellow to red young stems; we find this is rather susceptible to dieback, where the stem tips turn grey-brown in autumn. *C. stolonifera* (syn. *C. sericea*) *H5* (2.5m x 4m+) tough and sometimes invasive North American species with red stems. More manageable selections have yellow stems: **'Flaviramea'** bright-yellow stems, **'Kelseyi'** (75cm x 90cm) a dwarf form with red-tipped yellow stems, **'White Gold'** yellow-green stems, leaves with white variegation.

Corylopsis

H4 ❁ Related to *Hamamelis* (see page 55), this is another useful deciduous early-flowering shrub with pendent racemes of fragrant yellow flowers before the leaves unfurl in February–March. In Scotland it needs heat to ripen wood and flower well, so it does best in a warm south- or west-facing site, in a well-drained rich soil.

Corylopsis pauciflora

C. pauciflora (1.5m x 2m) is the best choice for a small garden, with pale-yellow flowers. *C. sinensis* (3–4m x 3–4m) lemon yellow, larger growing.

Corylus (hazel)

H5 Our native hazel, *C. avellana* (cobnut) ✉ is a familiar sight throughout Scotland, with its long yellow catkins in early spring and its toothed ribbed leaves, usually forming a dense, multi-branched shrub or tree to 3–6m x 3–5m. Nuts can be produced if there are male and female trees planted together, though most commercial nuts are produced from *C. maxima* (filbert). The nuts are eaten and distributed by red squirrels, woodpeckers and other animals. The common hazel is usually sold in garden centres as small hedging plants, while selected forms are pot grown to larger sizes. Hazels are fully hardy (*H5*), tolerate most reasonably drained soils in sun or part shade, and are usually trouble free. They can be coppiced (cut down to the ground) every few years to restrict their size. Remove suckers from the base of grafted forms.

C. avellana **'Aurea'** (6m x 5m) soft yellow leaves; *C.a.* **'Contorta'** (corkscrew hazel, Harry Lauder's walking stick) (4m x 4m) slow growing to 3m, with twisted branches, not to everyone's taste, but very effective with the catkins hanging from the twisted bare branches. *C. maxima H5* (6m x 3m) (filbert or commercial hazelnut) for gardens, the form **'Purpurea'** (3–5m x 2–3m) is one of the

Corylus avellana 'Contorta'   *Corylus maxima* 'Purpurea'

best purple-leaved shrubs with really dark rich-purple leaves and purple-tinged catkins and fruit; a promising new variety **'Red Majestic'** has the combination of corkscrew branches and red-purple leaves. **'Te-Terra Red'** red-purple leaves, edible nuts.

Cotinus coggygria (smoke bush)

H4 These are fine, popular foliage plants with coloured oval leaves and superb autumn colour, suitable for all but the coldest gardens, and requiring well-drained but moist soil, in at least part day sun for the best leaf colour. They produce masses of tiny white flowers in June–July, which from a distance give the effect of a haze of smoke. They are very effective shrubs to plant in mixed borders, providing structure and acting as an excellent foil for other flowers.

C. coggygria (3–5m x 3–5m) green leaves, generally free flowering; most garden forms have coloured leaves: **Golden Spirit** ['Ancot'] (2m) slow-growing with bright yellow leaves which don't burn in the sun, autumn colour is not very pronounced, seldom flowers, **'Royal Purple'** 🏆 (2–3m) relatively small wine-purple leaves which turn scarlet, **'Grace'** (3–5m) 🏆 if you have room for one cotinus, this is the best of them all, large reddish leaves which turn to a dramatic autumnal reddish orange, lasting several weeks, **'Young Lady'** (1–2m tall) a new dwarf green-leaved form that has just been released, said to be very free flowering from a young age.

Cotoneaster (climber)

This familiar tough plant is mainly grown for its red autumn berries. There are over 400 species worldwide, with a very complex taxonomy, varying from trees to creeping ground-covers. They are some of the most reliable berrying shrubs for Scotland, providing useful food for birds, and the toughest varieties will grow anywhere, flowering and berrying well in dry shade. The small white, pink-tinged flowers in spring are attractive and especially ornamental on some of the dwarf, compact forms. Many varieties such as 'Hybridus Pendulus' are top-grafted on to standard (2m) or half-standard (1–1.5m) stems, forming compact or weeping trees. It is best to rub out all swelling buds on the stems to keep a clean trunk. The stem may snap in snow or wind if the head is allowed to get too big, so thin and prune branches from time to time. Cotoneasters are one of the best choices for Scotland for formal training and for containers, as they include some of the toughest evergreens. They respond well to an occasional hard pruning if they outgrow their allocated space, but otherwise you can leave them alone. Fireblight is rare but can be fatal – if leaves blacken and shrivel, and remain clinging to the stem, cut out and burn the affected stem to at least 60cm below visible damage.

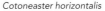

Cotoneaster horizontalis   *Cotoneaster frigidus* 'Cornubia'

Cotinus coggygria 'Golden Spirit',
'Royal Purple' and 'Grace'

Cotinus coggygria 'Grace'
(autumn colour)

Cotoneaster salicifolius
'Exburyensis'

Cotoneaster 'Hybridus Pendulus'

Deciduous varieties

C. horizontalis H5 (30–60cm x 2m+) ⚜ a spreading ground-cover and climber, probably the best-known cotoneaster with its herringbone-like branches with small glossy-green leaves which redden in autumn. The masses of white flowers are followed by small red berries. Very tough, it is ideal for north and east exposure, and will also grow in coastal sites. The variegated form (now *C. atropurpureus* 'Variegatus') *H5* has white edges to the leaves. Much larger is *C. bullatus H5* (to 3–5m x 2–3m) arching shoots and dark-green leaves which colour well in autumn, with dark-red berries, which are popular with finches, and excellent in Shetland.

Evergreen varieties (small)

There is a huge number of evergreen ground-cover cotoneasters, most of which are good garden plants. They flower and berry best in full or part day sun and will tolerate dry soils once established. They dislike frozen wet/heavy soil, especially in containers. The varieties listed below are equally tough with white flowers and red berries unless stated otherwise. Many of them can also be obtained grafted on to standard or half-standard stems, forming weeping trees.

C. congestus (70cm x 90cm) compact and slow growing, the form 'Nanus' (15cm x 50cm) even smaller. *C. conspicuus* (to 1.5m x 1m+) includes the form 'Decorus' lower growing to 30–60cm with arching stems. 'Coral Beauty' (1m x 2m) bright-orange fruit, a compact shrub often grafted as a half standard, *C. dammeri* (20cm x 2m+) ⚜ a vigorous ground-cover, spreading up to 60cm a year. 'Gnom' (30cm x 2m) prostrate, evergreen with red berries. *C. integrifolius* (45m x 1–1.5m) pink berries. *C. microphyllus* (75cm x 1–1.5m) tiny leaves. *C. procumbens* 'Queen of Carpets' (to 30cm x 1–2m), Avoid 'Skogholm' (60cm x 1–2m) as it produces few berries.

Evergreen or semi-evergreen varieties (larger)

These have attractive arching stems as they mature. Most of the larger evergreen varieties will suffer burned leaves in cold winds. *C. franchettii H5* (3m) semi-evergreen, arching branches, bright orange-red fruit. The species *C. frigidus* (tree cotoneaster) *H5* and its various forms are probably the most popular of the larger growers – they reach 2m x 2m in 5–8 years and can ultimately reach 10m x 5m; usually sold as the form 'Cornubia' ⚜ with large clusters of red berries, which performs well in Shetland. 'Hybridus Pendulus' (2–3m) evergreen or semi-evergreen, a small weeping tree, with red berries on long pendulous branches in autumn. *C. lacteus H4* (3–4m) often used as a hedging plant, with a dense habit and orange-red berries. *C. frigidus* 'Fructo-luteo' *H5* has creamy-yellow berries, as does *C. salicifolius* 'Exburyensis' *H4–5* (3–5m), while those of 'Rothschildianus' *H4–5* (3–5m) ⚜ are deeper golden yellow, and 'Pink Champagne' *H4–5* (5m) an evergreen, with arching branches, has pale yellow fruits. *C. simonsii H5* (4m) semi-evergreen, red autumn colour, orange-red fruits, good for hedging. Another fine red-berried selection is *C. x wateri* 'John Waterer' *H3–4* (5m) evergreen or semi-evergreen with large leaves, up to 10cm long.

Crinodendron hookerianum

Crinodendron
(Chilean lantern tree)

This Chilean shrub is becoming more widely grown these days with recent warmer winters, and it can be grown in a sheltered site, even in moderately cold gardens. In cold winters it may be badly damaged, but established plants will break well from the base. It likes moist but well-drained acid soil and is evergreen, so in cold gardens needs protection from a south- or west-facing wall. In the west it grows well as a stand-alone shrub.

C. hookerianum H3–4 (2–3m, U: 3–6m) ⚜ striking pendulous, lantern-like, crimson-red, bell-shaped flowers in early summer, dark-green evergreen leaves. There is a fine grove at Castle Toward, near Dunoon. It flowers best in a sunny site. 'Ada Hoffmann' has pink flowers and smaller narrower leaves, shy flowering. *C. patagua H2–3* (2–3m x 1–2m) shy-flowering, probably not worth growing in Scotland: a huge plant at Torosay on Mull rarely produces its small white flowers.

Cytisus and the broom family:
Agrocystus, *Genista* and *Spartium junceum*

⚘ Banks of native yellow broom brighten many a Scottish hillside in early summer. The vertical narrow dark-green stems form a semi-evergreen framework. Brooms do very well in poor, dry soil in full sun, dislike peaty/acid and wet soil and are best planted small, as they don't like being moved. They are a good choice if you have a rabbit or deer problem, as they are seldom touched. They can get woody and sparse with age and don't respond well to hard pruning, so are probably best considered a short-lived plant and replaced from time to time. There is now a huge range of colours to choose from, with the pea-like flowers often in two contrasting shades. Heights and spreads are similar.

C. x beanii H5 (60cm) deciduous, a good choice for the smaller garden, with bright yellow flowers, best cut back after flowering. 'Boskoop Ruby' *H5* (1.2m) deep crimson. 'Burkwoodii' *H5* (2–3m) cerise and crimson, edged yellow. 'Goldfinch' *H3* (90cm–1.2m) creamy yellow, flushed pink and red, early flowering. 'Hollandia' *H5* (1.5–2m) pale cream and cerise with darker wings, habit can be a bit untidy. 'Lena' *H5* (1.2–1.8m) ⚜ yellow, backed red, dark green leaves, upright but compact habit. *C. x praecox H5* (1.2m) pale yellow, good in Shetland; 'Alba' (syn. 'Albus', 'Multiflorus') *H5* (3m) white, 'Allgold' *H5* ⚜ dark yellow, 'Warminster' *H5* creamy yellow.

'Windlesham Ruby' *H5* (1.2–1.5m) flowers red, arching shoots. *C. scoparius* f. *adreanus* *H5* (1.5m) flowers yellow, flashed red. Very different from the above is *C. battandieri* (syn. *Agrocystus*) *H3–4* (2–4m) ⚜ ❀ from North Africa, usually grown as a wall shrub in Scotland, with silvery, silky leaves and pineapple-scented yellow flowers in June–July. Not for cold inland gardens but good near the east coast in a sheltered site, and can be grown as a free-standing shrub in the west. Fine example at Abriachan Garden on Loch Ness-side. *Chamaecytisus purpureus* (syn. *Cytisus purpureus*) *H4* (50cm) is a charming low grower with purple flowers in May; rabbits are rather partial to it.

Cytisus battandieri

Cytisus x *praecox* and
C. x *praecox* 'Alba'

Genista 'Lydia'

Genista Similar to *Cytisus* and enjoys similar conditions. The most commonly available forms are compact, and suitable for the rock garden or border.

G. hispanica *H4* (60cm x 1m) clusters of golden-yellow flowers in May–June, deciduous with tiny green leaves, spiny branches. **'Lydia'** *H4* (60cm x 1m) ⚜ pea-like, bright-yellow flowers in May and June, arching habit, tiny leaves, deciduous. *G. pilosa* 'Vancouver Gold' *H4* (60cm x 1m) deep-yellow flowers in May and June. *G. aetnensis* *H2-3* (3–5m x 2–3m) has very little in common with those listed before: it is a large rather scruffy upright shrub or small tree with narrow leaves and upright racemes of bright-yellow flowers in June–July, best grown near the sea.

Spartium junceum (Spanish broom) *H3* (1.5–2m+) ☠ Closely related to broom, this has slender green shoots forming an upright shrub, sparse if not pruned after flowering, with masses of pea-like bright yellow flowers in summer. It comes from dry areas of south Europe and is

less well suited to Scotland, requiring a well-drained sunny site. Plant and seeds are poisonous.

Daboecia see Heathers, page 55

Daphne

☠ ❀ With their attractive scented flowers, daphnes have a reputation for being difficult, but they do well in Scotland as long as you plant them in suitable soil. Don't kill them with kindness: they don't like rich, peaty soil, and nor should they be regularly fed or watered. Daphnes like poor gritty soil in full sun, and should be planted young, as they hate being moved. All parts of the plants are poisonous.

D. bholua *H3–4* (2–4m x 1.5m) ❀ if you want one daphne, this is probably it, as it is the finest scented winter-flowering shrub, with masses of pale pink-purple flowers in January–March. It is best grown against a wall or under the eaves of a house in a west or southern aspect. There are both deciduous and evergreen forms, but the pick of the bunch are the similar evergreen forms **'Glendoick'** and **Jacqueline Postill'** # and the deeper-coloured **'Sir Peter Smithers'**. *D.* x *burkwoodii* *H4* (1m x 1m) ❀ semi-evergreen with fragrant white flowers, flushed pink or purple, in late spring, and sometimes in autumn. There are several forms, some with variegated leaves; they all look sparse and scruffy in winter. *D. cneorum* *H5* (15cm x 50cm) ❀ spreading evergreen with strongly scented pink flowers; **'Eximea'** (20cm) ⚜ a vigorous form, crimson buds, deep pink flowers. *D. mezereum* *H5* (1.2m x 1.2m) the best-known and probably the toughest daphne, produces masses of deep pink (or white in f. *alba*) sweetly scented flowers in December–February on bare branches. Short-lived, and prone to virus infection where turns leaves yellow which

Daphne bholua

Daphne mezereum

Daphne tangutica

weakens or kills the plant, but birds freely spread around seeds so replacements tend to appear. *D. odora* (1.5m) ❊ relatively large leaves and white and purple-pink scented flowers in early spring. *D. tangutica* **H4** (1m x 1m) ⚜ ❊ relatively easy to grow, pink-purple scented flowers in May–June and sometimes through the summer; **D.t. Retusa Group** ⚜ more compact, to 75cm.

Decaisnea fargesii

Decaisnea fargesii

H3–4 (2–4m+ x 2–4m) This is a distinctly boring shrub until autumn, when it comes into its own with clusters of striking matt blue seed pods shaped like those of broad beans. It has long pinnate leaves and small, greenish-yellow flowers in early summer. It produces the best crop of 'beans' after a hot summer such as that of 2006. Easy to please, it likes moist soil in a fairly sheltered site.

Desfontainia spinosa

H3–4 (1–2m x 1–2m) ⚜ This South American Andes native has eye-catching red and yellow flowers and holly-like prickly leaves. Suitable for west-coast and sheltered inland and eastern gardens, although a cold winter might kill it in colder sites. The distinctive pendent tubular red flowers with yellow tips open on and off from mid-summer to autumn, seldom putting on a spectacular show, as they don't all open at once. The evergreen, spiny leaves clothe a fairly tidy plant, best grown in acid/peaty soil in sun or part shade.

Desfontainia spinosa

Deutzia

H5 (1–2m) Deutzias are an under-appreciated genus of plants, which grow very well in Scotland, and are tough, reliable and trouble free. The mass of small white, pink or purple-pink flowers open in early summer and many varieties have attractive peeling bark. Admittedly, they are bit dull when not in flower. They do best in well-drained soil in full sun or part shade, and they are suitable for hedging and screening, borders and woodland gardens. They don't need to be pruned every year, but old non-flowering wood can be cut out at the base and they can be cut back after flowering if they outgrow their space.

The taxonomy is complex and confused, but most commercially available deutzias are man-made cultivars. Those listed are fully hardy (**H5**); height and spread are roughly similar.

D. x *elegantissima* **'Rosealind'** (1.2m) pink flushed white. *D. gracilis* (1m) fragrant white flowers; includes the form **'Nikko'** (1.2m) compact with star-shaped white flowers. *D.* x *kalmiiflora* (1.5m) deep pink. **'Mont Rose'** (1.2m) purple-pink. **'Perle Rose'** (1–1.5m) purple buds, pink-white flowers. *D.* x *rosea* (90cm) white, tinged pink or red outside. **'Rosea Plena'** double pink, fading to white. **'Strawberry Fields'** (syn. 'Magicien') (1.5m) ⚜

Deutzia x *kalmiiflora*

Deutzia 'Strawberry Fields'

crimson flushed pink, one of the deepest in colour.

Dipelta see *Weigela*, page 109

Disanthus cercidifolius
see *Hamamelis*, page 55

Drimys
and *Pseudowintera colorata*

❊ These South American and Australian evergreens

Drimys winteri var. *andina*

with star-shaped small fragrant white flowers and black berries are useful plants for the Scottish west coast and islands, and mild or sheltered eastern gardens. Forming vigorous but dense and bushy shrubs, they flower in late spring and early summer, and are best planted in moist but well-drained soil in a sheltered position. Susceptible to *Phythopthora ramorum* in west coast gardens.

D. lanceolata **H2–3** (2–4m x 2m) deep-red shoots, black berries (with male and female plants); the peppery taste of the leaves discourages browsing animals. *D. winteri* **H2–3** (10m x 7m) ❊ large shiny leathery leaves, scented white flowers in summer. There are superb examples at Brodick Castle on Arran, Castle

Kennedy in Dumfries and Galloway and a fine collection in the Chilean garden at Benmore, Argyll; *D.w.* var. *andina H3–4* (30–40cm) is a slightly hardier, dwarf slow-growing form, suitable for the smaller garden, striking black or purple fruits are sometimes produced, especially if a clump of different clones is planted.

Pseudowintera colorata H2–3 (1m+ x 1m) This related plant is usually grown for its coloured and deer-resistant leaves, which are pale yellow-green, flushed pink with dark-red edges. It has small greenish-yellow flowers. For mild coastal gardens only, and does well in Shetland.

Elaeagnus pungens 'Maculata'

Elaeagnus

H3–4 These popular, tough garden plants are grown for their evergreen foliage. The white flowers mostly in late summer or autumn, are notable for their scent, not their size. The leaves are silvery on the underside, and many selections have attractive coloured variegation. Most garden centres offer a selection of *E.* x *ebbingei* and *E. pungens* cultivars, which are dense shrubs, best grown in full sun in well-drained soil. Remove reverted (green) shoots on the variegated varieties and break off suckers if plants are grafted. They are some of the main shelterbelt and buttress shrubs at Torosay Castle on Mull, and make good windbreaks for coastal gardens. What they don't like is frozen roots in waterlogged soil, especially in containers. Stem dieback and coral spot can cause problems; in both cases cut back to below any sign of infection. They reach 2–4m x 2–4m unless stated otherwise.

E. x *ebbingei H4* leaves dark green, slivery below; 'Gilt Edge' ⚜ leaves with dark green centres and yellow margins, 'Limelight' young leaves silvery, mature leaves green with paler-green and yellow centres, a new improved version of this **Gold Splash** ['Lannou'] with larger leaves and bolder variegation. *E. pungens* 'Maculata' *H4* ⚜ leaves with bold yellow splashes in the centre; 'Frederici' (1–2m) slow growing with small leaves with irregular cream patches and stripes. Less hardy, but useful for its tolerance of wind and salt spray, is *E. angustifolia* (oleaster) *H3* (4–6m) with silvery leaves and small cream flowers in summer; the form 'Quicksilver' (3–4m) is deciduous, a little less vigorous, and more bushy, with exceptionally silvery foliage.

Embothrium coccineum
(Chilean fire bush)

⚜ *H3–4* (3–7m+) If only this spectacular plant were easier to produce commercially, it would be in every Scottish

Embothrium coccineum

garden with a moderate climate. This South American beauty opens its clusters of fiery orange-red tubular flowers in late May–June and there are few sights to match a large plant in full flower. A multi-branched large shrub or tree, it grows well in the typical Scottish moist acid soil suitable for rhododendrons. There are good examples in many west-coast gardens, for instance at Kelburn Castle, Ayrshire, and Crarae in Argyll (in a windy site at the end of the drive). Its scarcity is because it resents being grown in containers and does not like to be moved. A plant definitely well worth searching out, though you may be shocked at the price.

E.c. var. *lanceolatum* with narrow leaves is said to be slightly hardier than the type; 'Inca Flame' has red flowers.

Enkianthus
and *Menziesia* and *Zenobia*

H3–5 Enkianthus is a rhododendron relative, well worth growing for both its flowers and fiery autumn colour. These fairly compact deciduous shrubs have masses of small hanging bell-shaped red, pink or white flowers in May–June. The small thin leaves colour up to fine shades of yellow, orange and red most autumns. They enjoy similar conditions to rhododendrons with moist but not wet peaty/acid soil.

Enkianthus campanulatus

E. campanulatus H5 (3–4m x 3–4m) probably the only one you'll find in a non-specialist garden centre or nursery; it can have white, creamy yellow, pink or reddish flowers. *E. chinensis H4* (4–6m x 2m) less hardy but has larger flowers. *E. deflexus H4* (3–4m x 3–4m) pink-veined cream. *E. cernuus* var. *rubens H4* (2m x 2m) slow growing with smaller leaves, flowers deep red-pink.

Menziesia ciliicalyx (now *Rhododendron cilicalyx*) *H4* (1m+ x 1m) Smaller growing than *Enkianthus*,

Zenobia pulverulenta

with similar small nodding purplish bells in May–June. Likes moist acid soil. Two fine forms are **'Ylva'** pink and **'Plum Drops'** purple.

Zenobia pulverulenta H5 (1–2m x 1–2m) ❉ A small deciduous or semi-evergreen shrub with white, aniseed-scented, bell-shaped flowers in early summer. The best forms, such as **'Misty Blue'** and **'Blue Sky'** have attractive grey-blue leaves.

Erica see Heathers, page 55

Escallonia
H3–4 (2–3m) A plant much used for hedging and windbreaks around most of Scotland's coastline, this is a versatile evergreen or semi-evergreen which can be shaped freely and which opens its masses of tiny white, pink or red flowers through long periods in summer. Pretty rather than spectacular, the hardier varieties (see below) are

Escallonia 'Apple Blossom', 'Pride of Donard' and 'Donard Seedling'

Escallonia laevis 'Gold Brian'

suitable for reasonably sheltered gardens inland in well-drained soil in full sun or light shade. For hedging, plant 50–75cm apart and clip after peak of flowering. They reach 2–3m x 2–3m unless stated otherwise.

'Apple Blossom' *H3* ♛ flowers pale pink to white in the centre and deeper pink on the outside. **'C.F. Ball'** *H4* bright red, one of the hardiest. The flowers of **'Donard Radiance'** *H3* are rich pink, **'Donard Seedling'** *H4* pink tinted white, **'Iveyi'** *H3* ♛ fragrant pure white. *E. laevis* **'Gold Brian'** (syn. 'Hopleys Gold') *H2–3* has golden-yellow young growth, pink flowers; for mild gardens only; *E.l.* **'Gold Ellen'** *H2–3* golden new growth with splashes of green variegation, bright pink flowers. **'Langleyensis'** *H3–4* bright rose pink, **'Peach Blossom'** *H3* peach pink with white centres, **'Pride of Donard'** *H3* light red. **'Red Elf'** *H3* compact, with dark-crimson flowers. *E. rubra* *H4* dark-crimson to pink; **'Crimson Spire'** deep-crimson; **var. macrantha** larger leaves, making a denser plant. *E. pulverulenta* *H2* is rarely offered commercially, white flowers, good on Mull.

Eucryphia
H3–4 These South American and Tasmanian plants are some of the most spectacular late-summer-flowering

shrubs. Evergreen, apart from *E. glutinosa*, forming vigorous, columnar, multi-stemmed large shrubs or small trees, ideally suited to acid soil and cool summers. The white flowers, sometimes with fragrance, have conspicuous yellow or orange-brown stamens, and open in July–September. Hill of Tarvit in Fife has some of Scotland's finest specimens. The more vigorous varieties grow 50cm–1m per year.

Eucryphia x *intermedia* 'Rostrevor'

E. cordifolia H3 (10m+ x 8m) the most handsome foliage, large saucer-shaped white flowers, does best on the west coast. *E. glutinosa H4* (5–10m x 5–7m) deciduous, single or double cup-shaped white flowers, the toughest and most wind-tolerant variety, not always easy to obtain. *E. x intermedia* **'Rostrevor'** *H4* (5–10m x 4–5m) smallish cup-shaped white flowers and small leaves, quite tough, good in a sheltered site on much of the east coast. *E. lucida H2–3* (3–5m+ x 2–3m) small-leaved and small-flowered, white, in June–July, best on the west coast; the clones **'Pink Cloud'** and **'Ballerina'** have small pink flowers with crimson centres; forms with variegated leaves such as **'Gilt Edge'** appear to be more tender. *E. x nymanensis H4* with shelter (10m+ x 6–7m) probably the finest choice, this handsome evergreen has large saucer-shaped flowers to 7cm across; of several forms, the best known is **'Nymansay'** ♛ but we also rate **'George Graham'**, which is slower growing and flowers younger.

Eucryphia x *nymanensis* 'Nymansay'

Euonymus
This large genus contains both evergreen creepers and deciduous trees, which, unless you take a close look at the distinctive fruits, may seem unrelated to one another. Both are useful for their ease of cultivation and toughness, although many of the evergreen plants can suffer from mildew. Vine weevils are partial to euonymus, and can seriously affect container-grown specimens, but rarely do serious damage to plants in the ground.

Deciduous trees and shrubs
These are mainly grown for their curious claw-like fruit capsules and fiery autumn colour. *E. alatus H5* (1.5m x 3m) ♛ outstanding red autumn colour, the flowers are tiny but the

corky wings on the stems and trunk are distinctive; *E.a.* 'Compactus' (1m x 2m) more compact. *E. europaeus* our native spindle, mainly cultivated as the form 'Red Cascade' *H5* (2m x

Euonymous fortunei, variegated form

Euonymus alatus (autumn colour)

Euonymus japonicus 'Silver Queen', Blondy and 'Microphyllus Aurea'

Euonymus europaeus 'Red Cascade' (fruit and autumn colour)

2m) ✯ reddish-purple fruits and bright red or purple leaves in autumn. *E. hamiltonianus* subsp. *sieboldianus H4–5* (3–5m x 3–5m) autumn leaves yellow and pink, seeds orange-red inside pink capsules. *E. planipes H5* (3–5m x 3–5m) red fruit and bright-red leaves.

Evergreen shrubs

These are excellent foliage plants, suitable for poor and dry soil. They do best in plenty of sun, especially the variegated forms. *E. fortunei H5* (60cm–1m x 2–3m+; can climb up a wall to 2–3m) is a fine tough dense evergreen foliage plant often used in containers and as low hedging; the flowers are minute, and the pink fruits are rarely produced. There are many named selections: most are good, so just choose the leaf effect you like: **Blondy** ['Interbolwi'] (60cm x 45cm) leaves with yellow blotch, prone to reversion, doesn't sprawl like some of the others, **'Canadale Gold'** (1m x 1.2m) golden-yellow margined, bright green leaves, **'Emerald Gaiety'** (1m x 1.5m) ✯ leaves with a creamy white edge, bronze in winter, **'Emerald 'n' Gold'** (60cm x 1m) ✯ leaves with green centres and irregular gold edges, **'Harlequin'** (60cm x 90cm) striking white and striped young growth, pink in winter, **'Kewensis'** (15cm x 1m+) very dwarf, suitable for rock garden,

with tiny leaves, **'Silver Queen'** (1–2m x 1–2m) bushy and upright, leaves with white margins, pink in winter, **'Sunspot'** (60cm x 90cm) dark green leaves with bold yellow blotches. *E. japonicus H3* (1–1.5m x 1–1.5m) considerably less hardy, good for coastal and west-coast gardens, where it can be used in hedging; *E. j.* **'Gold Pillar'** (50cm), leaves green and gold. Too many *E. japonicus* plants have been imported from Italy and sold to inland Scottish gardeners, where it is too cold for them. To confuse matters, there are lots of names for the same plants: 'Auropictus' should now be called 'Aureus', while 'Aureovariegatus' is now 'Ovatus Aureus', not to be confused with 'Microphyllus Aureovariegatus' . . . Never mind; just choose the pattern of variegation you like.

Exochorda macrantha 'The Bride'

H5 (2m x 3m) ✯ A tidy lax rounded deciduous shrub with arching branches which are covered with white flowers in May. It is tolerant of most soils and best in a sunny site.

Exochorda x macrantha 'The Bride'

Fallopia (Polygonum) baldshuanicum

Prune if you need to immediately after flowering, cutting back the flowering stems as far back as you like, prune later in summer and you'll be cutting off the following year's flower buds. In a sheltered site, it can make an attractive centrepiece as a weeping standard.

Fallopia baldschuanica

(syn. *Polygonum baldschuanicum*)
(Russian vine, mile-a-minute vine) climber
H5 (12m x as much of Scotland as you let it) This is probably the most rampant climber you can buy. Frankly, the only reason to plant it is to cover a large eyesore, as it is little more than a massive tangle of leaves with lots of small white flowers in late summer. Shoots that trail on the ground can take root and spread even further. Deciduous, with heart-shaped leaves, it is suitable for almost any soil in sun or shade and requires no regular pruning, except to stop the damn thing taking over your house and garden. It will grow and usually flower on a north-facing wall.

Fargesia see Bamboos, page 28

Fascicularia bicolor

Forsythia x intermedia, Kew

Forsythia Weekend

Fascicularia bicolor

H2–(3?) (50cm x 50cm) This extraordinary plant is a Chilean bromeliad which can be grown outdoors with a little care in mild gardens: it grows well at the Royal Botanic Garden Edinburgh, at Benmore, Argyll, and in sheltered raised beds by the house at Hill of Tarvit in Fife. The rosettes of spiky linear leaves have a central set of bright-red leaves which surround the white-blue flower. It is slow growing, needs gritty soil in full sun and seems to be hardier than previously thought, provided it is protected from winter wet and coldest weather. Some recommend planting at an angle to allow water to drain from the crown and selecting a site next to a south- or west-facing wall. It can also be grown in a container and kept in a cold greenhouse in winter. Rosa Steppanova grows it in Shetland in a clay drainpipe filled with gravel to keep the leaves off the ground.

Fatsia japonica

x fatshedera lizei
see *Fatsia japonica*, below

Fatsia japonica and
x fatshedera lizei

H3 (1–3m x 1–3m) *Fatsia japonica* is a rather sinister subtropical-looking evergreen shrub with palm-like light-green leaves and curious creamy-white flowers on stalks in late summer into autumn. It is useful for filling part-shaded corners. It does best in a sheltered spot because it is vulnerable to wind, frost damage and snow breakage. There are also variegated forms with white and golden edging on the leaves.

x fatshedera lizei H3
(2m x 3m) A loose spreading evergreen shrub with large ivy-like lobed leaves, a cross between *Fatsia japonica* and ivy. Flowers light green in autumn.

Forsythia

H5 (1–3m x 1–3m) If only it came in any colour but bright acid yellow. Forsythia are visible from miles away, it sometimes seems that every garden in every town has one or more of these. There is good reason for this, as it is one of the toughest and most reliable early-flowering shrubs. It was first collected in China by the roguish but talented plant hunter Willie Forsyth, from Oldmeldrum in Aberdeenshire, who later helped found the Royal Horticultural Society. It can be pruned and shaped, cut to the ground or let to run riot. It has masses of frost-resistant bright-yellow flowers on bare stems in February, March or April, depending on how cold or late spring is. The most profuse flowering comes from plants in full sun, though light or part shade will do. If you want to prune or thin shoots, do so straight after flowering to give plenty time for new flowering stems to be produced. Forsythias are fully hardy (**H5**), tolerant of most soils, including clay unless it is waterlogged. In still, damp spring weather, grey mould (botrytis) can affect flower buds, but rarely causes any serious damage.

Most of the commercially available clones are forms of **F. x intermedia** but they are usually just sold under the clonal name (2–3m x 2–3m) : **'Spectabilis'** very reliable and extremely free flowering, **'Lynwood Variety'** larger flowers than 'Spectabilis', **'Spring Glory'** a little more compact, to 1.8m, **'Fiesta'** leaves with cream and gold variegation, fairly compact to 1.8m, not very free-flowering, **Boucle d' Or** ['Courtacour'] (80cm x 80cm) suitable for a rock garden or container, **Mêlée D'Or** ['Courtaneur'] (1m x 1m) compact, light yellow, relatively late flowering, good autumn colour, **Weekend** ('Courtalyn') (1.8m x 1.5m) a French franken-forsythia, irradiated and mutated to form a compact very free-flowering variety – what would Willie Forsyth have said?

Fothergilla major

Fothergilla major
(syn. *F. monticola*)

H4–5 (1.5–3m x 1.5m) This is a fine slow-growing shrub with fragrant, white bottlebrush-like flowers in March– April, appearing prior to the leaves, and brilliant orange, red and yellow autumn colour. It does best in full sun or part shade in moist acid/peaty soil that does not dry out, and it is a good foil for rhododendrons, which like similar conditions.

F. gardenia (1m) is lower growing and most selected forms have attractive blue-green leaves, but the autumn colour is often not as good.

Fremontodendron

H3–4 (5–6m x 4m) A spectacular evergreen shrub with large deep yellow flowers in

Fremontodendron californicum

June–August. Once nicknamed the Sloane Ranger plant because it was planted against every Chelsea wall, it needs well-drained soil in a warm, sheltered, position, preferably on a south- or west-facing wall and in inland gardens may need extra protection in winter. In hot sunny summers such as that of 2006, it flowers for months. The furry indumentum on the leaves, consisting of needle-like hairs, is a skin irritant, so use gloves to handle or prune it.

F. californicum is less widely grown than the hybrid form **'Californian Glory'**, said to be the hardiest form, with impressively large flowers.

Fuchsia (hardy)

H3–4 Few plants give as much flower over such a long period as the hardy fuchsias, which can remain outside all year round. These differ from the tender bedding fuchsias, which need to be over-wintered in a heated greenhouse. There are thousands of named fuchsias, but only a limited number of reliably hardy ones. The distinctive pendulous flowers consist of coloured sepals and a coloured tube, which are often a different colour from the four petals that make up the bell-shaped corolla. Grow in moist but well-drained soil, in sun or light shade. In coastal gardens, hardy fuchsias tend to grow larger and larger each year, while in colder more inland gardens they tend to be cut back to ground level after cold winters. Wait until early spring to

Fuchsia 'Genii'

Fuchsia 'Lady Thumb'

Fuchsia magellanica 'Versicolor'

see where the growth buds sprout from and then cut away all dead stems. In cold gardens it is worth mulching the crown of the plant to protect it from frost, especially when young. *F. magellanica* in its various forms makes a fine informal hedge in coastal gardens. There are good examples surrounding the houses on the west-coast island of Iona and also on Skye. It is tolerant of salt spray and wind, and can be grown very close to the sea. Vine weevils and capsid bugs can be troublesome and some, including the 'Thumb' family, can get rust.

'Alice Hoffman' *H3* (60cm) semi-double rose pink and white flowers. **'Delta's Sarah'** *H3* white and purple. **'Genii'** *H3–4* (1.2m x 90cm) red shoots and lime-yellow foliage, small flowers cerise and reddish purple. *F. magellanica* *H4* (1–3m) depending on climate, probably the hardiest fuchsia and certainly the most common, especially on the west coast, and in Orkney and Shetland, where it is used for hedging, small, narrow deep red flowers with purple corollas, flowering late summer and into autumn; **var.** *alba* and **var.** *molinae* narrow white flowers tinged mauve; **var.** *aurea* yellow-green leaves. **'Versicolor'** *H3–4* (1.2m) red and purple flowers, foliage grey-green, pink tinted when young, with stripes of white variegation when mature. **'Lady Thumb'** *H3* (45cm) semi-double, light carmine and white, a good dwarf selection. **'Mrs Popple'** *H4* (1.5m x 90cm) the hardiest of the larger-flowered hybrids, an excellent choice, scarlet with purple-violet corollas. **'Phyllis'** *H3* (1–1.5m) semi-double and rose-cerise, another good choice for hedging in coastal gardens. **'Riccartonii'** *H4* (1–2m) one of the hardiest, leaves dark green with a bronzy sheen, narrow single scarlet and purple flowers, suitable for hedging. **'Son of Thumb'** *H3–4* (40cm) cerise sepals and lilac corolla. **'Tom Thumb'** *H3* (30cm) carmine sepals and tube with a purple corolla.

Garrya elliptica (silk tassel bush)
and *Itea*

H4 (3–4m x 3–4m) Silk tassel bush is the descriptive common name for *Garrya elliptica*, which can be grown as a freestanding shrub in mild gardens but is usually trained as a wall shrub. Vigorous with pinkish stems and dark-green leathery leaves, it produces long grey-green catkins in winter and early spring. The 20cm catkins on male plants are longer than the female ones, so most forms sold are male. It needs well-drained soil in full sun or light shade, and is best planted in a sheltered site; in eastern and central Scotland, a south- or west-facing wall is advisable. **'James Roof'** ❦ (male) the most popular clone,

Garrya elliptica

Gaultheria mucronata,
white and red

has particularly good catkins.

Itea looks similar to Garrya and fills a similar niche in the garden. The holly-like leaves are accompanied by long dense greeny-yellow/ cream catkins in late summer and early autumn.
I. virginica H4 (1.5–3m x 1.5–3m) deciduous and the hardiest species. *I. ilicifolia H3* (3–5m x 3–5m) evergreen. Both are usually grown on a warm wall in Scotland.

Gaultheria (including Pernettya)

These evergreen heather relatives occur on moorland and in rhododendron forest on mountains in many parts of the world. They range from tiny alpine creepers to vigorous medium-sized shrubs. The well-known winter-berried pernettyas have recently been reclassified within *Gaultheria*. All have small white or pale-pink flowers in spring and early summer but are mainly grown for their edible but mostly disappointingly tasteless blue, red or black fruits in autumn. They need moist but not waterlogged lime-free/peaty soil, and flower and berry best in at least part day sun.

G. cuneata H4 (30cm x 1m) dense and low with racemes of white flowers and white fruit. *G. mucronata* (formerly and still widely grown as *Pernettya mucronata*) *H4–5* (1m x 1m) ♣ a very popular winter-berrying shrub with small prickly leaves, small white flowers in spring and large fruit which usually lasts well for most of the winter. A male (which has white flowers but no fruit) is required to ensure good fruit set for the female plants which have berries in white, pink, purple or red. Prune long straggly shoots in winter or early spring to retain compact habit. All parts of the plant are poisonous. Forms include: **Bell's Seedling'** (said to be self-fertile), and **'Crimsonia'** red, **'Mother of Pearl'** (syn. 'Parelmoer') light pink, **'Snow White'** (syn. 'Sneeuwitje') and **'Wintertime'** white. *G. procumbens* (wintergreen) *H4–5* (15cm x unlimited) commonly sold in garden centres at Christmas for its large red berries, and often used as a container bedding plant, inclined to suffer from dieback. *G. shallon* (syn. Salal) *H4* (1.2m x 2m+) spreading by suckers, a vigorous thug which is out of control in wetter parts of western Scotland and should not be

planted there. In the drier east it makes a useful evergreen for woodland edges and borders. The urn-shaped pale pink flowers are followed by dark purple fruit in autumn. *G. shallon* is currently on a Scottish government 'Most Wanted' list of imported vandals, and it may become an offence to sell or plant it (see page 159). *G. x wisleyensis* (syn. *Gaulnettya*) *H4* (1m x 1m) compact, spreading, with pink (**'Pink Pixie'**) or white (**'Wisley Pearl'**) flowers in spring followed by purple-red fruit.

Genista see Cytisus, page 46

Griselinia littoralis

H3–4 (2–3m on the east coast, 5–8m x 2–3m on the west coast) This New Zealand native is a very popular coastal

Griselinia littoralis 'Variegata'
(RC-M)

hedging and shelter plant. It is a dense evergreen with attractive pale-green, leathery leaves which is easy to shape. If left unpruned on the west coast and western islands it can grow into a small tree with attractive bark. There is a fine example by the old castle at Castle Toward, near Dunoon and Wormistoune castle near Crail in Fife has a huge clump. You won't notice the tiny flowers, so this is essentially a foliage plant. Beware of growing this in mild, high rainfall west-coast gardens, as it can grow into an unmanageable leylandii-like thug and tends to seed everywhere. Good in Orkney, where few evergreens thrive in the wind. For gardens away from the coasts, laurel (see page 84) is probably a hardier bet as an evergreen screening plant. There are less vigorous variegated forms which can also make a fine hedge: **'Variegata'** (3m) leaves margined creamy white and streaked grey, **'Bantry Bay'** (3m) creamy-yellow splash in the centre of the leaf, **'Dixon's Cream'** (3m) leaves with bold splashes of yellow.

Halesia, Stewartia pseudocamellia and Styrax japonicus

These North American and Asian white summer-flowering large deciduous shrubs can all grow into substantial small trees in time. Their small white flowers are showy en masse, though they flower best with heat and shelter and can suffer from frost damage in inland gardens. They enjoy moist acid to neutral soil with some wind shelter and can also have good autumn colour, stronger in a dry cold September/October.

Halesia H5 Hanging white bells along the branches, lovely on a mature tree. *H. carolina* (3–5m+ x 5–7m+)

flowers late spring. *H. monticola* (snowdrop tree) (6–10m x 7m) white bells in late spring.

Stewartia pseudocamellia H4 (5–10m+ x 5–7m) Rose-like small white flowers, peeling pink-reddish-brown bark, needs a sheltered warm, sunny site.

Styrax japonicus H4 (3–6m+ x 3–6m+) Bell-shaped white (or pale pink) flowers, leaves yellow and red in autumn.

Halesia monticola

Hamamelis x intermedia 'Diane', 'Jelena' and 'Barmstedt Gold'

Hamamelis x intermedia 'Pallida' (RC-M)

Hamamelis mollis

Halimium see *Cistus*, page 35

x *Halimiocistus* see *Cistus*, page 35

Hamamelis (witch hazel)
and *Disanthus cercidifolius*
H5 ❀ When all else is frozen, one old faithful in winter–early spring is the hamamelis, with its frost-resistant flowers. The curious spidery or string-like ribbons of yellow, orange or red petals are held on bare branches, and most yellow forms are scented. The more or less oval, ribbed leaves often turn to fine oranges and yellows in autumn. These are expensive plants to buy, as they are grafted and take several years to reach saleable size, but they are tough and reliable – definitely worth the investment. Hamamelis need moist well-drained soil in sun or part shade, with some wind shelter. Watch out for

suckers from the rootstock and remove these. Expert Chris Lane advises pruning from time to time after flowers go over to retain tidy, dense and free-flowering plants. The dark-flowered selections are shown off best against a light background, such as a white wall or building. In mild winters, they can open as early as November, but typically by January to February they are at their peak. Those listed are fully hardy (**H5**) and reach 3–4m x 3–4m.

H. x intermedia some lightly scented; forms include '**Arnold Promise**' large-flowered yellow, '**Barmstedt Gold**' deep yellow, lightly scented, '**Diane**' dark red, '**Jelena**' coppery orange, '**Pallida**' ❦ ❀ perhaps the best of all, pale yellow with a sweet scent, '**Westerstede**' golden yellow. *H. mollis* ❦ ❀ very fragrant golden yellow.

Disanthus cercidifolius H4 (3m) tiny spidery red flowers in autumn, mainly grown for its fine fiery autumn colour. Does well at Dawyck, near Peebles, and former curator David Knott feels that it should be more widely grown.

Heathers, heaths and related genera
Few plants have more impact on the landscape of Scotland than heather: it carpets much of the high moorland and coastal slopes of the country. Scotland has three native heathers. The commonest is *Calluna vulgaris* (ling), which turns the hills purple in late summer, but you will also find *Erica cinerea* (bell heather) in drier sites, and the pink *E. tetralix*, which likes boggy conditions. A vast range of heather varieties is now available, many of which have striking coloured foliage, and there are some that flower almost any month of the year. The UK national heather collection at Cherrybank, Perth, has more than 900 different varieties. Heathers belong to the family *Ericaceae* (which includes rhododendrons and azaleas) whose members share a liking for acid or peaty soil. *Erica carnea* and *E. x darleyensis* cultivars will grow in neutral or alkaline soil. Heathers have traditionally been grown in heather beds with several varieties planted together, so as to contrast the flower and foliage colours. They can also be used in mixed borders and in troughs and containers. Heathers should be grown in full sun and, if possible, facing south. They are very wind tolerant but salt spray can damage the golden-leaved varieties. Plant in groups of three to five of each cultivar in a large bed, or singly in a small space. The Heather Society recommend using five plants per square metre in order to carpet the ground completely. The key to good-looking heathers is to shear them after flowering for the spring and summer varieties, cutting back to below the flowering heads. The autumn-flowering ones will need only an occasional tidy-up in spring. Most garden centres tend to sell only heathers coming into flower, which can mean that the full range of spring, summer and autumn varieties are not available at one time. There are several

Scottish specialist nurseries which stock a wide range. There are far too many named heather cultivars, many of which are hard to tell apart. Heathers can suffer from several pests and diseases, but they are generally quite easy to please.

Calluna vulgaris (ling) H4–5  probably Scotland's most popular native plant, and should perhaps replace the thistle as our national emblem. The purple flowers of the wild forms colour the late summer moorland of much of the country. Rosa Steppanova reports from Shetland that though the wild forms grow well, many cultivars, especially those with coloured foliage, tend to burn in strong winds and salt. There are hundreds of named forms, varying from 15cm to 50cm in height, flowering in late summer and autumn. We have grouped them by size.

Calluna vulgaris 'Alexandra'

Calluna vulgaris 'Hammondii Aureifolia'

Low (15–25cm x 30–50cm)
'Alba Plena' double white, 'Alexandra' deep crimson, 'Caerketton White' white, Scottish raised, 'County Wicklow' double shell pink, semi-prostrate, 'Cuprea' winter foliage copper-coloured, flowers lavender, 'Dark Beauty' compact, flowers red turning purple red, 'Dark Star' semi-double crimson, 'Darkness' crimson, compact, 'Foxii Nana' rarely flowers, but very compact, with bright-green foliage, 'Golden Carpet' mauve, foliage gold turning orange and red in winter, prostrate habit, 'J.H. Hamilton' very dwarf, double pink, 'Kinlochruel' ♥ one of the best double pure whites, foliage bronze in winter, 'Multicolor' mauve, copper foliage, flecked orange and red, but inclined to revert, 'Radnor' neat, double shell pink, 'Red Favorit' double crimson, 'Red Carpet' semi-prostrate, 'Serlei Aurea' white, greenish-yellow foliage with yellow tips in summer, 'Sir John Charrington' dark lilac-pink, foliage golden, turning reddish in autumn, 'Sister Anne' mauve, grey-green foliage, turning bronze in winter, low spreading habit, 'Spitfire' mauve, gold foliage, turning orange then red in winter, 'Sunset' lilac pink, gold foliage, red in autumn and winter, bronzing slightly in spring, 'White Lawn' prostrate, white, 'Winter Chocolate' lavender, gold foliage with pink tips in summer, bronze in winter.

Medium (30–40cm x 40–50cm)
'Allegro' ruby, 'Beoley Crimson' long bright-crimson flower spikes, 'Blazeaway' lavender, gold foliage turning reddish in autumn, 'Boskoop' lavender, foliage gold, turning reddish, 'Con Brio' ruby, foliage yellowish green, turning reddish, 'Drum Ra' white, 'Flamingo' mauve, young foliage pinkish red, 'Fred J. Chapple' lilac pink, foliage tips red, cream and pink, 'Gold Haze' white, foliage pale yellow all year round, 'Guinea Gold' white, yellow foliage all year round, 'Hammondii Aureifolia' white, light-green foliage with yellow tips, 'H.E. Beale' long spikes of double pink, an old favourite, tolerant of clay soil, 'Joy Vanstone' lavender, yellow-pinkish foliage in summer, orange-red in winter, 'Kerstin' foliage lilac grey, tipped red and yellow in winter, flowers mauve, 'Peter Sparkes' long spikes of double rose pink, one of the latest flowering, 'Robert Chapman' ♥ lavender, with gold foliage in summer, orange in autumn, red in winter and spring, prone to dieback, 'Spring Cream' white, green foliage with white tips in spring, 'Spring Torch' mauve, foliage with pink and red tips in winter, cream and pink in summer, 'Tib' double pink, early, rather open habit.

Calluna vulgaris 'H.E. Beale'

Tall (45–50cm x 50–70cm)
'Annemarie' double deep pink, 'Beoley Gold' ♥ white, golden foliage, 'Elsie Purnell' long spikes of double lavender, foliage grey-green, 'Firefly' deep mauve, foliage terracotta turning red in winter, 'Gold Flame' lilac, bronze and red foliage, 'Kirby White' white, foliage with yellow tips in spring, 'Red Haze' lavender, gold foliage in summer turning reddish bronze in winter, 'Silver Knight' mauve-pink, grey foliage, purple-grey in winter, 'Silver Queen' foliage silvery grey, flowers lavender, 'Velvet Fascination' white, downy silver-grey foliage, erect habit, 'Wickwar Flame' ♥ mauve, foliage golden in summer, orange-red in winter.

Erica There are more than 700 species of *Erica*. The hardy European species and their many hybrids and cultivars make excellent garden plants. Most of the rest come from South Africa and need greenhouse culture in Scotland.

E. arborea (tree heath) H3–4 ❄ is the tallest hardy heather and it can reach 3–5m x 3–5m or more. The honey-scented white flowers open in spring. Two smaller forms (to 2m) are the golden-foliaged 'Albert's Gold', which seldom flowers, and var. *alpina* (Nana). Prune to shape when young and trim after flowering. A fine plant for coastal Scotland, but probably a bit tender for cold inland gardens. *E. x veitchii* (*E. arborea* x *E.*

Erica arborea

Erica carnea 'Adrienne Duncan'

Erica cinerea (white)

Erica x *darleyensis* 'Ada Collins'
and 'Kramer's Rote'

Erica carnea 'Foxhollow'
(summer foliage)

Erica carnea 'Golden Starlet'

lusitanica) *H3* (to 2m) white flowers in winter and early spring.
E. carnea H4–5 (15–25cm x 40–50cm) purplish-pink flowers in
late winter (as early as December) and early spring, with mid- to
dark-green foliage. This is a very useful and tough plant for
early-season colour, as it flowers through snow and hard frosts. It
is tolerant of some shade and will cope with salt spray. Forms
include: **'Adrienne Duncan'** early with bronze foliage, **'Ann
Sparkes'** ✿ dark-golden foliage with bronze tips, pink flowers,
'Aurea' foliage gold, all year round, pink flowers, very compact,
'Bell's Extra Special' yellow, orange foliage a few pink flowers,
'Challenger' purple pink, **'December Red'** pink darkening to
near red in December–February, **'Foxhollow'** ✿ lavender, yellow
foliage tipped bronze or orange, **'Golden Starlet'** white, lime-
green foliage, **'Isabell'** white, **'King George'** compact pink,
'Loughrigg' vigorous, pink deepening to mauve pink, **'March
Seedling'** pink, February–May, **'Myretown Ruby'** ✿ pink
darkening to crimson, **'Nathalie'** deep bright purple, very good
colour, **'Pink Spangles'** shell pink, trailing habit, **'Rosalie'** bright
pink, compact, very good, **'Ruby Glow'** reddish pink, spreading
habit, **'Snow Queen'** pure white, compact, **'Springwood Pink'**
trailing, pink, **'Springwood White'** ✿ vigorous, trailing white,
'Vivellii' ✿ bronze leaves, deep-red flowers, **'Westwood Yellow'**
shell pink, yellow foliage, fairly upright habit.
E. cinerea (bell heather) *H4–5* (30–60cm, except the dwarf forms

indicated, x 50–80cm) ✉ This is the largest group of what can be
termed summer-flowering heathers, blooming June–September.
They are compact with dark green leaves with pink, white or
purple flowers. Forms include: **'Alba Minor'** (15–20cm) white
flowers, **'Apricot Charm'** yellow foliage turning orange in winter,
a few mauve flowers, **'C.D. Eason'** bright magenta, good ground-
cover, **'Eden Valley'** (20cm) lavender-pink fading to white,
bicolour effect, **'Fiddler's Gold'** lilac-pink flowers in late summer,
yellow-gold foliage with red tints, **'Glencairn'** magenta, foliage
with red tips, **'Golden Drop'** sparse mauve flowers, foliage
orange, fading to gold, turning deep red in winter, **'Knap Hill
Pink'** magenta-pink, **'Lilac Time'** (15cm) lavender, shy-flowering,
'P.S. Patrick' reddish-purple, **'Pentreath'** beetroot red, **'Pink Ice'**
(20cm) clear rose-pink, compact, **'Stephen Davis'** (20cm)
compact but erect habit, flowers deep magenta, **'Velvet Knight'**
flowers deep beetroot, with dark green foliage and an upright
habit. Other summer-flowering heathers include *E.* x *williamsii*
lilac-pink late summer into autumn, and the two forms **'Ken
Wilson'** clear magenta, fine colour, **'P.D. Williams'** growth yellow-
tipped. *E.* x *griffithsii* (50cm x 50cm) pale pink, yellow foliage, a
fine recent hybrid.

Erica x *darleyensis*
'George Rendall'

E. x *darleyensis H4–5*
(30–60cm x 60cm) flowering in
January–April is easy to please
and forms a dense vigorous
ground-cover which weeds find
hard to penetrate. Forms
include: **'Darley Dale'** foliage
tipped cream, pink flowers,
'Furzey' leaves tipped pink,
flowers purple-pink, **'George
Rendall'** pink darkening to
heliotrope, foliage tipped red,
fading to pink and cream,
'Ghost Hills' foliage light green,
tipped cream, flowers pink,
'J.W. Porter' purple on dark
green foliage with cream and

red tips in spring, not always very free-flowering, **'Jack H. Brummage'** purplish-pink, leaves orange-yellow, **'Jenny Porter'** pinkish white flowers, foliage with cream tips in spring, **'Kramer's Rote'** magenta flowers, bronzy foliage, **'Mary Helen'** pink flowers, with yellow foliage bronze in winter, **'Silberschmelze'** (syn. Molten Silver, Silver Beads) white flowers, foliage cream tipped in spring, tinged red in winter.

E. erigena (Irish heath) **H3–4** (1–2.5m x 1–2.5m) upright, with brittle stems, and flowers can be frosted, so better avoided in cold inland gardens and areas of high snowfall. Makes a fine low

Erica erigena 'Irish Dusk'

Erica erigena 'Golden Lady'

hedge in western coastal gardens, and usually flowers in winter (November to March/April). Forms include: **'Brightness'** lilac-pink, purple-tinged winter foliage, **'Golden Lady' H3** bright-yellow foliage, subject to wind and frost burn, **'Irish Dusk'** salmon to rose pink, with dark grey-green foliage, **'W.T. Rackliff'** white, compact, very fine.

E. x stuartii H4 (25–30m x 40–50cm) this Irish natural hybrid has lilac-pink flowers in June–September; **'Irish Lemon'** bright yellow young growth, **'Irish Orange'** orange tipped spring foliage.

E. tetralix H4 (25–30cm x 25–40cm) urn-shaped purple-pink or white flowers with narrow mouths July–October, does best in moist soil; **'Alba Mollis'** white, silvery-grey leaves, **'Con Underwood'** magenta, **'Pink Star'** (20cm) star-like pink flowers on the ends of the stems.

E. vagans (Cornish heath) **H3–4** (40–80cm x 80cm) forms neat compact hummocks which spread vigorously, with pink, mauve or white flowers in July–October/November. It needs well-drained soil and may be damaged in cold winters in inland gardens. It is very good in Shetland. Forms include: **'Birch Glow'** deep bright rose pink, with dark-green foliage, flowering two weeks later than other pinks, **'Cornish Cream'** off-white flowers in long racemes, **'Lyonesse'** the most popular white form, **'Mrs D.F. Maxwell'** deep reddish pink with dark-green foliage, very popular, **'Saint Keverne'** clear pink with dark-green foliage, **'Valerie Proudley'** sparse white flowers, bright-yellow new growth, subject to windburn and reversion.

Daboecia

Cassiope

Daboecia H3–4 (20–45cm x 40–60cm+) With relatively large bell- or urn-shaped purple, reddish, pink or white flowers in July–August and sometimes into autumn, these are charming ground-covers, more quirky and unusual than their relatives above. They are not as tough as most of the ericas and callunas and in inland gardens it is best to wait until spring before pruning out winter damage. They dislike drying out in summer. A haircut after flowering will help to maintain a compact habit.

D. cantabrica H4 (25–40cm x 50–60cm) forms include **'Atropurpurea'** deep purple, **'Bicolor'** flowers white, pink and red flowers, sometimes striped, **'David Moss'** white, **'Polifolia'** pale mauve, leaves grey-green, **'Praegerae' H2–3** cerise, semi-deciduous and looks scruffy, compact, not very hardy. **D. subsp.** *scotica* **H3** (25cm x 40cm) forms include **'Jack Drake'**, a ruby-red Scottish selection, **'Silverwells'** white, **'William Buchanan'** ❦ a vigorous, long-flowering purple-crimson, raised in Bearsden.

Cassiope H4 (10–25cm) With whipcord-like stems and masses of tiny white bells in May, these grow wild on Asia and North American mountain moorland. They like to have cool roots in peaty soil. The most-free flowering are the hybrids, raised in Scotland or north-east England: **'Edinburgh'** (25cm), **'Bearsden'** (10cm), **'Badenoch'** (10cm), **'Muirhead'** (10cm) ❦, **'Randle Cooke'** (15cm). You'd need a magnifying glass to see much difference between them.

Phyllodoce H4 Another heath relative, with pink, purple-pink or cream bell-like flowers on heather-like plants. They like peaty soil in sun, away from overhanging trees, and are inclined to die off with fungal disease. *P. aleutica* (20cm) cream flowers. *P. caerulea* (20cm) purple-pink. *P. empetriformis* (30cm) purple-pink.

Hebe

This huge genus of mostly New Zealand origin low shrubs are ideal for coastal gardens with the hardier varieties suitable for growing inland. The tiny flowers are borne en masse in racemes or spikes, in shades of purple, blue, reddish, pink or white in summer. Many have attractive coloured foliage and the compact varieties are good rock garden and container subjects. As a general rule, the smaller the leaf size, the hardier the plant. There are now far too many named varieties, many of which are disease prone and fare poorly in inland Scottish winters, the 2011–2012 winter saw most hebes killed away from the coast. The hardiest hebes are a group of white varieties which includes *H. ochracea* 'James Stirling' and *H. pinguifolia* 'Pagei'. Hebes grow very well in seaside gardens; nowhere is this better illustrated than in villages on the Fife coast such as Anstruther and Pittenweem, where it seems to be compulsory for every garden to have at least one, if not an entire hedge. Many hebes are also excellent in Shetland and Orkney. 'Blue Gem' is particularly popular there. The smaller compact mound-forming ones, such as *H. rakaiensis*, make good border-edge structural plants. Hebes grow best in gritty, well-drained soil, and they dislike winter waterlogging. Most need little or no pruning. Some are prone to mildew, which spots the leaves, particularly on crowded garden-centre benches with overhead watering; it is less of a problem in gardens. Height and spread are similar unless stated otherwise. The larger leaved varieties can reach 3m x3m or more in mild west coast gardens.

Hebe 'Autumn Glory'

Hebe 'Great Orme'

Hebe 'Pink Paradise'

H. albicans H3 (45cm x 60cm) white flowers in June–July, grey-green leaves; *H.a.* 'Red Edge' young leaves margined and veined red, rarely flowers, a form 'Super Red' has redder leaves. 'Autumn Glory' *H3* (90cm) leaves dark green with red margin, tinged bronze, habit rather open, dense racemes of small rich-purple flowers in late summer. 'Baby Marie' *H3* (40cm) lilac white in summer, compact with blue-green leaves. *H. brachysiphon H3–4* (2m) small white flowers; 'White Gem' a compact (1m) form. 'Bowles' Hybrid' *H2* (60cm) lavender purple in late summer, for mildest gardens only. 'Caledonia' (syn. 'E.B. Anderson') *H3* (50cm x 1m) flowers violet in late summer, young leaves red tinted. 'Champagne' *H2–3* (60cm) pale lilac fading to white. 'Emerald Gem' (syn. 'Emerald Green', 'Green Globe') *H2–3?* (30cm) very compact with tiny leaves, rarely flowers, mainly grown for its tight habit. *H. x franciscana* 'Blue Gem' *H3* (60cm x 1.2m) light mauve, widely grown and good in the north-west and Orkney, where it flowers for months and everyone seems to have one; 'Variegata' *H2–3* (syn. *H. elliptica* 'Variegata') cream-margined leaves, popular on the west coast. Goldrush [PBR] (60cm–1m) leaves yellow, green and pink, flowers pink. 'Great Orme' *H3* (1.2m) pink fading to white, young growth purple, open habit. Heartbreaker [PBR] *H3* (1m) dark-green leaves edged cream, turning red in winter,

a few mauve flowers. Lady Ann [PBR] variegated leaves, red flushing. Margret [PBR] *H3–4* (45cm x 60cm) sky blue fading to white, giving a two-tone effect, from spring to autumn. 'Midsummer Beauty' *H3–4* (2m) lilac purple fading to white in mid- to late summer, one of the hardiest of the larger growers. 'Mrs Winder' *H3* (1m) violet-blue, in spikes up to 10cm long in late summer, red-purple young growth on a compact, rounded bush, shy flowering, mainly grown for its foliage. 'Nicola's Blush' *H3* (60cm) pink fading to white in racemes up to 8cm long, in mid-summer and sometimes again in autumn, leaves tinged purple. *H. ochracea* 'James Stirling' *H4* (90cm) ❦ one of the hardiest and most unusual, an excellent choice with whipcord conifer-like stems with tiny yellow-green leaves and white flowers in June–July. 'Pascal' mauve, reddish leaves in winter. 'Pewter Dome' *H3–4* (60cm) white in June–July, grey-green foliage. *H. pimeloides* 'Quicksilver' *H3–4* (30cm x 60cm) light blue-mauve in early summer, silver-grey leaves. *H. pinguifolia* 'Pagei' *H4* (30cm x 90cm) ❦ another hardy choice, and a good ground-cover with blue-green leaves and small white flowers in May–June. 'Pink Elephant' *H3* (60cm) pink and copper variegation, white flowers. Pink Lady [PBR] *H3* leaves with red edge, flowers pale pink. 'Pink Paradise' *H3* pink and white flowers, 'Pink Pixie' *H3* (60cm) bright pink in mid- to late summer, can suffer from rust. Rosie [PBR] *H3* (60cm) pink. Purple Pixie ['Mowhawk'] *H3* (60cm) purple. *H. rakaiensis H4* (1m) large white flowers in June–July, sculptural plant with dense glossy foliage, similar to box. *H. salicifolia H2–3* (1.5–2m) an architectural narrow-leaved hebe, white summer flowers, good in mild coastal gardens. 'Sapphire' *H2–3* (1m) purple, narrow, red-tinged leaves. *H. topiaria H3* (1m x 2m) compact and bushy, white flowers.

H. vernicosa H3–4 (60cm x 1.2m) pale lilac to white in June, dark-green leaves. **'Wiri Charm'** *H2–3* (75cm x 50cm) deep rose purple. **'Wiri Mist'** *H2–3* (50cm x 80cm) white. **'Youngii'** (syn. 'Carl Teschner') *H3–4* (20cm x 60cm) violet-purple fading to white, in summer, compact with green leaves, sometimes red edged. A new range under the Addenda® banner have been released from a Danish nursery. **'Gretha'** dark purple, looks like 'Autumn Glory', **'Linda'**, **'Lisa'** both pink, **'White Lady'** small-leaved, small white flowers all probably 60–90cm+.

Hedera (ivy) (climber)

An extremely varied and versatile plant, hedera is one of the best evergreen climbers and one of the few that will do well on north-facing walls and in heavy clay soil. Ivies also make useful ground-covers, especially the native *H. helix* and *H. hibernica* (Irish ivy), which thrive in dense shade, where little else will grow, and they can become an invasive nuisance. Cambo, in Fife, use pet pigs to clear their ivy. Ivies do well in the Western and Northern Isles, though yellow-leaved varieties can be burned by salt spray. Ivy climbs upwards in its juvenile phase, growing outwards and more bushy at maturity (when it reaches the top of whatever it is climbing on), which means it can eventually fatally smother a tree. Ivies are mostly self-clinging, useful for climbing on walls, fences and trellis, but the roots penetrate mortar and can

cause serious structural damage. Though they flower, they are almost exclusively grown for their green or variegated foliage. The leaves are poisonous, and beware of the sap, which can cause irritation to skin.

Hedera algeriensis 'Gloire de Marengo'

H. algeriensis **'Gloire de Marengo'** *H3* (4–6m) a striking rampant foliage plant, named after Napoleon's horse, for sheltered and mild gardens with bold white variegation on the large pale leaves. *H. colchica H4* (5–10m+) vigorous with dark-green leaves, suitable for a large wall; the variegated forms are less vigorous (to 5m), including **'Dentata Variegata'** light-green leaves, mottled grey-green with creamy-white margins, **'Sulphur Heart'** (syn. 'Paddy's Pride') more vigorous with large gold-splashed leaves. *H. helix* (common or English ivy) *H4–5* (10m) is the native green ivy which smothers old trees and walls and it is rarely grown as a garden plant. Better to choose from the many more manageable cultivars, some of which are climbers or ground-covers, while others form small freestanding shrubs. While pretty tough, cold winds can burn some of the variegated

selections. The following are hardy (*H4–5*) unless stated otherwise: **'Buttercup'** (2m) slow growing, pale green in shade, bright yellow in sun, **'Erecta'** (1m) dark-green leaves, stiffly upright, not needing any support, **'Glacier'** (2m+) small triangular grey-green leaves with silver and cream variegation, **'Goldchild'** small grey-green leaves with yellow margins, **'Goldheart'** (syn. 'Oro di Bogliasco') (3m+) dark-green leaves with a splash or bright yellow, an excellent choice for a wall, **'Green Ripple'** striking, large five-lobed jagged-edged green leaves, **'Ivalace'** (1m) slow, and low growing, good ground-cover with medium-sized crinkled and curly-margined green leaves, **'Kolibri'** small white-variegated leaves, **'Little Diamond'** (60cm) a bushy plant with silvery and grey variegation, **'Midas Touch'** *H3* (1m) less hardy than most, small leaves with irregular golden

Hedera helix 'Goldheart' ('Oro de Bogliasco')

Hedera 'Sulphur Heart' ('Paddy's Pride')

variegation, **'Sagittifolia'** (1.2–2m) deeply cut, arrow-like green leaves. *H. hibernica* (Irish ivy) *H4* } a tough, vigorous climber to 10m and also a good ground-cover, with heart-shaped leaves and masses of small white flowers; forms include **'Deltoidea'** (5m) heart-shaped green leaves, **'Sulphurea'** (3m) leaves splashed with yellow, **'Variegata'** (5–10m) irregular yellow-cream variegation.

Helianthemum (rock rose)

H3–4 On a dreich Scottish summer's day, rock roses stubbornly refuse to open their flowers at all, unable to believe that this is what we call a summer. But don't be put off, as they are perfectly happy here, and in sunshine, the bright oranges, red and yellow flowers in June–July help us dream of the Mediterranean. Evergreen or semi-evergreen low shrubs, smaller than the related cistus (see page 35), they need lots of sun and very well-drained soil, and they are good in alpine troughs, raised beds and at the front of sunny borders. Do not over-feed them. With good drainage they are surprisingly hardy, but winter wet and heavy soil can kill them. The best for Scotland are hybrids of *H. apenninum, H.*

nummularium and *H. croceum*, two of which are native to parts of the south of England. The Scottish mountain series were bred by John Nicoll in Dundee. Abriachan Garden Nursery on Loch Ness lists over 50 varieties.

The following form spreading mats of 20–40cm x 20–40cm: **'Amy Baring'** deep yellow, **'Ben Fhada'** golden yellow with orange centres, **'Ben Heckla'** orange with scarlet centre, **'Ben Ledi'** deep purple-pink, **'Ben More'** orange with a darker centre, **'Cerise Queen'** bright double pink, **'Chocolate Blotch'** buff marked brown, **'Fire Dragon'** orange-scarlet, foliage greyish, **'Georgeham'** pink and yellow, **'Golden Queen'** bright yellow, **'Henfield Brilliant'** ⚜ brick red, greyish leaves, **'Jubilee'** double primrose yellow, **'Mrs C.W. Earle'** double scarlet, dark-

Helianthemum 'Cerise Queen', 'The Bride', 'Ben Fhada' and 'Ben Heckla'

Helianthemum 'Ben More'

Helianthemum 'Salmon Queen'

Hibiscus syriacus 'Blue Bird'

green leaves, **'Raspberry Ripple'** reddish pink edged white, dark-green foliage, **'Rose of Leeswood'** double pink, **'Salmon Queen'** bright salmon pink, **'Sudbury Gem'** deep pink with red centres, foliage greyish, **'Supreme'** crimson, foliage greyish, **'The Bride'** creamy white with yellow centres, **'Wisley Primrose'** pale yellow, **'Wisley Pink'** soft pink, **'Wisley White'** soft white,

H. lunulatum yellow with an orange base in June–July.

Helichrysum see *Olearia*, page 76

Hibiscus syriacus
H3(–4) (1.5 x 1.5m) An irresistible late-summer-flowering shrub with exotic trumpet-shaped flowers from August to October. Unfortunately the lack of summer heat in Scotland means that you won't see hibiscus thriving as in their native Mediterranaean climate, or even as they do in the south of England, but if you have a sheltered courtyard, or south-facing suntrap, they are well worth a try in well-drained soil. They leaf up very late in spring, so if they still look dead in May don't be too hasty to dig up and throw them out. *H. syriacus* has been cultivated in British gardens since the 16th century and there are hundreds of selected forms. They reach 1.5m x 1.5m unless stated otherwise.

'Blue Bird' (syn. 'Oiseau Blue') (2m x 1.5m) the best choice for Scotland as it sets flower buds with less heat than the others, bright blue with a small red centre. Very good at Glendoick in a sheltered courtyard.

Hippophae rhamnoides (sea buckthorn)
⚜ *H4* (2–4m+ x 3–5m) ✉
This is one of the best of all berrying shrubs, in terms of the sheer quantity of berries and the long season of colour: on a winter walk along the beach at Gullane, East Lothian, you will see a magnificent display of large orange-yellow berries crowding the branch ends and hanging on long after the leaves have fallen. The deciduous leaves are silvery green and narrow and the branches are thorny. The tiny white spring flowers are barely noticeable. This is an excellent seaside plant, tolerating wind and salt spray, and good for stabilizing sand dunes. It is also worth growing in gardens away from the coast, but be aware that it can be invasive in richer soils. Both male and female forms are needed to obtain good berrying; finding them may be difficult, as garden centres may not know which they are selling. A more certain method is to grow them from seed. The plant needs shaping from time to time: hard prune, removing old branches in late summer. Wear gloves, though.

Hippophae rhamnoides

Hoheria

Hoherias are a group fine large shrubs or small trees from New Zealand. They do best in milder regions or sheltered gardens, but with milder winters, they will do well over much of Scotland and should probably be more widely grown. All have clusters of sometimes scented white flowers in late summer. There is a superb specimen of *H. lyallii* in the walled garden at Dunninald, near Montrose, Angus, a huge *H. sextsylosa* at Hill of Tarvit, Fife and largest of all, the 'Glory of Amlwch' at Mount Stuart, Bute.

H. lyallii H3–4 (4–7m x 4–7m) deciduous with silvery leaves, showy white flowers a bit like cherry blossom. *H. glabrata* is almost identical and the two are often confused. *H. sexstylosa H3* (7m x 5m) ❋ evergreen with lance-shaped leaves, small star-shaped scented white flowers in late summer. The two most commonly offered evergreen cultivars/hybrids are **'Stardust'** *H3–4* (3–6m+) ❋ with small white flowers in summer, and **'Glory of Amlwch'** *H3* ❋ with slightly larger scented white flowers.

Holboellia see *Trachelospermum*, page 106

Humulus lupulus (hop)

H4–5 (3–6m) ⚘ This rampant climber will soon cover a wall,

Hoheria sexstylosa 'Stardust'

Humulus lupulus 'Aureus'
(golden hop)

shed, trellis or fence and, in theory at least, you could harvest your own hops from it for home-made beer. The green form, used for commercial beer production, is seldom offered as an ornamental, but the golden form **'Aureus'** is a popular garden plant. For best yellow foliage, grow in plenty of sun, in fertile, well-drained soil. The female forms produce the greenish-yellow fruits used for beer-making. It looks fabulous above and behind a statue at House of Pitmuies, Angus. Try growing a purple late-summer clematis through it.

Hydrangea

These are some of the best plants of all for late-summer colour. The mostly deciduous shrubs sell by the thousand, both for garden use and as houseplants. The large flower heads consist of a combination of small fertile flowers and larger flat ray florets. In many of the hybrids, the flatter sterile ray florets make up almost the whole flower, hence the name mopheads. There are a bewildering number of varieties to choose from, but only some do really well in Scotland, so it pays to hunt out the best performers. Hydrangeas do not like to dry out in summer and do best in moist, humus-rich soil – manure, compost and leaf mould are all good soil additives. In Scotland it is best to plant them in as much sun as possible for good flowering, but sheltered from cold easterly winds. All parts of the plants can cause mild stomach upsets if ingested, and sap can cause mild skin irritation. Vine weevils can cause leaf and root damage to hydrangeas, especially in pots. We are very grateful to Shelagh Newman at Holehird, the Lake District Horticultural Society garden in Cumbria, and Anne Greenall in Ayrshire, keepers of national collections, for extensive help in assessing hydrangeas. Anne Greenall's choice of the best for western coastal Scotland: *H. arborescens* 'Annabelle', *H. macrophylla* 'Altona', 'Mme Emile Moullière', 'Blaumeise', 'Blue Wave', Quadricolor', *H. paniculata* 'Limelight', *H. petiolaris*, *H. quercifolia* and *H. serrata* 'Preziosa'.

H. arborescens H4–5 (1.5m x 1.5m) one of the hardiest, with white flowers, suitable for cold and inland gardens, where it tends to die back to ground level each year. The form **'Annabelle'** ⚘ has huge trusses which are so large and heavy that they tend to bend over the foliage. A rarely offered form **'Discolor Sterilis'** has smaller flower heads and is recommended for western gardens, as it stands rain better. *H. aspera H3–4* (2m x 2m) characterized by velvety leaves and striking blue to purple fertile flowers and white-mauve sterile florets, does best in a sheltered site with wind protection, vulnerable to both late and early frosts, so not very successful in colder inland gardens, responds well to hard pruning if it gets too large or straggly; *H.a.* subsp. *sargentiana* (syn. *H. sargentiana*) mid- to late summer, large grey-green hairy leaves, flowers blue-purple,

Hydrangea arborescens 'Annabelle'

Hydrangea aspera Villosa

Hydrangea macrophylla

Hydrangea paniculata 'Grandiflora'

surrounded by white sterile florets; **Villosa Group** (syn. *H. villosa*) later flowering with haunting mauve and purple shades, almost fluorescent in shade, probably the best choice for general planting, as it is a little more manageable , perhaps a little hardier and does not grow so early in the season. *H. heteromalla H2–3* a vigorous summer-flowering giant with white flowers, **'Snow Cap'** is a fine form. *H. macrophylla H3/4–5* (1.5–2m x 1.5–2m) This is what most people have in their mind's eye when the word hydrangea is mentioned. It forms rounded deciduous shrubs with late-summer flowers ranging from white, through pink to reddish and purple. As most of Scotland has acid soil, the blue hydrangeas tend to be blue rather than the pink or muddy pink-blue mixture that tends to occur on limey or neutral soil. Pink hydrangeas are always pink, it is the blue ones which can change colour according to the soil pH. They are excellent in coastal gardens; the whole Scottish western seaboard is ideal for them and the typically peaty soil makes the blues really intense. In eastern and inland gardens they can suffer spring frost damage from time to time, which may cause no lasting damage but tends to reduce flowering. Hardier forms of *H. serrata* are often a better choice for coldest sites. In colder gardens faded flowers should be left on all winter and only pruned in spring once new growth starts. Look out for the garden on Edinburgh Road, Perth, which consists entirely of mophead hydrangeas. Many of those offered in the trade do poorly in Scotland, while there are many outstanding varieties that are sadly seldom sold in garden centres. There are lots of new varieties named every year, many produced for the houseplant trade, with double, star-shaped (Hovaria Series) or Fireworks Groups or picotee (Japanese Lady Series) flowers. Unfortunately most of these do not flower reliably in Scottish gardens, so are best avoided. *Hydrangea macrophylla* divides into two groups:

Hortensias or mopheads
H4–5 unless stated otherwise (1.5–2m x 1.5–2m unless stated otherwise) The flowers consist almost entirely of the flat ray or sterile florets. They usually have longer-lasting flowers than the lacecaps (see below) and they can be dried and used for flower arranging. We (the authors)

don't entirely agree on the merits of mophead hydrangeas: KC is a fan but RC-M thinks they should just stay in your granny's garden.

'All Summer Beauty' blue, flowering on new wood, so good in frost pockets, **'Altona'** dark purple-blue, wind and weather resistant, **'Ami Pasquier'** *H3–4* slow growing, blue-purple, needs shelter, **'Ayesha'** pale mauve or light blue, not that good in the north, **'Dark Angel'** [PBR] and **Red Angel** [PBR] pink-red with striking dark foliage, **Endless Summer** ['Bailmer'] [PBR] blue or pink, can flower on the new season's wood, so good in cold gardens, there is also a pink version and a white version (The Bride) which is later and seems less free-flowering, **'Europa'** purplish-blue (not much of a colour, to be honest), good for seaside, **'Forever Pink'** (1m x 1m) very fine pink flowers (you may need to add lime on peaty soil), low growing, long flowering period, **'King George'** rose red, **'Merveilla Sanguine'** (syn. 'Brunette') red purple, bronze-purple foliage, **'Mme Emile Mouillère'** white slightly tinted pink, one of the best of this colour, **'Zorro'** black stems, fine blue lacecap flowers.

Lacecaps
H(3)4–5 (1.5–2m in height and spread unless stated otherwise) These have a centre of a mass of small flowers surrounded by sterile or ray florets, classier than the more 'in-your-face' Hortensias or mopheads. **'Blaumeise'** (syn. 'Teller Blue') pale-blue fertile flowers, deep-blue sterile florets, tough, **'Blue Wave'** (syn. 'Mariesii Perfecta') very popular, rich blue to mauve with darker fertile flowers, **'Geoffrey Chadbund'** (syn. 'Möwe') (1.5m) light red surrounded by brick-red ray florets, **'Hamburg'** blue, **'Lanarth White'** free flowering, blue flowers surrounded by white ray florets, narrow leaves, a bit leggy, **'Libelle'** (syn. 'Teller White') late, with small blue flowers surrounded by white ray florets, habit rather leggy, **'Lilacina'** *H3–4* mauve to blue, **'Maculata'** *H3–4* leaves with a white variegated border, flowers pinkish white with a few ray florets, not free-flowering, **'Mariesii'** blue flowers with rosy-pink ray florets, **'Quadricolor'** *H3–4* leaves with cream, yellow and light green variegation, flowers white or mauvish pink, tolerant of salty winds, **'Rotschwanz'** (syn. Redstart), deep wine-red ray florets, **'Teller Blue/Pink/White'**, Dutch renamings of Swiss varieties, good in Scotland, **'Tricolor'** leaves variegated greenish-white and yellow, mauve pink fertile flowers, cream sterile flowers, **'Veitchii'** *H3–4* pure white, very vigorous and will often flower well in shade, needs shelter, **'White Wave'** (syn. 'Mariesii Grandiflora') bluish flowers with cream ray florets, tough and tolerant of salt spray.

Other species and varieties
H. paniculata H5 (2–3m+) The toughest and most versatile of all the hydrangeas, this will probably thrive the length and breadth of Scotland. The large panicles of creamy flowers open in late summer (July–August) and turn pink as they go over, hanging on into late winter. If cut back hard in spring, the flowers will be larger, and will then require some wind shelter to protect them. There are several fine selections: **'Grandiflora'** ❦ the commonest

with large flower heads 20–30cm long, **'Kyushu'** upright habit, a good choice for a confined space, **Limelight** [PBR] (1.5m x 1.5m) low and compact, greenish as it opens, **'Phantom'** (1.2m x 1.2m) new and outstanding, compact, flowering very young, with enormous greeny-white panicles in July–August, fading to pink, **Pink Diamond** ['Interhydia'] (1.8m x 1.8m), flowers pale pink, **'Unique'** early flowering, vigorous. New varieties, just coming onto the market include **'Big Ben'** very large flowers, **'Chantilly Lace'** early white turning pink, **Early Sensation** [PBR] early flowering, good autumn colour, **'Pink Lady'** white to good pink, **Pinky-Winky** ['DVPPinky'] flowers turn pink at the bottom, giving a two-toned effect, **'Silver Dollar'** large flowers, **Vanille Fraise** ['Renhy'] red stems, flowers maturing to pink and then red. Don't bother with **'Bombshell'** it is weak and poor.

H. petiolaris (syn. *H. anomala* subsp. *petiolaris*) **H4–5** (5–15m) ♥
A deciduous climbing hydrangea, a very adaptable plant which clings by aerial roots and can be used on walls, to hide eyesores, and will also climb tree trunks: a tree at Birkhill, Fife, has a climbing hydrangea growing at least 15m up the trunk. It can also be used as a spreading shrub. The dark-green leaves can colour

Hydrangea quercifolia

Hydrangea serrata 'Preziosa'

Hydrangea serrata 'Kiyosumi'

Schizophragma hydrangoides

Hydrangea paniculata 'Phantom'

Hydrangea petiolaris

well to yellow in autumn and the inflorescence, consisting of tiny white fertile flowers and flat-faced white ray florets, open in June–July. It is suitable for a shady or north-facing wall but it might not flower very freely in the low Scottish light levels. It is self-supporting once established, but best tied in as a young plant to help it take hold. **'Mirranda'** is a recently introduced form with yellow- variegated leaf edges.

The white-flowered evergreen climbing hydrangeas such as ***H. seemannii*** and ***H. serratifolia*** are not very hardy (**H2–3**), and need a warm wall in a sheltered western or south-western Scottish garden to flower well. ***H. quercifolia*** (oak-leaved hydrangea) **H4** (2m x 2m) ♥ is a striking foliage plant with leaves like giant oak leaves which colour up to bronze-purple in autumn, staying semi-evergreen in mild winters and coastal gardens. The conical panicles of white flowers open in July–August and turn purplish as they age. Some forms grow late

and tend to be frosted. Good coastal plant, wind and salt spray tolerant. Selections include **'Little Honey'** bright yellow-green leaves, **'Snowflake'** double white flowers age to pink, **Snow Queen** ['Flemigea'] upright panicles of flowers, ***H. serrata*** **H(3)4–5** is a smaller-growing, smaller-leaved and sometimes hardier version of *H. macrophylla* and some of the best hydrangeas for Scotland are forms of this species. It is less tolerant of wind and salt than *H. macrophylla*, so needs some shelter in seaside gardens. Most forms of this species are lacecaps (a mixture of fertile flowers and sterile florets), in mid to late summer – on a compact deciduous shrub. It will flower in shade better than *H. macrophylla*, but doesn't thrive in dry conditions. The following reach 60cm–1.5m x 60cm–1m unless stated otherwise. **'Preziosa'** (1.5m x 1.5m) ♥ one of the best, small mophead flowers which open whitish green, turning pink to red and finally purplish, sometimes with all the colours at once with flowers at different stages, excellent in eastern Scotland and seems pretty tough, **'Beni-gaku'** white flowers with few ray florets which age to pink in June–July, leaves reddish, **'Bluebird'** blue with pale blue ray florets, red autumn leaves, **'Diadem'** pale blue, leaves red in autumn, **'Golden Sunlight'** (syn. 'Golden Showers') young growth bright yellow-green, gradually fading to pale green, shy flowering, pink, **'Grayswood'** (2m x 2m) mauve with white sterile ray florets which turn deep red, good autumn colour, a bit leggy,

'Kiyosumi' (2m x 2m) reddish young growth, white sterile florets with pink picotee edging, 'Miranda' low, good in wind and salt spray, 'Tiara' pale pink, good autumn colour, habit a bit loose.

Schizophragma hydrangoides* H3–4** (3–6m+) This is a close relative, a self-supporting climber with white flowers with distinctive heart-shaped cream bracts. Suitable for most fertile soils, does best on a wall or sheltered site outside favourable areas but may take many years to flower. It is impressive on the terraces of Torosay Castle, Mull. **'Moonlight' *H3 less hardy, with variegated leaves, **'Roseum' *H4*** pink flowers.

Hypericum (St John's wort)
Yellow, yellow, yellow: no other colour seems to have been invented in hypericums. They are some of the best and most reliable of summer-flowering shrubs with flowers of various sizes, bright yellow with a cluster or yellow or orange stamens in the centre. In Scotland they do best in full sun, in well drained but not dry soil. Only the deciduous forms need pruning; they are best cut back hard in autumn. Others can be tidied up after flowering. KC thinks highly of most of them, while RC-M thinks that you can get bored of them very quickly and that their unfortunate sparse growth habit traps and then proudly displays whatever the wind throws their way – leaves, newspapers, pizza boxes. The species *H. perforatum* provides the anti-depressant St John's wort (which you'll end up resorting to if you plant too many of them – RC-M).

***H. aegypticum* H2–3** (50cm x 1.5m) for mild and west-coast gardens only, low spreading evergreen with small pale-yellow flowers in May–June. ***H. androsaemum* H4** (75cm x 1.5m)

Hypericum calycinum   *Hypericum* 'Hidcote'

deciduous with star-shaped yellow flowers to 2cm, followed by red-black fruit; the form **'Albury Purple'** has red-purple flushing to the leaves. ***H. calycinum* H4** (15cm x indefinite) evergreen with small yellow flowers grown as a vigorous ground-cover, spreading by runners, suitable for shady sites. It is so susceptible to rust

fungus that it is no longer sold in large numbers, though it still grows in some gardens without disease problems. **'Hidcote' H4** (1.2m x 1.5m) ❦ by far the best seller, an outstanding plant with large yellow flowers to 6cm across from July to September/October; semi-evergreen, likely to be damaged in hard winters in cold inland gardens, but will usually recover well if cut back; avoid the poor variegated form, which is unstable, inclined to revert and less hardy. ***H. x inodorum* H4** (1.2m x 1.2m) deciduous or semi-evergreen, small star-shaped yellow flowers, showy red-black fruit, mainly used for its fruit in flower arrangements; most forms, including **'Elstead'**, are very prone to rust, although **'Rheingold'** is said to be resistant. ***H. x moserianum*** (50cm x 60cm+) a dwarf ground-cover with deep yellow flowers, usually sold in the form **'Tricolor' *H3*** (30cm), white, pink and green variegated leaves, needs a sheltered site and not for cold and inland gardens. **'Rowallane' *H3*** (1.5m x 1.5m) an impressive plant for mild coastal gardens, similar to 'Hidcote' but with larger leaves and flowers.

Ilex (holly)
Hollies are great plants for Scottish gardens: they are some of the few evergreens to perform well in severe climates and some of a handful of larger shrubs which tolerate dry shade. They are useful for hedging, although the fallen leaves of the spiny varieties are a problem in small gardens, or where children play in bare feet. They are also excellent in woodland gardens for providing shelter under trees. The familiar red berries of our common native holly (*I. aquifolium*) are only part of the story: there are over 400 species worldwide, many of which do not resemble the typical 'holly' at all. The leaves of most of the garden-worthy hollies are evergreen and spiny or scallop-edged. There are male and female forms: both produce small white or cream flowers in spring but only females produce the red, orange or yellow berries. Females require a related male holly near by to pollinate them, except in the few self-fertile forms. Just to confuse the issue, some of the commonest male forms have foolishly been given female names and vice versa. Amongst the miscreants are 'Golden Queen' (male), and 'Golden King' (female). Lots of hollies have variegated foliage, some of which tend to produce reverted shoots, which are best removed. Hollies like well-drained, moderately fertile soil, and the green-leaved forms of *I. aquifolium* are tolerant of dry shade once established, but coloured-leaved forms need sunlight to retain the variegation. There are lots of slow-growing and dwarf hollies suitable for the shrub border and containers. Provide staking and/or artificial protection for young plants in exposed positions, and don't let them dry out until well established. Holly leaf miner can make unsightly trails on the leaves but don't do any serious damage (and are virtually impossible to treat), and scale insect can be a problem. Hollies in pots are far less hardy than those in the ground and the 2010–11 winters killed many

Ilex x *altaclerensis* 'Belgica Aurea'

Ilex x *altaclerensis* 'Golden King'

Ilex aquifolium 'Madame Briot'

container-grown plants: use bubble wrap to protect the roots.

I. x altaclerensis H3–4 vigorous, evergreen, a cross between the common English holly and the less hardy *I. perado* from the Azores. Most are tolerant of city pollution and seaside exposure, but for coldest inland gardens forms of *I. aquifolium* would be a better choice. Forms include **'Belgica Aurea'** (syn. 'Silver Sentinel') *H4* (8m x 3m) female, a handsome plant of erect habit with green leaves, margined yellow, producing few berries, **'Camelliifolia'** *H4* (6–10m+) female, conical habit, entire dark green leaves, purple stems, red berries, **'Golden King'** *H3–4* (6m x 5m) female, compact with grey green leaves with golden margins, sparse red berries, mainly grown for its foliage, **'Lawsoniana'** *H3–4* (6m x 5m) female, yellow-streaked green stems and leaves splashed yellow, berries red.

I. aquifolium (common or English holly) *H4–5* (10–20m x 6m) ✹ ✉ a dense, erect tree with spiny leaves and red (occasionally orange or yellow) berries in female forms, leaves variable in prickliness. This is one of the toughest evergreens, useful for hedging (planted 50cm–1m apart) and for providing shelter from biting north-east winds. There are hundreds of selections, all hardy (*H4–5*), varying in berry colour, leaf colour and degree of prickliness: **'Alaska'** female, prickly, green-leaved, very hardy and free-berrying, a good choice for hedging, **'Argentea Marginata'** female, of columnar habit, leaves with wide white margins, purplish pink when young, produces abundant red fruit, **'Argentea Marginata Pendula'** (6m x 5m) as above but with weeping branches, a good small garden specimen tree, **'Aurea Marginata'** (6m x 5m) female, slow growing with bushy habit, purple stems and spiny, yellow-margined leaves, a good fruiter, **'Bacciflava'** (syn. 'Fructo Luteo') (15m x 6m) female, dark-green leaves, yellow berries, **'Ferox'** (6m x 4m) male, 'the hedgehog holly', green, extremely prickly, with purple stems, and **'Ferox Argentea'** ✹ similar, with cream-margined leaves, for some reason both very prickly hollies that seem to be attractive to deer, **'Flavescens'** (moonlight holly) (6m x 5m) female, prickly leaves suffused with yellow on the young growth and remaining yellow most of the year if planted in plenty of light, red berries, **'Golden Queen'** (7–10m x 6m) male, spiny leaves broadly

margined gold, **'Golden Milkboy'** (3–6m x 4m) male, leaves with a large bold splash of yellow in the centre of the leaf, inclined to revert but very striking, **'Golden Van Tol'** (4m x 3m) female, self-fertile, but producing only a few red fruit, leaves margined yellow, one of the hardiest, **'Handsworth New Silver'** (5–8m x 5m) female, a dense columnar tree with spiny leaves with creamy margins and red berries, **'J.C. van Tol'** *H4–5* (6m x 4m) ✹ female, purple stems, non-spiny dark-green leaves, with slightly downward pointing branches, one of the toughest and self-fertile, so great if you have room for only one holly, **'Madame Briot'** (10m x 5m) dark-green leaves with prickly gold margins and dark-red fruit, very good habit, one of the best variegated forms, **'Myrtifolia'** (3–4m x 3m) male, small leaves with fine spines, **'Myrtifolia Aurea Maculata'** (3–4m x 3m) dark-green leaves with a gold centre, purple stems, slow growing, **'Pyramidalis'** (4–6m x 5m) female, of narrowly conical habit with yellow stems and few-spined green leaves, free berrying (there are also variegated and yellow-berried – 'Fructo Luteo' – forms), **'Silver Milkboy'** male and **'Silver Milkmaid'** female (both 4–6m x 4m), leaves with bold splashes of white variegation in the centre of the leaf, inclined to revert, **'Silver Queen'** (syn. Silver King) 5m x 4m) ✹ male, dense and upright with purple stems and spiny leaves with cream margins, young leaves salmon pink, **'Silver van Tol'** (3–4m x 3m), female but self-fertile, leaves margined creamy white.

I. crenata (box-leaved or Japanese holly) *H4–5* (5m x 3m) resembles a box more than a holly and it can be used in a similar role – as a tidy, compact shrub with glossy oval leaves. Female forms have small black berries. This is an extremely hardy plant, but it can suffer damage from unseasonal frosts. In the USA and Japan it is much used in topiary and hedges. Forms include: **'Convexa'** (syn. 'Bullata') (2m x 1.2m) female, dark-green leaves and free fruiting, **'Fastigiata'** (2m x 1m) narrow columnar habit (there is more than one clone around with this name), **'Golden Gem'** *H4* (1m x 1.5m) female, leaves golden yellow, shy flowering with only sparse black berries, best yellow colour in a sunny location, **'Variegata'** (4m x 2.5m) male, leaves yellow or marked yellow, shy flowering.

I. x meserveae (blue holly) *H3–4* (3m x 1.2m) is becoming more and more widely grown as it is slower than the large hollies listed above and has attractive blue-green foliage. Females have glossy red fruit. Less hardy than the native hollies, it likes some summer heat and tends to struggle a bit in wetter and coastal parts of Scotland. Forms include: **'Blue Angel'** *H3* female, dark-purple stems, bluish-green leaves, the least hardy of this group, **'Blue**

Ilex crenata 'Golden Gem'

Ilex x *meserveae* 'Blue Prince'

Jasminum officinale

Prince' male, spreading habit, **'Blue Princess'** female, large handsome leaves and abundant fruit.

Itea see *Garrya elliptica*, page 53

Jasminum (jasmine) (climber)

❊ Jasmine is best known as a white summer-flowering climber with exotic evening fragrance, but this is a large genus and many species are not scented and look quite different. There are rampant climbing scented jasmines and smaller shrubby ones, and they flower at various times of year. Winter jasmine (*J. nudiflorum*) is ideal for most of Scotland, while the others need a relatively mild climate or a warm sheltered site on a wall. All can be hard pruned after flowering to keep them in bounds.

J. beesianum H3 (3–5m) a vigorous twining climber, evergreen in mildest districts, otherwise deciduous, with fragrant pinkish-red flowers in June–July and black berries in winter. *J. humile* **'Revolutum'** *H3* (2–2.5m) fragrant deep-yellow flowers over a long period from spring to autumn; though this is a shrub rather than a climber, in Scotland it does best on or in front of a warm wall. *J. nudiflorum* (winter jasmine) *H4–5* (2–3m) ♟ popular winter-flowering shrub that is the toughest of the taller jasmines and opens its flowers as early as November in mild years; though not a climber, it is usually grown against a wall; the bright yellow frost-hardy flowers open on the leafless branches over several weeks;

'Mystique' is a newly introduced form with variegated leaves. *J. officinale* (common jasmine) *H3* (5–12m) the classic sweetly fragrant, white-flowered jasmine, a popular plant for the conservatory, but beware: this is a rampant spreading thug, particularly indoors. Better to grow it outdoors where cold snaps will bring it back down to earth. Deciduous and flowering in mid-summer to early autumn, it is best grown on a warm south- or west-facing wall, particularly in cooler areas. It may be hardier than we think, as there is a large happy plant on the south side of Tillypronie House at 300m in mid-Aberdeenshire. Forms includes *affine* white flowers tinged pink, **'Argentiovariegatum'** leaves margined creamy white, **'Aureum'** yellow leaves, but can look a bit sickly. Lots of new forms have been popping on to the market in recent years: **'Clotted Cream'** creamy-yellow flowers, **Fiona Sunrise** ['Frojas'] leaves flushed yellow, **'Inverleith'** a fine form from Edinburgh with red and white flowers. *J.* x *stephanense H3* (3–5m) fragrant pink flowers in June–July.

Kalmia

H5 ♟ Kalmias are mainly grown for their exquisite flowers: the usually deep-coloured buds gradually open out like miniature parasols in June–July over several weeks. Kalmias like an acid or peaty soil and in Scotland need full sun to bloom freely. They associate well with rhododendrons and other ericaceous and woodland plants. They are brittle and hard to handle, so be careful when planting them. All parts of the plants are poisonous.

K. latifolia (mountain laurel) *H5* (2–3m x 2–3m) is by far the best-known species, with thick evergreen leaves, which are inclined to yellowness. There are many fully hardy (*H5*) named clones; some of the best are **'Carousel'** white, with radiating bands of bright red purple, **'Freckles'** light pink with a circle of deep purple spots, **'Eskimo'** pure white, **'Galaxy'** star shaped, pink with burgundy markings, **'Heart's Desire'** deep red buds open to rich maroon, **'Mitternacht'/'Midnight'** dark reddish purple, the darkest we have seen, **'Minuet'** (a selection of var. *myrtifolia*) light pink with a broad cinnamon-maroon band, dwarf with smaller leaves, **'Ostbo Red'** an old favourite with red buds, pink flowers, **'Olympic Fire'**, red buds, pink flowers, good foliage, **'Peppermint'** red centre with

Jasminum nudiflorum

Jasminum beesianum

Kalmia, mixed colours

white and red stripes. *K. angustifolia* (sheep laurel) *H5* (1m x 1.2m+) small red-purple or white (**var. candida**) flowers in June, on a slow spreading, low shrub. Compact and easy.

Kerria japonica

H5 (2–2.5m x 3m+) This is a useful early-flowering shrub, very tough (hardy to at least -25°C) and suitable for anywhere in Scotland. Deciduous, with bright orange-yellow rose-like flowers, 4–5cm across, opening on the bare green branches from February to April, depending on the season and climate. Easy to please, and tolerant of moist soils, it is happiest in a well-drained site, in sun or part shade. Kerrias require little or no maintenance, though you can cut them back after flowering if required. They spread with suckers but are easily dug up if they outgrow allotted space.

There is only one species but several different fully hardy (*H5*) forms: '**Golden Guinea**' large, single flowers, '**Picta**' (syn. 'Variegata') (1.5m x 2m+) single flowers and leaves with white-variegated edges, but the least garden-worthy form in our opinion, shy flowering, liable to revert and suffer from dieback, '**Pleniflora**' (3m x 3m+) double deep-yellow flowers, the most popular form, vigorous suckering spreading habit.

Kerria japonica 'Pleniflora'

Kolkwitzia amabilis see *Wiegela*, page 109

Laurels, cherry see *Prunus*, page 84

Laurus nobilis (bay)

H3–4 (2–3m x 2–3m in 10–15 years, U: 10m x 8m) Most cooks like to have bay leaves to hand, and the shrubs can be carefully sculpted into pyramids and balls or just grown in the herb garden and kept compact by constant harvesting. Left unpruned, they grow into small trees. Evergreen, with dark green leaves and small yellow flowers, bays do best in a sheltered spot, in as much sun as possible. In mild west-coast gardens they can be used for hedging. Unprotected bays can be damaged or even killed in a really severe winter in eastern and inland Scotland. That said, they are reasonably tough once established. Growing the single-stem lollipop topiary bays that often flank smart townhouse doors is risky in all but the mildest areas of the country, because frost tears the exposed bark and disease soon sets in. Scale insect can cause problems – if the leaves look sooty and are sticky to touch, spray with a systemic insecticide.

Laurus nobilis (bay)

Likewise for red spider mite attacks. There is a yellow-leaved form '**Aurea**' which always looks ill.

Lavandula and *Teucrium fruticans*

Everyone loves lavender, or so it seems, as plants are sold by the thousand all over Scotland. Yet this is another plant that, far from its natural home in the Mediterranean, tolerates rather than relishes our climate. What lavenders like is well-drained, preferably neutral-limy, stony soil, in plenty of heat and sun and low rainfall; and they dislike winter wet and heavy soils. So how do they survive here at all? The truth is that in Scotland they tend to look sorry for themselves after a few years, suffering from dieback and worse, but while they are alive, they are good value, so view them as a short-term investment and you won't be disappointed. The fragrant purple, lavender, pink, blue or white flowers are produced over a long period in summer and attract bees and butterflies. The narrow greyish or silvery-green leaves are of course delightfully aromatic, used in cooking, pot pourri, drawer sachets, etc. Though lavenders can reach 1m in height, it is best to prune them annually to encourage bushy growth; this is probably best done

Lavandula angustifolia hedge at Carestown Steading

in April–May. One of the best places to grow them is under the eaves of the house, where they are sheltered from the worst deluge and get extra heat. They are good container plants, not least because if you go away on holiday and they don't get watered they usually come back from the brink after a good soaking. Lavenders suffer from several pests and diseases that cause dieback, but the weather is much more of a problem. Lavenders are best planted in early summer so that they can establish before winter.

Lavandula stoechas and L. angustifolia varieties

L. angustifolia (Old English lavender) *H3–4* (90cm x 90cm) the hardiest species and the best choice for Scotland. The dense spikes of flowers vary from pale to deep purple. Two old favourites are the compact **'Hidcote'** (60cm x 75cm) ♈ dark purple and **'Munstead'** (45cm x 60cm) blue, but there are now better choices available. Newer varieties include **'Arctic Snow'** (80cm x 90cm) white, **Blue Cushion** ['Schola'] (40cm x 50cm) deep blue, fading to pale blue, **'Havana'** (50cm) a good alternative to 'Hidcote' with larger flowers and healthier....? **'Imperial Gem'** (60cm x 75cm) purple, with particularly silvery foliage, said to be more disease resistant than 'Hidcote', **Lavenite Petite** [PBR] (35cm x 40cm) very compact habit, dark blue pompom-like flowers earlier than 'Hidcote' and 'Munstead', **Little Lady** ['Batlad'] (60cm x 60cm) purple-blue, **Little Lottie** ['Clarmo'] (45cm x 50cm) lilac pink, **'Loddon Blue'** (45cm x 60cm) blue, **'Loddon Pink'** (45cm x 60cm) soft pink, 90cm) white, **'Miss Katherine'** (60cm x 80cm) probably the best of the pink-flowered forms, **'Melissa Lilac'** (40cm x 50cm) impressive large lilac flowers, **'Nana Alba'** (40cm x 50cm) white, **'Royal Purple'** (75cm x 90cm) relatively tall, with fine purple flowers. **L. x intermedia** *H2–3* less hardy than *L. angustifolia*, looks very similar; Heavenly Angle [PBR 'Dowfangel'] (50cm) compact white, Heavenly Night ['Dowphnight'] (50cm) dark purple, Heavenly Scent ['Dowphscent'] (50cm) blue, **'Grappenhall'** (syn. 'Pale Pretender') (90cm x 90cm) lavender blue, vigorous, **'Grosso'** (90cm x 90cm) vigorous and tough, much used for commercial production of lavender oil, **'Twickel Purple'** (60cm x 60cm) violet fading to lavender, can be rather straggly, **Walberton's Silver Edge** ['Walvera'] *H3* ♦ (75cm x 75cm) pale purple, leaves edged with cream variegation. **L. stoechas** (French lavender) *H(2)–3* (60cm x 60cm) flower heads of purple or white with distinctive sterile bracts or tufts from the top of the flower,

Lavandula stoechas 'Fat Head'

sometimes a different shade than the flowers themselves; often flowers in late spring and then again in late summer. Very attractive and well worth extra care, this species requires even sharper drainage than the above, and will not survive waterlogged or heavy soil. A raised bed under the eaves of the house, or a container with very gritty soil, is ideal. There are so many forms on the market now; just go for the colours you prefer. **Blueberries and Cream** [PBR] (70cm x 70cm) dark purple with cream bracts, very striking, **'Fat Head'** *H3* (45cm x 50cm) plum-purple sterile bracts, one of the hardier forms and said to survive winter wet better than most, **'Helmsdale'** (60cm x 75cm) dark-purple bracts with purple flags and dark-green aromatic foliage, **'Kew Red'** (40cm x 45cm) cerise-crimson flowers with pale-pink bracts from April to first frost, rather tender, so give winter protection, **L.s. f. leucantha** (45cm x 50cm) white flowers, **'Madrid Pink'** (40cm x 45cm) very compact, pink-red, **'Madrid White'** (40cm x 45cm) white flowers and bracts, **subsp. pedunculata** (syn. 'Papillon') (90cm x 90cm) dark purple with red-violet sterile bracts, shorter flower spikes, **'Rocky Road'** [PBR] (60 x 60cm) deep purple with pink ears, **'Ruffles Boysenberry'** [PBR] dark pink with pale pink bracts, **'Snowman'** (40cm x 45cm) white, **'Tickled Pink'** (70cm x 80cm) fine pink flowers but poor habit and less hardy than most of the others, **'Tiara'** purple with cream bracts, **'Willow Vale'** (60cm x 75cm) grey-green foliage, long purple crinkly bracts. **L. viridis** and **L. lanata** very tender and probably not worth considering.

Teucrium fruticans (germander) *H2–3* (1–2m x 2–4m) A closely related shrub from the Mediteranean, which enjoys similar conditions to lavender: well-drained soil in full sun. It has a long flowering period with pale lavender-blue flowers in summer and autumn. The leaves are white on the underside. Not reliably hardy in much of Scotland, but good near the coast, does best in a sheltered site, against a south- or west-facing wall. It often suffers partial dieback in winter, so needs a good prune in spring. The form **'Azureum'** has dark-blue flowers and is less hardy.

Lavatera (mallow)

H(2)3–4 (1–2m x 1–2m) There are lots of good things about lavateras: they grow huge in one season and produce masses of saucer-shaped flowers in clusters up the stems, not unlike hollyhocks, in shades of purple-pink, pink or white, from July to October. The harsh purple-pink flowers of most forms are not to everyone's taste. The main drawback of lavateras is their lack of longevity, but as they grow so fast and flower so freely, it is not the end of the world if you lose one in a cold winter. Most garden lavateras are derived from **L. x clementii**, which is thought to be a cross of *L. olbia* x *L. thuringiaca*. Fleshy top growth is usually cut back by winter cold – not by much in mild conditions, but frequently to the ground in cold winters or severe climates. In more exposed positions, you'd do well to prune them before winter winds knock them over;

otherwise you can wait until spring to see where the young growth will come from. Most do well in coastal gardens. Plant them in late spring and summer rather than autumn or winter, unless you have a very mild climate. Hardiness *H3–4* and size 2m x 1.5–2m unless stated otherwise.

'Barnsley' attractive red-eyed, off-white flowers ageing to pink, but partly reverting to purple in the second season in our experience – cut these out, **'Baby Barnsley'** (1.2m x 1.2m) more compact and said not to revert to purple, **'Blushing Bride'** *H3* white with a pink eye, **'Bredon Springs'** (1.2m x 1.2m) pink, flushed mauve, **'Bressingham Pink'** pale pink, **'Burgundy Wine'** (1.5m x 2.5m) dark pink with darker veins, **'Candy Floss'** *H3* pale pink, **Chamallow** ['Inovera'] (1.5m x 1.5m) compact pink, new, **'Kew Rose'** (3m x 3m) bright pink, **'Lisanne'** *H3* (1m x 1.2m) dwarf with white flowers, **'Pavlova'** *H3* (1m x 1.2m) pastel-pink flowers with a white eye, **'Pink Frills'** *H3* pale-pink, crinkled flowers, **'Rosea'** (syn. *L. olbia* 'Rosea') deep pink, **'Red Rum'** dark red-purple, not all that attractive. *L. maritima* *H2–3* (1.2m x 1.2m), attractive pink or lilac-pink flowers with distinctive deeper veins, not very hardy; a plant for a mild coastal garden, it grows well in the East Neuk of Fife. *L. thuringiaca* **'Ice Cool'** *H3* (1.5m x 1.2m) pure white. The spectacular annual *L. trimestris* is grown as a bedding plant.

Lavatera 'Red.Rum', 'Rosea' and 'Barnsley'

Lavatera 'Baby Barnsley'

Leptospermum

H2–3 These New Zealand and Australian shrubs and trees can make excellent garden plants for mild west-coast and favourable east-coast gardens, and if you have a sheltered south-facing wall, they might succeed elsewhere. Most of the hardier forms are derived from *L. scoparium* (manuka) *H2–3* (2–3m x 2–3m) a fairly compact evergreen with narrow aromatic leaves borne on arching shoots, with cup-shaped red, pink or white double flowers in June–July. It is also sold as a houseplant. The white and pink forms seem to tolerate wet soils better than the red ones. There are some good examples at Colonsay House garden, Jura House walled garden, and Logan in Dumfries and Galloway. They do best in well-drained, not over-rich soil

in full or part day sun. They suffer from sooty mould in some climates, but we have not yet seen it in Scotland.

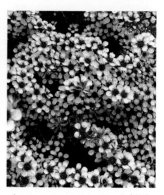

Leptospermum scoparium (pink)

Leptospermum scoparium (white)

'Appleblossom' *H2–3* light pink, **'Centaurus'** *H2* (1.5m x 2m) white with pinkish-red edges and red eye, **'Cygnus'** *H2* light pink with green centres, **'Electric Red'** [PBR] *H2* (1.5m x 1.5m) deep red, **'Gaiety Girl'** *H2* semi-double, deep pink outside, paler inside, **'Kea'** (50cm x 60cm) dense, with bronze foliage, low-growing, single pink flowers, **'Kiwi'** (1m x 1m) fine dark crimson flowers, young growth tinged purple, a fine form, suitable for a container or rock garden, **'Nichollsii'** *H2–3* crimson, foliage purple-tinged, **'Pompom'** double white, **'Red Damask'** *H2* double deep red long-lasting flowers, very fine, **'Snow White'** *H2* double white with a dark centre. *L. rupestre* *H3–4* (0.5–1.5m) usually prostrate, but sometimes mounding evergreen shrub with deep green leaves and small star-shaped white flowers in May–June, relatively hardy.

Leucothoe fontanesiana

H5 (1–2m x 2m) Try as we might, it's difficult to get excited about these plants, because they just don't do much. Yes, they are useful evergreens with coloured foliage and they produce small-urn-shaped white spring flowers in panicles, but they don't thrill, at any time of year. Similar to, and closely related to, pieris (see page 82), they like moist but not soggy acid soil in sun or part day shade. They have evergreen leathery leaves, often coloured. Selected forms include **'Rainbow'** dark-green leaves mottled cream and pink, **'Curly Red'** (*L. axillaris*) (1.2m) compact and slow, curled leaved turn red in winter, **'Rollissonii'** small narrow leaves, **Scarletta** ['Zeblid'] red-edged young foliage, with red-purple winter colour.

Leucothoe fontanesiana 'Scarletta' and 'Rainbow'

Leycesteria formosa

Leycesteria formosa

🌶 *H4* (2m x 3m) a weird and exotic-looking plant in flower, that's for sure, but it's actually fairly tough, vigorous and easy, and does well in most of Scotland. It can become a weed, spreading freely by seed. This thicket-forming deciduous shrub produces tapered leaves on hollow cane-like stems. In summer, the pendent spikes of white flowers appear, surrounded by prominent red-purple bracts. These are followed by red berries, which apparently pheasants love to eat. A yellow-leaved form, **Golden Lanterns** ['Notbruce'], has attractive leaves, but the flowers seem to be smaller and less freely produced.

Ligustrum (privet)

🌶 Suffering somewhat from a suburban image problem, privet is actually a large and varied genus, tolerant of most soils and particularly useful for hedging. The small tubular white flowers tend to smell unpleasant, and the leaves and black berries of most varieties are harmful if eaten. For hedging, the species most commonly used is *L. ovalifolium*. Like holly, privet is a hungry feeder, and it tends to dry out neighbouring soil; you can root prune with a spade to reduce this. For hedging, plant 30–40cm apart and clip twice a year to keep the height manageable and to maintain density and bushiness. It is wind tolerant and good for coastal planting.

L. ovalifolium H5 (2–4m x 2–3m) semi-evergreen in mild climates, otherwise deciduous, with oval dark-green leaves, and small white flowers in summer; coloured leaf forms include **'Argenteum' H5** leaves margined creamy white, **'Aureum' H5** (golden privet) (4m x 3m) leaves with bright yellow borders, **'Vicaryi' H3–4** a hybrid golden privet with yellow suffused leaves which turn purple-bronze in winter. *L. vulgare* (common privet) *H5* (3m x 3m) ✂ is a Scottish native, useful for hedging, screening and hedgerows, with green deciduous or semi-evergreen leaves, tiny white flowers and black fruits. Evergreen privet varieties include *L. japonicum* (Japanese privet) *H4* (2–3m x 2.5m) a dense evergreen with glossy dark green leaves and plentiful black berries. These are grown in thousands in Italy, often shaped in to balls and pyramids, and shipped over. They don't always seem to be very happy in Scotland, maybe partly because of the shock of moving north; they seem to grow better in hot dry countries. The form **'Rotundifolium'** (1–1.5m x 1.5m) has rounded, very leathery leaves. *L. lucidum* (Chinese privet) *H4* (3m x 2m) has very similar foliage to *L. japonicum* – the two are often confused; **'Excelsum Superbum'** is a very grandiose name for a form with yellow-margined leaves. *L. delavayanum H2–3* (2m x 3m) has small dark-green leaves; commonly offered by Italian growers, it is not hardy enough for most of Scotland, but makes a good hedge in mild areas.

Lonicera (honeysuckle)

There are over 180 species of *Lonicera*; the best known are the scented summer-flowering climbers, but there are also many shrubby species. Most have distinctive tubular flowers which are two-lipped, usually with five spreading lobes.

Climbing species and hybrids

❋ These grow in full or part day sun, in fertile, humus-rich, moist but not waterlogged soil. Climbing honeysuckles are deciduous, semi-evergreen or evergreen, the deciduous ones generally being the toughest. They can be trained on walls or fences or into other trees and shrubs (but cut back periodically, as they can strangle other plants). Most of them will climb by twining their stems round whatever support is available. They are dense and vigorous and the weight of a honeysuckle can be considerable, so don't rely on a flimsy structure to support them. If you can shade the roots it helps keep them moist in summer, which ensures vigour and best flowering. Evergreen varieties are best planted in spring; deciduous ones can be planted almost any time, but as usual, autumn planting will give quickest establishment. Pruning is only necessary to keep them in bounds or to remove damaged or diseased sections. This is best done immediately after flowering. Honeysuckles can suffer from aphid attacks and mildew (white patches on the leaves), both of which can be chemically treated.

L. x americana H4 (4–7m+/-) ❋ deciduous, flowers very fragrant white, fading to yellow, flushed red purple in July–September. Another plant commonly but incorrectly grown under this name is *L. x italica* ❋ fragrant pink and yellow flowers and purple young stems; it includes the form **Harlequin** ['Sherlite'] variegated leaves, edged with cream. *L. x brownii* **'Dropmore Scarlet' H4** (4m) orange-scarlet flowers, not scented, over several weeks in June–July, with rounded leaves; best grown in part shade to reduce attacks from aphids, and likes a warm site. **Golden Trumpet** ['Mintrump'] *H4* (3m) orange-yellow, *L. caprifolium H4–5* (6m) ❋ very fragrant, creamy-white to yellow flowers, flushed pink, in June–July, followed by red berries, large leaves. *L. etrusca H3–4* (3–4m) ❋ flowers tubular fragrant white, fading to yellow, flushed red, June–July, semi-evergreen, does best in full sun but not always a great performer in Scotland as it likes

Ligustrum ovalifolium, privet hedge, golden and green forms

Lonicera x heckrottii

Lonicera periclymenum 'Belgica'

Lonicera periclymenum
'Graham Thomas'

Lonicera periclymenum 'Serotina'

stems brown, leaves with a purple underside, flowers very fragrant, tinged purple on the outside, **'Superba'** (syn. 'Red Coral') scarlet. *L. periclymenum* (woodbine) *H4–5* (5–7m) ✉ ❀ a British native, found in parts of Scotland, and most people's idea of the 'typical' honeysuckle. It does well as far north as Shetland. The flowers are scented, white to yellow on the inside, often flushed red outside, in summer, followed by red berries. Usually sold as one of many named forms: **'Belgica'** (syn. Early Dutch) ❀ ♟ heavily scented pink and red flowers in May–June, and again in September after a hot summer, **'Graham Thomas'** ❀ ♟ very fragrant, cream, turning to yellow, with no pink or purplish tint, **'Red Gables'** similar to but more compact than 'Serotina', **'Serotina'** ❀ ♟ (Late Dutch) scented, red-purple outside, cream-yellow inside, July–October, more than one form of this in the trade, the best one has glaucous blue-green leaves, **'Sweet Sue'** selected by plantsman Roy Lancaster and named after his wife, similar to 'Graham Thomas' but with a larger inflorescence. *L. sempervirens H3* (2–4m) stunning unscented scarlet-orange flowers, yellow inside, over a long period, large oval leaves, for a warm sheltered site in mild gardens only. *L. x tellmanniana H3–4* (3–5m) bright copper-orange, not scented, in June and July, large oval leaves.

Shrubby *Lonicera*

L. fragrantissima H4 (2m x 3m) ❀ semi-evergreen, very early flowering, in winter and early spring, flowers fragrant, cream, red berries in summer. Very similar is *L. x purpusii H4* (2m) ❀ sweetly fragrant white flowers with yellow anthers in winter, rather gaunt habit, usually sold as the fine form **'Winter Beauty'**. *L. syringantha H4* (1–2m) ❀ is a little-known deciduous species that resembles a small daphne for its pink, sweet-smelling purplish-pink flowers in April–May; small green leaves, and a tidy habit; tough and easy, should be more widely grown. *L. nitida H4* (1.5–3m x 1.5–3m) a very popular evergreen with tiny leaves, looking like a box – hence the common names box-leaved honeysuckle or poor man's box. Small fragrant creamy-white flowers in spring, transparent blue berries. Commonly used for hedging and screening, plant 30–50cm apart and trim 2–3 times a year, with the occasional hard prune to keep in bounds. Reported to be unpalatable to deer. Forms include **'Baggesen's Gold'** (2m x 2m) a popular selection with golden-yellow summer leaves which turn yellow-green in

more sun and heat than we can give it; two popular selections are **'Donald Waterer'** flowers red, fading to orange-yellow outside, white inside, red stems, and **'Superba'** fragrant yellow flowers, flushed pink. *L. x heckrottii H4* (3–5m) ❀ deciduous or semi-evergreen with fragrant flowers, pink outside, orange-yellow inside, the most popular form **'Gold Flame' H4–5** deep pink and yellow. *L. henryi H3–4* (5–10m) evergreen, very vigorous, with hairy shoots and dark-green leaves, small yellow, purplish-red-tinged flowers in June–July, followed by black berries; inland, it needs a warm, sheltered site; the flowers last a very short time and are rather small. **Copper Beauty** [PBR] selection with shiny coppery new growth. *L. japonica H4–5* (8–10m) ❀ this is the toughest and most vigorous of the evergreen or semi-evergreen varieties, and it is rampant, useful for covering an eyesore. Flowers open over a long period from June onwards, fragrant, white, changing to yellow as they age, followed by blue-black berries. Forms include **'Aureoreticulata' H3** less hardy and less vigorous, leaves veined yellow, **'Cream Cascade'** ❀ a new selection with white and yellow flowers, **'Dart's World' H4** ❀ a relatively hardy selection with very fragrant flowers with strong red flushing, **'Halliana' H4** ♟ the most popular form, vigorous, with hairy young leaves, **'Hall's Prolific'** ❀ very similar to 'Halliana', **Mint Crisp** [PBR] (3m) leaves with white mottled variegation, flowers white fading to deep yellow, **var. *repens*** ❀

autumn and winter, **'Lemon Beauty'** leaves margined creamy white, **'Red Tips'** leaves deep-red purple when young, turning bright green, **'Silver Beauty'** leaves margined silver, **'Twiggy'** (1m) a dwarf version of 'Baggesen's Gold' with yellow leaves. *L. pileata H4* (60cm x 2.5m) a dense spreading semi-evergreen with tiny white flowers, followed by purple berries, mainly grown as a foliage plant for underplanting shady corners, a decidedly boring plant.

Lonicera nitida 'Lemon Beauty'

Luma apiculata see *Myrtus communis*, page 75

Magnolia

Almost unrivalled in flower, magnolias are some of the greatest show-offs of the plant kingdom. The reddish-purple, pink, white or pale-yellow goblet-shaped or star-shaped flowers in spring and early summer can provide a jaw-dropping spectacle: some west-coast gardens such as Glenarn have stunning displays. Lack of summer heat means that not all magnolias do well in Scotland, but most gardens can grow some of them. Choose with care for your conditions and you should have a spectacular display nearly every year. It's the deciduous varieties that are really worth growing in Scotland. Try growing *M. grandiflora* if you like, but you're unlikely to get much more than foliage interest, because there's not enough sustained heat in a Scottish summer for regular flowering. With March–May-flowering magnolias, there is always some risk of frosted flowers and growth, but this seldom does any lasting damage; it just causes huge disappointment when your beautiful blooms turn to a mass of brown mushy blobs overnight. Plant magnolias in as sunny a site as possible, definitely not under other trees, but with some wind shelter to protect flowers and young growth. Some magnolias have fragrant flowers – mostly the varieties with cup or goblet-shaped flowers; the Stellata types are only lightly scented, if at all. Magnolias like humus-rich moist acid soil and appreciate being mulched with manure. They don't need pruning, though you can cut back the shrubby ones if they get too big.

The large woodland species

These are all magnificent plants, but you need plenty of room, a sheltered garden and patience, as some take many years to flower. *M. campbellii H3–4* (3–5m, U: 10–15m) giant tree magnolia which in full flower is one of the most breathtaking sights of all; the only problem is that it takes at least 10–15 – and sometimes up to 30 – years to get the thing to flower. It is generally worth the wait, with large white to purple-pink tulip-like flowers on the bare branches in March–April, frost permitting. *M. denudata H4* (2–3m U: 10m) ❀ large shrub to small tree, cup-shaped pure-white fragrant flowers in April. *M. sprengeri* 'Diva' *H3–4* (3m, U: 10–12m) ❀ deep-pink fragrant flowers, up to 15cm across, in April.

The star magnolias

M. stellata (star magnolia) (3–4m x 4m) *H4(–5)* 🏆 free-flowering from a young age, these are broad but compact large shrubs with star-shaped flowers in white, cream or pale-pink shades. One of the best choices for Scotland – tough and suitable for smaller gardens. Selected forms include **'Centennial'** white with a pinkish cast, **'Gold Star'** the nearest to a yellow star magnolia, flowers pale creamy yellow, deeper on the outside, **'Jane Platt'** the best of the pink forms, pale pink, holding their colour, **'Rosea'** pale pink, **'Royal Star'** large white flowers, one of the hardiest,

Magnolia stellata

Magnolia x *loebneri* 'Leonard Messel'

Magnolia soulangeana

Magnolia soulangeana 'Susan'

'Waterlily' 🏆 later flowering, large white, with a pinkish cast. *M. x loebneri* (*M. kobus* x *M. stellata*) *H4–5* (6–8m) large shrub to small tree size, star-shaped, white to pale-pink fragrant flowers on bare branches. Forms include **'Leonard Messel'** purple buds open to pale pink, very fine, one of our favourites, **'Merrill'** a vigorous, broad, spreading tree with somewhat frost-resistant white flowers, several weeks later than most.

Hybrid magnolias with goblet-shaped flowers

M. soulangeana (*M. denudata* x *M. liliiflora*) *H4* (2–3m, U: 6m) ❀ broad, spreading large bushes or small trees, which can eventually grow too large for a small garden, flowers classic goblet-shaped, fragrant, white, pink or purple-pink, tough, but early flowers can be damaged by frosts. Forms include **'Alba'** (syn. 'Alba Superba') pure white, early, **'Alexandrina'** white inside and pink-purple outside, late, **'Brozzoni'** pale pink, white inside, the latest and largest-flowered of this group, **'Lennei'** rose-purple, said to be rather tender, but a good colour, **'Picture'** large leaves and flowers, white inside, purple outside and on base, very fine, **'Rustica Rubra'** dark reddish-pink, **'San José'** pink outer petals, cream inside. *M. liliiflora* **'Nigra'** *H4* (2–3m x 3–4m) goblet-shaped dark-purple red in May–June after the leaves have emerged, sometimes repeating through the summer, useful for its late flowering, but not as spectacular as *M.* x *soulangeana*. The **'Little Girl Hybrids'** (*M. liliiflora* x *M. stellata*) *H4–5* (2–4m) from the USA National Arboretum, a useful group for Scotland, slow and low growing with good flower colour: **'Ann'** deep reddish

Magnolia 'Star Wars'   *Magnolia 'Elizabeth'*

pink, cup-shaped opening out to star-shaped, **'Betty'** purplish red outside, inside white, opening from cup to star-shaped, **'Jane'** cup-shaped, very fragrant, purple-red and white, **'Ricki'** goblet-shaped, pink to purple pink, **'Susan'** ♛ the best-seller, goblet-shaped, purple-red, flowers are lop-sided, good but not spectacular. Other fine magnolia hybrids include **'Atlas'** (3–7m+) huge pink, up to 30cm across, **'Apollo'** (3–5m+) huge flowers, pale pink inside, deep purple outside, like a miniature *M. campbellii*, **'Black Tulip' H4?** (2–4m) heavily textured, deep burgundy, **'Galaxy' H4** (7–10m) tulip-shaped, reddish purple in April, on a fast-growing pyramidal-shaped tree which flowers young, **'Genie'** deep burgundy, compact habit, **'Heaven Scent' H4–5** (7–10m) ✿ cup-shaped, scented, pale pink, flushed deeper, one of the hardiest, **'Raspberry Ice' H4** (2–3m) pinkish white from deeper buds, long flowering season, **'Star Wars' H4** (3–7m+) large pink flowers, over several weeks, up to 15cm across, flowering at a young age, this is one of the finest magnolias we have seen, a sure best-seller. **'Vulcan' H4** (3–6m) very free-flowering pink.

The 'yellow' magnolias

H4–5 There are now dozens of named varieties, mostly bred in the eastern USA; they appear to be tough, but in a really cold winter may prove otherwise. Flowering in April–May in the UK, they tend to be creamy yellow here and there is some evidence that cold winters increase the intensity of yellow. **'Butterflies'** (3–6m) small creamy-yellow flowers appear before the leaves on an upright tree, **'Daphne'** (3–6m) one of the best yellows, deep colour and good habit, **'Elizabeth'** (5–10m) ✿ a pyramidal tree with greenish-yellow fragrant flowers, fading to cream, opening before leaves appear, **'Lois'** 93–6m) clear yellow, **'Yellow Bird'** (4–8m) light yellow, cup-shaped flowers are produced simultaneously with new leaves, slow growing, a good yellow for a smaller garden, **'Yellow Lantern'** (3–5m) pale yellow, the flowers appearing with the leaves, fastigiate habit.

Summer-flowering deciduous species

H4–5 ✿✿ (3–8m x 3–8m) *M. sieboldii* and *M. wilsonii* ♛ are very similar, forming large shrubs or multi-stemmed trees. These are an excellent choice for Scotland, as they avoid frost damage by flowering late. The almost overpoweringly sweetly scented nodding or pendent white flowers with red anthers open in June

(*M. sieboldii* sometimes flowers again in late summer) and are followed by eye-catching reddish seed pods. They are perhaps the best choice of magnolia for really cold inland gardens, but still requiring shelter from cold winds. There is a fine example of *M. wilsonii* at Arduaine Garden, Kinlochmelfort, Argyll. Rosa Steppanova reports that these are the two best magnolias for Shetland, and they are also the best choice for the north-east.

Mahonia

H4–5 ✾ These are very useful, tough, often statuesque shrubs with evergreen holly-like leaves held at the ends of the tall stems. The yellow fragrant flowers appear in winter and spring, followed by their apparently edible fruits, recommended by some for eating with muesli and porridge. The roots of *M. aquifolium* contain berberin and oxycanthin, used to treat skin and digestive disorders. Mahonias like moderately fertile, humus-rich, moist but well-drained soil in full or partial shade. They struggle in Orkney and Shetland. They don't need regular pruning, but if they get leggy, cut back 1–2 years' growth to a circle of leaves after flowering. They are good as specimen shrubs, and in shrub or mixed borders and in woodland, but you won't want to go barefoot where the prickly foliage drops.

M. aquifolium H5 (Oregon grape) (1m x 1.5m) a spreading, suckering shrub with yellow flowers in spring, followed by black

Mahonia aquifolium   *Mahonia japonica*

berries, suitable for making into jelly; the dark-green foliage, which often turns purple in winter, is subject to unsightly white mildew on leaves, especially in dry sites; forms include **'Apollo'** compact, bronze young growth, **'Atropurpureum'** particularly bronzy-purple winter foliage, **'Smaragd'** bright-green leaves all year. *M. x wagneri* **'Pinnacle' H4** (1.5–2m x 1.5m) similar to, but more upright than, *M. aquifolium*, with yellow flowers in late spring. *M. eurybacteata subsp. ganpinensis* **'Soft Caress' H4?** (1m) compact with narrow non spiky leaves, *M. japonica H5* (2m x 3m) ✿ a stiffly upright habit, dark-green sharply toothed leaflets, pale-yellow fragrant flowers in pendulous racemes sometimes partly hidden in the leaves, from December to early spring, followed by small, blue-black, ovoid fruit; *M.j.* **'Bealei'** flowers more erect, leaflets blue-green. *M. x media H4* (*M. japonica* x *M.*

lomariifolia) (3–5m x 3–5m) a cross that has produced the most popular garden varieties, erect habit with sharply toothed leaves, bright-yellow usually slightly fragrant flowers in upright and spreading racemes in November–March; varieties include **'Buckland'** fine flowers with some fragrance, **'Charity'** ✿ vigorous, some flowers hang down in the leaves, **'Lionel Fortescue'** early flowering, **'Winter Sun'** fairly compact, with fine erect racemes, young leaves flushed reddish.

Menziesia ciliicalyx see *Enkianthus*, page 49

Myrtus communis, Luma apiculata and *Ugni molinea* (myrtles)

❀ This is a somewhat neglected group of plants, now receiving more attention, partly because of the milder winters of recent years. They make good evergreen shrubs for coastal areas, as well as mild/sheltered inland sites. Botanists have removed many species long grown as *Myrtus* (myrtles) from this genus and placed them in five other genera including *Luma* and *Ugni*, with the consequence that many plants are circulating under two different names. There are some fine examples at Jura House Walled Garden, Arduaine Garden, Argyll and Cambo, in Fife.

Luma apiculata 'Glanleam Gold' flowers

Luma apiculata 'Glanleam Gold' bush (RC-M)

***Myrtus communis* H3** (2–3m x 2–3m) This has five-petalled scented white flowers with a mass of stamens, followed by black berries. This easy-to-please, dense evergreen shrub with aromatic leaves is an excellent plant for Scottish coastal gardens, particularly in the west. Tolerant of wind and salt spray, best in a sunny spot for good flowering. ***M.c.* 'Variegata'** (1m) leaves grey green, with thin white margins; **subsp. *tarentina* H3** (syn. 'Microphylla', 'Nana') (1.5m) smaller growing with much smaller leaves (to 2cm), flowers cream with pink tints, followed by white berries; ***M.c.* subsp. *t.* 'Microphylla Variegata'** (1m) leaves with white margins.

Luma apiculata (syn. *Myrtus luma*) ***H2–3*** (2m+, can reach 6–10m in mild areas) This has a mass of creamy white flowers from mid-summer to autumn, followed by black berries, on an upright bushy shrub or small tree with glossy dark-green evergreen leaves. Mature plants have attractive peeling cinnamon and white bark. A first-class plant for mild gardens, easy to grow, with a long flowering period. In favourable gardens it will self-seed. **'Glanleam Gold'** ***H2–3*** (1.5–3m) much slower growing, leaves with cream margins, pink tinged when young. A good container plant for mild gardens.

Ugni molinea (syn. *Myrtus ugni*) (Chilean guava) ***H2–3*** (1–1.5m x 1.5m) This has sweetly fragrant, white, pink-tinged flowers in summer, followed by edible black fruit, which are, according to Graham Stuart Thomas, 'of a delicious wild strawberry-like flavour'. Evergreen stiff dark leaves, suitable as a low hedge for mild gardens.

Nandina domestica (winter foliage)

Nandina domestica (heavenly bamboo)

H3 (2m x 2m) Despite the common name, this is not a bamboo but a relative of berberis. A stately semi-evergreen shrub with narrow pointed leaves which turn reddish-purple in autumn and winter, small white flowers in summer and red berries produced after a hot summer. Quantities of this plant are imported from Italy, and frankly it is not ideal for Scotland, as it needs more heat and sun than we can provide, but it can be grown successfully in containers, or in sheltered or mild gardens not too far from the coast. **'Pygmaea'** (syn. 'Nana') (1m) is more compact and slower growing. **'Firepower'** (50cm–1m) green leaves in summer, bright red in winter.

Neillia thibetica see *Physocarpus opulifolius*, page 81

Plants that are widely offered for sale in Scotland but should be left on the shelf

(mainly because of lack of summer heat)

- *Apple* 'Cox's Orange Pippin'
- *Azalea* (Japanese), most Indica, Kurume, Glenn Dale and other tender varieties; hardy ones are excellent
- *Camellia japonica* (most)
- *Campsis*
- *Cornus florida*
- *Magnolia grandiflora*
- *Olea* (olive)
- *Sophora*

Olea (olive) (RC-M)

Olea (olive)

H1–2 Have you noticed any large olive trees in Scotland, or eaten freshly picked olives at your local farmers' market? Thought not. So unless you live in some hidden part of this country, with a climate like that of the south of Spain, we suggest that you leave that olive in your local DIY store. Better still, walk out and go somewhere that offers suitable plants for Scotland.

Olearia

and *Cassinia leptophylla* subsp. *fulvida*, *Helichrysum* and *Ozothamnus*

These Australian and New Zealand 'daisy bushes' and their relatives are evergreen shrubs covered with masses of fragrant white (or pink or yellow) daisy-like flowers. Botanists keep changing their minds about which genus each belongs to, so the naming is a bit confused. These are excellent coastal and windbreak plants. *O.* x *haastii* is the toughest and can be grown throughout most of Scotland. The rest are rather tender, best in west- and east-coast seaside gardens, or at least not too far inland. They associate well with architectural 'spikies' like yucca and phormium, as well as with most other shrubs and flowers. All the tribe are tolerant of wind and salt spray and useful for hedging and screening; many are excellent in Orkney and Shetland. Some of them have quite ornamental foliage with toothed leaves and/or white felted leaf undersides. Grow in fertile, well-drained soil in as much sun as possible. The foliage can suffer damage from cold east winds, but this is mainly cosmetic. Most can be hard pruned if they get too large, and will break from old wood. There are thriving *O.* x *hastii* specimens right at the top of Edinburgh Castle (an 'exposed position' if ever there was one), as well as in several coastal gardens around north-east Scotland; and Dundee Botanic Garden, overlooking the Tay, has a huge collection of them. There are 130 species in all and numerous hybrids: those listed below include some of the tougher ones, forming rounded shrubs similar in height and spread, unless stated otherwise. Most of the rest are only suitable for mildest west-coast and island gardens: Garden Cottage Nursery, near Poolewe, Wester Ross lists almost 30 varieties.

O. avicenniifolia **H3** (3m) bushy shrub or small tree, late-summer flowering, small fragrant white flowers, good in Shetland. **O. x haastii H4** (2–3m x 2–3m) ✿ masses of fragrant white daisy-like flowers in July and August, on a dense grower with small dark leaves, felted on the undersides. The hardiest variety (but probably not for coldest inland gardens), it is very good on Orkney and Shetland, where it is used for hedging. **'Henry Travers' H2–3** (3m x 2m) is the most attractive in flower with relatively large lilac-blue daisies with white centres. Resents transplanting and does not break from old wood, so don't prune it. *O. macrodonta* (New Zealand holly) **H3** (2–5m+ x 2–4m) a vigorous shrub with aromatic, holly-like leaves, dark green, with white-silvery felted undersides and fragrant white flowers in June; a striking plant, excellent for coastal gardens, growing very large in mild west coast gardens. *O. phlogopappa* (daisy bush) **H3** (2m x 2m) you might not want to attempt to pronounce this . . . grey-green leaves, usually sold in named forms: **'Comber's Pink'** pink and **'Comber's Blue'** mid-magenta-blue, both of which look like May–June flowering Michaelmas daisies. *O.* x *scilloniensis* **H3** (2m x 2m) large (to 10cm) dark-green, wavy leaves, hidden by a mass of white flowers with yellow centres. *O. solandri* **H2–3** (2m x 2m) ✿✿ heather-like leaves, pale yellow very fragrant flowers in late summer. *O. traversii* **H3** (4–6m x 3–4m) one of the fastest-growing evergreen windbreaks for coastal gardens, so invaluable for windswept west-coast gardens, including Orkney, even in poor sandy soil. The white flowers are tiny, but it is a handsome foliage plant.

Cassinia leptophylla **subsp. *fulvida* H3** (2m x 2.5m) A bushy, rounded evergreen shrub with small, sticky, heather-like, yellow-green leaves, and masses of tiny white flowers in July. A good coastal plant, tolerant of wind and salt. Easily rejuvenated by a hard prune.

Helichrysum Most of the shrubs formerly grown under this name are now considered forms of *Ozothamnus*. The herbaceous varieties can be found on page 153.

Ozothamnus (including species formerly included in *Helichrysum*) This is another genus of Antipodean evergreen daisies with heather-like foliage and masses of small white daisy-like flowers. Most are rather tender and are particularly good by the sea, thriving in places like the west coast of Mull. They are best in well-drained soil in full sun. *O. coralloides* **H3** (60cm x 60cm) compact, with small scale-like leaves, on whipcord stems, flowers,

Olearia 'Henry Travers'

Olearia macrodonta

Ozothamnus rosmarinifolius

which are rarely produced, are yellowish white; often grown as a pot plant for the alpine house; **'County Park Silver'** silver-blue foliage. *O. ledifolius* (kerosene bush) *H3* (1m x 1m) a dense grower with yellowish shoots, glossy dark-green aromatic narrow leaves with yellow undersides, masses of tight white flowers from red buds in June. *O. rosmarinifolius H3* (2–3m x 1–2m) fairly compact, with rosemary-like dark-green leaves, woolly on the underside, fragrant white flowers in early summer; **'Silver Jubilee'** *H2* less hardy with silvery-grey leaves.

Osmanthus (syn. x *Osmarea*)

H3–4 ❀ These are useful evergreen shrubs, the hardiest of which are suitable for most of Scotland, although they might be damaged in the coldest inland gardens in a hard winter. The masses of small white flowers create a strong sweet scent, which carries for some distance. Most varieties are also used for hedging and even for topiary. They are good as specimens and in mixed borders, and like fertile, well-drained soil in full or part day sun. Shelter from cold east winds to avoid foliage burn.

Osmanthus heterophyllus 'Goshiki'

Osmanthus delavayi

O. x *burkwoodii H4* (3m x 3m) ❀ dense and rounded habit, with oval leaves to 5cm long, very fragrant cream-white flowers in April–May. *O. delavayi H4* (2–3m x 3–4m) ❀ ❦ an excellent plant with smaller leaves than *O. burkwoodii*, and more abundant flowers, pure white and more strongly fragrant. *O. heterophyllus H3* (3–6m x 3–6m) ❀ distinctive holly-like leaves and masses of small highly scented flowers in September–October, followed by black fruit; there are many popular forms of this with coloured foliage: **'Aureomarginatus'** (syn. 'Aureus') leaves margined yellow, **'Goshiki'** new growth bronze, leaves mottled and splashed creamy yellow and

Pachysandra terminalis, green and variegated

green, **'Gulftide'** interesting twisted leaves dark green, prickly, **'Purpureus'** young growth dark-purple–copper-beech coloured, fading to dark green, tinged purple, **'Variegatus'** leaves bordered creamy white.

Ozothamnus see
Olearia, page 76

Pachysandra terminalis
H5 (20cm x 2–3m)
Pachysandra terminalis is not one of our favourites. Granted it makes a dense ground-cover, but then so does a good layer of gravel. It is a rather uninspiring evergreen with dark green leaves, suitable for growing in dry shade and on dry banks. It is very good at covering these areas, but growth is rampant once it is established, and this is not a plant for small gardens. The clusters of tiny white flowers, which are disappointingly not scented, appear in February and March. Two lower-growing selections to 15cm high are **'Green Carpet'** ❦ finely toothed leaves and **'Variegata'** ❦ white margined leaves.

Paeonia (tree peony)
For herbaceous peonies, see page 212.

H4–5 The often stunning single or double flowers may not last long in driving Scottish wind and rain, but they are some of the most exquisite plants, and people pay huge sums for the latest and rarest varieties. The deciduous, divided foliage is dramatic in its own right, making them good specimen shrubs as well as valuable structure plants in a mixed border. Unlike their herbaceous counterparts, tree peonies have a woody stem, so maintain some framework above ground in winter. They have been grown as garden plants in China for thousands of years, and recently many more forms have been imported, not always correctly named, unfortunately. Tree peonies like rich, well-drained soil in full or part day sun, and do best sheltered from wind. Cut back after flowering to encourage bushiness, but beware of suckers from the rootstock: these should be broken off. Height and spread is similar unless stated otherwise.

P. delavayi H4–5 (1–2m x 1m) flowers small, single, dark red, in May, handsome leaves, suckering. *P. ludlowii* (syn. *P. lutea* var. *ludlowii*) *H4–5* (to 2m x 2m) ❦ large single yellow flowers in May. *P. rockii H4–5* (2m x 2m) ❀ palest pink to white scented flowers with purple-maroon blotches at the base of each petal. *P. rockii* hybrids, known as **Gansu Mudan** exist in a wide range of colours, in double and single forms. *P. suffruticosa H4–5* (2m

Paeonia ludlowii

Paeonia suffruticosa

x 2m) white, pink, red or purple flowers in May; of hundreds of varieties and hybrids, some of the most widely Japanese selections available include **'Godaishu'** semi-double yellow-centred white, **'Hana-Kisoi'** double deep red, **'Higurashi'** semi-double rich blood-red, **'Kinshi'** double yellow, **'Rimpo'** semi-double, maroon with yellow stamens, **'Taiyo'** semi-double, maroon-red, **'Yachiyo-tsubaki'** semi-double, two-toned pink, **'Yoshinogawa'** semi-double, blush pink.

Palms: *Trachycarpus fortunei, Phoenix canariensis* and *Chamaerops humilis*

This section includes palms which are suitable for growing outdoors, mostly only in mildest regions.

Trachycarpus fortunei H3–4 (3–5m+) This striking plant from

Chamaerops humilis

Trachycarpus fortunei

China is the hardiest palm and it can be grown successfully in many parts of Scotland. In a very cold winter it might completely defoliate, but it will usually recover. The palmate leaves (to 1m across) are deeply divided with often drooping tips. The mature trunk develops a thick furry texture, which increases the plant's exotic appeal. If you don't provide adequate wind shelter, the leaves shred and the whole plant looks a scruffy mess.

Phoenix canariensis H2–3 (2–3m x 2–3m in Torquay, but more

likely 1.2m x 1.2m in Scotland) is often grown as a houseplant, but can be grown reasonably well outdoors, probably best in a container which can be protected in cold spells outside mildest regions. *Chamaerops humilis (dwarf fan palm) H1–2* (1.5m x 1.5m) for mild gardens only or grow it in a container which can be brought inside in cold spells.

Parrotia persica (Persian ironwood)

H4 (3–5m x 4–6m, U: 7–10m tall) ♥ This forms a large spreading shrub or small tree, and is grown for its attractive flaky bark and coloured foliage. The leaves are deep red in young growth, dark green in summer, turning dark crimson and/or yellow in autumn. In January– February it may produce small spidery red and brown flowers in clusters along the bare branches,

most likely following a hot summer. The early flowers and growth are vulnerable to frost damage, so it does best in fairly sheltered gardens. There is a fine example at Cruickshank Botanic Garden, Aberdeen. **'Vanessa'** particularly good autumn colour, **'Pendula'** (1.5m x 3m) a compact weeping form.

Parrotia persica (autumn colour)

Parthenocissus (Virginia creeper, Boston ivy) (climber)

H3–5 A wall set ablaze in autumn by burgundy-red Virginia creeper or Boston ivy is one of the finest autumn spectacles. Both of these very popular climbers are self-clinging, with tendrils or disk-like suckers which adhere to brickwork or stone (without penetrating mortar as ivy does). You probably would not notice the tiny flowers with green petals or the berries, which can cause indigestion if eaten. Suitable for any well-drained soil, in sun or shade, and useful for north-facing walls. They are vigorous and can become a curse, as their tendrils reach your gutters, wrapping themselves round and clogging them up, so you may need to hack them back or pull them off the wall every so often. Megginch Castle, Perth and the Perth Swimming Pool complex both have spectacular and rather sobering 50ft walls of them, which are a blaze of colour in autumn.

P. henryana H3–4 (6–10m) three to five leaflets, green with conspicuous white markings, turning bright red in autumn, the least hardy variety, but handsome. *P. quinquefolia* (Virginia creeper) *H5* (10–15m) ♥ leaves consist of five oval toothed leaflets to 10cm long, turning brilliant red in autumn. *P. tricuspidata* (Boston ivy) *H5* (10–20m) ♥ very vigorous, three-lobed leaves turning brilliant red or purple in autumn; forms include **'Lowii'** small crisped leaves with three to seven lobes,

Parthenocissus quinquefolia

Parthenocissus tricuspidata
(autumn colour)

Perovskia atriplicifolia 'Blue Spire'

'Veitchii' purple young growth and purple-red autumn foliage.

Passiflora (passion flower)
(climber)

H1–3 Irresistible in flower, but unfortunately in Scotland most varieties need to be grown in a greenhouse or conservatory. A few varieties are hardy enough for most of coastal Scotland, and they are worth a try on a warm sheltered wall in colder gardens; take advantage of the increased warmth in towns and cities. They need well-drained soil in as much sun as possible.

The variety that produces the passion fruit, *P. edulis H1*, is for

Passiflora caerulea

greenhouse cultivation only. *P. caerulea H3* (5–8m) ♀ a fast-growing climber with slightly fragrant blue, white and purple flowers, darkest in the centre, with radiating stripes in July–September. Leaves and flowers are poisonous. In milder gardens it may remain evergreen and can flower well into autumn. Forms include 'Constance Elliott' *H3* white with pale blue or white filaments, 'Eden' *H2* new, fine purple flowers, flowering as a young plant, probably suitable for west coast gardens only.

Perovskia atriplicifolia (Russian sage)

H3–4 (1.2m x 1m) The common name is bizarre as it is neither Russian or a sage and it actually looks more like lavender, with long-lasting purple-blue flowers in late summer, aromatic foliage and striking grey-white stems in winter, this is a fine garden plant if you have the right conditions. It needs well-drained soil in full sun and dislikes

excessive winter wet. It is a good choice for coastal gardens, especially in sandy soil. In cold, inland gardens and those with heavy clay soil, it tends to be short-lived. Cut it back hard in late spring to encourage bushiness and good flowering. It does tend to end up sprawling in all directions however hard you try to prevent it.

Forms include 'Blue Spire' relatively large lavender-blue flowers, 'Filigran' very deeply cut leaves, fairly compact, 'Little Spire' (65cm) a lower-growing selection with deep purple-blue flowers.

Philadelphus (mock orange)

H4–5 ❋ The distinctive orange-blossom scent is the main feature of these shrubs, which do very well in Scotland. The fragrant single or double large or small white, four-petalled flowers with yellow stamens open in June and July. They are not the most exciting plants out of flower, so they work best in mixed borders with other seasonal interest. For consistent displays, it is well worth giving them a good prune every year or two. Cut out the old stems immediately after they have flowered, because next year's blooms are produced on the current year's growth. Philadelphus are mostly easy to please, needing at least part day sun to get a good crop of flowers, and preferring well-drained soils, although the vigorous ones seem to be relatively clay tolerant. Scone Palace, near Perth, has a fine collection.

'Avalanche' *H5* (1.5m) single white. 'Beauclerk' *H5* (2.5m) ♀ large single white, slight pinkish flush, very fragrant. 'Belle Etoile' *H4–5* (1.2m) ♀ arching habit, very fragrant single white with reddish-purple centres. *P. coronarius H4–5* (2–3m) small, very fragrant

Philadelphus 'Belle Etoile'

Philadelphus 'Snowbelle'

single white, good in dry soils; the form *P.c.* **'Aureus'** yellow young growth, turning yellow green, sometimes subject to sunburn, single white flowers, **'Variegatus'** rather sickly looking with somewhat misshapen leaves with broad white margins, single white flowers. **'Innocence'** *H4* (2–3m) medium-sized, very fragrant single to semi-double, **'Erectus'** (*P.* x *lemoinii*) *H5* (1.5m) upright but dense habit, small single, very fragrant white. **'Manteau d'Hermine'** *H4* (75cm x 1.5m) ❦ double, very fragrant, creamy white, low. *P. microphyllus H4* (1m x 1m) very fragrant small white flowers, small leaves, the most dwarf of the hardy varieties. **'Mrs E.L. Robinson'** *H5* (2–3m) very large single to semi-double. **'Silberregen'** (syn. 'Silver Showers') *H5* (1.2m) medium-sized single very fragrant flowers. **'Snowbelle'** *H5* (1.5m) double white. **'Sybille'** *H5* (1.2m) very fragrant large single white, very free-flowering. **'Virginal'** ❦ *H5* (2–3m) double, very fragrant pure white, vigorous.

Phlomis (Jerusalem sage)

H3–5 These evergreen perennials and subshrubs produce mounds of large bright green or grey-green, sage-like, wrinkled or woolly leaves and nettle-like, white, yellow and purple-pink flowers in whorls up the stems in summer. Neither of us is a great phlomis fan; we just don't find them very visually appealing, and we take comfort from Christopher Lloyd calling them 'grubby'. They prefer dry, poor soil in full sun, and will not tolerate exposure to strong winds. Late frosts can damage young growth and a hard winter can kill most of them in colder inland gardens. The felty grey-green leaves give a Mediterranean effect and they are drought-tolerant. They can be trimmed to shape after flowering.

Phlomis fruticosa

P. chrysophylla H3 (1m x 1m) golden yellow, leaves fade to yellow-green as the season progresses. *P. fruticosa H3(–4)* (1m x 1m) golden yellow, the most commonly grown variety. *P. italica H3* (1m x 50cm) upright in habit, with pink flowers and woolly leaves. *P. russeliana* (syn. *P. viscosa* Hort.) *H4* (1m x 60cm+) light yellow, large coarse leaves, a useful ground-cover, good at St Andrews Botanic Garden, Fife. *P. tuberosa H5* (1.8m x 1.2m) pink to purple with white throats, can tolerate some shade in a dry soil, making it useful under trees; *P.t.* **'Amazone'** *H5* (1.5m x 1m) lavender-purple from mid-summer to autumn.

Phoenix canariensis see Palms, page 78

Phormium (New Zealand flax)

H3 (2–3m x 2–3m) These striking architectural evergreens,

Phormium a variety of foliage forms

Phormium 'Dazzler'

forming dense, evergreen clumps of vertical sword-shaped leaves, are technically perennials but are more appropriately dealt with here. They make bold specimens and are good structural plants in borders. The tough, leathery, fibrous leaves sometimes have a metallic sheen, and they were traditionally used in New Zealand to make flax. Phormiums do well in coastal gardens, where they form spreading clumps, which can act as windbreaks – as in Orkney, for example. Mature plants produce spikes of small flowers in mid-summer. Plant in well-drained, moist soil, in full sun; they tend to rot at the crown in heavy soils and inland in cold wet winters. There are huge numbers of named forms; all seem about equally hardy (*H3*), so just choose the leaf colour you like best.

P. cookianum (2m x 3m) large green leaves to 1.5m long; **'Cream Delight'** leaves with broad cream central band, **'Tricolor'** leaves edged creamy yellow with a narrow red margin. *P. tenax* (3m x 3m) ❦ green leaves, flower spikes reach 4–5m; there are fine large old specimens at Royal Botanic Garden Edinburgh. Most of the following varieties are hybrids between the two species and grow to 1.5–3m x 1–3m: **'Alison Blackman'** leaves green and creamy yellow with narrow red margin, **'Apricot Queen'** yellow, tinged apricot, **'Bronze Baby'** bronzy, with drooping tips, **'Dazzler'** striped reddish-pink and deep red-purple, **'Evening Glow'** bright red and pink, **'Flamingo'** pink with red margins, **'Jester'** pink with green margins, **'Golden Ray'** leaves with yellow-orange margin, **'Maori Sunrise'** slender cream and light red leaves with bronze margins, **'Pink Panther'** pink margined red, **'Platt's Black'** very deep purple, **'Rainbow Sunrise'** bronze and pink, **'Sundowner'** large bronze-green with pinkish-red margin, **'Yellow Wave'** striped creamy-yellow and green with drooping tips.

Photinia (and *Stransvaesia*)

H3–4 *Photinia* and *Stransvaesia* have been merged together into *Photinia*, although most gardens and garden centres still use the name *Stransvaesia*. The evergreen *Photinia* x *fraseri* with dark-red young growth is a popular garden plant. All the commonly offered varieties of photinia are evergreen and pretty tough, but start rather early into growth, which can expose some leaves to late frost damage, which is more cosmetic than life threatening. Photinia like moist but well-drained soil in at least part day sun, and east winds should be avoided if possible.

P. davidiana (syn. *Stransvaesia davidiana*) *H4* (3–6m+) a vigorous evergreen that was more widely grown than it is now, but susceptibility to the fungal disease fireblight has reduced its popularity. Masses of white flowers in summer are followed by masses of long-lasting red fruit in autumn. The older leaves turn red in autumn before falling. Forms include: **var. *undulata* 'Fructo Luteo'** (2–3m) yellow fruit, **'Palette'** *H4* (3–5m) evergreen with lance-shaped leaves, splashed with irregular patches of creamy white and pink, small white flowers in summer – it looks a bit as if someone splashed paint over it. *P.* x *fraseri* **'Red Robin'** *H3–4* (2–3m+) ⚜ one of the most popular shrubs for British gardens over the last 20 years, though it can take a real battering in cold winters like 1981 and 2010–11, particularly if grown in containers. The bright reddish-brown young growth is very showy but comes early and can be frosted. It is very responsive to hard pruning, and to shaping into pyramids, columns and hedging. The small white flowers in April–May look like those of hawthorn or pyracantha. **'Canivily'** (1.5–2m) more compact with darker young growth. **'Curly Fantasy'** jagged edges to the leaves, less attractive in our opinion. **'Little Red Robin'** (1–2m) dwarf, with smaller leaves and said to keep the red leaf colour for longer. A good container plant. **Pink Marble** ['Cassini'] (2m) leaves streaked with pink on young growth, later white. **'Scarlet Blaze'** (2–3m) persistent red foliage.

Photinia davidiana 'Pallete'

Photinia x fraseri 'Red Robin'

Phygelius, various colour forms

Phygelius

H3 Virtually unknown to Scottish gardeners 20 years ago, these exotic South African shrubs are becoming very popular for their mass of long-lasting, pendulous clusters of narrow tubular flowers in typically warm shades of salmon, orange, yellow and pink, in summer. They are semi-evergreen, so often look bedraggled by spring and need tidying up. If the main flowering stems are cut back in mid-summer they will usually flower again from side shoots, sometimes lasting into October. They need full sun in a warm, sheltered site in well-drained soil and are sometimes attacked by sawfly, which shred the leaves.

P. aequalis (1m x1m) useful in a herbaceous border; there are many named forms and hybrids of it: **Somerford Funfair series** [PBR] several colour forms, including **'Coral'**, **'Cream'**, **'Wine'**, **'Yellow'**, etc., **'New Sensation'** magenta pink, **'Trewidden Pink'** pink, **'Yellow Trumpet'** creamy yellow. *P. capensis* (1m) orange to deep red. *P.* x *rectus* (1.5m x1.5m) taller than the above, good against a wall; **'African Queen'** pale red, **'Candy Swirl'** new, bicoloured pink and cream, **'Cherry Swirl'** deep red, **'Devil's Tears'** deep reddish pink, **'Ivory Twist'** white, **'Moonraker'** white, flowering all round the stems, **'Salmon's Leap'** orange, **'Winchester Fanfare'** reddish-pink, with yellow throats.

Phyllodoce see Heathers, page 55

Phyllostachys see Bamboos, page 28

Physocarpus opulifolius
and *Neillia thibetica*

H5 (1.5–3m x 1.5–3m) The tiny white to pale-pink flowers and small red berries in autumn make a reasonable display en masse, but this is a shrub grown mainly for its foliage, in yellow and purple-leaved forms. It makes a good structural back of the border plant, and the bark peels in an attractive way on mature specimens. The purple forms are surprisingly wind tolerant and we have seen excellent examples on the coast of Mull. Growing as wide as tall, it is fully hardy (*H5*), and should be planted in moist soil in full sun.

Physocarpus opulifolius 'Diabolo' and 'Dart's Gold'

'Angel Gold' yellow with copper flushing, 'Dart's Gold' striking bright-yellow young foliage, slowly turning green, red stems, **Diabolo** [PBR] leaves develop from bronzy green to an impressive dark-purple colour, **Diable d'Or** ['Mindia'] orange-bronze young growth, **Lady in Red** ['Tuilad'] purple-red leaves, pink flowers, less vigorous than 'Diablo'.

Neillia thibetica H4–5 (2m x 2m) This closely related shrub is grown for its arching racemes of pink flowers in June. A tough, easy, suckering shrub for full sun or part shade. It can be pruned after flowering if required.

Pieris
H4–5 There can't be many Scottish gardens without a pieris – these incredibly popular slow-growing evergreens have fine early spring flowers and many also have impressive bright-red young growth. They are excellent value, generally easy to please, with lily-of-the-valley-like, lightly scented white or pink flowers in panicles which open from attractive winter clusters of buds. Some varieties grow early in the year and are vulnerable to spring frosts, though this seldom does long-term damage. Frosted or old straggly plants can be rejuvenated by cutting them back hard, and variegated forms should have reverted shoots cut out. Pieris need acid/peaty soil in sun or light shade, sheltered from cold east winds. They are also suitable for containers, and once established they are relatively drought tolerant. Height and spread is usually about the same.

'Forest Flame' *H4* (2–3m+) the best-seller, with bright-red young growth which fades to cream and then turns green, white flowers, not all that freely produced; it comes into growth early and is very often frosted, making it look unsightly until a further flush of growth is produced. **'Flaming Silver'** *H3–4* (2–3m+) a sport of 'Forest Flame' but less hardy, leaves with a silvery-white margin, young growth red. *P. formosa* **'Wakehust'** *H3* (3m+) fine red young growth, but rather tender, flowers white. *P. japonica H5* (1–3m+) good for coldest gardens, as the bronze (or red in selected forms) young growth comes later; white or pink flower panicles; selections include **'Bonfire'** (1m) red young growth and masses of upright panicles of white flowers – this is almost certain to become a best-seller, **'Carnaval'** (1m) compact, leaves edged with a white margin, inclined to revert, vivid pink-red young growth, white flowers, sometimes produces a second flush of red growth in late summer. **'Katsura'** (1–2m) young growth deep burgundy red, flowers deep pink, **'Little Heath'** (60cm) dwarf, compact, leaves with white margins, shy flowering, **'Mountain Fire'** (1.5m) deep-red young growth mellows to chestnut brown, a good red-leaved form for cold gardens, **'Red Mill'** (3m) a rather rangy plant with dark-red young growth, flowers white, **'Valley Valentine'** (1–1.5m) flowers dark red, **'Variegata'** (1m) flowers white, rather lacking in vigour, so barely worth growing.

Pittosporum
Pittosporums, native to South Africa, Australia and New Zealand, are very widely grown in Mediterranean countries as hedging and in municipal plantings, as well as for flower arranging. Only a few are hardy enough for Scotland, where they are useful evergreens for mild coastal gardens, but probably not hardy enough for inland gardens far from the sea. They are grown mainly for their evergreen leathery leaves, which are variegated or purple in some forms, as the small, usually scented white, maroon or purple flowers are not very spectacular, though the fragrance can be strong. There are fine examples of *P. tenuifolium* at Achamore on the island of Gigha and in many other west-coast gardens, as well as Fife coastal gardens. They like well-drained soil in sun or light shade.

P. eugenoides **'Variegatum'** *H2* (5–10m) small tree with wavy-margined leaves to 13cm, cream to creamy-yellow margins, small, creamy scented flowers in summer, for mildest west-coast gardens only. **'Garnettii'** *H2* (3–5m) bushy, spreading shrub with greyish-green leaves, with creamy-white margins, small dark-purple flowers in spring. *P. tenuifolium H3* (4–8m x 2–4m) a widely grown plant with many forms; the wavy-edged leaves

Pieris 'Flaming Silver'   Pieris 'Mountain Fire'   Pittosporum 'Garnettii'   Pittosporum tenuifolium
                                                                                                   'Abbotsbury Gold'

contrast well with the almost black stems, and the small maroon flowers in spring are quite striking. This is an excellent coastal plant, though it can be burned by salt-laden gales, so it is probably best with a little shelter. It reaches small tree size where happy. Forms include **'Abbotsbury Gold'** (3m) leaves yellow with irregular green margins, fading with age, **'Collaig Silver'** (2–3m) black stems,

Pittosporum tobira

Polygala chamaebuxus

Potentilla fruticosa 'Abbotswood'

grey leaves with white margins, Scottish raised, **'Golden King'** (3m) light green-yellow foliage, **'Gold Star'** (2–3m) green and gold variegated leaves with yellow midribs and stalks, **'Gold Wave'** leaves with gold variegation, wavy margins, **'Irene Patterson'** (1.2m) slow growing with striking mottled green and white leaves, **'Limelight'** (2m) lime green with dark-green, non-wavy margins, **'Purpureum'** (3m) striking foliage plant, young green leaves become bronzy red-purple, black stems, not quite as hardy as others, **'Silver Queen'** (2–3m) leaves pale green with white margins, **'Tom Thumb'** (1m) a dwarf form with deeper bronze-purple leaves than 'Purpureum', young growth pinkish purple, very striking, autumn growth often green, **'Tandara Gold'** (3m) variegated green and gold. *P. tobira* **H2** (2–6m) more tender, with glossy smooth evergreen leaves, scented white flowers in late spring and early summer, does well in containers and can be clipped to shape.

Pleioblastus see Bamboos, page 28

Polygala chamaebuxus

H5 (5cm x 20cm+) ❧ This tough evergreen subshrub forms low-growing mounds of small leathery dark-green leaves and produces pea-like white and yellow flowers in late spring and early summer. It is ideal for the rock or peat garden, and good for growing amongst dwarf rhododendrons or heathers. It does not require any maintenance once established, apart from trimming to shape, but can suffer from fungal disease, causing partial defoliation. var. *grandiflora* (15cm x 30cm+) taller, bicoloured purple and yellow.

Potentilla fruticosa

For herbaceous potentillas, see page 217.

H5 This is an invaluable and dependable deciduous shrub (if not the most exciting), tough enough for almost any Scottish garden, with a very long flowering period from June to October. The small five-petalled saucer-shaped flowers range from white, through pink and yellow to orange and orange-red. It grows best in full sun, in well-

Potentilla fruticosa varieties

drained sandy or stony soil, and is well suited to containers. Some of the more vigorous ones tend to get a bit leggy and respond well to a good haircut in late autumn or winter. Shrubby potentillas also make an attractive low hedge. There are now far too many named forms, many of which are indistinguishable from one another, as a visit to one of the national collections confirmed. They thrive in a wide range of soils and conditions, preferring reasonable drainage and full sun. Fortunately, rabbits and deer seem largely to ignore them. They grow to 50cm x 50cm in 5 years, eventually 1m+ x 1m, unless stated; compact varieties are smaller and slower.

'Abbotswood' ❧ white, blue-green leaves, quite tall and vigorous, perhaps the best white, **'Daydawn'** ❧ creamy yellow, flushed orange-pink, **'Elizabeth'** ❧ bright yellow, prone to mildew, **'Goldfinger'** large deep yellow, blue-green leaves, **'Golden Spreader'** bright yellow, spreading habit, raised in Orkney, **'Goldstar'** large-flowered bright yellow, **'Grace Darling'** (30cm) peach pink, very compact, **'Hit for 6'** red-deep pink, raised by Peter Milne at Glendoick, **'Hopleys Orange'** orange, leaves with yellow margins, the best orange, **'Katherine Dykes'** (1–2m) primrose yellow, one of the largest, **'Knaphill'** yellow, **'Limelight'** (syn. 'Lemon & Lime') soft yellow near cream, deeper yellow in the centre, the best pale yellow in RHS trials, **Lovely Pink** ['Pink Beauty'] (30cm) single and semi-double pink, the best pink in RHS trials, **Marian Red Robin** ['Marrob'] red, deeper than 'Red Ace', spreading, the best of this colour, **'Medicine Wheel Mountain'** bright yellow, leaves blue-green, a fine choice, **'New Dawn'** large-flowered pink, the hardiest of this colour, **'Pink Beauty'** [PBR] semi doube pale pink, **'Primrose Beauty'** pale yellow, grey-green leaves, **Princess** ['Blink'] pale pink, **'Red Ace'** ❧ orange-red, fading to pink, **'Summer Sorbet'** pale creamy yellow, **'Sunset'** orange, fading to pink, **'Tangerine'** yellow, flushed pale orange-red, **'Tilford Cream'** creamy white, dense habit.

Prostanthera

These Australian mint bushes produce a mass of flowers in summer. Most of them are suitable for mildest gardens only, apart from *P. cuneata*, which is fairly hardy. There are good examples at Colonsay House, Isle of Colonsay.

P. cuneata H3 (30–90cm x 30–90cm) a fairly compact evergreen with small, aromatic leaves and white flowers with pink spotting in summer; grows best in well-drained soil in full sun, quite widely available in garden centres, not reliably hardy in cold inland gardens. **'Alpine Gold' H2–3?** pale-pink flowers and yellow-variegated leaf tips. **'Poorinda Ballerina' H2** (1m x 1m) flowers white with a yellow throat, prolific, for very mild gardens only. *P. rotundifolia H2* (2m x 2m) a mass of purple-to-lilac purple flowers in summer, almost obscuring the leaves; needs a sunny hot site, and suitable for mildest gardens only.

Prostanthera cuneata

Prunus (cherry laurel)

☠ It is hard to see how laurels can possibly be in the same genus as flowering cherries, but they are. These are very useful tough evergreen shrubs – or should that be thugs, as they are inclined to take over the garden and they are hard to get rid of once well established. They very happily sprout again, however hard you cut them back, and in mild climates they can layer and seed freely. Dense growing, with thick green, leathery leaves, laurels produce masses of tiny white flowers in upright spikes in spring and early summer. The shiny black fruits, which resemble cherries, are toxic to all but birds (who love them), so this is a shrub to avoid if there are young children and puppies around. This is a really useful shrub for massing in shade, under trees and along drives, and for making dense screens. The fleshy roots are easily killed by frost in containers, so you may need to insulate potted specimens in winter.
P. laurocerasus (cherry laurel) *H4–(5)* (3m x 2m after 10 years, U: 8m x 10m) ☠ dark-green oblong, glossy leaves, fragrant white flowers in April–May, followed by back fruit. **'Rotundifolia'** (5m x 4m) A bushy selection with shorter leaves, vigorous and good for hedging. For small gardens or a more manageable plant, choose one of the excellent slower-growing forms: **'Cherry Brandy'** (60cm x 1m+) very low, spreading habit, **Etna** ['Anbri'] (1.5–2m x 1–1.5m) coppery young shoots, **'Otto Luyken'** 1m x 1.5m) ♚ a superb compact form, with narrow leaves, suitable for the small garden and very fine in a container, **'Zabeliana'** (1m x 2.5m) a

Prunus laurocerasus

Prunus laurocerasus 'Otto Luyken'

low, spreading habit, almost ground-cover. *P. lusitanica H3–4* (Portuguese laurel) (3–5m, U: 10–20m x 10–20m) ☠ with dark leaves with red stems, this is a finer-looking plant, but less hardy than the above and potentially even more vigorous, with white flowers in June. It can be used for topiary. It can be damaged in inland gardens in cold winters. There is a superb mushroom-like domed specimen in the middle of the walled garden at Crathes Castle, Aberdeenshire. *P.l.* **'Variegata'** less vigorous, leaves with irregular creamy white margins.

Pseudosasa japonica see Bamboos, page 28

Pseudowintera colorata see *Drimys*, page 48

Pseudosasa japonica see Bamboos, page 28

Pyracantha (firethorn)

H3–4 (1.5–3m+ x 1.5–3m) These are a good choice as a manageable wall shrub for almost any Scottish garden and they are some of the best berrying shrubs of all, so good way to feed local wildlife. All varieties produce a mass of small white flowers in early summer, followed by long-lasting yellow, orange or red fruits in autumn. They are evergreen or semi-evergreen, with a stiff habit and vicious spines – alongside *Rosa rugosa*, mahonia, berberis and holly, pyracantha features on the police's recommended anti-burglar plant list. Suitable for any soils except boggy ones, they will grow on walls or fences facing in any direction, in sun or shade, although flowering and berrying is likely to be reduced on a shady north-facing wall. In cold gardens exposed to easterly winds, some shelter is advisable. They are not climbers as such (they don't cling), but pyracanthas grow well trained against walls or fences, tied to wires or trellis, although in the latter case, the shrub's weight or snow on top of it may eventually bring it down. They also make a fine free-standing shrub or hedge. The main problem is scab, an unsightly fungal disease which coats the leaves and berries in dark-green to black spots; it is particularly bad in a wet late spring and early summer. Resistant varieties

Pyracantha flowers

Pyracantha 'Orange Charmer' and 'Golden Charmer'

include 'Saphyr®' (three colours), 'Shawnee', 'Golden Charmer', 'Navaho' and 'Orange Charmer'. Fireblight (a fatal disease) and scale insects can also be a problem. Pruning can be done to shape the plant and to remove berries once they have dried up (wear thick gloves, though – it's not called firethorn for nothing). A light trim after flowering will help show the berries off come autumn. Hardiness varies, and heights and spreads are similar unless stated otherwise.

P. atalantioides **'Aurea' H3** (6m x 4m) very vigorous, berries yellow. *P. coccinea* **'Red Column' H4** (2–3m x 1m) early-ripening scarlet fruits. **'Dart's Red'** large red berries. **'Golden Charmer' H4** (3m x 2m) vigorous, berries bright orange-yellow, good foliage, resistant to scab. **'Harlequin' H3** (1.5m x 2m) leaves marked creamy white, flushed pink when young, red berries, needs a sheltered site. **'Mohave' H3** (4–5m x 3m) very vigorous, berries orange-red, long lasting as birds don't like them, fireblight resistant. **'Navaho'** (2–3m x 2m) orange-red, resistant to scab and fireblight. **'Orange Charmer' H4** (3m x 2m) deep orange berries, scab resistant. **'Orange Glow' H4** (3m x 2m) orange-red berries. *P. rogersiana* **H3–4** (3–4m x 1–2m) vigorous, spreading habit, orange-red berries; *P.r.* **'Flava'** yellow berries. **Saphyr Group H4** (3m x 2m) fireblight and scab resistant, three colour forms: **Jaune** ['Caudane'] yellow berries, **Saphyr Orange** ['Cadange'] orange berries, **Saphyr Rouge** ['Cadrou'] red berries. **'Shawnee'** (3m x 2m) orange-yellow fruit, colours early. **'Soleil d' Or' H4** (3m x 2.5m) reddish stems, fruit golden yellow. **'Teton' H4** (5m x 3m) small orange-yellow fruit.

Rhododendrons and azaleas

Rhododendrons are perhaps the most prevalent of all plants in the great Scottish gardens. Most west-coast gardens are dominated by them and Scotland holds several of the world's largest collections. Forming evergreen mounds (apart from the deciduous azaleas) of leathery green leaves, they produce spectacular flower displays, mainly in mid- to late spring, although there are rhododendrons that flower in almost any month of the

year. Some have outstanding foliage too. Botanists working at the Royal Botanic Garden Edinburgh have made Scotland the centre of the study of rhododendrons for 150 years. Scottish plant hunters, including George Forest, George Sherriff and members of the Cox family from Glendoick, have brought back hundreds of species from China and the Himalayas. And yes, there is of course 'the purple weed', *R. ponticum*, first introduced in the 18th century for game cover but now 'taking over' in areas of the high-rainfall west coast. We certainly would not recommend planting it (it is about to be made illegal to plant it at all – see page 159) although people still ask for it. It is important to point out that *R. ponticum* is the only problem plant out of a total of around 900 species, which range from tiny alpines to giant trees. None of the other species or 24,000 named hybrids are causing any environmental damage at all.

Rhododendrons and azaleas grow so well in Scotland because our soil and climate mimic the conditions they enjoy in the wild: peaty/acid soil, plenty of rainfall, cold but not extreme winters and cool summers. Almost all Scottish soil and water is acidic, so worries about whether you have the correct soil pH are usually unfounded. They are shallow rooting, and most soils can be improved for rhododendrons by adding organic matter such as leaf mould, compost (home-made or

Rhododendron 'Brambling'

Rhododendron 'Crane'

Rhododendron 'Egret'

Rhododendron fastigiatum

bought), composted bark or conifer needles to the top 30cm. You don't need to use peat if you don't want to: it has little or no nutrients, structure or mulching value. It is useful, however, as an acidifier and for containers. The rootball should be just below the surface when planting; any deeper and you may kill the plant. Rhododendrons need an open, reasonably draining soil mixture, with moisture and air to the roots. Many people gardening on heavy/clay soil struggle to provide these conditions, in which case the best thing to do is to build a raised bed above the heavy/clay soil, mixing the existing soil with plenty of organic matter/ericaceous compost.

Rhododendrons are long lived and so giving sizes for them is difficult. The more vigorous varieties will grow 30cm (12in) a year or more, often outwards as well as upwards, and so can eventually form giant bushes and trees, as can be seen in many Scottish gardens. Small-leaved varieties and azaleas can be pruned to keep them within bounds, but most of the large-leaved ones respond less well. In Scotland's relatively low light levels, most rhododendrons will not grow or flower well in deep shade or under trees. Tree roots will take the moisture and nutrients (particularly those of hungry feeders like beech and sycamore), and the lack of light will make plants straggly and shy flowering. Alpine (small-leaved) rhododendrons must be out in the open, as they hate to be under dripping from overhead branches, which rots the foliage. Rhododendrons can suffer from several pests and diseases, which in the main cause cosmetic rather than fatal damage. Most rhododendron failures are caused by incorrect choice of site, inadequate soil preparation and poor planting, and not by pest and disease problems. Mildews and rusts can be controlled with the same fungicides recommended for roses. Beware of vine weevil, particularly for plants in containers. The best choices for container growing are evergreen/Japanese azaleas, *R. yakushimanum* hybrids ('yak' hybrids), and *R. forrestii* and *R. williamsianum* hybrids. Ericaceous compost (which is the correct acidic pH for rhododendrons) should have extra grit or perlite added to it to improve the structure and maintain good drainage when used for container growing.

As there are over 900 species and 25,000 named hybrids, we have had to be very selective here. We have broken those listed down into categories: rhododendrons from smallest to largest, followed by the two azalea groups. Plants with the most striking and unusual foliage can mostly be found in the rhododendron species sections. Glendoick Gardens and Garden Centre, near Perth, is Scotland's rhododendron specialist. Of the many gardens to visit for rhododendrons, some of the best include the four gardens of the Royal Botanic Garden (Edinburgh, Dawyck, near Peebles, Benmore, in Argyll, and Logan), Glendoick, and many of the gardens of Argyll and Bute. Many rhododendrons spread outwards as much

as they grow upwards, so heights and widths are roughly similar.

Dwarf/alpine species and hybrids

H4–5 unless stated otherwise. Low-growing alpine plants for the small garden, rock garden or raised bed. Most smother themselves in flower and are dense twiggy growers, producing small scaly leaves, which should be grown away from the drips of trees. Many were bred at Glendoick by Peter and Kenneth Cox. Most of those listed here grow a little wider than high.

'Brambling' (90cm) brightest pink in April. *R. calostrotum* subsp. *keleticum* (20cm) flat-faced purple flowers in May–June. *R. campylogynum* **H4** (30cm) pink or purple thimble-like flowers in May. 'Curlew' **H4** (40cm) ⚜ bright yellow. 'Crane' (75cm) pure white. 'Dora Amateis' (60cm) white in April–May. 'Egret' (60cm) tiny white bells in May. *R. fastigiatum* (20–30cm) purple-blue in May, fine grey-blue foliage, very compact; 'Blue Steel' 'Intrifast', 'Indigo Steel' selected forms. 'Ginny Gee' (40cm) ⚜ pale pink, fading to cream, very free-flowering. 'Joachim Reich' (1m) Early double purple. Evergreen with good foliage. 'Lucy Lou' **H3–4** (60cm) pure white in March–April, furry leaves. 'Moerheim' (30cm) a loathsome muddy lavender, fit only for the bonfire. 'Night Sky' (60cm) fine purple-blue in April–May. 'Patty Bee' (30cm) pale yellow in early April. 'Penheale Blue' (1m) purple-blue in late April. 'Praecox' **H4** (1.2m) ⚜ lilac pink in March. 'Ptarmigan' ⚜ (20cm) masses of small frost-resistant white flowers in March–April, spreading habit. 'Quail' (30cm) Bright red buds open to deep reddish-pink. Compact. 'Razorbill' **H4** (50cm) clusters of tubular pink flowers. 'Ramapo' (45cm) ⚜ lavender pink, grey-blue foliage. 'Swift' (40cm) Yellow flowers, spotted red. 'Tinkerbird' **H3–4** (75cm) white, scented. 'Tree Creeper' (30cm) Two-toned pink and cream. 'Wee Bee' (25cm) two-toned pink. 'Wren' (20cm) creeping habit, very compact, fine yellow flowers in May.

Maddenia and related species and hybrids

H2–4 (30cm–3m) This extensive group of large-flowered and often sweetly scented species and their hybrids provide superb garden plants for west-coast gardens. Logan, in Galloway, Glenarn, near Helensburgh, and Arduaine in Argyll, have particularly spectacular examples. The hardiest, such as *R. edgeworthii* and *R. lindleyi*, can be grown out of doors in a sheltered site at Glendoick and other sheltered east-coast gardens. They can also be grown in the cool greenhouse and conservatory and brought into the house in flower. Most are epiphytic in the wild (growing on trees, logs and cliffs), so they need a coarse growing medium and sharp drainage: they do best in raised beds and old tree stumps, and must not be allowed to become waterlogged. Indoors, allow them to become a little pot bound. They can be hard pruned after flowering to improve habit. Most of these are available from specialist nurseries only.

R. edgeworthii H2–3 (1m) ✿ white or pale-pink scented flowers in May, handsome furry leaves. *R. formosum H2–3* (1.5m) ✿ fragrant white with a yellow flare, in May. **'Fragrantissimum' H2** (2m) ✿ scented white, in May, the best known, but so straggly it is hard to tame. **'Lady Alice Fitzwilliam' H2–3** (1.5m) ✿ scented white, in April–May, more compact than 'Fragrantissimum'. *R. lindleyi H2–3* (2m) ✿ stunning lily-like white scented flowers, very straggly. *R. maddenii H2–3* (1–2m) ✿ scented creamy flowers in June, spreading but fairly compact.

R. forrestii and *R. williamsianum* hybrids
H4–5 (60cm–1.5m) These two groups of low, compact

Rhododendron edgeworthii

Rhododendron lindleyi

Rhododendron 'Gartendirektor Rieger'

Rhododendron 'Linda'

Rhododendron 'Scarlet Wonder'

Rhododendron Wine and Roses [pinkros]

hybrids are free-flowering, compact and tough, and one of the best choices for containers. *R. forrestii* hybrids have waxy red flowers, while *R. williamsianum* hybrids have bell-shaped pink or cream flowers and oval leaves, bronzy when young.

R. forrestii hybrids: **'Carmen' H4** (30cm) deep red in May, compact, **'Elizabeth' H4** (1.2m) bright-red flowers in April–May, an old favourite but very prone to powdery mildew, **'Ruby Hart' H3–4** (75cm) dark red in May, fine deep-green glossy foliage, **'Scarlet Wonder' H5** (60cm) bright red in early May. *R. williamsianum* and its hybrids: **H4–5** (1–1.5m). *R. williamsianum H4* (60cm) the parent species: pink bells, rounded leaves, compact, early growth subject to frost damage inland. The hybrids are tougher: **'Bow Bells' H5** (1–1.5m) pink bells, ageing to pale pink, in lax trusses, **Everred** ['85/1C'] **H4** (60cm) dark red-purple flowers in April–May, stunning dark purple leaves, **'Gartendirektor Rieger' H5** (1.5m+) cream with red spotting, a fine choice, **'Linda' H5** (1m), deep rose-pink in May, light green leaves, **'Osmar' H5** (1.2m), lavender-pink bell-shaped flowers in May, tough, **'Ruby Hart' H3–4** (50cm) Darkest red floweers in early May. Dark green glossy foliage, compact. **Wine and Roses** ['Pinkros'] **H4** (1m) bright pink in April–May, leaves with a deep red underside.

'Yak' hybrids
H4–5 (1–1.5m, 2.5m for tallest x 1–1.5m), bred from the Japanese species *R. yakushimanum*, these have full rounded flower trusses similar to those of the large hybrids, but on small compact plants, usually with woolly indumentum on the leaves. Suitable for small gardens or containers.

'Bohlken's Lupinenburg' H5. The best purple-blue, with a paler greenish centre, **Bohlken's Snowfire H5** 80cm White with purple blotch. Slow growing. **'Cupcake' H4** salmon pink, **'Dopey' H4** bright red in early June, silvery new growth, **'Fantastica' H5** fine two-toned pink, in late May, one of the best, **'Golden Torch' H4** cream not gold, and not very good, **'Grumpy' H4** cream tinged pink, very compact with fine foliage, **'Loch Earn' H4** pale yellow, needs good drainage, **'Percy Wiseman' H5** pale pink-cream, **'Schneekrone'** (Snowcrown) **H5** cream, fading to white, with red spots, **'Sneezy' H5** deep pink fading to pale pink, **'Teddy Bear' H4** pale-pink flowers fade to white, good foliage, **'Titian Beauty' H4** loose trusses of red, compact with good foliage, *R. yakushimanum H5* (1m) ⚥ pale-pink buds open to white flowers, with darker spotting, late May–early June, very dense and compact with silvery foliage. Several yaks are not recommended: **'Dusty Miller'** (muddy colour), **'Flava'** (shy flowering, mildew), **'Kalinka'** (poor flowers), **'Silver Sixpence'** (poor foliage, disease).

Rhododendron species: Triflora, Heliolepida and Cinnabarina
(2–6m) Large-growing, vigorous species with small leaves,

Rhododendron 'Caroline Allbrook'

Rhododendron 'Cupcake'

Rhododendron 'Fantastica'

these are easy to grow and most are spectacularly free flowering. All can be hard pruned after flowering to keep them in bounds or improve habit.

R. augustinii H3–4 (3–6m) purple-blue in April–May, new growth prone to frost damage in inland gardens, **R. cinnabarinum H4** (2–3m) stunning and striking bell-shaped flowers in red, orange and yellow, unfortunately prone to powdery mildew so best sprayed during the growing season, **R. concinnum** Pseudoyanthinum Group **H5** (2–4m) a good choice for coldest sites with striking deep ruby-red flowers in April–May, **R. davidsonianum H3–4** (2–4m) a mass of pink in April–May, **R. lutescens H3–4** (2.5–3.5m) yellow in March–April, reddish-bronzy young growth, **R. oreotrephes H4** (2–3m) lavender, pink or cream in May, glaucous foliage, **R. rubiginosum H3–4** (3–6m) rose-lavender in March–April, vigorous, **R. yunnanense H3–4** (2–4m) pink or white in May, very spectacular; subject to bark split from unseasonal frosts in cold gardens and frost pockets.

Species for scent and/or fine foliage

H3–5 (2–4m) Most rhododendron species need some wind shelter and are at home in woodland conditions but not in too much shade. This is just a small selection of the best, most of which are available only from specialist nurseries.

R. arboreum H3–4 (4–6m+) the Himalayan tree rhododendron, flowers red though pink to white, leaves with silvery or reddish-brown indumentum on the underside, the red forms tending to

Rhododendron augustinii

Rhododendron cinnabarinum 'Roylei'

be the least hardy, **R. auriculatum H4–5** (3–5m x 5–7m) ❉ the latest of the larger species to flower, scented white flowers in August, grows very late in the season and is therefore vulnerable to early-autumn frosts, **R. barbatum H4** (2–4m) bright scarlet in early spring, fine peeling purplish bark, **R. bureavii H5** (2–3m) small pale pink-white flowers in late May–June, with very fine furry brown foliage, **R. calophytum H5** (3–5m) white to pale pink in February–March, large narrow leaves, **R. campylocarpum H4** (2–3m) yellow flowers, oval leaves, **R. decorum H4** (3–5m) ❉ pale pink or white, scented, tough and easy, **R. fortunei H5** (2–4m) ❉ pale lavender-pink scented flowers in late May and early June, **R. orbiculare H5** (2–3m) striking, smooth, almost rounded leaves and bright pink-purple flowers, **R. oreodoxa var fargesii H5** (2–4m) frost-resistant lilac-pink or pink flowers in March–April, **R. pachysanthum H5** (1–2m) pale pink to white in April, very fine silvery foliage, **R. thomsonii H4** (2–3m+) waxy red flowers, smooth, pinkish bark, prone to powdery mildew, **R. wardii H4–5** (2–3m) yellow in May–early June, needs good drainage. **R.yuefengense H5** (1–2m) low spreader with pink bells in June.

Scented plants

Lots of plants have scented flowers. Many of the best are winter flowering and some remarkably small flowers can produce very strong fragrances. Scent is often best at dusk and on warm and still days.

Buddleja	Primula veris (cowslip)
Choisya	Rhododendron
Corylopsis	'Loderi', R.
Cytisus battandieri	decorum
Daphne	R. luteum, R.
Fothergilla	arborescens
Hamamelis	Rosa (many)
Lonicera	Sarcococca
periclymenum	Syringa
Osmanthus	Viburnum (winter
Philadelphus	flowering)

Species: the 'big leaves' (SS *Falconeri* and SS *Grandia*)

(3–6m x 3–6m; some can reach 10m) This group of species are noble giants in every way, forming small trees with huge handsome leaves, lending a prehistoric subtropical effect to the garden. Most have an indumentum (layer of hairs) on the leaf undersides, and are superb garden plants as long as you can provide some wind shelter. West-coast gardens such as Achamore, Benmore, Brodick, Crarae, Glenarn and Arduaine have many

Rhododendron decorum

Rhododendron pachysanthum (foliage)

Rhododendron hodgsonii

Rhododendron macabeanum

Rhododendron wardii

fine examples. On the west coast they grow faster, but on the east coast they flower younger. You can expect to wait up to 10 years for the huge trusses of flowers in various colours.

R. arizelum H3–4 (3–5m) cream to pink trusses in March–April, leaves with woolly cinnamon indumentum, pink to reddish bark, *R. falconeri H3* (3–6m+) long-lasting huge cream trusses in late April–May, amongst the longest lasting of any species, very handsome leaves, *R. hodgsonii H4* (3m+) rose to magenta-purple flowers in April–May, peeling bark, one of the hardiest big-leaved species, worth trying in sheltered inland gardens, *R. kesangiae H4* (3–5m) pink, purple-pink or white in April–May, needs extra wind shelter, *R. macabeanum H3* (4–6m+) yellow with a purple blotch in March–April, very fine, there are two excellent specimens at the Royal Botanic Garden Edinburgh, *R. rex H4* (3–5m) pale pink to white with crimson markings in April–May, very handsome foliage, one of the best for cold areas, *R. rex* subsp. *fictolacteum* smaller leaves and flowers, equally good, *R. sinogrande H3* (4–6m+) creamy white in April–May, the largest leaves of all (up to 1m in length), best in mild, sheltered gardens, grows and flowers well at Glendoick.

Larger hybrid rhododendrons

This section contains hybrids mainly grown for their spectacular flowers. Most grow 2m x 2m or more in 10–20 years and the larger ones can attain well over 4m x 4m at maturity. Hardiness: *H5* hardy hybrids will generally take exposed sites and do well in cold and inland gardens; *H4* varieties can suffer wind damage and bark split in inland gardens if not given some shelter; *H3* varieties generally need favourable woodland conditions outside the mildest and west-coast areas. All yellow varieties need particularly well-drained soil: best to mound plant, or make a raised bed if the drainage is poor.

'Alena' *H5* (1.5m+) ❋ lightly scented pure white with yellow spotting in early May, **'Christmas Cheer'** *H4–5* (1.3m) ♛ pink fading to off-white in February–April, probably the best early-flowering hybrid, **'Crest'** *H3–4* (2–3m) pure yellow in mid-May, probably the most famous yellow hybrid, does best with some shelter, **'Cunningham's White'** *H5* (1.2–1.5m) white with a greeny-yellow centre in May, good in exposure and poor soil, two forms,

Rhododendron 'Cunningham's White'

Rhododendron 'Graziela'

one with larger trusses and leaves, **'Cynthia'** *H5* (2–3m) rose crimson in May–June, vigorous, **'Fabia'** *H3–4* (1.5m) orange salmon, in loose trusses in late May–June, does best with some shelter, **'Fastuosum Flore Pleno'** *H5* (2–3m) ♛ semi-double lavender in June, very tough, good for exposed sites, **Glendoick® Velvet** ['GLE018'] *H5* (1.5m) deep-purple

Rhododendron hybrids

Rhododendron 'Jean Marie de Montague'

Rhododendron 'Lem's Monarch'

flowers in May–early June, dense habit with reddish stems, **'Goldbuckett'** *H5* (1.5m) pale yellow with reddish spotting in May, needs good drainage, **'Golden Everest'** [EU PBR] *H5* (1m) Deepest yellow. Compact habit. **'Goldflimmer'** *H5* (1.5m) pinkish purple in June, leaves with internal splashes of yellow variegation, **'Goldkrone'** *H4–5* (1.3–1.5m) deep yellow flowers with red spotting in May, needs good drainage, **'Gomer Waterer'** *H5* (2m+) ❦ pale lavender-cream with a yellow flare in late June, one of the best later-flowering varieties, **'Graffito'** *H5* (2–3m) Pale pink flowers with a bold red blotch. Vigorous, upright habit. **'Graziela'** *H5* (1m) slow growing with pink flowers in May and striking narrow leaves, **'Hachmmann's Charmant'** *H5* (1.5m) White flowers edged purplish-pink with a red flare in May-June. **'Halopeanum'** *H5* (3m) Pink buds open white with red spots in May. Very vigorous. **'Horizon Monarch'** *H4* (2–3m) large trusses of pale yellow, blotched pink in May, thick leaved and sturdy, **'Jingle Bells'** *H4* (1.2–2m) pendent orange-yellow flowers with red centres in May, always attracts comment, **'Kali'** *H4–5* (1.5–2m) Dark purplish red with a deeper blotch. Dark foliage. A very striking, unusual colour. **'Lem's Monarch'** *H4* (3m x 3–4m) huge white, edged deeper pink in May–June, sturdy, a show-stopper, **'Loderi'** *H4* (3–5m) ❦ huge sweetly scented pale-pink, cream or white flowers, forming a tree, and needing wind shelter. **'Lord Roberts'** *H5* (2m) small rounded trusses of dark crimson with a small black flare in June–July, **'Maharani'** *H5* (2m) cream, tinged and spotted pink, in May, **'Marcel Meynard'** *H5* (2m) Striking darketst purple flowers. **'Markeeta's Prize'** *H4* (2m) large bright scarlet in May, sturdy, **'Metallica'** *H5* Blue-purple with a large almost black flare. **'Molten

Gold'** *H5* (1–1.5m) slow growing with bold yellow variegation, flowers small, pinkish purple in May–June, **'Mrs T.H. Lowinsky'** *H5* (1.5–2.5m) pale pink, with an orange-brown flare in June, a useful, tough, late-flowering choice, **'Nancy Evans'** *H4* (1.5m) deep yellow with orange flushing in May, one of the best hybrids of this colour, like all yellows needs sharp drainage, **'Nobleanum'** *H4* (1.5–2m) ❦ small trusses of pinkish-red in mild periods in December–February, the earliest hybrid to flower each year, **'Nova Zembla'** *H5* (2–3m) carmine-red in June, good for cold and exposed gardens, but not worth growing in milder areas, **'Pink Pearl'** *H4* (3–4m) pink fading to near cream in large trusses in May–June, on a tree-forming plant, **'Polar Bear'** *H3–4* (3–4m) ✽ scented white flowers in July–August, requires shelter from wind and unseasonable frosts, especially as a young plant, **'Rabatz'** *H5* (1.5m) Very fine red flowers with white stamens. **'Rasputin'** *H5* (1.5m) Rich deep purple, compact and spreading. **'Sappho'** *H5* (2–3m x 3–4m) white with a deep purple black blotch in early June, a straggly spreader and an old favourite, **'Sonata'** *H4–5* (1.5–2m) salmon orange edged red in small trusses in June, compact, **'Starbright Champagne'** *H4* (1.5–2m) cream with a deep red flare in the throat in May, compact with red young growth, **'Taurus'** *H5* (3–4m) fine red in April–May, handsome foliage and attractive red buds, **'Unique'** *H4* (1.5m) peach open to cream in April–May, compact, **'Vanessa Pastel'** *H3–4* (2m) cream flushed pink with a red throat in late May, needs a sheltered site, **'Virginia Richards'** *H4–5* (2–3m) fine salmon and cream, but very susceptible to mildew, so we no longer recommend it.

Deciduous azalea species and hybrids

H5 (1.5–2m) Hardy and relatively late flowering, these are ideal for virtually any Scottish garden, a particularly good choice for cold and inland gardens. Some are scented and most have good autumn colour. They are good in cold and windy sites except those marked as *H4*. They need protection from rabbits and deer when young.
R. arborescens ✽ small, sweetly scented white flowers in June–July. **'Arneson's Gem'** very fine orange fading to yellow. **Glendoick Scottish Mountain Series:** Double flowered in a range of colours: **'Ben Cruachan'** cream, pink edge, **'Ben Lawers'** deep pink, **'Ben Lomond'** pale pink, **'Ben Vorlich'** orange **'Ben Vrackie'** salmon pink, orange centre. **'Delicatissima'** *H4* ✽ cream tinged pink with yellow flare, scented. **'Exquisita'** *H4* ✽ cream flushed pink, orange flare, scented. **'Fireball'** orange-red, bronze young foliage. **'Gibraltar'** ❦ very free flowering, slow-growing orange. **'Gold Topaz'** deep yellow, bronze-purple young growth. **'Homebush'** balled trusses of double carmine pink, **'Klondyke'** bright yellow, bronze young growth. *R. luteum* (syn. *A. pontica*) ✽ ❦ small, scented yellow flowers, good autumn colour, vigorous and easy. **'Irene Koster'** ✽ pale pink, scented. **'Jock Brydon'** *H4* ✽ pink with a bold reddish blotch, scented, very vigorous. **'June Fire'** fine red, late June. **'Lemon Drop'** *H4* ✽ scented, small creamy yellow with reddish markings in June–July, glaucous foliage. **'Persil'** white with yellow flare. **'Rosata'** ✽ pale pink, scented. **'Soir de Paris'** ✽ pink with orange throat, lightly scented, neat

Deciduous azalea hybrids

Azalea luteum

Azalea 'Glendoick® Glacier'

Azalea 'Kermesina Rose'

low habit. **'Strawberry Ice'** peach-pink flushed yellow.

Evergreen azaleas
The best evergreen/Japanese azaleas for Scotland were raised in Germany and at Glendoick in Scotland. Many other evergreen azaleas are poor performers in Scotland because of insufficient hardiness or the need for intense summer heat to ripen their wood. Those listed below have been bred for tidy habit and good foliage retention in winter, as well as hardiness and freedom of flowering. Evergreen azaleas flower in late May and early June, and form mounds with height and spread similar, unless stated otherwise.

'Canzonetta' *H5* (30cm) hose-in-hose brightest pink, **'Chipmunk'** *H4–5* (30cm) bright-pink flowers in late June, slow growing, **'Elsie Lee'** *H4–5* (90cm) double lilac lavender, the most popular in this shade, **'Geisha Orange'** *H5* (50cm) salmon orange, low and compact, **'Girard's Hotshot Variegated'** *H4* (50cm) bright red, leaves with white-variegated margins, **Glendoick® Dream** [GLE005'] *H4–5* (50cm) double, ruffled purple, **Glendoick® Glacier** [GLE009] *H4–5* (50cm) double white, compact, **'Kermesina Rose'** *H5* (50cm) two-toned picotee flowers, rose pink with a white edge, **'Konigstein'** red-purple, compact with good foliage, **Maischnee** Large-flowered white in May. Compact. **'Marushka'** Carmine red, long-lasting. The finest dark reddish winter foliage. Compact. **'Mother's Day'** *H4* (1m) bright red, **'Opossum'** *H5* (50cm) deep reddish purple, compact with good foliage, **'Panda'** *H5* (30cm) pure white, probably the best-selling white azalea in the UK, **'Squirrel'** *H5* (50cm), masses of bright scarlet in June, neat habit and good foliage, **'Wombat'** *H5* (20cm x 1m+) a carpet of pink, good ground-cover. Amongst the azaleas that have proven not hardy in eastern and central Scotland but which are offered for sale in Scottish garden centres are **'Gumpo White'**, **'Gumpo Pink'**, **'Mary Helen'**, **'Salmon's Leap'** and many others.

Rhus typhina (sumach)
H5 (3–6m x 3–6m) ♣ ♠ This tough deciduous American tree or large shrub has striking foliage and good autumn colour. The large, pinnate leaves, up to 60cm long, turn brilliant

Azalea 'Squirrel'

scarlet, purple and orange in autumn. It can be cut back hard each spring to maintain as a shrub and it is prone to suckering, so you may need to cut these off from time to time if space is short. The sap can be an irritant. **'Dissecta'** finely dissected leaves, **'Tiger Eyes'** (2m x 3m) new, a dwarf, less invasive form which can be grown in containers.

Ribes (flowering currant)
H3–5 These are extremely tough, easy and adaptable deciduous shrubs, flowering in spring, suitable for anywhere in Scotland, tolerant of shade, drought and cold. First brought back from the USA by the plant hunter David Douglas, they look great with a carpet of daffodils underneath, and are also useful for informal hedging. They can be hard pruned after flowering to keep them in bounds, but can equally be left alone once established. At Glendoick they flower perfectly every year and have never been pruned or fed. The tougher ribes (*H5*) are some of the best spring-flowering shrubs for colder inland sites, as well as Orkney and Shetland. Heights and spreads are similar. Black, red and white currants and gooseberries are covered under soft fruit on page 146.

R. alpinum H4 (60cm) flowers sweetly scented, greenish yellow in erect racemes, the smallest-growing variety, reddish berries. *R. x gordonianum H5* (2m) ✿ fragrant red flowers with a yellow centre in dense pendent racemes in April, very tough,

Rhus typhina (autumn colour)

leaves sometimes with some autumn colour. *R. odoratum H4* (2m) clove-scented golden-yellow flowers in drooping racemes in April. *R. sanguineum H5* (2m) the most popular flowering currant, this is a useful plant for windbreaks and screening, for underplanting beneath trees and for the back of the shrub border, and it is extremely hardy, an excellent choice for spring colour in the coldest gardens. Frost-resistant flowers, bright pink to near red, in pendent racemes in March–April, followed by (non-edible) blue-black fruit. Often sold as seedlings, but there are also many named forms: **'Brockelbankii'** (1.2m) pale pink, striking yellow-green leaves which can suffer sunburn, suitable for a small garden, **'Elkington's White'**

Ribes sanguineum, pink and white forms

(2.5m) vigorous white selection, **'King Edward VII'** 🏵 (2m) dark red, late April to early May, **'Pulborough Scarlet'** (3m) 🏵 dark red with white centres, vigorous, **'Koja'** (1.5m) dark pink to bright red, **'Tydeman's White'** (2.5m) pure white. *R. speciosum H3* (2m) less hardy than the others with spiny shoots and dark-red flowers in March–April, occasionally producing gooseberry-like fruit.

Roses

Ah roses, roses, how can there be so many roses? Britain's best-loved plant, and yet they seem to be so much trouble: they tire out your soil, get attacked by all manner of bugs and diseases, and seem to need complex annual pruning and deadheading nearly every day. Well, this isn't strictly true – not for *all* roses at least. There is no doubt that the classic Hybrid Tea and Floribunda roses require some effort to achieve perfection, but there are lots of others, particularly the species and Shrub roses, which are easier to grow and less trouble to look after.

We surveyed lots of Scottish gardeners in order to come up with the selection of the best roses. There were hundreds of suggestions, but most agreed that reliability and ease of cultivation are the key characteristics. So we have shied away from listing many of the Johnny-come-lately roses named after 'B-list' celebrities and instead concentrated on the tried and tested, those roses with flowers that stand up to Scottish weather and leaves that don't hooch with blackspot, and which don't need too much pruning and feeding. In the wetter west coast gardens, black spot is particularly bad, and ironically, clean air is making it worse: sulphur from industrial pollution used to keep Glasgow's roses clean, but now you have to spray them. The Glasgow Rose Trial garden in Tollcross Park is a great place to see a wide selection, but be aware that these roses are sprayed regularly and disease resistance is not being tested, which we think is a pity. Global warming is another cause of increased rose disease: roses drop their leaves later and later in mild autumns, and then start growing in February and March, which means that you may have to start spraying much earlier than you used to. Recent articles by members of the National Rose Society have claimed that most modern roses are not prone to disease. They evidently have not spent much time in Scotland! Many yellow and orange-yellow roses have fussy genes and they are susceptible to frozen roots in heavy soil and containers, so it might be better to avoid these in coldest gardens and poor soils. James Cocker & Sons nursery in Aberdeen is the only significant contemporary Scottish rose breeder. This nursery has produced some of the greatest roses, including 'Silver Jubilee', which has won all the awards going. Scotland has quite a number of native roses: *Rosa canina, R. micrantha, R. pimpinellifolia, R. rubiginosa, R. sherardii, R. tomentosa* and *R. villosa*.

A note on rose names Most modern roses are protected by Plant Breeders' Rights [PBR], which means that they have two names, the second of which is usually a meaningless code, for example Kent ['Polkov']. We have omitted these code names to save space and avoid confusion.

Pruning roses Only Hybrid Tea roses should be pruned fairly hard; most other roses will respond well to the previous season's growth being shortened by two-thirds to half their length. Don't over-do it: it is better to under-prune than to cut off too much. If in doubt, leave alone. Dead and old wood can also be cut out. Don't worry about the old advice of cutting above a bud, or sloping cuts, experiments have shown that it makes no difference. Timing can be important: Ramblers and vigorous Climbers can be hard pruned after flowering or in autumn, but most other roses are best pruned in spring – not too early, though, as you don't want the resultant soft growth to be frosted: late February to late March for coastal, mild and sheltered gardens and early to mid-April for colder, inland gardens.

Abbreviations: ♦ = fairly disease resistant ♦♦ = very disease resistant. ❀ = fragrant ❀❀ = very fragrant.

Bush roses: Hybrid Teas and Floribundas
H4–5 (60cm–1.2m x 50cm–1m) This section includes what most people think of as the 'typical' rose: the classic long pointed bud, which opens to a double flower with many layers of petals. Hybrid Teas have the largest individual flowers and are the best for cutting. Floribundas are also known as cluster-flowered roses, having groups of smaller flowers produced more prolifically over a longer period. Hybrid Teas are the most formal of roses, traditionally

planted in rows in beds. They branch poorly, forming sparse, gaunt bushes, especially if they are diseased, and they are hard to integrate into the garden alongside other plants. They need careful pruning and deadheading, and almost all need regular spraying against black spot and mildew. Wind and rain can do a lot of damage to their flowers too. Floribundas are tougher, better in wet weather and less particular about how they are pruned, so unless you want perfect large blooms for cutting, Floribundas make better garden plants.

Roses in this section marked ♦ are the healthiest in this category, but even these will need spraying, especially for black spot in wet summers. If you don't want to spray, or if you live in western Scotland, you would probably be better off choosing healthier species and Shrub roses. Most roses in this category grow to 60–90cm, those described as tall will reach over 1m in height and those described as low or compact will reach 40–60cm. They spread as wide as they grow tall. Roses are greedy plants: they need feeding regularly, with either manure or granular fertilizer. It is well known that bush roses should not be replanted in a bed where roses have previously been grown, unless the soil is changed, because of what is known as rose replant disease or rose sickness. Most Shrub and species roses do not seem to suffer from this, which suggests that the over-breeding of modern roses may be the cause of it.

Half-standard and standard roses are grafted on stems 50cm–1.5m high. Almost any rose can be top grafted as a standard, and you can now find bush, patio and weeping (that is, ground-cover) standards. They need to be carefully staked, kept out of strong winds and pruned carefully to ensure that the head does not get too large.

HT = Hybrid Tea, FL = Floribunda.

'Abbeyfield Rose' (HT) ♦ small-flowered rosy-pink, light fragrance, tough: the best performing bush rose at Biggar Park, central Scotland, at an altitude of 250m above sea level, 'Absolutely Fabulous' (FL) ❊❊ Sweetly scented yellow, 'Alec's Red' (HT) ❊❊ ♦ ▼ cherry red with outstanding fragrance, flowers can be weather marked, 'Alexander' (HT) ♦ clear red, rain resistant, tall, 'Amber Queen' (FL) ♦ amber yellow, fragrant, low growing and very free flowering, not very rain or wind resistant, sometimes suffers from mildew, 'Arthur Bell' (FL) ❊❊ ♦ ▼ deep yellow, fading to cream, excellent scent, long flowering season, tall, 'Bewitched' (FL) ❊ pink, good fragrance, 'Birthday Girl' (FL) yellow and red, light scent, 'Blessings' (HT) ♦ coral pink, slight fragrance, good rain resistance, long flowering season, 'Blue for You' (FL) ❊ mauve, good scent, 'Blue Moon' (HT) ❊❊ double pale lilac-blue, very fragrant, horrible unnatural colour, prone to mildew, 'Twice in a Blue Moon' is much better, 'Braveheart' (FL) coral-salmon, slightly fragrant, 'Britannia' (HT) golden apricot, slight fragrance, repeat flowering, 'Buxom Beauty' (HT) ❊ ♦ large flowered, pink/magenta with outstanding fragrance, fairly

vigorous and tall, 'Champagne Moment' (FL) ❊ ♦ sweetly fragrant pale yellow-cream, low and compact, 'Champagne Cocktail' (HT) ❊ pink and yellow, scented, Chandos Beauty (HT) ❊❊ apricot pink, highly scented, 'Chicago Peace' (HT) pink, copper and yellow, slightly fragrant, tall, 'Chinatown' (FL) ❊ ♦ deep yellow, flushed pink, fragrant, 'City of Leeds' (FL) deep salmon-pink with little fragrance and rather prone to disease, but very free flowering and vigorous, Cleopatra (HT) ❊ Crimson with orange, scented, 'Dawn Chorus' (HT) ♦ deep orange, flushed yellow, slight fragrance, vigorous, 'Deep Secret' (HT) ❊❊❊ ♦ very dark red, probably the deepest of all, very fragrant, 'Easy Going' (FL) golden amber, slight fragrance, mildew prone, 'Ena Harkness' (HT) ❊ Bright red, fragrant, 'English Miss' (FL) ❊❊ ♦ soft pink, edged deeper, fragrant, quite weather resistant for a rose of this

colour, bushy habit, 'Especially For You' (HT) ❊ rich yellow, very fragrant, quite tall, 'Eternal Flame' (FL) bright orange and yellow, 'Fascination' (FL) ❊ shrimp pink, fragrant, 'Fellowship' (FL) ♦ deep orange, slight fragrance, long flowering season, tough, 'Fragrant Cloud' (HT) ❊❊ one of the strongest fragrances of all, coral red, but rather susceptible to black spot and mildew, 'Fragrant Memories'

Rose 'Arthur Bell'

(HT) ❊❊ ivory, very fragrant, 'Freedom' (HT) chrome-yellow, slightly scented, vigorous, 'Friend For Life' (FL) carmine-pink, fragrant, 'Fyvie Castle' (HT) ♦ light apricot, amber and pink, 'Garden News' (FL) apricot blend, very fragrant, 'Glenfiddich' (FL) ♦ golden amber with light fragrance, long flowering season (bred by Cocker), 'Golden Beauty' (FL) ♦ amber yellow, sweetly fragrant, good disease resistance, gold medal Glasgow Rose trials 2006, 'Golden Memories' (FL) ♦ semi-double, golden yellow, lightly scented, 'Golden Wedding' (FL) rich golden yellow, fragrant, 'Gordon's College' (FL) ❊ ♦ coral-salmon, good fragrance, purplish young growth, 'Grandpa Dickson' (HT) ♦ pale lemon-yellow, slight fragrance, good rain resistance, rather sparse growing and needs good soil preparation, as do most of this colour, 'Great Expectations' (FL) ❊ apricot pink, very fragrant, 'Greetings' (FL) H5 deep mauve-purple, slight fragrance, very tough, 'Halcyon Days'(FL) ♦ semi-double pale pink, 'Happy Anniversary' (FL) salmon pink, fragrant, 'Happy Retirement' (FL) soft pink, slight fragrance, 'Her Majesty' (FL) apricot, peach and pink, fragrant, 'Hot Chocolate' (FL) new, a rather odd russet-orange, scented, 'Iceberg' (FL) ▼ pure white, slight fragrance, the most popular white Floribunda, very free flowering, best lightly pruned, which helps reduce disease, to which it is prone, 'Ice Cream' (HT) ❊ ♦ ivory, fragrant, dark bronze-green foliage, tinted coppery red when young, 'Ingrid Bergman' (HT) large dark red, slight fragrance, needs good soil preparation, the best-selling red in the UK, 'Irish Eyes' (FL) yellow and scarlet blend, slight fragrance, 'Just Joey' (HT) ❊ ♦ copper-orange, fragrant, petals ruffled, long flowering, low, spreading habit, **'Korresia'** (FL) ❋ ♦ bright yellow, fragrant, long flowering period, probably the best yellow bush rose, **'Lady Marmalade'** Rose of the Year 2014 (FL) orange, good scent, **'Lady Rose'** (HT) ❋ soft red, fragrant, **'Many Happy Returns'** (FL) ❋ ♦ blush pink, fragrant, early flowering, spreading habit, **'Margaret Merril'** (FL) ❋❋ white, very fragrant, probably the best scented white Floribunda, but somewhat disease prone, **'Masquerade'** (FL) yellow buds open salmon and turn to red, slight fragrance, needs to be deadheaded, somewhat disease prone, which has reduced its availability, but a famous rose, **'Mischief'** (HT) ❋ fragrant coral salmon, very prone to rust so now seldom available, **'Mountbatten'** (FL) ❋ ♦♦ golden or mimosa yellow, fragrant, tall, good disease resistance, **'National Trust'** (HT) ♦ crimson red, no fragrance, **'Nostalgia'** (HT) ❋ an outrageous red and white bicolour, red on the back and outside, fragrant, **'Oranges and Lemons'** (FL) *H3* ♦ yellow striped orange, strikingly attractive or in very bad taste, depending on your point of view, slightly fragrant, rather tender, **'Pascali'** (HT) white shaded cream, slight fragrance, good rain resistance, but a sparse grower and prone to blackspot, **'Peace'** (HT) golden pink, slight fragrance, tall and should not be hard pruned, susceptible to black spot, **'Peacekeeper'** (FL) orange/yellow blend, slight fragrance, **'Pomponella'** (FL) lightly scented rich pink, **'Prima Ballerina'** (HT) ❋❋ cherry pink, very fragrant, susceptible to mildew and not a reliable flowerer, best avoided, **'Princess of Wales'** (FL) ♦ pure white, slight fragrance, fairly disease resistant, **'Queen Elizabeth'** (FL) ♦ light pink, slight fragrance, a good cut flower, very tall, over 2m, **'Red Finesse'** (FL) carmine-red, slightly scented, compact, gold medal Glasgow rose trials 2006, **'Remember Me'** (HT) ♦ large coppery orange, blended yellow, in clusters, slightly fragrant, **'Remembrance'** (FL) ♦ scarlet, slightly fragrant, long flowering season, some mildew, **'Renaissance'** (HT) ❋❋ blush pink and cream, flowers in clusters, some disease problems, **'Rhapsody in Blue'** (FL) ❋❋ ♦ purple fading to slate blue, almost certainly the closest yet to a blue rose with good scent and some disease resistance (sometimes classified as a Shrub rose), **'Rob Roy'** (HT) large flowered, red, upright habit, **'Rose Gaujard'** (HT) ♦ rose red and cream, with slight fragrance, good in poor soils and flowers are rain resistant, **'Royal William'** (HT) ❋❋ ♦ deep crimson, well scented, robust, tall and disease resistant, **'Ruby Wedding'** (HT) ruby red, slight fragrance, small flowered, rather prone to disease, **'Ruby Wedding Anniversary'** (FL) bright red, lightly scented, **'Samaritan'** (HT) ❋❋ amber peach to pink, very fragrant, **'Scent-imental'** (HT) ❋❋ cream with pink stripes, very fragrant, very vigorous to 1.5m, **'Scent-sation'** (HT) ❋❋ ♦ soft peach pink, very fragrant, **'Sexy Rexy'** (FL) ♦ extremely free flowering, shell pink, slight fragrance, fine despite the name, needs wind shelter, **'Sheila's Perfume'** (FL) ❋ yellow and red, good scent, **'Silver Anniversary'** (HT) ❋ ♦ pure white, fragrant, a good choice for disease resistance, **'Silver Jubilee'** (HT) ♦♦ 🏅 🏆 pink-peach, fragrant, perhaps the best Hybrid Tea for disease resistance (bred by Cocker) highly recommended, **'Silver Wedding'** (HT) creamy white, slightly fragrant, **'Simply the Best'** (HT) ♦ ❋❋ coppery orange, very fragrant, **'Southampton'** (FL) ♦ apricot-orange, flushed red, slight fragrance, vigorous, **'Special**

Rose 'Korresia'

Rose 'Rhapsody in Blue'

Rose 'Scent-imental'

Rose 'Scent-sation'

Anniversary' (HT) ❋❋ rich rose pink, very fragrant, **'Sunblest'** (HT) ♦ golden yellow, slight fragrance, **'Super Star'** (HT) vermillion-orange, good for cutting but a poor garden plant, prone to disease, best avoided, **'Super Trouper'** (FL) orange, lightly scented, **'Sunset Boulevard'** (FL) ❋ rosy salmon, fragrant, **'Tequila Sunrise'** (HT) ♦ yellow, edged scarlet, slight fragrance, **'The Jubilee Rose'** (FL) dark red, **'Thinking of You'** (HT) deep crimson, fragrant, **'Tickled Pink'** (FL) ♦ ❋ pink, scented, healthy, Rose of the Year 2007, **'Toprose'** (FL) ♦ golden yellow, slight fragrance, low growing with bushy habit (bred by Cocker), **'Troika'** (HT) ♦ ❋ orange-bronze, shaded red, fragrant, good rain resistance and healthier than most of this colour, **'Trumpeter'** (FL) bright scarlet, slight fragrance, **'Twice in a Blue Moon'** (HT) ♦ ❋❋ lilac, very fragrant, a replacement for 'Blue Moon' with much better disease resistance, the 'People's Choice' Glasgow rose trials 2006, **'Valencia'** (HT) ❋❋ buff-orange with golden shadings, very fragrant, **'Valentine Heart'** (FL) ❋ lilac pink, fragrant, **'Velvet Fragrance'** (HT) ♦ ❋❋ deep crimson, very fragrant, long flowering period, fairly tall, **'Warm Wishes'** (HT) *H3* ♦ ❋❋ very fragrant peach-coral, bushy, good wind and rain resistance, **'Whisky Mac'** (HT) ❋❋ very fragrant golden apricot, very susceptible to disease so no longer recommended, **'Yesterday'** (FL) silvery pink, fragrant, **'You're Beautiful'** (FL) pink, lightly scented, Rose of the Year 2013.

Climbing Roses and Ramblers
H(3)4–5 (3–15m+ x 2–6m) Climbing and rambling roses are, at their best, simply one of the most spectacular sights

Rose 'Sexy Rexy'

Rose 'Silver Anniversary'

Rose 'Silver Jubilee'

Rose 'Warm Wishes'

almost white centre, unscented, very spectacular in flower, but very rampant and suffers from mildew, *R. banksia* 'Lutea' (Rambler) **H3** (8–10m) a vigorous evergreen rose for mild climates, frilly primrose-yellow flowers in May–June, **'Bantry Bay'** (Climber) (2–3m) ♦ semi-double pink, slight fragrance, long flowering season, not very vigorous, good mildew resistance, **'Breath of Life'** (Climber) (2–3m) ❄ double light apricot, fragrant, not very vigorous, almost a Patio Climber, **'Bridge of Sighs'** (Climber) (2–3m) ❄ ♦ semi-double, golden amber, scented, **'Climbing Arthur Bell'** (Climber) (4.5m) ❄❄ ♦ deep yellow, very fragrant, **'Climbing Iceberg'** (Climber) (3m) pure white, slight fragrance, needs spraying for mildew, **'Compassion'** (Climber) (3m) ❄❄ ♦ apricot pink, very fragrant, repeat flowering, can suffer disease in late summer, **'Crème de la Crème'** (Climber) (3–4m) ❄❄ very fragrant, cream-white, **'Crimson Cascade'** (Climber) (3m) ❄ semi-double bright crimson, fragrant, repeat flowering, stiff upright habit, **'Danse du Feu'** (Climber) (3m) orange-scarlet, turning purple as flowers age, flowers well on a semi-shaded north wall, almost unscented, **'Dublin Bay'** (Climber) (2–3m) crimson, slight fragrance, good repeat flowering, not very good at climbing, sometimes remaining a bush, prone to blackspot, **'Ena Harkness'** (Climber) (4m) ❄❄ double deep red, scented, **'Félicité Perpétue'** (Rambler) **H5** (4–5m) ♦ ⚜ double creamy white with a slight scent, almost evergreen, very tough and will flower in semi-shade, one of the most disease-resistant ramblers, **'Galway Bay'** (Climber) (3m) ♦ large double pink, slight fragrance, **'Gloriana'** (Patio) (to 2.5m) ❄ lavender purple, scented, summer into autumn, **'Gloire de Dijon'** (Climber) (4m) ruffled double buff yellow-cream, slight fragrance, subject to mildew, an old favourite, **'Golden Showers'** (Climber) (2–3m) ❄ ⚜ fragrant double golden yellow, long flowering season, not too vigorous, good disease resistance, probably the best yellow Climber overall, though the name does it no favours, **'Handel'** (Climber) (4–5m) striking double two-tone cream and pink with slight fragrance, flowers over a long period, quite rain resistant, needs spraying for disease, **'High Hopes'** (Climber) (3.5m) ❄ ♦ double pink, some fragrance, good in less than ideal soils, **'Iceberg Climber'** (Climber) (3m) pure white, slight fragrance, needs spraying for mildew, **'Kiftsgate'** (*R. filipes*) ⚜ (Rambler) (7–10m) ❄❄ single very fragrant creamy white, over 2 weeks, probably the most rampant rose you can buy, don't consider it unless you have a large tree or shed to cover with it, **'Lavinia'** (Climber) (3m) ❄ large double pink, fragrant, repeat flowering,

in the garden. Most are very free flowering, some over a long period. Ideal for covering the walls of the house, they are also excellent for growing on pillars, arches and pergolas and over fences. Patio climbers (marked 'Patio') are less vigorous, reaching 2–2.5m or so, and more suited for a small garden or growing in a container. Most roses need sun to flower well, so avoid north-facing walls. A drawback of many climbing roses is that they are inclined to become bare at the bottom, with all the leaves and flowers at the top. This can only really be cured by pruning old stems regularly to encourage new basal growth, or by training branches laterally. If you cut back too hard, it encourages suckers from the rootstock which need to be removed.

Rambling roses can be the most spectacular of all. They are more vigorous, less able to support themselves, and may need more pruning and maintenance than the modern Climbers if you are short on space. Ramblers are usually not repeat flowering and are generally rather prone to disease, but the best ones are invaluable for growing up trees, large walls or houses or covering ugly buildings. All listed below are rated **H4–5** unless stated otherwise.

'Albertine' (Rambler) (4–5m) ❄ ⚜ salmon-pink in early summer, very fragrant, reddish young foliage, prone to mildew and flowers are easily damaged by heavy rain, **'Aloha'** (Climber) (2.5m) ❄ ♦ salmon pink, fragrant, repeat flowering, flowers are quite rain resistant, **'American Pillar'** (Climber) (4.5m) bright pink with an

Rose 'American Pillar'

Rose 'Iceberg'

Rose 'Dublin Bay'

'Laura Ford' (Patio) semi-double, yellow, pink tinged with age, over several months, a very good plant, usually covered in flower, **'Love Knot'** (Patio) (2m) ♦ bright crimson, quite bushy, **'Maigold'** (Climber) (4.5m) ❄❄ ♦ very fragrant bronze-yellow flowers, in late May and early June, one of the first to flower, the thorns are vicious, **'New Dawn'** (Climber) (3m) ❄ small semi-double shell pink, fragrant, flowers all summer, on a vigorous plant with shiny leaves, some disease, **'Open Arms'** (rambler) (2.5m) shell pink, light scent, **'Paul's Himalayan Musk'** (Rambler) (7m) double pale pink fading to off white, very vigorous, don't plant in a confined space, it needs lots of room, **'Paul's Scarlet'** (Rambler) (4m) scarlet crimson in mid-summer, not repeat flowering and rather prone to disease, but still a popular choice, **'Penny Lane'** (Climber) *H5* (2–3m) ❄ ♦ champagne blush, fragrant, repeat-flowering, one of the hardiest climbers, **'Pink Perpetue'** (Rambler) (3m) carmine-pink, slight fragrance, **'Rambling Rector'** ⚥ (Rambler) (6–9m) ❄❄ cream with a yellow centre, very fragrant and extremely rampant, with hips in autumn, a good woodland plant, **'Schoolgirl'** (Climber) *H4* (3.5m) ♦ apricot/orange, fragrant, rather leggy and sparse, not very tough and not always the most free flowering, **'Seagull'** (Climber) (4–6m) white, slight fragrance, flowers once only, very spectacular, ideal for covering eyesores and scrambling up trees, **'Sparkling Scarlet'** (Climber) (4.5m) bright scarlet, slight fragrance, **'Starlight Express'** (Climber) (2.5m) dark pink, fragrant, **'Star Performer'** (Patio) (2.5m) ❄ satin pink, scented, very free-flowering, **'Summer Breeze'** (Climber) (4m) ♦ single rose pink, good scent, **'Summertime'** (Patio) (2–2.5m) ❄ double, creamy yellow, scented, **'Summer Wine'** (Climber) (3m) ❄ semi-double, deep pink-bright red, scented, **'Super Excelsa'** (Climber) (3.5m) rose/crimson, slight fragrance, **'Warm Welcome'** (Patio) (2m) ♦ orange red with a slight scent, more spreading in habit than the other patio climbers, **'Wedding Day'** (Rambler) (6m+) ❄❄ ♦ small, cream fading to pinky white, very

Rose 'Danse du Feu'

Rose 'Maigold'

fragrant flowers in July–August, very vigorous, **'Zéphirine Drouhin'** (Climber) (3.5m) ❄❄ ⚥ semi-double carmine pink, very fragrant, repeat-flowering if deadheaded, thornless, subject to disease.

Patio roses

H3–4 Essentially these are low-growing Floribunda roses, which reach around 40–50cm in height and have small leaves and masses of flowers in clusters over a long period. Most have little or no scent. They are becoming more and more popular for containers and small gardens, and can also be used for low hedges. They should be pruned in spring: cut back approximately half the growth length and remove old and dead wood. Feed regularly in containers to encourage a long flowering period.

Rose 'Paul's Himalayan Musk'

Rose 'Zépherine Drouhin'

'Baby Love' ♦ single yellow, **'Bianco'** white, **'Butterscotch Dream'** as in the name, **'Carefree Days'** light pink, **'Caribbean Dawn'** semi-double orange-pink and yellow-orange mix, **'Charmant'** ❄ ♦ double pink with yellow-white centres and cream-white reverse, delicate sweet fragrance, **'Diamond'** semi-double pure white, **'Champagne Dream'** cream and yellow, **'Cider Cup'** ♦ deep apricot, quite large, good for cutting, **'Conservation'** rose pink, **'Coral Reef'** coral pink, **'Cream Dream'** cream, **'Dream Lover'** ❄ lilac pink, fragrant, **'Drummer Boy'** bright red, **'Fab'** ❄ one of the few with a good scent, pink, **'Flirt'**, double deep pink with white centres and yellow stamens, **'Flower Power'** ❄ peachy salmon, fragrant, **'Golden Anniversary'** bright yellow, **'Golden Jewel'** golden yellow, **'Hand in Hand'** vermilion-red, **'Happy Birthday'** ❄ pale yellow, fragrant, **'Happy Times'**, cerise, **'Honeybunch'** ❄ ♦ yellow flushed salmon, fragrant, **'Lovely Meidiland'** neon pink, no fragrance, **'Magnolia Dreams'** cream, **'Mandarin'** orange and yellow, **'Nice 'n' Easy'** pink, **'Paradise'** orange and yellow, **'Peter Pan'** orange-red, **'Pretty Polly'** ♦ shell pink, very free flowering, **'Pure Magic'** orange/gold, **'Queen Mother'** ♦ shell pink, a good choice for disease resistance, **'Ray of Sunshine'** ♦ small-flowered yellow, semi-double (bred by Cocker), **'Ring of Fire'** amber, edged red, **'Ruby Anniversary'** red, **'Ruby Ruby'** ruby-red, **'Scarlet Patio'** scarlet-red, **'Shine On'** pink-orange, **'Shining Light'** golden apricot, long flowering period (bred by Cocker), **'Snowcap'** pure white, **'Stardust'** ❀ lilac, fragrant, **'Strawberry Fayre'** ❀ cream and red, fragrant, **'Sugar Baby'** ❀ rich pink, fragrant, **'Sugar & Spice'** pale pink, **'Sunseeker'** ♦ mandarin red with a yellow eye, long flowering period, **'Sweet Dream'** ❀ ♦ apricot-salmon, fragrant, on a disease-resistant and bushy plant, the best-selling Patio rose, flowers are weather resistant, **'Sweet Lemon Dream'** lemon yellow, **'Sweet Magic'** ❀ ♦ orange-gold, fragrant, **'Sweet Memories'** ❀ lemon yellow, fragrant, **'Sweet Wonder'** dark apricot, **'The People's Princess'** medium pink, **'The Ribbon Rose'** pink, **'Vermilion Patio'** vermilion-orange, **'Wee Jock'** bright crimson-scarlet, **'Yellow Dream'** lemon yellow, **'Yellow Patio'** rich yellow.

Miniature roses
(20–30cm) Often sold as houseplants or for containers, Miniature roses are very often sold by colour only and with

Rose 'Carefree Days'

Mixed Patio roses

Rose 'Sweet Dream'

no name given. They have tiny leaves and flowers; most are rather disease susceptible and weak, so they tend to be treated as bedding and thrown out when finished. They have little or no scent.

Ground Cover roses
H4–5 (30cm–1m x 1–2/3m) These dense, bushy, spreading shrub roses can be used as ground-cover with masses of usually small flowers in large sprays – good for containers, banks and raised beds. Most are tough and fairly disease resistant, and some are repeat flowering. These are a good choice for Scotland, being low maintenance and mostly quite weather resistant. The sizes given here are for typical height x spread.

'Amber Cover' (50–75cm x 75cm) double cream, orange and yellow, **'Arctic Sunrise'** (30cm x 60cm) white, no fragrance, **'Blenheim'** (70cm x 1m) ❀ white, fragrant, **'Broadlands'** (50cm x

80cm) yellow, some fragrance, **'Cherry Cover'** (50–75cm x 75cm) ❀ semi-double bright red, scented, **'Flower Carpet Amber'** (70 x 80cm) orange, yellow, **'Flower Carpet Coral'** (80cm 1.2m+) single coral pink, very attractive, **'Flower Carpet Gold'** (60cm x 80cm) double buttercup yellow, too new to evaluate, **'Flower Carpet Pink'** (50cm x 1m) ♦ double pink, very popular, **'Flower Carpet White'** (50cm x 90–1.2m) ❀ ♦ semi-double pure white, very reliable and disease resistant, **'Flower Carpet Sunshine'** (60cm x 1m+) pale yellow, not as good as the others and prone to blackspot, **'Flower Carpet Red Velvet'** (60cm x 1–1.2m) single rich dark-red, **'Flower Carpet Ruby'** (60 x 60cm) dark red, long flowering, **'Flower Carpet White'** (50cm x 90-1.2m) ❀ ♦ semi-double pure white, very reliable and disease resistant, **'Magic Carpet'** (50cm x 1.5m) lavender, fragrant, **'Norfolk'** (60cm x 60cm) ❀ bright yellow, fragrant, **'Pathfinder'** (60cm x 90cm) vermilion, some fragrance, **'Pheasant'** (1m x 2–3m) ❀ double deep pink, scented, in early summer, not repeat flowering, very vigorous, good for covering large areas, **'Playtime'** (70cm x 1.2m+) ❀ pink, good fragrance, **'Pretty in Pink'** (60cm x 1.2m) ❀ light pink, good fragrance, **'Red Trail'** (20cm x 1.m) bright red, light scent, very low **'Rosy Cushion'** (80cm x 1.2m) cluster-flowered shrub, pink with white eye, some fragrance, **'Yellow Cover'** (50–75cm) double yellow.

Shrub roses
H4–5 In many ways, this section is where the future of rose cultivation lies. Despite the fact that many of these were bred long ago, their toughness, their disease resistance and the fact that they don't need to be carefully pruned make them an attractive proposition for many gardeners. Many are wild species or only a generation or two away from them. These are plants that look after themselves, are suited for less formality and associate better with other plants, growing in shrub borders, in woodland or as hedging. Many of the hybrids are repeat flowering. In many ways they have much more character too: apart from the diversity of flower form, some have interesting foliage, others have autumn colour and many have impressive autumn hips. We make no secret of the fact that we think these are some of the best roses to grow, particularly on the west coast, where rainfall is high and

Rose 'Flower Carpet Coral'

where floribundas and hybrid teas are particularly prone to blackspot. It is well worth visiting the Garden of Historic Roses at Drum Castle in Aberdeenshire to see their collection of 400 species and Shrub roses.

Several categories of roses are included here. The old-fashioned fragrant Gallicas and Damasks flower in mid-summer but are mostly not repeat blooming. Scots roses were mostly bred in Scotland from *Rosa pimpinellifolia* and are free flowering, mostly scented, but not repeat flowering. Most modern Shrub roses are repeat blooming if they are deadheaded. Many of these (called English Roses, but don't let that put you off) were bred by David Austin and can be recognized in garden centres in their dark-green square pots. They cost quite a bit more than other roses, and only some of them are worth growing: the heavy flowers of many fail to stand up to the weather. We are grateful to Michael Mariott from David Austin Roses for help with selecting the best of their range.

The number-one rose for Scotland is undoubtedly *Rosa rugosa* and its forms and hybrids. We can't over-praise this wonderful plant – disease resistant, flowers all summer, scented, huge reddish hips, wind, salt spray and drought resistant, good for hedging, needs no pruning or feeding. This rose should not be planted outside the garden, however, as it can be invasive, spreading with numerous suckers to form thickets. Jennifer Cunningham in her very

Rose 'Flower Carpet White' and 'Flower Carpet Pink'

Rose 'Kent', 'Wiltshire', 'Sussex', 'Suffolk' (County Series)

exposed garden on windy Easdale Island, Argyll, where waves break over the house during storms, told us that *Rosa rugosa* shelter was the key to being able to garden there at all.

Hardiness ratings are **H4–5**, height and spread measurements are similar, and flowers are double, unless stated otherwise.

'A Shropshire Lad' (Austin) (1.5m) ❀ soft apricot pink, fragrant, vigorous and heatly, can be used as a short climber. *R. x alba* **'Alba Maxima'** ('The Jacobite Rose') (2m) ❀❀❀ white with creamy centre, very fragrant, also flowers in semi-shaded woodland conditions, grey-green foliage, disease resistant and tough. **'Belle de Crécy'** (Gallica) (1.3m) ❀❀❀ ♦ pink-purple in mid-summer, very fragrant, grey-green leaves. **'Ballerina'** (1–1.5m) ♦ masses of single small pink flowers with a white eye, repeat flowering, with a light, musk-like scent, good disease resistance. **'Benjamin Britten'** (Austin) ❀ (1m) deep reddish-pink, fragrant. **'Blanc Double de Coubert'** (Rugosa) (1.5m) ♦♦ ⚜ large, sweet-smelling white from June to early autumn, outstanding disease resistance, rather

sparse and upright and flowers don't stand up to much rain. **'Bonica'** *H5* (1m) ♦ pale pink, slightly fragrant, ground-covering habit. **'Boscobel'** (Austin) (1.2m) very fine salmon-pink excellent fragrance, disease resistant, **'Buff Beauty'** (1.2–1.5m) pale apricot, lightly fragrant, very free-flowering, attractive bronze young foliage. **'Buttercup'** (Austin) (1.3m) ❀❀ single rich yellow, rain resistant, very fragrant, heathly foliage. *R. canina* (dog rose) *H5* (3m+) single white or pink in June–July, with red hips ripening in autumn. Used for hedging, found in wild hedgerows and tolerant of neglect. **'Cardinal de Richelieu'** (Gallica) (1.2m) ❀ rich reddish-purple, fragrant, mid-summer. **'Comte de Chambord'** (Portland) (1m) ❀❀ ♦ deep pink, very fragrant, long flowering season. **'Constance Spry'** (Austin) (2m) fragrant pink, somewhat subject to mildew. **'Cornelia'** (musk) (1.5m) pink, tinted apricot, from early to late summer, fragrant, rain resistant, good for hedging. **'Crown Princess Margareta'** (Austin) ❀ (1.5m) double apricot, fruity scent, good disease resistance, **'Duchess of Portland'** (1m) single red, with conspicuous anthers, slight fragrance. **'Evelyn'** (Austin) (1m) ❀ light apricot, fragrant, bushy habit. **'Falstaff'** (Austin) (1.3m) ❀ dark crimson fading to rich purple, fragrant, very striking colour. **'Felicia'** (Hybrid Musk) (1.5m) ❀❀ apricot pink, very fragrant, with a very long flowering season, good for hedging. **'Frau Dagmar Hastrup'** (Rugosa) (1m) ❀ ♦♦ ⚜ fragrant, single pink, very tough (in constitution as well as in pronunciation), long flowering season which huge hips, makes a good hedge and tolerant of salt spray. **'Frühlingsgold'** (2m) ❀ ⚜ semi-double large fragrant flowers in early summer, very free-flowering on long arching shoots, but flowers last only a fortnight. **'Frühlingsmorgen'** single bright pink with yellow stamens, in early summer, arching shoots. *R. gallica* var. *officinalis* (syn. 'Crimson Damask') (1m) ❀ semi-double pinkish red, fragrant, long used for perfume; for *R.g.* var. *o.* **'Versicolor'**, see 'Rosa Mundi'. **'Gentle Hermione'** (Austin) (1.2m) double two-toned pink flowers of the old rose type, which David Austin says is particularly rain resistant. **'Geoff Hamilton'** (Austin) (1.5m) ❀ ♦♦ soft pink, scented flowers over a long period, vigorous. **'Gertrude Jekyll'** (Austin) ❀❀ ⚜ (1.2m) large double deep pink with a strong scent, but a rather sparse habit, so best at the back of a border, prone to mildew, voted Britain's favourite rose in 2005. *R. glauca* (syn. *R. rubrifolia*) (2–3m) small single deep-pink

Rosa x alba 'Alba Maxima'

Rose 'Blanc Double de Coubert'

Top 10 Roses for Scotland

Choosing roses can be a bit of a challenge as there are so many. But there are undoubtedly some outstanding candidates and these would be our top 10 listing, taking disease resistance, scent and toughness/reliability as the key criteria.

Species & Shrub

R. moyesii 'Geranium' red with showy hips.

R. xanthina 'Canary Bird' bright yellow in May-June.

Rosa rugosa the toughest, most trouble free rose, purple or white scented flowers.

'Rose de Recht' disease resistant and fragrant deep pink.

Flower Carpet TM disease resistant, require no pruning and flower over a long period. Best forms are 'Pink', 'White' and 'Red Velvet'.

Bush Roses

'Arthur Bell' & 'Korresia' best yellow floribundas.

'Rhapsody in Blue' amazing purple colour.

'Silver Jubilee' peach pink, fragrant, disease resistant.

Climbers

'Rambling Rector' rampant, and amazing.

'Helen Knight' (2m) small single clear yellow in late May–June, fern-like leaves, slight fragrance, similar to 'Canary Bird'. **'Jacques Cartier'** (Portland) (60cm) ❀ light pink, old rose type, repeat flowering, fragrant. **'Jacqueline du Pré'** (2m) ivory white, early, prickly stems. **'Lady of Megginch'** (Austin) (1.2m) deep pink. **'Marjorie Fair'** (1m) pink and red bicolour with no fragrance, repeat flowering and bushy grower, easy. **'Mary Rose'** (Austin) (1.2m) ❀ rose pink, scented and good in less-than-ideal soil conditions. **'Madame Isaac Pereire'** (2m) ❀❀ ⚱ an old Bourbon rose with tightly packed purple-pink very fragrant flowers, sometimes misshapen and so heavy that it needs staking or tying in, prone to disease. **'Molineux'** (Austin) (1m) ❀ double yellow, orangey tones, musky fragrance, good had proven good in Scotland, upright growth habit. ***R. moyesii* 'Geranium'** (2m) single bright red in May and June, needs full sun for good flowering, slight fragrance, very showy orange-red hips, good in Shetland. **'Nevada'** (2m+) large flowered single creamy white in June, thornless, very vigorous, prone to blackspot, **'Penelope'** (Hybrid Musk) (1.5m) ❀ shell pink fragrant, repeat flowering if deadheaded, good mixed border shrub. ***R. pimpinellifolia*** (60cm x 1.5m) ♦ single white flowers on a suckering dense spreader with very thorny stems, good by the sea and for hedging and screening. **'Queen of Sweden'** (Austin) (1m) double light pink, good in wet areas as flowers are not too heavy and growth is sturdy. Good disease resistance. **'Rosa Mundi'** (syn. *R. gallica versicolor*) (Gallica) (1m) pale pink, striped crimson and splashed cream, slight fragrance but suckering and subject to mildew. **'Roseraie de l'Hay'** ***H5*** (Rugosa) (2m) ❀ ♦♦ star-shaped flowers with white centres and yellow stamens, and attractive red hips in late summer, attractive glaucous purple foliage, reddish violet, almost thornless stems, flowers don't last long, but an outstanding foliage plant, good in Orkney, Shetland and throughout Scotland, including coastal gardens. **'Golden Wings'** (Scots) (1.5m) ❀ single or semi-double light primrose yellow, scented, repeat flowering. **'Graham Thomas'** (Austin) (1.5m) ❀❀ pure yellow, very fragrant, named after the great shrub rose expert, needs wind shelter, long flowering at Glendoick. **'Harlow Carr'** (Austin) ❀❀ (1.2m) double pure rose pink, good fragrance, disease resistance and repeat-flowering.

Rose 'Graham Thomas' (Austin)

'Rosa Mundi' (syn. *R. gallica versicolor*)

Rose 'Gertrude Jekyll'

Rosa glauca

Rosa moyesii

Rosa rugosa

Rosa rugosa 'Alba'

Rosa xanthina 'Canary Bird'

wine-red sweetly scented flowers, disease resistant, tough, good in poor soils and for hedging. **'Rose de Rescht'** *H5* (Damask) (2m) ♦ fragrant deep fuchsia-pink clustered pompom flowers, disease resistant, good in exposed gardens. *R. rugosa H5* (2–3m) ❀ ♦♦ ♛ single purple, pink or white ('Alba') #, fragrant, repeating blooms with huge ornamental red hips in autumn, tough, disease and wind resistant, excellent by the sea, vigorous (maybe too vigorous), probably the most versatile rose of all, happy from Galloway to Shetland (St Abbs Head near Berwick is covered with it); **'Scabrosa'** a bright mauve-pink form. **'Sophy's Rose'** (Austin) ❀ (90cm) double light crimson, tea fragrance, fairly short and upright, rain-resistant flowers, very good repeating and healthy foliage. **'Teasing Georgia'** (Austin) (1.5m) double yellow with orange tones, reliable, arching habit or can be used as a climber. **'The Fairy'** (75cm x 1m) double pale pink in late summer, occasional disease. **'The Mayflower'** (Austin) ❀ double pink, resistant to rust and mildew, excellent choice for Scotland. **'The Pilgrim'** (Austin) (1–1.5m) ❀❀ vigorous, sweetly fragrant, double lemon yellow, paler edges, can be used as a climber. **'Wild Edric'** (Austin rugosa hybrid) (1.2m) ❀❀ extremely healthy, deep velvety pink, very fragrant, long flowring. Best variety at the Pencoed trials in South Wales where there is about 60in of rain a year. *R. xanthina* **'Canary Bird'** (3m) ♦ ♛ single bright yellow in May–June, attractive ferny foliage, disease resistant, arching growth, good for hedges.

Rosmarinus officinalis (rosemary)

H2–3(4) (1–2m x 60cm–1.5m) Rosemary is one of the tougher of the culinary herbs and its aromatic evergreen leaves can be used all year round for flavouring lamb, pork and chicken. There are a wide variety of forms, from vigorous upright varieties which can be used for specimen shrubs and hedging, to dwarf and ground-cover forms which can also be grown in containers. The flowers – loved by butterflies and bees – appear in shades of mauve, purple, pink or white along the stems in May–June, and often again later in summer. Like most plants from dry areas, rosemary prefers a well-drained soil in full sun. Some will tolerate wetter, heavier soils, but waterlogging will kill them. Rosemary can be a long-lived plant in coastal gardens, but without protection inland you

may lose even the tougher forms (hardy to at least -10°C) in a severe winter. It is best to plant in late spring to allow the roots to grow into the surrounding soil. Occasional pruning may be required to shape, which is best done after flowering in early summer. Height and spread measurements are similar.

R. officinalis *H2–3(4)* (1–2m) purple-blue, **var.** *albiflorus* white, **'Aureus'** leaves with some yellow variegation, looks sick, **'Benenden Blue'** (syn. 'Corsican Blue') *H2* (1m) early, gentian blue, for mildest gardens only, **'Fota Blue'** *H2* (60cm) a tender semi-prostrate form with dark blue flowers, **'Lilies Blue'** (1.5m) Scottish-raised, blue, **'Goriza'** (1.5–2m) upright habit, large-leaved, light blue, **'Majorca Pink'** *H2–3* (1m) tender, with arching stems and pink flowers, **'Miss Jessopp's Upright'** *H3–4* (2m) the best-seller, vigorous and upright,

Rosmarinus officinalis 'Fota Blue'

light mauve blue, a good choice for hedging and one of the hardiest, **'McConnell's Blue'** (syn. 'Mrs McConnell') (60cm) dwarf, spreading, with dark blue flowers, **'Primley Blue'** *H3(4)* (1m) clear blue, **'Prostratus Group'** *H2–3* (60cm) spreading forming trailing mats, for mild gardens only (several forms including **'Deben Blue'** and **'Capri'**), **'Roman Beauty'** (50cm) dwarf, good in pots, **'Roseus'** (90cm) lilac pink, **'Severn Sea'** *H2–3* (1m) violet blue, spreading habit, rather tender, **'Sissinghurst Blue'** *H3* (1.2m) upright habit, rich blue, **'Tuscan Blue'** *H2* (1.5m) upright, large light green leaves with a nutmeg scent, sometimes flowers in winter, tender.

Rubus (ornamental brambles)

So much time is spent trying to get rid of unwanted brambles that you may not see much point in paying money to get 'fancy' ones, but there are several fine non-invasive *Rubus* that are well worth garden space. The raspberry, tayberry, loganberry, etc. (see page 147) are also forms of *Rubus*. Some ornamental *Rubus* have fairly vicious thorns, others have none, and most of the ornamental ones have edible but sometimes tasteless fruit. Some have striking white winter stems and others are useful ground-covers. The white-stemmed varieties are best hard pruned in spring, but beware of the thorns.

'Benenden' *H4* (3m+) deciduous and thornless with single, rose-like white flowers with yellow centres in May along the arching branches. **'Betty Ashburner'** *H4* (30cm x 2–3m) an evergreen ground-cover with heart-shaped leaves and small white flowers in summer, less invasive than *R. tricolor*. *R. biflorus* *H3–4* (3m) an erect deciduous prickly shrub mainly grown for its striking chalky white winter stems, white flowers

Rubus 'Benenden'

Rubus tricolor

in summer followed by edible yellow fruit, leaves white-felted on the underside. *R. cockburnianus H4* (2.5m) a vigorous deciduous species with arching prickly stems of purple overlaid with a brilliant white bloom in winter, small flowers of little merit, needs plenty of space; given the unfortunate nickname *Rubus coke-can-ianus* through its use in municipal plantings, where no one is willing to negotiate the prickly stems to retrieve litter; **Goldenvale** ['Wyego'] yellow leaves, less invasive. *R. spectabilis* (salmonberry) *H5* (1.8m x indefinite) a rampant American native that has gone wild in parts of Orkney, Lewis and elsewhere; The Scottish Executive is likely to declare it illegal to plant it (see page 159); much better and not invasive is the form **'Olympic Double'** (2m) large double magenta-rose flowers in April, a thicket-forming deciduous shrub with slightly prickly stems. *R. thibetanus H4* (2m) a suckering deciduous species with silvery grey ferny leaves and young winter stems with a blue-white bloom, flowers small, purple, in late spring. *R. tricolor H4* (60cm x 2–3m) an evergreen ground-cover with trailing stems and dark-green bristly leaves, white flowers in July, followed by edible (quite nice) red berries; this is one of the few good ground-covers for dry shade and will even grow under beech trees.

Ruscus aculeatus (butcher's broom)
H4 (75cm x 1m) A native low evergreen shrub, mainly grown for its bright red berries, which are plentiful provided there is a male form near by. It's sometimes grown as a low prickly leaved hedge (one of which I recall being thrown into at school – KC) and is useful for its tolerance of dry shade.

Ruta graveolens (rue)
H4–5 🌢🌢 An evergreen shrub with aromatic blue-green leaves and small yellow flowers in summer, usually sold as the form **'Jackman's Blue'** (60cm x 60cm), with particulary glaucous foliage. All parts of the plant are toxic if eaten and the leaves are a skin irritant.

Ruscus aculeatus

Ruta graveolens (RC-M)

Salix (willow – the shrubby varieties)
H5 Willows seem to take whatever conditions they land in – boggy or heavy soil, exposure to wind, salt spray or extreme cold – and many can be rooted by cutting a bit off and sticking it in the ground. They range from tiny alpines suitable for troughs to large vigorous bushes and trees (see page 139 for the tree species). All have catkins, which are important food for bees in early spring. Despite their versatility, shrubby willows are under-used in gardens; more than 15 willows are native to Scotland, so perhaps they are not considered refined enough, but willows can make very fine garden plants and they will grow where almost nothing else will. They tend to look haggard in late summer, with fungal diseases on the leaves, but these seldom cause any lasting harm. Willows are often the easiest plants to establish for shelterbelt and buttress planting, making gardening possible and enjoyable in some of the most extreme climates such as Shetland, Orkney, the Western Isles and the northern coastline. All those listed below are very tough (*H5*).

S. x boydii (50cm x 30cm) 🏅 a gnarled upright, slow-growing shrub with grey-green leaves, good for the rock garden and

Salix x boydii

Salix integra 'Hakuro-nishiki'

Salix lanata

trough, where it resembles a miniature tree. **S. gracilistyla 'Melanostachys'** (2–3m x 2–3m) a vigorous grower with distinctive black catkins. **S. hastata 'Wehrhahnii'** (1m x 1.5m) 🌿 a deciduous species with rounded leaves that colour in autumn, silvery male catkins in April. **S. helvetica** (1m x 1m) a slow-growing shrub with grey-green leaves and silky silver-grey catkins that turn yellow in March–April. **S. hookeriana** (3–5m x 2–3m) very fine silvery-white catkins in winter, vigorous large shrub or small tree, outstanding resistance to salt spray. **S. integra 'Hakuro-nishiki'** (1.5m x 1.5m) leaves streaked white, young leaves white, pink tinged (not to everyone's taste), often grafted on stems ranging in height from 30cm to 2m. **S. lapponum** (1.5m x 1.5m) ✉ grey, downy leaves, silky grey catkins. **S. lanata** (50cm–1m) ✉ 🌿 felted leaves, striking yellowish green in March–April, extremely hardy. **S. magnifica H4–5** (2–3m x 2m) the most handsome-leaved willow, leaves to 20cm long, but needs a little shelter. **S. purpurea 'Nana'** (syn. 'Gracilis') (2m x 2m) ✉ narrow grey-purple leaves, small catkins. **S. repens 'Argentea'** (1m x 2m) grey-green narrow furry leaves, silvery catkins in April–May. **S. reticulata** (10cm x 30cm) ✉ 🌿 prostrate spreading willow which roots as it spreads, yellow catkins with pink tips.

Sambucus (elder)

H5 🌿 The common elder grows all over the UK, and forms a large open shrub or small tree with frothy cream-coloured flower heads in early summer, followed by bunches of purple-black autumn berries. The garden versions have coloured leaves and are tough ornamentals, great as specimens and for shelterbelt and buttress planting in exposed situations. There are good examples on the very exposed Sutherland coastline gardens around Tongue. They will grow in almost any soil, and can be cut back to keep them to the size you want. The only drawback is the rather unpleasant smell of the leaves. The flowers and berries of *S. nigra* can be made into wines and cordials, but take care because the uncooked fruit can cause severe indigestion, and some people have an allergy to the foliage. Elders seem to be rabbit proof. All mentioned are fully hardy (**H5**) and reach 2–3m x 2–3m, unless stated otherwise.

S. nigra (6m) ✉ the common elder, which grows wild over much of Scotland, white flowers in June–July, followed by black fruit in late summer and autumn; selected forms include **'Aurea'** leaves yellow, stalks pink flushed, somewhat subject to sunburn, **'Aureomarginata'** yellow-margined dark green leaves, **Black Beauty** ['Gerda'] (3–4m x 3–4m) pink flowers, deep purple leaves,

Black Lace ['Eva'] cream-pink flowers and blackish-red berries, exotic-looking black-purple, fern-like deeply divided leaves, a bit like those of a Japanese maple, **'Guincho Purple'** dark-green leaves turn black purple, then red in autumn, flowers pink tinged, f. *laciniata* sometimes known as the parsley-leaved elder, free flowering with very dissected green leaves. **S. racemosa 'Plumosa Aurea' H5** 🌿 yellow, scented flowers in June, followed by poisonous scarlet berries, finely cut bright-yellow leaves, sometimes sunburned; **'Sutherland Gold'** is similar but slightly more greenish yellow, less prone to sunburn.

Santolina chamaecyparissus (cotton lavender)

H3–4 (60cm x 90cm) The common name cotton lavender

Sambucus racemosa 'Sutherland Gold' and 'Black Lace'

Santolina chamaecyparissus

sums up the effect of this plant's aromatic narrow filigree grey leaves and the mass of button-like bright-yellow flowers in summer. Santolinas are good front-of-border and edging plants, their fluffy grey foliage acting as a foil for more colourful plants. They form fast-growing mounds, but don't live very long, tending to become scruffy and woody after about 5 years, when they are best replaced. Not very hardy, nor good in wet, cold sites or heavy soil, they are definitely most successful near the coast, where they can be used for hedging, planted 30–40cm apart. Greywalls Hotel in Gullane, East Lothian, has a fine border of it.

There are several named selections **H3–4** (60cm x 90cm unless stated otherwise): **'Lemon Queen'** pale yellow, **'Nana'** (20cm) dwarf, suitable for the rock garden, **'Pretty Carol'** compact with greyish foliage, **'Primrose Gem'** pale primrose-yellow. The species **S. rosmarinifolia** (syn. *S. viridis*) **H3** has bright-green foliage and light-yellow flowers, but is less hardy than *S. chamaecyparissus*.

Sarcococca

H3–5 ❄❄ It is the strong scent of this winter-flowering ground-cover that makes this a popular plant (because it's certainly not got much visual appeal – RC-M). Known as Christmas box, its tiny star-like clusters of tubular white flowers open in mid-winter on a spreading, evergreen shrub with narrow, pointed leaves, with occasional black fruit in summer. They are useful for their tolerance of dry shade.

S. confusa H5 (1m x 1m) dense and shrubby. **S. hookeriana H3–4** (1.5m x 2m) the hardiest form; **var. digyna** very narrow leaves.

Sarcococca confusa   Sarcococca hookeriana

S. humilis H3–4 (60cm x 1m) flowers pink tinged, dwarf and compact. **S. ruscifolia H3** (1m) less hardy than the other species, with broader leaves.

Sasa palmata see Bamboos, page 28

Schizophragma hydrangoides
see *Hydrangea*, page 62

Skimmia
H3–4(5) ❊ This is a very useful medium-sized, evergreen, mound-forming shrub, providing months of interest in winter and associating well with other shrubs and plants, particularly woodlanders such as rhododendrons and hellebores. Skimmias are tough, tidy, compact, virtually maintenance free and good in containers. (That said, they can be a bit over-used in smaller gardens, but that's just my opinion – RC-M.) They grow well in moist but well-drained acidic soil, and better in shade than hot sun, which can turn the leaves yellowish. Both male and female varieties are required for berries, except in the case of the self-fertile *S. reevesiana*. The male forms have colourful large clusters of reddish buds through winter, before opening out into tiny scented white flowers in spring. The females have smaller flowers but produce long-lasting red berries, which ripen in autumn. Because they tolerate cold particularly well, they give great colour and structure through the most dreich autumn and winter weather. The compact smaller varieties look great in window boxes too, giving a long consistent display. Skimmias are particularly useful for towns and cities because they tolerate drought and air pollution well. Heights and spreads roughly similar.

S. x confusa 'Kew Green' H4–5 (1m) male, creamy-white fragrant flowers in spring. **S. japonica H4** mostly sold as selected forms:

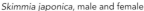

Skimmia japonica, male and female   Skimmia japonica 'Rubella'

'Fragrans' (1–1.5m) ❊ male, fragrant white flowers, **'Kew White'** (70cm) female, fruits creamy white, slow growing, **'Magic Marlot'** (1m) [PBR] male, leaves with cream variegated edges. **'Nymans'** (1–1.5m) female, bushy and vigorous, with freely produced large red berries, **'Rubella'** (1m) ❊ ♛ male, red buds open to white flowers in March–May, a good pollinator, **subsp. reevesiana** (1–1.5m) ❊ female, self-fertile, fragrant white flowers and red berries, **'Veitchii' H4–5** (syn. 'Foremanii') (1–1.5m) ❊ female, fragrant white flowers, large leaves, bunches of red fruit, said to be one of the hardiest.

Solanum (climber)
H2–3 (3–6m) ♛ These potato and tomato relatives (you can see the relationship in their flowers) are fine climbers for sunny walls and frameworks in relatively mild and sheltered gardens. In eastern Scotland they are often grown on the walls of houses for the extra heat/protection. The five-pointed blue or white flowers with yellow beak-like centres open in July–September. They are fast growing, scrambling climbers, which die back to the ground in winter in colder gardens but remain partially evergreen in milder areas. All parts of these plants can cause severe indigestion if eaten.

Solanum crispum

S. crispum H3 (3–6m) fragrant lilac-purple blue, followed by non-edible yellow fruit; **'Glasnevin'** (3–6m) deep purple-blue, selected for its long flowering season. **S. jasminoides** (syn. *S. laxum*) **H2** (3–6m) less hardy, fragrant palest blue-cream flowers with yellow centres, suitable for mildest west-coast gardens only, but a good conservatory plant in cold areas; **S.j. 'Album'** pure white, **S.j. 'Variegatum'** leaves with yellow variegation.

Sophora microphylla Sun King

Sophora

H1–2 An Antipodean large shrub or small tree, with racemes of exotic bright-yellow pea-like flowers, and small divided dark-green leaflets. Compact selections of **S. microphylla** have recently been offered by nurseries. **Sun King** ['Hillsop'] (2–3m) is a bushy dwarf with small leaflets and yellow pea flowers in winter. We're not convinced that Scotland always gets enough summer heat for this member of the pea family to flower well, although Chip Lima rates it for central Scotland. There are some fine (and flowering) small *S. microphylla* trees at Mount Stuart on Bute and a few other mild west-coast gardens. They are best sited in full sun and well-drained soil, and can be trained against a warm sheltered wall.

Sorbaria sorbifolia

Sorbaria

H4–5 These very attractive, large and vigorous deciduous shrubs resemble giant white-flowered astilbes, bearing dense panicles of small white flowers in mid-summer. Sorbarias spread slowly, and tend to sucker, so are best given plenty of room, looking fine in woodland or waterside plantings. They tolerate most reasonably drained soils in sun or semi-shade. They tend to hold on to their dead flowers, which you may want to prune off.

S. sorbifolia **H5** (2m x 3m) thicket-forming, impressive in flower; **'Sem'** (1m x 1.5m) yellow foliage with bronzy pinkish young growth, it can look a bit sickly. *S. tomentosa* var. *angustifolia* (syn. *S. aitchisonii*) **H4** (4m x 3m) white flowers in summer.

Sorbus reducta see page 140

Spartium junceum see *Cytisus*, page 46

Spiraea

Spiraeas are a very attractive and versatile range of deciduous shrubs, forming mounds of thin foliage, and masses of small pink or white flowers in spring or summer. The taller ones make good specimen or back-of-the-border plants. Spiraeas are tough, suitable for even the coldest gardens; in Scotland they do best in well-drained soil in full or part day sun. Prune after flowering to keep tidy, or to reduce in size. There are several suckering species and hybrids which are invasive in areas of high rainfall and should not be planted at all on the west coast. These include *S. douglasii*, *S. salicifolia*, *S.* x *pseudosalicifolia*, *S.* x *billardii* and several others. Those listed below are fully hardy (**H5**), and have similar height and spread measurements, unless stated otherwise.

'Arguta' (syn. 'Bridal Wreath') (1.5–2.5m) slender arching shoots with small leaves and masses of clusters of tiny white flowers in May: a wonderful plant. *S. japonica* (40cm–2m) depending on the variety, flowering in June, July or August; the yellow-leaved forms tend to get mildew (grey spotting) on the leaves in late summer; forms include **'Anthony Waterer'** (1.5m) leaves margined creamy white, flowers dark pink, **'Candlelight'** (60cm) dwarf with yellow young leaves and good autumn colour, pink flowers, **'Firelight'** (60cm) deep-pink flowers in July–August, orange-red young growth turns to bright yellow and pale green, **'Goldflame'** (60cm–1.2m) pink flowers in July–August, orange-red young growth turns yellow and then pale green, some reversion, **'Gold Mound'** (30–50cm) pale-pink flowers in July–August, leaves yellow, sometimes sun scorched, inclined

Spiraea 'Arguta'

to revert, **'Golden Princess'** (40cm x 60cm) rose crimson with orange-red to yellow young leaves turning pale green, **'Little Princess'** (40cm) small crimson flowers, green leaves, **Magic Carpet** ['Walburna'] (70cm–1m) leaves red-orange, fading to greeny yellow, **'Shirobana'** (60cm) a curious mixture of white and pink flowers in July–August, **'White Gold'** (60cm) white flowers from June to August,

Spiraea japonica 'Gold Mound'

Spiraea nipponica 'Snowmound'

yellow leaves gradually turn to pale green, may scorch in full sun. **S. nipponica 'Snowmound'** (1–1.5m) ✻ showy white flowers in June against dark-green leaves. **S. salicifolia** (1.8m) a tough, vigorous suckering shrub, useful plant for extreme and windy climates, but should not be planted in mild wet west-coast areas because of invasiveness, pink flowers in summer, will grow in boggy sites. **S. x vanhouttei** (1.5–2m) clusters of white flowers in June, leaves toothed; **'Pink Ice'** (1m) white in April–May, young growth pink turning to white, then mottled white and green.

Stewartia pseudocamellia
see *Halesia*, page 54

Styrax japonicus see *Halesia*, page 54

Symphoricarpos (snowberry)
H5 (2–3m x 2–3m) ♟ The snowberry is a rather coarse deciduous suckering shrub, more useful for its tolerance of poor dry soils, shade and wind than for its ornamental value. It has insignificant flowers, but relatively showy clusters of white or pale pink berries. These last well into winter as they don't seem to interest birds. The berries cause indigestion if eaten and the sap can cause skin irritation – hence the common name 'itchy berry': schoolchildren have a nasty habit of squashing them down each other's backs. It was planted as game cover in lots of Scottish estates, and has naturalized and become invasive in places. It is no longer widely commercially available,

Symphoricarpos albus

though it has its merits: you can even grow it under sycamore and it does well in Orkney. All are fully hardy (*H5*), and benefit from a good pruning from time to time, thinning out old shoots and even cutting the whole bush back hard.

S. albus (1–1.8m) an invasive species that is naturalized in parts of Scotland, originally planted for game cover; not recommended for garden use. **S. x chenaultii 'Hancock'** (50–70cm x 1–2m) a low-growing form with small purplish-pink berries. **S. x doorenbosii 'Mother of Pearl'** (1–1.5m x 1.5–2m) berries white, flushed rose pink. **S. x doorenbosii 'White Hedge'** (1.5m x 1.5–2m) long-lasting white berries in clusters. **S. orbiculatus 'Foliis Variegatus'** (2m x 2m) leaves edged with yellow, popular with flower arrangers, berries small, needs a hot sunny site.

Syringa (lilac)
With their sweet early-summer fragrance, and unmistakable large clusters of flowers, lilacs have long been some of the most popular garden shrubs. All are deciduous and range from small shrubs to trees. Most are tough and easy to grow, and the vigorous hybrids are sometimes used for hedging and screening. They do best in full or part day sun in reasonably fertile, well-drained soil. They are very hardy, but soft new growth can be frost damaged, which can cause dieback and grey mould; it is

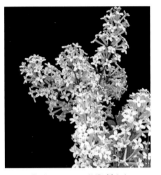
Syringa meyerii 'Palibin'

best to cut back to clean green wood. All can be deadheaded after flowering, when weak, congested or diseased shoots should also be removed, and they will usually benefit from a feed. All are fully hardy (*H5*), flowering in May–June.

Syringa vulgaris cultivars

S. emodii *H4–5* (3–5m x 3m) pale-lilac flowers with an unpleasant smell. **S. x josiflexa 'Bellicent'** *H5* (3m x 2m) ✾ loose panicles of fragrant, bright rose-pink flowers. **S. meyerii 'Palabin'** (1–2m x 1–2m) ✻ smaller shrub, lilac-pink flowers, sometimes grafted on a half-standard or standard stem. **S. x persica** (2m x 1.5m) ✾ one of the finest of all lilacs, forming an arching, graceful shrub with narrow pointed leaves and small panicles of scented, soft lilac flowers. **S. pubescens** subsp. *microphylla* **'Superba'** (1–2m x 1–2m) ✾ very fragrant, pink flowers, sometimes again later in summer, needs full sun in well-drained soil; subsp. *Patula* **'Miss Kim'** (2m x 1.5m) ✾ scented purplish-lilac flowers, fading to off white, dark-green leaves with wavy edges. **'Red Pixie'** (1.5m x 1.5m) ruby red, fading to light pink. **S. vulgaris** (4–7m x 3–5m) ✾ the common lilac, makes a fine specimen given enough room, but is not well suited to the small garden – it grows upwards and outwards, forming a huge suckering, swamping bush. **S. vulgaris** and its forms have large heart-shaped leaves up to 10cm long. There are lots of single- and double-flowered selections, most forms of which are grafted. Suckers can be a problem, particularly after a rejuvenative pruning; they should be wrenched rather than cut off. Forms include **'Aurea'** pale pinkish-yellow young growth, pink flowers, **'Belle de Nancy'** double mauve-pink, **'Charles Joly'** double dark purple, **'Congo'** single deep reddish-purple, **'Esther Staley'** red buds open single lilac pink, **'Firmament'** single light blue, **'Katherine Havemeyer'** double lavender blue, **'Maud Notcutt'** single pure white, **'Madame Lemoine'** ✾ double white, **'Mont**

Tamarix

Blanc' single white, **'Primrose'** pale creamy yellow in small panicles, less vigorous than the others, **'Red Prince'** purple-red, **'Sensation'** purple edged with creamy white, **'Souvenir de Louis Spaeth'** claret-red, reliable performer, **'Vestale'** single pure white.

Tamarix

H2–3 With feathery plumes of pink flowers and tiny leaves on slender branches, tamarix are popular for seaside planting in the East Neuk of Fife, and coastal gardens in Dumfries and Galloway, for example, as they are very wind and salt-spray resistant, suitable for hedging and windbreaks. They look a bit like giant heathers, like well-drained soil in full sun and are best pruned regularly. They grow well in Scotland, but don't always flower well, probably due to lack of summer heat and we're not convinced that they are really worth growing: they always look a bit sad, bare and thin in pots in garden centres.

T. ramosissima (2–4m x 2–4m) rose pink in August, prune in early spring; *T.r.* **'Pink Cascade'** pink; *T.r.* **'Rubra'** deeper pink. *T. tetrandra* light pink in early June; flowers on the previous year's wood, so should be pruned after flowering if required.

Teucrium fruticans see *Lavandula*, page 68

Trachelospermum, Campsis and other climbers

You'll find climbers such as *Trachelospermum*, *Campsis*, *Akebia* and *Holboellia* offered for sale in garden centres round Scotland. They may grow well and cover walls in relatively mild and sheltered gardens, but lack of summer heat means that they seldom flower as well as they do further south, so we don't really think that they merit garden space for most of us.

Campsis x tagliabuana

Trachelospermum H2 (3–5m) ❀ White periwinkle-like, sweetly scented flowers; can be successful in mild gardens on a warm wall and may flower well after hot summers. *T. asiaticum H2* (3–5m) creamy white-yellow in late summer, evergreen. *T. jasminoides H2* (3–5m) pure-white flowers in July–August; *T.j.* **'Variegatum'** leaves edged white; **'Wilsonii'** leaves purplish in winter.

Campsis (trumpet vine) *H2–3* This spectacular deciduous climber, with trumpet-shaped orange or red flowers in late summer to autumn, clings to walls and fences with aerial roots. While it is hardy on the west coast and in east-coast seaside gardens, it needs hotter summers than Scotland's to flower well. *C. radicans* (2–5m+) orange-red; f. **'Flava'** yellow, **'Indian Summer'** new, orange, striped red. *C. x tagliabuana* 'Madame Galen' (3–8m) orange-yellow tubes and red lobes.

Akebia quinata H2–3 (3–10m) Purple flowers, palmate leaves, fruit in autumn with male and female plants.

Holboellia latifolia H2–3 (3–7m) Leaves with three to seven leaflets, white or purplish flowers, in spring/early summer. This is flowering well for some, now that summers are warmer, though you may have to wait a few years. Purple fruit can be produced if both male and female plants are present.

Trachycarpus fortunei see Palms, page 78

Ugni molinea see *Myrtus communis*, page 75

Ulex (gorse)

✉ One of Scotland's best-known wild plants: the bright yellow sweetly scented flowers of gorse cover vast areas

Ulex europaeus

of the countryside, and nowhere better than the cliffs alongside the M90 heading north from the Forth Bridge. The very prickly stems make it a good plant for hedgerows and to prevent short-cut taking. Gorse grow best in poor soils in full sun.

The common gorse *U. europaeus H5* seeds freely and will grow to 1–2m in size, with bright yellow flowers in May–June and sometimes again later in the summer. Recent mild winters have meant that it flowers in winter too; sometimes it can be full out in February. You don't often see it for sale, as it grows everywhere anyway. A better garden plant is the double form **'Flore Pleno'** which reaches a height of 75cm–1m and does not seed itself. *U. gallii* **'Mizen'** *H3–4* collected and selected by KC's parents Peter and Patricia Cox on a windswept Irish headland makes a superb spreading shrub, seldom more than 30cm tall, with bright yellow flowers in late summer. Not as tough, it can be damaged by a severe winter in eastern Scotland.

Vaccinium
(including blueberry and cranberry)
H3–5 These heath relatives include a wide range of low and medium-sized, mostly evergreen spreading shrubs with urn-like white flowers and usually edible berries (including blueberries and cranberries). Enjoying similar conditions to rhododendrons (moist acid soil in sun or light shade), vacciniums usually flower in late spring and summer.

V. corymbosum (blueberry) *H5* (1–1.5m x 1–1.5m) small white or pinkish flowers in May are followed by sweet blueberries, which are excellent eaten raw or cooked, but which will be eaten by birds unless netted. Deciduous leaves turn red in autumn. The best-selling form is **'Bluecrop'** which fruits well in Scotland. *V. delavayi H3* (30cm x 45cm) compact with bronze young leaves,

Vaccinium glaucoalbum

dark and shiny with age, pretty pinkish flowers. *V. floribundum H3* (1m x 2m) a dense spreading evergreen with dark-green leaves, pink-tinged white flowers in June and edible red berries. *V. glaucoalbum H3–4* (60cm x 1m) handsome bluish-grey leaves, large black fruit. *V. macrocarpon H5* (30cm x 45cm) (cranberry) small, drooping pink flowers in June followed by red, edible fruits; evergreen with small dark-green leaves. *V. moupinense H4* (60cm x 1m) evergreen, with glossy dark-green leaves, tiny red-brown flowers and edible purple-black berries. *V. vitis-idaea* **'Koralle'** ✉ *H5* (20cm x 50cm) small bell-shaped white flowers, tinged pink in June–August, followed by large, brilliant, red berries (does best with more than one clone); evergreen, suckering, spreading and sometimes invasive.

Viburnum
There are viburnums for almost every garden and for almost every month of the year, some with spectacular flowers and many with ornamental berries too. The flowers are small and white, cream or pink, sometimes scented, produced in clusters and often very showy. They are a versatile tribe – as specimens, providing border structure or for hedging – and don't require much maintenance. Most of the popular evergreen species are hardy but need some protection from cold winds. The deciduous species are mostly tough (*H5*) and can be pruned to keep them the size you want. All like well-drained but moist soil in sun or dappled shade. Reports from Orkney and Shetland indicate that they don't do very well there. Heights and

Viburnum x bodnantense 'Dawn'

Viburnum davidii

Viburnum davidii berries

spreads are similar unless stated otherwise. Sadly fungal diseases seem to be attacking viburnums, particularly the winter flowering deciduous ones, and their popularity is decreasing.

V. x bodnantense **'Dawn'** *H4* (2–3m) ⚘ deciduous, with sweetly scented, long-lasting pink flowers during mild periods from November to February, oval, dark-green, toothed leaves; *V. x burkwoodii H5* (2m) clusters of sweetly scented white flowers in March–May, dark-green shiny leaves – semi-evergreen, can look a bit sickly in winter with drooping dead leaves; selected forms include **'Anne Russell'** a compact form, pink in bud, opening white, **'Mohawk'** dark-red buds, opening white, orange autumn-leaf colour, **'Park Farm Hybrid'** relatively large pink-tinged flowers and a spreading habit, growing wider than high. *V. x carlcephalum H5* (1.5–2m) pink buds open to richly scented clusters of white flowers in May, deciduous with grey-green leaves often colouring in autumn. *V. carlesii H5* (1.2–1.5m) ✻ widely planted garden shrub, pink buds open to very fragrant white flowers in spring, deciduous with rounded grey-green leaves often turning red in the autumn; named forms include **'Aurora'** flower buds reddish, open pale pink, *V. davidii H4* (1–1.5m) ⚘ a popular tough compact evergreen, handsome dark-green leaves, unspectacular white flowers in June; the long-lasting blue fruit on red stalks are only produced on female plants pollinated by a male (unfortunately, most garden centres can't tell you which sex their plants are); **'Eskimo'** *H5* (1.5m) a fine semi-evergreen hybrid with balls of pure white flowers in June. *V. farreri* (syn. *V. fragrans*) *H4–5* (3m) ✻ pink buds open to somewhat frost-resistant fragrant white flowers, November–February, on the bare deciduous branches, toothed, dark-green leaves, bronzy when young; *V.f.* **'Candidissimum'** light-green leaves and white flowers. *V. x juddii H5* (2m) ✻ sweetly scented, pink-tinged

Viburnum plicatum 'Lanarth'

Viburnum tinus

Vinca major 'Variegata'

Vinca minor f. alba,
'Atropurpurea' and 'Illumination'

white flowers in spring, deciduous with grey-green leaves, often turning red in the autumn. **V. opulus** (guelder rose) *H5* (3m) lacecap-like white flower heads in early summer, long-lasting round red autumn fruits, lobed leaves redden in autumn, deciduous. Sap-sucking insects tend to attack young growth which rolls up; forms include **'Aureum'** leaves yellow, inclined to burn, **'Compactum'** a low-growing form to 1–1.5m, **'Roseum'** (syn. 'Sterile') ball-shaped green flowers turn to creamy white in summer, **'Xanthocarpum'** (3m) yellow fruit. **V. plicatum H5** (1.5–3m) probably the best viburnum of all, showy flower heads of white sterile florets in May–June, deciduous with dark-green leaves reddening in autumn; a statuesque tiered shrub, with many selected forms: **'Grandiflorum'** large flower heads, **'Lanarth'** vigorous with branches less tiered than those of 'Mariesii', **'Mariesii'** ⚜ tiered horizontal branches, very decorative, **'Pink Beauty'** sterile florets change to pink as they age, **'Summer Snowflake'** flowers produced into late summer, very similar to **'Watanabe'** (syn. 'Nanum Semperflorens') (1–2m) slow growing with tiered branches and a long flowering period through summer. **V. rhytidophyllum H4–5** (3m) a strong structural evergreen shrub with dark-green, heavily veined leaves, creamy-white flowers in May and June, occasional red-black fruits; Needs protection from cold winds. **V. sargentii H5** (2–3m) the hardiest viburnum, deciduous, with maple-like leaves and white flowers with purple anthers in June; **V.s. 'Onondaga'** purple young leaves and showy flower heads of white sterile florets. **V. tinus H4–5** (1.5–3m) one of the most reliable winter-flowering shrubs, a fine dense, evergreen species with plentiful small white flowers in late autumn to early spring and blue-black berries; pretty tough, but may be damaged in coldest inland gardens, tolerant of some shade, and good in coastal areas; named forms include **'Eve Price'** ⚜ flowers with a carmine pink blush, **'French White'** vigorous, flowers white, **'Gwenllian'** compact, flowers pink flushed white, **'Purpureum'** young leaves tinged reddish-purple, **'Variegatum'** *H3* leaves with yellow variegation on margins, less vigorous and less hardy.

Vinca (periwinkle)

⚘ Some of the best and most versatile of all ground-cover plants, with a long flowering period from late spring to autumn, and tolerant of a wide range of soil and light conditions. Vincas do well under light tree/shrub cover, but beware of the vigour of the larger-growing forms of *V. major*, which are too thuggish for the small garden. The five-petalled flowers look like propellers and vary in colour from purple and blue through pinkish to white, with a few double forms too. There are several forms with variegated leaves. Semi-evergreen, the spreading shoots can root at the tip, forming an ever-expanding carpet, which can be pruned or dug out annually to keep in bounds. All parts of the plants can cause stomach upset if eaten.

V. difformis H3–4 (30cm x 60cm) pale lilac-blue to white flowers in autumn, winter and spring, less vigorous and less hardy than the others, tends to die back to the ground in cold areas; **V.d. 'Jenny Pym'** lilac-pink edged white, **V.d. 'Ruby Baker'** pink-purple. **V. major H5** (50cm x 2–3m) (greater periwinkle) flowers blue, 4cm across, rampant, needing plenty of room; **'Maculata'** blue, leaves with splash of gold variegation, **'Variegata'** ⚜ leaves with creamy-white variegation, **'Wojo's Gem'** blue, leaves with bold creamy-yellow variegation. **V. minor H5** (10–20cm x 1m+) (lesser periwinkle) less rampant, smaller and lower growing than *V. major*, flowers blue-purple, spring and sometimes all summer; f. alba white, **'Alba Variegata'** white, leaves splashed and edged creamy white, **'Argenteovariegata'** bright blue, grey-green leaves, splashed and edged cream, **'Atropurpurea'** plum purple, **'Aureovariegata'** bright blue, leaves variegated yellow, **'Azurea Flore Pleno'** double blue, **'La Grave'** (syn. 'Bowles Variety') azure blue, **'Gertrude Jekyll'** white, **'Illumination'** blue, leaves bright yellow, edged green, very striking, good in a hanging basket, **'Multiplex'** double reddish purple.

Vitis (vine) climber

H3–4 If you want regular grapes to eat in Scotland, you'll need to grow them under cover, so they are not included in this book. This section covers ornamental vines, which climb with tendrils and are grown for their striking large leaves, similar to those of Virginia creeper. There are good examples at Falkland Palace gardens and Cambo Fife and at Craigieburn near Moffat. The flowers are usually insignificant, while the fruits are attractive but inedible. They are ideal for covering arches, growing up poles and covering walls and fences; for best leaf colour, site them in full or part day sun. It is advisable to prune them in winter to avoid sap 'bleeding'. Mildew can make a mess of vines, *V. vinifera* in particular.

V. **'Brant'** *H3–4* (4–7m) palmate leaves, grapes rarely produced outdoors in Scotland, mainly grown for its bronzy-red autumn colour. *V. coignetiae H4* (5–10m+) ❀ a vigorous deciduous climber with dark-green deeply veined leaves which colour a magnificent dark red in autumn. *V. vinifera* **'Purpurea'** *H4* (4–7m) leaves five-lobed, toothed, greyish turning a handsome plum purple in autumn, it also produces unpalatable purple fruit. Can suffer mildew.

Vitis coignetiae

Weigela
and *Kolkwitzia amabilis* and *Dipelta*

H3–5 Weigelas are not the world's most exciting shrubs but they are hardy, easy and trouble free, and flower over several weeks. They should be more widely planted, particularly some of the new varieties with coloured leaves. The foxglove-like flowers range from deep red through pink to white or yellow. They like moist, well-drained fertile soil, and in Scotland they flower best in full sun, although they'll grow happily in light shade. The golden-leaved forms may suffer sunburn in hot summers. Prune to shape by cutting stems after flowering, and also remove old stems completely to the ground. Heights and spreads are similar in most varieties.

W. florida H5 (2.5m) flowers dark pink outside, pale pink to white inside; forms include **'Foliis Purpureis'** (1m) ❀ compact and slow growing, leaves purple-green, **Monet** ['Verweig'] (40cm) purple-pink flowers, white and pink variegation, low, **'Tango'** (60cm) deep pink, foliage bronze, **'Variegata'** (2m) ❀ grey-green leaves with

Weigela florida (two colours)

white margins. *W. middendorffiana H3* (1.5m) flowers sulphur yellow, peeling bark, needs a sheltered site as its early growth is frost vulnerable. *Weigela* **cultivars** *H5* (2–2.5m unless stated otherwise) flowering in May–June and sometimes repeating later: **'Abel Carrière'** dark-purplish red with yellow throat, **'Briant Rubidor'** (2m) leaves yellow-green, flowers ruby red, **'Bristol Ruby'** dark red, the best of the dark-red varieties, **'Eva Rathke'** (to 1.5m) compact, dark crimson, **'Kosteriana Variegata'** (1m) pink with cream-edged leaves, **'Midnight Wine'** (60cm) a new selection with pink flowers and dark purple leaves, **Moulin Rouge** ['Brigela'] red, variegated leaves, **Naomi Campbell** ['Bokrashine'] purple leaves, red flowers, **'Newport Red'** rich crimson, **'Pink Poppet'** (30–60cm) low growing, flowers pink, **'Red Prince'** dark red, long flowering, very tough, **Wine and Roses** ['Alexandra'] deep pink, with purple leaves.

Kolkwitzia amabilis (beauty bush) *H5* (2–3m x 3–4m) ❀ impressive in full flower, and similar to weigela in stature, size and cultivation requirements. It forms an open shrub with soft grey-green leaves and a mass of smaller pale-pink flowers in June. Malleny gardens near Edinburgh has some magnificent examples. The most commonly available form is **'Pink Cloud'**.

Kolkwitzia amabalis 'Pink Cloud'

Dipelta Another related plant with striking fragrant pale-pink to white, yellow-centred spring flowers, and the added bonus of attractive peeling bark and attractive winged fruit/seed capsules. *D. floribunda H4* (4m x 4m) flowers pale-pink marked yellow. *D. yunnanensis H4* (3m x 4m) arching habit with white flowers marked orange.

Wisteria

❀ A free-flowering mature wisteria is one of the most spectacular sights in the garden, but it takes the right grafted variety and a suitably warm, sunny site for success in Scotland. The year 2007 was a great one for wisteria, following the hot summer of the previous year. A wisteria can be grown on the wall of a large house, over a pergola or on a free-standing support, or allowed to scramble through a big tree, where it is less likely to need constant pruning. The racemes of fragrant pea flowers, which tumble down like waterfalls in shades of purple-blue, lavender, pink and white, open in May–June, and are followed by green seed pods. The fresh green deciduous foliage is attractively divided. While it may be tempting to buy a cheap seedling at a garden centre, you will have to wait many years for flowers and you might find these disappointing. Better to buy a grafted named form – the graft is usually quite obvious near the base of the plant. Wisterias are long lived and quite greedy plants, so they need plenty of soil to get their roots into. The further north you are, the more important the quantity of heat and sunshine is – not enough and you'll just get leaves, so make sure you plant in a suntrap.

Pruning wisterias is a somewhat contentious subject: traditionally long shoots were shortened in late summer to encourage flowering, with a further pruning in February–March to show the flowers to full advantage, and especially to keep the shoots away from windows on the walls of a house. The RHS now advises that wisterias

can just be left with no pruning and the difference in flowering seems to be negligible. You'll find firm advocates for both schools of thought.

Gardens prone to late frosts may not succeed in regular flowering, as cold snaps tend to cause flower buds to drop and in extreme cases can wilt the whole raceme. Non-flowering wisterias can be encouraged with

Wisteria sinensis

superphosphate or sulphate of potash. Do not apply high-nitrogen feeds, as these encourage leaf growth rather than flowers. There are fine wisterias in the walled garden at Tyninghame, in East Lothian, and at Manderston, in the Borders.

W. brachybotrys (silky wisteria) *H4* (4–9m) fragrant violet to white flowers in June, silvery foliage; **'Shiro-kapitan'** (syn. *W. venusta alba*) ✿ very fragrant white. *W. floribunda H4* (5–9m) ✿ fragrant flowers in a huge colour range, usually sold as named forms: **'Alba'** (syn. 'Shiro Noda') white, tinted lilac, **'Issai'** purplish blue, **'Lipstick'** white and pink mixture, **'Macrobotrys'** lilac blue, **'Peaches and Cream'** pale rose-pink, **'Rosea'** pale pink with darker throat, **'Snow Showers'** white, **'Violacea Plena'** (syn. 'Black Dragon') double purple. *W. sinensis H4* (5–9m) ✿ lilac blue to white, fragrant; **'Prolific'** lilac blue to pale violet, one of the best and most free-flowering, **'Purple Patches'** dark and light mauve.

Yucca

A fine architectural plant, forming clumps of evergreen sharp-pointed sword-like leaves, which are stiffer and less flexible than those of the cordylines and phormiums. Tall stems of large and impressive white bell-like flowers are produced in summer. Yuccas grow slowly, ideally in well-drained, gritty soil in full sun.

Y. filamentosa H3–4 (75cm–1m x 75cm) ✿ a slow, low-growing,

clump-forming plant, suitable for the smaller garden or container, white flowers in late summer on spikes up to 2m long; **'Bright Edge'** leaf margins yellow, **'Variegata'** leaf margins white. *Y. flaccida H3* (75cm x 75cm) low growing with blue-green leaves fringed with threads, white flowers in spikes up to 1.5m high; **'Golden Sword'** leaves margined yellow, **'Ivory'** flowers ivory, green tinged. *Y. gloriosa H4* (1.5m+ x 1.5m) the hardiest species, leaves to 60cm long, white flowers in summer on spikes up to 2m; **'Variegata'** leaves margined and striped creamy white. *Y. recurvifolia H3* (1.5–2m x 1–2m) forms a small multi-branched tree with lance-shaped blue-green leaves and white flowers on stems up to 2m tall.

Yucca flaccida 'Golden Sword' (RC-M)

Yushania anceps see Bamboos, page 28

Zenobia pulverulenta see *Enkianthus*, page 49

Climbers for north-facing walls
North-facing walls usually get little or no sun, so few climbers will flower well until they reach the top of the wall. It is therefore better to concentrate on growing foliage plants. This list contains the best performers.

Cotoneaster horizontalis	Parthenocissus
Pyracantha	Hydrangea petiolaris
Hedera	Lonicera japonica 'Halliana'

CONIFERS

✉ Scottish native plant ⚘ Scottish Gardenplant Award
☠ irritant or toxic; ☠☠ extremely irritant or toxic if ingested
❄ fragrant; ❄❄ very fragrant
♦ disease resistant; ♦♦ very disease resistant

Conifers sometimes suffer from a bad press these days, probably because of their over-use in suburban gardens and the problems of out-of-control leylandii hedges. But they are some of the toughest, most varied and most useful plant groups. They have had a huge influence on the wild landscape and gardens of Scotland: Scots pine is one of Scotland's most important native trees, while the countryside is dominated by commercial plantings of spruce, larch and other conifers. Scottish plant hunters such as David Douglas and Archibald Menzies introduced many important conifer species to Europe by, and if you drive up the A9 from Perth to Pitlochry through the Atholl estates you will see one of the best demonstrations of good conifer planting anywhere. Many Scottish gardens have significant collections and UK champion trees: Blair Castle and Scone Palace, (Perthshire), Dawyck (near Peebles), Ardkinglas, and Mount Stuart (Argyll and Bute) are just some examples. The tallest tree in the UK is currently the Douglas fir at Reelig Glen, near Inverness which overtook a tree at Ardkinglas which lost its top. Much used for hedging and shelter as well as in borders and containers, conifers can be found to suit any Scottish garden, and most do very well here. The few conifers that don't perform well tend to be tender species found at low altitudes and those such as *Cupressus* (cypress) from climates with hot summers and/or consistent cold winters, which are fooled by the stop–start nature of Scotland's seasons.

For information on hedging, see page 122.

Conifer growth rates and sizes

What everyone wants to know is: how big does it get? The answer is that there is no answer. A conifer grows upward and/or outward at a fairly steady rate, from a few millimetres to 1m or more per year, as long as it is happy and healthy. So a better question to ask is: what is the annual growth rate? You can estimate this by inspecting a conifer in a garden, or by looking at a small specimen at a garden centre. Find the growing tip and work your way down the stems until you arrive at a brown or woody part: the distance from tip to this point is the annual growth rate. So if the conifer grew 30cm this year, it will probably grow 30cm next year and the year after that. A small plant in a pot is simply a miniature version of the mature plant: it will grow into a larger version of what you see in front of you, at a steady rate, faster in milder west-coast gardens than in the drier east. No one has come up with a conifer

that grows to 2m and stops. Most conifers will reach 2m, it is just that some such as leylandii only take 2 years to reach this height while others take 20 years or more. But all will just carry on growing year after year, so you will have to prune them to keep them to a specific height or width. If you want to see what so-called 'dwarf' conifers really grow into after 30–40 years, visit the walled garden at Benmore in Argyll, where many of them are now towering specimens.

For larger-growing trees, two heights/sizes are given here: the size you can expect after 10 years or so, and an ultimate height (U) after 20–30 years.

Abies (fir)

The firs are a large and varied group of usually handsome trees, ranging in height from some of Britain's tallest trees (*A. grandis* and *A. nordmanniana* at 50–60m) to dwarf selections that are slow growing and suitable for the rock garden or trough. The green or bluish-green needles are stiff, aromatic and usually white- or grey-striped on the underside. Firs grow very well in Scotland, as they prefer moist acid soil and cool or cold winters. Many have spectacular coloured cones, but you may have to be patient, as some are not produced till the tree reaches over 20 years of age.

Abies grandis at Ardkinglas, Argyll (RC-M)

A. balsamea (balsam fir) **H5** can reach 15m but is usually grown in its dwarf forms **'Nana'** and **'Hudsonia' H5** (60cm–1m x 75cm–1m) rounded bushes with deep-green foliage. **A. concolor** (white fir) **H5** (4–6m in 10 years, U: 25m+) a large columnar/pyramidal tree usually with blue-grey needles, tolerant of dry soils; **'Compacta'** (1–2m) irregular habit, steely blue, **'Violacea' H5** (2–4m, U: 15m) a conical tree with glaucous blue foliage. **A. grandis** (giant fir) **H4** introduced by Scottish plant hunter David Douglas, this is a fast-growing giant, reaching 30–50m in a favourable site; Britain's tallest is at Ardkinglas in Argyll. **A. koreana** (Korean

Abies balsamea 'Nana'   Abies koreana

fir) **H5** (2–3m in 10–15 years, U: 5–10m) ⚜ an outstanding tough and stately conifer which will grow large in time, useful for its large purple cones from an early age; forms include **'Flava'** (syn. 'Aurea') (1.2–1.5m) dwarf, with yellow young needles, can look sick and starved, but some people like it, **'Silberlocke'** (2–3m, U: 10m) leaves twist to reveal the silver underside, slow growing. *A. nordmanniana* (Caucasian or Nordman fir) **H5** (5–6m, U: 30m) ⚜ familiar as the best-selling Christmas tree, this is a handsome and potentially very tall tree with dark green needles, dusty white below; smaller is **'Golden Spreader'** (60cm x 1m, U: 3–5m) low, striking golden-yellow foliage. *A. pinsapo* (Spanish fir) **H4** (3m, U: 4–8m+) slow growing, drought and clay soil tolerant; **'Glauca'** with fine blue needles is the most common form. *A. procera* (noble fir) **H5** (10–20m, U: 40–70m) one of the tallest conifers, fine in a large garden; more suitable for most is the slow-growing form **'Glauca'** (5–10m) with fine blue foliage; there is also a prostrate form, which grows to less than 1m in height if vigorous upright shoots are pruned out.

Araucaria araucana (monkey puzzle)

H4–5 (2–3m, U: 10–20m+) ⚜ The monkey puzzle is so named as its shedding lower branches and spiky bark would, in theory, prevent a monkey from climbing it. Introduced from its native Chile, it was perhaps over-planted in the early 20th century and became a bit of a joke, but it is now back in vogue again. You may be shocked by the price of a reasonable-sized specimen, as it is slow growing when young. The foliage is dark green and prickly, on a tough and statuesque tree with branches all the way to the ground when young. It needs protection from cold winds, which tend to cause brown patches. It makes a stunning specimen tree, but bear in mind that it will get too large for a small garden.

Araucaria araucana (RC-M)

There is a superb monkey puzzle avenue at Castle Kennedy in Galloway.

Cedrus (cedar)

The kings and queens of conifers, cedars are handsome, stately trees with striking foliage and an architectural form. There are dwarf selections suited for the smaller garden, but the species themselves get very large and have the annoying habit of shedding branches in snow and gales. Cedars do best in open, sunny sites in well-drained soil. Their tiered growth looks spectacular in silhouette, with the sun behind.

Cedrus atlantica and C. libanii   Cedrus deodora 'Golden Horizon'
at Culzean

Cedrus libanii

C. atlantica Glauca Group (blue cedar) **H5** (4–8m x 2–3m in 10–20 years, U: 30m) ⚜ a very fine specimen conifer with silver-blue foliage on wide spreading branches; **C.a. 'Fastigiata'** (3–5m, U: 15–25m) a more narrow, upright habit, **C.a. 'Pendula'** (1–3m) weeping, suitable for training along a wall or over an arch, or for ground cover. **C. deodara** (deodar) **H4** (3–5m, U: 25–30m) ⚜ the least hardy of the three species, young growth can be cut by spring frosts, probably best in gardens not far from the coast, young foliage bluish grey on attractive drooping stem tips; **C.d. 'Aurea'** (3–5m+) golden-yellow young growth, slow growing, **C.d. 'Blue Dwarf'** (50cm–1m) a compact and slightly irregular shape, with grey-blue foliage, **C.d. 'Feelin' Blue'** (35cm–1m) a weeping dwarf, ideal for the rock garden, with bright blue foliage in spring and summer, **C.d. 'Golden Horizon'** (1m x 2m+) bright golden-yellow needles in summer, arching spreading branches, cut out any vigorous upright shoots, **C.d. 'Karl Fuchs'** (3–5m, U: 15–20m) said to be the hardiest selection, narrow, upright habit with silver blue-grey foliage. **C. libani** (cedar of Lebanon) (3–5m, U: 30m) ⚜ many fine old specimens in Scotland, but today not as widely planted as the

Plants for clay soils

Many Scottish gardeners have to contend with clay soils, especially those in flat valleys such as the Carse of Gowrie between Perth and Dundee. Clay soils are heavy, often tending to set and crack when too dry. Regular waterlogging, compaction and lack of air around the roots can kill many plants (see page 14), and the easiest way to deal with clay is to garden on it, rather than in it. Many plants can be far more successfully grown in raised beds, a minimum of 30cm high, containing lighter, free-draining topsoil or compost, held in by wood, rocks, cobbles and other materials. Or use containers.

Trees and shrubs (including climbers)
Aucuba japonica
Aesculus
    hippocastanum
Berberis darwinii, B.
    stenophylla
Chamaecyparis
    lawsoniana cvs
Cornus alba
Cotoneaster
Cryptomeria
Drimys winteri
Hamamelis
Humulus lupulus
    aureus
Metasequoia
    glyptostroboides
Philadelphus
Populus
Pyracantha
Quercus robur
Ribes sanguineum
Roses (but dislike
being waterlogged)
Salix, including S.
    hastata, S. caprea,
    S. matsudana, S.
    chrysocoma
Sambucus racemosa
Syringa vulgaris
Taxodium distichum
Viburnum opulus, V.
    bodnantense
Vitis coignetiae
Weigela florida

Perennials
Ajuga reptans
Aruncus dioicus
Aster novae-angliae,
    A. novi-belgii
Astilbe
Aruncus
Astrantia
Carex elata
Digitalis
Ferns, including
    Osmunda regalis,
    Polystichum
setiferum
Filipendula ulmaria
Gunnera manicata
Helenium
Hemerocallis
Hosta
Houttuynia cordata
    'Chamaeleon'
Inula hookeri
Iris laevigata
Lythrum salicaris
Mimulus
Monarda
Persicaria affine
Primula florindae,
    P. japonica
Rodgersia
Rudbeckia
Solidago
Trollius

Bulbs
Camassia
Chionodoxa
Fritillaria meleagris
Galanthus nivalis

others; dark-green needles on horizontal branches, heavy foliage on branch ends can cause snow damage; *C.l.* **'Sargentii'** (50–75cm x 1–3m) weeping or cascading habit, needles glaucous green, suitable for growing over a wall or bank, or training as a bush.

Chamaecyparis (false cypress)

Chamaecyparis lawsoniana cultivars at Benmore

After leylandii, these are by far the most popular conifers in Britain. The *RHS Plant Finder* lists over 300 varieties with a bewildering array of shapes and foliage colours and from minute rock garden types to vigorous upright growers ideal for hedging. The flowers and cones are small and scarcely noticeable. While hardy, many of them burn in cold or salt-laden east winds, particularly yellow-leaved varieties, and they are vulnerable to damage from wet snow: knock it off if you can. When newly planted, try to provide enough shelter to prevent wind rock or else the roots may never manage to establish into the soil, and growth will be stunted. They like moist but well-drained soil in sun or part shade. Variegated and yellow varieties produce the brightest foliage colours in full sun: in shade it tends to go green.

C. lawsoniana (Lawson cypress) *H5* with a growth rate of 30–60cm per year; ultimately the more vigorous forms can reach 20–30m. Many make striking and tidy specimen plants for the border, with smaller ones being more suited to the rock garden. Many are ideal hedging plants, less vigorous than leylandii so a bit easier to control. Plant hedging plants 75cm–1.5m apart and trim little and often, rather than hard prune, as they won't break well from old wood. Forms include: **'Alumii'** (4–6m, U: 15m) blue-green, narrow conical habit, **'Alumigold'** (3–5m, U: 10–12m) less vigorous, young growth tipped yellow, **'Bleu Nanteis'** (1–2m, U: 5–8m) slow growing, silvery blue, **'Broomhill Gold'** (3m, U: 10–15m) deep yellow fading to yellow-green, cone-shaped habit, **'Chilworth Silver'** (1–2m, U: 5–8m) silvery blue, slow growing,

Chamaecyparis lawsoniana 'Golden Wonder'

Chamaecyparis lawsoniana 'Pottenii'

Chamaecyparis lawsoniana 'Stardust'

Chamaecyparis pisifera 'Filifera'

'Columnaris' (2–3m, U: 10–15m) ♣ narrow, columnar habit, bluish-grey foliage, a good choice for the Italian look, 'Columnaris Glauca' deeper grey-blue, 'Ellwoodii' (2m, U: 7m+) ♣ blue-grey young leaves and intense winter colour, dense conical habit, very widely planted, 'Ellwood's Gold' (1–1.5m, U: 3–4m) ♣ very popular, a sport of 'Elwoodii' with yellow young growth, used for hedging, can be burned by wind and salt, Ellwood's Pillar ['Flolar'] (1m, U: 3–4m) blue-grey, slow growing with a tight columnar habit, suitable for a container or small garden, 'Ellwood's Golden Pillar' as above with bright-gold summer foliage, 'Erecta Viridis' (3m, U: 10–15m) dense and fairly tidy, green, 'Fletcheri' (2–3m, U: 7–10m) ♣ greyish blue-green foliage, a good choice for a medium-vigour hedge, 'Gimbornii' (50cm–1m) slow growing and rounded, bluish-green needles, good for the rock garden, 'Golden Pot' (1–2m) slow growing, soft bright yellow, columnar habit, 'Golden Wonder' (3–4m, U: 10–15m) a fine tough bright yellow, broadly conical, 'Grayswood Feather' (2–4m) a narrow column of dark-green feathery foliage, 'Green Globe' (15–30cm) dwarf and slow growing, very dense, rounded habit, remove any long shoots, 'Green Hedger' (3m, U: 10–15m) rich green, dense conical habit, a good hedging choice, 'Intertexta' (3m, U: 10m) a striking upright specimen, irregular drooping branches with a cedar-like habit, 'Ivonne' (3m, U: 10–20m) bright-yellow foliage, 'Kilmacurragh' (3m, U: 10–15m) dark green, very narrow columnar, resembling the narrow Italian cypress, 'Little Spire' (2–3m, U: 5–6m) narrow column, dark-

green irregular foliage, 'Minima Aurea' (syn. 'Aurea Densa') (30cm x 30cm, U: 1–2m) good for a rock garden, slow growing, bright yellow all year round, round topped and rigid in habit, 'Minima Glauca' (50cm, U: 2m) bun-shaped dwarf, with blue-green foliage, ideal for a container, 'Nana Albospica' (75cm–1.25m) a compact bun of bright cream, unique, 'Pelt's Blue' (2–3m: U: 10m) narrowly conical habit with bluish foliage, 'Pembury Blue' H4 (3m x 1.5m, U: 10–15m x 3m) very fine blue foliage, a little tender, conical habit, 'Pottenii' (2.5–3m, U: 15–20m) soft feathery green foliage, a good hedger, but may break or splay in snow, 'Pygmaea Argentea' (30cm–1m) a very slow grower, dark green with creamy white tips, 'Silver Threads' (1.5–2m, U: 5–10m+) foliage streaked silver and cream, 'Stardust' (2m, 7–10m) a fine slow-growing choice with golden foliage and narrowly conical habit, 'Stewartii' (3m, U: 10–15m) more vigorous than 'Stardust', one of the best golden forms, good for hedging, of conical habit, 'Summer Snow' (1.5m, U: 7–10m) tips of new growth white, gradually turning green, fairly slow growing, 'White Spot' (2.5m, U: 7–10m+) foliage grey-green, young growth flecked with white, 'Wisselii' (3m, U: 10–15m+) a fast-growing slender grower with blue-green foliage and a mass of tiny male flowers (strobili) in spring, 'Yellow Transparent' (1–2m, U: 3m+) pale yellow foliage, bronze-yellow in winter, 'Yvonne' (2m, U: 4–6m) flattened sprays of bright yellow summer foliage, conical habit.

C. nootkatensis 'Pendula' H5 (2–3m, U: 10m+) ♣ a very attractive weeping conifer with deep-green foliage which seems to hang off the branches. It takes a good number of years before the weeping effect shows up well. It is tolerant of damp soils and looks particularly fine beside water. It creates a restful melancholy mood and is one of my favourite trees (RC-M), with fine specimens at Dawyck, near Peebles.

C. obtusa H5 (5m x 2m, U: 10–20m) This very tough Japanese species with aromatic foliage is usually grown in its numerous dwarf and slow-growing selections. It is relatively drought tolerant but may burn foliage in cold east winds. Forms include 'Crippsii' (3–5m, U: 10–15m) young foliage bright yellow, very handsome; may need to be staked or trained when young to develop a leader: trim straggly side branches, 'Fernspray Gold' (1.25m x 1.5m, U: 2m) very attractive sprays of golden yellow ferny foliage, 'Nana' (10–30cm x 15–60cm) ♣ very slow growing, dark green, flattened sprays, forming an irregular rounded globe, often wrongly named, 'Nana Gracilis' (60cm x 45cm) forming an irregular pyramid, dark-green foliage in scallop-shaped sprays, one of the best dwarf conifers, 'Nana Lutea' as above but with bright-yellow foliage all year round, 'Nana Aurea' similar but faster growing, 'Pygmea' (50cm x 80cm: U: 2m) not really a pygmy as it can get quite large, green with bronzy winter foliage, 'Templehof' (1m, U: 3m) dense conical habit, light-green fan-shaped foliage, bronzy in winter, 'Tetragona Aurea' (2–3m, U: 12–18m) moss-like golden foliage, on an irregular, angular plant which forms a large tree in time, best in full sun.

C. pisifera H5 The species itself, which can reach 20m+, is seldom offered. Instead, there is a range of fine dwarf forms ideal for the smaller garden, which like moist, well-drained soils and resent waterlogging: **'Boulevard'** (1–2m x 50cm–1m, U: 5–8m) soft silvery-blue foliage, squat, pyramidal habit, very popular, best trimmed occasionally to keep a tight shape, **'Filifera Aurea'** (1m x 1m, U: 3–7m+) the thread-leaf cypress is one of my favourites (KC) with long trailing golden-yellow shoots giving a striking mop-like or shaggy-dog effect, occasional sunburn, **'Filifera Nana'** (50–1m) dwarf green-leaved version of the above with thread-like pendulous foliage, **'Nana'** (15–30cm) light green with some yellow in summer, **'Nana Aureovariegata'** (15–30cm x 30cm) very compact and slow growing, dark green with yellow flecks, **'Plumosa Aurea'** (1m, U: 2.5–4m) soft feathery yellow summer foliage, **'Squarrosa Sulphurea'** (1m) soft bright-yellow young foliage, pyramidal habit with longer shoots protruding, **'Sungold'** (50cm x 50cm) yellow thread-like foliage in summer, greener in winter, slow growing, stands full sun.

C. thyoides prefers boggy and soggy soil, though strangely not heavy clay soil. All the commonly grown forms are dwarf selections: **'Andelyensis'** *H5* (1m, U: 3–5m) columnar habit with bluish-green foliage, bronze in winter, **'Ericoides'** *H4* (70cm, U: 1.5–1.8m) feathery grey-green foliage turns deep purple in winter, perhaps not for coldest inland gardens as cold and wind can burn the foliage badly and it is subject to snow-damage, **'Rubicon'** (1–1.5m) compact, winter foliage plum purple.

Cryptomeria japonica (Japanese cedar)

H4–5 In common with many conifers, the full-sized wild forms of this species, which reach 40m, are seldom grown; instead, the dwarf and slow-growing selections are far more popular. It is happy in most moist, reasonably well-drained soils, sheltered from coldest east winds. The distinctive, cord-like foliage turns bronze in winter and the larger tree-forming selections develop a trunk with a red peeling bark. Like yew, this conifer responds well to hard pruning and will break from the trunk. All are *H5* unless stated otherwise.

'Bandai-sugi' (2m) rounded and dense with congested blue-green foliage, bronze in winter, **'Elegans'** *H4* (2–3m, U: 15m) soft feathery juvenile foliage deep purple-bronze in winter, forming a tree unless pruned to keep bushy, not as hardy as the dwarf forms, **'Elegans Compacta'** (2m) dwarf and compact with bronze winter foliage, **'Elegans Aurea'** (2m, U: 10m) foliage yellow-green, **'Globosa Nana'** (80cm, U: 3m) dwarf, forming an irregular dome, **'Golden Promise'** (50cm–1m) green with golden tips, bronze-purple in winter, **'Sekkan-Sugi'** (syn. 'Sekkan') *H4* (2m, U: 10m+) golden yellow, needs shelter to avoid burned foliage, **'Spiralis'** (1m, U: 5m) an oddity with light-green needles spiralling around the branches, best trimmed to obtain a bushy habit, **'Vilmoriniana'** (40–80cm) very slow growing and of globular habit with green foliage in summer turning reddish purple in winter.

Cupressus (cypress)

H3–4 Scotland's climate is far from ideal for most cypress, which prefer hot and dry, Mediterranean-like climates.

C. arizonica 'Blue Ice' *H4* (3–5m, U: 6–10m) striking silver-blue foliage on a narrow columnar plant with ascending branches, we found this growing well in Aberdeenshire, and inland, so it must be fairly tough. *C. macrocarpa* 'Goldcrest' *H2–3* (3–5m x 1–2m, U: 10m) a narrow column of dense upright habit with rich yellow feathery juvenile foliage, often grown as a patio pot plant, bedding or houseplant, not reliably hardy away from the coast. *C. sempervirens* the tall columnar Italian cypress, tends not to grow well in Scotland: the only place we saw it growing well was at Balcarres in south Fife. It is better to use narrow forms of *Chamaecyparis* or *Juniper* for a similar effect.

x Cupressocyparis leylandii (leylandii)

H5 (8–10m, U: 30–40m) Needing no introduction, this ubiquitous man-made hybrid is both the most popular and the most reviled conifer in Britain. It is estimated that over 60 million have been sold in the UK, so that's one for each of us. There is actually nothing wrong with it in the right place, as it makes a superb tall columnar specimen tree and a vigorous hedge or screen. The problems arise when it is used to make a hedge in a small or town garden. As it

Cryptomeria japonica 'Bandai-Sugi'

Cryptomeria japonica 'Globosa Nana'

Cupressus arizonica 'Blue Ice'

x Cupressocyparis leylandii (RC-M)

can grow 1m per year, it is simply too much work for most people to keep in bounds, so it inevitably gets too big, casting a huge shadow, blocking neighbours' light and taking all the moisture from the surrounding soil. It will not break well from old wood, so if you hack the sides, leaving bare patches, it seldom grows back, which accounts for the butchered look of many hedges. Once you let the hedge get too tall, you'll need a crane and a tree surgeon to cut it. If you want a more manageable hedge, there are many other conifers to choose from (see page 123). Leylandii certainly has its uses: it is very versatile and tolerant of most soils and coastal conditions, though in very windy sites it can blow over. Apparently it harbours lots of ladybirds in winter. For a screen or hedge, plant 75cm–1.25m apart.

'Castlewellan' *H4* (6–8m, U: 20–25m) less vigorous with greeny-yellow foliage; badly burned over much of Scotland in the 2010-11 winters so less hardy than the green form.

Ginkgo biloba

Ginkgo biloba
(maidenhair tree)
H5 (4–8m, U: 20–30m) ⚕
This ancient Chinese deciduous tree with no close relatives is a relic of the age of dinosaurs. Forming an upright, ungainly columnar shape, it has distinctive, two-lobed fan-shaped leaves, which colour up yellow in autumn before dropping off. Flowering is rare and fruiting even rarer in Scotland, which is probably just as well, as the fruit smell putrid. It is tough and quite easy to please in well-drained soils with some wind shelter. Don't prune it, as it does not respond well. All sorts of claims are made for extracts from the leaves, including increasing blood circulation and treatment for dementia. There are variegated and weeping forms available from specialist nurseries.

Juniperus (juniper)
and *Microbiota decussata*
The toughest and most versatile of all conifers, there are junipers suitable for every climate from the Hebrides to the mountain peaks of the Highlands. Most forms sold in garden centres are the spreading ground-cover types, but there are lots of taller, tree-forming varieties too. Some have prickly foliage while in others it is soft, and most will produce the well-known juniper blue or purple-black 'berries' used in cooking and for making gin. Most junipers require well-drained soil in full sun. The Latin names *J. chinensis*, *J. x media* and *J. x pfitzeriana* are used

somewhat interchangeably, so just ask for the cultivars by name ('Old Gold', Blue Star', etc.). Junipers are good for dry banks and thrive on neglect once established; they can also be pruned to keep in bounds. Rabbits and deer rarely eat them.

J. chinensis H5 mainly grown in selected forms: **'Blaauw'** (1.2m x 1m, U: 3m x 2m) deep blue-green, **'Blue Alps'** (1.5m x 1.2m, U: 6m x 4m) vigorous bushy grower with prickly blue-green foliage, nodding tips, **'Expansa Variegata'** (1m x 3m) scattered creamy-white flecks in the green foliage, **'Kaizuka'** (1.5m x 1.5m, U: 5m x 3m+) an irregular, upright and spreading grower, which can be pruned to shape, with bright-green foliage, **'Plumosa Aurea'** (1m) ascending yellow branches, good winter colour, **'Pyramidalis'** (1.5m x 45cm, U: 5–8m) this is a misnomer as it actually forms a tight blue-green column. *J. communis* (common juniper) *H5* ♦ this very prickly subject grows wild in Scotland and over a vast swathe of the northern hemisphere, and numerous selected forms of every shape and colour have been made, including **'Compressa'** (30cm x 10cm, U: 1m) ⚕ upright habit, green prickly foliage, very slow growing and neat, suitable for rockery or container, protect from cold winds and salt spray, **'Depressa Aurea'** (60cm) spreading with semi-erect branches, yellow young growth, bronze in winter, **'Green Carpet'** (10–30cm x 1–3m+) ⚕ a very fine tight green prostrate ground-cover from Norway, **'Hibernica'** (Irish juniper) (2m x 30cm, U: 6m+) ⚕ forming a tight narrow column with silver-blue foliage, good in formal gardens, **'Repanda'** (30cm x 2–5m+) ⚕ dark green, bronzy in winter, roots as it spreads, a good ground-cover. *J. conferta* (syn. *J. rigida* subsp. *conferta*) (shore juniper) *H5* (30cm x 1.5–5m+) a spreader with prickly green foliage, needing good drainage, excellent for seaside; *J.c.* **'Blue Pacific'** greenish-blue. *J. horizontalis* (creeping juniper) *H5* a fine ground-cover with soft foliage in many colours, best

Juniperus squamata 'Blue Carpet'

Juniperus 'Old Gold'

pruned when young to increase density; forms include **'Andorra Compact'** (40cm x 1–3m+) feathery green, bronze in winter, **'Bar Harbor'** (30cm x 3–8m) bluish-green, purplish in winter, **'Blue Chip'** (50cm x 3m+) bright blue, **'Golden Carpet'** (10cm x 1–5m) slow growing, yellow-green, **'Prince of Wales'** (15cm x 3–5m) green, tinged blue, purplish in winter, **'Wiltonii'** (15cm x 2–5m) soft bright blue, purplish in winter, very fine. *J. x pfitzeriana/J. x media H5*

Juniperus x pfitzeriana 'Carbery Gold'

Juniperus recurva var. *coxii*

Juniperus virginiana 'Grey Owl'

Juniperus squamata 'Blue Star'

Juniperus 'Sulphur Spray'

well to pruning, **'Blue Star'** (40–60cm x 40cm–1.5m) 🏆 an excellent choice for the smaller garden with bright blue-green leaves, also grown grafted on a stem, **'Holger'** (30–60cm x 3–5m) yellow young growth, whitewashed yellow-green in summer, green in winter, unusual and striking. ***J. virginiana*** 'Grey Owl' (50cm x 3m, U: 2m x 6m+) 🏆 a fine vigorous plant with attractive blue-grey foliage and grey berries.

***Microbiota decussata* H5** (30cm x 1.2m) This Siberian juniper relative is extremely tough with flattened sprays of foliage, which turns bronzy in winter. In very cold weather the leaves turn brown and it can look dead. Prefers well-drained soil. Suitable for the severest parts of Scotland.

Larix (larch)

H5 Larix are some of the few deciduous conifers. The new spring foliage is a beautiful and intense pale green, gradually deepening to dark green, and finally turning a lovely clear yellow in autumn, before the needles drop. Not forming too dense a canopy, larix are a fine choice for providing dappled shade in a large garden. Sadly Japanese larch has been badly affected by *Phytophthora ramorum* in Scotland and large forestry plantations have needed to be felled.

L. decidua (European larch) (10–15m in 20 years, U: 20–30m) 🏆 widely planted all over Scotland as a forestry tree, only used in large woodland gardens. ***L. kaempferi*** (Japanese larch) (2–3m, U: 10–15m) grey-green needles, most commonly grown in its dwarf forms such as 'Blue Dwarf' (75cm) and Diane (1.5m). **'Pendula'** growth rate 50cm per year, would be prostrate were it not usually grafted on a 1–2m stem, giving rise to a very attractive weeping tree.

semi-prostrate, taller than *J. horizontalis,* very tough, many colour forms, some more vigorous than others: **'Carbery Gold'** (1–1.5m x 1–3m) bright-yellow young growth, yellow in winter, bowl-shaped habit, **'Gold Coast'** (75cm–1.5m x 1.5–3m+) semi-prostrate with bright-yellow young foliage, vigorous, **'Gold Star'** (70cm x 1.2m) bright-yellow young growth, yellow in winter, **'Mint Julep'** (1–3m x 1.3–3m+) a fairly upright spreading habit with fine green foliage, **'Old Gold'** (70cm x 1.2m) 🏆 the most compact and slow growing of the yellows, holding colour all year, **'Pfitzeriana'** (syn. 'Wilhem Pfitzer') (1m x 2m, U: 3m x 5m) 🏆 rangy, vigorous grower, green foliage with drooping tips, **'Pfitzeriana Aurea'** (1.2m x 1.8m) irregular graceful habit, foliage yellow-green in summer, fading slightly in winter, **'Sulphur Spray'** (1–1.5m x 1–3m+) foliage suffused creamy yellow, unusual and striking. ***J. procumbens*** 'Nana' *H5* (15–30cm x 1.5–5m+) a fine ground-hugging plant good for containers and for growing over walls, with bright-green foliage. ***J. recurva*** var. **coxii** *H4* (2m, U: 10–15m) a beautiful weeping juniper making a fine specimen tree with grey-green needles, named after Ken Cox's grandfather, Euan. ***J. sabina*** 'Tamariscifolia' *H4* (50cm x 1m, U: 1m x 3m) a flat-topped spreader with aromatic dark-green foliage, sometimes susceptible to dieback. ***J. scopulorum*** **'Skyrocket'** *H5* (2–3m, U: 5–10m) a distinctive pencil-thin columnar grower with blue-green foliage, giving the Italian cypress look; **J.s.** **'Blue Arrow'** slower growing and tighter in form and less intensely blue. ***J. squamata* H5** only cultivars are widely grown: **'Blue Carpet'** (40–60cm x 1.5–5m+) 🏆 a fine tough mounding spreader with silver-blue young growth and purple-blue winter colour, responds

Larix decidua

Larix decidua (RC-M)

Metasequoia glyptostroboides

Metasequoia glyptostroboides (dawn redwood)

H3–4 (5–7m, U: 20–40m) ♥ Despite the somewhat unpronounceable name, this is a handsome, tough deciduous conifer with feathery light-green foliage which turns golden bronze in autumn, with a flaking, cinnamon-brown bark. It makes an attractive cone-shaped specimen tree, preferring moist but not waterlogged soil; the foliage can be damaged by late frosts. **'Gold Rush'** less vigorous with bright-yellow summer foliage, which can suffer sunburn.

Microbiota decussata see *Juniperus*, page 116

Picea (spruce)

H5 The most familiar species of this large genus is Norway spruce (*P. abies*), much used as a Christmas tree, and Sitka spruce (*P. sitchensis*), planted in huge numbers all over Scotland by the Forestry Commission. There are also many smaller-growing forms with fine foliage, suitable for small and medium-sized gardens. Spruce really like moist cool climates, so some of Britain's largest specimens are found in Scottish gardens. Spruce aphid has caused damage in recent years, defoliating plants or sections of plants, usually in winter, even in isolated areas such as Shetland. It may be necessary to do preventative spraying. All are dully hardy (**H5**), unless stated otherwise.

Picea abies 'Nidiformis'

Picea abies (Norway spruce) (5–10m, U: 30–50m) a tall conical tree, long cones, usually grown in gardens in one of the selected forms: **'Inversa'** vigorous, usually top-grafted or trained up a stake as a weeping tree, **'Little Gem'** (15–20cm) dark green, globe shaped, **'Nidiformis'** (25–50cm x 50–80cm) ♥ very slow growing and compact, good for rock garden and containers. *P. breweriana* (Brewer's weeping spruce) **H5** (1–2m, U: 10–20m) ♥ one of the most strikingly beautiful of all conifers, slow growing when young, eventually forming a wide tree with weeping branchlets, very fine at Tillypronie in Aberdeenshire, and Dawyck, near Peebles, two of Scotland's coldest gardens. *P. glauca* var. *albertiana* grown in numerous selections, all compact and neat with small brown cones: **'Alberta Blue'** (60cm x 30cm,U: 3–5m) blue-green foliage,

Picea breweriana

Picea glauca var. *albertiana* 'J. W. Daisy's White'

Picea pungens 'Glauca Prostrata'

Picea pungens

prune out any green shoots, **'Alberta Globe'** (30cm x 30cm, U: 1m x 1m) very slow growing, squat habit, **'Conica'** (1m x 50cm, U: 3–5m) may be the world's best-selling conifer, as it is very neat and ideal for small gardens, with no pruning required for a perfect cone and attractive bright-green young growth, **'J.W. Daisy's White'** (60cm–1m) rather outrageous, with striking cream young growth, fading to pale yellow, then green. *P. mariana* **'Nana'** (20–30cm) a tiny compact blue-green bun, ideal for troughs. *P. omorika* (Serbian spruce) (5–7m, U: 20m+) ♥ handsome with dark-green needles, silvery on the underside, dropping branches, fine cones, very tough, resistant to pests and diseases; a weeping form **'Pendula'** has sharply downward-pointing branches. *P. pungens* (Colorado blue spruce) mostly grown in intense silver-blue-leaved selections, which are ideal and striking plants for any garden; most are grafted and slow growing, so expect to pay more for these than most other conifers: **'Erich Frahm'** (2m x 1m, U: 8–10m+) cone-shaped with fine blue foliage, **Glauca Group** and **Glauca Prostrata** (1–2m) selections which will grow 15–30cm per year, some more upright than others, **'Globosa'** (50cm–1.5m) ♥ slow growing and mounding habit, ideal for small gardens, **'Hoopsii'** (2m x 1m, U: 5m+) ♥ possibly the finest for foliage, bluish-white needles, pyramidal habit, **'Koster'** (2–3m, U: 10m) ♥ slow growing, narrowly conical, with curved silver-blue needles.

Pinus (pine)

Mostly **H5** The long needles of pines, held in clusters of two to five, make them easy to recognize. Apart from the native Scots pine, many other species grow very well, providing useful wind shelter on coasts and hills, and there are also compact forms suitable for the smaller garden. Pines do well in dry, sandy, rocky/well-drained sites; only a few will tolerate wet and heavy soils. Many have attractive bark and showy flowers and cones. Be aware that the vigorous varieties get extremely large (15–20m+). All listed are fully hardy (**H5**), unless stated otherwise.

P. bungeana (1.5m, U: 10m+) usually a multi-stemmed tree with stiff sharp needles, yellow-brown cones, outstanding peeling multi-coloured bark, likes hot summers. *P. heldreichii* (syn. *P. leucodermis*) **'Compact Gem'** (1m x 60cm) slow growing, compact, with bright-green new growth, blue cones; *P.h.* **'Satellit'** (1.5m x 90cm) glossy dark-green foliage forming a narrow conical tree, *P.h.* **'Smidtii'** (25–50cm x 25–50cm, U: 2m x 2m) dark needles, domed congested habit, very slow growing. *P. nigra* (European black pine) (10–30m) dark-green needles, growing very large, useful for coastal shelterbelts. *P. mugo* the well-known European mountain pine is the most widely grown dwarf pine. There are many forms: the larger ones will grow to 1m or so in 10–15 years, ultimately much bigger; the prominent winter buds and cones are most attractive, as are the new growth tips as they enlarge. Most are spreaders, growing wider than high: **'Gnome'** (50cm x 75cm, U: 1–2m) slow growing, **'Humpy'** (50cm–1m) neat with dark needles and prominent buds, **'Mops'** (50cm–1m x 50cm–1m) ⚜ dense, with grey-green needles, fine winter buds, **'Ophir'** (60cm x 30cm, U: 2m) needles tipped yellow in summer turn bright gold in winter, compact, **Pumilio Group** (50cm–1m) variable in habit, some prostrate, others more upright, cones purple, winter buds whitish, **'Wintergold'** (50cm) yellow needles in winter. *P. parviflora* Glauca Group (2–3m x 2m, U: 10m+) blue-grey needles and blue-green cones, upright habit. *P. patula H2* (2m x 50cm, U: 6–10m) blue-green needles and weeping branches, only suitable for mildest west-coast gardens. *P. radiata H3* (Monterey pine) (10–15m, U: 20–40m) a fast-growing tree much used in Scottish west-coast gardens for providing shelter from winds and salt spray, fissured

Pinus wallichiana

dark-brown bark and glossy pale-coloured cones; there is a superb example at Kelburn Castle, near Largs, Ayrshire. *P. sylvestris* (Scots pine) (6–10m, U: 20–30m) ⚜ Scotland's ancient pine forests are mostly long gone but this is such a versatile, wind-tolerant and shapely plant that is planted in large numbers over much of Scotland. It does not generally do well in Orkney or Sheltland. Conical when young, becoming flat-topped, attractive pinkish red bark. Named forms include: **Aurea Group** needles yellow in winter, **'Chantrey Blue'** (2–4m) slow growing, with bluish needles, **Fastigiata Group** (2m+ x 50cm, U: 8m+) form with narrow columnar habit, blue-green needles, a striking plant, **'Inverleith'** (2–3m, U: 5–10m+) tall and vigorous, growing about 30cm a year, with creamy-white variegation on the needles, **'Watereri'** (1m x 1m, U: 3–5m) slow growing, blue-grey needles. *P. wallichiana* (4m x 1.5m, U: 15–20m+) ⚜ beautiful long blue-green needles, sticky cones, very attractive.

Platycladus see *Thuja*, page 121

Podocarpus nivalis

Podocarpus

H3–4 (60cm x 80cm, U: 1–2m) This southern-hemisphere conifer has been gaining lots of attention in recent years with selections with coloured foliage, though many of the bronze-leaved ones look dead or burned for part of the year. They are tidy spreaders with berries on female forms.

Pinus mugo 'Wintergold'

Pinus sylvestris 'Fastigiata Group

Podocarpus: typical winter foliage

Podocarpus: young growth on one of the yellow-leaved forms

County Park Fire [PBR] new growth white-pink, winter foliage bronze. *P. nivalis* 'Killworth Cream' pale creamy foliage especially in winter. 'Spring Sunshine' cream turning to yellow young growth, bronze in winter. *P. lawrencei* 'Blue Gem' new growth creamy white, turning to blue-green. *P. salignus H3* (5–10m+) handsome, willow-like dark-green leaves, best in mild and western gardens, though it does survive (just) in a cold Aberdeenshire garden.

Pseudotsuga menziesii at Scone Palace

Pseudotsuga menziesii
(Douglas fir)

H4–5 (3–5m, U: 25–50m, in the wild it can reach 90m) This giant was discovered in North America by Archibald Menzies and introduced by David Douglas, both Scottish plant hunters. Dark-green aromatic needles on a broadly conical tree, useful for large spaces, parks, stately homes and palaces but not recommended for small gardens. It tends to develop a slightly uneven or lop-sided shape, which is not unattractive. The two tallest trees in Britain are giants of this species growing at Reelig Glen near Inverness and the Hermitage, near Dunkeld, and there are also some superb examples at Scone Palace, Perthshire.

Sciadopitys verticillata

Sciadopitys verticillata
(Japanese umbrella pine)

H4–5 (1–1.5m, U: 5–10m+) A slow-growing conifer with handsome narrow dark-green needles giving a porcupine-like effect. It can produce small cones. Plant in moist but well-drained soil in sun or part shade. Although it can get large in time, it is slow growing, so suitable for a small garden. There are many fine examples in west-coast gardens.

Sequoiadendron giganteum
(wellingtonia, big tree) and *Sequoia sempervirens* **(Californian redwood)**

H5 ❧ The wellingtonia (4m+ x 2m+, U: 25–40m) has been planted all over Scotland: Benmore in Argyll has a fine avenue of them, there is a magnificent line at House of Dun near Montrose, while Cluny in Perthshire has the one with the widest girth in the UK. Easily recognized by their size and their soft furrowed reddish bark, they are also easily confused with the Californian redwood (*Sequoia sempervirens*), a very similar tree, but with harder bark. Horticultural students are often taught to tell the difference

Sequoiadendron giganteum avenue at Benmore

by punching the trunk: if your hand hurts afterwards, it's a redwood. Site both carefully, as they do of course get very large: don't plant these 'time bombs' in places where their size will cause problems later. The biggest tree in the world, 'General Sherman', is a wellingtonia, and the oldest trees in the world are Californian redwoods. They are pretty wind tolerant but the tops tend to be blown out eventually by storms.

There are also slow-growing and dwarf versions of wellingtonia: 'Glaucum' (5–15m) narrowly conical habit with glaucous leaves, 'Pendulum' growth rate 30cm per year, a strange-looking plant with erratic habit and pendulous branches with hang down parallel to the main trunk, described by Adrian Bloom as 'a living sculpture'.

Sequoia sempervirens (5–8m, U: 25–40m) Very tall in its native California (over 100m). Fast growing, good in moist acid soils. There is a fine pair at Taymouth Castle, Kenmore, on Loch Tay.

Taxodium distichum (RC-M)

Taxodium distichum
(swamp cypress)

H5 (4–6m, U: 20m) One of the few conifers that likes to grow in moist or soggy soil or at a pondside. It is best to plant it on a slight mound, so that the crown of the plant remains dry. Deciduous, the leaves often colour to a rich orange-brown in autumn, leaving a striking winter framework of branches and a trunk with red-brown bark.

Taxus baccata (yew)

H5 (2m x 1m, U: 10–20m, growing 25–40cm per year) ♦ ☒ ❧ This British native is extremely long lived: the Fortingall Yew in Perthshire is said to be over 3,000 years old. There are huge and spectacular layering yews, which spread by radiating branches taking root, at Ormiston and Whittinghame, East Lothian, and several other sites in Scotland. Yews are one of Britain's few native evergreen trees and they have been used around churchyards, and for hedging, for generations. Yews have dark green needles and are tidy and compact growers which can be pruned

Taxus baccata: clipped yews, at Malleny Gardens

right back to the trunk; they will almost always freely sprout again. The female plants will produce scarlet berries (containing poisonous seed) in autumn if pollinated by a male. Choose male forms to avoid berries. English yew (*T. baccata*) makes one of the most impressive formal hedges and topiary subjects, its tightly knit foliage creating a dark-green wall, which provides a perfect foil. Yews will grow in sun or shade in free-draining soil but avoid heavy or waterlogged sites.

T. baccata cultivars include **'Adpressa Variegata'** (syn. 'A. Aurea') (60cm–1m) male, slow growing, new growth yellow, mature leaf edges yellow, **'Dovastonii Aurea'** (2.5m x 1.5m, U: 8–10m) male, with irregular habit and weeping branchlets, yellow-margined foliage, **'Fastigiata'** (Irish yew) (2m x 50cm, U: 8–10m) a broad column with steeply ascending branches, male and female forms exist, **Fastigiata Aurea Group** (2m x 50cm, U: 8–10m) golden-yellow young growth, yellow all year in sun, **'Fastigiata Aureomarginata'** as above with green leaves edged yellow, **'Standishii'** (1.5m, U: 5–8m) female, slow growing, upright habit, fine golden-yellow foliage, very fine, **'Summergold'** (50cm x 1m, U: 1–2m x 3–6m+) male, low and spreading with golden foliage all year round, brightest in summer. *T. x media* **'Hicksii'** (2m, U: 10m+) female, dark green, vigorous, used for hedging, abundant red berries.

Thuja (and Platycladus orientalis)

Useful for hedging and specimen plants, thujas are similar to *Chamaecyparis*, with aromatic foliage in soft sprays, and enjoying moist but well-drained soil. Some people suffer a skin allergy to the foliage and rabbits seem particularly fond of eating them.

T. occidentalis H5 is grown in numerous cultivars: **'Danica'** (30cm x 30cm, U: 1m) dense compact globular habit, **'Holmstrup'** (1.2m x 50cm, U: 5–8m x 2.5–3m) slow growing with dark-green foliage, narrow conical habit, **'Rheingold'** (1m, U: 3–4m) a best-seller with golden-yellow summer foliage which is bronzy orange in winter, forming a conical bush, juvenile foliage is feathery, mature foliage lacy, **'Smaragd'** (2m x 60cm, U: 6–8m+) a fine hedging plant with lacy green foliage and a pyramid shape, **'Sunkist'** (1.5m x 90cm, U: 5–8m) golden yellow young foliage, **'Tiny Tim'** very slow growing. *T. orientalis* (syn. *Platycladus orientalis*) H3–5 botanists have seen fit to remove this to a new genus, *Platycladus*, but as most growers have ignored this, we are retaining it here as *Thuja*. Cultivars include **'Aurea Nana'** H4–5 (60cm x 40cm) compact rounded habit, yellow summer foliage, bronze yellow in winter, **'Rosedalis'** H3–4 (40–80cm) a compact, slow-growing egg-shaped bush, soft yellow young foliage, turning green and then purple in cold winters, best in a sheltered position. *T. plicata* (western red cedar) H5 aromatic

Thuja occidentalis 'Danica', Threave

Thuja occidentalis 'Smaragd'

Thuja orientalis 'Aurea Nana'

Thuja occidentalis 'Rheingold'

foliage, easy to please, mostly grown in the forms **'Atrovirens'** (5m, U: 20–30m) dark-green foliage, probably the best hedging conifer for Scotland, less vigorous than leylandii, breaking from old wood (so easier to prune) and more tolerant of heavy soils, should be more widely grown, plant 60cm apart, **'Copper Kettle'** (50cm–1m) a mixture of yellow and copper foliage, **Daniellow** [PBR] (2–3m x 1m) very bright yellow foliage, said not to bun in sun, **'Rogersii'** (50cm x 50cm, U: 1m) dense with gold and bronze foliage, **'Stoneham Gold'** (1m, U: 3–5m) green with coppery gold young growth, **'Zebrina'** (3m x 1.5m, U: 10m+) pyramidal habit, green foliage striped yellow.

Tsuga (hemlock)

Tsuga canadensis 'Jeddeloh'

H5 These graceful trees have tiny dark green needles and small pendulous cones and range from giant trees to compact mounds.

T. canadensis (3m x 1m, U: 15m) a large multi-stemmed tree. Forms include **'Cole's Prostrate'** (30cm x 60cm, U: 30cm x 1.5–2.5m) spreading and prostrate with blue-green foliage, **'Fantana'** (2m) fan-like branches, slow growing and bushy, **'Jeddeloh'** (30cm, U: 1m) light-green foliage bright green in spring, squat habit, **'Minuta'** (15cm x 15cm, U: 75cm) very slow growing, congested foliage, bun-like habit, **'Pendula'** (annual growth rate 15–20cm height variable), overlapping, drooping branches, needs to be trained up to the height desired, otherwise prostrate. *T. heterophylla* (10–20m in 20 years, U: 40m) a vigorous handsome tree with dark-green needles and green cones, tinged purple, used for vigorous hedging and to provide shelter.

HEDGES, SCREENS AND SHELTERBELTS

✉ Scottish native plant ♀ Scottish Gardenplant Award
☠ irritant or toxic; ☠☠ extremely irritant or toxic if ingested
❀ fragrant; ❀❀ very fragrant
♦ disease resistant; ♦♦ very disease resistant

Hedges are used for many things: to provide privacy, to define a boundary or screen an unsightly object, to provide shelter from prevailing winds or to divide a garden into sections. Hedges can be formal, regularly clipped into shape, or informal and just left to grow naturally. Traditional hedgerows are made up of a mixture of different plants such as hazel, hawthorn and rose. The best and cheapest way to plant a hedge is using bare-root plants in winter and early spring. At other times of year, plants will be containerised and usually considerably more expensive.

Choosing your hedge or screen

You can, in theory, make a hedge or screen out of almost any tree or shrub, or a mixture of them. But it makes sense to carefully consider what qualities you need: height required, whether evergreen/semi-evergreen or deciduous, ease of maintenance/frequency of cutting required, whether you want flowers, berries, thorns and other desirable or undesirable characteristics. Take into account the climate, soil type and situation. For example, if the site is very exposed or badly drained, choice will be more limited. If you are not sure, have a look at neighbouring gardens and you'll probably see the type of hedge you require.

Hedges need good and even soil preparation. If part of the hedge run is waterlogged, or in dry shade under trees, some plants will struggle or fail and you will get uneven growth. Yew, beech and many other hedging plants need well-drained soil that does not dry out, especially when plants are young. Newly planted hedges need to be watered regularly and in exposed situations may require artificial protection in order to aid establishment.

Hedges for a shelterbelt To protect exposed gardens from cold and strong winds it is best to consider planting two to three or more lines of mixed trees and shrubs (provided you have the space), perhaps a mixture of deciduous and evergreens. Pine, leylandii, willow, beech, hazel, hawthorn, laurel, flowering currant and *Rosa rugosa* are just some examples. If space is limited, a single line of either the same or mixed planting will still be effective.

Hedges for exposed coastal situations open to salt-bearing sea winds. **Evergreen**: *Brachyglottis, Elaeagnus x ebbingei, Griselinia littoralis, Olearia.* **Deciduous**: *Fuchsia, Rosa rugosa, Hippophae rhamnoides* (sea buckthorn).

Hedges for heavy/clay **Evergreen:** *Berberis darwinii, Ilex aquifolium* (common holly), *Cotoneaster, Escallonia, Osmanthus delavayi, Potentilla fruticosa, Prunus laurocerasus, Prunus lusitanica.* **Deciduous:** *Ribes sanguineum, Spiraea.*

Deciduous flowering hedges *Potentilla fruticosa, Ribes sanguineum, Deutzia, Weigela, Rosa, Forsythia.*

Griselinia hedge (RC-M)

Tough evergreen hedges for cold, exposed situations
Ilex (holly), *Prunus* (laurel), *Taxus* (yew).

Tough deciduous hedges (all *H5*) *Fagus* (beech),
Crataegus (hawthorn), *Carpinus* (hornbeam).

Hedges to encourage wildlife The best hedges for
wildlife are traditional hedgerows, with a mixture of
species providing nesting/shelter and food for birds,
animals and insects. Some of the most commonly used
plants are: *Rosa canina* (dog rose), *Crataegus* (hawthorn),
Corylus (hazel), *Prunus* (blackthorn), *Sorbus* (rowan).

Conifers for hedging
You can use almost any upright conifer for hedging, but
the following are amongst the most popular. The typical
height given is for a regularly pruned hedge. The ultimate
height is what will be achieved if the hedge is not regularly
pruned. Prune in summer when the hedge is growing (if
possible), or in spring. Most conifers are reluctant to break
from old wood, so don't let them get out of control. Yew
(*Taxus*) is the exception: it can be cut back to the trunk.

Chamaecyparis hedge (RC-M)

CONIFERS FOR HEDGING						
Name	Foliage colour	Typical height	Ultimate height	Annual growth rate	Spacing	Soil
x *Cupressocyparis leylandii*	Green	3–5m+	10m+	75cm–1m	75cm–1.2m	Well drained
x *C.l.* 'Castlewellan'	Yellow	3–5m+	10+m	70–90cm	75cm–1.2m	Well drained
Chamaecyparis lawsoniana	Green, blue, yellow	3–5m+	5–8m+	30–60cm	75cm–1m	Well drained
C.l. 'Ellwood's Gold'	Yellow-green	1–2m	2–4m	20cm	40–60cm	Well drained
Taxus baccata (yew)	Green, golden	1–3m	5-10m+	15–30cm	60cm	Well drained
Thuja occidentalis 'Smaragd'	Green	2–3m	3–6m	25cm	60cm	Any
Thuja plicata 'Atrovirens'	Green	3–5m	5–10m	60cm	60cm	Any

THE MOST POPULAR HEDGING TREES AND SHRUBS

HEDGING PLANTS	Evergreen (E) or Deciduous (D)	Growth rate per year once established	Typical spacing	Typical hedge size (height x width)	Pruning
Fagus sylvatica Beech	D	Medium 30–50cm	30–60cm	2m x 1.2m	Once, summer
Berberis darwinii Berberis	E	Medium 20–40cm	45cm	1.5–2.5m x 1m	Once, summer
B. thunbergii cvs Dwarf berberis	D	Slow under 20cm	30cm	30–45cm x 45cm	Once, summer
Buxus Box	E	Slow 10–20cm	20–30cm	30–60cm	1–3 times, summer
Prunus laurocerasus Cherry laurel	E	Medium 30–60cm	1m+	2m x 1.5m	Once, summer
Escallonia	E	Medium 30cm	75cm	2–3m x 1.5m	Once, summer
Crataegus monogyna Hawthorn	D	Fast 40–60cm	45–60cm	2.4m x 1.2m	Twice, early and late summer
Corylus avellana Hazel	D	Fast 40–60cm+	45–60cm	2.1m x 1.5m	Once, summer
Ilex Holly	E	Slow 15–30cm	45–60cm	2.4m x 1.5m	Once, summer
Carpinus betulus Hornbeam	D	Medium 30–50cm	45–60cm	2.4m x 1.2m	Once, summer
Prunus lusitanica Portugal laurel	E	Slow 15–30cm	1m+	2m x 1.5m	Once, summer
Ligustrum ovalifolium Privet	E/D	Medium 30–50cm	30cm	1.5–2.4m x 1.2m	2–3 times, spring–summer
Rosa rugosa Rose	D	Medium 30–60cm	45–60cm	1.5–2.1m x 1.2m	Once, early spring

Flowers	Autumn and winter interest	Spines or thorns	Tolerant of
No	Leaf colour	No	Wind
Yes	Foliage and early flowers	Yes	Shade
Tiny	Autumn colour	Yes	Dry soil
Tiny	Shiny dark foliage	No	Dry soil
Yes	Foliage	No	Wind, salt, shade
Yes	Foliage	No	Wind, salt,
Yes	Berries	Yes	Any soil
Catkins	Nuts, catkins	No	Wind
Tiny	Berries	Spiny leaves	Wind
Tiny	Autumn colour	Yes	Wind, salt, Any soil
Yes	Berries	No	Wind, salt
Yes	Coloured or green leaves	No	Shade/ any soil
Yes	Hips	Yes	Wind, salt, almost anything

Berberis thunbergii hedge (RC-M)

Holly hedge (RC-M)

Privet hedge (RC-M)

Formal yew hedging at Tyninghame walled garden, East Lothian

ORNAMENTAL TREES

✉ Scottish native plant ❦ Scottish Gardenplant Award
☗ irritant or toxic; ☗☗ extremely irritant or toxic if ingested
❀ fragrant; ❀❀ very fragrant
♦ disease resistant; ♦ ♦ very disease resistant

Scottish native trees

✉ *Alnus glutinosa, Betula pendula, Corylus avellana, Crataegus monogyna, Fraxinus excelsior, Malus sylvestris, Pinus sylvestris, Populus tremula, Prunus padus, Prunus avium, Quercus robur, Quercus petraea, Salix alba, Sorbus aria, Sorbus aucuparia, Ulmus glabra*

Most gardens have room for at least one tree: even the smallest garden can accommodate a slow-growing tree or one grown in a container. Trees provide scale, structure, privacy, shelter, shade and an environment for wildlife. Trees have a feel-good factor – some people want to hug them. They are long lived and therefore a long-term investment, and they create much of the atmosphere and microclimate of a garden. Not all trees are good news; many gardeners have to suffer the ill effects of greedy mature trees such as sycamores, not to mention leylandii, often in neighbouring gardens. Trees can be a time bomb: they may seem a good idea when small, but they can get so large that, if planted in the wrong place, they can become a blight or headache, and they are expensive or almost impossible to control or remove. Choose carefully, however, and you should ensure that a tree brings you years of pleasure. If space is limited, you might consider coppicing, where the tree is cut back hard each year or two, producing masses of young shoots and leaves (poplar, catalpa, ash, willow and others are suitable). It is an excellent way of keeping trees compact and manageable. Alternatively, buy top-grafted weeping trees, which never get any taller than the height of the stem (cotoneasters, for example).

There is no doubt that autumn, winter and early-spring planting is advisable for trees. A tree needs to get its roots established before it can stand up to wind and put on any significant new growth. It must not be allowed to dry out in the first few growing seasons and it will need extra care, especially if planted in late spring or summer. Good soil preparation is crucial, so prepare a large hole with added compost and organic matter. Try to plant when the soil is not too wet, to avoid compaction and ruining the soil structure. Soak the rootball before planting, dunking it if necessary, and water in well to settle in the soil. Stakes are usually required for the first few years to stop wind rock and the breaking of fresh young roots. Current wisdom is that a tree stake should be about a third of the length of the trunk (less in the case of semi-mature size). The short stake allows the main stem to flex in the wind and gradually

become strong enough to withstand winds unsupported. The stake should be positioned on the prevailing wind side of the tree (usually the south-west) to minimise damage caused by the bark rubbing against it. Bark is a tree's protective skin, which keeps diseases out, and if this is broken, an entry point is created for potentially fatal infection. Proper rubber tree ties are shaped in a figure of eight and can be let out as the trunk thickens. In a really windy site, two or three stakes may be needed to anchor the tree. Top-grafted trees should be staked at the height of the graft. Use artificial protection such as woven plastic to protect young trees until they get established, and use tree guards to stop rabbits and deer barking the trees. If you want to grow copses, hedges or plantations of common and native trees, it is best to buy these as whips, bare-rooted in the winter (they come in bundles of 10, 25 or 100 plants and are relatively cheap). Two Scottish tree specialists are the Tree Nursery, Cairndow in Argyll, and Kirkdale Tree Nursery, near Inverurie in the north-east.

Trees and shrubs with striking bark and stems

Bark: *Acer griseum* (cinnamon, peeling), *Acer davidii* (white and green striped), *Betula utilis* var. *jacquemontii* (white), *Eucalyptus* ssp., *Prunus serrula*, (red-brown, peeling), *Rhododendron thomsonii, Rhododenron barbatum*.
Stems: *Acer palmatum* 'Senkaki' ('Sangu-kaku'), *Cornus alba* 'Elegantissima' (red stems), *Cornus alba* 'Sibirica' (coral-red stems) *Cornus alba* 'Flaviramea' (yellow-green stems), *Rubus biflorus* and *Rubus thibetanus* (white stems), *Phyllostachys* (bamboos) with black or yellow stems

Acer palmatum and *Cotinus* 'Grace'

Cornus alba (RC-M)

Trees and shrubs with best and most reliable autumn colour in Scotland

Autumn colour is variable in Scotland: a few trees are brilliant every year but others require a crisp dry autumn to colour well. The ones on this list generally colour up very well every year.

Acer palmatum 'Ösakazuki', *Acer rubrum*, *Berberis thunbergii*, *Betula* (most), *Cercidiphyllum japonicum*, *Cotinus* 'Grace', *Euonymous europaeus*, *Euonymus alatus*, *Fothergilla*, *Larix*, *Parrotia persica*, *Partenocissus*, *Rhus typhina*, *Rhododendron (azalea) luteum* and other deciduous azaleas, *Sorbus* 'Joseph Rock', *Viburnum plicatum*

Acer (maple)

Every garden needs an acer or two: from the irresistible leaves and form of the dwarf Japanese maples to large

Acer shirawasanum 'Aureum'

Acer palmatum forms

forest trees, this enormous genus contains hardy deciduous trees with fine foliage, fiery autumn colour and attractive bark. Most acers have insignificant flowers and usually winged fruits (familiar to children as 'helicopters') and require moist, well-drained, soil in sun or part shade. The snakebark maples such as *A. capillipes* have attractively striped bark, usually with green and white striations, and the paperbark maple (*A. griseum*) has peeling bark.

Japanese maples

H3–5 Japanese maples are forms of *A. palmatum*, *A. japonicum* and *A. shirawasanum* and are extremely popular garden plants. There are hundreds of named forms, mostly with tongue-twistingly charming Japanese names.

Although they are perfectly mid-winter hardy, plants can be severely damaged by late frosts and cold east winds, particularly when young. A protective covering such as fleece is advisable on frosty nights if there is vulnerable fresh young growth. They grow well in a cold inland garden at Ardverikie, between Spean Bridge and Newtonmore, with the protection of a walled garden.

Acer 'Sango-kaku' ('Senkaki')

Varieties with dissected leaves are particularly vulnerable to wind damage on young growth, so provide a sheltered site. Scale insects can cause problems: treat with a systemic insecticide if necessary. Japanese maples can be grown in containers with some wind shelter, ideally using a mixture of John Innes No. 3 and ericaceous compost. Most forms are grafted, so remove any suckers from below the graft union.

A. palmatum (2–5m after 10–20 years) leaves green or red, five-to-seven-lobed, often with good autumn colour. Seedling-raised plants vary in size, vigour and leaf colour. Numerous forms include **f. Atropurpureum** deeply lobed red-purple leaves, red in autumn, **'Aureum'** leaves finely cut, leaves yellowish green, flushed red, good yellow autumn colour, bushy habit, **'Bloodgood'** (5m x 5m) ♛ dark red five-to-seven-lobed leaves, turning bright red in autumn, one of the best and toughest, getting large in time, **'Burgundy Lace'** (5m x 5m) deeply cut rich red-purple leaves, one of the most vigorous of the fine-leaved varieties, **'Butterfly'** (3m+ x 1.5m) small green leaves margined white and pink, inclined to revert, **'Deshojo'** (2.5m x 2.5m) red young leaves turning green. **A.p. var. dissectum** (1–2m x 2–3m) ♛ mound forming with very finely cut leaves, forms a dome-shaped shrub: if you want a low-growing one, choose a plant that is weeping at 30–45cm high, for taller plants and standards, train the trunk up a stake to the desired height. There are many fine selections: **Dissectum Atropurpureum Group** red-purple leaves, **Dissectum Viride Group** green, turning orange-yellow in autumn, **'Garnet'** (2–3m) ♛ dissect leaves remain deep red-purple till autumn. **'Inaba-Shidare'** (3m) deep purple, good autumn colour, **'Orangeola'** (3–4m) relatively large red leaves turning bronze then orange, weeping, **'Ornatum'** (3m) leaves green, tinted bronze, **'Seiryu'** (3–5m) deeply dissected green leaves, excellent autumn colour. **'Fireglow'** (3m) large red-purple leaves, rich crimson in autumn, **'Katsura'** (2–3m) five-lobed leaves, bright orange-yellow when young, yellow and orange in autumn, **'Orange Dream'** (2–3m) greenish-yellow, margins red, very striking, **'Orido-Nishiki'** (3–5m) young growth red and white, green leaves margined pink and white, bark creamy white and pink, young shoots red, unusual and a good performer, **'Ösakazuki'** (5m x 4m) ♛ outstanding fiery scarlet autumn colour year after year, green summer leaves, vigorous, **'Red Pygmy'** (1–3m) dark red-brown young foliage, fading to green, **'Sango-kaku'** ('Senkaki') (6m x 5m) five-lobed leaves yellow-green with bright red winter shoots, tough vigorous and easy, good for winter interest, **'Shaina'** (2–3m+) dwarf version of 'Bloodgood', reddish-purple leaves, **'Shindeshōjō'** (2–3m) five-

Acer capillipes (bark) (RC-M)

Acer platanoides 'Crimson King'

Acer griseum (bark)

lobed, young leaves bright red, fading to green speckled white and pink, orange-red in autumn, **'Shishagashira'** (2–4m) slow-growing, upright habit with dense deep green leaves, yellow in autumn, **'Shishio'** (2.5m) leaves green, young growth and autumn colour red, **'Trompenburg'** (3–4m) deep-purplish red young leaves, deeply-cut, rolled edges, green in summer, red in autumn, tougher than the dissectum types.

A. japonicum H5 (3–10m) seven-to-ten-lobed leaves, less finely cut than *A. palmatum*, green, turning red in autumn. A multi-stemmed tree of rounded habit, usually grown in selected forms: **'Aconitifolium'** (3m x 3m) deeply cut green leaves which turn deep red in autumn, an excellent small garden tree, **'Vitifolium'** (5m–10m) vigorous with vine-shaped green leaves colouring well in autumn.

A. shirasawanum 'Aureum' (syn. *A. japonicum* 'Aureum') (3m x 2–3m, U: 5m+ x 5m) beautiful pale yellow-green leaves, foliage may burn in mid-summer, slow growing, red and green seeds, autumn colour usually poor, **'Autumn Moon'** soft-yellow leaves, suffused bronze-orange, more resistant to burning.

Other maples

A. buergerianum H5 (3–4m, U: 10m) three-lobed dark-green leaves, usually orange and red in autumn, yellow flowers, good bark. *A. campestre* (field maple) *H5* (3–4m, U: 8m+ x 4m) ✻ often used in rural hedges, with lobed leaves with yellow autumn colour, tolerant of waterlogged sites. Cultivars include: **'Carnival'** (2–3m, U: 5m x 3–4m) leaves, edged white and splashed grey-green, **'Pulverulentum'** (5m) leaves, heavily splashed creamy green, **'Royal Ruby'** (10m+) dark-red leaves. *A. capillipes H5* (snakebark maple) (4–10m) three-lobed, green leaves turn brilliant red and orange in autumn, bark striped white and red-brown to green. *A. cappadocicum* 'Aureum' *H5* (to 10m x 5m+) young leaves red, turning rich yellow in autumn; *A.c.* 'Rubrum' (10m x 5m+) young leaves red, turning green and then bright yellow in autumn. *A. x conspicuum* 'Silver Cardinal' (snakebark) (3m) white-striped bark, leaves blotched and streaked with white and pink when young,

flushed red. *A. davidii* (5–10m x 5m) (snakebark) dark-green leaves, yellow, red and purple in autumn, bark green, striped white, red seed capsules; *A.d.* **'George Forrest'** ✻ a popular clone with spreading habit and red leaf stalks. *A. griseum* (paperbark maple) (5–10m) ✻ a fine tough, slow-growing tree with very fine peeling red-brown bark, small leaves turn red in autumn; Ian Christie has a fine group thriving in an exposed site near Kirriemuir, Angus. *A. grosseri* var.

Acer negundo 'Flamingo'

Acer pensylvanicum
(bark and autumn colour)
at Dundee Botanic Garden

hersii H5 (3–5m, U: 8–10m) (snakebark) arching branches, shallowly lobed leaves turn red in autumn, bark blue-green, marbled with white. *A. negundo* (box elder) *H5* (4–6m, U: 15m) mainly grown in the following cultivars, which are often hard pruned to keep as shrubs/bushes (all tend to revert, so cut out green shoots): **'Auratum'** (syn. 'Aurea') leaves bright yellow, **'Elegans'** leaves variegated green and bright yellow, **'Flamingo'** leaves green and silvery white, pink-edged when young, **'Kelly's Gold'** bright yellow leaves, **'Variegatum'** leaves white-margined, very prone to revert. *A. pensylvanicum H5* (4–6m x 2–3m) (snakebark) bark striped green and white, lobed leaves turn bright yellow in the autumn. *A. platanoides* (Norway maple) *H5* (5m, U: 15–25m x 8–15m+) a very large, tough tree with large toothed leaves, insignificant flowers in spring, yellow autumn colour. There are many less vigorous, more garden-worthy selections (all reach 3–5m in 10 years; only ultimate heights are given): **'Crimson King'** (15m) handsome dark-crimson leaves, reddish in autumn, **'Crimson Sentry'** (12m) narrow upright habit with deep red-purple leaves, prone to mildew in late

Plants for windy sites inland

Plants may need extra help to establish in very exposed sites: use artificial materials such as fencing or woven plastic. Trees should be securely staked (see page 126).

Trees and conifers
Acer platanoides,
A. pseudoplatanus
  cultivars
Alnus glutinosa, A.
  incana
Betula
Chamaecyparis
  lawsonia
Crataegus monogyna
Fagus sylvatica
Juniperus horizontalis,
  J. squamata
Larix decidua

Pinus sylvestris
Querus robur
Sorbus aucuparia, S.
  aria
Tilia cordata

Shrubs
Azaleas (deciduous)
Aucuba
Bamboos
Berberis (deciduous)
Buddleja davidii
Cornus alba
Cornus canadensis

Corylus
Cotoneaster
Cytisus (except C.
  battandieri)
Deutzia
Forsythia
Hippophae
  rhamnoides
Ilex aquifolium
Kerria japonica
Pinus mugo 'Mops'
Potentilla fruticosa
Prunus laurocerasus
Pyracantha coccinea
Rhododendron
  'Cunningham's
  White',
  'Cunningham's
  Blush', 'Fastuosum
  Flore Pleno'
Rosa pimpinellifolia,

R. rugosa
Salix alba (and others)
Sambucus niger
Spiraea
Symphoricarpos
Ulex
Viburnum opulus
Weigela

Perennials and bulbs
Achemilla mollis
Anaphalis
Aster alpinus
Bergenia
Brunnera
Euphorbia
Polemonium
Veronica spicata

summer, **'Drummondii'** (12m) leaves green with a broad cream margin, **'Laciniatum'** (20m) deeply cut (claw-like) bright-green leaves, **'Schwedleri'** (15m) young leaves crimson-purple, fading to dark green. **A. pseudoplatanus** (syacmore) **H5** (15–30m x 15–20m) large green, leaves, yellow in the autumn, very tough, grows well in most soils, suitable for exposure; however, this is also the bane of thousands of gardeners. It is so greedy that you can't grow much under it, and it sows seedlings and drops black sticky secretions everywhere – in small and town gardens sycamores should be cut down immediately. But it is well worth growing as the best broadleaved tree for coastal planting: it will tolerate salt spray and very exposed sites, though in Shetland it needs some shelter to get going. There are several less vigorous cultivars which make better garden plants: **'Brilliantissimum'** (3m x 3m) slow growing, leaves salmon pink when young, turning yellow-white and finally green, looks spectacular in spring and anaemic in summer, and then colours in autumn, **'Leopoldii'** (10m) leaves open yellowish pink, fading to green with paler speckles, **'Prinz Handjéry'** (3m x 3m) slow growing, leaves salmon pink when young, purplish beneath, turning yellow and green, **'Simon-Louis Frères'** (10m) leaves creamy white and pink when young, pale green splashed white in summer,

Acer platanoides 'Drummondii'

'Worley' (10m+) leaves open soft yellow, deepen to golden yellow, then pale green, yellow in the autumn. **A. rubrum** (Norway maple) **H5** (4–6m x 3–4m, U: 20m) dark-green leaves, turning bright red in autumn. Selected forms include: **'Red Sunset'** good autumn colour, **'October Glory'** **H4** slower growing, less hardy, long-lasting colour in autumn. **A. rufinerve H5** (5–8m) (snakebark) broadly columnar habit, arching branches, bark striped green and white, green, three-lobed leaves red and yellow in autumn. **A. saccharinum H4** green, lobed leaves, silvery beneath, vigorous, often has good autumn colour, large tree, needs wind shelter. **A. tataricum** subsp. *ginnala* **'Flame'** (5–10m) slender arching branches, three-lobed leaves, good autumn colour.

Acer pseudoplatanus 'Brilliantissimum'

Aesculus (horse chestnut)

H4–5 ♨ The common horse chestnut provides conkers and makes a fine tough and easy-to-please deciduous specimen tree for the large garden or park. Better for medium and small gardens are some of the less vigorous selected forms. All have distinctive palmate leaves and long spikes of flowers known as candles. All parts of the plants are poisonous to humans and animals. An insect pest, horse chestnut leafminer moth (*Cameraria ohridella*), plus leaf scorch disease and bleeding canker, are threatening horse chestnut trees in the south of the UK.

Aesculus hippocastanum

A. x carnea 'Briottii' *H5* (10m x 6m, U: 20m x 15m) flowers deep pink, glossy leaves. *A. hippocastanum* (horse chestnut) *H5* (10m, U: 25m x 20m) ♨ a handsome, very large tree with white flowers in early summer and conkers in autumn; a form 'Baumannii' has double flowers but no conkers, which might be disappointing. *A. indica* (Indian horse chestnut) *H4* (3–5m, U: 15m x 15m) a fine large tree with pink-flushed flowers in June–July, with bronze new growth and rich autumn colour, inclined to seed too freely round the garden; 'Sydney Pearce' is an outstanding pink-flowered selection. *A. x neglecta* 'Erythroblastos' *H4* (6m x 4m, U: 15m) mainly grown for its leaves which emerge pink, fading to yellow and then green with good autumn colour, rarely flowers (yellow), quite slow growing, suitable for the smaller garden. *A. parviflora* (buckeye) *H4–5* (2–3m) not a tree this one but a multi-stemmed suckering shrub, with white flowers in late summer, bronzy young foliage. *A. pavia H5* (2–3m x 2–3m) a useful shrubby tree suitable for the small garden with bright red flowers and handsome leaves with good autumn colour.

Alnus (alder)

H5 A group of very useful, tough, quick-growing deciduous trees which thrive in poor, wet or waterlogged soil and in exposed sites. They are useful as 'nurse trees', used to protect other less vigorous young trees and then thinned or cut down. They produce showy catkins (best in male forms) in early spring, small cones in autumn, and many have handsome foliage and attractive fissured bark at maturity. Alder are invaluable in windswept areas such as the Outer Hebrides, Orkney and Shetland, where trees are usually hard to establish; try to obtain seedlings of local provenance. Less ornamental species such as *A. rubra* and *A. sinuata* are particularly useful in such climates; the latter has excellent resistance to salt spray.

Alnus glutinosa

A. glutinosa (common alder) *H5* (5–8m x 2–3m, U: 10–15m+) an excellent native tree for wet soils, river and pond banks and bogs, with yellow catkins on the male plants. Forms include 'Aurea' yellow leaves, 'Imperialis' (3–5m) a neat and handsome slow-growing conical tree with deeply cut 'feathery' leaves, 'Laciniata' leaves deeply cut. *A. incana* (grey alder) (6m x 2m, U: 15m) red-yellow catkins in April, leaves greyish beneath; 'Aurea' young shoots and leaves yellow, turning pale green.

Betula (birch)

H5 These are graceful deciduous trees with outstanding handsome white or brown bark, yellow catkins in spring and small, toothed triangular leaves, which usually colour well in autumn. Birches are versatile plants, tolerant of wind and sun, enjoying moist or sandy soil. Some, such as *B. pendula*, can tolerate wet and heavy soils. Most are extremely hardy and suited for almost any Scottish garden, but they may blow down in very windy sites. You can wash white-barked forms with soap and water to keep them shiny and gleaming. The Royal Botanic Garden Edinburgh has a fine collection, as does Auchgourish, near Aviemore. The best choice for Orkney and Shetland is the native *B. pubescens*; the others seem to struggle.

B. albosinensis (5–7m, U: 15–20m+) bark cream at first then pinkish red-brown, peeling; *B.a. var. septentrionalis* bark a marbled effect – orange-brown, peeling to under-layer of pinkish-grey – leaves dull green. *B. alleghaniensis* (syn. *B. lutea*) (5–7m, U: 20m) leaves coated in fine hair, turn bright yellow in early autumn, peeling yellow-brown bark. *B. ermanii* (5–7m, U: 20m) peeling, pinkish white warty bark; 'Grayswood Hill' a fine white-barked selection, 'Polar Bear' often multi-stemmed with fine white bark, leaves heart-shaped. *B. nigra* (red birch) (10m, U: 20m x 12m) wide, spreading habit with pinkish young bark, peeling brown with age, angular leaves with glaucous undersides. *B. papyrifera* (paper birch) (5–7m, U: 20m+) slender upright habit, narrow leaves, yellow in the autumn, white bark peels like papery sheets, very attractive. *B. pendula* (silver birch) (5–7m, U: 18m) ♦ bark silvery white marked with black, yellow autumn-leaf colour, catkins to 6cm. They are often seen with harmless but disfiguring 'witches' brooms', which look like giant birds' nests but are caused by a fungus. Garden forms of silver birch include 'Fastigiata' narrow upright habit, 'Golden Beauty' pale greenish yellow scorch-resistant leaves, 'Laciniata' and 'Dalecarlica' two very attractive forms often confused, both with deeply cut leaves, but only the former has drooping branches, 'Purpurea' (5–10m) purple leaves, tends to lack vigour, 'Tristis' very attractive

Betula pendula 'Golden Beauty'   Betula utilis var. jaquemontii (bark)

Castanea sativa (sweet or Spanish chestnut)

H5 (5–10m, U: 30m) the sweet or Spanish chestnut is a vigorous, deciduous broadly columnar tree with oblong glossy leaves which colour to yellow in autumn, suitable for well-drained soils in full sun. Opening in July, the heavily scented cream flowers are like erect catkins. In their native Mediterranean, they are usually followed by edible chestnuts in a spiny casing, but lack of summer heat means that in Scotland fruiting is rare. There are a number of ancient 'heritage' sweet chestnuts in Scotland, well over 350 years old, most of which look rather bedraggled, though the oldest of all, at 28m in height, and planted in 1550 at Castle Leod, Strathpeffer, Highland, is in fine shape. **'Albomarginata'** white-edged leaves, **'Variegata'** leaves with broad yellow variegation.

pendulous branches, **'Youngii'** dome-shaped habit with weeping branches. *B. pubescens* (3–5m U: 10–20m) ♦ slower growing than silver birch, this is excellent in wet, poorly drained and northern regions, such as Orkney and Shetland. **'Royal Frost'** (3–5m, U: 10m) a form of *B. szechuanica* with purple leaves and white bark, new, but looks promising, said to be the best of this type, *B. utilis* (Himalayan birch) (4–6m, U: 18m) bark colour copper-brown to grey-pink, **'Fascination'**, fine bark and very long catkins, **'Grayswood Ghost'** brilliant white bark, glossy leaves. **Var. jacquemontii** ⚘ the most popular birch for gardens because of the stunning white bark, leaves clear yellow in autumn, good as a multi-stemmed tree, **'Snow Queen'** (syn. 'Doorenbos') bark coppery brown peeling to white, **'Jermyns'** good bark, vigorous, fine long catkins, **'Silver Shadow'** large drooping leaves, very fine bark, quite slow growing.

Catalpa bignonioides (Indian bean tree) and *Paulownia tormentosa* (foxglove tree)

H3–4 (2–3m as shrub, 5–10m+ as tree) The striking Indian bean tree has handsome leaves and a fantastic name. In theory, it produces white foxglove-like flowers with yellow and purple markings in late summer, but you will have to wait 25 years or more for them to appear and they only appear following a sustained warm summer. They are followed by the characteristic long hanging seed pods. There are fine examples of catalpa in the Culzean walled garden in Ayrshire, and at Ardmaddy in Argyll. In all but the warmest parts of Scotland, catalpas are probably better coppiced (cut back hard) or stooled (cut down to ground) in winter, and kept as shrubs. The spectacular, large, heart-shaped leaves, which do not appear until June, need a sheltered site to look their best. **'Variegata'** leaves marked with creamy white, **'Aurea'** leaves yellow-green. *C. x erubescens* **'Purpurea'** young shoots and leaves dark purple.

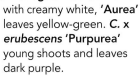

Carpinus betulus (hornbeam)

H5 (5–10m, U: 25m) An excellent choice for Scotland, this tough deciduous tree, related to birch, has distinctive ribbed leaves which turn yellow and orange in autumn, and green catkins followed by winged nuts. It is suitable for a wide range of soils, including chalk and clay, and is quite commonly used for hedging (plant 40–60cm apart and top at 2.5–4m or more) and pleaching (training). **'Fastigiata'** and **'Frans Fontaine'** are handsome forms, both with a narrow fastigiate habit.

Carpinus betulus

Catalpa bignoniodes 'Aurea'

Castanea sativa

Paulownia tomentosa (foxglove tree) Has similarly large leaves and produces large foxglove-shaped purple flowers in summer, but like catalpa, it much prefers a warmer climate than we can provide.

Cotoneaster (tree forms) see page 45

Crataegus (hawthorn, snow in May)

H5 As well as the well-known native hawthorns of hedgerows, this genus contains many excellent tough deciduous garden trees with fine early-summer flowers and sometimes showy red autumn berries (haws).

Crataegus laeviegata
'Crimson Cloud'

Crataegus monogyna (berries)

'Don't cast a clout [discard your winter clothing] 'til May is out' refers to the seasonal opening of the massed, white, sweetly fragrant hawthorn flowers – a traditional herald of summer proper and source of its other common name, snow in May. Most have sharp thorns, which make them challenging to cut as hedges, and not much fun to tread on barefoot on lawns. Grows best in sun, but otherwise tolerant of most soils and conditions: wind, seaside, heavy soils. They make superb fully hardy (**H5**) shelterbelt plants in coastal or exposed inland areas. They also make very attractive relatively compact specimen trees. Heights and spreads are similar, unless stated otherwise.

C. arnoldiana (3m, U: 5–8m) white flowers, lobed leaves, showy cherry-like red fruit. **C. crus-galli** (3–4m, U: 8m x 10m) white flowers with pink anthers in June, fine red berries. **C. laevigata** (Midland hawthorn) (3–4m, U: 5–8m) clusters of white, pink or red flowers in May, red haws, usually grown as the following cultivars, which produce little or no fruit: **'Crimson Cloud'** crimson with white-yellow eye, **'Paul's Scarlet'** double scarlet, **'Plena'** double white, **'Rosea Flore Plena'** double pink. **C. monogyna** ♦ the common hawthorn makes an attractive tree, or a thorny hedge, with good autumn colour and shiny dark-red berries which are very valuable food for birds and animals; for hedging, space 40–60cm apart. **C. persimilis** 'Prunifolia' (3–5m, U: 8m x 10m) handsome shiny leaves, orange-red berries and good autumn colour, suitable for hedging and security barriers.

Davidia involucrata
(handkerchief or dove tree)
H5 (5–10m or more) ✱ Introducing this famous Chinese tree was the main goal of plant hunter Ernest Wilson's 1899 expedition. Fairly slow growing, with a domed crown, it can get very large in time and is mainly grown for the white bracts that hang down below the tiny white flowers in May–June – although you may have to wait 10 years or more to see the first ones. It grows best in a sheltered, sunny site in moist but not boggy soil: it dislikes

Davidia involucrata

drying out in summer. There is a beautiful specimen at The Crichton in Dumfries and two at Glendoick.

Eucalyptus
(gum tree)
'They remind me of old ladies washing their hair', the late and colourful Tory MP Nicky Fairburn once remarked to me (KC) about eucalyptus on a tour of Glendoick. I've never forgotten it. Only a small number of these well-known Australian trees do well in Scotland; the rest are too tender or need more summer heat. Dundee Botanic Garden has groves of the hardier species, while Crarae and Arduaine in Argyll, and Logan, in Dumfries and Galloway, have fine collections of the more tender ones. Eucalyptus are well worth growing for their attractive grey-blue leaves and fine peeling bark, though they have a tendency to grow too fast and then blow over. After 10–15 years, the trees may bloom with creamy-white flowers. The leaves of most species, apart from *E. gunnii*, taste horrible to rabbits and deer. Menthol derived from the leaves is used to treat colds and flu. The roots can damage foundations, so keep them away from buildings. The juvenile foliage is bigger and brighter than the mature foliage, and at Glendoick we found that cutting them back hard was a good option, producing more bushy, multi-stemmed trees and more persistent juvenile leaves. It is suggested that this should be done at a height of about 1m, or at ground level.

The hardiest species are **E. coccifera H4** (10–15m) white to white-grey bark, **E. dalrympleana H3(–4)** (15–20m) creamy-white bark, **E. gunnii H4** (10–20m) whitish-green bark shedding to reveal

Eucalyptus gunnii (young growth)

Eucalyptus pauciflora subsp. *niphophila* (bark)

greyish-green young bark, blue juvenile foliage fading to dusty green, *E. pauciflora* subsp. *niphophila H4* (4–6m) ✤ narrow, long, thick leaves, and fine, striped brown and white bark, probably the best choice for Scotland. Other species will grow in mildest west-coast and island gardens.

Fagus sylvatica (beech)

H5 Thought to have been introduced by the Romans, beech is one of Britain's most majestic deciduous trees as well as a very popular hedging plant. Turning a fine golden yellow in autumn, it also produces one of the largest and densest leaf canopies, making beech woods very dark places, in which nothing much grows at ground level after spring. Gardening under beech trees is therefore very hard work, as few plants will grow. Requiring a well-drained but moist soil in reasonable sunshine, it's a very tough plant, generally suitable for anywhere in the UK apart from very windy sites. Beeches tend to thrive for 250 years and then go into terminal decline, with limbs falling and trunk rotting. Although technically deciduous, juvenile beech hedges with regular clipping retain the brown leaves often well into spring, which is useful for privacy. Plant 30–60cm apart for a hedge typically 2m tall, and prune annually in summer. Let the beech hedge at Meikleour, Perthshire, be a warning of what can happen if you forget to prune: it's now the world's tallest hedge at 30m.

F. sylvatica (green beech) (6m x 3m, U: 25m x 15m) ✤ with bright-green young leaves, turning to dark green, golden to copper in autumn. There are numerous fine selections: **'Asplenifolia'** (fern-leaved beech) leaves narrow, deeply cut, **'Dawyck'** (Dawyck beech) ✤ a narrow columnar tree to 7m,

Fagus sylvatica Purpurea Group

Fagus sylvatica 'Dawyck Gold'

originally discovered at Dawyck, near Peebles, **'Dawyck Gold'** (10–15m) columnar habit with bright-yellow young leaves, pale green through the summer, **'Dawyck Purple'** narrow columnar habit to about 10m with deep purple leaves, **'Pendula'** (weeping beech) (5m, U: 18m x 10m+) forming curtains of hanging branches which can root into the soil, **Purpurea Group** (copper

beech) (6m x 3m, U: 25m x 15m) leaves first appear copper brown in spring, become purple in summer, copper yellow in autumn, a large magnificent tree especially with the sun rising or setting behind. Forms of copper beech include **'Purple Fountain'** (5m) slender habit, purple-leaved, weeping branches, **'Purpurea Pendula'** (5m) attractive purple-leaved small weeping tree, **'Riversii'** (5m) large, handsome, deep purple leaves, the best of the purple-leaved forms, **'Rohanii'** (5–8m, U: 20m) narrow, deeply cut, fern-like purple leaves, fading to purplish green. **'Zlatia'** (5–8m, U: 20m) slow growing, golden-yellow young leaves turning to bright green.

Fraxinus (ash)

H4–5 Ash are fast-growing deciduous trees tolerant of most soils and can be used for screening: most are not suitable for small gardens, as they are so vigorous and greedy that other plants struggle to grow beneath them. They can be coppiced to keep them under control. The opposite pinnate leaves are easily recognized, as are the 'keys' or bunches of seeds, which stand out in winter hanging from the bare branches. The flowers are insignificant except in *F. ornus*. A devastating disease *Chalara fraxinea* (ash dieback) arrived in the UK in 2012-2013 and is likely to spread to most parts in the next few years. It is usually fatal and could potentially do for ash like Dutch elm disease did for elms. For more details see www.forestry.gov.uk/chalara.

Fraxinus excelsior 'Pendula' at Threave

Fraxinus seeds or 'keys'

F. angustifolia **'Raywood'** *H4* (5–8m, U: 20m) compact, leaves reddish purple in autumn. *F. americanum* **'Autumn Purple'** *H5* similar to *F.a.* 'Raywood' but broader crown and darker leaves. *F. excelsior* (common ash) *H5* (10m, U: 20–30m) ♦ dark-green leaves, black buds; **'Aurea Pendula'** (3–6m) small weeping tree, yellow autumn colour, **'Jaspidea'** (5m, U: 10–15m) young shoots and winter twigs yellow, **'Pendula'** (weeping ash) (10–15m+ x 5–10m) long shoots to the ground, less vigorous. *F. ornus* **'Obelisk'** *H4* (3m) a compact form of manna ash with fine fluffy scented white flowers in early summer.

Gleditsia triacanthos 'Sunburst'
see *Robinia pseudoacacia* 'Frisia', page 139

Juglans regia
(walnut)
H3–4 (10m, U: 20–30m)

Juglans regia (walnut)

Walnuts form handsome deciduous trees, worth growing for the pinnate leaves, bronzy when young, turning greyish, and the catkins. Ripe, edible walnuts are rare in Scotland except in hot summers such as that of 2006, and we find that grey squirrels get most of them before we do. If you want regular cropping, it might be worth growing them against a south- or west-facing wall. Grow in sun in deep fertile, well-drained soil in a sheltered site; not suitable for inland gardens and frost pockets. Damage to growth and bark can lead to fungal disease such as coral spot. **'Buccaneer'** and **'Broadview'** are self-fertile; most other clones need to be grown in pairs if they are to set fruit/nuts.

Laburnum
H5 ☠ Most people are familiar with laburnum's long pendulous golden-yellow flowers in May–June, hanging from the branches of a vigorous deciduous tree, with pea-like seed pods usually forming in late summer. Laburnums need well-drained soil in full sun. All parts of the plants, particularly the seeds, are poisonous. They are prone to various diseases (especially bacterial canker), but they will usually regenerate if diseased branches are cut out. Cawdor Castle, Nairn, has a fine laburnum walk surrounding its maze. Those listed form small, usually weeping trees and are fully hardy (*H5*).

Laburnum watereri 'Vossii'

L. alpinum 'Pendulum' (2–3m, U: 4–6m) long, drooping clusters of lightly scented yellow, pea-like flowers in early June; usually top-grafted and weeping from this height. **L. anagyroides** (2–3m, U: 6–8m) bright yellow, less widely available than the forms below, but the best performer in the far north, including Orkney and Shetland. **L. x watereri 'Vossii'** (2–3m, U: 4–6m) ☒ trailing clusters of golden-yellow flowers in June; few seeds are produced.

Liquidambar styraciflua (sweet gum)
H4 (3–5m, U: 10–20m) At their best these are handsome deciduous trees with distinctive maple-like foliage and very fine red and purple autumn colour. Unfortunately mild and damp Scottish autumns tend to encourage late growth, which is often frosted before it colours up, especially in inland gardens, and we also find them subject to snow breakage and wind damage. The greenish-yellow flowers are inconspicuous and the bark is ridged and corky. **'Lane Roberts'** deep-red autumn colour, possibly the most reliable, **'Silver King'** leaves

margined white, **'Variegata'** leaves mottled and striped yellow, **'Worplesdon'** leaves with narrow lobes, orange and yellow in autumn.

The other *Liquidambar* species are less widely grown.

Liquidambar styraciflua

Liriodendron tulipifera (tulip tree)
H4 (5–10m, U: 20m+) The distinctive leaves of this statuesque deciduous specimen tree look as if they have been chopped off at the ends. The tulip-like, pale greenish-white flowers are produced only on mature trees and usually only after hot summers. It can have fine yellow autumn colour, and tends to prefer a sheltered, fairly warm site There are fine specimens at the Hirsel in the Borders and the House of Pitmuies in Angus.

Liriodendron tulipifera

'Aureomarginatum' leaves with yellow margins, can be pruned to keep as a shrub, **'Fastigiatum'** a selection with a narrow erect habit.

Malus (crab apple)
H5 Although only a few varieties produce edible fruit suitable for jelly making, there are a huge variety of ornamental malus with showy flowers and ornamental fruit of various colours, which make fine trees for small and larger gardens. Five-petalled, usually fragrant, white, pink or near red flowers open in April, May or June, followed by long-lasting reddish, orange or yellow fruit

in autumn. The dark-flowered varieties contrast very well with the paler flowering cherries (*Prunus*). Some varieties also produce fine autumn-leaf colours. Best planted in at least part day sun, they can tolerate light or heavy but not waterlogged soils. For the varieties suitable for making into jelly, fruit flavour is best if the fruit is allowed to remain on the tree until after first frosts. Malus are subject to scab, a fungal disease which covers the fruit, leaves and twigs in grey scabby layers and is particularly severe in damp weather. Many modern varieties are very resistant (marked here RR) or fairly resistant (R) to scab. Malus varieties are sometimes grafted on to a dwarfing (M27) rootstock, which will restrict the height to around 2m. M27 trees need extra care, careful staking and good drainage, and they should be clearly labelled at a garden centre or nursery. Many crab apples make excellent pollinating partners for eating and cooking apples, which is useful if space is at a premium. All listed are fully hardy (**H5**), and heights are similar to spreads, unless stated otherwise.

Admiration ['Adirondack'] (3m) (RR) a fine dwarf disease-resistant variety with white flowers in April and long-lasting bronzy-red fruits. ***M. baccata*** (3–5m, U: 10–15m) (RR) one of the most vigorous varieties, white flowers in April, fruit red or yellow. **'Butterball'** (6m) (RR) white flowers, yellow fruit, spreading, arching branches. **'Coral Burst'** (1–2m) (RR) very dwarf, double pink with darker reserve, small bronze fruit, suitable for patio. **Coccinella** ['Courtarou'] (3–4m, U: 5–7m) (RR) flowers purple-pink, purple leaves, fruits crimson, good scab and fireblight resistance. ***M. coronaria* var. *dasycalyx* 'Charlottae'** (5–9m) large, semi-double, shell pink-violet, scented flowers, leaves turning red in autumn, large green fruit, somewhat prone to canker. **'Donald Wyman'** (5–8m) (R) white flowers, the longest lasting of all in fruit, which are small and red. **'Evelyn'** (*M. ioensis*) single, pink very fragrant flowers, purple leaves, very good autumn colour. **'Evereste'** (4–7m x 3–6m) outstanding, flowers pale pink to white in April–May, long lasting, small orange-yellow fruits, often used as a pollinator for apples. ***M. floribunda*** (5–10m) red buds open to pale pink-white flowers on a spreading bush, masses of yellow fruits, unfortunately very susceptible to scab, so does best in the east. **'Golden Gem'** (5–9m) masses of sweetly scented pure-white flowers in April, long-lasting small yellow fruit, a good apple pollinator. **'Golden Hornet'** (*M. zumi*) (4–7m+) ✤ (R) a popular old favourite with white flowers in spring followed by large bright yellow fruits. **'Gorgeous'** (3–5m) (R) pure-white flowers, glossy red fruit, slow growing. **'Harry Baker'** (5–9m) (RR) large dark-pink flowers, large ruby-red fruit, very good for making jelly. ***M. hupehensis*** (5–9m) a vigorous spreading tree with fragrant white flowers and red, cherry-like fruit. **'Hyde Hall Spire'** (2–3m), columnar habit, green-yellow fruit, **'John Downie'** (6–8m) ✤ white flowers, bright orange and red fruits, the most popular variety for jelly making, but susceptible to scab. **'Laura'** (3–5m) a dwarf with fastigiate habit, two-tone pink and white flowers, purple leaves and maroon fruit good for making jelly, a

Malus 'Golden Hornet'

Malus 'John Downie'

Malus 'Royalty'

Malus 'Sun Rival'

little scab susceptible. **'Liset'** (4–6m) (R) purple young growth, reddish-pink flowers, small blood-red fruits, the most disease resistant of this type. **'Profusion'** (4m) leaves purple fading to bronzy, dark purple-pink flowers, small cherry-like reddish-purple fruit, subject to canker and mildew. **'Red Obelisk'** (6m) (RR) white to pink flowers, red spring foliage, red fruit, narrow upright habit, good disease resistance. **'Red Sentinel'** (4–7m) white flowers, very persistent, long-lasting deep-red fruits in large clusters, used for Christmas decoration. **'Royal Beauty'** (2–2.5m) a small weeping tree with copper-red young growth, deep pink-purple flowers, small dark-red fruits, prone to canker and scab. **'Royalty'** (4–7m) dark-purple leaves and flowers, but subject to disease and no longer recommended. **'Cardinal'** (R) is similar but more disease resistant. **'Scarlett'**® (to 5m) shiny purple young growth, vivid orange/red in autumn, deep-pink flowers. ***M. x scheideckeri* 'Red Jade'** (2–4 x 6m) a weeping tree, white flowers, flushed pale pink, small red fruits, prone to scab. **'Snowcloud'** double white flowers, a few yellow fruits, narrow, upright habit. **'Sun Rival'** (3m) (RR) probably the best weeping crab apple, semi-weeping habit, pink buds opening to white, bright red fruits, very disease resistant. ***M. toringoides*** (syn. *M. bhutanica*) (4–8m) creamy-white flowers in May, fruits, red or yellow. ***M. tschonoskii*** (4–6m, U: 12m) large single white-tinged-pink flowers in May, sometimes produces small greenish-yellow fruits, downy young leaves, fine red and yellow autumn colour (hence the nickname bonfire), rather subject to scab.

Nothofagus (southern beech)

Originating from Chile and Tasmania, nothofagus are fine and handsome trees, not that widely planted in gardens but suitable for much of Scotland. They do particularly well in Argyll: Crarae has a national collection, Benmore in Argyll has a hillside of them, and Stonefield Castle Hotel garden on the Kintyre peninsula has some of the UK's biggest. They seem very well suited to Shetland and could be more widely grown in the Western Isles. They can reach over 30m in their native habitats, but in cultivation they are smaller. They grow best in moist western gardens and in the east not too far from the coast. Inland they tend to have young growth frosted. They include some elegant evergreens, as well as some of the UK's finest autumn-colouring deciduous garden trees (Sheffield Park in Sussex is set on fire every year by them). The flowers and fruit are inconspicuous.

N. antarctica H4–5 (5–10m+) deciduous with yellow autumn colour, the most widely and hardiest grown species, herringbone-like branches, irregular habit, often with a twisted trunk. *N. dombeyi H3–4* (5–10m+) evergreen with finely toothed leaves. *N. obliqua H4–5* (5–10m+) deciduous, yellow and red autumn-leaf tints, vigorous.

Paulownia tomentosa see
Catalpa bignonioides, page 131

Platanus (plane)

H5 Planes are large, hardy deciduous trees, making fine specimens for parkland and also urban squares and wide streets. They have attractive maple-like leaves, and insignificant flowers, followed by small spiky fruits. Some have striking flaking bark on the trunk, giving a mottled effect. Planes tolerate most soils, except waterlogged ones.

Platanus x hispanica

P. x hispanica (London plane) *H5* (10m, U: 30m) a common street tree, particularly in London, well known for its fine bark with dark and light patches – a bit like the fur of a piebald horse. *P. orientalis* (10m, U: 30m) deeply lobed dark green leaves, sometimes with red autumn colour.

Platanus orientalis

Populus alba

Populus x candicans 'Aurora'

Populus (poplar)

H5 Poplars are large, tough, versatile deciduous trees which make good shelterbelt planting for large gardens. They are suitable for almost any soil as long as it is not waterlogged. Poplars grow very fast, and have invasive root systems, which can break foundations and drains, causing problems near houses or roads unless they are hard pruned or pollarded to keep them in check. They are often planted in rows for large hedges or to mark field boundaries. Some varieties are susceptible to the sometimes fatal disease bacterial canker. Poplar rust, and poplar leaf and shoot blights, can also cause problems.

P. alba (5–10m, U: 30m) leaves grey-green with a white, woolly underside, yellow in autumn, suckering, leaves make an attractive rustling sound in the wind; *P.a. 'Richardii'* a slow-growing yellow-leaved form often grown as a shrub by hard pruning each winter. *P. x candicans* (syn. *P. x jackii*) *'Aurora'* (5–10m+, but usually pollarded to keep as a shrub) like the hostess trolley, this plant is a symbol of 1970s suburban hell; the heart-shaped balsam-scented young leaves are splashed pink and white, turning green in summer, susceptible to canker. *P. nigra* (10m, U: 25m+) glossy leaves, strong ascending branches forming a dome; *P.n. 'Italica'* (Lombardy poplar) columnar habit, prone to fungal disease. *P. tremula* (aspen) (5m, U: 20m+) ♦ a Scottish native with grey-green leaves that rustle in the wind, long grey catkins in early spring, usually yellow autumn colour, tends to be relatively short lived but regenerates with numerous suckers; very useful in the Northern Isles, as it is good in wind and salt spray.

Prunus (flowering cherries, almonds, etc.)

H4–5 Flowering cherries and almonds have the 'ahh' factor, which makes them some of the most popular garden trees. The masses of pink or white flowers in spring, usually on bare branches, may not last long, but they are certainly spectacular. Many varieties are slow growing or weeping, and are suitable for small gardens or containers; some are fragrant, some have coloured foliage and good autumn colour, and a few have attractive bark. Some also make good hedging plants – there are beautiful purple cherry plum hedges at Crathes Castle in Aberdeenshire, House of Pitmuies in Angus and Earlshall in Fife, and the town of Helensburgh in Argyll and Bute is an unforgettable sight in spring, when the streets are lined with pink cherry blossom. All prunus grow best in full sun and well-drained soil, and they tend not to live long in peaty west-coast gardens with high rainfall. Almonds (*P. dulcis*) particularly require a warm, sheltered spot. The main downside of *Prunus* is their susceptibility to silver leaf and bacterial canker, which causes dieback and is sometimes fatal. Both enter the tree through weather damage or pruning scars and it is important to keep such damage to a minimum by providing wind shelter and keeping pruning to a minimum (it is best done in summer). The toughest are probably the native cherries and *P. serrula*. Many are grafted and prone to suckering, particularly where roots rise just beneath a lawn surface. Suckers should be cut out with a clean, sharp pair of secateurs. There are hundreds of varieties, and only the most popular are covered here. They are fully hardy (*H5*) unless stated otherwise.

Prunus 'Accolade'

Prunus 'Amanogawa'

Flowering cherries

'**Accolade**' (2m, U: 6–8m) semi-double, deep pink in March–April, good autumn colour. '**Amanogawa**' (2.5m, U: 8m) a narrow, erect tree, useful for confined spaces, semi-double, slightly fragrant, slightly muddy pale-pink flowers in late April–early May, bronze young growth, leaves prone to shot hole. *P. avium* (gean,

Prunus 'Cheal's Weeping'

Prunus incisa 'Kojo-no-mai'

wild cherry) *H5* (4m, U: 15–20m x 10m) ♦ a large Scottish native tree with white flowers in April–May, sometimes produces deep-red cherries, leaves red and yellow in autumn, also useful as a hedgerow plant as far north as Orkney; '**Plena**' is a form with double pure-white flowers. '**Chocolate Ice**' (syn. 'Matsumae-fuki') (3–5m) single white, with bronze young growth. *P. incisa* (Fuji cherry) (3m, U: 6m) pink buds open to small white-pink-flushed flowers in March, leaves sharply toothed, a large shrub or small tree, suitable for the small garden and often pruned after flowering to keep shape, most have good autumn colour; forms include '**Kojo-no-mai**' (1m or less) with zigzagging shoots and pale-pink flowers in April, popular for containers, '**Praecox**' early, opens in February, '**Shôgetsu**' (syn. 'Blushing Bride') semi-double white, '**Snow Showers**' (1–2m) usually top-grafted, weeping, with pure-white flowers in April–May, '**The Bride**' white with red anthers. **Fragrant Cloud** ['Shizuka'] (3–5m, U: 7–8m) large white semi-double fragrant flowers in May, vigorous. '**Kanzan**' (3m, U: 6–10m x 6–10m) some of the largest cherry flowers, purple-pink to 5cm across, in April; this is a very popular tree, not withstanding its vulgar Barbara Cartland qualities; leaves are coppery red when they unfurl, fading to green, yellow in autumn. '**Kiku-shidare-zakura**' or '**Cheal's Weeping**' (2m, U: 4m) one of the most popular weeping forms, with arching branches, excellent for a small garden, double, deep-pink flowers, 4cm across, in April, young growth bronzy. '**Kursar**' (2.5m, U: 5m) clusters of small deep-pink flowers in early April, long leaves, bronzy when young, good autumn colour, as has its seedling '**Collingwood Ingram**' with deeper flowers. '**Okame**' (2.5m, U: 5m) small carmine flowers in March, longer lasting than most, leaves reddish in autumn. *P. padus* (bird cherry) (3m, U: 10m) ♦ small almond-scented white flowers in pendent racemes in May, bitter black fruits popular with birds; the form '**Watereri**' has longer-than-normal flower spikes. '**Pandora**' (2.5m, U: 6m) single large shell-pink flowers in March–April on ascending branches, young growth bronze red, often good autumn colour. *P. pendula* (2–2.5m) weeping, forming an umbrella-shaped tree, often top-grafted to keep it small; '**Pendula Rosea**' tiny blush-pink flowers in March–April; '**Pendula Rubra**' single deep carmine-rose flowers in March–April. '**Pink Perfection**' (3m, U: 6m) ascending

Prunus 'Royal Burgundy'

Prunus x subhirtella 'Autumnalis Rosea'

Prunus 'Taihaku'

Prunus serrula (bark)

habit forming a vase-shaped tree with double pale-pink flowers in clusters in April–May, young leaves bronze. **'Royal Burgundy'** a form of 'Kanzan' with purple-bronze leaves. *P. sargentii* (3m, U: 15–20m x 10–15m) ♛ large, with clusters of single pink flowers in March–April, young leaves bronze red, good autumn colour, attractive chestnut-brown bark. *P. serrula* (2.5m, U: 5m) ♛ small single white flowers in May, mainly grown for its outstanding spectacular reddish-brown peeling bark; the House of Pitmuies, Angus has fine examples. **'Shirofugen'** (3m, U: 8–10m) long-lasting double white, ageing to pink in April–May, young leaves coppery, good autumn colour. **'Shirotae'** (syn. 'Mount Fuji') (2m x 2m, U: 4m x 4m) fragrant white flowers in long clusters in April, feathery leaves, spreading or weeping habit. **'Shôgetsu'** (2m x 2.5m, U: 5m x 8m) semi-double fringed white flowers in April–May, feathery leaves, spreading habit. **'Spire'** (3m, U: 10m) upright vase-like habit, clusters of pale pink flowers in April, good autumn colour. *P. x subhirtella* **'Autumnalis'** (3m, U: 8 x 8m) ♛ a popular autumn- and winter-flowering cherry with masses of small pale-pink flowers in mild spells from November to March; *P. x s.* **'Autumnalis Rosea'** ♛ deeper semi-double pink flowers. **'Taihaku'** (great white cherry) (3m, U: 8m x 10m) the Rolls-Royce of cherries, stunning large single pure white flowers in April–May, young leaves coppery red; Glendoick has the oldest in Scotland.

'Ukon' (2.5m, U: 7m) flowers large semi-double cream, tinged green, in April, bronzy young leaves, red-purplish in autumn. *P. x yedoensis* (syn. 'Yoshino') (3m, U: 12m x 8–10m) clusters of lightly scented, pale-pink to blush-white flowers March–April, spreading with arching branches; *P. x y.* **'Shidare-yoshino'** (3m) pale pink, weeping habit.

Flowering almonds, peaches, plums

Mostly smaller growing and shrubbier than the cherries; many are popular in containers. *P. x blireana* (2m, U: 4m x 4m) a good choice for the small garden, double pink in April, coppery-purple leaves. *P. cerasifera* (cherry plum) usually sold as coloured-leaved forms, which are often used as hedging; **'Hessei'** (2–3m) small white flowers in March, leaves pale green, becoming bronze-purple splashed creamy white, yellowish or pink on the edges, shrubby habit; **'Nigra'** (3–5m) ♛ small pink flowers, March–April, leaves and stems blackish purple, turning bronze purple, also makes a good specimen tree, **'Pissardii'** (purple-leaved plum) (3–5m) single pale pink-white flowers in March–April, leaves dark red to deep purple. *P. x cistena* (2m) similar to *P.c.* 'Pissardii' and often used for hedging, with white flowers and dark-red leaves. *P. glandulosa* (Chinese bush cherry) pink; **'Alba Plena'** (1.5m) double white, a small rounded shrub, needs a warm site, often grafted on half- or quarter-standard stems.

Pyrus salicifolia 'Pendula'

Pyrus
(ornamental pears)
With masses of small white flowers, silvery leaves and often good autumn colour, these are popular garden plants, hardy and tolerant of drought and most soils. The silver weeping pear (*P. salicifolia* 'Pendula') is a very versatile large shrub or small tree, which can be clipped into formal globes or domes, or left as a weeping specimen. An Cala garden, on the Isle of Seil, and the House of Pitmuies in Angus, have good examples.

P. calleryana 'Chanticleer' (5m, U: 15m) a vigorous tree forming a tall narrow column, white flowers in March–April, green leaves, colouring red-purple in autumn. *P. salicifolia* 'Pendula' (silver weeping pear) (3–5m x 3–5m, U: 10m) ♛ small creamy-white flowers in April, willow-like silvery leaves, forming a dense mound of weeping branches. Similar, but more free-flowering, is *P. elaeagnifolia* 'Silver Sails' (syn. *P. kotschyana*) with erect thorny branches and greyish leaves.

Quercus (oak)
H3–5 Apart from a few evergreen species, the majority of

oaks are large-growing deciduous trees that need plenty of room. Scotland's two native oak species, *Q. petraea* and *Q. robur*, provide some of our mightiest native trees. They have been recorded at well over 500 years of age and occasionally as much as 1,000 years old, but most of the original forests were felled for timber. The old saying goes that it takes an oak tree 200 years to grow, 200 years to mature and 200 years to die. There are still a few remnants of the Cadzow Oaks, at Hamilton High Parks in Lanarkshire, and a fabulous collection of sessile oak (*Q. petraea*) at Cawdor Castle near Nairn. Most oaks have distinctive lobed leaves, inconspicuous flowers and hard little acorns that can give you a sore head in autumn if you stand beneath the trees. Oak powdery mildew can often cover new shoots and can stall growth in young trees, but rarely causes long-term damage.

Quercus coccinea

Quercus frainetto

Quercus ilex (bark) at Logan

Quercus robur 'Concordia'

Q. cerris (turkey oak) *H4* (5–10m, U: 30m) the fastest-growing oak for the UK, good for seaside and inland, with rough lobed leaves and acorns on mature trees; '**Argenteovariegata**' leaves with conspicuous creamy edges – striking and in very bad taste! *Q. coccinea* (scarlet oak) *H3* (U: 8–10m x 4–6m) glossy, deeply lobed, dark green leaves, often turning a glowing scarlet in the autumn, deciduous, insignificant flowers, fast growing, autumn colour in acid soil in full sun; the form '**Splendens**' has particularly fine scarlet autumn colour. *Q. frainetto H4–5* (5–8m, U: 25–30m) multi-lobed, large leathery leaves. *Q. ilex* (evergreen oak) *H3–4* (6m x 5m, U: 30m) an evergreen oak with holly-like dark-green, leathery leaves, shiny above, dusty below; yellow catkins in June, followed by small acorns; not suitable for cold and inland gardens, good for coastal planting. *Q. palustris* (pin oak) *H5* (5–10m, U: 30m) deeply lobed, glossy leaves, usually red in autumn, slender branches drooping at the tips, tolerates wet soil. *Q. petraea* (sessile oak) *H5* (4–6m, U: 20–30m) ♦ a long-lived native tree, most common in the west of Scotland and excellent in coastal areas, large leaves, acorns without stalks. *Q. robur* (English oak) *H5* (4–6m, U: 20–30m x 30m) ♦ ❦ despite the common name, this is also native to Scotland, particularly in the east; most ancient oak trees are this species, leaves orange in autumn; forms include '**Concordia**' (3–5m) a small slow-growing tree, leaves bright yellow young growth, turning yellow-green, **f. fastigiata** '**Koster**' narrow columnar habit. *Q. rubra* (red oak) *H5* (5–10m, U: 30m x 20m) ❦ large-lobed leaves, usually reddish in autumn, fast growing, smooth trunk; '**Aurea**' (3m, U: 15m) yellow-green leaves, inclined to sunburn.

Robinia pseudoacacia 'Frisia'
and *Gleditsia triacanthos* 'Sunburst'

H3–4 (3–5m, U: 10m+) *Robinia pseudoacacia* 'Frisia' is an attractive tree with golden pinnate leaves and pea-like fragrant, white flowers in summer if there is sufficient heat. It is better suited to hotter and drier climates than Scotland. Give it a warm sheltered site with well-drained soil. It makes a small garden specimen tree and is very popular in the south of England. The brittle branches can be damaged in windy weather.

Robinia pseudoacacia 'Frisia'

Gleditsia triacanthos '**Sunburst**' *H3–4* (3–5m, U: 10–12m) A fast-growing tree with bright-yellow young growth, fading to pale green in summer, colouring to yellow in autumn. The white flowers are insignificant. Very common in southern England as a suburban garden tree, but less popular in Scotland, where it needs a well-drained sunny site.

Salix (willow)

H(4–)5 These tough, versatile, often very vigorous deciduous trees have fluffy catkins in early spring and are suitable for most soils. Many are excellent for wet areas, ponds and riverbanks, and can grow in sun or part shade.

The combination of the new growth and catkins in spring gives a wonderful pale yellow-green effect, which stands out well against a dark background. Some willows are susceptible to willow scab and rusts, which can make the late summer leaves rather unsightly. Dieback caused by cankers and insect attacks are also possible. For the shrubby willows, see page 101. All are fully hardy (*H5*) unless stated otherwise.

Salix x sepulcralis var. *chrysocoma*

Salix caprea 'Kilmarnock' ('Pendula')

S. alba (4–6m x 2–3m, U: 20m) slender, yellow-green drooping branches, narrow, pointed silvery leaves, slender catkins in spring; **'Aurea'** bright-yellow leaves, slow growing and usually pruned as a shrub, var. *vitellina* young shoots orange-yellow, usually cut back hard in spring to keep as a shrub; **'Britzensis'** (syn. 'Chermesina') orange-red winter branches. **S. babylonica** var. *pekinensis* **'Tortuosa'** (syn. *S. matsudana* 'Tortuosa') (contorted willow) (2–5m+) pale-green leaves, twisted stems which stand out in winter. **S. caprea** **'Kilmarnock'** (syn. *S. caprea* 'Pendula') (goat, pussy or Kilmarnock willow) (1–3m+) dark-green leaves, greyish below, usually grafted on a stem 1–2m in height, from which it weeps with stiffly pendulous branches. **'Erythroflexuosa'** (syn. 'Golden Curls') *H4–5* (2–5m x 2–5m) pale-green curled leaves on twisted, pendulous orange-yellow shoots very effective in winter, needs well-drained soil. **S. pentandra** (3–10m) a spreading bushy tree, oval leaves, catkins produced after the leaves in spring, good in Shetland. **S. x sepulcralis** var. *chrysocoma* (5m x 5m, U: 15m x 15m) the well-known golden weeping willow often found at river- and pondsides; the long thin yellow shoots cascade down to the ground, with narrow bright-green leaves and yellow catkins in spring; very vigorous, not suitable for small gardens, and the thirsty invasive roots can wreak havoc with drains and foundations.

Sophora see page 103

Sorbus (rowan)

If there is one tree more than any other suited for Scottish gardens large and small, it has to be sorbus. Our native

Sorbus aria 'Lutescens'

rowan (*S. aucuparia*), with its familiar red berries, is one of a huge number of sorbus that can be grown in Scotland. Apart from the ground-covering *S. reducta*, sorbus are small to medium-sized trees with attractive deciduous foliage, and most have bunches of long-lasting fruits in autumn, which can last for months at a time of year when gardens often need colour. Dawyck, near Peebles, St Andrews Botanic Garden in Fife and Ardchattan Priory in Argyll all have fine collections.

Sorbus like moist but well-drained soil and suffer in drought, especially when young. They can be divided into two groups: those with entire leaves (Aria section) and those with pinnate leaves, divided into many pairs of small leaflets (Aucuparia and Micromeles sections). All listed are fully hardy (*H5*), unless stated otherwise.

Aria section (whitebeam)
H5 (4–6m x 2–4m, U: 15–25m) Now removed to their own genus by some authorities, but still *Sorbus* to most people, the whitebeams are distinguished be their entire leaves, which are characterized by silvery-white undersides that flash in the wind. They grow well as far north as Orkney and Shetland with some shelter.
S. aria a multi-stemmed tree with young growth and leaf underside silvery white, leaves yellow in autumn, small creamy flowers in spring, red berries; **'Lutescens'** ⚘ a popular choice, conical habit when young and orange-red berries, **'Majestica'** relatively large leaves, **'Chrysophylla'** less vigorous with yellow young growth. **S. intermedia** (4–6m, U: 7–10m) young growth silvery, orange-red fruit. **S. thibetica** **'John Mitchell'** almost rounded leaves, fruit orange-yellow.

Aucuparia and Micromeles sections
H5 Most of the trees in this section have tiny pinnate leaves, casting relatively little shade, so they are good for underplanting with other shrubs and perennials and some of the best trees to grow with rhododendrons. They all produce a mass of tiny white-cream flowers in May and

June, followed by masses of berries. Birds seem to eat the red-berried forms first, so go for pink, yellow and white if you want a long-lasting display. Most also have fiery orange, yellow or deep-red autumn colour.

Sorbus berries   *Sorbus* 'Joseph Rock'

S. aucuparia (rowan) (3–5m, U: 10–12m) ♦ one of Scotland's commonest trees, the berries are an excellent food source for birds, often multi-stemmed, fruit red; selected forms include 'Asplenifolia' narrow habit, deeply cut ferny leaves, 'Sheerwater Seedling' narrower habit than the type, fruit orange-red. *S. cashmiriana* (4m x 3m, U: 5–7m) ❦ flowers tinged pinkish, long-lasting white fruit, grey-green leaflets, yellow in autumn, one of my favourite small garden trees (RC-M), good as far north as Shetland with wind shelter; 'Rosiness' a form with speckled pink fruits. *S. commixta* (3m, U: 10m x 7m) fruits orange-red, surprisingly good in Shetland; 'Embley' outstanding autumn colour and masses of fruit, 'Ravensbill' curved blue-black winter buds, good autumn colour. 'Copper Kettle' orange berries, good autumn colour. 'Eastern Promise' pink berries, ferny leaves, good autumn colour. *S. hupehensis* ❦ and *S. coxii* (3m, U: 8m) berries long lasting, white, pink tinged, good autumn colour, good for the small garden; 'Pink Pagoda' a form with pink berries. 'Glendoick® Spire' red berries, upright columnar habit, 'Glendoick® White Baby' large white berries, slow growing, shrubby. 'Joseph Rock' (4m, U: 7–9m) ❦ clusters of small pale-yellow berries; a seedling of this, 'Autumn Spire', has deeper yellow berries and a narrower, more fastigiate habit. *S. koehneana* (syn. *S. fruticosa*) (2m) ❦ a multi-stemmed shrub or small tree with masses of fine white berries. *S. randaiensis* (3–5m) outstanding with very long-lasting red berries. *S. reducta* ❦ not a tree but a spreading suckering shrub to 60cm with rose-pink berries and good autumn colour. *S. sargentiana* (3–5m x 3–5m, U: 10m) larger leaves than most, with sticky buds and bunches of orange-red berries, usually quickly eaten by birds, fiery autumn colour. 'Signalman' bright orange fruits, neat shape. *S. vilmorinii* (2–5m x 2–5m) ❦ attractive ferny foliage, rose-red fruits changing to white-flushed-pink, a fine slow-growing and fairly compact tree, good in Shetland with some wind shelter.

There are lots of new named forms coming onto the market, most of them are good.

Tilia (lime)

H5 Lime trees buzz in summer with the huge number of insects attracted to their fragrant cream-yellow flowers; unfortunately, though, some lime flowers are toxic to bees. These large deciduous trees with heart-shaped or rounded leaves form a stout trunk. One downside of limes is secretions that drop from aphids, which live on the leaves, leaving a sticky mess, so they are best planted away from cars and roads. The other negative aspect is the growth from the base (epicormic growth), which needs to be removed from time to time if you want to see the trunk. All listed are fully hardy (*H5*).

T. cordata (small-leaved lime) (4–7m, U: 20m) leaves heart-shaped, flowers in late summer; 'Winter Orange' has orange-red winter stems and is often cut back each year and grown as a shrub. *T. x euchlora* (4–7m, U: 20m) dark-green rounded toothed leaves, shiny above, dusty below, arching branches. *T. x europaea* (common lime) (4–7m x 2–3m, U: 40m) a very large grower, suitable for large gardens and parkland, the trunk tends to send

Tilia x *europaea* (mature size)   *Tilia* x *europaea*

out numerous shoots from burrs, which are usually removed; 'Wratislaviensis' less vigorous with striking pale-yellow young leaves, often pleached or coppiced to keep to a manageable size. 'Petiolaris' (weeping silver lime) (8–12m, U: 20–30m) a graceful columnar tree with weeping branches, pointed, heart-shaped leaves, with silver undersides. *T. platyphyllos* (broad-leaved lime) (4–7m, U: 30m+) large softly hairy leaves, native to England; the clone 'Rubra' has red winter shoots.

Ulmus (elm) and *Zelkova*

H5 Dutch elm disease (DED) may have denuded most of the UK of the once common elm tree but there are still fine old trees in northern Scotland, for instance in towns and villages in Orkney, and there are now varieties available that appear to be resistant to this insect-borne

Ulmus x *hollandica* 'Dampieri Aurea'

disease. Elms have tiny flowers and leaves with good autumn colours, and make handsome specimen trees.

U. glabra (wych elm) *H5* (5m, U: 25m+ x 20m) This is unfortunately susceptible to DED, but some selected forms are said to be more resistant: **'Camperdownii'** (2m x 2m, U: 5–7m x 5–7m) discovered at Camperdown House (now a country park) in Dundee, a slow-growing compact form with pendulous branches, forming a domed head (there are two fine specimens at the Cruickshank Botanic Garden in Aberdeen), **'Lutescens'** (5m, U: 20m+) leaves yellow-green, open shape. An alternative to risking native elms is a new hybrid of three Asian species: **'Triumph Elm'**® forms a tree that resembles an English elm but is DED resistant. *U.* x *hollandica* 'Dampieri Aurea' *H5* (4m x 2m, U: 10m) toothed leaves golden yellow. *Zelkova* Closely related but resistant to DED. *Z. serrata H5* (4–6m, U: 15–30m) small oval toothed leaves, bronze or red autumn colour, often suckering at the base. **'Kiwi Sunset'** *H5*? (3–5m in 10–15 years) an umbrella-shaped slow-growing selection with golden leaves which do not scorch. Too new to evaluate fully, but promising.

Trees for wet soils

Although there are many trees that will grow successfully in soils that are permanently moist, few can survive really boggy or waterlogged conditions. Even for the list here, it is advisable to plant on a slightly raised mound and let the roots grow down into the wet soil.

Acer campestre (field maple), *Alnus* (alders), *Liquidambar styraciflua* (sweet gum), *Metasequoia glyptostroboides* (dawn redwood), *Populus* (poplars), *Salix* (willows), *Taxodium distichum* (swamp cypress).

Trees and shrubs for shelter
in Orkney, Shetland, the Western Isles and other windswept treeless areas
Once many of these islands and headlands were well wooded, but now most of the tree cover is long gone and it is very hard to establish trees and shrubs. Experience has shown that local provenance is important in re-establishing tree species. In Orkney and Shetland islanders are trying to raise rowan, hazel and other species from seed from local native stock. Wind, salt spray, boggy soil, extreme acidity, cold, lack of summer heat, rabbits and deer can all be factors that make trees hard to establish. Planting bare-root stock in small sizes in spring is sound advice. Willows (*Salix*) can be grown from direct-stuck hardwood cuttings.

Deciduous trees
Acer pseudoplatanus
Alnus glutinosa, A. rubra, A. incana
Salix species: *S. alaxensis, S. pentandra, S. caprea, S. viminalis,* etc.
Sorbus aucuparia (local provenance)

Conifers
Larix kaempferi
Pinus contorta (Alaskan types)
Picea sitchensis (Sitka spruce)

Shrubs
Cotoneaster bullatus
Fuchsia magellanica
Hippophae rhamnoides
Prunus spinosa
Ribes sanguineum
Rosa canina, R. rugosa
Salix (shrubby varieties)

FRUIT

TREE FRUIT

Apples, pears and plums can all be excellent in Scotland, given the right growing conditions, but make sure that you choose the right varieties. Some just won't fruit well in Scotland, while others seem to do better in one part of the country than another. The further north you go, the more the shelter that is required. Most fruit north of Aberdeen, away from the favourable Moray Firth, is grown on walls or with other shelter. If space is short, cordons (single stems planted at 45 degrees on a wall) allow several varieties to be grown. All fruit trees should be staked when young, until the trunk is strong enough to withstand wind and heavy fruiting; trees on dwarf rootstocks (see below) should be staked, even when mature.

Fruit-tree pruning is often considered a mystery, but it is not that complex. When trees are young, pruning is done to create a balanced goblet-shaped head on the tree. Subsequent pruning is used to keep the tree in bounds and to rejuvenate from time to time. Apples and pears can be pruned at any time, though traditionally this was done when the tree was dormant. Fruit on dwarf rootstocks should be only lightly trimmed. For cordons, fans and espalier pruning it is best to consult a specialist book. One advantage of summer pruning is that you can

Apples and pears

thin and/or remove diseased fruit at the same time. Thinning fruit after the natural June drop (see Apples, below) helps the tree to maintain energy levels and reduces the tendency to produce biennial cycles of bumper crop followed by barren crop. Stone fruit trees (cherries, plums, etc.) should be pruned lightly in late spring or summer, but avoid winter pruning, which can let in disease.

The fungal disease of scab is the scourge of apple and pear growing in Scotland. It causes unsightly greyish blisters on the leaves, branches and the fruit itself. It is worst in wet areas (the west coast) and during wet springs and early summers. If you want clean fruit, stick to the most disease-resistant varieties, or spray preventatively against scab with mancozeb or myclobutanil, from when new growth appears until May–June. Organic gardeners can use copper and sulphur sprays. The sometimes fatal disease of bacterial canker affects plums, and fungal canker can affect apples and pears. These diseases are most prevalent in areas of high rainfall and/or sites with poor drainage, so improve drainage and/or select disease-resistant varieties.

A wide range of fruit trees are available from specialist nurseries Tweed Valley Fruit Trees in The Borders and Appletreeman in Perthshire. We are very grateful to some of Scotland's foremost fruit experts, Willie Duncan, John Butterworth and Jim McColl, for their considerable assistance with this section. You'll find a lot more detail in *Fruit and Vegetables for Scotland* by Kenneth Cox and Caroline Beaton.

Apples

H4–5 Apples (*Malus domestica*) are suited to Scotland, and there are plenty of fine varieties to choose from. Fred Last, in his foreword to John Butterworth's excellent booklet *Apples in Scotland*, quotes an estimate that there are 140,000 apple trees in Edinburgh alone. We have no idea who counted them all. But – and it's a big but – not all apples fruit well in Scotland; choice of variety is crucial. Most of the supermarket apples such as 'Granny Smith' 'Cox's Orange Pippin' and 'Golden Delicious' need more heat than Scotland has to ripen and are not worth growing, although you may find them for sale in outlets that should know better. To be successful in Scotland, an apple needs to be able to set fruit and ripen at relatively low light levels and cool summer temperatures. The difference in summer temperatures between the north coast of Scotland and the Borders can be as much as that between the Borders and London, so some apples successful in south Scotland struggle in the north. John Butterworth reports considerable regional variations in where apples grow best in Scotland: 'Galloway Pippin' seems to grow best in the south-west, for example.

To set fruit, most apples need their flowers to be pollinated by insects carrying pollen from a different variety growing near by. Some apples are partially self-fertile but all fruit better with a partner. Winds and spring frosts can both prevent pollination, so try to avoid growing in frost pockets and very exposed sites. The pollinating tree can be an apple or a crab apple, and it needn't be in the same garden (although it should be within 100m or so). It may be stating the obvious to say so, but the two (or more) apples need to flower at the same time. We don't recommend early-flowering apples, as they are more often frosted. Family trees with several varieties grafted on a stem are a possible solution is space is tight, but you need to ensure that they are pruned to prevent the most vigorous variety (usually Bramley) from taking over.

To increase fruit size and decrease disease it is often advisable to thin fruit, particularly when trees are young. This can be done 3–6 weeks after flowering; aim for one or two fruits per cluster. The earlier this is done, the larger the remaining fruit will become. Cooking apples can be thinned to 15–22cm apart on the branch. Alternatively, thin fruit after the June (or July in the north) drop. This is when some fruit naturally falls off the tree: it is the tree's own method of conserving energy and not exhausting itself in over-production. At Glendoick, we never get round to thinning the fruit on our old apple trees, and this results in small fruit but seemingly little reduction in flavour. Some apples store better than others. The late-ripeners generally keep longer: 'Discovery' is poor, while 'Fiesta' and 'Egremont Russet' are said to be amongst the best.

Store apples in a cool, dark, frost-free place and maintain good air circulation around the fruit to reduce rotting. Avoid trying to store bruised or heavily blemished fruit because rots will set in, which will spread.

Scotland has lots of fine orchards and historic collections of apples. Good examples include Drumeldrie, Pitmedden and Fyvie Castle in Aberdeenshire, Auchinleck in Ayrshire, Hercules' Garden at Blair Castle in Perthshire, Kellie Castle, Aberdour Castle, Newburgh in Fife, and Priorwood in Melrose.

Apples are grafted on a variety of rootstocks, which affect vigour and ultimate size. The most common are:

MM 106 Medium-large tree, 3–5m in 10–20 years. Needs staking as a young plant but then self-supporting.
MM 26 Semi-dwarf, grows to 2–3m. Needs staking, or to be grown against a wall.
MM 27 Very dwarf, suitable for small garden or pot, not very vigorous, and needs good drainage and a stout stake to protect from wind and snow damage. Not very drought tolerant. Fruit is smaller than normal and a heavy crop should be thinned to prevent breakage.

The following list contains most of the best commercially available apple varieties for Scotland. Early-ripening varieties are usually ready in September in Scotland; the remainder ripen in October. If the weather turns cold early, the later-ripening varieties may not have time to fully develop their best flavour. Eaters (also called dessert apples) are sweet to taste when ripe, whereas cookers are sourer, needing sugar when eaten and usually used to make baked apples, pies, crumbles, etc. Varieties marked ♦ are the most resistant to disease such as scab.

Ballerina apples: columnar habit to 3m with few or no side

Apple 'Ellison's Orange'

Apple 'James Grieve'

branching, excellent for the small garden, fruit experts are usually dismissive of the taste, but they look great; **'Bolero'** (eater) greenish yellow, early, **'Polka'** (eater) green and red, September–October, **'Moonlight'** (eater) ♦ yellow-green, **'Sunlight'** (eater) orange, mid season, **'Blenheim Orange'** (eater) triploid, so needs two pollinator partners, large orange and green fruit, **'Bloody Ploughman'** (eater) This apple, raised in the Carse of Gowrie is a fine red variety, best in E. Scotland. It was named after a ploughman who was caught stealing the apples and was shot by a gamekeeper. **'Bramley's Seedling'** (cooker) ❦ large green-yellow apples; this is a great 'tank' of an apple, very vigorous, takes a while to produce its enormous heavy fruit and though pollinated by other apples, it does not work as a pollinator, so you need to grow two different varieties with this. **'Bramley Clone 20'** a little less vigorous and with a higher yield; Jim McColl recommends it. **'Charles Ross'** (eater/cooker) a versatile apple, stores well and good for cooking as well as eating. **'Chivers Delight'** (eater) sweet flavour, may be hard to obtain; Willie Duncan's choice for flavour and good storage. **'Discovery'** (eater) ♦ ❦ bright red, early, probably the number-one apple for Scotland (does better in the north of the UK); John Butterworth, Willie Duncan and Jim McColl all recommend this; it does not store well, so eat off the tree. **'Rosette'** is a pink fleshed version, **'Egremont Russet'** (eater) ❦ early flowering, cream, tinged yellow, good flavour, keeps well, scab prone in the west, but good in the east. **'Ellison's Orange'** (eater) Cox-like fruit, scab-resistant. **'Falstaff'** (eater) heavy cropping, not the hardiest and somewhat prone to scab. **'Fiesta'** (syn. 'Red Pippin') (eater) ❦ sweet, reddish orange, Cox-like flavour, good in Scotland and north England, keeps well, subject to canker in some areas, one of Jim McColl's favourites. **'Galloway Pippin'** (cooker) late, raised in Galloway where it is still popular. **'Greensleeves'** (eater) golden yellow fruit, partially self fertile, **'Grenadier'** (cooker) ♦ early with good scab resistance but poor storage; good on west coast, according to John Butterworth. **'Hereforshire Russet'**, (eater) tastes like Cox, **'Howgate Wonder'** (cooker) ❦ tough, red over yellow, sometimes scab susceptible; Jim McColl and John Butterworth recommend it. **'James Grieve'** (eater) ❦ red and

Apple 'Worcester Permain'

green, crisp and juicy, a good pollinator, an old Scottish favourite, does better in the east than the west, but perhaps superseded by less scab-susceptible varieties. **'Katy'** (eater) ♛ sweet red, early, from Sweden, skin rather thick, good in the west. **'Limelight'** (eater) ♦ yellow-green, crisp, free cropping and compact. **'Lord Derby'** (cooker) ♦ mid-season, good disease resistance. **'Red Devil'** (eater) ♦ scarlet, good flavour. **'Red Falstaff'** (eater) crisp and juicy, very heavy yield, frost-resistant flowers, good storage. **'Red Windsor'** (eater) ♦ very hardy, Cox-like flavour, early ripening. **'Scotch Bridget'** (cooker/eater) cream, crisp, a Victorian Scottish apple, usually used for cooking but can be eaten off the tree some years. **'Scotch Dumpling'** (cooker) large, with fine flowers, ripens early. **'Scrumptious'** (eater) very good taste, popular with children, frost hardy in flower, fruit stays ripe on tree for long time; one of Jim McColl's picks, but John Butterworth reports that it is scab prone in the west. **'Spartan'** (eater) dark red sweet fruit, prone to scab, particularly in the west. **'Sunset'** (eater) ♦ sweet-sharp flavour, stores well, fairly disease resistant. **'Worcester Permain'** (eater) ♛ sweet, juicy orange-red fruit, early ripening, best eaten straight off the tree; John Butterworth and Willie Duncan recommend it highly, but Jim McColl has no time for it. Resistant to mildew but can suffer scab.

Pears

Most pears fruit well in Scotland, provided the blossom is not frosted, though in wet summers and high rainfall areas trees suffer from severe scab, which will need to be sprayed. Some are self-fertile or partly self-fertile (as indicated below), others require a pollinator. Triploids cannot pollinate other pears so you need to grow these with two other varieties to ensure pollination of all three. Quince A rootstocks produce large trees up to 3–4m while Quince C is a somewhat dwarfing stock giving a slightly less vigorous (2–3m) tree. In colder areas, pears may need the warmth of a south-facing wall to protect blossom and for fruit to ripen fully. All can be considered H4-(5) except where marked; the plant is tougher but the flowers are vulnerable to frost in cold inland gardens.

'Beth' (self-fertile) early, conical, pale yellow, juicy, sweet, compact tree, heavy cropper from a young age; a Jim McColl choice. **'Beurre Hardy'** round conical fruit, light-green skin, tender, sweet, juicy flavour, vigorous and upright, a poor pollinator, needs a warm site and takes a few years to bear fruit. **'Concorde'** ♛ (partly self-fertile) good flavour, compact, heavy cropping; Willie Duncan's choice as the most reliable, and a Jim

McColl pick. **'Conference'** ♛ (self-fertile) the most popular pear in the UK, and perhaps the best for Scotland as it sets fruit even if frosted, good flavour, fairly compact, heavy cropper. **'Doyenne du Comice'** the best flavour of all, but needs a warm, sheltered site and a pollinator, vigorous, scab prone. **Invincible** ['Delwinor'] *H5* (self-fertile) not the best flavour, but the best for severe climates, as it can flower a second time if frosted, very free fruiting from a young age. **'Jargonelle'** one of the best for the west, but triploid, so needs two pollinator partners. **'Merton Pride'** sweet and juicy, triploid, needs two pollinator partners. **'Williams' Bon Chretien'** yellow skin, juicy flesh, good for bottling, spreading habit, heavy cropper; a new sport of this, with red skin, **'Sensation'** should also be good. There are several other locally popular pears, somewhat harder to track down commercially: **'Crawfurd'** common in Newburgh area, Fife, early ripening, **'Bristol Cross'** mid-season, said to be good in west Scotland climates.

Plums
and damsons and gages

Plums generally fruit well in Scotland but they can be short lived because of canker and silver leaf. They are heavy cropping from a young age, and all listed below are self-fertile, so you need only one. It is most practical to grow them against a wall, to avoid breakage from heavy fruiting and for ease of netting from birds and wasps. It may be necessary to thin fruit, to avoid exhausting the tree and starting a bumper/barren biennial cropping cycle. Prune in summer if required after fruit set, but not in winter, because of the risk of disease. The commonest rootstocks are 'St Julien A' for a full-sized plum (3–4m) and 'Pixy' for a semi-dwarf tree (to around 2.5–3m).

Plums and gages

'Czar' ♛ sharp flavour, usually used for cooking, early fruiting, tough, spring frost and shade resistant, susceptible to silver leaf. **'Excalibur'** similar to 'Victoria' with larger fruit, **'Jubilee'** similar to 'Victoria, but a little earlier. **'Marjorie's Seedling'** sweet but not the best taste, good for cooking, late ripening, long-lasting fruit, vigorous and upright, heavy cropping. **'Opal'** reddish-purple fruit, tastes like 'Victoria' but less susceptible to bacterial canker, so we would recommend this instead. **'Victoria'** (Victoria plum) the most popular plum, heavy cropping, but very susceptible to canker so often short lived.

Damsons These have smaller fruit but are tougher and more disease resistant, and can be used as a windbreak or hedge. They need to be cooked and made into jam, wine or gin. **'Farleigh Damson'** (self-fertile) the most reliable fruiter for Scotland. **'Merryweather'** is also good in cold and exposed locations and has larger fruit.

Gages These are not as successful as plums in Scotland, as they need more shelter and warmth, and they may take years to start fruiting and then may not fruit every year. Apart from perhaps the Moray Firth coast (and other localized suntraps), we would not recommend them for the northern half of Scotland. **'Cambridge'** (self-fertile) is probably the best. Others worth trying are **'Dennistons'** green, **'Early Transparent'** yellow, very sweet, **'Oullins'** yellow, takes a few years to start fruiting, quite late ripening, **'Jefferson'** yellow.

Cherries

Cherries

These are usually fan-trained against a wall, so they can be easily netted against birds. For smaller gardens, we recommend buying cherries on 'Gisela 5' rootstocks, as they fruit younger and more heavily on a less vigorous tree/bush. For a larger tree, buy trees on the 'colt' rootstock. Whatever the size, cherries need a rich, fertile soil and regular feeding. All the cherries below are self-fertile. They don't require pruning unless you need to restrict growth; just tie in the young branches.

'Morello' 🌣 dark-red cooker, very hardy. **'Stella'** 🌣 dark-red sweet, eating cherry, fruit inclined to split. **'Summer Sun'** dark red, sweet, with good frost tolerance good in colder more exposed locations. **'Sunburst'** sweet black fruit. **'Sweetheart'** dark red, late, heavy fruiting. **'Lapins'** (syn. 'Cherokee') sweet, dark red, good flavour, heavy cropping and seldom splitting; this recent introduction is Willie Duncan's choice as the best cherry for east Scotland.

Apricots, peaches, figs and other tree fruit

Scotland's summers are too short and too cool for most other tree fruit to crop reliably outdoors, and they are best grown indoors. That said, recent hot summers have meant that we have seen figs ripening outdoors in Aberdeenshire and grapes at House of Pitmuies, Angus, so never say never; but in our experience the taste of outdoor Scottish apricots, peaches and figs does not match that of those from hotter climates. If you want to try growing them, find a suntrap on a south-facing wall and use fan-trained trees.

SOFT FRUIT (berries and currants)

Until recently, Perthshire and Angus boasted the world's largest concentration of strawberry and raspberry production, much of the produce being canned or made into jam in Dundee. Berry picking was an annual 'holiday' for many city dwellers. There are still many producers in Scotland, but no longer on the same scale, and much of the picking is done by migrant labour from elsewhere in Europe. Now the fruit is produced in tunnels, planned to ripen over a long period and grown mainly for supermarkets. The major soft fruit research is carried out in the James Hutton Research Institute (formerly called the SCRI) in Invergowrie, by Dundee, where the tayberry and many raspberry, strawberry and blackcurrant varieties were bred. James McIntyre & Sons' Moyness Nurseries in Blairgowrie and J. Tweedie in Galloway have a fine range of soft fruit, available by mail order if you live far away.

Blackberries (brambles) and hybrid berries

Brambles, of course, provide free fruit all over Scotland in late summer and early autumn. There are thornless versions which you may prefer to grow in the garden, as they are easier to pick. **'Black Satin'**, **'Loch Ness'** and **'Oregon Thornless'** are all good, but the flavour is not as fruity as that of the wild ones. Alternatively consider one of the hybrid berries, mainly crosses between a bramble and raspberry: **'Loganberry'** *H5* thorny and best for cooking, **'Thornless Variety'** as it sounds, **'Tayberry'** *H4* reddish purple, larger and sweeter, can be damaged by cold winds, bred at the SCRI.

Blueberries (*Vaccinium corymbosum*)

H4–5 (1.5m) These are handsome deciduous shrubs with white flowers in spring, blue berries in summer and the added bonus of fine autumn colour. Blueberries like well-drained, acid (peaty) soil. Netting against birds in the fruiting season and planting more than one variety ensures good berrying. As plants mature, winter pruning will keep them in shape. Sawfly can strip the plant of leaves.

Vaccinium corymbosum (blueberry)   *Vaccinium corymbosum* (blueberry) (autumn colour)

'Bluecrop' by far the most popular variety, large, light blue berries with good flavour, orange autumn colour, 'Grover' late fruiting, 'Jersey' keeps well, good fresh or cooked, 'Patriot' vigorous, hardy, excellent flavour.

Cranberry see *Vaccinium*, page 107

Currants

Ninety-five per cent of all **blackcurrants** in the UK end up in Ribena and similar juices. But they do, of course, have other uses, eaten fresh, pulped, or made into jams and sauces. Blackcurrants are pretty tough, but are usually grown in netted cages to keep birds off. Mildew can cause problems. Most varieties were bred at SCRI, near Dundee and are named after Scottish peaks: **'Ben Alder'** small, juicy berries, resistant to mildew, **'Ben Connan'** large fruit,

'Ben Lomond' late flowering so good in frosty areas, some mildew, **'Ben Sarek'** large berries, **'Ben Tirran'** late flowering, large fruit.

Redcurrants are less popular, but fine for cooking, in jams, jellies and summer pudding, and for setting jams of other fruit. The old favourite is **'Laxton's no. 1'** which is early fruiting (July). **'Red Lake'** a little later fruiting.

Red and black currants

White currants, usually 'White Versailles', are not widely grown but ripen in July–August and are good for pies and jams.

Gooseberry

Gooseberries

H5 (1m x 1.5m) Amongst the hardiest of all fruit: you should be able to grow gooseberries almost anywhere in Scotland. (Their thorns also make them one the toughest fruit to pick: my worst summer job ever was picking gooseberries for a week and I earned more scratches than pennies – RC-M.) They like a fertile, well-drained but not dry soil and will fruit in partial shade, even on a north-facing wall. You may need to net fruit against birds from May to July/August, and some recommend thinning fruit in May. Prune in winter, or after fruiting is finished, and remember to wear thick gloves. The main troubles are mildew (turns leaves white), and sawfly

larvae (strip the leaves).

'Careless' pale fruit, some disease resistance, 'Invicta' compact and free fruiting, can be container grown, 'Leveller' can be eaten raw when very ripe, very good taste, 'Martlet' a new red dessert gooseberry, sweet flavour, heavy cropping, good disease resistance to both mildew and leaf spots, said to be suitable for organic cultivation. 'Pax' almost thornless, mildew resistant, 'Whinham's Industry' red fruited, the best variety for a shady site, can suffer from mildew.

Rhubarb see *Rheum*, page 221

Raspberries

These are another excellent crop for Scotland and many of the best known varieties (including the 'Glens') were

raised at the Scottish Crop Research Institute (now called James Hutton Institute) near Dundee. Raspberries fruit in summer, most fruiting on canes produced the previous year except for one or two late/autumn varieties such as 'Autumn Bliss', which fruit on canes from the current year, so they should be cut to ground each year. Raspberries need well-drained soil, and are often planted on a ridge if soil is heavy. They are generally planted with posts and wires to support them, normally in single or double rows. Plant canes about 40cm apart. When newly planted, cut down old canes to ground level in spring, and then to ground level again when all fruit is picked. They should be fed at planting time and then annually (general fertilizers like Growmore or rose fertilizer are good). Raspberries succumb to virus and should be replaced after about 10 years. Replant new stock in another part of the garden.

Raspberries

'All Gold' autumn fruiting, yellow, 'Autumn Bliss' late fruiting (August) on current season's wood, needs a sheltered sunny site, 'Glen Ample' spine free, mid–late July, 'Glen Coe' the first purple raspberry! Bred in Scotland, it will really brighten up the dinner table, 'Glen Ericht' not the best taste but root rot resistant so good for poor soils, 'Glen Moy' spine free, good flavour, 'Glen Prosen' spine free, needs rich soil, a good all-rounder, 'Malling Admiral' spine free, disease resistant, needs wind shelter, 'Octavia' late July, 'Polka' perhaps the best of the autumn varieties, 'Tulameen' late July, long season, good flavour. 'Cowichan' mid-season, good root

Strawberry 'Cambridge Favourite'

rot resistance.

Strawberries

H4 Strawberries do well in Scotland and usually taste much better from the garden, as you can pick them ripe and eat them straight away, whereas supermarket strawberries are often picked green. The traditional wisdom is to plant runners in late summer/autumn and container-grown plants in autumn or spring, and then not to let them fruit in the first season. Take off the flowers and runners to obtain a really dense plant, which will fruit well the following season (up to 1kg). Strawberries need to be in plenty of sun, and in not too acidic a soil (some may need a dose of lime), and you may need to net ripening fruit to keep birds and

children off. Rain is the great enemy, as it rots the fruit. Use a mulch of straw, black polythene or strawberry mats to keep the fruit out of contact with the ground, or grow them in raised beds or containers. Vine weevil grubs are serious root-eating pests. After 3–4 years, fruiting will decrease and it is best to dig out the plants and start again. The flowers can be frosted in cold inland gardens, resulting in no fruit, so you may need to cover them.

These days most people eat nothing but **'Elsanta'**, which the supermarkets love, as it lasts well on the shelf. A perfectly good fruit if picked ripe, but all too often it is picked green and ripened inside, which means it tastes mildly of turnips. **'Cambridge Favourite'** is probably the most widely grown older variety, with good flavour, mid-season and heavy cropping, but prone to virus. Slightly later ripening is **'Pegasus'**, which many believe to the best of the recent introductions. If you plant a mixture of varieties you can have a long season of fruit. Varieties known as everbearers or perpetuals fruit into July and August, but are less hardy, produce smaller fruit and fruit well for only 2–3 years.

Berried treasure: the best berrying trees and shrubs for Scotland

Berries and hips are both ornamental and in most cases beneficial to birds and animals in winter. The best berry set is usually after hot summers such as that of 2006. Some berries are eaten by birds as soon as they are ripe, while others, less tasty to wildlife, hang on well into winter.

Cotoneaster horizontalis, C. hybrida pendula, etc.
Gaultheria (Pernettya) mucronata (male needed)
Ilex (male needed near by)
Hippophae rhamnoides
Malus (crab apple) (needs pollinator)

Pyracantha
Rosa species but not hybrids
Sorbus aucuparia and Chinese species S. hupehensis, S. cashmeriana, etc.
Skimmia reevesiana and S. japonica (male needed)
Viburnum opulus, V. davidii (needs male)

Plants for boggy soil, pond margins and streamsides

Although we don't cover aquatic plants, such as water lilies, in this book, we cover most of the key waterside plants that like to have their roots permanently or semi-permanently moist. The best ones for Scotland include:

Astilbe
Caltha
Carex (some)
Eupatorium
Filipendula
Gunnera
Hosta
Iris ensata
Ligularia
Lysichiton (invasive)

Mimulus (invasive)
Phalaris (invasive)
Primula japonica and P. florindae
Rheum
Rodgersia
Insectivorous plants (Sarracenia etc.)
Trollius

PERENNIALS, ALPINES AND BULBOUS PLANTS

✉ Scottish native plant ⚘ Scottish Gardenplant Award
☠ irritant or toxic; ☠☠ extremely irritant or toxic if ingested
❁ fragrant; ❁❁ very fragrant
♦ disease resistant; ♦ ♦ very disease resistant

Acaena

H4–5 This popular alpine or carpeting ground-cover with potentilla-like leaves is characterised by soft burr-like seed heads, which can stick to clothing; the flowers are insignificant. Plant in full sun in well-drained soil, or between paving slabs, but beware, as it is vigorous, rooting as it spreads, and can swamp out other alpines. Do not plant *A. ovalifolia* or *A. novae-zelandiae*, as they are rampant weeds.

Acaena caesiiglauca

A. buchananii (10cm x 50cm+) a vigorous evergreen ground-cover with bluish-green leaves, spherical burrs in summer. *A. microphylla* 'Kupferteppich' (Copper Carpet) (5cm x 60cm) very low growing, evergreen, copper- to bronze-tinted green leaves, small red spherical burrs. *A. caesiiglauca* (10–15cm) blue-grey leaves, small brown burrs. *A. saccaticupula* 'Blue Haze' (20cm x 60cm) brown flower heads on reddish stems in late summer, blue-grey leaves.

Acanthus

(bears' breeches)
H3–4 (1–1.5m x 60–90cm). Acanthus is a bold accent plant, useful as a specimen or as a repeated structural plant in a border, with glossy dark-green leaves in an unmistakable sculpted form. The mauve and white summer flower spikes are equally dramatic. The leaf shape has adorned pots and amphoras from Ancient Greek and Roman times. Hardy once established, it seems to grow in almost any soil, though it prefers a warm sunny well-drained spot and in cold/inland gardens should be protected with a mulch in the first winter. It will grow but not flower well in shade in Scotland. Think carefully about the planting

Acanthus spinosus

position, because the roots are long and brittle, making it tricky to move once established, and the broken roots tend to sprout new plants. Mildew can also be a problem during long dry spells.

A. hungaricus (syn. *A. longifolius*) *H4* deeply cut, matt-green leaves, white to pale-pink flowers. *A. mollis* *H3/4* ⚘ semi-evergreen with matt-green leaves and white-pink, mauve-hooded flowers from June to August; forms with broad leaves are known as **Latifolius Group**. *A. spinosus* *H3/4* ⚘ the most aristocratic, with large glossy, viciously spiny, deeply cut leaves, spikes of mauve and white flowers in summer; less vigorous than the others.

Achillea (yarrow)

One of the mainstays of the herbaceous border, achillea has feathery foliage and wonderful flower plates composed of tiny florets. It flowers in summer in a broad range of colours (the *RHS Plant Finder* lists over 100 varieties) from red, orange and pink to yellow and white, but many of them fade out to muddy colours as the flowers age. Christopher Lloyd calls these colours 'extremely disagreeable', which is a bit of an exaggeration. The flowers are useful for drying. Achilleas do best in full sun and a well-drained soil and are often short lived, particularly in heavy soils. Most are upright in form, although there are also some tiny alpine gems for the rock garden. Divide them in spring if they become shy flowering and congested. Most are pretty tough and suitable for most of Scotland; the only ills likely to afflict them are aphids and mildew during prolonged dry spells. The taller varieties may need staking in exposed positions. Hardiness is *H4–5* unless stated otherwise; those marked as *H4* can rot off in cold wet winters.

A. millefolium and *A. filipendulina* cultivars and hybrids; spread approximately 50cm, unless stated otherwise: forms include: 'Apfelblüte' *H4* (60cm) pale pink, 'Cassis' (70cm) deep cerise, 'Coronation Gold' *H4* (1m) 'Gold Plate' *H5* (1.2m) ⚘ and 'Cloth of Gold' *H5* (75–90cm) ⚘ all yellows, 'Cerise Queen' *H5* (75cm) very vigorous magenta-pink, 'Credo' *H4* (1.2m) creamy yellow, 'Fanal' *H4* (75cm) crimson, fading to brown, throughout summer, 'Feuerland' *H4* (1m) impressive rosy red, fading to yellowish, 'Lachsschönheit' ('Salmon Beauty') *H4* (90cm) salmon pink, 'Lilac Beauty' (syn. 'Lavender Beauty') (60cm) lilac, fading to cream, 'Martina' (60cm) large pale yellow, greyish foliage, 'McVities' (60cm) biscuit yellow fading to cream, 'Mondpagode' (Moon Pagoda) (90cm) creamy white, 'Moonshine' *H4* (60cm) ⚘ bold yellow throughout summer, semi-evergreen silvery grey feathery foliage, needs regular dividing, or it is short-lived, **'Paprika' H5** (70cm) orange-red, greyish foliage, **'Red Velvet'** (60cm) pure red, good colour, **'Rose Madder'** (30–50cm) bright salmon pink, said to be winter-wet resistant, low growing, **Summer Fruits Group** 60cm red, salmon, lemon forms, **Summer Pastels Group** (60–90cm) colours mixed, **'Summerwine'** (70cm) deep reddish purple, **'Terracotta' H4** (60cm x 60cm) brownish orange fading to pale yellow, slivery, fern-like leaves, if you only want one, try to get this, **'Walther Funcke'** (60cm) orange red.

A. ptarmica (sneezewort) *H5* (75cm x 90cm+) white daisy-like

Achillea, five colours   Achillea ptarmica 'The Pearl'

flowers, dark-green leaves, can be invasive; a better garden plant is **'The Pearl' H5** (70cm x 90cm+) ☙ small white pompoms above tight dark-green feathery-edged leaves; **'Boule de Neige'** is similar. *A. nobilis* subsp. *neilrichii H4* (45cm x 45cm) is a neater, white achillea with grey leaves which can run around a bit. *A. siberica* var. *camschatica* **'Love Parade' H5** (60cm) soft pink flowers, handsome glossy foliage.

Dwarf varieties
These are more suitable for rockery and border front, growing under 20cm in height, and spreading approx. 25cm. *A. x huteri* (15cm) white, needs full sun and good drainage. **'King Alfred'** (10cm) silver foliage, sulphur yellow in spring. *A. lewisii* **'King Edward' H5** (10cm) a good plant for pots and the rock garden, grey-green leaves on woody stems, tiny buff-yellow flowers.

Aconitum (monkshood)

H5 🌿🌿 These are striking and tough plants for Scottish gardens, but they have their sinister side, with all parts of the plants being highly toxic; they were used in olden times for poisoning arrows. Aconites like sheltered, cool moist conditions and will tolerate full sun or light shade. Mostly later flowering than their relatives the delphiniums, they form clumps of divided leaves and send up spikes of hooded purple, blue or white flowers in summer and early autumn. It is not a bad idea to prune them in spring to encourage bushiness and slightly later flowering. They are tough (*H5*), generally trouble free and relatively low maintenance. All flower in July–August/September unless stated otherwise and spread approx 30-50cm.

Aconitum carmichaelii 'Arendsii'   Aconitum x cammarum 'Bicolor'

'Bressingham Spire' (90cm) ☙ violet blue, with deep glossy leaves, sturdy. *A. carmichaelii* **'Arendsii'** (1.2m) ☙ rich blue hooded flowers, September–October, *A.c.* **'Royal Flush'** (60cm) fine blue flowers, leaves reddish in spring, *A.c.* **'Spätlese'** (1.2m) pale blue. **'Ivorine'** (90cm) ☙ the earliest flowering, creamy white in June–July, deeply lobed leaves, does best in cool moist climates, needs to be divided regularly. *A. napellus* (monkshood) (1–2m) variable, hooded indigo-blue flowers, sometimes sows itself around; subsp. *vulgare* **'Albidum'** white, flushed greyish. **'Spark's Variety'** (1.2m) ☙ deep blue. **'Stainless Steel'** (90cm) white-eyed blue flowers and blue-grey foliage. *A. x cammarum* **'Bicolor'** (1.2m) blue and white, June–July. There are also several climbing species: the most common is *A. hemsleyanum* (2–3m+) twining with vine-like leaves, variable purple or blue flowers in mid-late summer.

Actaea (*Cimicifuga*) (bugbane, snakeroot)

H5 🌿🌿 Botanists have recently merged *Cimicifuga* into the genus *Actea*, much to many gardeners' displeasure. The common name bugbane refers to the insect-repellent smell produced by the foliage. Clump forming, with attractive divided leaves, actaeas associate well with most plants. They can be slow to establish and prefer rich, moist, free-draining soil and a sheltered spot in light shade. They occasionally suffer from rust and black spot, and the leaves can scorch in dry soil, leading to poor growth. Mainly late summer and autumn flowering, they reach 75–90cm x 60–90cm unless stated otherwise. The berries of *A. alba*, *A. rubra* and *A. spicata* are very poisonous and the sap can cause skin irritation.

A. matsumurae **'White Pearl'** (1m) arching stems, narrow sprays of white flowers. *A. pachypoda* creamy white in late spring, autumnal red berries. *A. racemosa* (*Cimicifuga simplex*) (1.5m) ❀ fragrant white flowers in late summer. *A. rubra* fragrant white flowers in late spring, red berries in summer. *A. simplex* (1–2m) ❀ white, scented flowers in long arching spikes in August–September; this is a really fine plant and should be more

Actaea (Cimicifuga) 'Brunette'

widely grown, particularly in the numerous dark-leaved forms kown collectively as **Atropurpurea Group**: **'Brunette'** ⚜ leaves and stems purple-red, **'Hillside Black Beauty'** dark purple-black leaves, **'James Compton'** purple-green leaves, **'Pink Spike'** pinkish flowers, very dark foliage.

Agapanthus

These are fabulous South African exotic-looking plants which produce great globes of blue, purple, mauve and white flowers. Unfortunately, most prefer a warmer climate than ours and few of them thrive inland in Scotland without extra winter protection. Having said that, we found a clump growing at Tillypronie, above Ballater, in one of the coldest areas of Scotland. Agapanthus are excellent in coastal gardens, both east and west. The fleshy strap-shaped leaves are also attractive, and complement the flowers, which come in late summer, between July and September or later. Some are hardier than others, with the evergreen ones generally the most tender, and all do best with some protection in winter until well established. Agapanthus make good focal points and are particularly effective in pots and containers, giving you the added insurance policy of being able to bring them under cover for the winter. If you leave pots outside you might need to insulate them to stop them freezing. They don't like to sit in cold damp soil and need adequate drainage and full sunshine to flower well. Planting under the eaves of a house on the south side is often successful. The *RHS Plant Finder* lists over 200 varieties, so we only cover the most common varieties, which spread 60–90cm, unless stated otherwise.

Agapanthus campanulatus, dark form

Avoid **A. africanus H2** as it is tender, unless you live in the most favourable west-coast areas. **A. campanulatus H3–4** (60cm–1.2m) narrow, greyish-green leaves, flattish trusses of blue, the commonest species in gardens in its various forms including **var.** *albidus* (60cm) ⚜ white, **subsp.** *patens* (45cm–1m) smaller heads of wide open light-blue flowers, flower colour varies from pale to deep blue. There are now a huge number of named hybrids; the following are only a selection of what is available, most *H3*: **'Black Pantha'** (60cm) blue-black, **'Enigma'** [PBR] (75cm) bicolour white with blue base, **'Headbourne Hybrids'**

Agapanthus campanulatus, pale blue form

H3–4 (60cm) ⚜ somewhat variable but many of the toughest varieties are from this group, **'Jack's Blue'** (1.5m) one of the tallest, purple-blue trumpets, **'Lilliput'** *H3–4* (15cm) deep blue, a wee delicate gem for a sheltered spot, **'Navy Blue'** (60cm) very fine dark blue, **'Northern Star'** (60cm) 2 toned deep blue, **Silver Moon** ['Notfred'] (40cm) pale blue, white-striped leaves, **'Snowdrops'** (75cm) tiny white flowers, **'Streamline'** (50cm) mid-blue, **'Timaru'** (80cm) deep blue, **'Tinkerbell'** *H2–3* (40cm) semi-evergreen variegated leaves, infrequent pale blue flowers, **'Windsor Grey'** muddy grey-blue, not very nice.

Agastache see *Monarda*, page 209

Ajuga reptans (bugle)

H5 ✉ (15–25cm x 50cm–1m+) This Scottish native is a tough and useful sun or shade-tolerant ground-cover, thriving underneath trees and shrubs. Evergreen or semi-evergreen, the leaves have a leathery almost reptilian texture, and are dark green, deep purple or multi-coloured, though coloured foliage forms often revert to green. The spring flower spikes are blue, in some hybrids brighter and stronger than others. Ajuga like a fertile, moist, humus-rich soil, although they will tolerate some dryness. They do well all over Scotland from Galloway to Shetland. They are vigorous and spreading, and can become a pest in a small space. Ants spread the seeds so seedlings pop up anywhere.

Ajuga reptans 'Atropurpurea'

'Arctic Fox' grey or cream with dark-green edge, bright-blue flower spikes, **'Atropurpurea'** (15cm x 45cm) ⚜ dark purple, tinged bronze, **'Braunherz'** glossy bronze-purple leaves and deep-blue flowers, good for winter colour in tubs, **'Burgundy Glow'** ⚜ pink and cream foliage, bright-blue flower spikes in late spring, **'Catlin's Giant'** (25cm x 90cm) ⚜ a vigorous spreader, forming mats of purplish leaves with bright-blue flowers, **'Multicolour'** purple-green leaves splashed yellow, small blue flower spikes in late spring, **'Variegata'** (syns. 'Rainbow', 'Tricolor') grey-green leaves, mottled cream, pale-blue flowers in late spring.

Alcea (hollyhock)

H5 (1.5–1.8m x 60–90cm) A classic summer cottage garden and herbaceous border plant, producing unmistakable nearly 2m-high spikes of disc-shaped flowers. The trouble with most hollyhocks is that they are extremely susceptible to rust (brown-red blotches on the leaf underside), which tends to lead to disfigured plants by the end of summer. You can spray with fungicide or just let nature take its course. Hollyocks are pretty tough but not long lived (often biennial); they prefer a fertile soil with plenty of feeding, and a warm sunny position.

Alcea

Most readily available hollyhocks are varieties of **A. rosea**, flowering from June to August and producing rough-textured mid-green leaves: **'Red/Pink'** (1.5m) single pink-red, **'Nigra'** (1.5m) single, deep burgundy, **Chater's Double Group 'Peach'**, **'Rose'**, **'Scarlet'**, **'Violet'**, **'White'** and **'Yellow'** (all 1.8m) double flowers in colours matching their names. **A. x kitaebella 'Parkallee'** has cream semi-double flowers, said to be resistant to rust as is the yellow **A. ficifolia** (2m+) with fig-shaped leaves.

Alchemilla (lady's mantle)

H5 Named after the alchemists' search for the Philosopher's Stone, because you can see all the colours of the rainbow inside water droplets trapped between the hairs on the plants' leaves, alchemillas flower in late spring and summer, and then seed everywhere, so deadhead quickly if you want to control them. They like most soils apart from the very dry or very wet. They may get a bit of mildew and the odd aphid attack, but nothing that is likely to be fatal. Alchemilla is a great plant for combination planting, as both flowers and foliage are a good foil for any colour.

Alchemilla mollis

A. mollis H5 (45cm x 60cm) ✿ airy sprays of sulphur-yellow flowers in June, downy grey-green palmate leaves, inclined to flop after flowering. The common name is lady's mantle, but don't be deceived by this suggestion of delicacy because this is as tough as old boots and can be a bit of a thug. It seems to thrive almost anywhere – borders, pots, between paving slabs, the semi-shade beneath shrubs . . . it would probably thrive on the fast lane of the M8 motorway if given the chance. It can also make a good cut flower. The best form is **'Robusta'** with a tidier, less floppy habit. **A. conjuncta** (syn. *A. alpina*) *H5* (15cm x 30–40cm) fine silvery foliage and yellow flowers in summer, a useful plant for the rock garden, associating well with campanulas. **A. erythropoda** *H5* (15cm x 20–30cm) yellow sprays of flowers throughout summer, scallop-edged grey-green leaves.

Alstroemeria (Peruvian lily)

☘ This exotic-looking border plant flowers intermittently between June and September in a broad range of colours. The hardiest alstroemerias are found wild in Chile and Peru, and they need a fertile well-drained soil and a sunny, sheltered position out of the wind. They should be planted deeply (20cm or more) so that the frost does not reach them; alternatively mound up the soil or apply a protective winter mulch. They don't transplant easily, and may become invasive – their very deep roots mean that they are hard to get rid of once they are established. Young growth is likely to be checked by late frosts in cold gardens. All parts of the plants may cause skin allergy. Heights and spreads are similar unless stated otherwise.

Alstroemeria

A. aurea (syn. *A. aurantiaca*) *H3–4* (60–75cm) fine orange, short lasting and sometimes shy flowering, and beware: it can run amock – on Mull, for example, it seems to be running away down the street. **A. psittacina** (syn. *A. pulchella*) *H2–3* (1m x 50cm) deep red and green. **Ligtu Hybrids** *H3–4* (50cm) ✿ in a wide range of flower colours, mainly oranges and pinks. **Little Princess Hybrids** (20–40cm) a range of fine dwarf hybrids in colours from cream, through yellow, orange and red. **Princess Series** (to 1m) tall, long flowering, white, pink or orange.

Other cultivars

H3 (80cm–1.2m x 1m+) There are dozens of named hybrids, and seedling strains, so it is perhaps best to choose them in flower at your local nursery or garden centre. Some are tall and will need support. Some of the most widely available are **'Apollo'** white, tinged yellow with a burgundy spot on the top petals, **'Blushing Bride'** soft white blushed pink, **'Bonanza'** cerise pink, **'Elvira'** soft striped pink, **'Evening Song'** small flowered, deep burgundy, **'Golden Delight'** deep yellow, **'Lucinda'** light purple, **'Orange Gem'** sturdy, orange, **'Orange Glory'** deep orange, **'Red Beauty'** a vigorous spreader, crimson June–August, **'Spitfire'** red, leaves with cream variegation, **'Yellow Friendship'** *H3–4* pale yellow, white tips.

Alyssum (and *Aurinia*)

H5 These rock garden and border edge gems form low spreading mounds and produce masses of yellow (or pink) flowers in late spring and early summer. The white-flowered alyssum is an annual, used for bedding. They are easy to grow, best in full sun, and with a little luck, they will seed themselves into crevices and old stone walls. Easy to please, they don't require any maintenance apart from deadheading and an occasional trim to shape.

Alyssum saxatile

A. montanum (15cm x 15cm) ❋ ☗ masses of scented yellow flowers above a carpeting mound of hairy grey-green leaves. *A. saxatile* (syn. *Aurinia saxatilis*) **'Gold Dust'** (23cm x 30cm) ☗ chrome yellow flowers above grey-green mats. This plant associates well with aubretias and spring bulbs, **'Citrina'** *H5* (23cm x 30cm) lemon yellow, *A.s.* **'Variegata'** (23cm x 30cm) leaves with white margins. *A. spinosum* var. *roseum* (30–50cm x 50cm) pale to deep rose pink.

Anaphalis (pearl everlasting)
and *Helichrysum*

H5 (60–90cm x 60cm) Anaphalis is a useful ground-cover with greyish silver leaves for sun or shade with masses of small white flowers in late summer, used for cutting and drying. Most silver-foliage plants like hot dry soils, but this prefers moisture and so is ideally suited to Scotland. Graham Stuart Thomas recommends it for growing with Japanese anemones.

A. margaritacea (60cm high) ☗ and *A. triplinervis* (90cm high) ☗ are the most commonly sold species. The latter is used extensively in the parterres at Drummond Castle, Perthshire.

Helichrysum H3 Rather like coloured versions of pearl everlasting, these have clusters of long-lasting tiny daisy flowers in spring, which have been described as being 'like miniature shaving brushes'. They have aromatic (smelling strongly of curry) silvery leaves and one species, *H. italicum*, is the well-known herb known as curry plant. Coming from South Africa, they need well-drained soil in full sun and dislike rich or heavy soil and winter wet, so they may not be long lived in Scotland.

H. italicum (For curry plant, see Herbs, page 195.) New hybrids include **Amber Cluster** [PBR applied for] pale yellow and salmon, **Pink Sapphire** [PBR] pink, **Ruby Cluster** ['Blorub'] reddish-pink buds, fading to yellow, silvery leaves, **'Schwefellicht'** (Sulphur Light) yellow.

Anchusa azurea
and *Cynoglossum nervosum*

H3–4 One of the 'bluest' blues available, the early-summer flowers are like those of a giant gentian-blue forget-me-not in appearance, contrasting well with poppies, bearded iris and daisies. Tending to have a rather untidy habit and often requiring staking, with hairy lanceolate leaves, this prefers well-drained soil and full sun. Cut back after flowering to encourage further blooms and to encourage perennial basal rosettes. It tends to be short lived, but often self-seeds.

Anaphalis triplinervis   *Anchusa azurea* 'Feltham Pride'

'Dropmore' (1m x 60cm), **'Little John'** (40cm x 40cm), **'Feltham Pride'** (1m x 60cm), **'Loddon Royalist'** (1.5m x 50cm) large bright-blue flowers, **'Opal'** (1.2m x 60cm) light blue, red stems.

Cynoglossum nervosum H5 (1m x 60cm) Another useful member of the same family: intense blue flowers in summer, clump forming with hairy leaves, a good plant for the woodland garden.

Androsace

A range of alpines in the primrose family, mostly with tiny woolly leaves in rosettes. The tiny flowers on long stalks are pink, red, lavender or white. They need a dry, gritty soil and good drainage but do not like to dry out, *A. lanuginosa* (10cm x 20cm) pink in late summer, trailing. *A. sarmentosa* (10cm x 10cm) pink, April–June. *A. sempervivoides* (2–4cm x 5cm) tiny, pink with a yellow eye in spring.

Androsace sempervivoides (RC-M)

Anemone

Every garden should have some anemones. They are mostly showy, tough and easy to please, varying in size from tiny to vigorous and spreading. Anemones can be roughly split into spring-flowering and late-summer-flowering groups. The spring anemones, most of which come from woodland or moorland regions, prefer a well-drained, moist, humus-rich soil in full or part shade. The late-summer (Japanese) anemones, which flower from August to October, prefer a warm, sunny, sheltered spot in well-drained soil; once established, they can spread vigorously.

Anemone blanda

Anemone coronaria

Anemone nemorosa

Anemone x hybrida, pink and white forms

Spring-flowering species and hybrids

A. blanda H5 (10–15cm x 30cm) ❦ small purple, blue, pink or white daisy-like flowers in February–March. ***A. coronaria H3–4*** (25cm x 30cm) blue, red, white, brightly coloured cultivars, need a good baking and well-drained soil. These two are sold as dried tubers in late summer, which need to be soaked before planting (the right way up of course, when you can figure it). The remainder are woodlanders for moist soil: ***A. nemorosa H5*** (15cm x 30cm) ❦ British native wood anemone, nodding bells in white and blush pink in late March–April; **'Alba Plena'** double white, **'Allenii'** ❦ large-flowered blue, **'Bowles Purple'** lilac, later than most, **'Robinsoniana'** ❦ lavender blue. ***A. ranunculoides H5*** (15–20cm x 30cm) similar to *A. nemorosa*, yellow, flowers a little later in spring. ***A. rivularis H5*** (15cm x 30cm) ❦ vigorous, white with violet reverse in spring, moist but not soggy soil, fine lobed foliage. ***A. sylvestris H5*** (45cm x 30cm) single white with a yellow centre in May. ***A. trullifolia H4*** (20cm x 20cm) ❦ varies from white-flushed pale blue to deep blue, the latter being the most desirable, flowering in May– June and sometimes again later in the summer. **Wild Swan**, H4 (50cm), white flowers with blue

backs in summer. Some of these species and forms are only available from specialist nurseries (try the annual Gardening Scotland show).

Late-summer-flowering species and hybrids

H5 (forms of *A. hupehensis* or *A. x hybrida*), spreading gradually (50cm–1m or more), especially in sandy soil; deep rooted, they dislike being moved once established; forms include **'Hadspen Abundance'** (60cm) ❦ single deep rose-pink, **'Bressingham Glow'** (45cm) semi-double ruby red, **'Honorine Jobert'** (1m) ❦ fine single white, but rather tricky and dislikes cold and damp, **'Königin Charlotte'** (1m) ❦ large single pink, flowers damage easily in rain, prone to eelworm, **'Lady Gilmour'** (syn. 'Crispa') (60cm–1m) irregular pink flowers, crisped foliage, **'Pamina'** (50cm) double deep pink, **'Praecox'** soft pink, **'Robustissima'** (*A. tomentosa*) (60cm) pink, very vigorous, sometime invasive, **'September'** (syn. 'September Charm') (60cm) ❦ semi-double rose pink, **'Whirlwind'** (90cm) semi-double white.

Anthemis see Daisies, page 171

Aquilegia (columbine)

H5 This is a hardy, tough, easily grown cottage garden and border favourite, tolerant of a wide range of soils and light conditions and suitable for anywhere in Scotland as far north as Shetland (where they do very well). The curiously spurred flowers in almost every colour and combination of colour appear in May–June, and are thrown up above the elegant divided leaves. There are both single and double forms, the single being more striking. Associating well with grasses and most herbaceous plants, aquilegias are relatively maintenance free, although aphids and mildew can cause problems. Aquilegias tend to be short lived, living for 2–3 years, but normally seed freely. They hybridise and spread rampantly and promiscuously, so if you want to keep selected forms

Aquilegia, three colour forms

pure, you will need to keep them isolated in one part of the garden. Most spread 30–45cm.

Dwarf species such as ***A. alpina*** (20–60cm) blue, and ***A. pyrenaica*** violet blue, and hybrids of them, make wonderful rock

Aquilegia vulgaris 'Nora Barlow'

garden plants. They prefer very well-drained soil and part shade, and can require some skill to grow. The following are larger growing and easy to please: **Biedermeier Group** (35cm) compact dwarf, upright-facing flowers in many colours, **'Blue Admiral'** (90cm) deep blue, **'Dragonfly'** (75cm) long-spurred flowers in a range of pastel shades, above ferny grey-blue foliage, **McKana Group** (75cm) large-spurred flowers in a wide range of colours, held above feathery glaucous leaves. **Star Group** (50cm–1cm) red, white and yellow. *A. vulgaris* (granny's bonnet) (90cm) ✄ mostly shades of blue-purple, this favourite British native has been much selected and hybridized: **Vervaeneana Group** (45–60cm) short spurred, blue, pink or white, mainly grown for the yellow leaves, mottled green and grey, **var. *stellata* Barlow Series** (75cm) double flowers in a range of deep colours, held above grey-green divided leaves, **'Nora Barlow'** ✿ striking combination of red, pink and green, **A.v. 'William Guinness'** (60cm) dark maroon (almost black) and white. **'Clementine Series'** (35cm) doubles in a wide range of colours. **Songbird Series** (75cm) very fine, preferring cool, northern climates, glaucous leaves; forms include: **'Blue Jay'** (blue and white), **'Cardinal'** (red), **'Dove'** (white), **'Goldfinch'** (yellow). **Winky Series** (50cm), crowded stems of bicolours, white with blue, purple or red; some people think them in bad taste.

Arabis (rock cress)
and *Erinus alpinus*

(10–15cm x 30–50cm) These rock garden, path-edge and wall-crevice gems both form low spreading mats, flowering in spring and early summer. They are easy to grow, and semi evergreen. Arabis have loose rosettes of often grey-green toothed leaves and are tolerant of dry conditions.

Arabis alpina 'Rosea', 'Snowcap' and 'Spring Charm'

A. alpina subsp. *caucasica* **'Flore Pleno'** *H4* one of the toughest, grows almost anywhere, with double white flowers; *A.a.* subsp. **'Schneehaube'** *H4* large single white, **'Variegata'** *H5* white/green leaves and white flowers, less persistent than the others. *A. ferdinandi-coburgi* **'Old Gold'** *H4* green leaves striped gold with white flowers. *A. procurrens* **'Variegata'** *H5* white-variegated leaves and white flowers.

Erinus alpinus H4 ✿ Mass of small pink flowers, a fairly compact alpine for crevices and troughs. Tends to be short lived but can seed around.

Armeria (sea pink or thrift)

A. maritima (thrift) grows wild in Britain on sea cliffs, and makes a great plant for seaside gardens and well-drained rock gardens and troughs in full sun. Spread slowly to 15cm or more.

Armeria maritima

A. juniperifolia *H2–3* (8cm) evergreen cushions of sharp green leaves, pompom-like pale pink flowers in spring–early summer; *A.b.* **'Bevan's Variety'** *H2–3* (8cm) ✿ deep pink, excellent. *A. maritima* *H5* (10cm) ✄ evergreen cushions, white to pink flowers in summer; forms include *alba* (10cm) white, **'Splendens'** reddish pink, **'Vindictive'** *H5* (10cm) ✿ a rather strange name for a fine plant, long flowering, deep rose-pink with blue-green leaves. **'Nifty Thrifty'** pale leaves, pink flowers.

Artemisia (mugwort, wormwood)
and *Euryops acraeus*

Artemisias are low-growing silvery foliage subshrubs and perennials that are grown mainly for their fine silvery white leaves, highly aromatic in some varieties, which are an excellent foil for other plants. They are happiest growing out of the wind, in full sunshine in light, well-drained soil. They can stand cold temperatures but can fail to come through the winter or be severely damaged by early frosts and snow. Most artemisias flower, but not in a way to write home about, and some recommend cutting them back before they flower to get a new flush of foliage instead. If plants get straggly or mildew strikes, the best course of action is a good trim: fresh healthy foliage will generally result. Don't do this too late in the season as it can kill the plants. Don't overfeed – they do well in poor soils; taller varieties may need staking, especially in rich or fertilized soils. Artemisias spread 60–90cm unless stated otherwise.

A. abrotanum (80cm) aromatic narrow grey-green leaves. *A. absinthium* **'Lambrook Silver'** (90cm) *H4* a long-cultivated medicinal plant, used to flavour drinks such as Pernod, with simple silvery-green leaves; *A.a.* **'Lambrook Mist'** *H3–4* (80cm) divided silvery-white, silky leaves, slightly less hardy. *A. lactiflora* **Guizho Group** *H3–4* (1.5m) intriguing jagged-edged, purple-green leaves and fairly attractive white flowers in late summer, somewhat mildew and rust prone, and you may lose it in winter. *A. ludoviciana* **'Silver Queen'** *H4* (1.2m) ✿ leaves near white, few flowers; *A.l.* **'Valerie Finnis'** (75cm) silvery-green willow-like

Artemisia ludoviciana 'Silver Queen'

Artemisia 'Powis Castle'

leaves, almost white in spring, prone to mildew. **'Powis Castle'** (60–90cm) very elegant filigree silvery leaves and grows into a pleasing mound shape. *A. stelleriana* **'Boughton Silver'** (60cm) one of the hardiest, but does not like prolonged winter wet, and forms carpets of deeply lobed silvery, almost white foliage that is more effectively evergreen than the others; an excellent foil for dwarf bulbs. *A. schmidtiana* **'Nana'** (10cm x 30cm) evergreen with silvery leaves and tiny yellow flowers, does best in well-drained soil with grit/pebbles around base.

Euryops acraeus **H3–4** (50cm) Has equally silvery foliage, and showier yellow daisy flowers in May–June. Requires a warm site in very sharply draining soil.

Aruncus see *Astilbe*, below

Aster

There are more than 600 species of *Aster*, the best known of which are the Michaelmas daisies, which give a late great splash of colour in September and October. They are amongst the most accommodating and attractive of late-summer and autumn-flowering border plants, although mildew can be a problem for *A. novi-belgii* varieties particularly in dry summers. Asters have daisy-like flowers, mostly in the pink-purple spectrum, tolerate most soils except waterlogged ones, and like full sun or light shade. Some are clump forming and others creep along the ground. The taller ones may need staking in rich soils and exposed gardens. Asters spread 45–60cm unless stated otherwise. Botanists have recently moved some species to a genus *Symphotrichum* but most people will still call them asters.

A. amellus **H5** (45–60cm) the Italian aster, mauve, August–September, coarse grey-green leaves, rather straggly and sparse at first but will make a good clump in time, a fine plant which should be more widely grown, as it does not suffer from mildew; *A.a.* **'Brilliant'** *H5* (60–75cm) bright purple-pink, *A.a.* **'King George'** *H5* (60–75cm) ⚜ violet-blue. *A. alpinus* **H3–4** (20cm) ⚜ dwarf, violet and yellow in June–July, full sun, good drainage. *A. divaricatus* (white wood aster) **H4–5** (40cm) starry white flowers on almost black stems in September and October; it prefers a moist soil in partial shade so is very good for naturalizing under trees and shrubs. *A. ericoides* (heath aster) **H4–5** (90cm x 30cm) from the American prairies, drought tolerant, clumps of thin dark-green leaves, flowering September–November, does not require splitting up; the varieties *A.e.* **'Blue Star'** *H4–5* (blue), *A.e.* **'Golden Spray'** *H4–5* (white, yellow centre) and *A.e.* **'Pink Cloud'** *H4–5* (purple-pink) are especially good garden plants. *A. x frikartii* **'Mönch'** *H5* (90cm) ⚜ long-flowering with lavender-blue flowers in July–October, rough grey-green leaves, mildew resistant, dislikes cold, wet soils, best planted in spring. **'Kylie'** (1.2m) pale pink in arching sprays in autumn, mildew resistant. *A. lateriflorus* **'Horizontalis'** *H5* (50cm x 30cm) spreading habit, pale-lilac flowers in September–October, narrow leaves; *A.l.* **'Prince'** (50cm) pink, young leaves bronze-purple. **'Little Carlow'** (to 1.2m) lavender, in late summer–autumn; Michael Wickendon, Carole Klein and others rate this as outstanding, largely mildew resistant. *A. novae-angliae* **H5** (1m) flowers from August to October on stiff stout stems, thin leaves; These are resistant to powdery mildew, but they need dividing every 3–4 years: **'Andenken an alma Pötschke'** bright salmon pink, fine, susceptible to tarsonemid mites (and would you dare ask for it with a name like that?), **'Barr's Pink'** large flowered, deep violet-blue with orange centres, **'Harrington's Pink'** pale salmon-pink, **'Herbstschnee'** pure white, **'Purple Dome'** (30cm) violet-purple, late. *A. novi-belgii* hybrids **H5** include some fine autumn-flowering garden plants, but they are a magnet for powdery

Aster novi-belgii

mildew, and tarsonemid mites which eat the flower buds can be a problem; amongst the most popular are **'Audrey'** (30cm) bright lilac-blue, **'Heinz Richard'** (30cm) pink, some mildew resistance, **'Jenny'** (30cm x 30cm) violet-purple, **'Lady in Blue'** (30cm) double lilac-blue, **'Marie Ballard'** (90cm) double powder blue, **'Schneekissen'** (25cm x 30cm) white. The **Island Series** are claimed to be mildew resistant: **'Bahamas'** rose red, **'Barbados'** violet, **'Samoa'** purple, **'Tonga'** red. *A. pilosus* var. *pringlei* **'Monte Cassino'** *H5* (60cm x 30cm) masses of starry white daisies in October–November, good for cutting, needs sharp drainage. *A. sedifolius* **'Nanus'** *H5* (30–45cm x 30cm) a mass of starry mauve flowers in August–September, mildew resistant.

Astilbe
and *Aruncus*

H5 The attractive ferny foliage of astilbes and their frothing, colourful plumes of red, pink or white make these tough perennials particularly good for Scottish gardens. They are easy to grow and wind tolerant, and they don't need staking. Astilbes like a moist humus-rich soil in sun or part day shade, although in shade they may not flower very freely and they look ragged and burned if allowed to dry out. They are low maintenance, resenting disturbance once established, though beware of vine weevil grubs, which love munching the roots. Early spring growth can be checked by frost, but this seldom affects the summer flowers. They look particularly good massed beside water, and can take a border position in full sun, provided the soil is kept moist. Fine displays can be seen in the gardens at Carnell and Culzean Castle in Ayrshire, lining the borders at the walled garden at Hatton in Aberdeenshire, and at the national collection at Holehird, in Cumbria. There are over 200 varieties listed in the *RHS Plantfinder*, which is about 150 too many: just choose the flowering time, colour and height you want, as most of them are perfectly good. Binny Plants near Edinburgh has a wide selection. Astilbes spread 60–90cm unless stated otherwise.

Astilbe x *arendsii* and *A. japonica* hybrids flower from July to August in a range of colours: **'Amethyst'** (90cm) lilac pink,

Astilbe, mixed

'Bressingham Beauty' (90cm) ✤ rich pink, **'Bumalda'** (75cm) white, bronze leaves, **'Deutschland'** (65cm) early white, **'Federsee'** (60cm) rosy red, said to be more drought tolerant than most, **'Fanal'** (60cm) ✤ deep red, the most popular red, and one of the best, **'Irrlicht'** (50cm) and **'Snowdrift'** (60cm) white, **'Lollipop'** (70cm) light purple-pink, dark stems, early, one of Billy Carruthers' (of Binny Plants) choices, **'Rheinland'** (60cm) ✤ purplish pink, early, **'Venus'** (90cm) bright pink. *A. chinensis* varieties are later flowering, from August–October, and relatively tolerant of sun and drier soils: *A.c.* var. *pumila* (30cm x 30cm) ✤ is smaller with lilac pink flowers, *A.c.* var. *taquetii* **'Purpurlanze'** (90cm) erect purple plumes, *A.c.* var. *t.*

Aruncus dioicus

'Superba' (1.2m) purple-rose flowers in August–October, fine foliage, *A.c. var. t.* **'Visions'** (50cm) strong purple. *A.* x *rosea* **'Peach Blossom'** (60cm) peach-pink. *A.* x *crispa* **'Lilliput'** (20cm x 25cm) small, salmon pink, crinkled dark foliage, 'probably the most beautiful dwarf Astilbe on the planet' (Billy Carruthers). *A. simplicifolia* and its hybrids are fine dwarf varieties with bronzy leaves: **'Bronze Elegance'** (syn. 'Bronce Elegans') (25cm x 25cm) bronze-purple foliage, rosy pink flowers in June–August, **'Sprite'** (45cm) ✤ one of the best dwarf varieties, pale pink feathery spikes, with dark reddish-green leaves, **'Willie Buchanan'** (20cm x 15cm) ✤ a gem for the rock garden with pale pink-creamy white flowers and burgundy-tinged dark leaves, named after the Bearsden gardener. Younique Series (50cm–1m) several colours, said to be particularly free flowering.

Aruncus **H5** These resemble tall, early-flowering white astilbes, and are tolerant of more sun and drier soil. They are happy massed in a woodland or waterside situation, and they look very fine with blue meconopsis. *A. aethusifolius* **H5** (30cm x 60cm) dwarf, with attractive deeply cut, fern-like leaves, small spikes of small white flowers in June–July. *A. dioicus* (goatsbeard) (1.5m x 1.2m) ✤ frothy white flower plumes, attractive dissect leaves. The form **'Kneiffii'** **H5** (90cm x 45cm) is lower growing, with bronzy young growth. *A. dioicus* grows well all over Scotland, even in coldest gardens. If male and female forms are planted together, seedlings may come up in swarms; you may be able to obtain only male or female plants. Be wary of planting this in mild areas with high rainfall – Mull, for instance – as it may get out of control.

Astrantia (masterwort)

H5 (40–90cm x 60–90cm) The distinctive and long-lasting flowers always attract attention, and this is an almost indestructible, fully hardy all-rounder in Scottish gardens. It's great for the semi-shade beneath open trees and shrubs, and also good as a border plant in full sun. Forming small to medium-sized mounds of attractively divided leaves, it is easy to grow in any reasonably moist soil. Astrantia is low maintenance, and pretty trouble free, although it tends to seed around. The flower heads on multi-headed stalks are surrounded by attractive papery bracts, in June–July, often continuing into August, especially if cut back after the first flush of flowering. The paler white-flowered varieties take on a luminous quality in a shady corner and are very effective amongst goatsbeard, white foxgloves and other pale-flowered perennials. The red forms do best in full sun, and are usually less vigorous than the white ones, associating well with centranthus, bronze-leaved grasses and plants with dark foliage.

'Buckland' (75cm) small pink flowers, tipped green. **'Hadspen Blood'** (75–90cm) blood red. *A. major* (60–90cm) white, tinged green or pink, includes the forms **'Claret'** (75–90cm) ✤ wine red, variable, **'Gill Richardson'** (75cm) rich crimson, **'Lars'** (60cm) dark red, **'Primadonna'** (90cm) pinky red, Roma [PBR] (90cm) pink with dark centre, 'very special' (Elizabeth MacGregor of Ellenbank nursery), *A.m. rosea* (60cm) pink, subsp. *involucrata* **'Shaggy'** (syn. 'Margery Fish') (75cm) large white flowers tipped green, very fine, *A.m. rubra* (60cm) plum red, *A.m.* **'Ruby Wedding'** (60cm) ✤ ruby red, dark stems, the best of all, but make sure you get the real thing, *A.m.* **'Sunningdale Variegated'** (80cm) leaves splashed and striped cream and yellow, with greenish-white flowers. *A. maxima* (60cm) pink, usually June flowering, fine but a little harder to please, resents drying out in summer, needs richer soil. **'Moulin Rouge'** (45cm) almost black-red with a spot of green.

Aubretia deltoidea

H5 A creeping alpine with masses of purple or reddish flowers in late spring and early summer, aubretia seems to be able to grow and seed itself almost anywhere. A tiny crevice can be enough to sustain a substantial plant, and a vertical display on a wall can be very impressive. It is worth

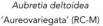

Aubretia deltoidea
'Aureovariegata' (RC-M)

Aubretia deltoidea

Bergenia 'Baby Doll'

Bergenia 'Silberlicht'

giving it a good haircut after flowering. It doesn't appear to enjoy Shetland's weather or very acidic soil much.

A. deltoidea (5cm x 15cm) lavender purple, spreading mats; **'Aureovariegata'** (5cm x 15cm) lavender purple, mats of yellow-edged green leaves, **'Argenteovariegata'** (5cm x 15cm) is similar with grey-edged leaves, **'Bressingham Pink'** (5–8cm x 30cm) deep pink, **'Dr Mules'** (5cm x 30cm) one of the oldest, evergreen toothed green leaves and large double deep purple flowers, **'Kitte Series'** (10cm) large flowers, several shades, **'Red Carpet'** (5–8cm x 30cm) deep red.

Aurinia see *Alyssum*, page 153

Bergenia (elephants' ears)

H4–5 With their large, glossy, leathery leaves, these are great structural evergreen herbaceous plants for borders and for massing under the semi-shade of trees and shrubs. Hardy, and clump forming, they flower in a range of reddish pink to white shades in early spring and, along with hellebores, they provide useful colour when the rest of the garden is just waking up. Bergenias are happy in most soils, in sun or shade, flowering best in sun. With age they squat and spread, sometimes refusing to flower much except round the margins of a clump, so you may need to dig them up and divide. The leaves, which are dark green, turning reddish in winter in some forms, can get battered and tattered in strong winds, and they will suffer in very dry conditions. In heavy frosts the leaves crumple and wilt, usually bouncing back up again when it warms up, but foliage and flowers can be damaged. Most are hardy, suitable for anywhere in Scotland. Rosa Steppanova advises very well drained soil to succeed with them in Shetland, to avoid winter rotting. Greenbank Garden near Glasgow has a national collection; former head gardener Jim May picks out *B. purpurescens* 'Bressingham White' and 'Silberlicht' as outstanding performers in a cold spot with regular late frosts. Most spread gradually to form clumps of 60–90cm or more and are *H4–5* unless stated otherwise.

'Abendglut' (25cm) semi-double magenta. **'Baby Doll'** (30cm) pale pink. **Ballawley hybrids** (60cm) grow best in part shade, glowing carmine-red on red stems, good winter colouring.

'Beethoven' (40cm) fine white. **'Bressingham Ruby'** (30cm) red-pink flowers, compact, fine red winter colour. **'Bressingham White'** *H3–4* (30cm) ♥ white, neat habit, Billy Carruthers' (of Binny Plants) and Jim May's choice as the best white. *B. cordifolia* (45cm) sprays of mauve-pink; *B.c.* **'Purpurea'** (30cm) ♥ a good ground-cover, magenta flowers, large leaves purplish in winter. **'Morgenröte'** (45cm) deep carmine-pink, sometimes repeat flowers in summer. *B. purpurescens* (syn. *B. beesiana*) (30cm) purple-red, bright beetroot-red leaves in winter. **'Silberlicht'** (30cm) ♥ white, gradually turning pink, winter leaves tinged reddish, said to be less hardy than most, good at Greenbank near Glasgow; Christopher Lloyd couldn't stand it. **'Sunningdale'** (30cm) deep red-pink, reddish winter foliage. **'Wintermärchen'** (40cm) deep pink, deep-green leaves, reddish in winter. **'Winterzauber'** (25cm) pink, outstanding red winter foliage, good at Greenbank.

Brunnera macrophylla

H4–5 (30–45cm x 45–60cm). This is a tough, useful ground-cover for shady areas beneath trees and shrubs, which can also be used as a border plant. The heart-shaped leaves are rough textured with interesting colour variations, developing more character as they age, and forming mats above which sprays of tiny blue forget-me-not-like flowers appear in spring. It prefers part shade but copes in full sun provided the soil is cool and moist. Exposure to strong/cold winds can cause leaf scorch, particularly with variegated leaf forms. Though there are other species, garden forms of Brunnera are all derived from *B. macrophylla* ♥ and are easy to grow.

Brunnera macrophylla 'Jack Frost'

'Dawson's White' (syn. *B.m.* 'Variegata') *H4* wide rounded cream-variegated leaves, bright-blue flowers, **'Hadspen Cream'** *H4* bright blue, leaves with a broad cream edge, **'Jack Frost'** *H5* (30cm x 45cm) ♥ silvery leaves with green veins, deep-blue flowers, **'Langtrees'** *H5* similar flowers to 'Jack Frost', leaves dark green, spotted silvery grey, **'Looking Glass'** *H5* (30cm x 45cm) leaves silvery grey with faint green veins.

Invasive Species Legislation:
invasive and undesirable plants
There is new EU legislation coming through Scottish government to cover plants and animals which are or may have become a problem due to their invasiveness and their ability to smother native flora or cause other undesirable consequences such as silting up rivers and streams or causing skin allergy.

1. Section 14A. A list of plants which may not be sold or planted anywhere in Scotland.

Several rampant water plants
Fallopia japonica (Japanese knotweed)
Heracleum mantegauianum (giant hogweed)
R. ponticum (likely to be added 2007–8)

2. Schedule 9, 3.1. This is a list of plants which can spread out of control and it is proposed to make it illegal to 'cause them to grow' in the wild. These are plants which have caused or may cause environmental damage in areas where they spread unchecked. Plants such as *Rubus spectabilis*

should be re-assessed and placed on the section 14A list above. Some plants on this list are particularly problematic on the milder and wetter part of the west coast, while they may be relatively harmless on the drier eastern side of the country. We doubt anyone will ever be prosecuted under the above legislation, but it does serve as a warning of possible effects on the environment.

Alchemilla mollis
Allium paradoxum
Allium triquetrum
Aster aggregate
Buddleja davidii
Cotoneaster species
Crocosmia
Fallopia – all species
Gaultheria shallon
Gunnera
Hyacinthoides hispanica (Spanish bluebell)
Hippophae rhamnoides
Impatiens balsamica
Lamium galeobdolon argentatum
Lavatera arborea
Lysichiton americanum
Persicaria wallichii
Rosa rugosa
Rubus spectabilis
Rubus armeniacus
Spiraea x pseudosalicifolia, S. x billardii
Symphoricarpus albus

Plants for moist shade
Provided the soil is not waterlogged, nor the shade too dense, moist shade can support a wide range of plants. Shade under the edges of the crowns of trees and large shrubs is ideal, whereas right underneath the middle of a dense tree such as beech will be too dark and too dry for almost all plants. The north sides of walls often provide sites with moist shade.

Shrubs
Aucuba
Bamboos
Berberis
Buxus sempervirens
Callicarpa
Desfontainea
Gaultheria
Hydrangea
Ilex
Mahonia
Osmanthus
Prunus laurocerasus and *P. lusitanica*
Rhododendron and Azalea (dappled or part day shade only)

Perennials
Alchemilla mollis
Arum italicum
Astrantia
Bergenia
Brunnera
Dicentra
Digitalis
Dodecatheon
Ferns
Gunnera
Heuchera
Hosta
Luzula sylvatica
Tiarella
Tricyrtis
Trillium

Bulbs
Camassia
Cardiocrinum
Galanthus
Eranthis
Narcissus (species)

Bulbs, tubers and corms

No garden in Scotland should be without bulbs – from the humble happy spring crocus and snowdrop, to exotic-looking woodland treasures such as the giant Himalayan lily (*Cardiocrinum*), and the show-stopping alliums and summer-flowering lilies. Bulbs are particularly useful for extending the season (both early and late) and for growing in between shrubs and plants in borders. In most cases, they have a dormant period below ground, allowing their neighbours room to grow and flower. Annual topdressing with compost or well-rotted manure just as they are dying down will keep them happy. Bulbs, rhizomes, tubers and corms are included in this section, although iris (tuberous) and crocosmias (corm) are perceived more as herbaceous plants than bulbs, and have their own entries. There are hundreds of daffodils and tulips to choose from – worthy of a book on their own – and they are dealt with only briefly here. Bulbs and related plants that are tender and need lifting in winter, such as dahlias, chrysanthemums, cannas, etc., are not covered.

Allium cristophii

Allium H3–5 A large genus including onions, garlic and chives (***A. schoenoprasum*** – see page 196), as well as many highly ornamental species, which form clumps of strap-shaped leaves and flower mostly in May–June. The flower heads form a large spherical globe of many tiny individual flowers. Alliums prefer full sunshine and a well-drained soil. Slugs, river voles and white rot can cause problems; in the latter case, bulbs should be lifted and destroyed. In general they should be planted 15cm deep. The taller varieties are useful for the middle of a border. A few members of this genus, e.g. *A. moly* and *A. neapolitanum*, can become a pest as they spread and seed everywhere. ***A. caeruleum H3–4*** (80cm) small blue flower heads, ***A. carinatum* subsp. *pulchellum H3–4*** (60cm) drooping purple flower heads. ***A. cernuum H5*** (70cm) loose hanging pink and white flower heads; best form is **'Hidcote'**. ***A. cristophii H5*** (1.2m) large spheres of star-shaped purple flowers. ***A. giganteum H5*** (2m) large dense purple-pink flower heads. ***A. hollandicum* 'Purple Sensation' *H5*** (90cm) violet-purple. ***A. karataviense H5*** (20cm) wide exotic glaucous leaves, large late-spring pale-pink flower heads. ***A. schubertii H5*** (60cm) large flower heads of purple-pink starry flowers, **'Gladiator' *H5*** (1.5m) enormous purple-pink spherical flower heads, **'Globemaster' *H5*** (80cm) deep-purple flowers.

Arisaema* (cobra lily) *H3–5 ☠ This curious, Gothic mini-monster is loved by some but found sinister by most. The flower consists of a hooded pitcher known as a spathe, which is usually striped and often has curious 'ears' or 'tails' on its end, and a spadix, which grows inside and contains the floral parts. Arisaemas generally like moist but not wet conditions in woodland, or part day shade. There are around 170 species and you are likely to need to try specialist nurseries for most of them. ***A. candidissimum*** (30cm) the most widely grown species, variable, spathe usually white to pale green. ***A. flavum*** (50–75cm) spathe yellow, will tolerate drier conditions.

Arum italicum 'Marmoratum'

Arum* (cuckoo pint, lords and ladies) *H4–5 ☠ A very useful clump-forming plant for naturalising in shady sites beneath trees and shrubs. The often attractively mottled leaves appear from the tubers in autumn, followed by spikes of bright red poisonous berries. The pale greeny-white spathes (flowers) appear in spring. They prefer well-drained, rich soil, and benefit from a protective winter mulch in cold areas. Plant 7.5cm deep. ***A. italicum H4–5*** (25cm) arrow-shaped white-veined leaves, bright orange-red berries; **'Marmoratum'** (syn. 'Pictum') attractively mottled green and white leaves.

Asphodelus albus H3–4 (90cm) Starry white flowers on stems in late spring and early summer, likes well-drained soil in full sun, mulch in colder gardens in winter. ***A. lutea*** has yellow flowers.

Camassia* (quamash) *H5 These summer-flowering bulbs produce clumps of thin sword-like leaves, above which rise showy flower spikes, densely packed with star-shaped flowers in shades of white, blue and purple. Camassias prefer heavy moist soils with reasonable drainage, and tend to perform better in west-coast gardens rather than east. They must not be allowed to dry out in spring and summer, and should be planted 15cm deep and 15cm apart, in autumn. They can be naturalized in moist meadows. ***C. cusickii*** (70cm)

Camassia cusickii

soft lavender blue. *C. leichtlinii* (1.2m) violet-blue or creamy white. *C. quamash* (80cm) large flowers in blue, purple or white shades.

Cardiocrinum giganteum (giant Himalayan lily) H4

(2–3m) ❀ This fabulous bulb thrives in Scotland's cool climate, producing tall spikes of large heart-shaped green leaves which spiral up the stem to the exotic, heavily fragrant cream-coloured trumpet-shaped flowers with deep purple throats. The bulbs should be planted just below the surface in autumn, about 90cm apart. The bulb below the flowering stem dies after flowering, but there are usually offsets, which should be detatched in late summer and replanted. It takes about 5–6 years to flower from seed, so to ensure continuity it is best to have a clump of bulbs of various sizes. It prefers a rich, moist soil with adequate drainage, and is susceptible to late spring frosts and slugs and snails. It should not be allowed to dry out in the growing season, and will benefit from a winter mulch in colder areas. **var.** *yunnanense* produces slightly shorter flower spikes and bronze-green leaves.

Cardiocrinum giganteum (RC-M)

Chionodoxa luciliae (blue)

Chionodoxa (glory of the snow) H5 (10–20cm)

Beware of this early-spring charmer, because it can become a menace, seeding everywhere. In the right place, however, its bright flowers brighten up late winter and early spring. Chionodoxas thrive in most soils and are good for naturalizing at the edge of borders or in light shade beneath trees and shrubs. They should be planted in groups, about 5cm deep, in autumn. They are fully hardy (*H5*) and usually trouble free. The two species listed are now considered a single variable entity, but both names are used. *C. luciliae* (syn. *C. gigantea*) (10cm) large blue flowers with a white eye. *C. forbesii* (syn. *C. luciliae*) (20cm) generally smaller white-eyed deeper blue flowers; *C.f.* **'Pink Giant'** (20cm) white-eyed pink flowers.

Colchicum (autumn crocus)

Colchicum (autumn crocus, naked ladies) H5 ☘

Not a crocus at all, this is a wonderful, tough and easy plant which provides autumn colour, with huge crocus-like floral goblets in warm shades of pink, mauve and creamy white. The flowers appear naked without the large green clumps of leaves, which come up in spring. Colchicums prefer well-drained soil in full sun, and should be planted 10cm deep in late summer. The foliage has a tendency to flop over and smother small neighbouring plants. All parts of the plants are poisonous. *C. autumnale* (15cm) deep pink or white; **'Album'** white. *C. byzantinum* pale mauve. **'Lilac Wonder'** a rich warm lilac. *C. speciosum* shades of pink; **'Album'** white. **'Waterlily'** (15cm) very showy double lilac-pink.

Convallaria majalis

Convallaria majalis (lily of the valley) H5 ☘☘ (15cm)

The tiny white spring bells pack a considerable punch in their scent. Creeping rhizomes form small clumps, which are great for naturalizing in the lightly shaded woodland edge conditions around trees and shrubs. They like a rich soil with adequate drainage – avoid wet or boggy areas. Plant the rhizomes pointy end up, just below the soil surface, in autumn, and just wait for them to spread gradually. All parts of the plant are extremely toxic. **'Flore Pleno'** is a double version.

Crocus H4–5

A harbinger of spring with their instantly recognizable funnel-shaped flowers, which open wide in the sun. They are great for naturalising in lawns and at the edge of borders, preferring a sunny position in well-drained soil. They should be planted 7.5cm deep (10–15cm in very light sandy soil) in autumn, and can be left alone for years. Birds have an annoying habit of attacking yellow-flowered crocus, and black thread can be tied to sticks to deter them. Mice and squirrels like the taste of the corms, especially when they are newly planted; if this becomes an issue, try placing chicken

Crocus (spring flowering)

Cyclamen coum (RC-M)

Cyclamen hederifolium (RC-M)

wire over them. There are hundrerds of both small- and large-flowered forms; just choose the colours you like.

Cyclamen H3–5 ❄ This large genus includes some very hardy autumn and late-winter-flowering garden plants, as well as some very attractive houseplants. Cyclamen form clumps of often prettily marbled ivy- or heart-shaped leaves, which appear after or with the purple, pink and white flowers. Plant them in either full sun or partial shade, in well-drained soil, a few centimetres below the surface, and then leave them alone. Vine weevil can cause problems; infestations should be treated with insecticide or nematodes if necessary. The varieties listed reach 8cm x 10cm+, unless stated otherwise. **C. cilicium H3** white or purple in autumn. **C. coum H4–5** deep mauve-pink or white in winter to early spring. **C. hederifolium H4–5** shades of pink, late summer and autumn, good for naturalising in light woodland shade. **C. purpurascens H4** purple-pink fragrant flowers in summer and autumn. Dwarf cyclamen sold for October and November flowering under names such as **'Miracle' H2** are not reliably hardy and need to be over-wintered in a greenhouse or cold frame except in mild areas.

Eranthis hyemalis (winter aconite) H5 (10cm) With its attractive yellow flowers and low-growing clumps of divided leaves, this is one of the first plants to flower in February, and it is a great foil for snowdrops. The tubers should be planted 2.5cm deep in well-drained moist soil, in full sun or light shade.

Eremurus (foxtail lily) H2–4 (2m) The dramatic towering spikes of densely packed flowers held above strap-

Eranthis hyemalis (winter aconite)

shaped leaf clumps, can make superb border specimens. They often need staking and hate wind. Hardiness is variable, and their early growth makes them susceptible to frost damage. A protective straw mulch will help in all but the mildest Scottish gardens. Plant them a couple of centimetres below the soil surface in a sunny position, in well-drained soil. **E. himalaicus H4** pure white. **E. robustus H3–4** pink. **E. x isabellinus H2–3 'Cleopatra'** peachy orange; **Ruiter hybrids** shades of orange, beige, cream or white.

Erythronium revolutum 'White Beauty'

Erythronium (dog's-tooth violet) H5 Spring flowering, with beautiful pendent flowers in a range of pink, yellow and white shades, erythroniums spread gradually. They are great for naturalising in the light shade beneath trees and shrubs, as well as in the rock garden or border edge. They are easy to grow in any moist well-drained fertile soil, and form small to medium-sized clumps of often attractively spotted foliage. Don't buy dry bulbs after September, as they should be planted and growing roots by then. Much better to beg a few bulbs in late summer from a friend as the foliage is dying back, or buy them potted in spring. They grow well in Shetland. **E. dens-canis** (20cm) pink, purple or white, attractive foliage. **'Pagoda'** (35cm) nodding yellow flowers, slightly spotted green leaves. **E. revolutum** (25cm) pink, reflexed flowers; **'White Beauty'** (E. californicum) (30cm) very fine, multiplying quickly, pretty, reflexed cream-white flowers, excellent under rhododendrons.

Eucomis (pineapple flower) H2 This exotic-looking late-summer flower resembles a pineapple, with a little crest

Eucomis comosa (RC-M)

of leaves on top of the creamy-white flower spike, and is worth trying in the milder areas of Scotland. The bulbs should be planted a few centimetres below the soil in spring, in well-drained soil, in full sun. Protect with mulch in winter. *E. bicolor* (40cm) green or cream flowers with faint purple edges. *E. comosa* (60cm) white flowers on purple-spotted stems; the form **'Sparkling Burgundy'** has leaves and bracts tinged reddish.

Fritillaria imperialis 'Lutea'

Fritillaria meleagris (RC-M)

Galanthus (snowdrop)

Fritillaria H3–5 A varied genus, including some wonderful small to medium-sized spring-flowering garden plants. In general, they prefer a well-drained soil, in full sun or part shade. *F. camschatcensis H5* (60cm) rich purple-black, plant 15cm deep in rich soil. *F. imperialis* (crown imperial) *H4* (to 1.5m) a showy rather vulgar border plant, leaf-topped flower spike, packed with drooping orange, yellow (**'Lutea'**) or deep red (**'Rubra'**) bells; plant 20cm deep in autumn. *F. meleagris H4–5* (snake's head fritillary) (30cm) snakeskin-patterned flowers in shades of purple, pink and white, Good for naturalizing in grass (although it can be fickle), should be planted 15cm deep; Rosa Steppanova does well with it in Shetland.

Galanthus (snowdrop) H3–5 One of the first plants to flower after Christmas. There are many wonderful snowdrop displays in Scotland, with Cambo in Fife being perhaps the best known. Though they look perfectly at home here, snowdrops actually come from Turkey and other parts of Europe. They form small clumps of strappy leaves with stems of nodding white and green flowers in winter (about 12–15cm high), disappearing entirely by the end of June. Plant bulbs 10–15cm deep in late summer or early autumn, no later than September, or buy 'in the green' in late spring, after flowering. Plant in fertile, well-drained soil in light shade. Do not buy wild-sourced bulbs; buy only those from cultivated stock. *G. nivalis* (common snowdrop) *H5* white with a green splash; **'Flore Pleno'** double. Galanthophiles – yes, there is even a name for snowdrop fanatics – collect other species and dozens of expensive named forms, some of which flower at odd times of year. It's a shame they can't seem to find any colour other than white . . .

Galtonia candicans

Hyacinthoides non-scriptus (bluebell)

Galtonia **(summer hyacinth)** *H3–4* (1.2m) A beautiful plant with late summer white or pale green flowers, best suited to areas of Scotland not too far from the coast, although worth trying with a protective mulch in colder regions. Galtonias form clumps of strap-shaped green leaves, and should be planted 15cm deep in full sun or light shade, in rich, well-drained soil. Galtonia is used in bold plantings at Manderston, near Duns, in the Borders, and Kellie Castle in Fife has a fine border of them combined with catmint. *G. candicans* ❈ spikes of scented white bells in August. *G. viridiflora* flowers pale green.

Hyacinthoides **(bluebell)** *H5* ❈ Bluebell woods are one of Britain's great wild-flower displays. Bluebells also make robust and versatile garden plants, although they can spread beyond their desired location. The bulbs form clumps of fresh green strap-like leaves, with scented blue, mauve or white flower spikes in late spring. They should be planted 10–15cm deep in autumn, in sun or part shade, in moist but not boggy, humus-rich soil. The vigorous, seemingly larger and more erect flowering Spanish bluebell is more invasive than the English type (more graceful with nodding stems), and it is likely to become illegal to naturalise these. Both reach 30cm.

H. hispanica (Spanish bluebell) blue, white or pink. *H. non-scriptus* (English bluebell) scented blue, pink or white flowers on stems that bend near the top.

Hyacinthus H4 🜨 ❋ These bulbs produce pretty, scented (sometimes sickly sweet) flower spikes, in white, cream, pale yellow, orange, deep or pale pink, blue or purple, instantly recognizable from Christmas baskets or park bedding schemes. They can be useful garden plants,

although perhaps they do not associate as well with other plants as other bulbs do. Plant garden hyacinths about 15cm deep in full sun or light shade, in any well-drained soil. Take care when handling the bulbs, as they can cause skin irritation.

Hyacinths

Leucojum (snowflake) *H2–5* These 'giant snowdrops' form clumps of fresh green sword-like leaves, above which appear the spikes of nodding green-tipped white bells in spring and late summer. They prefer a moist soil with adequate drainage, and a position in light shade. They vary in size and hardiness, and should be planted 7.5cm deep, and then left undisturbed. *L. aestivum* (summer snowflake) *H5* (60cm)

Leucojum vernum (RC-M)

flowers in late spring; *L.a.* **'Gravetye Giant'** slightly bigger. *L. autumnale* (autumn snowflake) *H2–3* (15cm) bears autumnal pink-tinged white flowers on thin stems. *L. vernum* (spring snowflake) *H5* (10cm) flowers in spring.

Lilium H3–5 ❋ Fabulous, versatile and showy plants, great for growing in borders or pots and for cut flowers. Lily bulbs produce stems of grassy to broad green leaves, at the tops of which appear the dramatic, often strongly scented flowers, in a wide range of colours, in trumpet, turk's cap, or open-faced shapes. Hardiness is difficult to gauge, as some lilies are short lived, and most are susceptible to a diverse selection of viral and fungal ills, as well as animal attacks from slugs, rots, lily beetle and vine weevil. The naming of lilies is another fun adventure for the poor gardener, and there are many distinct groups, including Asiatic, Martagon hybrids, Candidum cultivars, American cultivars, Longiflorum cultivars, Trumpet cultivars, Oriental cultivars, Regale group and Tigrinum group. There are huge numbers of hybrids that do very well in Scotland. The following species are amongst the

Lilium speciosum var. album

Lilium 'Stargazer'

most widely available. Most will not survive in permanently cold, damp soils, and as a precaution should be planted with sharp grit or sand beneath the bulb. Plant most of them 15–20cm deep. *L. candidum* (Madonna lily) *H2–3* (1–2m) ❋ fragrant trumpet-shaped white flowers in summer, and prefers full sun and alkaline soil, not for cold gardens. *L. duchartrei* white with purple spots, and *L. lankongense* rosy purple (both *H5*, 60cm) spreading and easy; flowering in summer. *L. formosanum var. pricei H5* (60cm) white trumpet flowers with purple markings in late summer, prone to virus and split corollas. *L. henryi H5* (2m) reflexed turk's-cap orange spotted flowers in late summer, prefers alkaline soil. *L. lancifolium* (syn. *L. tigrinum*) **'Flore Pleno' H5** (1m) a variable tiger lily with double pink to orange purple-spotted turk's-cap flowers in late summer. *L. mackliniae H5* (40cm) drooping bell-shaped purple-pink to pale-pink flowers in early June. *L. martagon* (turk's cap lily) *H5* (1.5m) many-flowered stems of dusky-pink, purple or white (album) spotted turk's cap flowers in summer. *L. regale* (regal lily) *H5* (to 2m) ❋ sweetly scented white with yellow centres in summer, plant just beneath the soil surface, in a sunny position. *L. speciosum var. rubrum H5* (1.5m) ❋ heavily scented, deep carmine-pink, spotted flowers with reflexed petals in late summer.

Muscari

Muscari (grape hyacinth) *H3–5* (15–20cm) Grape hyacinths are great little blue or white-flowered spring bulbs to group at the front of borders or naturalise beneath open shrubs such as roses. They do, however, have a tendency to spread everywhere, and once you've got them, you can't get rid of them. They prefer a sunny position in any soil with reasonable drainage.

Plant 7.5cm deep in autumn. **M. armeniacum H5** deep blue; **'Valerie Finnis' H5** strong sky blue. **M. azureum H3–4** pale blue; **M.a. 'Album'** white. **M. latifolium H3–4** (25cm) deep violet-blue.

Narcissus (daffodil), large-flowered hybrids

Narcissus 'Jetfire'

Narcissus (daffodil) H5 As redolent of spring as the bluebell, daffodils are some of the easiest garden plants to grow. They form clumps of thin strap-like leaves, and send up taller stems carrying their mainly yellow flowers in spring. It is advisable to leave the messy yellowing foliage after the blooms have gone, because these leaves are storing food for next year's flowers. Clumps may need lifting and dividing when they go 'blind' with masses of leaves and few flowers appearing. They should be planted in autumn, with the amount of soil above them roughly equal to double the height of the bulb. Daffodils like sunny or lightly shaded sites, in a rich, moist soil with adequate drainage. Slugs can cause problems, as can basal rot, eelworm and narcissus yellow stripe virus. In the case of pronounced viral infections, lift and destroy the infected bulbs. Many Scottish gardens have fine daffodil displays in spring, including Brodie Castle in Morayshire, Braco in Perthshire and Greenbank Garden near Glasgow. They are rabbit and deer proof. There are many charming low-growing varieties for the small garden, border and rockery. Varieties include: **'Quail'**, **'Pipit'**, 'Rip Van Winkle', **'Tête à Tête'**, etc. If you want to naturalize daffodils in grass, the best are the vigorous types such as **'King Alfred'**. Many of the commercially available daffodils sold in garden centres are grown in eastern Scotland by Grampian Growers: you may see the fields in flower in spring in the Forfar, Brechin and Stonehaven areas.

Nerine (Guernsey lily) H3–4 These deep-pink and white bulbs are useful for late-season colour. They form large clumps of strap-shaped leaves, with flower spikes in September–October with up to eight flowers per stem. They need good drainage and do best in Scotland against

Nerine bowdenii

a south- or west-facing wall. Greywalls in Gullane has a superb double border of them. Nerines will also tolerate poor soils, but do not like to dry out when in growth. Plant the bulbs in early spring so that the neck stands above the soil, in a well-drained site or a raised bed. **N. bowdenii** (60cm) is the toughest of the tribe, pink flowers with curved petals; **N.b. alba** is the slightly pink-flushed white form. The others are for mild gardens only.

Scilla siberica

Scilla H3–4 Cheery small spring bulbs, good for naturalising at the front of borders or in grass. They produce narrow strap-like leaves, and frost-resistant flowers in shades of purple, blue, pink and white in early spring. Plant 5cm deep in early autumn, in any moist well-drained soil, in sun or light shade. No maintenance required, other than control of excessive self-seeding. All parts of the plants are poisonous. **S. bifolia H4** (15cm) many-flowered spikes in early spring, in shades of violet-blue, pink or white. **S. mischtschenkoana** (syn. *S. tubergeniana*) (12cm) pale purple. **S. peruviana H3** (20cm) striking deep-mauve flower heads in early summer; benefits from a protective mulch in colder gardens. **S. siberica** (14cm) deep violet-blue.

Trillium chloropetalum

Trillium (wood lily, wake robin) H5 These fascinating woodlanders are well suited to Scottish conditions, with clumps of distinctive and often patterned leaves and irresistible flowers, in a range of colours, in April–May. They thrive in rich, moist, well-drained soils, in shady conditions, and the rhizomes should be planted 10cm deep in late summer or from pots in spring. They spread slowly, forming impressive drifts in time: those at the Royal Botanic Garden Edinburgh and at Cluny House in Aberfeldy, Perthshire, are the envy of many gardeners. Keep an eye out for slugs. All those listed are fully hardy (**H5**) and reach 45cm x 30cm unless otherwise stated. *T. cuneatum* deep-red flowers, mottled leaves. *T. erectum* upright deep reddish purple. *T. grandiflorum* large white flowers which fade to pink. *T. luteum* yellow flowers, mottled leaves, not very vigorous. *T. ovatum* (50cm high) pure white upright flowers. *T. rugelii* nodding white flowers below the leaves, the most vigorous and quickest to spread.

Tulipa (tulip) Almost everyone loves tulips, with their brightly coloured goblet-shaped flowers in spring. They like free-draining soil in a sunny position. Most larger hybrids tend to weaken if not lifted and replanted each year, unless you can create a sunny bed with excellent drainage; we don't cover these varieties in this book. There are, however, some dwarf species and hybrid tulips which can be naturalized (planted and left *in situ* where they will slowly multiply) in well-drained, sunny soil about 10cm deep. *T. bakeri* 'Lilac Wonder' (15cm) bright pink, May. *T. humilis* 'Eastern Star' (10cm) magenta with a yellow eye, late May. *T.*

linifolia (30cm) red, April–May. *T. praestans* 'Fusilier' (45cm) with its early-spring multi-headed stems of orange-red flowers. The orange-yellow *T. praestans* (30cm) orange to scarlet in April–May, multi-headed; 'Fusiler' a fine red form. *T. sprengeri*

Tulips, red and yellow

(45cm) red-orange in early summer, one of the latest. *T. tarda* (15cm) yellow and white, tinged green. *T. turkestanica* (20cm) March–April, cream, unpleasantly scented. The two best groups of hybrids for naturalizing are **Kaufmanniana hybrids** (15–20cm) March–April flowers in many colours, mottled leaves, and **Greigii hybrids** (25cm) with mottled leaves and May-flowering single flowers; an example is 'Red Riding Hood' deep red.

Caltha palustris
(marsh marigold, kingcup)

Caltha palustris

H5 ✉ Marsh marigolds or kingcups can be found in boggy ground, pondsides and streamsides all over Scotland. They are moisture-loving, mound-forming plants, good for bog gardens or pondside planting, with bright yellow or white flowers in spring. *C. palustris* **H5** (25–40cm x 25cm) ♥ yellow flowers; more popular in gardens are the double yellow 'Flore Pleno' ♥ with longer-lasting flowers, and the white form *C.p. alba* ♥.

Campanula cochleariifolia and *C. carpatica*

Campanula
(bell flower)
and Platycodon
(balloon flower)

H2–5 *Campanula* is a variable genus of more than 300 species, ranging from stately border plants such as the 2m-high *C. lactiflora* hybrids to low-growing gems like the 10cm 'Birch Hybrid'. The bell-shaped flowers appear in a range of blues, mauves, purples, pinks and whites, from spring to late summer. Campanulas dislike strongly acidic (very peaty) or permanently wet soil. The taller varieties form large clumps and produce flower spikes from June to August; they may need staking and are happiest in a sunny position, in free-draining soil. The lower varieties are mat forming, and good for border edges, the rock garden, crevices, troughs and walls. The taller campanulas benefit from the old flower stems being cut back to soil level after flowering. Mildew and rusts can cause problems on some varieties; avoid too much fertilizer and overhead watering, and/or use a fungicide. Keep an eye out for slugs too and treat accordingly.

Taller varieties

(50cm–2m high) *C. alliariifolia* **H3** (syn.'Ivory Bells') (60cm x 45cm) nodding creamy-white flowers and heart-shaped grey-green leaves, may not survive colder inland gardens. *C. glomerata* 'Superba' **H5** (60–90cm x 1m) ♥ a vigorous, somewhat rampant grower with rounded heads of large purple flowers; forms include 'Alba' white, 'Caroline' white flushed lilac. *C.* 'Kent Belle' **H4** (1.2–1.5m x 45cm) deep-violet glossy bells, prone to rust, habit floppy. 'Sarastro' (50cm) deep purple, outstanding. *C. lactiflora* **H5** (1.2–1.5m x 60cm+) masses of purple, blue, lavender, pale-pink or white bells; 'Alba' ♥ white, 'Loddon Anna' **H5** (1.5m) ♥ pale pink, 'Prichard's Variety' (1m) ♥ violet-blue, the bluest form 'Superba' ♥ violet-blue. As well as being eye-catching border plants, *C. lactiflora* varieties can be naturalized in grass. The dwarf form 'Pouffe' is weak and not impressive (Christopher Lloyd calls it 'revolting'). *C. latifolia* **H5** (90cm–1.2m x 60cm) very tough, flowers in spikes in shades of purple, blue and white; forms include 'Brantwood' violet-purple, var. *alba*, white, var. *macrantha* rich violet-purple. *C. latiloba* **H5** (1m) stiff erect stems with cup-shaped flowers along them in July–August, rather coarse, best at the back of the border and good in woodland gardens; forms include 'Percy Piper' purple,

Campanula 'Kent Belle'

Campanula lactiflora 'Loddon Anna' and 'Prichard's Variety'

'Hidcote Amethyst' lavender, and 'Alba' white. *C. persicifolia H5* (1m x 30cm) evergreen, or semi-evergreen, with long thin rich-green leaves and slender, wiry stems of nodding cup-shaped flowers, ranging in colour from purple to white: they benefit from staking to prevent them from going horizontal and they can get rust; forms include: var. *alba* white, 'Bennett's Blue' double blue, 'Chettle Charm' [PBR] nodding flowers, white tinged blue, 'Telham Beauty' light blue. *C. pyramidalis* (2m) H4 Tall spikes of blue or white flowers in June–July, cut back after flowering, usually biennial, *C. takesimana H5* (50cm x 1m+) tubular white hanging bells, suffused pink, spotted red within, in July–September on arching stems, likes moist soil in semi-shade, can spread vigorously; 'Elizabeth' a selection with deeper plum-pink flowers.

Lower-growing varieties

'Birch Hybrid' *H5* (10cm x 30cm) large open deep-violet blooms in summer. *C. carpatica* 'Blaue Clips' *H5* (usually sold as 'Blue Clips') (30cm x 30cm) mounds of toothed green leaves, masses of blue flowers throughout summer, often short-lived; the white form is 'Weisse Clips'/'White Clips'. 'G.F. Wilson' *H5* (10cm x 15cm) neat mounds of yellow-green leaves, masses of large upturned violet bells. *C. cochlearifolia H5* (8cm x as far as you let it) nicknamed fairy thimbles, spreads by runners which produce rosettes of tiny leaves and masses of lavender, white or pale-blue thimble-like flowers, good in paving and walls. 'Elizabeth Oliver' pale lavender form, *C. garganica* H4 (5cm x 30cm) star-shaped blue or purple flowers in summer; *C.g.* 'Dickson's Gold' leaves greenish yellow. 'Isabella Blue' (30cm) free flowering blue in summer, *C. portenschlagiana H5* (15cm x 1m+) a vigorous ground-cover (as well as needing vigour to pronounce it), deep-blue bells all summer, good in walls, paving cracks and crevices. Can be invasive; the form 'Catharina' is better behaved. *C. poscharskyana* 'E.H. Frost' *H5* (10cm x 1m) is another mouthful, a spreading ground-cover which can climb up low walls, with star-shaped white flowers, seeds freely, can grow in shade, 'Stella' H5 (10cm x 1m) fine dark-blue form; Blue Waterfall ['Camgood'] fine blue. *C. punctata H5* (30cm x 1m+) cream to mauve bells in late summer, spotted red inside, can spread vigorously and invastively; 'Hot Lips' white speckled

crimson, *C.p.* f. *rubriflora H5* (30cm x 45cm) narrow-mouthed hanging bells, cream, flushed purple, with red spots inside, f. *rubriflora* 'Bowl of Cherries' deep purplish red. *C. rotundifolia* (harebell) *H5* with delicate blue bells on slender stems, the native harebell is an attractive feature of Scotland in July–August, on roadside verges in well-drained soil, and it can be encouraged to seed in grass. 'Samantha' (20cm x 40cm) long flowering April–September, fragrant violet flowers, creeping habit.

Cardamine see *Hesperis matronalis*, page 196

Catananche caerulea (cupid's dart)

H3–4/5 (60–90cm x 30–45cm) This is a useful, pretty perennial with wiry stems, grey-green toothed leaves and daisy-like flowers with serrated edges, in shades of violet, blue and white with a deeper centre, flowering throughout the summer. Best in a well-drained site in a sunny position, and not long lived, peaking in the second and third years, so it is usually necessary to replant every few years; it is easily raised from seed. In heavy and wet soils it is best considered an annual. We have found it thriving in Dumfries and in parts of north-east Scotland. 'Alba' white, 'Major' vigorous with larger flowers than the type.

Celmisia

H3–4 (30–50cm x 30cm) It is a funny thing that while researching this book we found that almost every garden in eastern Scotland seems to have a celmisia or two, but

Catananche caerulea

Celmisia semicordata hybrid

you don't often see them for sale. The source is usually a division from a friend, and they always seem to be the same type, *C. semicordata* (or hybrid of it), with pointed stiff, leathery, silver-green leaves, white on the underside, with white daisy-like flowers with yellow centres in late spring–mid-summer. Whatever it is, it should be given a clonal name. It enjoys a sunny site in well-drained soil, and performs best with grit or gravel around the crown. If you want one, you probably need to beg divisions from someone with a large clump.

Centaurea (cornflower, knapweed, dustymiller) and *Stokesia laevis*

H5 This large genus, in the aster family, contains several excellent species, grown for their long-lasting thistle-like flowers and appealing silvery foliage. Centaureas are mound forming in habit, and some can be invasive. They prefer a sunny site, in well-drained soil, but will grow in most soils as long as they are not waterlogged. Maintenance is easy; congested clumps can be lifted and divided every few years. Some suffer from mildew, but this tends to happen as they are dying down, so just cut them back. The British native cornflower (*Centaurea cyanus*), is a delightful addition to wildflower meadow areas with dazzling electric blue flowers. The native lesser knapweeds (*Centaurea nigra*) are valuable pollinator plants for meadows.

Centaurea macrocephala

Centaurea montana

C. dealbata H5 (90cm x 60cm) bright-pink flowers all summer if regularly deadheaded, needs staking; the form **'Steenbergii' H5** (75cm x 60cm) grey-green deeply cut foliage, rose-red flowers all summer, makes a good cut flower, but can be invasive. **C. hypoleuca 'John Coutts' H5** (50cm x 50cm) deep rose-purple, similar in habit to *C. dealbata*, forming thick clumps. **C. bella H5** (25cm x 25cm) a long-lived rock garden gem, requiring good drainage and full sun, leaves with white hairs beneath, flowers bright pink in mid-summer. **C. macrocephala H5** (90cm x 60cm) a rather rank, coarse plant, with yellow flowers with brown papery bracts surrounding the petals which are useful for cutting and drying. **C. montana H5** (90cm x 60cm) tough, with blue flowers in early summer, leaves covered in white hairs; selected forms: **'Alba'** white, **'Amethyst in Snow'** white with purple-blue centre, **'Carnea'** palest pink, **'Gold Bullion'** blue, yellow leaves, **'Parham'** deep amethyst-blue. **C. ruthenica H5** (1.2m x 45cm) a great back-of-the-border plant for late summer colour, sulphur-yellow thistle-like flowers from July onwards, which are good for cutting.

Stokesia laevis **(Stoke's aster) H3–4** (30cm–1m x 30–45cm) frilly daisy-like flowers on stalks in summer and forms evergreen clumps of dark green narrow, pointed leaves. It

needs full sun in well-drained acid soil that does not dry out; waterlogged and heavy clay soil is usually fatal. Mulching will help protect crowns in colder inland gardens. **S. laevis** (50cm x 50cm) lavender blue; the following are garden cultivars: **'Alba'** (35cm) white, **'Blue Star'** (50cm) larger dark lavender blue, **'Mary Gregory'** (30cm) creamy yellow, **'Omega Sky Rocket'** (1m) bright lavender-blue, later flowering, September–October, the tallest form, may need staking, **'Purple Parasols'** (30cm) fluffy purple blue; **'Silver Moon'** (40cm) silvery white flushed rose.

Centranthus ruber and *Valeriana* (valerian)

These two closely related genera are both commonly referred to as valerian.

***Centranthus ruber* H4** (75cm x 60cm) An almost indestructible clump-forming perennial, amongst the easiest to grow of all garden plants. A Continental European native, it has now naturalized in parts of western Britain, and is becoming common on walls and roadsides in parts of Dumfries and Galloway, Ayrshire and places with similar climates. The crimson, strong reddish-pink or white tiny individual flowers make up impressive panicles, which open all summer long. The foliage is glaucous grey-green and fleshy. Centranthus prefers free-draining soil and full sun, and is useful for borders, path edges, walls or paving. It will seed itself all over the place if the conditions are right, and the flowers attract moths and butterflies. It tends not to be long lived in cold, wet and inland gardens. **C. ruber** crimson to reddish-pink flowers; **C.r. 'Albus'** off-white, **C.r. var. coccineus** deep purple-red.

Centranthus ruber

Valeriana **(valerian) H5** These attractive fully hardy summer-flowering perennials make good companions for a wide range of plants, and are useful in cottage and woodland gardens. They form medium-sized clumps of fresh-green divided foliage and produce clusters of small tubular flowers in shades of white and pink. They prefer a sheltered site in full sun or part shade, in well-drained soil. The common valerian (*V. officinalis*) attracts cats, which you may find undesirable. **V. officinalis** (1.2m x 1m) spikes of pink and white flowers in summer. **V. phu 'Aurea'** (40cm x 40cm) young yellow foliage if planted in a sunny site, which mellows as the season progresses, tiny white summer flowers; mainly grown as a foliage plant for summer bedding.

Chelone (turtle head)

H5 Forming upright, small to medium-sized clumps, with

toothed leaves, chelones produce their distinctive, long-lasting, slightly sinister, hooded flowers in shades of purple/pink and white in August–September when most perennials are going over. Very tough, suitable for anywhere in Scotland, they don't mind damp, even waterlogged soil,

Chelone obliqua

and look great spreading beside water, where they can become invasive. They also do well in the herbaceous border.

C. glabra (1m x 2m+) a vigorous spreader with dense spikes of white flowers; *C.g.* 'Black Ice' white form with a dark purple beard. *C. obliqua* (60cm x 60cm) deep pink-purple flowers; *C.o.* 'Alba' white form, *C.o.* 'Praecox Nana' (30cm x 45cm) reddish purple, a dwarf form.

Chiastaphyllum oppositifolium see *Sedum*, page 225

Chrysanthemum see Daisies, page 171

Cimicifuga see *Actaea*, page 150

Cirsium see Thistles, page 229

Codonopsis

These are twining and climbing campanula look-a-likes with similar blue, purple or white flowers. By far the most widely grown is *C. clematidea H4–5* (60–80cm) nodding pale-blue flowers in June–July, a non-climbing species, which likes well-drained soils. The climbing species such

Codonopsis clematidea (RC-M)

as *C. grey-wilsonii* (syn. *C. forrestii*) (to 90cm) are generally available only from specialist nurseries but are well worth seeking out for useful late-summer colour, looking fine scrambling over shrubs. They are not difficult to grow from seed.

Coreopsis see Daisies, page 171

Corydalis

H5 The ferny foliage and brightly coloured, spurred, spring and early-summer flowers make many species of corydalis fine and versatile garden plants. Once

established, many of them will self-seed everywhere, which can be either attractive or a pain in the neck. Most prefer to be left undisturbed once planted (although you might prefer to disturb them once they start to spread). Scotland's cool summers are ideal for growing many varieties that might struggle further south where summers are hotter and drier. Individual plants spread at least 25–30cm and can seed around making huge clumps.

C. cashmiriana H5 (15cm) ❦ vivid blue in spring, leaves blue-green. *C. cheilanthifolia H5* (30cm) ferny bronze-tinged green foliage and bright-yellow flowers in May–June; good for rocky crevices in sun or shade, but can be a nuisance seeding

Corydalis flexuosa (RC-M)

everywhere. *C. elata H5* (45cm) light blue, fragrant, fine foliage, an excellent plant. 'Tory MP' ❀ a hybrid between *C. elata* and *C. flexuosa*; Longacre Plants explain that 'it is true blue and goes on and on' – hence the name. For political reasons, it may not catch on in Scotland... *C. flexuosa H5* (30cm) ❦ introduced from China in the

Corydalis solida 'George Baker'

1980s this is now a very popular garden plant; many named forms have been selected but as they seed everywhere, there is no way to keep these pure, so don't worry too much about which form you get, as they are mostly good: finely cut blue-green leaves and masses of blue flowers in spring and then sporadically in summer: 'Blue Panda' turquoise-blue, 'China Blue' ❦ sky blue, 'Père David' mid-blue, leaves grey-green, 'Purple Leaf' deep-green purplish leaves and bright-blue flowers. 'Golden Panda' a horrible form with yellow leaves, should have been destroyed – it just looks sick. *C. lutea H5* (40cm) this yellow-flowered species seeds itself freely in paving cracks and walls and flowers on and off all summer; the foot of the walls of Kellie Castle in Fife is a mass of it. *C. solida* 'George Baker' *H5* (15cm x 15cm) divided leaves and deep rosy-red flowers in spring; *C.s.* 'Dieter Schacht' deep pink.

Crambe

Crambe are characterized by some of the smallest flowers relative to the leaf size of any plant. They are useful border subjects, especially for coastal gardens, preferring well-drained soil in full sun.

C. maritima (sea kale) *H4* (60cm x 60cm) one of the few plants that can grow on a shingle beach, this has been cultivated as a vegetable since the 16th century but also makes a reasonably

Crambe cordifolia

Crambe maritima

attractive mound-forming plant, good for seaside gardens, with magnificent silvery-green wide, curved and lobed leaves, and large heads of small fragrant white flowers in summer. If you want to eat it, it should be blanched by covering with a pot or barrel in spring: the leaves can then be eaten like spinach. *C. cordifolia H5* (2m x 1.2m) ❋ 🌣 mounds of large crinkly lobed leaves, purple-tinged in spring, and branched sprays of masses of tiny scented white flowers May–July. It prefers a deep, rich, well-drained lightly acid or alkaline soil, in full sun or light shade. Everything about *C. cordifolia* is big, and it needs plenty of space, but it makes a great feature beside water, combined with grasses, or as a specimen planting. Mildew can be a problem in long dry summers or in dry soils, and slugs can turn lower leaves into skeletons. Christopher Lloyd claimed that the scent was 'reminiscent of drains' – evidently he had sweet drains. Some Scottish gardeners have told us they just can't keep it alive.

Crocosmia (montbretia)

H3–4/5 Late summer would not be the same without the firey flowers of crocosmia, in shades of red, orange, pink and yellow, borne on exotic-looking spikes above the leaves. The vertical sword-shaped leaves grow in clumps and provide a good foil for mound-forming perennials. Plant the corms 7–10cm deep in well-drained but not dry soil. Congested clumps should be dug up and divided from time to time to ensure plenty of flowers. They are easy to please and some of the older varieties can be invasive on the west coast, where they spread out into the wild along walls and ditches, but most modern varieties behave better. The braes of Portpatrick, on the Galloway coast blaze orange with them in late summer. A hard wet winter in heavy soil can kill them, especially when newly planted; established clumps are tougher. Hardiness varies somewhat with the small-flowered ones, deep colours such as 'Lucifer' being the most hardy (*H4–5*) and the large-flowered yellows more tender (*H3*). If you plant dry corms in spring, they tend to take a year to settle down before flowering; they are also available container grown. The naming of crocosmias is a 'seething mess' (according to Christopher Lloyd), so unfortunately you may not receive exactly what it says on the label. Most will spread to form clumps 50–70cm+ wide.

The species *C. masonorum H4–5* (80cm) orange, a bit of a thug, *C. paniculata H3* (1.2m) orange-red, and *C. pottsii H4* (1m)

orange-red and the hybrid *C. x crocosmiiflora H3–4* (which has yellow genes from *C. aurea*) have given rise to a huge range of cultivars, including: **'Carmin Brilliant'** (70cm) red with yellow throat, **'Citronella'** (60–75cm) lemon yellow with red markings, often misnamed, not always long-lived ,**'Columbus'** (60–80cm) strong yellow, with red markings, **'Dusky Maiden'** (50cm) deep orange, bronzy leaves, **'Emily Mackenzie'** (60–75cm) large flowered, deep orange with crimson throat, not always too easy, useful for its late flowering, **'Gerbe d'Or'** (60–75cm) tubular, yellow, **'George Davison'** (syn. 'Golden Fleece') early, bright yellow, **'Golden Ballerina' H3** (70cm) large flowered, orange-red, **'Honey Angels'** (45–60cm) yellow with a faint white stripe in the throat, **'Jackanapes'** (60–75cm) bicolour red and buff yellow, **'Lucifer' H4–5** (1.2m) 🌣 tall, brilliant flame red, may need some support to stop it splaying outwards, one of the most popular, **'Solfatare' H3** (45–60cm) 🌣 suitable for mild gardens, bronze-tinged leaves and warm apricot-yellow flowers, **'Spitfire'** (70–80cm) orange-red, very fine.

Crocosmia 'Solfatare', C. masonorum and *C. 'Lucifer'*

Crocosmia 'Lucifer'

Cyananthus

Low growing with trailing stems, these Himalayan plants are very happy in Scottish gardens and useful for their late flowering in late summer and autumn. They like moist acid soil in part day sun, and will struggle in hot, dry conditions. They thrive under dwarf rhododendrons and similar. You may have to go to an alpine specialist to find one for sale. *C. lobatus* (10cm x 40cm) 🌣 bright blue. *C. microphyllus* (5cm x 20cm) tiny leaves, purplish blue flowers.

Cynara cardunculus see Thistles, page 229

Cynoglossum nervosum see *Anchusa azurea*, page 153

Dactylorrhiza

These hardy orchids, some of which are native to Scotland, are perhaps the easiest to establish in the garden, and they are beautiful and versatile garden plants. They form small to medium-sized clumps of narrow attractively spotted foliage, and produce white, pink or purple flower spikes in late spring and early summer. In most parts of Scotland, hardy orchids benefit from a protective winter mulch, and prefer a well-drained, moist, rich soil in light shade or planted between shrubs. Slugs can cause problems, and they are sometimes attacked by a fatal stem rot, which turns the plant into a grey mush. Dactylorrhizas reach 70cm–1m x 30–45cm unless stated otherwise.

Dactylorrhiza (RC-M)

D. elata (robust marsh orchid) *H3–4* ♈ prefers damp soil, and has spotted leaves and pink flowers. *D. foliosa* (also called *D. maderensis*) *H3–4* ♈ green leaves and purple to pink flowers. *D. fuchsii* (common spotted orchid) *H4–5* (45–60cm high) ✉ pink, variable leaves. *D. maculata* (heath spotted orchid) *H4–5* ✉ white, pink and purple shades. These species cross readily and many of the plants that are sold under these names are hybrids, which are often more vigorous and better garden plants.

Daisies

We have taken the liberty of treating these together, partly as they have much in common, but also because taxonomists keep changing the names, as you will see. The mid to late summer-flowering daisies are stalwarts of the grand border and smaller mixed bed, providing colour after most perennials have reached their peak. They usually form tufts and clumps of foliage and produce stalks of either single or several flowers at varying heights. In general, they like well-drained lightly acidic soil and full sun. Some of the taller varieties benefit from staking and most benefit from deadheading; and the late summer ones can be hard pruned in late spring to encourage bushiness and late flowering. In general, they should be cut down to soil level in autumn and regularly dug up and divided to maintain vigour.

Anthemis tinctoria

Anthemis (chamomile) (For the herb, see page 195.) With ferny foliage and cream or yellow flowers over several weeks, these provide a good foil for the blues and silvers of other perennials and shrubs. Plant in full sun and avoid heavy soils, as they don't live long in them. *A. punctata* subsp. *cupaniana H3–4* (30cm x 30cm) white daisy-like flowers with yellow centres in summer, finely cut silvery leaves, dislikes winter wet so short lived in colder, wetter gardens. *A. sanctijohannis H5* (90cm x 45cm) masses of orange-yellow

Anthemis tinctoria 'E.C. Buxton'

flowers in summer; cut back after flowering to encourage healthy leaf rosettes for winter, but usually only lives for two years or so. *A. tinctoria H3–4* (90cm x 50–90cm) by far the most popular species and there are dozens of fine named selections and hybrids with cream or yellow flowers with deeper centres in July–August. In rich soils they get leggy and tend to flop over. They can be cut back in early summer to produce sturdier plants, which flower later and longer. Two good stocky Scottish selections are '**Cally Cream**' and '**Cally White**' available from specialists only. More commonly available are '**E.C. Buxton**' ♈ pale lemon-yellow, '**Grallach Gold**' a good yellow, but short lived, '**Kelwayi**' bright yellow with finely divided leaves, '**Sauce Hollandaise**' pale cream with yellow centres, '**Wargrave Variety**' pale yellow.

Chrysanthemum ♱ (60–1.2m x 60cm) What has happened to this genus probably takes the biscuit for confusing name changes: not only are former chrysanthemums now dispersed to seven other genera (*Ajania, Leucanthemum Rhodanthemum*, etc.) but a few years back the remainder were renamed *Dendranthema* and then after an outcry returned to *Chrysanthemum*. Still under this name are several fine hardy border plants, as well as the specialist florists' and exhibition varieties, which are not covered here. The most relevant garden plants are late-flowering varieties of *C.* x *rubellum*, which are an alternative to late-summer asters with purer shades of pink, red and oranges. They flower best in a dry autumn; they can go mouldy in wet ones. The foliage and sap can be a skin irritant. '**Clara Curtis**' *H4* (60cm) clear pink, '**Duchess of Edinburgh**' *H3–4* (60cm) semi-double wine red, '**Emperor of China**' *H4* (1.2m) deep pink, very late, lax habit, **Fanfair Series** (90cm) many colour forms, '**Innocence**' *H3–4* (80cm) pale pink, '**Winning Red**' *H4* (70cm) single red.

Coreopsis (Tickseed) *H3–4* (40–60cm x 30–45cm) These popular daisies prefer a sunny, well-drained spot and are generally fairly short lived, which can make assessing hardiness a little difficult. Cutting them back in late summer to encourage fresh growth will increase the likelihood of over-wintering being successful. The yellow or pink flowers on their wiry stems, often all summer long, are very popular as cut flowers. Huge numbers of new ones in many colours have come onto the market, some as yet untested in Scottish winters.

C. grandiflora a popular species, so inclined to die in winter that it is best considered an annual, or a biennial at best; forms include **Big Bang Series**, (40-60cm) some amazing flower combinations, **'Mayfield Giant'** (75cm) brilliant yellow from June to September, **'Early Sunrise'** (45cm) ❦ double yellow, prone to mildew, **Flying Saucers** ['Walcoreop'] (45cm) golden yellow, **'Sonnenkind'** ('Baby Sun') (40cm) deep yellow with red centres. C.

Coreopsis grandiflora 'Sonnenkind'

Coreopsis verticillata

Echinacea purpurea

Echinacea purpurea 'White Swan'

lanceolata 'Sterntaler' (40cm) yellow with brown centres.

C. rosea **'American Dream'** (60cm) small starry rose-pink flowers, finely divided leaves, inclined to die off in winter. *C. verticillata* the variety most likely to be long lived in gardens; forms include **'Grandiflora'** (60cm) small starry rich-yellow flowers, finely cut leaves, **'Moonbeam'** (50cm) pale lemon-yellow, grows best in a fertile soil and in hot summers, **'Zagreb'** (40cm) compact, deep yellow.

Doronicum (leopard's bane) (45cm–1m x 30–40cm+) The earliest to flower of the yellow daisies in April–May, with heart-shaped leaves, taking over from the daffodils, as Graham Stuart Thomas observes. The form **'Little Leo' H4** (30cm) semi-double, bright-yellow daisy-like flowers, seems to be churned out by the million by Dutch nurserymen, though some think the rarely offered **'Miss Mason'** (45cm) is a better option. Both like moist soil in sun or shade. *D. orientale* **'Finesse'** (50cm) and **'Magnificum'** (50cm) both golden yellow. The taller species *D. pardalianches* (1m) light yellow, a vigorous and sometimes invasive

species which has naturalised in parts of Scotland.

Echinacea **(purple cone flower)** *H3–4/5* (50cm–1.2m x 50–75cm) Echinaceas are some of the most striking of all the daisies and they are definitely a 'plant of the moment'. They like a sunny position in well-drained soil and form clumps, which should be cut back to ground level in autumn. Dutch and American breeders are introducing dozens of new, sometimes outrageous varieties, coming soon to a garden centre near you but beware as many are vulnerable to rotting in wet and heavy soils and are more suited to eastern Scotland than the west. The white-, yellow- and orange-flowered forms are more inclined to die off in winter than the pink ones, and some of the new varieties may prove to be useless in Scotland.

E. pallida **H5** (1.25m) rose, pink or white florets that droop attractively from the central cone in July–September. *E. purpurea* **H3–4** radiating pink-purple ray florets, and a bold orange-brown cone-like centre in July–August/September, thin, slightly toothed leaves, probably the best choice for Scotland; many named forms, including **'Bressingham Hybrids'** (90cm) variable deep pink, **'Fatal Attraction'** (1m) purple-pink, **'Kim's Knee High'** [PBR] (50cm) pink, **'Jade'** (65cm) white, green centres, **'Leuchtstern'** (1m) purple-red, flat petalled, **'Magnus'** (1.2m) purple, more horizontal and less drooping petals than most, **'Primadonna'** (90cm) white and pink **'Razzamataz'** (75cm) double pink, poor in rain as flowers are too heavy, **'Rubinstern'** (1m) carmine-red, **'The King'** (60cm) vibrant pinkish crimson, **'Vintage Wine'** (85cm) purple-red, **'Alba'**, **'White Swan'**, **'White Lustre'**, **'White Star'** (70–90cm) all white or off-white, with an orange-brown cone. A new one **'Fragrant Angel'** [PBR] is said to be very fine. There are several new orange and yellow cultivars bred from *E. paradoxa* which we find are seldom long-lived and need sharp drainage and a warm sunny site: examples include **'Tangerine Dream'** (orange), **'Tomato Soup'** (red).

Erigeron (fleabane) (15)25–80cm x 50–60cm) These are useful, easily grown and tough border plants, flowering in mid-summer, and often again in autumn, suitable for a sunny spot. There are dozens of varieties, including some gems for the rock garden. **'Adria'** *H4* (60cm) lavender blue. **'Dimity'** *H4* (25cm) bright pink, divide regularly. **'Dunkelste Aller'** (Darkest of All) *H4* (60cm) deep blue with yellow centres. **'Foersters' Liebling'** *H4* (80cm) semi-double pale pink, grey-green leaves. **'Quakeress'** *H4* (80cm) lilac pink, floppy habit, needs staking, can flower into November. **Alpine species:** *E. karvinskianus H3(4)* (15cm) low-growing, tiny white flowers, ageing to pink,

loves to be grown in cracks in walls; very pretty, yes, but can become a bit of a pest in mild gardens, as it seeds everywhere; it is very fine on the terraces at Logan, in Dumfries and Galloway. Another dwarf is *E. compositus H3–4* (15cm), which is really a large-scale lawn daisy with white, pink or pale blue flowers and may seed all over the place.

Erigeron 'Azurfee' and 'Quakeress'

Gaillardia x *grandiflora* (blanket flower) *H4* Ever more outrageous, these sumptuous and exotic (or tacky, depending on your taste,) plants produce some of the brightest, most multi-coloured flowers of all the daisy family. They prefer full sunshine and well-drained soil, and may need staking in exposed situations. They are inclined to rot at the base and tend not to be all that long lived (3–4 years is a normal lifespan), but they grow fast and put on a good display in the first year. Gaillardias may need some winter protection in colder areas – a light straw mulch placed over the dormant crowns in late autumn, for example. Cut back old growth before applying the mulch. Deadhead and cut back to prolong flowering. They spread approx. 30–45cm: **'Burgunder'** (60cm) deep wine-red flowers, June–October, glaucous, narrow leaves. **'Dazzler'** (60cm) golden yellow with red centres. **'Kobold'** (syn. 'Goblin') (35cm) similar flowers to 'Dazzler' but more compact. Some of the newer varieties seem particularly inclined to die off in winter, so beware. There are also many annual varieties.

Helenium *H4–5* Some of the best daisies of all for Scotland. These have striking flowers in the orange-red and yellow spectrum, mostly in July–August and into

Gaillardia x *grandiflora* 'Dazzler'

September, with fringed petals and a brown or yellow centre, known as a boss. They are bushy perennials, preferring sunny, well-drained but not dry soils. Some need staking, especially in rich soils, and congested clumps need dividing. There are at least 50 named varieties; most are good, and they spread 60–90cm: **'Bressingham Gold'** (1m) bright yellow. **'Butterpat'** (1m) deep yellow, yellow boss, one of the best yellow forms; there are several clones circulating under this name. **'Dunkelpracht'** (syn. 'Dark Beauty') (1.2m) dark red-brown. *H. hoopesii* (1m) yellow daisies in early summer. **'Moerheim Beauty'** (1m) ⚜ glowing orange-red, dark-brown boss. **'Pumilum Magnificum'** (60–90cm) yellow. **'Rotgold'** (syn. 'Red and Gold') (1–1.2m) variable red and yellow. **'Rubinzwerg'** (80cm) dark red, self-supporting, does not need staking.

'Sahin's Early Flowerer' (90cm) long flowering, orange fading to yellow, attractively streaked orange, opening in July, needs staking. **'Wyndley'** (80cm) ⚜ orange-yellow, July–August.

Helenium 'Moerheim Beauty' and Rudbeckia

Helenium 'Moerheim Beauty'

Helianthus 'Lemon Queen'

Helianthus These are almost indestructible perennial sunflowers which are easily grown in sunny positions in most free-draining soils. They are useful for their late flowering, well into September for most varieties. Taller ones usually need staking, and they are vigorous and spreading and can become invasive. They spread approx. 60cm: **'Capenoch Star'** *H5* (1.5m) large lemon-yellow flowers; apparently lots of misidentified plants are sold under this name. **'Gullick's Variety'** *H5* (1.5m) deep yellow classic-looking sunflowers. **'Lemon Queen'** *H5* (to 2m) lemon yellow. **'Loddon Gold'** *H4–5* (1.5m) vivid lemon yellow, with double centres, particularly vigorous. **'Monarch'** *H4* (2–3m) large bright yellow, inner disc of brick-red, giant and dramatic, but it might take over, so beware in a small garden.

Heliopsis subsp. helianthoides var. scabra (oxeye) H5 (1m x 1–2m) Another set of tough and easy yellow daisies for the late-summer herbaceous border. They can get leggy and require staking; alternatively cut them back hard in June, which makes them flower later on shorter stems. The most popular are **'Benzinggold'** (1m) bright yellow, **'Light of Loddon'** (1m) semi-double bright yellow with a raised centre, **'Sommersonne'** (90cm) deep yellow with a brown centre. **H. var. h. Lorraine Sunshine** ['Helhan'] **H4** (1m) bright yellow, extraordinary leaves are silvery white with green veins, striking but a bit odd, needs good drainage and rather lacking in vigour compared to the others.

Heliopsis helianthoides var. scabra 'Light of Loddon'

Inula H5 These robust daisies are excellent in Scotland, with flat-topped deep-yellow daisy flowers in summer. They have escaped over the garden wall in parts of Mull, where they are rabbit and deer proof. They range from low and compact to giants for the back of a border. **I. ensifolia** (50cm x 30cm) deep yellow, mid-summer, on wiry stems; a dwarf form **'Gold Star'** reaches no more than 30cm high and across. **I. helenium** (1–2m x 1m) a giant, does best in a woodland or wild garden, huge dense woolly leaves (to 80cm long), pale-yellow flowers, very fine at Balcarres, Fife. **I. hookeri** (50–70cm x 60cm) pale yellow, lance-shaped leaves, excellent in Shetland and Western Isles, will colonize even poor soils. **I. magnifica** (to 1.8m x 90cm) deep yellow, handsome large hairy leaves, purple-striped stems, for the back of the border.

Inula hookeri

Leucanthemum (ox-eye, Shasta daisy) Formerly known as chrysanthemums, these are excellent and easily grown white-flowered daisies. **L. x superbum H5** (30cm–1m x 45–60cm) A superb showy border plant with many forms, single and double white flowers with yellow centres in mid-summer, tough and easy – just lift and divide congested clumps every few years. Some of the new ones have flowers which are so heavy they flop over in wind and rain, **'Aglaia'** (1m) semi-double, **'Alaska'** (1m) white single, **'Ester Read'** (60cm) semi-double white, **'Phyllis Smith'** (1m) single white with very narrow florets, **'Silberprinzesschen'** (45cm) single white, **'Snowcap'** (40cm) single white, **'Sonnenschein'** (Sunshine) (80cm) single creamy yellow, **'Fiona Coghill'** (60cm), **'T.E. Killin'** (1m) and **'Wirral Supreme'** (1m) 🏵 fully double whites, need shelter or support for the heavy flower heads. **L. vulgare 'May Queen'** (syn. 'Maikönigen') **H5** (60cm x 45cm) is a large-flowered form of our native ox-eye daisy, and wonderful for naturalising in wild-flower meadows.

Leucanthemum x superbum, single and double forms

Leucanthemum x superbum

Rudbeckia (coneflower) H3–5 These are outstanding subjects for late summer colour, ranging from compact to giant; all have yellow, daisy-like flowers with dark centres and need full sun and well-drained but not dry soil. Many have a very long flowering period.

R. fulgida var. deamii H5 (90cm) bright yellow with a black centre, July–September, hairy greyish leaves; **R.f. 'Goldsturm' H5** (90cm) 🏵 striking deep yellow with conical black centres, July–September, narrow rough leaves, by far the best form, outstanding; **Little Gold Star**, lower growing to 40cm. **R.f. var. speciosa** (60cm) a range of single and double yellow flowers. **R. hirta** (black-eyed Susan) **H3** (30–100cm) striking yellow to orange flowers but beware: most of these do not survive the winter and are best considered annuals. **R. laciniata 'Goldquelle' H5** (90cm) double, deep yellow, August–October, divided leaves, slugs love it. **R. laciniata 'Herbstsonne' H5** (1.8m) the giant of family, for the back of the border or against a wall, broad-petalled bright yellow with conical, green centres, on long stems in August–September. Looks much

Rudbeckia laciniata 'Herbstsonne' and R. fulgida 'Goldsturm'

better in the garden than in the garden centre and is best pruned in late spring to encourage branching.

Tanacetum coccineum* (syn. *Pyrethrum coccineum*)** This bushy perennial with feathery leaves seems to have fallen from favour a bit, perhaps because of its loose floppy habit. A haircut after first flowering often results in a second show of flowers on sturdier stems. They reach approx. 75cm x 45cm, and should be divided every few years in summer or spring, but not in autumn. **'Eileen May Robinson' *H5 pink with yellow centres, **'James Kelway' *H5*** cream, ageing to pink, **'Robinson's Pink'** single pink. *T. vulgare* (tansy) with yellow flowers is often found in grassy meadows.

Tanecetum (Pyrethrum) coccineum 'Robinson's Pink' and 'James Kelway'

Telekia speciosa* (syn. *Buphthalmum salicifolium*) *H4 (90cm–1.2m x 24–60cm) This is a striking, tall border plant with fragrant yellow daisy flowers any time from June to September. Preferring moist soil, it tends to hang on to its dead flowers, so you may need to give it a good haircut, unless you like the black skeletons to remain into winter.

Darlingtonia californica see **Insectivorous plants, page 199**

Delphinium

H5 🌠 True border statesmen, delphiniums have been classic herbaceous border plants for as long as anyone can remember, though if we are honest they are a bit of pain, needing mollycoddling, staking, pruning and replanting. But once you have seen the borders at House of Pitmuies in Angus, you'd do anything to have the same… Forming mounds of cut green foliage, from which up to 3m-high flower spikes in shades of blue, purple, pink and white rise in early to mid-summer, delphiniums prefer fertile well-drained soil in a sunny position, and they will struggle in cold, wet clay or dry sandy soil. Staking is most definitely required for the taller plants, especially in windy sites. Slugs love them, unfortunately, and they are prone to mildew and almost every other disease you have heard of. Cut off the dead flower spikes and feed the plants to encourage secondary autumn flowering. All parts of the plants are harmful if eaten. There are dozens of named clones which come and go from year to year, so few are listed here. Delphiniums are usually classified in three groups.

Belladonna Group *H4* (1–1.2m x 60cm) loose-branched spikes of single flowers early to late summer: **'Blue Bees' *H5*** (1.5m x 60cm) sky blue, **'Lamartine'** purple-blue, **'Wendy'** gentian blue. *D. grandiflorum* varieties are very similar to the above, usually grown as annuals, at best biennial; **'Blue Butterfly'** is one of the best known.

Elatum Group *H5* (1.5–2.2m x 1m) the largest group, available in small, medium and tall forms, in a range of purples, violets, blues, whites and mixtures in summer. These include most of the longest-lived varieties, their longevity helped by heaping grit over the crowns in winter to keep the slugs off. You may need to go to specialist nurseries to find named clones.

Pacific hybrids *H3–4* (1.2–1.5m x 60cm) short lived, usually grown as annuals or biennials, in mixed colours. Some of the best known include **Astolat Group** lilac and pink, **Black Knight Group** mostly dark blue with a black centre, **Blue Bird Group** bright blue with a white eye, **Cameliard Group** lavender blue with white eye, **Galahad Group** white, sometimes lacking in vigour, the **Guinevere Group** lavender rose, the **King Arthur Group** (dark blue with a white centre) and the **Summer Skies Group** (pale blue with a white eye). **'Magic Fountains'** hybrids

Delphinium

H3-4 (90 x 60cm) dwarf range suitable for front of borders in a range of midnight to light blues, violet and pink to white. Compact and bush growing. **'Red Caroline' *H3-4*** (1m x 60cm), recent introduction with double red flowers.

Dianthus (pinks)

H3–4 ❋ ❋ These are low-growing mat and cushion-forming plants, with narrow greyish leaves. They have single or double buttonhole flowers, in a huge range of colours in summer, and most have a sweet clove scent. They are great border-edge and rock garden plants, but they prefer alkaline soil, so for much of Scotland they appreciate lime added to the gritty compost, or to be mulched with limestone chips. In acid soil they tend to live for no more than a few years. Whatever the soil, drainage seems to be the key. They thrive between paving stones, in raised beds, and with flat stones placed beneath their foliage. Mix grit and sand into the planting compost but use little or no fertilizer, as they dislike over-feeding. Wet weather and/or poor drainage tend to lead to rotting at the base of the plant. They also suffer from other fungal problems such as rusts, so you may need a regular fungicide-spraying programme and rabbits can demolish them. We have seen dianthus flourishing in many parts of Scotland, in both mild

Dianthus, mixed colours

Dianthus 'Whatfield Joy', 'Fusilier'
and 'Pike's Pink'

and cold climates, including parts of Dumfries and Galloway, and Aberdeenshire. Deadheading or cutting for the house prolongs flowering and they should be trimmed when blooms have finished, to encourage compact growth habit. Hardiness is hard to quantify: they are probably *H5* in ideal conditions and *H3* in heavy soil with poor drainage. All are well scented unless stated otherwise.

Believe it or not, there are over 30,000 registered *Dianthus* and more are released each year, so we have made no attempt to cover any more than the most popular and Scottish-raised varieties. Dianthus can be divided into several categories. Border carnations are tallest, up to 60cm, often clove scented. Old-fashioned pinks (up to 50cm) bloom once only, in early summer, while the modern pinks usually flower in several flushes from spring to autumn. The smallest are the alpine pinks (to 10cm x 10cm), which carpet the ground. We do not cover the annuals or tender varieties grown under glass. Heights and spreads are similar unless stated otherwise.

D. alpinus (10cm) ♥ pink, white or purple with darker eyes. 'Bridal Veil' (30cm) ❀ double white with a red eye, *D. deltoides* (20cm) ♥ pink, June–September. 'Flashing Light' (syn. 'Leuchtfunk') brilliant cerise-red. *D. gratianopolitanus* (syn. *D. caesius*) 'Cheddar Pink' (15cm) ❀ loose grey-green mats, pale pink. 'Devon Cream' (35cm) creamy yellow, unscented. 'Doris' (30cm) ❀ double pale pink with darker centres. 'Gran's Favourite' (30cm) ❀ white streaked mauve, weak stemmed, needs support. 'Inshriach Dazzler' (15cm) ♥ Scottish-raised, single fringed deep magenta. 'Joy' semi-double carmine-pink, good in containers as it cascades over the edge; there are also white ('White Joy') and pink ('Rose Joy') versions. 'La Bourboule' (5cm) single deep pink, said to be one of the neatest and easiest to grow. 'Little Jock' (10cm) ❀ ♥ semi-double deep pink with a purple eye. 'Nyewood's Cream' (8cm) creamy white. 'Mrs Sinkins' (30cm) ❀ ♥ frilly edged white, often lop-sided. 'Old Spice' (30cm) salmon pink, fringed, fragrant. 'Pike's Pink' (15cm) pale pink, lightly scented. 'Starry Eyes' (10cm) white and purple, long

flowering. 'Tatra Blush' ❀ selected by Michael Wickendon at Cally, fine fringed cream-white. 'Tickled Pink' (20cm) lavender pink. 'Whatfield Can-Can' (10–15cm) ❀ double pink. 'Whatfield Gem' (10–15cm) ❀ ruby red, frecked white. **Star Series** from Whetman are highly rated in RHS trials, but only some have scent: 'Brilliant Star' (15cm) ❀ white, burgundy eye, 'Evening Star' (10cm) double deep pink with darker eye, 'India Star' (20cm) ❀ pink with darker eye, 'Neon Star' (30cm) ❀ cerise, 'Night Star' (30cm) maroon and pink, 'Pixie Star' (20cm) pink with darker eye.

Diascia and *Nemesia*

These colourful South African plants are grown as annual bedding for their summer flowers. Some varieties can be

Diascia, pale pink form

grown outdoors all year round in relatively mild climates in soil with sharp drainage, even at Glendoick we have managed to keep them going for several years. With one of the longest flowering periods of all, from early summer to the first frosts, and with bright-coloured flowers, they are good value. In colder inland and east-coast gardens or where soil is heavy, they are best grown in containers and brought indoors in winter. Deadhead and cut back to encourage long flowering.

Diascia H2–3 (25cm x 30cm) 'Appleby Apricot' apricot, 'Hopleys' pink, 'Ice Cracker' white, 'Ruby Field' fairly compact, coral red. 'Salmon Supreme' quite hardy.

Nemesia fruticans (syn. *N. caerulea*) *H3* (20–50cm x 20–50cm) Pink, blue, lavender or purple flowers all summer long. 'Amelie' *H2–3* (20cm) pink with a soft vanilla scent. 'Raspberries and Cream' as it sounds.

Dicentra (bleeding heart, Dutchman's breeches)

H4–5 Their delicate ferny foliage and gently dangling late-spring and early-summer flowers may suggest tenderness, but these are very tough deciduous woodlanders from North America which are ideally suited to Scottish gardens. A favourite with children (and young-at-heart adults), *D. spectabilis* on first inspection looks like a lovelorn heart bleeding, but turn it upside down and you see a naked lady about to take her bath! Dicentras like plenty of moisture in the soil and grow in sun or dappled shade. They are happy spreading under trees and shrubs, and associate well with rhododendrons. Slugs can be a problem, and late frosts can burn young foliage, but otherwise they don't need much attention. Clumps can be divided from time to time and you may need to restrict the more vigorous types in smaller gardens, as they can spread to 2m across or more. Height and spread are similar unless stated otherwise.

D. spectabilis (now *Lamprocapnos spectabilis*) *H4* (75–90cm) ☼ the tallest, red and white lockets in May–June. Early into growth, so susceptible to spring frost damage, and requiring wind shelter or support of shrubs to stop it being blown flat; *D.s. alba* (60cm) ☼ the pure white form, less vigorous with paler leaves. *D. cucullaria H3–4* (15cm x 30cm) compact with small white yellow-tipped flowers in March–April that look like trousers dangling in the wind, needs sharp drainage, dies back in summer. *D. eximia H5* (60cm) magenta-rose, grey-green leaves, very tough; forms include '**Spring Morning**' (30cm) pink, grey-green ferny foliage, '**Snowdrift**' white. *D. formosa H5* (35cm) magenta-rose, tends to seed around; '**Aurora**' white, long flowering period. There are lots of dicentra hybrids, with new ones coming on to the market all the time (all *H5*): '**Adrian Bloom**' (45cm) carmine-red, finely cut grey foliage, '**Bacchanal**' (30cm) pale-green leaves and fine dark purplish-red flowers, **Candy Hearts** [PBR] (30cm) reddish pink, long flowering, grey foliage, **Ivory Hearts** [PBR] (30cm) white, foliage grey, long flowering, '**King of Hearts**' (30cm) ☼ the best recent introduction, rosy pink, finely cut, soft grey-green foliage, compact, '**Luxuriant**' (30cm) cerise-pink, '**Pearl Drops**' (syn. 'Langtrees') (30cm) creamy white, pink tinted, blue-green foliage. '**Stuart Boothman**' (45cm) ☼ carmine, attractive grey-green leaves.

Dicentra spectabilis and white form, 'Bacchanal' and 'Stuart Boothman'

Dictamnus albus var. purpureus

Dictamnus albus

H4 (90cm x 50cm) ☠ This herbaceous perennial is also known as burning bush because of the volatile oils in the flowers and seed pods, which can in theory catch fire, but which in practice are more likely to cause skin irritation. Christopher Lloyd, often one for a bit of mischief, recommends lighting the flowers with a match, for the 'gassy noise and delicious aroma'. Star-shaped white flowers from June to August, with aromatic, divided leaves; does best in full sun in a warm corner, in well-drained soil. Hard to propagate, so not widely available. **var.** *purpureus* soft mauve-purple.

Dierama (angel's fishing rod)

H3–4 (60cm–1m high) A bit of a new kid on the block, and very much a vogue plant, this South African gem is well worth the extra care it requires. The graceful, arching slender stems are tipped with pink or white bell-like flowers in July–August above long, narrow, greyish-green, evergreen leaves. They require a sheltered sunny site with a moist, but well-drained gritty soil, and will die in heavy soil and waterlogged conditions. They do well in gravel gardens and between paving. Best planted in spring and summer, never in autumn and winter, they take a few years to form a decent clump, so you have to be patient, but once you get them going in a place they like you'll get forests of seedlings. They can be somewhat mixed and variable in commerce, as named clones are being unscrupulously propagated from seed. They also look a bit thin and disappointing in a small pot; you need to be patient. Some of the best forms include: '**Guinevere**' (1m x 1m) white. *D. pendulum* (60–90cm x 60–90cm) pink, grey-green leaves, perhaps less hardy than the others. *D. pulcherrimum* (1–1.5m+ x 1m) pale to deep rose-pink; '**Merlin**' (1m+ x 90cm) dark purple, very striking. *D. igneum* (60cm–1m x 75cm) lilac.

Digitalis (foxglove)

H3–5 ☠ (1.2m x 30cm) Everyone knows the British native foxglove, *Digitalis purpurea*, and along with the many

Dierama pulcherrimum

Dierama 'Guinevere'

other *Digitalis* species and varieties, it makes a very good garden plant. Foxgloves form rosettes of rough-textured leaves, from which rise up to 2m+ flower spikes throughout late spring and summer. They tolerate most soils, even the poorest, but are happiest in a woodland edge situation, in rich, moist, fertile soil. Our native *D. purpurea* is normally biennial, and tends to self-seed freely. Most foxgloves are tough and maintenance free, and their poisonous nature makes most of them unattractive to rabbits. Strong winds can flatten them, so some support may be necessary.

D. ferruginea H4 (1.2m) pale bronze June–August. *D. grandiflora* (syn. *D. ambigua*) *H5* (60cm) ☼ soft yellow in summer, not very long lived. *D. laevigata H3* (1m) prefers alkaline soil and

Digitalis purpurea and
D.p. f. *albiflora*

produces exotic yellow flowers, speckled and striped purple-brown. **D. lanata H3** (60cm) creamy yellow tinged with a purplish hue, May–July. **D. lutea H5** (60cm) creamy yellow, May–July. **D. x mertonensis H5** (60cm) ❦ spikes of salmon pink, June–September. **D. parviflora H4** (60cm) reddish brown, silky leaves; **'Milk Chocolate'** (60cm) reddish brown with purple veining. **D. purpurea H5** (1.2–1.5m) ✉ purple-pink June–August, our native species, biennial, but seeds freely; forms and seed strains include **f. albiflora** white, takes on a ghostly glow in shade, **Excelsior Group** a range of colours, **'Primrose Carousel'** yellow with red spotting, said to come true from seed, **'Sutton's Apricot'** apricot, **'Tinkerbell' H3–4** yellow, sometimes perennial, grows well at Abriachan, Loch Ness.

Dodecatheon (shooting stars, American cowslip)

Dodecatheon meadia

H5 Fascinating, hardy low perennials suitable for sun or light shade, best in conditions that imitate the woodland edge habitat in which they thrive in the wild in North America. Dodecatheons form ground-level rosettes of grey-green leaves and produce spikes of pink, purple or white blooms in spring. The flower petals are reflexed skywards and the stamens and stigma point soilwards, making a perfect shooting star. They prefer moist well-drained soil, and can withstand drought in summer, often disappearing below ground by August. Congested clumps with reduced flowering should be divided. Vine weevils can be a problem.

D. jeffreyi (50cm x 30cm) magenta, lavender or white, May–June. **D. meadia** (20cm x 15cm) pale pink, April–May; **D.m. alba** (20cm x 15cm) white. **D. pulchellum** (15cm x 10cm) deep rose-pink, May–June; **'Red Wings'** (20cm x 15cm) deep carmine-red.

Doronicum see Daisies, page 171

Draba

A tiny alpine inclined to get lost in the garden unless planted in a trough. It forms a dome of mossy foliage with tiny yellow flowers held on long stalks. The most commonly available species is **D.**

Draba aizoides

aizoides H5 (8cm x 15cm) with greyish leaves and yellow flowers in spring.

Echinacea see Daisies, page 171

Echinops (globe thistle)

H5 These are statuesque plants with mounds of thistle-like leaves, and deep blue-purple or white spheres or globes of flowers in summer on long stems, which attract bees and butterflies. Echinops are pretty easy-going plants, tolerant of most soils except waterlogged ones, and preferring a sunny site. If they get mildew or become ragged, just give them a haircut. They do best in poor soils, and spread about 60cm unless stated.

E. bannaticus 'Taplow Blue' (1.2m x 60cm) powder blue, July–September, grey-green leaves with white undersides.

Echinops ritro

E. ritro (90cm–1.2m x 45cm) ❦ grey-blue flowers, July and August; **E.r. subsp. ruthenicus** (1m x 40cm) bright blue, leaves with white underside; **'Veitch's Blue'** (80cm–1m x 60cm) particularly bright blue flowers. **E. sphaerocephalus 'Arctic Glow'** (60cm–1m x 50cm) white June–August, grey leaves; some people think it looks sickly.

Echium (viper's bugloss)

Echium candicans

H2–3 These exotic-looking plants, mostly from the Canary Islands, kept turning up in all sorts of sheltered nooks and crannies all over coastal Scotland – from the Hebrides to Logan, in Dumfries and Galloway, to a sheltered stairwell at Dunrobin Castle, Golspie, in Caithness. They are relatively easy to grow in full sun in any well-drained soil, and form subtropical-looking clumps of long thin dark-green leaves, from which rise tall (2m+) flower spikes in shades of blue-mauve and white. They are very attractive to bees and butterflies, but the foliage may cause skin irritation. They need shelter from cold winds, but will tolerate seaside conditions. Most clumps die after flowering but with luck the plants will set seed. Whitefly can be a nuisance.

E. candicans H2 (1.5–2m) mauve-blue, perennial. *E. pininana H3* (2m+) deep violet-blue flowers, sometimes forming towering (3m+) inflorescences, probably the hardiest of the bunch but short lived. *E. russicum H2* (60–90cm) dark red, treat as biennial exotic front-of-border specimen in mildest areas only. *E. vulgare H2–3* (60–90cm) deep blue, best treated as an annual.

Epimedium

H4-5 (25–30cm x 30–45cm) With small distinctive cup-shaped flowers in spring, and attractive leaf markings, these are fine low-growing plants for Scottish gardens everywhere. They are easy to grow and, although they will tolerate dry shady situations where not much else will grow, they prefer rich moist soil in partial shade. They can be left alone for years once established and don't suffer any particular pest and disease problems. All flower in April–May, and over time will spread forming substantial colonies. The smaller ones also make good rock garden plants. It is worth cutting back old foliage to show off the flowers better. The spidery flowers are rather small and we think these are somewhat over-praised plants which are more attractive in close-up photographs than in real life. You can apparently make a medicinal tea with some epimedium leaves, though we can't say that we've tried it. Vine weevil are attracted to them, particularly in containers.

Epimedium x rubrum and E. x versicolor

E. grandiflorum H4 (30cm) ✤ deep pink with white spurs, deciduous, pale-green leaves; *E.g.* 'Lilafee' (25cm) small dark purple-violet flowers, deciduous, leaves brown tinged as they appear; *E.g.* 'Rose Queen' (30cm) deep pink, deciduous, heart-shaped leaves, tinged brown when young. *E. x perralchicum* 'Frohnleiten' *H4* (30cm) ✤ yellow, semi-evergreen, bright-green heart-shaped leaves that turn bronze in winter. *E. pinnatum* subsp. *colchicum H5* (30cm) yellow flowers, evergreen, heart-shaped leaves. *E. x rubrum H5* (25cm) ✤ rather dark and inconspicuous crimson flowers, deciduous, leaves bronze when young. *E. x versicolor* 'Sulphureum' *H5* (30cm) ✤ pale-yellow flowers, deciduous, leaves tinged red in spring and autumn. *E. x youngianum* 'Niveum' *H5* (25cm) white, deciduous, bright-green leaves, tinged red at the start and end of the season, forming neat clumps, *E. x y.* 'Roseum' pink-purple flowers. Fans of *Epimedium* also tend to like the closely related but less impressive *Vancouveria* from North America.

Erigeron see Daisies, page 171

Erinus alpinus see Arabis, page 155

Eryngium (sea holly)

An irresistible architectural plant, in the carrot family, very much in vogue, with metallic grey-blue holly-like leaves and flower cones surrounded by holly-like bracts. Bees and butterflies love them, and they are great for flower arranging and drying. Sea hollies prefer light, free-draining soils in full sun and they often succumb to winter wet in heavy and poorly drained soils, particularly when newly planted. A gravel mulch can help prevent this. Not all are hardy enough for cold gardens, and some are naturally short lived, but they often self-seed. They are probably best planted in late spring and early summer and usually some need support to stop them flopping over. There are dozens of newly named selections coming out every year.

E. agavifolium H3 (1.5m x 60cm) a spiky contender with green sword-like toothed leaves, evergreen in mild winters, relatively small green thimble-like flowers in July–October. *E. alpinum H5* (60–75cm x 30cm) ✤ purplish-blue flower cones with blue metallic bracts from June–August, green heart-shaped leaves. *E.*

Eryngium bourgatii 'Pico's Blue'

bourgatii 'Graham Stuart Thomas' *H5* (45cm x 30cm) ✤ silver-blue thistle-like flowers in June–August, deeply cut grey-green leaves; *E.b.* 'Picos Blue' (50cm x 50cm) ✤ blue flowers and stems. *E. giganteum* (Miss Willmott's ghost) *H5* (1.2m x 75cm) spectacular, with grey-green thistle-like leaves and late-summer flowers of a haunting pale grey-green, with a metallic sheen, biennial, but it usually self-seeds around the garden; 'Silver Ghost' (60cm) ✤ has narrower leaves and very silvery bracts. *E. x oliverianum H5* (60cm–1m x 60cm) ✤ large heads of blue and lavender-blue thistle-like flowers in late summer, held above jaggedy mid-green leaves, usually needs staking. *E. planum H4* (50cm–1m) characterized by

Eryngium giganteum (Miss Willmott's ghost) (RC-M)

the oval/egg-shaped basal leaves, bluish-toothed spiny flowers, inclined to grow leggy and fall over; the best-known form is 'Blaukappe' (60cm x 45cm) rich blue. **Blue Hobbit** (30cm) compact form. *E. variifolium H4–5* (45cm x 25cm) smaller with green thistle-like flowers in mid-summer, striking white-veined green leaves, suited to the rock garden or front of border. *E. x zabelii H4* (60–70cm x 50cm) a variable hybrid with grey-green or blue flowers; two fine forms are 'Donard Variety' with grey-blue flowers and silvery foliage, and 'Jos Eijking' with fine blue-tinted flowers.

Erysimum (perennial wallflower)

H3-4/5 (30–60cm x 30–60cm) ✿ Not as popular as they once were, these evergreen, sometimes perennial wallflowers are grown for their small but long-lasting scented flowers, which appear on and off from April to August. Deadhead flowers with secateurs regularly to prolong flowering all summer. They form low-growing mounds and are easy going, provided the soil is well drained and not too acidic/peaty. They are short lived, suffering from club root and subject to virus infection, which weakens them, and can become straggly after a few years, when it's best to replace them – cuttings root easily.

'Apricot Twist' *H4–5* (60cm) shades of apricot, light-green leaves, **'Bowles' Mauve'** *H4* (60cm) lilac, grey-green foliage, needs wind shelter, very long-flowering season, **'Constant Cheer'** *H4–5* (30cm) maroon, narrow dark-green leaves, **'Sweet Sorbet'** a rather nauseous combination of mauve and orange, as is **Jenny Brook** [PBR]. *E. linifolium* **'Variegatum'** *H3* (60cm) mauve-purple, long and narrow cream-striped green leaves, rather tender, best in mild western gardens. **'Cotswold Gem'** is a little hardier.

Erysimum 'Bowles' Mauve' and 'Apricot Twist'

Eupatorium

H5 These are large, stately but sometimes thuggish perennials, which are easy to grow, provided you've got the space and the right conditions. They form large clumps of serrated, sometimes nettle-like leaves, above which appear the densely packed late-summer pink-purple flower heads, which attract butterflies. They tend to seed around when happy. They are very attractive massed beside water and good in woodland gardens, and they associate well with grasses. They like moist but not waterlogged soil, and prefer a fair amount of sunshine to flower well.

Eupatorium rugosum 'Chocolate'

Aphids can cause problems. Prune after flowering or cut back hard in spring. A haircut in midsummer forces flowers later on shorter stems. *E. purpureum* (joe pye weed) *H5* (1.8m x 90cm) pink-purple flower heads in August–October, above coarse-leaved foliage, which grows in whorls around purple stems; *E.p.* **'Atropurpureum'** *H5* (1.8m x 90cm) pink flowers, purple stems and purple-flushed leaves; **subsp.** *maculatum* stems spotted purple, fatter flower clusters. *E. rugosum* **'Chocolate'** *H5* (1m x 90cm) creamy white flower heads July–September, deep purple leaves and stems, needs a hot summer to flower in Scotland.

Euphorbia (spurge)

⚘ Currently much in vogue, the euphorbias are a huge and varied clan (over 2,000 species), and it may be surprising to know that many species look like cacti and that another is the Christmas favourite, poinsettia. There are large numbers of garden-worthy spurges, which include shade-loving rampant ground-covers, medium-sized architectural evergreens, such as *E. characias* subsp. *wulfenii*, and exotic specimens like the large *E. mellifera* and small *E. myrsinites*. Some are late-winter and early-spring flowering; others flower in summer. In general, the larger summer-flowering euphorbias like full sun and free-draining soil, and the winter-flowering ones like part shade and moist soil. *E. amygdaloides* var. *robbiae* will tolerate dry shade. Take care when handling euphorbias because the milk-white sap (containing euphorbic acid) can cause eye and skin irritation.

E. amygdaloides (wood spurge) a ground-cover which seeds freely, usually grown in its coloured-leaf forms: **'Purpurea'** *H5* (30cm x 30cm+) clumps of variable purple-mahogany leaves and yellow-green flowers in April–May, tends to get mildew by late summer, **'Blackbird'** deep-purple leaves, **'Craigieburn'** ⚘ reddish-brown stems and leaves and light acid yellow flowers, *E.a.* var. *robbiae H4* (45–60cm x 60cm+) ⚘ lime-green flower bracts in late spring which sit on what look like little plates, glossy dark-green foliage, a rampant ground-cover, seemingly resistant to mildew, good for dry shade under trees. *E. characias H3-4* (90cm–1.2m x 1m) evergreen, attractive mounds of grey-green foliage with yellow-green flowers, March–May, not the hardiest species and often short-lived but tends to self-seed; **'Black Pearl'** lime-green-yellow flowers with intriguing black centres. **'Blue Wonder'** (75cm) compact variety with blue-grey foliage. *E.c.* **Silver Swan** ['Wilcott'] green and white leaves and flowers, the most striking variegated euphorbia we have seen; *E.c.* **subsp.** *wulfenii H3-4* (1.2m x 1m+) ⚘ yellow-green flowers in April–June, fine grey-green foliage, many named selections, some of the best of which are **'Humpty Dumpty'** (70–90cm x 45cm) a slightly smaller version, and **'Lambrooke Gold'** (1.2m x 1m) deep yellow. **Excalibur** ['Froeup'] (75cm x 60cm) striking red spring foliage on pinky-red stems, long-lasting yellow flowers, fine autumn foliage, not invasive. *E. cyparissias H4–5* (40cm x 1–2m+) yellow flowers, reddish autumn leaves, rampant, invasive and not for the faint-hearted, but good in a wild garden. *E. griffithii* **'Dixter'** *H5* (75–90cm x1m++) ⚘ carpets of dark green leaves flushed wine red, deep orange-red flower bracts in summer, rampant and sometimes invasive; *E.g.* **'Fireglow'** *H5* (75–90cm x 1m) ⚘ orange with green leaves. *E. x martinii H3–4* (60cm x 60cm+) a variable hybrid, evergreen, reddish-green leaves and green flowers in March–May, needs

Euphorbia amygdaloides

Euphorbia griffithii 'Fireglow'

Euphorbia 'Redwing',
'Blackbird' and 'Silver Swan'

Euphorbia characias subsp.
wulfenii (RC-M)

shelter and prone to mildew. **Redwing** ['Charm'] (40cm x 40cm) compact form, dark-red foliage, full sun. *E. mellifera H2* (1.2–1.5m x 1m+) ❄ an exotic shrubby evergreen species for mild west-coast gardens, with glossy green leaves and pinkish-brown honey-scented flowers in May. *E. myrsinites H4* (15cm x 60cm+) ⚜ a sun-loving evergreen succulent with fleshy blue-grey spiky leaves and yellow flowers in May–June, sprawling habit. *E. palustris H5* (1m x 1m) also likes full sun, and has yellow-green leaves and yellow-green flowers in June–July. *E. polychroma H5* (50cm x 50cm) ⚜ bright-yellow flowers in spring, sometimes gets mildew. *E. schillingii H4* (90cm–1.2m x 30–60cm) lime-green

flower heads in July–October, leaves with a distinctive pale central rib, needs a sunny site. *E. sikkimensis H4* (1m) deciduous, long leaves with red margins, yellow flowers in summer. *E. wallichii H4* (50cm x 50cm) orange-yellow flowers in summer, deciduous, not always correctly named.

Euryops acraeus see *Artemisia*, page 155

Plants for dry shade

Low light levels and summer dryness make dry shade one of the tougher problem areas for gardeners. It suits only a fairly select number of plants, and establishing plants under trees can be difficult, especially trees such as beech and sycamore, which are both greedy and cast a very dense shade. Digging between roots can be hard work, and it's often worth creating planting pockets with good compost to replace impoverished soil. Leylandii hedges are also bad news, as they take so much moisture from the soil for up to 2m either side, or more. The north side of a leylandii hedge is a particularly poor place to garden. Most plants with coloured and variegated foliage tend towards green in deep shade. In general, planting is best done in autumn, once first rains have come. Everything should be regularly watered until roots are well established.

Shrubs
Aucuba japonica
Cornus canadensis
Euonymus fortunei
Hedera hibernica
Hypericum 'Hidcote'
Ilex aquifolium
Lonicera pileata and
L. nitida
Mahonia
Pachysandra
  terminalis
Prunus lusitanica and
  P. laurocerasus
Rhododendron
  decorum and R.
  yunnanense
Ribes
Rosa x alba 'Alba
  Maxima'
Rubus
Ruscus aculeatus
Sarcococca humilis
Skimmia japonica
Symphoricarpos
Vinca

Perennials
Anemone x
  hybrida/japonica
Astrantia
Brunnera macrophylla
Convallaria majalis
Epimedium
Digitalis (foxglove)
Dryopteris filix-mas
  (fern)
Geranium
  macrorrhizum, G.
  phaeum and others
Helleborus
  argutifolius, H.
  foetidus
Lamium
Luzula (grass)
Maclaeya
Pulmonaria
Tiarella cordifolia
Viola odorata

Bulbs
Eranthus (aconite)
Cyclamen
Galanthus (snowdrop)
Hyacinthoides
  (bluebell)

Ferns (hardy)

Ferns have been around on our planet longer than almost any other plant – they even pre-date the dinosaurs. They usually occur wild in woodland, usually in dappled shade, and are ideal for damp, shady corners of the garden. There is a huge variety of leaf (pinnae) and frond shapes. Some are evergreen, while others die back to a crown. Those lucky enough to garden in the milder and wetter west coast of Scotland can grow giant tree ferns; you can grow these in a sheltered site elsewhere with some artificial protection. Ferns are back in fashion again, though not quite on the scale of the Victorian craze for them: the restored Ascog Fernery on Bute is a testament to that era. Most ferns prefer to be planted in moist humus-rich, slightly alkaline soil and appreciate the addition of leaf mould. Leave the dead foliage of ferns in winter to protect the crowns. Ferns are more or less pest and disease free; most problems are cultural – fronds crisping up from the tips, for instance, is caused by the roots drying out and/or cold winds. Some *Asplenium*, *Dryopteris* and *Polypodium* are tolerant of dry shade, but will need regular watering to become established. Rosa Steppanova finds many ferns do very well in Shetland.

Dicksonia (tree ferns) at Logan

Tree fern wrapped for winter

Tree ferns

Only a handful of these are suitable for growing outdoors in Scotland. *Dicksonia antarctica H3* (2–6m x 2–4m) is by far the most popular, as it is the hardiest. You can buy them as small slow-growing seedlings or more expensively as logs imported from Tasmania, which will burst into life when watered at the top. The base of a log needs to be dug into the ground to keep it steady. Semi-evergreen, usually partly dying back in winter; in colder sites the trunk, and the fronds gathered and fleece-wrapped in mid-winter. *D. fibrosa H2–3* from New Zealand is slightly smaller and a little less hardy. *D. squarrosa H2* is suitable (but still risky) for mildest west coast gardens only, or can be grown indoors.

Hardy terrestrial ferns

Height and spread are simlar unless stated otherwise: single measurements given are for height.

Adiantum (maidenhair ferns) *A. aleuticum* and *A. pedatum H4–5* (30–40cm x 30cm) ❦ are two almost identical, clumping deciduous species with lance-shaped mid-green fronds on glossy black/brown stems. Grow best in dappled shade in well-drained soil with some wind shelter.

Asplenium scolopendrium

Asplenium (spleenwort) *A. scolopendrium* (hart's tongue fern) *H4–5* ✉ ❦ evergreen, moisture loving but needs good drainage, best with some shade. Hair-splitting enthusiasts have named over 450 different varieties; two of the commonest are **Cristatum Group** (50 x 60cm) strap-shaped, leathery green fronds, crested at the tips, and **Undulatum Group** (30cm x 40cm) fronds with wavy margins. *A. trichomanes* (15cm x 20cm) ❦ semi-evergreen, lance-shaped pinnate fronds on black stalks.

Athyrium nipponicum
(Japanese painted fern)

Athyrium (lady fern) *H5* (80cm–1.2m x 45–60cm) A very tough and widely grown deciduous fern for cool and shady sites *A. filix-femina* ❦ delicate, lace-like foliage; **Cristatum Group** (1m high) finely cut and crested fronds; **Cruciatum Group** very narrow pinnae that overlap at right angles like crosses; **'Frizelliae'** (Irish tatting fern) fronds with bead-like pinnae, finely toothed margins. *A. nipponicum var. pictum* (syn. *A.n.* 'Metallicum') (Japanese painted fern) (20–30cm high) this deciduous, spreading fern is one of the most striking, as it has coloured leaves, needs a moist, shady site, long, arching fronds marked dark red, silver and grey; **'Silver Falls'** silvery, dissected leaves, vigorous.

Blechnum (hand fern) *B. chilense* (often confused with the similar and equally fine *B. tabulare*) *H3–4* (1m x 1.2m+) One of the most handsome ferns, a spreading evergreen with stiff foliage, excellent in many west-coast gardens and worth trying in a sheltered site elsewhere. *B. penna-marina H4–5* (20cm x 30cm+) ❦ a spreading evergreen with dense tufts of fronds, forming a ground-cover for damp shade. *B. spicant H5* (30–50cm) ❦ evergreen with leathery leaves, forming a rosette with a circle of upright and outward-facing fronds.

Cyrtomium fortunei

Cyrtomium fortunei (Japanese holly fern) *H3–4* (30–60cm x 25cm) An evergreen fern with an upright habit and holly-shaped leathery pinnae with smooth margins; not all that hardy and best with winter protection away from the coast.

Dryopteris affinis 'Cristata'

Dryopteris (buckler fern) H4–5 These are mostly fairly large ferns with bold shuttlecock-like fronds; there are ten species native to Scotland. **D. affinis** (golden male fern) *H5* (90cm) ✉ this native fern tolerates more sun and wind than most, common in wetter parts of the country, with shuttlecocks of more-or-less evergreen, lance-shaped fronds, pale green when young, with a yellow midrib; **Crispa Group** (30cm) pale-green, twisted, congested fronds; **'Cristata'** (king fern) (to 1.2m x 90cm) the largest-growing form. **D. cycadina H4–5** (45–60cm) erect habit. **D. dilatata** (syn. *D. austriaca*) (broad buckler) **H5** (1–1.5m) robust and good for naturalising with dark-green, broad-based fronds on long, bright-green stalks; the form **'Crispa Whiteside'** has crisped pinnae. **D. erythrosora H4** (60cm) ❦ tufts of triangular fronds, young growth copper-red, does best in a sheltered moist site, a striking choice. **D. filix-mas** (male fern) **H5** (1m) ✉ ❦ a common wild fern, semi-evergreen, good in sun or shade; there are many selections: **'Crispa Cristata'** fronds crested and crisped (which means the edges look a bit ragged), **'Cristata'** ❦ the crested form, **'Linearis'** a form with fewer pinnae, giving a sparse, rather airy appearance. **D. wallichiana H4** (1m+) shuttlecocks of yellow-green young fronds, turning dark green, midribs covered in dark-brown scales, perhaps the most handsome *Dryopteris*.

Gymnocarpium dryopteris (oak fern) **H5** (30cm x 45cm+) ✉ A Scottish native with soft fronds on creeping rootstocks, forming dense mats, which grows well in rocky or stony soil, on roofs and walls; there are fine examples on rooves at Pitmuies in Angus. **'Plumosum'** fronds feathery and broader.

Matteuccia struthiopteris (ostrich fern, shuttlecock fern) **H4–5** (1.2m) ❦ A beautiful and spectacular large deciduous fern for damp shade, with erect shuttlecocks of bright green, excellent for the moist Scottish woodland garden. It can spread rather vigorously for a small garden.

There is a fine grouping by the pond at Torosay Castle on Mull.

Onoclea sensibilis (sensitive fern) **H5** (60cm x 60cm+) A deciduous, sometimes invasive spreader for waterside or woodland with arching pale-green to pinkish-bronze young fronds; the male fronds die back with the first frosts, leaving only the female ones.

Osmunda regalis

Osmunda regalis (royal fern) **H5** (1–1.5m x 1m) ❦ The largest growing of the hardy ferns, with huge, bright green fronds up to 1.5m long with brown tassel-like tips, covered in fertile spores, fine golden autumn colour. This looks very handsome beside water and in a container, as long as it is not allowed to dry out. **'Cristata'** fronds and pinnae with crested tips, **'Purpurascens'** (1.2m) slower growing, young fronds flushed purple.

Polypodium vulgare H5 (30cm x 1m+) ✉ A spreading evergreen fern often found colonizing mossy trees, logs and rocks, with deeply cut, leathery fronds; one of the few that will tolerate dry shade.

Polystichum (shield fern) Handsome ferns with golden scales. **P. aculeatum** (hard shield fern) **H5** (60cm x 45cm) evergreen, with stiff leaves, which unfurl and curl over backwards, does not like rich deep soils, does best in shallow stony sites. **P. munitum** (sword fern) **H4–5** (90cm x 1.5m) shuttlecocks of dark green, glossy, lance-shaped fronds of spiny-toothed pinnae. **P. polyblepharum** (Japanese tassel fern) **H4–5** (50–60cm) ❦ evergreen with sturdy dark-green shuttlecocks covered in golden hairs, for sun or light shade. **P. setiferum** (soft shield fern) **H5** (1.2m) ✉ handsome and evergreen with intricately dissected soft lance-shaped fronds; can be grown in sun in Scotland, but don't allow the soil to dry out; there are many selected forms with tongue-twisting names, such as **Divisilobum Group** spreading with finely cut fronds, with narrowed and leathery segments, **Plumodivisilobum Group** with four-pinnate overlapping fronds, and **Plumosomultilobum Group** a mouthful which means 'with feathery or mossy fronds'. **P. tsussimense**

Polystichum setiferum

H4–5 (20–30cm) a neat evergreen fern (with another impressive name), for shade, rock garden or container.

Filipendula purpurea 'Rubra'

Filipendula (meadowsweet) and *Sanguisorba*

H5 Filipendulas are tough, moisture-loving, airy plants with masses of frothy tiny pink or white flowers in summer. *F. ulmaria*, our native meadowsweet, can be found in roadsides and ditches all over Scotland, and self-seeds freely. The plant has many traditional medicinal uses: the flowers can provide a natural painkiller (salic acid, used for aspirin) and can also be made into a country wine, so potentially provides both the hangover and cure. All varieties thrive in moist boggy soil in full sun and they are ideal subjects for wild and woodland gardens, as well as pond and streamsides. They have attractive finely cut leaves and the flowers have a musky, slightly sickly fragrance.

'Kahome' (60cm x 45cm) deep rose pink. **F. purpurea** (1.2m x 60cm) frothy heads of tiny purple-red flowers; **F.p. 'Elegans'** pink. **F. rubra 'Venusta'** (1.8m x 1.2m+) flat frothy rose-pink flower heads from early to mid-summer. **F. ulmaria H5** ✉ ❄ (90cm–1.2m x 1m+) our native meadowsweet, scented creamy-white flower clusters in mid-summer, good for naturalizing beside water; **F.u. 'Aurea'** (30cm x 30cm) yellow-green leaves, subject to sunburn; **F.u. 'Variegata' H5** (60cm x 30cm) leaves with a central splash of yellow, tends to revert; **F.u. 'Flore Pleno' H5** (45–60cm x 45cm) larger, double flowers in sprays. **F. vulgaris 'Multiplex' H5** (75cm x 30cm) ❄ clusters of scented double creamy-white flowers and finely cut foliage.

Sanguisorba tenuifolia

Sanguisorba (burnet) H5

These clump-forming perennials have attractive foliage and bottlebrush-like flower spikes in mid- to late summer. They are easy to grow in any reasonably moist soil in full sun, but are vigorous, becoming invasive in some situations. They grow naturally in wet meadows, like our native meadowsweet. Trim after flowering to keep in shape, but otherwise they can be left alone for years. **S. albiflora** (90cm x 60cm) drooping plumes of white. **S. canadensis** (1.2–2m x 75cm) white, toothed leaves. **S. obtusa** (60cm–1.2m x 60cm) drooping fluffy rose-crimson flowers, grey-green leaves. **S. tenuifolia** (1m+) drooping catkins of pink or white ('Alba'). **'Tanna'** (1m x 45cm) tight dark red late-summer ball-shaped flowers, grey-green ferny foliage, needs staking. **'Pink Tanna'** pink.

Fragaria (alpine and ornamental strawberries)

H5 Less fussy than their over-hybridized cousins (see page 148), these are tough, pretty and small. They are rather rampant ground cover plants that spread over the soil by runners, and are happy in most soil conditions and situations, apart from deep shade and waterlogged soil. The dreaded vine weevil larvae love munching the roots; otherwise they are pretty trouble free, although birds and mice have an annoying habit of stealing the fruit just before you are about to pick them. Flowers white, pink or red, in spring and summer; they spread widely (60–90cm or more).

Fragaria 'Pink Panda'

Pink Panda ['Frel'] (15cm) large pink flowers May–November, rarely produce fruit, divided green leaves. **Red Ruby** ['Samba'] (15cm) large red flowers, occasional fruit. **F. vesca** (wild strawberry) (10cm) ✉ small white flowers in May–June followed by small but flavoursome strawberries; **'Variegata'** leaves with white edging, less vigorous, inclined to revert.

Francoa (bridal or maiden's wreath)

H2–3 (75cm x 60cm) Traditionally used in bridal wreaths, this saxifrage relative has long-lasting, graceful stems of pink, purple or white flowers above rounded, deeply lobed, mid-green leaves. Seed heads add interest later in the year and are good food for birds. Rather tender, suitable for mild and coastal gardens with well-drained soil, it thrives at Torosay Castle in Mull and places with a similar climate. Don't allow it to be crowded out by its neighbours, it can't deal with the competition. **F. sonchifolia** is the commonest variety, usually as **'Rogerson's Form'** purple flowers, spotted with maroon; there is also a white form, **'Alba'**.

Francoa sonchifolia 'Alba'

Gaillardia see Daisies, page 171

Galega officinalis (goat's rue)

H5 (90cm–1.2m x 1m) This very tough plant from the Middle East is now naturalized in parts of southern England. It has spikes of small, pea-like, lilac-pink flowers in June–July, and the leaves are divided into oval leaflets. It has a rather loose flopping habit, so does best with support from other plants. It requires full sun and well-drained soil, and it is easy to please, though it resents being moved, seeming particularly at home in Dumfries and Galloway. *G.o.* **'Alba'** is a fine white form. *G. x hartlandii* **'Alba'** is very similar with a slightly more upright habit and larger flowers, **Coconut Ice** ['Kelgal'] ❋ cream-pink, coconut-scented, leaves white edged, **'Lady Wilson'** bicoloured mauve and white.

Galega officinalis 'Alba'

Gaura lindheimeri

Gaura lindheimeri

H3–4 (1–1.2m x 45–60cm) This erect perennial, with lance-shaped leaves and late-summer racemes of white or pink tubular flowers, resembling butterflies, has become quite widely available in garden centres. It is useful planted towards the back of borders or in drifts near water, and prefers a sunny site in moist but well-drained soil. Gauras can be short-lived, even annual in cold heavy soils, and they are prone to (harmless) leaf spotting, preferring a climate drier than that most of Scotland offers.

G. lindheimeri flowers white; forms include **'Corrie's Gold'** (*H3*) white flowers, yellow-variegated leaves, **Passionate Pink** [PBR] deep magenta pink, **'Siskiyou Pink'** pink, dark purple-green leaves, **'Whirling Butterflies'** a great name, white, **'Crimson Butterflies'** (1m) dwarf, pink, crimson leaves.

Gentiana (gentian)

H4–5 This variable genus includes many alpine gems for the rock garden, as well as some interesting taller clump-forming plants for woodland and the herbaceous border. The trumpet-shaped flowers are mostly bright blue, and some are evergreen. Most gentians love the cool wet climate of Scotland. The autumn carpeting types are outstanding, and need sun for at least part of the day to flower well and for the petals to open fully. Most prefer slightly acidic, moist, free-draining, humus-rich soil, which makes them ideal company for dwarf rhododendrons. A few, such as *G. acaulis*, will tolerate alkaline soil, and *G. lutea* prefers it. Aphids and vine weevil can cause problems. Some of the smaller alpine gentians can gradually become congested, which causes poor flowering or patches which yellow and die back. These are best split up in early spring and replanted.

Taller gentians

These include *G. asclepiadea* (willow gentian) *H4–5* (60–90cm x 60cm) ✿ willow-like leaves, arching sprays of deep-blue flowers in August–October; there is also a white form **'Alba'**, and a pink form **'Rosea'**. *G. septemfida H5* (15–20cm x 20–30cm) ✿ blue or purplish blue with white stripes, August onwards, prostrate or ascending stems, tolerates clay soil; var. *lagodechiana* almost prostrate stems. *G. lutea H5* (1.5m x 60cm) a dramatic-looking plant with hollow stems as thick as arms, whorls of leaves, around which nestle yellow flowers in summer.

Gentiana asclepiadea, white and blue forms   *Gentiana sino-ornata*

The smaller gentians

H4–5 (5–10cm x 5–10cm+) *G. acaulis H5* ✿ deep-blue trumpet flowers in spring and sometimes again in autumn. *G. verna* upright-pointing rich-blue flowers in May–June. Both these are evergreen. *G. saxosa* upright white crocus-like flowers in summer, evergreen. *G. sino-ornata* (5cm x 30cm+) ✿ rich-blue flowers in September, evergreen, glossy tufted, needle-like leaves. This needs a good moisture supply and should be divided every 3–4 years to maintain vigour. There are numerous fine Scottish and Welsh hybrids flowering in September, bred from *G. sino-ornata* and related species; they differ in fairly minute details of striping and shading in the flower: **'Blue Silk'** deep blue, striped violet inside, one of the finest, **'Cairngorm'** compact, short blue trumpets, **'Inverleith'** rich blue, trumpet-shaped flowers striped darker on the outside – apparently the plant in commerce under this name is an imposter, **'Lucerna'** vivid deep-blue flowers, **'Shot Silk'** highly rated, one of the deepest blues with purple markings, **'Strathmore'** pale sky-blue trumpets on long stems. *G. x* *macaulayi* **'Kidbrooke Seedling'** large blue flowers; **'Kingfisher'** (5cm) vivid blue, orange stamens; **'Wells Variety'** pale blue, striped, very fine at the Royal Botanic Garden Edinburgh.

Geranium (cranesbills)
and *Erodium*

H4–5 Every garden should have a few hardy geraniums: few plants are tougher, more versatile and more reliable, with fine dislays of colour and long flowering periods. Not to be confused with bedding 'geraniums' which are actually pelargoniums, the herbaceous geraniums include a huge range of plants suitable for Scottish gardens. They form ground-covering mounds of often very attractive leaves, and flower in a range of colours – purples, blues, pink and whites – some in early spring, others in summer through to the first frosts. They tolerate most soils except heavy waterlogged ones, and do best either in sun or part shade, depending on species and variety. Some excellent new varieties have been raised on Orkney by Alan Bremner. Some geraniums are relatively rabbit-proof while rabbits massacre others. They are not prone to slug or snail damage, though vine weevils like the roots and a few suffer mildew or rust. The many Scottish woodland gardens with little colour in summer would be greatly improved with carpets of geraniums under their rhododendrons. Scotland has several native species (cranesbills) including *G. pratense*, *G. sanguineum* and *G. sylvaticum*. In herbaceous borders you may need to stake geraniums to stop them flopping over. In a more informal setting as ground cover this may not be necessary. They can also be allowed to trail over walls and down banks.

All fully hardy **H5**, with similar height and spread, unless stated otherwise. **'Ann Folkard' H4–5** (60–90cm) ❦ is a border show-stopper with bright magenta, black-eyed flowers in June–October, does best in full sun, sprawling, foliage inclined to yellow. **'Anne Thomson'** is very similar to 'Ann Folkard', still sprawling but slightly more compact with better foliage. *G. x antipodeum* **'Pink Spice'** (20cm) rose pink, bronze foliage. **'Bertie Crûg' H3** (15cm) magenta-pink, bronzy leaves, creeping. **Black Beauty** ['Nodbeauty'] (25cm) violet-blue-mauve, June–July, leaves dark purple, gradually changing to green. **'Brookside'** (90cm) large deep violet-blue flowers with a paler eye, June–September, divided leaves, very good. **Blue Sunrise** ['Blogold'] (25cm) sprawling, leaves yellow-green, flowers blue, veined purple. *G. x cantabrigiense* (30 x 45cm) dense mats of carpeting semi-evergreen, aromatic foliage which colours in autumn, tolerant of moist or dry shade, white, pink or purple flowers in May–June, several clones: **'Biokovo'** white tinged pale pink, not always easy to please, **'Cambridge'** soft mauve, **'Karmina'** bright pink, **'St Ola'** white, long flowering, from Orkney. *G. cinereum* **'Ballerina'** (15cm) ❦ cup-shaped pale-pink to white flowers, deeply veined with purple, thriving in sun or part shade, good for the rock garden, path or border edge; other forms include **'Carol'** purple-pink, **'Purple Pillow'** (12cm) red-purple, darker veins, with a dark

Geraniums, mixed

Geranium macrorrhizum
'Ingwersen's Variety', 'Bevan's
Variety' and 'Album'

eye, needs good drainage, **Rothbury Gem** ['Gerfos'] pink with darker veining and centre, long flowering, semi-evergreen, **Rothbury Red** [PBR applied for] pink, bronze foliage. *G. clarkei* (45cm) finely cut leaves, best in full sun, flowers in loose clusters from June onwards, best cut back mid-summer for a second flush of flowers, various colours: **'Kashmir Green'** a new introduction, white, veined green, **'Kashmir Pink'** (pink), **'Kashmir Purple'** (purple), **'Kashmir White'** ❦ white veined purple. *G. dalmaticum* (15cm x 50cm+) ❦ semi-evergreen, leaves colouring in autumn, pale to bright pink flowers with red anthers, sharp drainage required. *G. endressii* (60cm) bright pink with notched petals, all summer long, clumps of wrinkled foliage, full sun; a new form **'Beholder's Eye'** more compact with large saucer-shaped flowers, June–August, and good autumn colour. *G. himalayense* (30–45cm) saucer-shaped blue to purple flowers with white centres in June and sometimes again in late summer, good in dry shade; forms: **'Gravetye'** ❦ deep blue, **'Irish Blue'** paler blue with reddish-purple centres, **'Plenum'** (25cm) small double purple-pink. **'Johnson's Blue'** ❦ clear-blue flowers all summer, deeply lobed leaves. *G. macrorrhizum* (30–40cm x 1m+) an invaluable thick carpeter for dry shade, thriving beneath trees and shrubs, with bronze and scarlet autumn colour, flowering in May–June, pink with red sepals; several colour forms: **'Album'** ❦ white, **'Bevan's Variety'** deep magenta, red sepals, **'Ingwersen's Variety'** ❦ soft rose pink. *G. maculatum* (spotted cranesbill) (60cm) mauve-pink in spring; selected forms with dark leaves include **'Elizabeth Ann'** and **'Espresso'**. *G. maderense* **H2–3** (1m x 90cm) a large-growing species, for mild gardens only, or indoors, with ferny foliage, bright-pink flowers; at Glendoick it escaped from the greenhouses and now grows outside. *G. x magnificum* (45cm x 60cm) rich purple-violet with heavy veining, forms dense clumps, good ground-cover. **'Orion'** (80cm) lavender-blue, deeper veins, pale centre, June to August, finely cut leaves, **'Orkney Pink'** (30cm x 50cm) one of Alan Bremner's best, trailing stems with deep pink-cerise flowers May–September, leaves bronze, needs good drainage. *G. x oxonianum* (90cm x 90cm–2m) a vigorous ground-cover with small pink flowers June–September, repeat flowering (best if cut back during the season), deeply lobed palmate leaves, semi-evergreen in mild climates, many selections: **'A.T. Johnson'** silver pink, **'Claridge Druce'** lilac pink, grey-green leaves, **'Southcombe Star'** pink, strap or narrow petals, **'Wargrave Pink'** (45cm) ⚜ clear salmon-pink flowers all summer long. **'Patricia'** (70cm x 45cm) lilac pink with a dark centre, June–September, five-lobed green leaves, a Bremner hybrid from Orkney. *G. phaeum* (30cm–1m) ⚜ excellent for spreading underneath shrubs or in shady beds, tolerant of dry shade, with distinctive small deep-purple flowers with reflexed petals in late spring and summer; forms include **'Album'** white, **'Samobor'** (75cm) dark-purple flowers in spring and a few in summer, leaves boldly marked with brown, one of the best for foliage. *G. pratense* (60cm) violet-blue flowers, June–August, deeply cut and lobed leaves, can suffer from mildew; forms include **'Mrs Kendall Clark'** pink with pale veins, at least three plants go under this name, **'Plenum Caeruleum'** double lavender blue, **'Plenum Violaceum'** (45cm) double violet, **f. albiflorum** white, **'Striatum'** (syn. 'Splish Splash') white-streaked lavender blue, **Summer Skies** ['Gernic'] double pale lilac-blue and white, a bit muddy-looking, inclined to rot off in flower in wet weather, **Victor Reiter Group** (15–60cm) purple flowers, dark-purple leaves; there are many forms and strains including **'Midnight Reiter'** very dwarf, the darkest leaves, rather lacking in vigour. *G. psilostemon* (1.2m x 90cm) ⚜ one of the most vigorous species, striking bright crimson-magenta flowers with a black centre in summer, loose habit. *G. renardii* (35cm) ⚜ white or lavender with purple veins, very attractive,

Geranium 'Rozanne'

Geranium pratense 'Mrs Kendall Clarke'

(40cm) purplish pink over a long season. *G. subcaulescens* (formerly a subspecies of *G. cinereum*) magenta with a black eye in summer. *G. sylvaticum* (90cm x 60cm) ✉ UK native, pink-purple flowers in May–June, seven-lobed leaves, rabbits apparently like this species; the forms **'Album'** white, **'Amy Doncaster'** fine blue with a white eye, **'Mayflower'** violet-blue with a white eye. **'Tanya Rendell'** (15cm x 60cm) red-purple with white eyes, bronzy foliage. *G. versicolor* (syn. *G. striatum*) white, veined magenta, in June and spasmodically to autumn, evergreen shiny leaves with red markings. *G. wallichianum* **'Buxton's Variety'** (25cm x 90cm) ⚜ deep blue with white centres in late summer and autumn, one of the latest to flower, dark-green leaves colour red in winter. *G. wlassovianum* (60cm) rather small purple-pink flowers with darker veins in late summer, leaves bronzy, turning red in autumn.

***Erodium* (heron or stork's bill)** These useful if somewhat underwhelming clump-forming rock garden plants from southern Europe are similar to the lower-growing geraniums with small flowers. They

Geranium psilostemon

Geranium renardii

Erodium x *variabile* 'Bishop's Form'

May–June, full sun, compact, trailing. *G.* x *riversleaianum* (20cm x 90cm) pink-reddish flowers in June–September, leaves greyish green, dies back completely in winter; forms include **'Mavis Simpson'** pale pink, needs sharp drainage, tricky on the west coast, **'Russell Prichard'** ⚜ carmine-red. **Rozanne** ['Gerwat'] **H3–4** (50cm x 75cm) one of the best of all for its intense blue flowers with white centres and long flowering period from late June to first frosts, sprawling habit; **'Jolly Bee'** looks almost identical. *G. sanguineum* (25cm x 45cm) deep magenta-pink, June–August, rounded, deeply divided, dark-green leaves, good ground-cover, needs a sunny, well-drained site; forms include **'Album'** white **'Max Frei'** deep magenta, **'Purple Flame'** deep purple, **var. striatum** ⚜ rose pink. **'Spinners'** (45cm x 60cm) purplish-blue flowers in May–June, deeply lobed leaves, **'Sirak'**

flower throughout the summer and like full sun and moist, but well-drained soil. They benefit from deadheading and from dividing every so often to maintain vigour; some are inclined to seed too freely and become a pest. *E. chrysanthum* **H3** (25cm x 25cm) ferny grey foliage, sprays of pale-yellow flowers in spring and summer. *E. manescavii* **H4** (45cm x 60cm) deep pink, ferny blue-green leaves, inclined to seed all over the place. *E.* x *variabile* **H4** (20cm x 40cm) small white to bright-pink flowers in summer and early autumn on a compact cushion-forming plant, leaves with scalloped edges; forms include **'Album'** white, **'Bishop's Form'** bright pink, **'Roseum'** pink with red veins.

Geum

H5 These tough clump-forming perennials have small red, orange or yellow flowers on long slender stalks in May–September, and are easy to grow. They are not the world's most breathtaking garden plants – Christopher Lloyd calls them 'stringy', which is a fair comment – but the long flowering period is invaluable: if deadheaded or cut back they will flower all summer long. They prefer full sun and moist but well-drained soil, and the taller varieties may need staking. They can be short lived, dislike drought in summer and if not divided every 3–4 years the flowering tends to decrease. They spread to approximately 30–60cm:

Geum 'Lady Stratheden' and 'Mrs J. Bradshaw'

'Borisii' (30cm) bright orange-red, hairy rounded leaves. *G. x borisii* yellow flowers. 'Fire Opal' (75cm) double orange flushed scarlet on purple stems. 'Georgenberg' (30cm) single yellow, 'Lady Stratheden' (60cm) ♧ double yellow. 'Mrs J. Bradshaw' (60cm) ♧ double red, often not long-lived. Totally Tangerine [PBR] (60cm) apricot orange. *G. montanum* (15cm) a rock garden species from the Alps with bright-yellow flowers, followed by fluffy seed heads.

Plants that attract butterflies, moths and bees

Aster novi-belgii	Hydrangea
Buddleja	Lavandula
Astrantia	Linaria
Ceanothus	Mentha
Clethra alnifolia	Nepeta
Digitalis	Perovskia
Echinacea	Salvia
Echinops	Scabious and Knautia
Eryngium	Sedum spectabile
Escallonia	Solidago
Eupatorium	Spiraea
Helleborus (flowers	Thymus
before most plants,	Verbascum
providing vital	Verbena bonariensis
food)	Veronica

Grasses, sedges and rushes

There is no doubt that grasses have caught the imagination of gardeners and garden designers over the last few years and that, after extensive breeding programmes, there are grasses suitable for any garden size or location. We hear rumblings amongst style gurus that grasses are now over-used, but in Scotland they are still a relatively recent innovation for most gardeners. As well as the waving heads and leaves in summer, well-planted displays of grasses can look magnificent well into winter, particularly with frost on the seed heads and stems. From the huge pampas grass down to the diminutive forms of *Carex* and *Festuca*, they provide a good leaf contrast and foil for other flowers, and many form specimen plants in their own right. The best grasses don't need much attention once they are established and they associate well with other perennial plants, in what is known as prairie-style planting. Many grasses are striking subjects for containers and flower arrangers love their long-lasting flower spikes. Some grasses need to be split up every few years, but the only maintenance most grasses need is cutting them down when they start to die back. This is best done in spring, rather than winter. Most grasses do well in poor soils and they should not be over-fed, or else they may not flower well. Many grasses have bronzy, bluish grey or yellowish foliage and/or flowers and it is well worth seeking out a range of foliage colours. Grasses are generally not suited to shady sites; they need to be out in full sun to flower well and to maintain a sturdy, compact habit. Not all grasses do well in Scotland: lack of summer heat and cold, wet winters cause some to be badly frosted or to rot away. Gravel mulches may help some of these through the winter. Most grasses require sharp drainage and will not last long in clay, waterlogged or peaty soils. Anyone looking for inspiration for gardening with grasses should visit Cambo in Fife in late summer. Binny Plants, Cally Gardens and Quercus Garden Plants have a good range of grasses for sale. Heights and spreads are similar, unless stated otherwise.

Acorus gramineus (sweet flag) *H5* Vigorous, semi-evergreen grass, usually grown in boggy soil or as a pond marginal, though it can also used as a border plant and will grow well in any soil that does not dry out: on the north side of a wall, for example. It can spread rather vigorously, but the garden forms listed below are usually more manageable, and all are excellent in Scotland. The flowers are insignificant and most forms are grown for their coloured foliage. They may need dividing and replanting if the centre becomes bare. 'Hakuro-nishiki' (15cm) ♧ bright golden-yellow variegation with green flashes, 'Ogon' (25–50cm) ♧ golden-yellow leaves, 'Variegatus' (50cm) ♧ slender leaves striped green and white.

Briza media (quaking grass) *H5* (30–70cm) ✉ ♧ Blue-green leaves with bristly margins, panicles of heart-shaped pale flowers which rattle in the breeze and turn yellow in summer, tolerant of heavy and poorly drained soils. Good for drying. Will self-seed.

Calamagrostis **(reed grass)** *H4–5* An elegant, architectural grass with long-lasting flowers that look good well into winter, best in moist soil in sun. Cut them to the ground in spring before growth begins. *C. x acutiflora* **'Karl Foerster'** (1.8m) flowers pink-bronze fading to white – Christopher Lloyd rates this as 'the most valuable ornamental grass'; **'Overdam'** (1.2m) leaves with pale-yellow margins and stripes, flowers purplish. *C. arundinacea* (1.5m) arching mounds of narrow green leaves turning orange and red in autumn. *C. brachytricha* (75cm) upright heads of pink tinged white flowers.

Carex **(sedge)** *H3–4(5)* Sedges differ from true grasses in their solid, usually triangular stems. Generally not as spectacular in flower as the grasses, but many are invaluable for their foliage, which is often coloured or variegated. Many are not reliably hardy for coldest inland gardens. Scotland has almost 60 native species of sedge and the *RHS Plantfinder* lists over 250 varieties, so it can be difficult to know which ones to try. Those listed below are the ones most commonly available, but many others are equally good. *C. berggrenii* *H3* (10cm) a miniature grass with a neat tufted habit, leaves can be blue-green, greyish or reddish brown, ideal for containers, the rock garden and at the front of a border, should not be allowed to dry out. *C. buchananii* *H3–4* (60cm x 90cm) red-brown arching leaves, brown flowers in summer, very

Carex buchananii (RC-M)

attractive but not all that hardy. *C. caryophyllea* **'The Beatles'** *H4–5* (15cm) tufts of dark-green narrow leaves, shaggy yellow-green flowers in spring. *C. comans* *H3–4* (20cm) one of the most attractive of all sedges; **bronze form** fine hair-like arching bronze leaves with slight curls to the ends, self-seeds everywhere; other forms include **'Frosted Curls'** (60cm) pale silvery-green leaves curling at the tips, green flower spikes turning brown in summer, very fine, but not long lived in wet, heavy soil, **'Milk Chocolate'** (60cm) leaves light brown, orange and green tints in autumn. *C. conica* **'Snowline'** *H3* (15cm x 25cm) semi-evergreen with white-margined green leaves forming dense clumps, small purple-brown flowers in early summer, likes moist or wet soil. *C. dipsacea* **(teasel-like sedge)** *H3* (75cm) narrow dark-green leaves in dense clumps, bristly dark-brown to

black flowers in late summer; **'Dark Horse'** a selected form with dark winter foliage. *C. elata* **'Aurea'** (syn. 'Bowles' Golden') *H4* (40–60cm) a tough deciduous sedge with narrow arching yellow-green leaves with brown flowering spikes in summer, likes moist or wet soil. *C. flagellifera* *H3–4* (75cm–1m) dense clumps of green or reddish-brown leaves, light-brown flower spikes, similar to *C. comans*. *C. grayi* *H4–5* (50–75cm) erect clumps of broad dark-green leaves, green flowers followed by attractive star-like seed heads, used for flower arranging. *C. kaloides* (75cm x 1m) shades of greens, yellows and bronze depending on exposure to sun. *C. morrowii* *H3* (40cm) evergreen with stiff leaves, bulrush-like flowers; the most popular forms are **'Fisher's Form'** (50cm) leaves striped and margined cream, flower spikes green and brown, **'Ice Dance'** (to 60cm) deep green with strong white edges, **'Silver Sceptre'** (25cm) leaves margined

Carex oshimensis 'Evergold'

silvery white, flowers cream in early summer, best with some shade, **'Variegata'** (30cm) leaves margined white, drought tolerant. *C. oshimensis* **'Evergold'** *H4* (to 50cm) evergreen with a low, clumping habit, leaves dark green with a bold cream-yellow central stripe, likes moist soil. **'Everest'** (to 50cm) bright green with neat white stripes, **'Everillo'** (to 50cm) bright gold foliage holds its colour best in part shade. *C. pendula* **'Moonraker'** *H4* (to 1.4m) a selected form of a Scottish native plant with white and cream young leaves, fading to yellow-green, arching pendulous catkin-like flowers and seeds. *C. phyllocephala* **'Sparkler'** (30–50cm x 1m) evergreen, with purple stems and cream-edged dark-green leaves which shoot out in all directions, spreading habit, needs moist but well-drained soil. *C. pseudocyperus* (75cm–1.2m) strap-like green leaves and somewhat pendulous green flowers, moist soil, good pond marginal. *C. riparia* **'Variegata'** *H4* (1m) ideal for wet places and stream- and pondsides, but rampantly invasive, so beware of using it in a small garden, leaves striped or almost completely white, tall flower spikes in summer, can be planted in water to a depth of 50cm. *C. siderosticha* *H4* deciduous slow spreader which needs damp soil; two popular selections are **'Shima-nishiki'** (15cm) gold-variegated overlapping leaves, and **'Variegata'** (30cm) leaves margined and striped white, flushed pink in spring. *C. testacea* *H3* (to 50cm) leaves dark green to bronze, dense, tufted habit, flowers dark brown, needs moist but well-drained soil. **'Lime Shine'** (to 50cm) lime green upright habit with slightly arching leaves.

Chionochloa conspicua

Chionochloa H3 (tussock grass) This is perhaps our favourite grass, but it is hard to find, you'll have to go to a specialist. It is a really handsome New Zealand grass for a sunny site in well-drained (but not dry) soil in mild or sheltered gardens. We have seen excellent specimens at Abriachan on Loch Ness and at Balcarres in Fife. The flowers are particularly good for drying. *C. conspicua* (1–2m) broad leaves, plumes of creamy-yellow flowers, like a more tasteful and less thuggish pampas grass. *C. rubra* (75cm) dense tussocks, narrow stiff reddish-bronze leaves, takes a few years to start flowering.

Cortaderia selloana (pampas grass) H3–4 (2–3m x 1–2m+) Pampas grass seems to be back in vogue now, and with good reason: the handsome leaves and fluffy flower heads provide some of the best plants for autumn and winter interest. Variegated forms are shy flowering. Pampas are aesthetically more pleasing amongst other plants than grown in an island bed in a lawn 1970s style. An established clump is pretty tough but cold or wet winter can kill a newly planted specimen, so we have given it an H3–4 rating. They like well-drained soil, are drought tolerant once established and in Scotland do best in

Cortaderia selloana (pampas grass)

plenty of light. Make sure you give yours room to expand, as trying to move an established pampas grass is like wrestling with a great white shark. Foliage needs chopping from time to time; some even recommend setting fire to it. (Personally, I'd recommend setting fire to all pampas, as I can't stand them anywhere – RC-M.) They are amazingly wind tolerant for a plant of this size, growing right by the beach in Aberdeenshire and the east Neuk of Fife, amongst other places. **'Albolineata'** (2m) leaves with white margins, **'Aureolineata'** (2.2m) leaves with yellow margins, shy flowering, **'Pumila' H4** (1.5m) compact, said to include the hardiest forms, **'Rendatleri'** (2.5m) plumes of silver-purple flowers, weak stemmed, **'Rosea'** (2–3m) variable, plumes silvery white with a pink flush, **'Splendid Star'** (70cm) flower spikes to 1.2m, new, said to be the hardiest of the smaller-

growing, yellow-leaved forms, **'Sunningdale Silver' H2–3** (2–3m) a tall form with wind-resistant stems, needs hot sun to flower well. *C. richardii* **H2–3** (2–3m in ideal conditions, more commonly 1.2–1.5m) is less hardy, earlier flowering and slightly lower growing.

Deschampsia cespitosa 'Northern Lights'

Deschampsia (hair grass) H3–4/5 Evergreen grasses with graceful thread-like leaves and often very impressive flower spikelets. The most commonly sold varieties were selected in Germany and are tough, probably suitable for any Scottish garden. Some of the few grasses that will flower in some shade, they will grow in damp or dry soil and the only maintenance they need is the flowers cutting down in early spring. *D. cespitosa* (leaves to 60cm, flower heads 1–2m) useful for mass planting, long flowering season, good for flower arranging; forms **'Bronzeschleier'** plumes of bronze-purple flowers to 1m high, **'Goldgehänge'** (45cm) flower panicles golden yellow, **'Goldtau'** (syn. 'Golden Dew') (75cm) low and compact, flower spikelets reddish brown, ageing to yellowish, **'Northern Lights'** (40cm) variegated leaves in autumn, shy flowering, soft golden flower heads in June–August. *D. flexuosa* **'Tatra Gold'** (40cm) bright golden-green leaves, small bronze flowers.

Elymus magellanicus (RC-M)

Elymus magellanicus H4 (60cm–1.2m) Little known, this is one of the bluest of all the grasses and it looks irresistible in summer. Semi-evergreen in mild climates, it needs cool nights and so does better in Scotland than further south. It needs very well-drained soil and the foliage can rot if wet for long periods, but it is hardy otherwise. Recommended for coastal gardens, gravel beds and containers.

Festuca (fescue) H4 (40–50cm) The fescues include striking ornamentals as well as a main component in lawn seed mixes. Free-draining soil is required or else they may succumb to winter wet. Shear after flowering to keep tidy and over-crowded clumps will need dividing. They don't tend to age very well. *F. amethystina* (60cm) fine blue-green leaves and fawn spring flowers. *F. glauca* (40cm)

Festuca glauca 'Blaufuchs'

pale blue thread-like leaves, bluish flowers in spring; **'Azurit'** (30cm) very blue leaves, **'Blaufuchs'** (Blue Fox) (25cm) bright blue, **'Elijah Blue'** (30cm) silvery blue, **'Golden Toupee'** (30cm) (it's hard not to picture this on top of someone's head) yellow-green leaves, yellowish flowers in summer.

Hakonechloa macra 'Alboaurea' (RC-M)

Hakonechloa macra H4 (40cm x 60cm) This is a slow-spreading deciduous Japanese grass with graceful, arching stems and bamboo-like leaves that turn pinkish and reddish in autumn. Elliot Forsyth recommends growing it in containers. **'Aureola'** yellow and pale-green striped leaves, **'Alboaurea'** yellow with thin stripes of green and some white splashes.

Holcus mollis **'Albovariegatus'** *H4–5* (30cm x 50cm+) A low spreader of soft blue-green leaves with creamy white margins, pale-green flowers. Do not allow to seed, as it is invasive. It tends to die back in patches and is best cut back in late summer. You can even use it to make variegated lawns.

Imperata cylindrica **'Rubra'** (syn. 'Red Baron') (Japanese blood grass) *H2–3* (40cm x 30cm) One of the most spectacular and widely available grasses, but it is not very hardy and is not likely to survive long in gardens away from the coast. A winter mulch can help protect the crown. It has red pigment in the leaves developing from the tips downwards, most intense in the late summer, and occasional white flowers in late summer. Needs well-drained but not dry soil in full sun. Divide and replant every three years (if it lives that long).

Juncus (rush) Most of Scotland's 21 species of rush are found in bogs and watersides, but one or two selected forms make eye-catching plants for moist borders and containers. *J. decipiens* **'Curly-wurly'** *H4* (15cm) evergreen except in coldest winters, spiralling/coiled leaves and stems, tiny flowers. *J. effusus* f. **'Spiralis'** (corkscrew rush) *H4* (50cm) spiralled dark-green stems, forming a tangle, small brown flowers in summer; **'Gold Strike'** (30cm) straight-stemmed, green with a single yellow stripe down the stem.

Koeleria glauca (blue hair grass) *H3–4* (40–60cm x 30cm) This hedgehog-like tufted grass grows and flowers early in the season. It is inclined to die back in hot or dry weather, while in wet summers it may put on a second flush of growth. It has striking blue-green leaves and upright flower panicles of light blue-grey-green flowers, later creamy white.

Luzula (wood rush) Wood rushes are useful ground-cover plants with flowers that are often dried for flower arranging, but they can spread further than intended. **L. nivea** (snowy wood rush) *H4–5* (60cm) ⚘ green hairy leaves, evergreen in milder climates, lax flower clusters off-white, a useful ground-cover, best in sun, inclined to self-seed. *L. sylvatica* (greater wood rush) *H5* (30–80cm) ⚔ tussock forming, spreading by rhizomes to form a dense mat, leaves dark green, flowers brown in summer; cultivars include **'Hohe Tatra'** (syn. 'Aurea') (60cm) greenish yellow, bright green in winter in sun, **'Marginata'** (syn. 'Variegata') leaves with cream margins.

Milium effusum 'Aureum'

Milium effusum **'Aureum'** (golden wood millet) *H4* (40–60cm) ⚘ This grass, a form of the grain crop millet, has shocking bright yellow-green young foliage and produces sparse flowers in summer. It grows well in most situations, especially in moist soil and woodland, and often self-seeds.

Miscanthus (silver grass) *H3–5* This genus of mainly deciduous grasses provides many of the finest garden plants, with tall graceful leaves and long-lasting soft, fluffy plumes of flowers, often with several 'fingers', which open in late summer and often persist well into winter. Late-flowering varieties may well not open in cold or early autumns, particularly in inland gardens. Heavy and waterlogged winter soils are not suitable for most of them: they thrive in well-drained soil in full sun and flower best after hot summers. Cut down the old flower heads in mid-winter or early spring, the later the better in cold gardens. Divide in spring if clumps become congested. Most of the best varieties for Scotland were bred by Ernst Pagels in Germany (and have obvious German names). *M. nepalensis H2-3* (Himalayan Fairy Grass) (1.2m) green arching foliage with attractive fingery, airy cream flowerheads, needs a sheltered spot. *M. sacchariflorus H3* (2.5–3m) known as the sugar cane miscanthus, this is a giant which is sometimes used as a hedge in mild gardens, rather rampant, so beware; shy flowering in cool summers. *M. sinensis H4–5* (unless stated otherwise) (1–4m) very

Miscanthus sinensis

variable, many cultivars: **'China'** (90cm) a low, arching selection, flowers reddish turning to silver, **var. condensatus 'Cabaret' H3–4** (2m) broad leaves green, striped white down the centre, shy flowering, **var. c. 'Cosmopolitan'** (2m) broad, white and green striped leaves, **'Ferner Osten'** (leaves to 7cm, flowers to 1.5m) leaves with cream midrib turning orange in autumn, flowers dark red with white tips, fading to beige, a striking choice for flowers and foliage, **'Flamingo'** (1–2m) plumes of purple-pink, tipped white, good in autumn, **'Gracillimus'** (1.2m) leaves narrow, curved, with white stripes, flowers rarely produced, **'Graziella'** (1.5m) vigorous and easy to establish, with silvery-white flower heads and fine autumn colour after frosts, **'Grosse Fontäne'** (2m) brownish flowers, fairly wide leaves, **'Kaskade'** (1.8m) arching habit with purple-brown flowers on tall stems, turning silvery, reddish autumn-leaf colour, **'Kleine Fontäne'** (1.5m) red arching/drooping flowers turning silver, **'Kleine Silberspinne'** (75cm) white-veined narrow leaves, flowers reddish, fading to silver, a fine dwarf selection, **'Little Zebra'** (45cm) the smallest of the selections with horizontal yellow banding, **'Malepartus'** (1.8m) dense with upright red flowers, broad leaves purple-red in autumn, a little untidy, **'Morning Light'** (1m) narrow white-margined leaves, upright habit, seldom flowers, **'Nippon'** (1.2m) compact form with narrow leaves turning orange in autumn, silver-pink flowerheads late summer fading to silver -white, **'Septemberrot' H4** (2m) reddish-brown

Miscanthus 'Zebrinus'

flowers above broad green silver-centred leaves, **'Silberfeder'** (2–3m+) a giant with broad leaves which colour well in autumn, flowers reliably, pinkish fading to white, needs wind shelter, **'Silberspinne'** (1.2m) a tall architectural grass with plumes of a reddish tinge fading to silver, **'Strictus'** (1.8m) (porcupine grass) dense clumps of narrow green leaves with horizontal bands of creamy yellow, hardier than 'Zebrinus', **'Variegatus'** (1.5m) leaves creamy white with pale green bands, one of the finest for foliage but seldom flowers, **'Zebrinus' H3–4** (1–2m) green leaves

with horizontal gold banding, seldom manages to open its silvery-buff flower heads.

***Molina caerulea* (purple moor grass)** (1–2m x 30–60cm) ✉ Deciduous with dense clumps of linear green leaves with purple bases with long-lasting purple flowers from spring to autumn on yellow stems. **'Edith Dudszus'** (1m) a low selection with purple flowers on dark-red stems, good yellow autumn colour, **'Moorhexe'** (80cm) a low form with grey-green leaves and flowers from July onwards, yellow leaves in autumn/winter, **'Variegata'** (50cm) cream and green striped leaves, flowers dark purple, **'Karl Foerster'** (1m) flowers purple, **'Transparent'** (2m) good late-summer and autumn yellow foliage, **'Windspiel'** (1.8m) flowers golden, good autumn colour. Plants under the name **subsp. aruninacea** tend to have striking yellow autumn colour.

Ophiopogon planiscapus 'Nigrescens' (RC-M)

***Ophiopogon planiscapus* 'Nigrescens' H5** (25 x 30cm) ⚜ Actually not a grass at all, but it looks like one, forming slow-growing spreading clumps of evergreen black leaves (fading to green in shade) with spikes of lilac flowers in summer.

***Panicum virgatum* (switch grass) H4** (1–2m) A narrowly upright dense, deciduous grass with purplish stems and weeping panicles of purple-green flowers in late summer and autumn. Grow in fertile well-drained soil in full sun; cultivars tend not to flower well on heavy soils. **'Heavy Metal'** (1.2–1.5m) stiff metallic blue-grey leaves, turning yellow in autumn, flowers pink, **'Rubrum'** (1m) narrow leaves, tinted red in autumn, chestnut-brown flowers, **'Squaw'** (1m) strong red autumn colour, flowers pink-purple, **'Warrior'** (1.2m) dark flowers, bronze-tinged leaves, good red autumn-leaf colour.

***Pennisetum* (fountain grass) H2–3** One of the most attractive grasses in flower, with dense bottlebrush- or foxtail-like fluffy purple or white racemes, good in arrangements. Unfortunately pennisetums are not amongst the hardier grasses; they are best grown in gardens not too far from the coast, and need well-drained soil. In cold gardens, the crowns are best mulched in winter to protect them. Plant and divide clumps in spring rather than autumn. Scotland's lack of summer heat means that only a few varieties flower well. *P. alopecuroides* (1–1.5m) narrow leaves turning golden yellow or pinkish in autumn, bottlebrush flowers in August and September; **'Hameln'** (50cm) a compact selection with fine flowers. *P. orientale* (60cm) flower spikes pinkish, like pipe cleaners. *P. setaceum* **'Rubrum'**

(red fountain grass) *H2* (1.5m) dark-purple foliage and plumes of pink-purple flowers, very attractive, but it is tender so it is grown as an annual in most of Scotland; Elliot Forsyth at Cambo even lost it in a cold greenhouse. *P. villosum* (50cm) not easy to over-winter in Scotland, but can be grown as an annual, long-lasting plumes of rabbits' tail greenish-white flowers in late summer.

Phalaris arundinacea var. *picta* (gardener's garters) *H5* (1m x the entire border before you know it) A rampant, attractive green-and-white striped evergreen grass, tolerant of part shade and most soils except very dry ones. It is useful for covering a moist pondside bank.

Stipa calamagrostis

Stipa (feather grass) One of the finest of all grasses, with fountains of flower heads that tremble in the wind, in mid- to late summer, usually lasting well into winter. Best grown in well-drained soil in full sun, apart from *S. arundinacea*, which can take heavier soils and light shade. **S. arundinacea** (syn. *Anemanthele lessoniana*) *H3* (1m x 1.2m) cascading purplish-green flowers in late summer and evergreen arching leathery dark-green leaves which turn orange-brown in autumn and winter, not very hardy and best in mild and coastal gardens, prone to rust. **S. calamagrostis** *H4* (1m) arching blue-green leaves, nodding feathery silvery-purple flowers. **S. gigantea** (giant oats) *H4* (2–2.5m) ⚜ A magnificent grass with lax clumps of semi-evergreen leaves up to 70cm long and tall spikes of long-lasting silvery

Stipa tenuissima

purplish-green flowers which turn golden in winter; needs sharp drainage and shelter from winds, which can flatten it. Best split and divided every 4–5 years to ensure good flowering: replant the fresh juvenile parts found around the clump edge. **S. tenuissima** (pony tails) *H4* (60cm–1m) tall, clump forming, requiring good drainage, long-lasting silky green flower heads which billow in the wind when well grown, but in rich soils and wet weather it tends to collapse into a soggy heap. Self-sows but resents being

moved and divided, so usually viewed as short lived.

Uncinia rubra *H3* (30cm) An evergreen grass with deep reddish-brown leaves and dark-brown to black flowers, not very hardy, needing protection from frosts and winds. *U. uncinata* 'Rubra' is very similar and the two are often mixed up.

Gunnera manicata (young leaves and flowers)

Gunnera

This South American giant has the largest leaves you can grow outdoors in Scotland – they are truly magnificent – and it graces stream and pondside plantings all over the country. One of the best examples is the tunnel at RBG Logan in Dumfries and Galloway, which you can walk though; children love it. It does well in a sheltered site as far north as Orkney and Shetland. There are also several small creeping species.

G. manicata *H3–4* (2m x 2–3m+) ⚜ giant, palm-like, leathery leaves up to 2m x 2m, with stout, prickly stems; flowers, in brownish spikes, tend to be hidden below the leaves. It likes constant moisture and it is most easily established by digging a section from an existing clump; this requires two people, a sheet of thick polythene, stout wellies and brute force. Seed-grown plants in pots in garden centres take several years to develop the large leaves and are more tender as young plants. In cold gardens, mulch the crowns in winter: the dying autumn leaves are ideal for this purpose. *G. tinctoria* (2m x 2m+) is slightly smaller growing and perhaps a little hardier. *G. magellanica* (15cm x 1m) a creeping ground-cover with small leaves, tiny green flowers, orange fruit, tolerant of clay and soggy soil.

Gypsophila paniculata 'Bristol Fairy'

Gypsophila
(baby's breath)
Popular with flower arrangers, the masses of white flowers on airy stems look excellent in the garden too. *G. paniculata* 'Bristol Fairy' *H5* (1.2m x 1m) double white flowers en masse on a network of wiry stems in summer. Deep rooted, it does not like being moved once established. It prefers well-drained and poor soils.

Heavy and peaty soils tend to be too wet and rich and full of slugs which eat the growing tips. There are also dwarf and pink forms. It can sometimes be obtained as dormant crowns in early spring. Two much smaller alpine varieties are **G. cerastoides H4–5** (5cm x 15cm) greyish leaves, white flowers with purple veins and centres, in spring and early summer, for rockery, and **G. repens** (20cm x 30–50cm) ✻ white or pink flowers on stalks held above the semi-evergreen mat-forming plant. Both these like gritty, well-drained soil; in a raised bed or trough is ideal.

Hacquetia epipactis

H4–5 (6–10cm x 15–20cm) ✻ This unassuming but tough dwarf ground-cover is ideal for woodland and for growing under other shrubs, as it likes part or full shade. It forms a spreading, mounded clump with tiny greenish-yellow flowers in early spring, resembling a winter aconite, though it is actually an umbellifer (cow parsley family). Grow in rich moist soil, where it may well seed around. There is also a variegated form **'Thor'** with leaves streaked and margined creamy white.

Hacquetia epipactis

Helleborus

Helleborus orientalis hybrids

☙ Invaluable for providing winter and early-spring colour, hellebores are mostly undemanding and easy, once established. Flowers vary greatly in colour and the range of shades and shapes available increases all the time. Breeders ought also to concentrate on getting the flowers to stand up, as the attractively spotted flowers tend to droop. They form mounds of attractive foliage, reaching around 60cm in height, and do best in moist well-drained fertile soils, in part shade. They are useful for massing beneath trees and shrubs and associate well with spring bulbs and other woodland plants. Hellebore black spot disease is a cosmetic inconvenience for the modern hybrids but is killing colonies of *H. foetidus* in many parts of Scotland. It is suggested that all old foliage be removed in November to reduce the spread of the disease. Hellebores may also suffer the occasional aphid attack. Though they are tough, late-spring frosts can cause considerable foliage damage in colder and inland gardens after a period of mild weather. Hellebores do not like being moved once established, and are hard to divide, but may self-seed

round the garden. All parts of the plants are poisonous and foliage may be a skin irritant.

H. argutifolius (formerly *H. corsicus*) **H4** (60cm x 90cm) ✻ an architectural, semi-shrubby evergreen with sprays of apple-green flowers in February–May, lobed and toothed grey-green leaves. **H. foetidus** (stinking hellebore) **H5** (60–90cm x 60cm+) ✉ ✻ a Scottish native, evergreen, with deeply cut dark-green leaves, light-green to cream red-tipped flowers from late winter to spring; the crushed leaves smell unpleasant, hence the name; will seed around freely on dry banks; unfortunately prone to a black spot foliage disease, which can be fatal; **H.f. 'Wester Flisk Group'** purple stems and a deeper red tip to the flowers, selected at Flisk on the River Tay. **H. x hybridus/H. orientalis** (lenten rose) **H4–5** (to 50cm) ✻ nodding cup-shaped flowers in varying shades of white, pink and purple, sometimes dark spotted. There are lots of good strains – Ashwood, Ballard's, Kaye's – and now there are also numerous spotted, dark-purple, two-toned, yellow and double hybrids – Queen Series, Lady Series, etc. – coming on to the market; just choose the colours you prefer: if you are lucky, you can select plants in flower. Evergreen or semi-evergreen, with divided shiny mid-green leaves. **H. niger** (Christmas rose) **H5** (30cm x 40cm) ✻ white nodding flowers, mid-December–March, very fine, not always as easy to please as the hybrids, sometimes short-lived. **H. x sternii 'Blackthorn Group' H3–4** (50cm x 50cm) ✻ green flowers, stained pinkish or purple, stems purple, leaves veined attractively.

Helenium see Daisies, page 171

Helianthus see Daisies, page 171

Helichrysum see Anaphalis, page 153

Heliopsis subsp. *helianthoides* var. *scabra* see Daisies, page 171

Hemerocallis (day lily)

H5 The day lilies are so named because – you guessed it – the flowers last only a day. But don't let that put you off, because these plants produce a huge number of sometimes scented flowers day after day for several weeks or even months, usually in July and August, in a huge range of flower shapes and colours. The rush-like leaves – the tougher varieties are evergreen – are also attractive and form small to medium-sized fresh-green clumps, which contrast well with other herbaceous perennials. They like moist but well-drained, loose (not compacted) soil, tolerate salt spray, and a sunny, warm site ensures the best flowering. You can apparently eat the flowers and foliage, but the gaudy hybrids might just shock your guests into leaving if you serve them up. Day lilies should be fed regularly and divided every 5–6 years to maintain vigour. They are fairly tough, and resilient to most pests and diseases, though in the USA they have been struck down with rusts and other problems, which will doubtless arrive here in due course. There are now a staggering 50,000 named day lilies, and more are churned out each year, mostly by American enthusiasts. Frankly, once you have the main colours, in singles and doubles, and in regular and dwarf sizes, you probably have all the palate you need. But don't be surprised if your local nursery has varieties you can't find listed in any books. Most are perfectly good. The scent is most pronounced in yellow and night-flowering cultivars, which open in late afternoon, but the perfume is often poor in Scotland because of cool summer night temperatures. All hardy **H5**, with the same height and spread, unless stated otherwise.

'**Bonanza**' (75cm) ❋ pale orange with maroon centre, fragrant. '**Burning Daylight**' (75cm) frilled orange. '**Catherine Woodbury**' (80cm) ❋ blush pink, scented. '**Children's Festival**' (60cm) peach, apricot throat. *H. citrina* (80cm–1m) slightly fragrant, yellow, narrow, slender flowers. '**Corky**' (70cm) pale yellow, brown on the outside. '**Cream Drop**' (50cm) ❋ scented, creamy yellow. *H. dumortieri* (60cm) orange to deep yellow in early summer. '**Eenie Weenie**' (25cm) small, yellow, long flowering time. '**Frans Hals**' (60cm) bicoloured yellow and brick red. '**Gentle Shepherd**' (75cm) pure white. '**Golden Chimes**' (1m) golden yellow, tall. '**Joan Senior**' (60cm) creamy white, green throat ('favourite white' – Elizabeth MacGregor of Ellenbank nursery). *H. lilioasphodelus* (syn. *H. flava*) **H4** (70cm) ❋ scented yellow, early. '**Little Wine Cup**' (50cm) small flowered, deep red. '**Luxury Lace**' (80cm) creamy pink with a green throat. '**Pink Damask**' (80cm) warm pink, yellow throat. '**Stafford**' (70cm) deep red, with a yellow throat. '**Stella d'Oro**' (30–45cm) ⚜ an excellent front-of-border plant, deep yellow, orange throated, one of the best, though flowers can be hidden in the foliage '**Summer Wine**' (60cm) maroon red.

Hemerocallis 'Stella d'Oro', 'Catherine Woodbury', 'Gentle Shepherd' and 'Bonanza'

Hepatica

H5 (15–20cm x 25cm) Hepaticas slowly form low-growing clumps of attractive deeply lobed leaves and early-spring blue, pink or white flowers of an almost perfect beauty. They are very useful for the edge of shrub borders and rock garden positions, in well-drained soils in part day or dappled shade, and are also popular in pots kept in alpine houses and cold frames. Clumps can be divided from time to time.

Hepatica nobilis

H. acutiloba pointed lobed leaves, deep lilac blue, occasionally white or pink shades. *H. nobilis* (syn. *H. triloba*) ⚜ three-lobed leaves with the central lobe flushed purple, flowers in variable shades of pale to deep blue, pink or white, occasionally ⚜ double. *H. transsylvanica* ⚜ slightly taller than *H. nobilis*, white, pink or mauve-purple flowers.

Herbs

As well as having medicinal and culinary qualities, many herbs make attractive garden plants. Many herbs are annuals or are usually treated as such in Scotland: basil, borage, cardamon, caraway, chervil, coriander, dill, lemon grass, purslane, rocket and sweet marjoram are all examples. We cover only the perennial (or biennial) and shrubby herbs. Many of these form attractive small to medium-sized mounds for the mixed border. Parsley (*Petroselinum crispum*) is a biennial, but rather tough in the second year, easily raised from seed, as are many of the herbs. Lavender (*Lavandula*, page 68), rosemary (*Rosmarinus*, page 100) and bay (*Laurus nobilis*, page 68) are covered in the shrubs section. Many herbs are tough survivors in the wild, and can be pretty ruthless thugs in a garden setting. Mint, borage and comfrey can be particularly hard to control. Herbs generally do best in full sun in well-drained soil and are well suited to containers, which can also be a useful way of keeping them in bounds. Beware of planting herbs too early in the season: the soft growth, advanced under protection, is all too easily scythed by late frosts. Late April and early May is the time to start planting them out, later in frost pockets. Scotland has several herb specialists. Scotland's largest herb specialist is Poyntzfield herb nursery on the Black Isle.

Herb garden (RC-M)

Parsley

Angelica (*Angelica archangelica*) H5 (2.5m x 1m) ❋ An architectural if sinister plant, useful in the border, large deeply divided green leaves, large round flower heads of sweetly scented greenish-white flowers in May–June. It likes a moist soil and is biennial, dying after flowering.

Bergamot (*Monarda fistulosa*) H5 (1.2m x 45cm) Lilac-mauve flower bracts from summer to autumn, held above aromatic leaves. The garden hybrids (see *Monarda*) also have scented leaves.

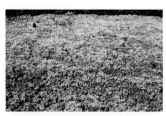
Chamomile lawn in the Star Garden at Cawdor Castle (RC-M)

Bettany see *Stachys officinalis*, page 228

Double-flowered chamomile (*Chamaemelum nobile* 'Flore Pleno') H4 (8cm x 30cm) Small double daisy-like white flowers in summer.

Lawn chamomile (*Chamaemelum nobile* 'Treneague') H4 (6cm x 15cm) Evergreen with finely divided aromatic leaves; spreads nicely between paving slabs or as a 'lawn'.

Chives (*Allium schoenoprasum*) H5 (30cm x 30cm) Forms an attractive clump of grassy hollow stems/leaves and produces purple flower heads all summer long.

Comfrey (*Symphytum officinale*) H5 (1m x 1m) Green lance-shaped leaves and summer flower clusters of white, pink or purple, used to make organic liquid fertilizer. See also *Symphytum*.

Fennel (*Foeniculum vulgare*)

Fennel (*Foeniculum vulgare*) H5 (2m x 45cm) Soft green feathery foliage and flat yellow flower heads in summer. The bulbs can also be eaten. **Bronze fennel (*F. vulgare* 'Purpureum')** with darker foliage makes an excellent foil for other herbaceous flowers in mixed borders.

Horseradish (*Armoracia rusticana*) H5 (90cm x indefinite) ⚘ Large, thick, crinkled green leaves. Use the roots to make the well-known condiment. Likes well-drained soil in sun. Leaves can cause skin irritation.

Hyssop (*Hyssopus officinalis*) H2–3 (80cm x 90cm) Dense spikes of violet-blue summer flowers, which are very attractive to bees, with small lance-shaped leaves.

Needs well-drained soil in full sun. Does not live long, and tends to rot off in winter, but seeds itself freely. Of limited use in the kitchen.

Lovage (*Levisticum officinale*) H5 (2m x 1m) Deeply divided leaves and flat greenish-yellow flower heads in summer. Use leaves, roots and seeds for soups, salads. Has medicinal properties.

Marjoram (French) (*Origanum onites*) H5 (45cm x 45cm) Golden-green oval leaves and clusters of pale-pink summer flowers.

Mint (*Mentha spicata*) H5 (60cm x 1m+) Oval leaves and mauve flower spikes in summer. There are many different varieties with different flavours: most are rampant spreaders so they are often grown in pots to keep them under control.

Golden marjoram (*Origanum vulgare* 'Aurea')

Oregano (*Origanum vulgare*) H4–5 (45cm x 45cm) An attractive dark-green mound-forming border plant with aromatic leaves and clusters of bee-attracting mauve flowers through summer. **Golden marjoram (*O. vulgare* 'Aureum')** golden leaved, a pretty front-of-border plant, and good in a lasagne.

Sage see *Salvia officinalis*, page 222

Tarragon (French) (*Artemisia dracunculus*) H2–3 (90cm x 45cm) Aromatic long thin leaves. Needs very good drainage and tidying up in winter. Not long lived. Russian tarragon is tougher and easier but not so good for cooking.

Thyme see page 229
Hesperantha see Schizostylis, page 225

Hesperis matronalis (sweet rocket) and *Cardamine*

H4–5 (50–90cm x 45cm) ❋ *Hesperis*, a member of the mustard family, is a cottage garden favourite with erect stems of fragrant lilac-purple or white 4-petalled flowers in late spring and early summer. Individual plants are not long-lived but it seeds around freely and often escapes from gardens, naturalizing itself on roadsides and in woodland. The genus will tolerate full sun or light shade in moist or dry soils. Double-flowered forms 'Plena' and

Hesperis matronalis

'Flore Pleno' are also sometimes available. *Cardamine* (bitter cress or lady's smock) *H5* Closely related and similar in appearance, this attractive, shade-loving, deciduous perennial has purple, pink, white or pale-yellow flowers in early spring. It also includes a couple of rampant weeds, such as *C. hirsuta*, the dreaded hairy bittercress. Cardamines prefer a cool climate, and some may disappear below ground for a summer dormancy period. They are easy to grow in any shady situation in fertile, moist but well-drained soil. Many are useful as ground-covers beneath shrubs and trees. *C. macrophylla* (75cm x 60cm) a beautiful, tall variety, clusters of pink flowers. *C. pentaphylla* ❦ (30cm x as far as you let it) lilac pink in early spring, a vigorous spreader, beautiful pinnate leaves, a good ground-cover for shady areas. *C. pratensis* (30–60cm x unlimited) is our lilac-flowered native lady's smock, and should only really be planted in gardens to naturalize in 'wild' damp meadows and ditches; the double-flowered *C.p.* 'Flore Pleno' is less invasive.

Heuchera

and x *Heucherella*, *Tiarella* and *Tolmiea menziesii*
H5 Heucheras, and their relatives covered here, are small mound-forming perennials which make great ground-covers and fine specimen plants too, suitable for borders and containers. Most have coloured or 'painted' foliage

Heuchera and x *Heucherella*, varied leaf colours

and most have candelabras of tiny but attractive flowers on long wiry stems, produced en masse in summer, sometimes as early as April or as late as October. Some of the new coloured-leaved hybrids flower poorly and are mainly grown for their leaves. Heucheras thrive in full sun or shade, which makes them useful in many different garden situations. They associate well with many herbaceous plants in the border, and prefer a moist, free-draining soil. Unfortunately vine weevil larvae make a beeline for them, so be particularly careful if growing in containers: you would be advised to use an insecticide to treat the soil. They are generally tough,

though they can look tatty and sad after prolonged cold and damp winters, or as they get too old. There are large numbers of new varieties pouring out of America and elsewhere. Many are just variations on a theme; some are fine while others are weak and sickly and should have been burned at birth ('Amber Waves' for example). All are fully hardy *H5*, forming clumps of foliage reaching 35–45cm x 40–50cm, with flower spikes 70cm–1m high, unless stated otherwise.

Beauty Colour [PBR] a 'nonsense' name (who comes up with them?), leaves greyish with dark-green edges and veining. **'Berry Smoothie'** pink and red leaves, **'Black Beauty'**, **'Blackout'**, **'Black Bird'** three new dark foliage selections said to be the darkest; time will tell which is best, **Caramel** cream-orange-brown leaves. **Chocolate Ruffles** (25cm) evergreen, large ruffled leaves which are brown on top and purple underneath, pink flowers in -summer. **Cinnabar Silver** metallic purple leaves turning to silver, short spikes of red flowers. **'Ebony and Ivory'** dark foliage, white flowers. **Ginger Ale** foliage amber, flowers creamy. **Green Spice** [PBR] dark grey-edged silver leaves with strongly contrasting purple veins, flowers insignificant. **'Leuchtkäfer'** (syn. 'Firefly') ❃ tiny red scented flowers, rounded green leaves. **'Licorice'** bronze-purple, almost black, **'Lime Ricky'** and **'Key Lime Pie'** very similar, white flowers, leaves pale lime green. *H. micrantha* **'Palace Purple'** ❦ evergreen deep-purple leaves, white flowers, vigorous and easy, a good choice for less than ideal conditions. **'Marmalade'** probably the best of the orange-cream-bronze foliage varieties, does not sunburn, flowers white. **Mint Frost** mint-green leaves, 'frosted' silver, pink flowers. **Obsidian** black-purple leaves, compact, tiny cream flowers; many consider this the best of the dark-foliaged varieties and we agree. **'Peppermint Spice'** pink flowers, bronze and pale-green leaves with dark-green edges. **Peach Flambé** foliage salmon pink suffused red. **'Plum Pudding'** ❦ coral flowers, glossy burgundy foliage with a silver tint. **Raspberry Ice** pink flowers, red and silver leaves. **Silver Lode** bronze and silver leaves, flowers white. **'Silver Scrolls'** silver with bronze veining, white flowers. **'Silver Shadows'** silvery burgundy with red veins. *H. sanguinea* **'Snowfire'** leaves with green and white variegation, flowers rose red. **'Stormy Seas'** vigorous, with evergreen shiny ruffled red leaves, tall spikes of tiny maroon-green flowers. **'Sugar Frosting'** burgundy with silver markings, white flowers.

x *Heucherella H5* (40–50cm x 50cm) These hybrids between *Heuchera* and *Tiarella* are mainly grown for their patterned foliage. The spikes of tiny white or pink flowers appear in spring–summer. They enjoy similar cultural conditions to those enjoyed by heucheras and share the weevil problem but don't suffer from rust, and many fine new forms have been released since the last edition. **'Alabama Sunrise'** golden, veined red, orange in Autumn, small white flowers, **'Burnished Bronze'** bronze leaves, pink flowers, vigorous. **'Brass Lantern'** maple-shaped leaves yellow and red, deeper in Autumn, white flowers, red stems, **'Kimono'** palmate leaves marked silver, purple and green, turning silvery pink in winter, white flowers. **'Quicksilver'** purple-silver leaves with bronze veining, pale-pink and white flowers in May–June. **'Solar Power'** yellow green leaves with reddish veins, white flowers, **'Stoplight'** yellow and green leaves with a red centre. **'Sweet Tea'** orange-bronze with darker veins, white flowers, **'Tapestry'** deeply cut maple-like leaves purple in the centre, green margins, pink flowers.

Tiarella (foam flower) *H5* Americans love their foam flowers, but they are not nearly so widely grown in the UK, where they should be better known. They are useful non-invasive ground-covers which will tolerate dry shade. The palmate or maple-like leaves are green, usually with patterned markings. The flowers are tiny, star shaped, white or pink, in small feathery spikes in spring or summer. Height and spread are similar. **'Ink Blot'** (30cm) green leaves with darker centres, pink flowers, **'Iron Butterfly'** (40cm) leaves with dark stripe across centre, white flowers.

Tiarella cordifolia

'Mint Chocolate' (35cm) lobed leaves striped maroon, cream flowers. **'Morning Star'** deeply cut palmate leaf with bold brown marking, pink-tinged flowers. **'Pink Bouquet'** (30cm) bronzy leaves, pink flowers. **Pink Brushes** (30cm) pale pink fading to white, green and red leaves. **Pink Pearls** (40cm) pale pink, leaves bronze in autumn. **'Spring Symphony'** fine foliage, fragrant pink flowers. *T. cordifolia* (20cm) heart-shaped mottled or striped leaves. **'Ninja'** (25cm) serrated matt green leaves, with a central maroon-brown blotch, and white flowers. *T. wherryi* (25cm) evergreen, green leaves turn bronze-red in autumn, white flower spikes from May–July; *T.w.* **'Bronze Beauty'** green leaves suffused bronze all year.

Tolmiea menziesii (piggyback plant) *H5* Similar to *Heuchera*, enjoying similar conditions, forming clumps of attractive leaves, with spikes of tiny nodding chocolate-brown and green flowers in spring. It spreads vigorously by producing plantlets in the leaf veins. Fine planted between shrubs in a semi-shaded position in a wild garden. **'Taff's Gold'** (50cm x 30cm) green leaves mottled cream and gold.

x *Heucherella* see *Heuchera*, page 197

Hosta

H5 Recent years have seen a huge amount of interest in hostas: the *RHS Plantfinder* lists over 800 varieties. Not everyone likes them, but they are amongst the best foliage plants for the garden, producing clumps of leaves in a wide range of greens, blues, golds and variegations. The white, mauve and pale blue/purple flowers in late summer can be very pretty, but the leaves are the main attraction, and some growers cut the flowers off. Hostas completely disappear below ground in winter, which helps give them great hardiness. They do very well in Shetland, and we have seen them thriving all over the country, though they can suffer windburn in exposed sites. Hostas like deep rich soils with plenty of moisture and adequate drainage. Most books recommend planting them in shade, but in Scotland most hostas are perfectly happy in sun, apart from the pale yellow forms, and you may find the white and golden leaves turning green in deep shade. As most gardeners know, slugs are hostas' biggest enemy, and can turn a wondrous foliar display into a sorry skeletal mess, so try preventative measures where possible (grit, slug pellets, etc.). Rabbits, deer, mice and voles like eating hostas, so you may need to net/fence them, particularly when small; and you may be surprised to know that they are used in Japanese cooking picked, steamed and in soups. Once established, they can be left alone for years, or divided (after 5–6 years or so), if you want to increase stock: just lift

(left to right) *Hosta* cultivars 'Frances Williams', 'Great Expectations', 'Emerald Tiara' and 'Patriot

and rip them apart, replanting pieces of root with three to five 'eyes'/resting buds. Hostas also make fine container plants, as long as they are not in too much hot sun or allowed to dry out. With so many named varieties, it is simply a case of selecting the leaf form you like. Those listed below are some of the most common and well tested. All are fully hardy (*H5*).

'August Moon' (60cm x 90cm) large crinkled golden leaves, white flowers. **'Aureomarginata'** (1m x 1m) 🏅 emerges in early spring; large oval leaves with white (yellow at first) margins, purple flowers. **'Big Daddy'** (90cm x 60cm) huge grey-green slug-resistant leaves, lilac flowers. **'Fire and Ice'** (75cm x 90cm) creamy-white leaves with green-splashed margins, scented lilac flowers, slow growing. *H. fortunei* var. *albopicta* (45cm x 30cm) 🏅 starts the season with strong butter-yellow leaves, splashed green, which mellow as summer progresses, flowers lilac; *H.f.* var. *aureomarginata* (45cm x 30cm) 🏅 green leaves with a yellow margin, lilac flowers. **'Francee'** (60cm x 45cm) dark-

Hosta sieboldiana

Hosta: a range of leaf forms

green, white-margined leaves, pale-lavender flowers. **'Frances Williams'** (75cm x 60cm) ⚜ large yellow-margined, deeply ribbed blue-green leaves and mauve flowers. **'Ginko Craig'** (20cm x 45cm) low growing, white-edged green leaves and purple flowers. **'Gold Edger'** (20cm x 30cm) a useful dwarf plant with light yellow-green leaves and pale lilac flowers. **'Gold Standard'** (60cm x 45cm) yellow-green with a darker margin, compact. **'Golden Tiara'** (20cm x 30cm) compact, green leaves edged gold, deep purple flowers in mid-summer. **'Hadspen Blue'** (40cm x 30cm) blue-green leaves, stronger blue in shade, less vigorous than most of this colour, lavender flowers. **'Halcyon'** (45cm x 30cm) ⚜ impressive silver-grey leaves, lilac-purple flowers. **'Honeybells'** (90cm x 60cm) ❁ scented mauve flowers in mid-summer, mid-green leaves. **'Krossa Regal'** (90cm x 1m) lilac flowers, dramatic large grey-green leaves with a wavy edge. **'June'** (45cm x 30cm) striking yellow and grey-green foliage, pale lilac flowers, reported to be slug-resistant. *H. lancifolia* (50cm x 60cm) small dark-green pointed leaves, lilac flowers in early autumn. **'Minuteman'** (60 x 90cm) dark-green leaves edged pure white, lavender flowers. **'Patriot'** (55cm x 90cm) dark-green white-edged leaves, lavender-blue flowers. **'Royal Standard'** (90cm x 45cm) ⚜ fragrant white flowers August–October, mid-green foliage. **'Shade Fanfare'** (40cm x 30cm) leaves green with a white margin in shade, the green turning yellow in sun. *H. sieboldiana* (75cm x 60cm) leaves variable, large, to 30cm long, grey-blue, more resistant than most to slug damage, flowers indifferent, white, flushed lilac; it often ends the year with bold yellow autumn colour; *H.s.* **'Blue Angel'** (70cm x 60cm) ⚜ fine blue leaves, white flowers; *H.s. var. elegans* (75cm x 90cm) ⚜ large blue-green puckered and ribbed leaves, pale-lilac flowers, one of the finest and most striking of all hostas in our opinion, more than one form in the trade. **'Sum and Substance'** (75cm x 60cm) ⚜ large glossy greeny-gold leaves and lavender flowers. *H. undulata* (45cm x 40cm) dramatic wavy green leaves with a central splash of white, pale-lilac flowers, *H.u. var. albomarginata* (syn. 'Thomas Hogg') (60cm x 45cm) glossy green white-margined leaves, lilac flowers. *H. venusta* (7.5cm x 15cm) the tiniest species, suitable for rock garden, trough, etc., heart-shaped green leaves, lilac flowers. **'Wide Brim'** (45cm x 30cm) green leaves with a wide yellow margin and lavender flowers.

Houttuynia cordata

H4–5 (30cm x indefinite) This is a potentially wonderful foliage plant if you've got a lot of ground to cover, but it can run rampant through a border or waterside planting. You can treat it as a vegetable and eat the leaves raw or cooked, but we are somewhat put off by its common name 'dog breath'. It forms spreading low-growing clumps of deciduous pointed leaves (which smell of oranges) and produces small yellow flowers with larger surrounding white bracts in mid-summer. It prefers part shade and a moist soil, and is more invasive in these conditions, although it must be said that dry soils don't seem to hinder it much.

Houttuynia cordata 'Chameleon'

'Boo-Boo' leaves silver-grey, edged crimson, turning pink-red in autumn. **'Chameleon'** the most common form, green leaves with a red margin, splashed yellow; it can revert (we saw a clump in St Andrews, Fife, over 2m across, which had almost completely reverted), so pull up green sections. Flame, orange, yellow and green leaves. **'Flore Pleno'** flowers are cones of white petals.

Iberis (perennial candytuft)

H5 (15–30cm x 30–60cm) Iberis produce low-growing mounds of deep-green, narrow, lance-shaped leaves; they prefer well-drained soil in full sun or light shade, and will seed around where happy. They benefit from a trim after flowering, but don't do it in winter or you'll not get many flowers the following spring. *I. sempervirens* mass of small white flowers; *I.s.* **'Schneeflocke'/'Snowflake'** ⚜ eye-catching large-petalled white flowers, *I.s.* **'Weisser Zwerg'** large white flowers with thin outer petals radiating from an inner core.

Iberis sempervirens 'Snowflake'

Insectivorous plants

Insect-eating plants have long been a fascination, and many of us have tried to grow and usually killed Venus fly-traps on windowsills. Insectiverous plants have adapted to eating insects because they do not get enough nutrients from their stagnant water habitats. There are several garden-worthy and surprisingly hardy insectivorous plants, which you can attempt to grow outdoors. It might give you satisfaction to know that they also eat midges and wasps, although unfortunately not enough to have much impact. Insects are trapped in the pitchers of *Darlingtonia* and *Sarracenia* (pitcher plants) and are slowly digested in the bottom. Come September, a macabre collection of skeletons will be found 'swimming' in the pitchers. These plants are quite a challenge to please in the garden, whatever those who sell them claim. They come from humid areas and most need permanently moist soil, probably doing best in an artifical bog, lined with polythene, planted in a mixture of sphagnum peat and perlite, in part day shade. Avoid fertilizer and alkaline water. They usually go dormant for the winter.

Darlingtonia californica (cobra lily) H2 (45cm x 45cm+) Green, mottled curved white pitchers with dark 'whiskers' drooping from under the top; there are fine examples at Brodick Castle on Isle of Arran.

Darlingtonia californica (cobra lily) (RC-M)

Sarracenia flava (pitcher plant) H4 (45cm x 45cm+) Yellow-green pitchers, marked red, and nodding yellow-green flowers in late spring. **S. purpurea H4** (30 x 30cm) evergreen rosettes of leaves and purple-tinged green pitchers; has gone native in Ireland and Cumbria and is rather rampant, and the same may be happening in Scotland; a great midge-eater. **S. x areolata H4** (40–60cm x 40–60cm) pink flowers in spring followed by white and purple-veined green pitchers, the colour of which intensifies through the season.

Assorted Sarracenia

Inula see Daisies, page 171

Iris
H3–4/5 ⚥ This is a very large genus with many species and thousands of named hybrids. We have divided most of this entry into two – iris that prefer dry soil and those that prefer moist – and we also give a brief mention of the dwarf and alpine irises. All will grow in acid or alkaline soil except for *I. ensata*, which needs acid soil. Experts may criticize this over-simplification, but our aim is to aid selection and planting for those confused by the huge range on offer. In general, iris form small to medium-sized clumps of usually deciduous but occasionally evergreen, sword-shaped leaves, and produce large sculptural flowers which consist of petals that stand on top of the flower (standards) and petals that droop (falls). Unless stated otherwise, the iris listed are **H5**. If you want to move them, Graham Stuart Thomas advises doing so soon after flowering to allow new root growth. Iris are poisonous and some can cause skin irritation.

Bearded Iris (RC-M)

Iris for dry, sun-baked soil (bearded or flag iris, I. germanica)
H4–5 It has to be admitted that these well-known and much loved iris are easier and more free flowering in England, where summers are hotter than they are in Scotland. East Lothian and the Fife coast, which have the sunniest and driest climate, seem to be the places where they do best. There are fine bearded iris at Shephard House, Inveresk, Macplants and Tyninghame Walled Garden in East Lothian, and Wemyss Castle, Fife. If you have a good site for them, they are worth trying elsewhere; for example, they grow well at Cortachy Castle, Angus, which has a fine sun-baked border backed by a wall. The key is to plant them with their rhizomes on top of the soil in a warm sunny site; 2007 was a great year as they had a good baking in 2006. If they stop flowering, then dig them up and divide in early autumn, shorten the leaves to help them re-establish. Don't let ground-covers grow over them, as the rhizomes do best with direct sun on them. In addition, they dislike acid soil, so for much of Scotland it may be useful to apply lime to reduce acidity. There are a huge number of hybrids in every conceivable flower colour, some of which are scented. A few of the best, graded according to size, are as follows. Individual measurements given are for height.

Tall Bearded (90cm–1.2m x 50cm) June flowering, pale-green sword-like leaves; as they are planted half out of the soil, they tend to fall over in wind, so need staking (which often looks ugly). **'Berkeley Gold'** (1m) rich yellows. **'Black Swan'** (85cm) darkest purple, near black. **'Blue Rhythm'** (1.2m) mid-blue. **'Blue Shimmer'** (1.2m) ❀ white mottled with blue, scented. **'Braithwaite'** (85cm) pale lavender standards, blue-purple falls.

'Chantilly' (1m) ruffled lavender pink with yellow falls. 'Helga' (90cm) orange-yellow. 'Jane Phillips' (1.2m) ✿ light blue, scented, consistently good in Scotland. 'Kent Pride' (85cm) ✿ chestnut brown, with white and yellow blaze, scented. 'Ola Kala' (80cm) canary yellow. 'Quechee' (90cm) ✿ red-purple, scented. 'Rajah' (90cm) ✿ reddish purple and yellow, spicy scent. 'St Crispin' (90cm) ✿ pale yellow, scented. 'White City' (90cm) ✿ white, slightly flushed blue, scented.

Dwarf Bearded (25–30cm x 15cm) Compact, pale-green sword-like leaves, flowering in spring and early summer. 'Amber Queen' coppery yellow, April–May. 'Blue Demin' mid-blue. 'Blue Pygmy' purple, veined white, June. 'Cherry Garden' purple-maroon, darker veins. 'Green Spot' white with a green spot, April–May. You may read about 'remontant' or reblooming iris, which flower a second time, but unfortunately Scottish summers are not hot enough to allow this to happen, so we would not recommend them.

I. foetidissima H4 (45cm x 60cm) ⚑ is a wonderful architectural evergreen for dry shady spots where not much else will grow. It forms clumps of green sword-like leaves, and pale-purple flowers, followed by striking seed pods which split open to show off the orange-red seeds in autumn. The variegated form, with striking white-striped leaves, is worth seeking out.

Iris for moist soil

These are many and varied but they require either wet or moist soil. They dislike having their rhizomes dry out, so unlike the surface-planted bearded iris, these should have their rhizomes buried, so plant then in the normal way for perennials.

Iris ensata, white

Iris that like wet soil *I. laevigata* H5 (50cm x 50cm+) lavender-blue flowers in early summer, prefers moist soil, including shallow water and bog gardens, and will tolerate alkaline conditions; forms include 'Snowdrift' (60–90cm), white early-summer flowers, thriving in the shallow water of the pond margin, 'Variegata' (45cm) lavender-blue, cream and grey-green leaves. *I. ensata* (formerly *I. kaempferi*) H5 (90cm x 60cm) ⚑ large flowered and one of the most beautiful, purple, lilac or white flat flowers, three to four per stem, in June–July, which iris expert Claire Austin aptly describes as 'like floppy handkerchiefs'; most do well in pond and stream

Iris pallida
'Argentea Variegata'

margins, in sun or part shade, and they dislike limy soil; forms include 'Rose Queen' small-flowered rose-pink, probably a hybrid with *I. laevigata*, lower-growing than most, 'Moonlight Waves' white with green centre, 'Variegata' purple, leaves with white stripes. *I. pseudocorus* (native flag iris) H5 (90cm–1.2m x 60cm+) ✉ common all over Scotland, this will spread vigorously, and is sometimes invasive in moist soils and ponds, producing deep-yellow flowers, with brown marking, in early summer, above green sword-like leaves; forms include 'Golden Fleece' plain-yellow flowers, 'Variegata' ⚑ yellow/green-variegated young leaves, yellow flowers.

Iris chrysographes

Iris pseudoacorus 'Variegata'

Iris that like moist but not wet soil *I. chrysographes* H5 (40–50cm x 30cm) ⚑ flowers in pairs, dark reddish purple to near black, clumps of slender rush-like leaves, tolerant of part shade or full sun; the most popular forms, known as 'black' ⚑ are very dark purple, which look black without sun on them. *I. douglasiana* H4 (60cm x 50cm) the easiest to grow of the so-called Pacific Coast irises, evergreen with lavender or lilac flowers in May. *I. forrestii* H4–5 (40cm x 40cm) ⚑ yellow, marked brown, spreading clumps, flowers well in Scotland. *I. graminea* H4–5 (45cm x 30cm) purple flowers in May–June, dark leaves, moist soil in full sun. *I. pallida* H4–5 (60cm x 60cm) flowers in early summer, prefers well-drained soil and full sun, tolerates alkaline soils; forms include 'Argentea Variegata' ✿ sword-like grey-green leaves with white variegation,

scented lilac-blue flowers, sometimes shy flowering, **subsp. pallida** very attractive, scented lavender-blue flowers, grey-green leaves, 'Variegata' lilac-blue scented flowers, gold-variegated leaves. *I. sanguinea* 'Snow Queen' *H5* (90cm x 40cm) tolerates dry soils, has rush-like green leaves and white flowers in early summer with a yellow blotch. *I. setosa H5* (20–80cm x 30cm+) purple with white and yellow veining, variable in height and vigour, likes damp ground; forms include 'Baby Blue' (50cm) dwarf, blue with white markings, 'Blaulicht' (80cm x 30cm) mid-blue, **var. arctica** (15cm x 15cm) dwarf form, purple flowers in May–June. *I. sibirica H5* (90cm–1.2m x 50cm–1m) particularly good in Scotland, and perhaps the best iris of all for general planting, with rush-like vivid green leaves, flowering in June–July; this and its many cultivars prefer full sun or part shade, in moist soils, but will tolerate dry soils in part shade; 'Butter and Sugar' white with a yellowish centre,

Iris sibirica
'Dreaming Yellow'

'Caesar's Brother' clear blue-veined flowers, 'Cambridge' light blue with darker veining, 'Dreaming Yellow' yellow-cream, 'Flight of Butterflies' ♥ rich blue, 'Papillon' pale blue, 'Perry's Blue' mid-blue, 'Ruffled Velvet' reddish purple with yellow veins, 'Silver Edge' vibrant blue, narrowly edged white, one of the best Sibiricas. 'Teal Velvet' reddish purple, 'Tropic Night' dark purple, 'White Swirl' ♥ white with gold centres. **Spuria hybrids** (60cm–2m) May–June

flowering, shades of purple, blue, yellow and white, need warm, sun-baked neutral or alkaline soil, some are very tall. *I. unguicularis H3–4* (50cm x 50cm) evergreen, lavender-blue flowers in late winter, rather untidy summer foliage; not all that easy to please, it needs a warm, sunny well-drained site in poor soil. *I. lazica H3* similar, small purplish flowers in early spring, with broader leaves.

Dwarf and alpine bulbous iris

Early-flowering varieties such as **I. reticulata** and **Juno Iris** are usually planted in autumn, sold as dry bulbs. They need very good drainage and are often not long lived. They are fine in containers and can be over-wintered in greenhouses and frames.

Kirengeshoma palmata

Kirengeshoma palmata (yellow waxbells)

H4 (75cm–1m x 1m) ♥ A woodland perennial, forming a large dense clump, with reddish-purple stems, large palmate leaves and pale-yellow, bell-shaped flowers in late summer. It is a good choice for growing in rhododendron gardens as it likes moist, rich acidic soil. It may suffer from the attention of slugs and its leaves shrivel and burn if it allowed to dry out, so keep away from greedy trees.

Knautia macedonica see *Scabiosa*, page 224

Kniphofia
(red hot poker)

H3–4 Everyone knows the distinctive red hot pokers. The best known is the common species *K. uvaria*, which has red flower buds at the top of the tall spikes, lower down in shades of orange and then yellow – hence the name red hot poker. But there are also cream, green, red, and brown varieties, and the changing colours and two-toned effects are part of the appeal. These stately plants make impressive border specimens, forming small to medium-sized clumps of grassy, sometimes sword-like, arching foliage. Kniphofias come from South Africa and the long, often wet Scottish winters do not suit them that well. They are promiscuous and many so-called 'species' sold are in fact garden hybrids. Recent hot and dry summers coupled with mild winters have seen them thrive in many Scottish gardens, and several Fife gardens have good collections. To help them get established, add sand or grit to the planting mix and mulch newly planted clumps, taking care not to smother the leaf crowns. Michael Wickenden from Cally Gardens, Dumfies and Galloway, specializes in these plants and he suggests not cutting back any foliage until spring, because the dead leaves will help protect the crowns in winter. Flower heads can be cut back as soon as they go over. They can suffer devastating attacks of violet root rot in wet acid soil in hot summers (it has wiped out whole collections), although this may not have reached Scotland yet. They prefer full sun, and are best planted in spring or early summer in colder gardens. Many are excellent seaside plants, tolerant of salt spray. Kniphofias flower in July–October; those marked 'late' generally do not open until September. Most are marked as hardy to *H3(–4)*; they are actually more cold hardy than this, but typical Scottish winters with long cold wet spells or, worse, alternate freezing and thawing, reduces their hardiness considerably. They spread 45–60cm unless stated otherwise, sizes given are the heights of the flower spikes.

'Atlanta' *H3–4* (1.2m) bicolour, red and yellow, very fine. 'Bee's Lemon' *H3–4* (1m) citron yellow with a green tinge, late. 'Bees Sunset' *H3–4* (1m) tangerine. 'Brimstone' *H3* (60cm) green in bud, opening yellow, late. *K. caulescens H3–4* (1.2m) reddish pink, late, grey-green leaves, vigorous and may need regular lifting and splitting for congested clumps; this has naturalized in some areas around the Firth of Forth. 'Dorset

Knifophia 'Atlanta', 'Drummore Apricot', K. caulescens and 'Tawny King'

Lamium maculatum 'Beacon Silver' and L. galeobdolon variegatum

Lamium maculatum 'Red Nancy'

Tough and trouble free, they can be left undisturbed for many years. They prefer reasonably drained soils and part shade. Lamiums spread by runners and some can be invasive, particularly L. galeobdolon.

L. galeobdolon (60cm x indefinite) yellow flowered, rampant, good in damp and heavy soils; **L.g. 'Hermann's Pride'** (40cm x 30cm) better behaved, silvery-green leaves, yellow flowers which tend to be somewhat hidden in the leaves. **L. maculatum** (20cm x 1m) red-purple, white or pink flowers, leaves mottled or veined white; forms include **'Beacon Silver'** pink, silvery leaves with a dusky purple tinge, **'Pink Pewter'** silvery-green leaves, soft-pink flowers, **'Roseum'** leaves with a central silver splash, flowers mauve, **'White Nancy'** white flowers, silvery-green leaves, rampant, **'Red Nancy'** deep pink. **L. orvala** (60cm x 30cm) large matt-green leaves, deep pink and purple flowers, non-invasive, forming clumps.

Sentry' *H3* (1m) greenish to yellow. **'Drummore Apricot'** *H3* (75cm) early, orange-yellow. **K. galpinii** *H3–4* (60–75cm) fiery orange; the form usually sold under this name is in fact *K. triangularis*. **'Green Jade'** *H4* (1.5m) striking and unusual, opening green, fading to cream, one of the largest and most vigorous. **K. hisuta 'Firedance'** *H3* (40cm) red turning yellow, **'Ice Queen'** *H3–4* (1.5m) green buds, cream flowers. **'Jenny Bloom'** *H3–4* (60cm) cream and coral pink, lacking in vigour. **'Little Maid'** *H4* (60cm) pale yellow to white, June–September, prolific flowering, relatively hardy. **'Nancy's Red'** *H3* (60cm) vermilion. **K. northiae** *H4* (1.5m) a giant, rather gaunt evergreen species with huge leaves, pale-yellow flowers. **'Percy's Pride'** *H3–4* (1m) yellowy green. **Popsicle Series** (50cm) Lemon, Mango, Papaya... as they sounds, **K. rooperi** (syn. 'C.M. Prichard') *H3–4* (1.2m) orange-red and greenish yellow, in rounded rather than the usual long spikes, very late – too late for some gardens. **'Royal Standard'** *H4* (1.2m) red buds opening yellow. **'Sunningdale Yellow'** *H3* (90cm) yellow, early. **'Tawny King'** *H3–4* (1.2m) intriguing brown flower buds which open cream. **'Timothy'** *H3* (70cm) soft salmon peach and cream, fine in several Fife gardens. **'Toffee Nosed'** *H3–4* (1m x 30cm) apricot-brown buds, pale-cream flowers. **K. triangularis 'Light of the World'** *H3(–4)* (60cm–1m) glowing golden orange. **'Wrexham Buttercup'** *H3–4* (1.2m) the best of the tall yellows. **K. uvaria** *H3–4* (1.2–2m) (red hot poker) this species, or hybrids of it, with coral-orange flowers turning creamy at the bottom of the spike, is the one that has gone native in some parts of Scotland. It is a bit coarse for the garden, especially as its foliage is untidy. The form **'Nobilis'** can reach as much as 4m in height. It is very tough and we found it growing well even in extremely cold north-eastern gardens. There are several hybrid series bred from this species with a variety of orange and yellow flowers. These include **Royal Castle hybrids** (1m) and **Fairyland hybrids** (60cm).

Lamium (dead nettle)

H5 Lamiums are not very exciting and most are considered weeds, but a small number of varieties are very useful ground-covers, particularly for shady areas beneath trees and shrubs. They form mats of attractive often attractively marked foliage and produce two-lipped mauve, pink, yellow or white flowers in April–June or July.

Lathyrus (everlasting sweet pea)

H3–4 (30cm–2m x 30cm) Related to the much-loved annual sweet pea (*L. odoratus*), but unfortunately not scented, the everlasting sweet peas are clump-forming or twining and climbing perennials that flower from June to September. They have matt-green trilobed leaves and are surprisingly hardy as long as they are grown in well-drained soil in a sunny spot. They can escape outside the garden and naturalize in hedgerows, as we have seen in Dumfries and Galloway.

Lathyrus vernus

L. aureus (60cm) small yellow-orange flowers, over a long period from May onwards, non-climbing. **L. latifolius** (2m+) climbing, with blue-green leaves, flowers from summer to autumn, several forms: **'Red Pearl'** deep red-pink, **'Rosa Perle'** varying pink shades, **'White Pearl'** white flowers, often tinged pink. *L. vernus* (30cm x 30cm) non-climbing, with clumps of soft ferny leaves, a useful floriferous ground-cover beneath trees and shrubs; forms include **'Alboroseus'** pink and white, **'Rainbow'** multi-coloured: pale pink to red and purple.

Leontopodium alpinum (edelweiss)

H4–5 (15cm x 25cm) A well-known alpine which inspired the irritating song of the same name. Narrow greyish-green leaves, starry white flowers in summer. Likes full sun in well-drained soil. Perhaps the best form is the compact **'Mignon'**.

Leontopodium (edelweiss)

Leucanthemum see Daisies, page 171

Lewisia

H4 This is a useful small perennial for growing between rocks and in the crevices of stone walls, anywhere with very sharp drainage and an acidic soil. Lewisias form rosettes of mostly evergreen grey-green succulent leaves and produce brightly coloured flowers in late spring and summer. They are cold hardy, but constant moisture

Lewisia cotyledon, mixed hybrids

on the leaves and crowns in winter can lead to rotting. A layer of gravel as a mulch around the neck of the plant helps to prevent problems, as does planting them sideways in cracks in walls. They tend to be most successful in the drier east of Scotland. They do best in full sun, and they can be grown in pots and kept rain-free in a frame or alpine house, or under glass shelters. Aphids and vine weevils can cause problems.

L. cotyledon hybrids (15–30cm x 20–40cm) are amongst the most reliable and easiest for general garden planting: **Ashwood strain** a range of warm pinks, oranges and yellows, **Sunset Group** shades of reddish orange and orange-yellow, **'Little Plum'** (15cm x 10cm) ☘ dwarf, with varying shades of reddish-pink large-petalled flowers, more resistant than most to winter wet, **'Little Peach'** peachy fading to cream, **'Pinkie'** pink. *L. nevadensis* (5cm x 10cm) deciduous, white flowers, narrow leaves. *L. pygmaea* (8cm x 10cm) pink with yellow and white centres. *L. rediviva* large silky pink flowers, best covered in winter. *L. tweedyi H2* beautiful

large soft pink and yellow flowers, best covered in winter as it is not very hardy and hates winter wet.

Liatris spicata

H5 (60–90cm x 30cm+) With its tufts of green grassy leaves and poker-like bottlebrush flower spikes in July–September, *Liatris spicata* is a most attractive border plant. Preferring moist, but well-drained soil in a sunny position, it requires little maintenance, other than deadheading at the end of the season. Congested clumps can be divided. It provides good cut flowers if they are harvested when half open, and they can also be

Liatris spicata

dried. The default flower colour is mauve, but selected forms are more popular: **'Alba'** white, **'Floristan Violett'** purple, **'Kobold'** deep purple-mauve, early, compact.

Libertia see *Sisyrinchium*, page 227

Ligularia

H5 These popular plants for damp and moist soils have impressive foliage and 'in-your-face' deep yellow or orange flowers. Most forms are vigorous and spreading, so they are useful in woodland and water gardens; they are often grown with astilbe, rodgersia and gunnera. The daisy-like orange or yellow flowers appear in

Ligularia 'Othello'

July–September, carried on stems above attractive often deeply cut foliage, which sometimes has an exotic deep purple tinge. Most are tough and hardy enough for anywhere in Scotland. The main enemies are slugs and snails, which can shred foliage. All are fully hardy (*H5*) and height and width are similar, unless stated otherwise.

L. dentata in its cultivars makes the finest garden plants: **'Britt-Marie Crawford'** (1.5m) ☘ magnificent black leaves, discovered in the gardens at Naughton House near Wormit, north-east Fife, a superb garden plant, tolerant of drier conditions than most, with bright golden-yellow daisies and chocolate-brown leaves, **'Desdemona'** (1.2m) ❦ tall spikes of orange-yellow flowers, leaves dark brown when young, with reddish-purple undersides, **'Othello'** (1m) almost identical, upper surface more purple coloured. **'Gregynog Gold'** (60–90cm) heart-shaped green leaves, golden-orange flowers, very fine. *L. przewalskii* (1.2–1.8m) ❦ deeply cut dark-green leaves, purple-green stems, long thin spikes of tiny yellow daisies. **'The Rocket'** (1.5m) ❦ large heart-shaped serrated-edged green leaves, spikes of yellow flowers. *L. x yoshizoeana* **'Palmatiloba'** (1.8m) handsome large lobed leaves, tall racemes of golden flowers.

Limonium (sea lavender, statice)

H3–5 The sea lavenders are variably hardy, but do particularly well in coastal gardens, forming small to medium-sized clumps of leathery, sometimes evergreen dark-green leaves. They produce airy sprays of flowers in late summer and autumn, which make attractive 'everlasting' dried-flower displays. Limoniums prefer full sun in a well-drained soil, and they may rot in heavy soils. They are drought tolerant once established. Occasional deadheading and trimming to shape will keep them looking good, and watch out for mildew in dry summers.

L. bellidifolium H3 (20cm x 10cm) useful for the rock garden, evergreen, dome-shaped with trumpet-shaped blue flowers, needs to be kept dry in winter so best covered with a cloche. *L. platyphyllum* (syn. *L. latifolium*) **'Blue Cloud'** *H5* (30cm x 45cm) blue-mauve; **'Violetta'** violet-mauve.

Linaria purpurea 'Canon Went' (toadflax)

H5 (60–90cm x 10–15cm) A selected form of the eastern European version of our native toadflax with spender pale-pink flower spikes in July–August, and greyish-green leaves. It thrives in poor soils and is useful for its long flowering season and its attractiveness to bees. It self-seeds but you may get violet or purple seedlings as well as pink ones.

Linaria purpurea 'Canon Went'

Lithodora diffusa (syn. Lithospermum diffusa)

H4 (15cm x 60cm–1m) Grown for its mass of small blue flowers in May-June and sometimes all summer long, this spreading rock garden and border edge plant needs a sunny position in well-drained soil. It forms loose lumps of evergreen dark-green foliage, which can be trimmed

Lithodora diffusa 'Heavenly Blue'

immediately after flowering to keep it compact. **'Alba'** white, **'Heavenly Blue'** ❦ dark blue, very popular, **'Grace Ward'** dark blue, **'Star'** white-edged blue flowers, tends to revert to blue.

Lobelia

H2–3/4 ☙ A variable genus of often spectacular but generally rather short-lived plants, most of which hail from the Americas. Unlike the well-known cascading blue annual lobelia, the perennial varieties form upright clumps up, with flowers up the stems in July–September. They like full sun in moist well-drained soil, and will tolerate some frost, but don't like a combination of prolonged winter wet and cold temperatures. If in doubt, protect with a winter mulch of organic matter, or lift and store for the winter as you would dahlias or gladioli. Regular lifting and division prolongs the life of *L. cardinalis*. Slugs and snails are rather keen on lobelia, and the plants can be affected by a virus transmitted by aphids. All parts of the plants are poisonous and sap can cause irritation to eyes and skin. Lobelias listed below rate as *H2–3/4* with some winter protection (mulch).

L. cardinalis (80cm x 30cm) blood-red, purple-green leaves, short lived (usually 2–3 years), but one of the reddest reds of any plant, **'Queen Victoria'** dark-purple leaves, fading to dark green, showy scarlet flowers in late summer, *L. siphilitica* (50cm x 30cm) clear blue, although the name is hardly a selling point. *L. x speciosa* The most popular garden hybrids are forms of this variable hybrid: **Fan Series** *H3* (60cm x 20cm) short-lived, often annuals or biennials, flowers in pink to red, **'Hadspen Purple'** (90cm x 30cm) rich, dark and vibrant velvety flowers on tall sturdy stems, long flowering period, **'Ruby Slippers'** (45cm x 30cm) clumping, ruby-garnet, fan-shaped flowers in June–July. **'Pink Flamingo'** (1m x 30cm) spikes of pink, **'Russian Princess'** (1m x 30cm) deep magenta-red, crimson leaves. **'Tania'** *H4* (1m x 30cm) hot magenta with bronze-flushed foliage; **'Vedrariensis'** (1.2m x 30cm) deep purple, dark-green foliage. *L. tupa H2* (2 x 1m) a fine vigorous Chilean species for mild gardens with long racemes of orange-red flowers, downy leaves, may need staking and best with wind shelter.

Lobelia cardinalis 'Queen Victoria'

Lupinus (lupin)

H5 ⚘ A classic border perennial, attractive in leaf and flower, forming mounds of fingered foliage above which are produced candelabra-like, densely packed flower spikes in June–July which have a curious peppery scent. Lupins are tough (although yellow-flowered varieties can be a little fragile), but they start into growth early, so beware of planting them in cold areas before frost danger has passed. Better still, plant in autumn. They prefer a sunny site in well-drained soil, but will tolerate some shade. They should be cut back after flowering, and divided if congested. They tend to seed around, so deadhead to avoid this. Slugs and snails can cause problems, as can mildew and a fatal disease, anthracnose. Worst are aphid infestations, particularly of the voracious North American lupin aphid, which can kill the plant. Lupins were first brought to Europe from North America by Scottish plant hunter David Douglas. There are some wonderful patches of them alongside the M90 motorway between Edinburgh and Perth, and even a healthy patch growing in the shingle by the River Dee at Aboyne, Aberdeenshire. Lupins are sold as seed strains (series) or as named varieties. All parts of the plants are poisonous.

L. arboreus H3 (1–2 x 1–2m) the so-called tree lupin, but more of a small shrub really, with tiny leaves and small yellow flower in spring and early summer; it needs a well-drained sunny site and seeds itself freely in gravel at Glendoick. **Band of Nobles Series**

Lupinus Gallery Series

(80cm–1.2m) available as mixed colours and named forms, including: **'Chandelier'** bright yellow, **'My Castle'** brick red, **'Noble Maiden'** white, **'The Chatelaine'** pink and white, **'The Governor'** deep blue and white, **'The Page'** brick red. **Gallery Series** (50cm) useful lower-growing strain, available by colour: blue, pink, yellow, red, white. **Russell Minarette Series** (60cm) good colour range.

Lychnis (catchfly) and *Silene* and *Saponaria*

H4–5 Lychnis are hardy, brightly coloured summer-flowering plants, forming mats of rough-textured leaves. Most require staking in rich soils or exposed situations, and prefer well-drained fertile soil in sun. *L. coronaria* varieties will grow in poor soils. Keep an eye out for aphids and you will find insects stuck to the leaves in summer – hence the name catchfly.

L. x arkwrightii **'Vesuvius'** *H5* (30cm x 30cm) deep purple-bronze leaves, fiery orange flowers, tolerant of light shade, short-lived. *L.*

Lychnis chalcedonica

Lychnis coronaria 'Alba'

chalcedonica (90cm x 50cm) deep-red flowers shaped like miniature Maltese crosses, one of the purest reds for mid-summer borders, *L.c.* var. *albiflora* white. *L. coronaria* (75cm x 50cm) ⚘ silvery hairy leaves, startlingly bright crimson-magenta flowers over a long period. Short lived in heavy soils, best considered a biennial, but tends to seed freely, so rip up the old ones as they become woody. On one of our research trips we passed a garden in rural Aberdeenshire that consisted entirely of two colour forms of this; the owner explained that he'd just bought the house and up it came. Forms include **'Alba'** white flowers tinged pink, **'Angel's Blush'** white with pink centres, **Atrosanguinea Group** blood red, **'Gardener's World'** (50cm) double crimson, non-seeding. *L. flos-cuculi* (ragged robin) *H5* ✉ the familiar wild flower with bright star-shaped purplish-pink or white flowers, good for woodland gardens and pond margins, liking damper soil than the other varieties; **Jenny** ['Lychjen'] fluffy double pink, striking, **'White Robin'** or **'Alba'** pure white. *L flos-jovis H4* (30–60cm x 30–50cm) matt forming with pink, white or scarlet flowers, grey woolly leaves, needs sharp drainage. *L. x haageana* (30cm x 30cm) short-lived, bright orange, often sold as **'Lumina Red'** and **'Lumina Orange'**. *L. viscaria* (catchfly) *H5* (50cm x 30cm) rather shocking magenta-pink notch-petalled flowers all summer, slowly creeping habit; there are reddish, purplish and double pink ('Plena') selections.

Silene (campion, catchfly) *H5*

Closely related to *Lychnis* and sharing a common name, *Silene* are characterized by the swollen calyx (the lowest part of the flower) and include our native red and white campions, which are recommended only for wild gardens. Most garden varieties are clump forming, for the rock garden or border, flowering in spring and early summer and and prefer full sun in well-drained soil.

Dwarf and rock garden varieties

S. acaulis **'Mount Snowdon'** (2.5cm x 15cm) A rock garden gem with tiny mats of dark-green leaves and stemless white flowers. *S. schafta* (15cm x 10cm+) a great plant for the front of the border, with dark-green mounds of foliage and bright magenta-pink flowers throughout summer. *S. uniflora* (syn. *S. maritima*) (sea

Silene uniflora

campion) (15cm x 20cm) forms an attractive mat of thin glaucous leaves with white flowers; cultivars include **'Druett's Variegated'** cream-margined leaves, **'Rosea'** pale pink, **'Robin Whitebreast'** double white.

Larger growers
S. dioica (80cm x 30cm) This is our native red campion, which will self-seed everywhere. One of many better-behaved garden forms is **'Flore Pleno'** more compact with double deep-pink flowers.

Saponaria (soapwort) (80cm x 50cm) These form a useful group of plants; the smaller varieties flower later than most alpines, in summer, while the taller varieties add colour to tired late-summer borders. The alpine varieties do best in gritty compost. Cut back after flowering to maintain a compact habit. **'Bressingham' H4** (10cm x 30cm) deep pink, good for troughs and rockeries. **S. officinalis H5** (1.2m x 1–2m) lightly scented campion- or phlox-like flowers in colours ranging from red to white, in late summer, a bit invasive and can be scruffy and untidy, but good for the back of the border; the most popular forms are the double-flowered **'Alba Plena'** white, **'Rosea Plena'** pink and **'Rubra Plena'** reddish pink. **S. ocymoides** (10cm x 50cm) known as tumbling Ted, this low spreader can seed everywhere and provides a carpet of pink-purple summer colour similar in effect to that of alpine phlox; less invasive than the type are the forms **'Alba'** white and **'Rubra Compacta'** dark red.

Saponaria 'Bressingham'

Lysichiton (skunk cabbage)
H4–5 The name skunk cabbage refers to the smell of the flowers, which has evolved to attract pollinators. It does not do justice to these regal waterside plants. They form medium-sized spreading clumps of large, deciduous, leathery green banana-like leaves and produce wonderful flowers (spathes) in yellow and creamy white, in spring. They can be rampant: in some west-coast areas such as parts of Argyll they have

Lysichiton americanum at Glenwhan (RC-M)

seeded and formed such thick clumps that they have clogged streams and ponds, and they even grow rampantly in tidal salt water, as at the edge of West Loch Tarbert, Argyll, so beware. They are happiest in full sun or part shade in damp/boggy ground where their roots can find water. They take a few years to get settled in and to flower. All parts of the plants are poisonous and can cause skin irritation.

L. americanum H5 (1m high) yellow. **L. camtschatcensis H4** (75cm high) pure white. Creamy-white-flowered hybrids between the two species are also quite common.

Lysimachia (loosestrife)
H3–4/5 A very variable genus with lots of good summer-flowering garden plants, including vigorous clump-formers and spreading ground-covers. They prefer full sun or part shade, in moist but well-drained soil. Some, such as *L. nummularia* and *L. punctata*, can become invasive, but nothing that a dose of weedkiller or a hoe can't take care of.

L. atropurpurea H4 (45cm x 45cm) deep claret-red, almost black flowers, metallic silver-green leaves. **L. ciliata 'Firecracker' H4–5** (1.2m x 1m+) thriving in part shade in a moist soil, small yellow flowers, deep-brown leaves, can be annoyingly invasive. **L. clethroides H4–5** (1 x 1m) vigorous, with attractive arching sprays of tiny white flowers from mid- to late summer, vigorous, needs plenty of space; **L.c. 'Geisha'** leaves variegated, less vigorous. **L. ephemerum H3–4** (1m x 30cm) tolerant of light shade and needs moist soil, smooth grey-green leaves, small white, purple-tinged flowers in mid-summer; may require winter protection in colder areas. **L. nummularia 'Aurea' H5** (2.5cm x 1m+) known as golden creeping Jenny, a low spreader, starting the season with cheery golden leaves which gradually fade to yellow-green, yellow flowers; thrives in shade and will rapidly cover the ground, often used as a bedding plant. **L. punctata** (garden loosestrife) **H4–5** (60cm–1m x 1m+) attractive summer yellow flower spikes above mid-green leaves, can become invasive, good in woodland and at pondsides;

Lysimachia punctata

L.p. 'Alexander' (60cm x 50cm) yellow, with green/cream variegated leaves, sometimes marked purple, less vigorous.

Lythrum (purple loosestrife)
H5 Useful, fully hardy, tall perennial for borders, ponds and bog gardens, preferring a sunny aspect in wet soil. Lythrums form clumps, with rather harsh, willowherb-like bright pink-purple flowers in July–September. They are used in prairie-style planting designs with grasses and other vigorous perennials. They are tough and easy to please – perhaps a bit too easy, so deadhead 'lest they sow the parish with their spurious offspring', as Arthur Johnson observed.

Lythrum salicaria

L. salicaria (75–90cm x 60–75cm) ✉ magenta-pink, clashing with everything, selected forms are kinder on the eye; 'Blush' ☘ light pink, the most attractive form, 'Feuerkerze' deep rose red, 'Robert' strong rose red. In the USA this has gone rampantly wild and is a menace, now banned from sale: not a problem here where it is native. *L. virgatum* (1m x 50cm) deep purple-red, less prone to self-seeding; 'Dropmore Purple' deep purplish-pink, 'Rosy Gem' pink flushed purple, 'The Rocket' deep pink, dark-green leaves, will grow in partial shade.

Macleaya (plume poppy)
H5 (to 2.5m x 1m+) An easily grown, hardy 'architectural' perennial, forming clumps of large lobed or scalloped grey-green leaves, above which arise in late summer the tall plumes of tiny airy white or pale-pink flowers. Macleayas prefer sunshine but will tolerate some shade; the whole plant can take on a haunting ghostly appearance in a shady corner. They like a fertile well-drained soil and are normally fairly free of pests and diseases. The varieties are often wrongly named, and they are hard to distinguish out of flower.

M. cordata creamy-white flowers, deeply lobed grey-green leaves. *M. microcarpa* 'Kelway's Coral Plume' coral-pink flower spikes, large rounded leaves; can become invasive in lighter sandier soils.

Macleaya cordata

Maianthemum (formerly *Smilacina*) (false Solomon's seal)
H5 You are still more likely to find these under their old name of Smilacina. They are attractive medium-sized woodlanders, good for massing beneath shrubs and trees in moist semi-shade. The large fresh green leaves appear on opposite sides of arching stems, similarly to those of Solomon's seal. The frothy or fluffy flower heads of tiny white flowers appear above the clumps of foliage in spring and summer, followed by red autumn fruits. They like humus-rich, moist acidic soil with adequate drainage and prefer semi-shade. Keep an eye out for caterpillar attacks, which can shred the leaves, and rabbits, which find the young growth tasty. Those listed below are fully hardy *H5* and in ideal conditions will spread further than the measurements given.

Maianthemum (Smilacina) racemosum

M. racemosum (*Smilacina racemosa*) (90cm x 50cm) ❄ scented white flowers, leaves yellow in autumn, red berries, can seed over-freely. *M. stellatum* (*Smilacina stellata*) (60cm x 50cm) glaucous leaves, smaller starry white flowers in loose clusters; beware, as in light soil it can get out of control.

Malva see *Sidalcea*, page 226

Mazus reptans see *Mimulus*, page 209

Meconopsis (Himalayan blue poppy)
H3–5 One of the great joys of Scottish gardens, these Himalayan and Chinese plants are probably more at home here than anywhere else, much to the envy of more southern gardeners. Moisture and cool summers are what they like. Many Scottish gardens such as Branklyn and Crarae, and nurseries such as Cally, Ian Christie and Glendoick, are famous for their displays. Meconopsis produce large disc-shaped flowers in early summer, most famously in deep intense blue but also in many other colours. They like a cool sheltered site, out of the strongest winds, and a rich woodland soil, in sun or part shade. They are best planted small, in autumn or early spring, so that they can become well established before flowering. Don't choose plants in flower or coming into flower as they are unlikely to prove perennial. Scottish plant hunters such as George Forrest and George Sherriff, and more recently Ron McBeath, Ian Christie and Peter and Kenneth Cox, have introduced many new forms and species from the wild.

Blue poppies
H4–5 (rosettes 30–40cm, flowers to 1m) the perennial blue poppies are quite easy to grow in moist soil, rich in organic matter, as long as the plants are not allowed to dry out. Divide congested clumps in spring or autumn every few years.

Meconopsis betonicifolia (blue)

M. betonicifolia (*M. baileyi*) ⚜ the best-known species, with rich-blue flowers; **var. alba** pure white, comes true from seed if kept isolated, **'Hensol Violet'** violet-purple. *M. grandis* large deep blue-purple flowers in May, some forms set fertile seed; **'Jimmy Bayne'** ⚜ huge blue flowers, needs to be increased by division, as it does not set seed; **'Slieve Donard'** ⚜ is very similar. **'Lingholm'** (formerly *M. x sheldonii*) ⚜ spectacular large flowers, a fine rich blue, comes true from seed. The blue poppies are rather mixed up in the trade, and Evelyn Stevens from near Dunblane has been trying to identify and separate the numerous forms via a group of *Meconopsis* experts and by conducting trials.

Meconopsis 'Lingholm'
(*sheldonii* x)

Monocarpic Group
H3–4 These species are normally biennial, forming an attractive rosette with silvery or golden hairs on the foliage in the first year, flowering in the second or third year with spikes, up to 2m high, with up to 50 or more flowers, and then dying. The seed can easily be collected to raise further plants. The monocarpic species appreciate a fair amount of fertilizer. The various species have hybridised freely in gardens, so *M. napaulensis* or *M. regia* hybrids, with attractive silvery rosettes, tend to be mixed yellows, reds and pinks, flowering in June–July. *M. paniculata* yellow. *M. wallichii* pale blue-lavender in July.

M. cambrica H5 (Welsh poppy) (40cm x 30cm) bright yellow flowers in April–May, ferny foliage, self-seeds merrily all over the garden but is pretty enough to be forgiven.

Mimulus (monkey flower)
and *Mazus reptans*
Some of the most colourful garden perennials for moist soils, but beware, as you may find that some of the larger species take over the garden. The characteristic snapdragon-like flowers splay open at the mouth and are often spotted in the throat. Most species require moist but well-drained soil; *M. luteus* and *M. ringens* are bog plants, which grow best in shallow water. Mimulus can be short lived but they are easily raised from seed or cuttings; in Scottish gardens some can be treated as self-perpetuating annuals as they will self-seed each year and they can spread indefinitely when they are happy.

M. aurantiacus (syns. *M. glutinosus*, *Diplacus glutinosus*) *H3* (1m) evergreen with orange, yellow or purple flowers, best in full sun. *M. cardinalis H3* (90cm) scarlet with yellow spots, tolerant of dryish soils. *M. cupreus* **'Whitecroft Scarlet'** *H3* (10cm) scarlet. *M. lewisii H2/3* (60cm) pink, tolerant of relatively dry soils. *M. luteus H3–4* (30cm) yellow, with red spotting ('vulgar!' says Christopher Lloyd), but beware, as this is a rampant weed in mild gardens which can clog streams and ponds as impatiens (balsam) does; do not plant on the west coast. **'Orkney Gold'** *H3* (30cm) double yellow. *M. ringens H4* (90cm) lilac blue; dwarf spreading varieties include **'Highland Orange'** *H3* (10cm) deep orange, May–September, **'Highland Red'** *H2* (10cm) ⚜ red, May–September, not hardy inland but will seed around.

Mimulus ringens 'Highland Yellow' and 'Highland Red'

Mazus reptans H4 (5cm x 30–50cm) This is closely related, with two-lipped purple or white ('Albus') flowers in summer. A ground-hugging carpeter for full or part day sun; does best in a rock garden.

Monarda (bergamot) and *Agastache*
H5 Monardas (see also Herbs, page 195) are fully hardy border stalwarts that produce medium-sized clumps of aromatic foliage (the bergamot fragrance of Earl Grey tea) and distinctive flowers in a range of colours throughout summer. They need well-drained soil in full sun and they are rather brittle, so need some wind shelter. Cutting them back in early summer gives longer and later flowering and often sturdier plants. The purple cultivars are more drought tolerant than the reddish ones. The main drawback is that most varieties are subject to mildew, which whitens the leaves and makes them unsightly. Some newer cultivars, many such as 'Comanche' and 'Cherokee' named after American Indian tribes, are somewhat mildew resistant, but these are only just coming on to the market and none is a good red. Christopher

Lloyd reckons that monardas suffer from 'replant' disease, so they should not be put back in the same spot when clumps are divided. All are fully hardy (**H5**), and reach 60–90cm x 50cm unless stated otherwise**.**

'**Aquarius**' (60cm) pale lilac, low, mildew resistant. '**Balance**' deep pink, mildew resistant. '**Beauty of Cobham**' rosy pink, small dark-green leaves. '**Blaustrumpf**' (Blue Stocking) violet-purple, roots as it spreads, partly mildew resistant. '**Cambridge Scarlet**' ⚜ fine blood-red flowers, somewhat variable, prone to mildew. '**Croftway Pink**' rose pink. '**Fishes**' (syn. 'Pisces') pale pink, mildew resistant. '**Gardenview Scarlet**' best performing red in recent RHS trials, only recently available. '**Mahogany**' deep red-brown, roots as it spreads. '**Prärienacht**' (Prairie Night) rich violet-purple. '**Schneewittchen**' (syn. 'Snow Maiden') white, self-rooting stems. '**Squaw**' scarlet, some mildew resistance, yellow-green leaves. '**Twins**' ('Gemini') pink, some mildew resistance.

Monarda 'Cambridge Scarlet'

Agastache (giant hyssop) H2–3 Another member of the labiate (mint) family with aromatic leaves; some varieties have culinary or medicinal use. Like most of their relatives, these are sun-lovers requiring well-drained soil. Most are not very hardy and tend to be short-lived – a winter mulch will help protect crowns in colder climates. Some are inclined to seed around too freely. '**Blue Fortune**' **H2–3** (70cm x 30cm) purple-blue, July–September. '**Firebird**' **H2** (60cm x 40cm) aromatic glaucous leaves and spikes of pinkish-orange flowers. **A. foeniculum H3** (1–1.5m x 90cm–1m) a stately plant, liquorice/mint-scented leaves and lavender-blue flowers; often hybrids crossed with the similar A. rugosa are offered under this name. **A. mexicana H2** (60cm–1m x 30–45cm) flowers, white, pink spotted, intoxicating to bees, but unfortunately the plant looks not unlike a stinging nettle; a form **Red Fortune** [PBR] with red flowers is said to be hardier than the type. **A. rugosa 'Liquorice Blue' H3** (1m x 45–60cm) small blue liquorice-scented flowers, this species is the most tolerant of damper or heavy soils.

Musa basjoo (banana)

H2–3 (2–3m+ x 2–3m) There is nothing quite like the large, lush green foliage of bananas, and garden designers have been including so-called hardy bananas in their tropical designs for the last few years. *Musa basjoo*, the Japanese banana, is probably the best one to try in Scotland. It has large bright-green leaves, arching from the main stem, and yellow and brown

Musa basjoo at Culzean Castle (RC-M)

flowers, followed by small inedible bananas. There are some fine examples at Culzean Castle in Ayrshire, and it will grow in mild west coast gardens. It might be worth trying elsewhere with a bit of extra protection in winter: strip off the leaves in autumn and wrap around the stem porous insulation such as straw, which needs to be covered on top to keep it dry. Alternatively keep it in a pot and move it indoors in winter. Bananas must have wind shelter to avoid shredded leaves. You can prune the leader to encourage branching if the plant gets too tall. If the main trunk of an established plant is frozen, all may not be lost, as there are often offsets underground which will allow new plants to develop. The hardiest form is said to be '**Sakhalin**'.

Nemesia fruticans see *Diascia*, page 176

Nepeta (catmint)

H3–4/5 Nepetas are some of the easiest and most useful garden plants available, irresistible to bees and cats, especially in the case of catnip (*N. cataria*), which has a stupor-inducing smell that gives some felines a serious 'high'. Nepetas form carpeting mounds of grey-green aromatic, often hairy foliage, and produce masses of purple, blue, pink, yellow or white flower spikes throughout late spring and summer. They thrive in any well-drained soil in sun or light shade, doing best in poor soils as rich ones cause them to grow too vigorously and flop over. They struggle in constantly wet soils and may rot in cold, wet, inland gardens, so we have downgraded their hardiness ratings slightly. Otherwise they are pretty resilient, and can be used as a tougher alternative to lavender in cold gardens, suffering fewer disease and weather problems. Many Scottish gardens use Nepeta to great effect: these include Dunrobin Castle in Sutherland, Glamis Castle, Angus, Inveresk Lodge and Tyninghame Walled Garden, East Lothian. The more vigorous varieties can be trimmed after flowering, or in mid-summer if they get straggly; this will encourage further flowers later in the season. Some of the white and pink varieties are rather 'underwhelming' in flower; the blues are more effective.

They can be lifted and divided every 4–5 years, but few gardeners bother. In cold gardens, leave the dying foliage over winter before cutting to shape in spring. Heights and spreads are similar unless stated otherwise.

N. x faassenii H4–5 (45cm) soft lavender blue, May–October, grey-green foliage, one of the hardier varieties; forms include **'Kit Kat'** (40cm) dwarf, dark purple-blue, **'Six Hills Giant'** (90cm) 🏆 small violet flowers, June–October, one of the most vigorous. *N. govaniana H4* (90cm) pale-yellow flowers in July–September; unlike the others, this likes a moist, shady site; good in woodland gardens. *N. grandiflora*

Nepeta subsessilis 'Candy Cat'

'Dawn to Dusk' H4–5 (25cm+) lavender-blue flower spikes in June–July; if sheared will often flower again. *N. longipes H4–5* (90cm x 60cm) taller growing, grey-green toothed leaves, lavender-blue flowers. *N. nervosa H4* (50cm) tight spikes of bright purplish blue, low, spreading habit. *N. racemosa* **'Snowflake' H4–5** (30cm) white, grey leaved, for the front of a border; *N.r.* **'Walker's Low'** (60–90cm) powder-blue flowers, grey foliage, repeat flowers if cut back mid-season. *N. sibirica* **'Souvenier d'André Chaudron'** (syn. 'Blue Beauty') *H5* (50cm) dark lavender-blue, perhaps the hardiest, and can be invasive, sending out underground runners. *N. subsessilis* (90cm) bright blue, flowers last into autumn; forms/hybrids include **'Candy Cat'** light rosy purple, **'Cool Cat'** pale lavender.

Nepeta hedge at Anne's Street, Edinburgh

Oenothera (evening primrose, sundrops)

H3–4 These are useful summer-flowering clump-forming perennials of varying size. Many are scented and open late in the afternoon, each flower lasting only a few hours. Growth can be a little bit straggly but they still make useful plants for the border edge and they flower over several weeks, particularly if deadheaded / pruned back. Most will happily seed themselves around in any sunny, well-drained not too fertile soil. They tend to be short-lived in wet and heavy soils. They flower from June to September unless stated otherwise.

O. fruticosa **'Fyrverkeri'** (syn. 'Fireworks') (45cm x 30cm) deep red buds open to clear yellow flowers, dark reddish-green leaves;

Oenothora fruticosa

subsp. *glauca* light yellow flowers, broad leaves, the form **'Erica Robin'** bronze-flushed leaves. *O. macrocarpa* (syn. *O. missouriensis*) (15cm x 40cm) a sprawler with light yellow flowers and narrow dark-green leaves. *O. speciosa* **'Siskiyou'** (20cm x 30cm) ❀ fragrant soft pink, with yellow centres on individual stems, dislikes winter wet. *O. versicolor* **'Sunset Boulevard'** (60cm x 30cm) clusters of orange-yellow flowers, deepening to reddish orange, in June–July, short lived or annual.

Omphalodes

H4–5 This is one of the best low-growing shade-tolerant ground-covers: its bright deep-blue forget-me-not flowers associate superbly with dwarf rhododendrons, trilliums, wood anemones and other woodland spring bulbs. But you may have to hunt around to buy it, as it is not always easy to find in garden centres. Omphalodes form clumps of semi-evergreen hairy leaves, and are tough plants, easy to please if you can keep slugs off them, and suitable for the rock garden and between paving stones.

Omphalodes cappadocica

O. cappadocica H4–5 (10–25cm x 1m or more) small bright-blue flowers with a white eye; forms include **'Cherry Ingram'** (to 25cm high) taller, more vigorous with larger brighter-blue flowers, **'Lilac Mist'** (15cm high) paler lilac-blue, **'Starry Eyes'** (15cm high) bright blue with off-white edging, tends to revert to blue. *O. verna* is slightly smaller than *O. cappadocica* but tolerates a wider variety of soils and flowers earlier; *O.v.* **'Alba'** white.

Onopordum see Thistles, page 229

Osteospermum jucundum

H3–4 (10–50cm x 30cm+) This is not to be confused with the tender osteospermum bedding plants with ever more garish daisy flowers. This used to be known as *Dimorphotheca* but botanists have merged that genus into *Osteospermum*. *O. jucundum* is a useful perennial, semi-evergreen species, from which have been bred a range of cultivars with white, pink or purple flowers in mid- to late summer. Being South African, it likes a warm well-drained site and it is surprisingly hardy as long as it does not get wet feet in winter. We saw it growing successfully all over Scotland, including Invergordon (Ross-shire) and Aberdeenshire (even well inland), so it must be tougher than many people think. Deadhead to prolong flowering.

Osteospermum jucundum 'Compactum', 'Westwood' and 'Cannington Roy'

O. jucundum mauve-pink to magenta-purple daisy flowers; **'Blackthorn'** deep purple, **'Cannington Roy'** white ageing to mauve-pink, deeper reverse, **'Compactum'** (10–20cm x 20–30cm) neat habit, **'Lady Leitrim'** white with purple-tinged reverse, said to be one of the hardiest but can be a bit straggly.

Ourisia

H4 From the woodlands of the Andes and New Zealand, these are happier in the cool damp conditions of Scotland than further south. Creeping and rooting as they spread, with pink or red flowers in early summer, they love a damp, mossy log by a streamside, although they can sometimes be shy flowering. **O. coccinea** (20–30cm x 20–30cm+) pure red. **'Loch Ewe'** (20cm x 20cm+) bright pink. **O. macrophylla** (30–60cm x 45cm+) white flowers, scalloped leaves. **'Snowflake'** (10cm x 20cm+) white.

Ourisia 'Loch Ewe'

Oxalis

H2–3 The genus *Oxalis* includes some rock garden gems and good front-of-border plants, as well as some pernicious weeds. Most oxalis form small clumps of grey-green foliage and produce comparatively large flowers, which open to flattened discs in sunshine but 'roll up' in cloud and at night. If you have the right conditions for them (well-drained soil in full sun), they are pretty undemanding.

O. adenophylla H3 (5cm x 10cm) one for free-draining soil, in a rock garden for instance, with beautiful pink blooms, fading to white, with a purple eye, in May–July. **'Ione Hecker' H3** (5cm x

Oxalis adenophylla (RC-M)

10cm) pale purple-blue flowers in summer. **O. magellanica H4** (8cm x 20cm+) bronze-green leaves and white flowers from spring to summer, good in woodland conditions; **O.m. 'Nelson'** (syn. 'Flore Plena') tiny double white flowers. **O. tetraphylla 'Iron Cross'** (syn. *O. deppei*) **H3** (30cm x 20cm) deep reddish-pink flowers, leaflets with a large purple blotch at their base.

Paeonia (herbaceous)

H3–5 No garden should be without a peony or two, with those sumptuous, often fragrant blooms held proud over mounds of attractively cut leaves. They also make great, if short-lived, cut flowers for the house. Most are fully hardy and much tougher than they look: we found *P. lactiflora* varieties flowering happily by the petrol station at Dalwhinnie in the Highlands, at 358m, in one of the severest climates in Scotland. Peonies thrive in any fertile soil in sun or part shade, and once they are established, can be left alone for 20 years or more. They don't much like being moved; if you really have to, it is best to try in autumn. They can suffer from blight/wilt, especially in pots and when newly planted, but they generally recover if cut back. Do not plant them too deeply ('eyes' just below the soil surface) and do not over-feed, as both will result in poor flowering. A winter mulch, with organic matter, and a handful of feed will help keep them healthy. Peony flowers need wind shelter and the taller and double-flowered varieties benefit from staking. All listed below are pretty tough and reliable. Others species such as *P. cambessedesii* from Majorca needs more heat than most of Scotland can offer, although Bob Mitchell manages to get it to flower in south Fife. Binny Plants in West Lothian offers the largest selection of peonies in Scotland, while some of the best displays are the borders at Manderston, near Duns, Tyninghame House walled garden, near Dunbar and The Murrel in Fife. For tree paeonies, see page 77.

P. lactiflora hybrids **H5** (70–90cm x 60–90cm) there are hundreds of these, in various flower forms – single, anemone form (with petalloid stamens), semi-double or double, flowering in June–July. Most have some fragrance, the strongest are marked in the text. Some of the most popular of the many named hybrids include: **'Bowl of Beauty'** large anemone-form carmine-red with a mass of cream stamens, fragrant, **'Duchesse de Nemours'** large fragrant double white, **'Felix Crousse'** (syn. 'Victor Hugo') large double carmine-red, **'Festiva Maxima'** large ruffled double white with red at the base, **'Kansas'** double red, Billy Carruthers'

Paeonia lactiflora 'Duchesse de Nemours'

Paeonia mairei

Papaver nudicaule

Papaver orientale 'Mrs Perry' and 'Allegro'

(of Binny Plants) choice for this colour, **'Karl Rosenfield'** dark double carmine-red, **'Lady Alexandra Duff'** ❃ double white flushed lavender, scented, **'Monsieur Jules Elie'** large double silvery rose, **'Mrs Frankin D. Roosevelt'** ❃ fragrant, double pale pink, late, **'Sarah Bernhardt'** ❃ ⚘ large double, fragrant, apple-blossom pink, flower heads very heavy, **'Dinner Plate'** is said to be an improved version, **'Shirley Temple'** ⚘ large, densely packed double pink, holds flowers well, **'White Wings'** single white, light scent. The newer **Coral Series** of hybrids are irresistible; these include **'Coral Sunset'** and **'Coral Charm'** early flowering with very attractive semi-double coral-peach-pink flowers in late May–June. Specialist nurseries only. *P. mairei H4–5* (60cm x 60cm) introduced from the wild by Peter Cox of Glendoick, seems to be one of the best species for the garden, with large purple-pink flowers. *P. mlokosewitschii H5* (1m x 75–90cm) ⚘ known as 'Molly the witch' as the Latin name is such a mouthful, blue-green foliage, short-lasting large single pale yellow, in May. *P. officinalis H4* (60–80cm x 60–80cm) ❃ flowers magenta-purple, sickly scented, leaves sometimes turn autumnal red, usually commercially available in the two double forms, particularly good in Scotland: **'Rosea Plena'** double bright pink, fading to off white, **'Rubra Plena'** double deep red, rather too heavy for the stems especially after rain.

Papaver (poppy)

H5 One of the most popular garden plants, with showy summer flowers in a wide range of colours, held above mounds of deciduous foliage. There are many popular annual garden species and strains such as *P. commutatum* (ladybird poppy), the corn poppy and the opium poppy. The poppies covered here are the Iceland poppies (*P. nudicaule*) and the Oriental poppies (*P. orientale*). Both are best grown in full sun, in well-drained soil. The flowers of Oriental poppies do not last long, especially in wet and cold weather, are difficult to stake and are followed by an unsightly mass of floppy foliage, which dies back in July, leaving a gap in the border. But don't let that stop you, because the flowers look fabulous. Aphids can cause problems, and poppies don't tend to live for ever, so you may have to start again after a few years.

P. nudicaule (syn. *P. croceum*) (Iceland poppy) (30cm x 30cm) single flowers in a range of oranges, yellows, peaches and creams; usually grown as a biennial, but easy to raise from seed; there are numerous strains. *P. orientale* (Oriental poppy) (50–80cm x 25–40cm) orange-scarlet single flowers in May–July, held above coarse deeply cut mid-green leaves. A huge number of varieties have been raised from this species; some of the most popular include **'Allegro'** large single bright orange-red, **'Beauty of Livermere'** large bright crimson, black markings, self-supporting, **'Black and White'** large white with black centres, **'Cedric Morris'** large salmon pink with a black base to the petals, **'Curlilocks'** ruffled orange-red with black centres, **'Lilac Girl'** lavender, crumpled edges, **'Louvre'** white, with black centres and pink shading, **'Mrs Perry'** soft salmon pink, black basal markings, **'Patty's Plum'** a glorious rich deep plum-purple, fading in strong sun, not one of the most perennial, **'Perry's White'** ⚘ white blushed pink with black blotches, **'Picotée'** ruffled white with salmon edges, **Pizzicato Group** (50cm) a seed strain with flowers ranging from cream to red, low-growing, **Place Pigalle** [PBR] white with a red edge, **'Raspberry Queen'** deep pinky red, unblotched, **'Türkenlouis'** fringed deep scarlet orange with dark centre, **'Watermelon'** pale pinkish purple.

Parahebe perfoliata see *Veronica*, page 232

Penstemon

H3–4 Some of the best perennials for long-lasting, late-summer colour, penstemons are semi-evergreen clumping plants, sometimes with woody stems, with spikes or clusters of mini-foxglove-like tubular flowers from June often right up until first frosts. Despite their

North American origins, the world centre of penstemon breeding until the 1960s was at the firm of John Forbes of Hawick in the Borders. They like fertile, moist, but well-drained soil. Although most penstemons are fairly cold hardy, they are prone to rotting in heavy soils and in long, wet winters, and to being damaged or killed by sudden drops in temperature before they have hardened off. The winter of 2005–6 saw the demise of lots of penstemons, even in relatively mild gardens in south-west Scotland. One important tip is not to cut them back until late spring – the old foliage will offer winter protection – although dead flowers can be removed without cutting into greenery. Mulching may help, but may also cause basal rotting. As a rule of thumb, the larger the leaf, the more tender the variety; if in doubt, take a few cuttings in summer. At best, expect to replace them every few years. Most will spread to 50cm or more. *H3* unless stated otherwise, though in heavy soils they are more realistically *H2*.

Penstemon
'Apple Blossom'

'Alice Hindley' *H2* (60cm–1m) mauve-violet-blue, evergreen. **'Apple Blossom'** (45cm) soft pink, evergreen. *P. barbatus* (90cm) rose red; there are many seed strains in mixed colours, including **Cambridge Mixed** compact to 30cm, and var. *praecox* f. *nanus* (40cm) mixed colours. **'Blackbird'** (60cm) evergreen, deep purple, white-throated. **'Burgundy'** *H2* (40cm) claret, tender. **'Countess of Dalkeith'** (60cm) purple with a white throat, raised in Scotland. *P. digitalis* 'Husker Red' (60cm) *H4* bright red, handsome bronzy foliage, one of the hardiest. **'Evelyn'** (45cm) small light pink. **Fruit of the Forest series** (60cm): **'Blackberry Ice'** deep purple, **'Blueberry Ice'** blue, **'Raspberry Ice'** reddish pink. **'Garnet'** (syn. 'Andenken an Fredrich Hahn' – we can see why they decided to rename that one!) (90cm) deep red, dark-green evergreen foliage. *P. heterophyllus* 'Catherine de la Mare' *H4* (60cm) lilac blue; **'True Blue'** is almost identical. **'Hidcote Pink'** *H3–4* (60cm) pink with dark veins in the throat, considered hardier than most. **'King George V'** (60cm) large scarlet flowers with a white throat, dark green evergreen foliage, Hawick raised. **'Mother of Pearl'** (60cm) ivory, flushed mauve. **'Osprey'** (60cm) white with a pink throat. **Phoenix Series** (75cm) flowers pink or red with white centres,

Penstemon 'King George V'

P. pinifolius (20cm x 15cm) low-growing gem, evergreen, thin leaves, bright orange-red flowers, liable to die off in winter; the form **'Mersea Yellow'** is yellow. **'Raven'** (60cm) purple with a striped throat. **'Schoenholzeri'** (90cm) scarlet. **'Sour Grapes'** (60cm) greyish purple and blue, flushed green. **'Stapleford Gem'** (60–90cm) lilac-purple, white throat, **'Thorn'** (60cm) large white flowers with a pink edge. **'White Bedder'** (45cm) white, also known by six other names.

Persicaria

H3/4–5 ⚘ Formerly known as *Polygonum*, these excellent garden plants will cover the ground, spreading almost indefinitely, in sun or part shade, and produce pink or red flowers in summer, often over a very long season. Some have leaves with attractive autumn colouring too. They like some moisture in the soil, and are more or less maintenance free. Hardiness is variable. The sap can irritate skin and cause mild indigestion if ingested.

Persicaria 'Donald Lowndes'

Heights and spreads are similar.

P. affinis H3–4/5 (30cm) matting deciduous ground-cover with a very long flowering period, June–September; forms include **'Darjeeling Red'** *H4/5* (25cm) ⚘ lower, deep red, July–August, **'Donald Lowndes'** *H4* ⚘ pale pink, darker with age, reported by some to be tender in inland gardens, **'Superba'** ⚘ pale pink, almost red when mature. *P. amplexicaulis H5* (50cm–1.2m) pink-red flowers in July–September, dock-like leaves, can be a bit over-vigorous for small gardens, but it is an excellent easy plant with a long flowering season and we think it should be more widely grown; selected forms include **'Alba'** white, **'Atrosanguinea'** dark red, **'Firetail'** bright red, **'Inverleith'** (50cm) crimson. *P. bistorta* 'Superba' *H5* (75cm) ✉ ⚘ a selected form of the Scottish native, clear pink

Persicaria virginiana 'Painters' Pallete', Variegata Group and *P. microcephala* 'Red Dragon' ⚘

spikes all summer, leaves like a docken, a bit of a weed, really; at least you can eat the leaves, apparently. *P. campanulata H3* (90cm) small pink bell-shaped flowers, June–September. *P. microcephala* 'Red Dragon' *H4* (60cm) spear-shaped leaves dark red and green with a grey 'V' in the centre, small white flowers, needs some shelter and do not allow to dry out, a fine foliage plant. *P. vacciniifolia H3/4* (20–30cm) a creeper with bright-pink flowers in August–October, best grown in a warm sheltered spot away from winter wet; can be invasive. *P. virginiana* 'Painters' Palette' *H3/4* (60cm) non-flowering, cream-, brown- and pink-variegated leaves, not very tough, leaves inclined to brown in cold/very sunny weather.

Phlomis see page 80

Phlox

There are many garden-worthy phlox varieties, ranging from small alpine gems to medium-sized border plants, as well as the popular annual bedding phlox *P. drummondii*.

Woodland, low and alpine phlox

A mass of flowers from early spring to early summer, most with needle-like leaves, forming semi-evergreen mats or carpets. The very dwarf ones do best in full sun, and are ideal for the rock garden or large containers/troughs in well-drained soil; the larger ones are more suited to dappled or part day shade/woodland. *H5* unless stated otherwise.

P. adsurgens 'Wagon Wheel' (10cm x 30cm) wheel-shaped narrow-petalled pink flowers in summer, a bit temperamental. *P. amoena* 'Variegata' (syn. *P.* x *procumbens* 'Variegata') (10 x 60cm) deep pink, leaves with cream margins. *P. divaricata* (35cm x 50cm) lavender-blue to pale-violet star-shaped flowers on tall slender stems in early summer, suitable for woodland ground cover, and will seed around; there are lots of named forms including 'Blue Dreams' lilac blue, 'Chatahoochie' deep lilac with a reddish eye, long flowering, best in full sun in Scotland, 'White Perfume' fragrant white. *P. douglasii* (8cm x 30cm) very easy and one of the best all-round alpines for Scotland, with a wide variety of forms in many colours, including 'Boothman's Variety' lavender with a darker centre, 'Crackerjack' ♛ brilliant magenta, 'Eva' pinkish lavender, 'Ice Mountain' white, flushed pale violet, 'Red Admiral' ♛ deep crimson. *P. subulata* (moss phlox) (8cm x 30cm) many forms ranging from light or dark purple to near red, pink and white, most seem good; some of the most popular

Phlox divaricata 'White Perfume' and 'Blue Dreams'

Phlox subulata 'Apple Blossom' and 'Tamaongalei' ('Candy Stripes')

include 'Amazing Grace' pale pink with a deeper eye, habit a bit lax, 'Apple Blossom' white, 'Emerald Cushion' lavender blue, 'McDaniel's Cushion' vigorous, bright pink, 'Tamaongalei' (syns. 'Candy Stripes', 'Kimono') white streaked deep pink. *P. stolonifera* (creeping phlox) *H4* (10–15cm x 30cm+) evergreen ground-cover for moist soil in sun or shade, pink or purple flowers in early summer, forms include 'Blue Ridge' pale lilac blue, a bit tricky, 'Fran's Purple' purple, 'Home Fires' deep pink.

Border phlox

The border phloxes flower from mid to late summer and are easily grown in any fertile, free-draining but not over-dry soil in sun or part day shade (add lots of dung, advises Christopher Lloyd). Most *P. paniculata* can suffer from mildew, causing lower leaves in particular to turn white and fall. Some new varieties have some resistance. They are also susceptible to eelworm, which disfigure the flowers and foliage; if you have an eelworm infection, it is best to remove phlox for a few years. It is worth pinching the growing tips out in May to encourage bushiness when plants are young. The variegated varieties are truly shocking when foliage and flowers are together – those style gurus at Sissinghurst disbud them to avoid ladies swooning. How considerate! There is a fine phlox border at Floors Castle walled garden.

P. carolina 'Bill Baker' *H4* (50cm x 40cm) pink flowers in early summer. *P. maculata H3–4* (80cm–1m x 50cm) ❄ cylindrical flower heads of fragrant flowers in summer, shiny mid-green leaves, more or less resistant to mildew, and even more floriferous and slightly earlier-flowering than *P. paniculata* – they should be grown more; 'Alpha' lilac-pink, 'Natascha' shocking pink and white striped, 'Omega' white with a lilac eye, 'Rosalinde' deep pink. *P. paniculata* hybrids *H3–4* (60cm–1.2m x 60cm) ❄ conical flower heads of scented flowers in July-September, in a bewildering array of colours, some also have variegated leaves. There are over 150 varieties listed in the *RHS Plantfinder*, including: 'Balmoral' rosy lavender, 'Bright Eyes' clear pale pink with a red eye, mildew resistant, 'Brigadier' bright salmon-orange flowers with a red eye, 'Europa' white with a carmine eye, 'David' clear white, good scent, good mildew resistance, 'Eva Cullum' clear pink with a magenta eye, 'Eventide' late, lavender blue, Feelings Series ('Fancy Feelings', 'Midnight Feelings', etc.) long-lasting, narrow, strap-petalled flowers in various colours, likely to become popular, good for flower arranging, some mildew resistance, 'Franz Schubert' purple, white edging, mildew resistant, Goldmine [PBR] showy yellow-variegated foliage, deep magenta, good, mildew

Phlox paniculata: four varieties

resistance, **'Harlequin'** variegated cream and green leaves, and reddish-purple flowers, **'Katrina'** lavender with a large white eye, **'Laura'** violet-blue with a white eye, **'Lilac Time'** (syn. 'Amethyst') violet, **'Little Laura'** (70cm high) a dwarf version of 'Laura', mildew resistant, **'Monica Lynden-Bell'** pink to white, **'Mother of Pearl'** white flushed light pink, **'Mount Fuji'** white, very fine, **'Norah Leigh'** small rather feeble pale-lilac flowers, leaves splashed cream, **'Prince of Orange'** salmon orange-scarlet, late, **'Sandringham'** deep pink with darker centre, **'Skylight'** pale blue, **'Starfire'** red, purple-tinged leaves, good colour but not very vigorous, **'Tenor'** early red, **'White Admiral'** ❦ pure white with a green eye, late, long flowering season, **'Windsor'** (60cm high) carmine-pink, darker eye.

Physalis alkekengi var. franchetii

Physalis alkekengi var. franchetii
(Chinese lantern)
H5 (1m x 60cm+) The Chinese lantern is grown mainly for its decorative autumnal red fruits, surrounded by protective orange calyces. These 'lanterns' make attractive dried flowers, and are useful for providing late-season colour. The white summer flowers are tiny and rarely noticed. The upright stems are produced from underground spreading rhizomes. It prefers a slightly alkaline, moist soil, in full sun, where it can spread to the point of becoming invasive. Unfortunately slugs are rather inclined to eat the young shoots. All parts of the plant except the fruit are toxic and the foliage may cause skin allergy.

Physostegia (obedient plant)
H4 A rather curious upright and vigorously spreading evergreen with toothed leaves and white or pink-purple, tubular, mid to late summer flowers with two lower lips. The common name, obedient plant, refers to the fact that if you move or bend the flowers, which are on 'hinged' stalks, they remain in place. It requires little maintenance except to be cut back or tidied after flowering, and can become invasive in moist, rich soils, spreading much further than the clump size listed below.
P. virginiana H4 (1m x 60cm+) rose purple; cultivars: **'Alba'** and **'Summer Snow'** (50cm x 60cm+) white, **'Vivid'**

Physostegia virginiana 'Alba'

(30–60cm x 60cm+) dark lilac pink, **var. *speciosa* 'Variegata'** (1m x 60cm+) pink-purple, white-edged leaves, tends to revert.

Podophyllum
H3–5 ❦ Specialist perennial growers have recently begun to list lots of exciting newly introduced *Podophyllum* from China, often wrongly named. These woodland plants are related to *Berberis*, though you'd never guess. Some species have amazing medicinal properties, more of which are being discovered, but the plant is generally toxic, so don't try home medication. Preferring moist soil, most are tough, though young growth can be frosted. The foliage markings can be most attractive. Height and spread are similar.

Podophyllum hexandrum

P. hexandrum (syn. *P. emodii*) **H4–5** (60cm) pink flowers held above the leaves which are often attractively marked with bronze patterns, red fruit in autumn. *P. peltatum* (May apple) **H5** (40cm) nodding white or cream flowers tend to be hidden under the leaves, large plum-like yellow fruit in late summer, inclined to spread. *P. aurantiocaule* **H3–4** (40–50cm) white flowers below the leaves, red fruit, first introduced from China by John Roy on one of Ken Cox's expeditions and grows well in Scotland on both east and west coasts.

Platycodon grandiflorus see *Campanula*, page 166

Polemonium (Jacob's ladder)
H3–5 Polemoniums are short-lived but very free-flowering and easily pleased perennials, which are prone to self-seeding everywhere, which can be either a blessing or a curse. They enjoy well-drained soil in a sunny position and will do well in cold gardens. Species of *Polemonium* have been used over the years to treat many maladies including fevers, palpitations, hysteria, toothache, dysentery, insect bites, syphilis and rabies. They have blue/purple or peach-apricot flowers; some are a mixture, with pairs of finely divided leaves. They can suffer from mildew. Most will seed or spread to form clumps of 30–60cm+ across. Most are **H4–5** but one or two are more tender (marked).

P. boreale **'Heavenly Habit'** (30cm) violet-blue with a yellow eye in summer, compact habit, long flowering period if deadheaded. **Bressingham Purple** ['Polebress'] (60cm) lavender blue, young growth deep purple. *P. caeruleum* (45–60cm) ❦ attractive divided light green foliage, lavender-blue flowers with central

Polemonium reptans 'Blue Pearl'
(right) and P. reptans (left)

Polygonatum x hybridum

orange stamens, in May–August; forms include: **Brise d'Anjou** ['Blanjou'] lavender blue, yellow-edged variegated leaves, not as easy to please as the others, **'Album'** white flowers with central orange-yellow stamens. **P. carneum 'Apricot Delight' H3–4** (60cm) divided green foliage, pretty apricot/lilac flowers. **P. cashmerianum** (80cm) pale lavender, in tall spikes; most plants sold under this name are incorrectly identified. **'Hopleys' H3–4** (75cm) ❀ fragrant pale mauve fading to white, does not seed around, mildew prone. **'Lambrook Mauve'** (45cm) bluish mauve, reddish stems, almost evergreen foliage, sterile so does not seed around. **P. pauciflorum H3–4** (30–45cm) trumpet-shaped peach flowers, with flared yellow ends, slightly scented, in May–July. **P. reptans** (40cm) pale-blue pendulous tubular flowers in May–June, good in woodland and semi-shade in moist soil; forms include **'Blue Pearl'** (20cm) low growing, light blue, **Stairway to Heaven** [PBR] (40cm) cream-edged foliage with a pink flush, blue flowers in May–July, the strongest growing of the variegated polemoniums.

Polygonatum (Solomon's seal)
and Uvularia grandiflora
H4–5 ⚘ Solomon's seal is an attractive plant, useful for spreading near the front of borders or around the base of shrubs, with pendulous stems of attractive finely cut grey-green leaves and drooping flowers in late spring and early summer. It's easy to grow in any cool shady spot and doesn't require much maintenance once established. It can, however, be susceptible to the ravages of slug and voracious sawfly caterpillar attacks in early summer, which can strip entire stems by the time you've noticed anything amiss. Leaves are poisonous.

P. biflorum H5 (60cm x 90cm+) green-white flowers followed by black fruit. **P. hookeri H4–5** (10–15cm x 15cm) a good rock garden plant with lilac-pink bell-shaped flowers. **P. x hybridum H5** (60cm–1.2m x 1m) arching stems with greenish-white flowers; **P. x h. Striatum** (syn. 'Variegatum') **H5** (60cm x 60cm) cream striped leaves. **P. odoratum H5** (60cm x 90cm) ✉ fragrant white flowers with greenish tips; **var. pluriflorum 'Variegatum'** (60cm x 60cm) leaves spotted and striped ivory, pairs of dangling cream

flowers; this is one of the most attractive polygonatums, the new stems coloured red when emerging in spring.

Uvularia grandiflora H4–5 (30–60cm x 30cm) ⚘ Related to *Polygonatum*, but differing in its more bell-shaped flowers, which are yellow (in **var. pallida** cream-pale yellow), opening in May–June. It enjoys humus-rich woodland-type soil with some shelter and slowly forms clumps.

Potentilla (cinquefoil)
and Waldsteinia ternata (golden strawberry)
H5 The herbaceous potentillas are not quite as well known as their shrubby cousins, but they are equally useful and in many ways classier garden plants. One or two are vigorous spreaders which can become invasive in small gardens. They flower best in full sun, often for long periods if deadheaded, and all are fully hardy but can be short lived. They have strawberry-like mid-green leaves, and flower in June–September unless stated otherwise. *Waldsteinia* are very similar.

P. alba (8cm x 8cm) a vigorous mat-former with white flowers. **P. atrosanguinea** (50–90cm x 50cm) deep red, dark-green leaves. **'Gibson's Scarlet'** (45cm x 45cm) ⚘ clump forming, single bright-red flowers with black centres, probably the best red-flowered variety. **P. x hopwoodiana** (45cm x 60cm+) one of the more long-lived potentillas, clusters of delightful, long-lasting, two-toned pink flowers with dark centres. **P. megalantha** (30cm x 15cm) clumps of hairy palmate leaves, deep-yellow flowers in May–July. **P. nepalensis 'Miss Willmott'** (30–45cm x 30cm) single rose pink, darker eye; **P.n. 'Ron McBeath'** (30cm x 30cm) very compact, carmine-rose, named after the Scottish plant hunter and alpine expert. **P. recta var. sulphurea** (50cm x 60cm) clump forming with pale-yellow flowers. **P. recta 'Warrenii'** (45cm x 30cm) golden yellow. **P. thurberi 'Monarch's Velvet'** (60cm x 45–60cm) velvety reddish-pink, darker eye, long flowering. **P. x tonguei** (5cm x 25cm) an attractive vigorous, mat-forming rock garden or border edge plant with apricot flowers, with dark centres, prone to rust.

'William Rollinson' (40cm x 30cm) semi-double, orange, yellow on the reverse. **'Yellow Queen'** (30cm x 30cm) fine bright-yellow semi-double.

Waldsteinia ternata H5
(10cm x 30cm+) ⚘ A useful creeping semi-evergreen ground-cover, which looks and behaves like a strawberry, spreading by runners, with yellow flowers in late spring and early summer. Does best in sun and reasonably moist

Waldsteinia ternata (top) and
Potentilla x hopwoodiana

soil, but will tolerate dry shade and can be grown on dry banks. Congested clumps with reduced flowering can be divided and replanted.

Pratia pedunculata

Pratia pedunculata

H4–5 (2cm x 1m+) This Australian mat-forming perennial is useful for its mass of tiny star-shaped pale-blue flowers in late spring and summer, which can last several months. Low growing but spreading with both overground and underground rooting stems, it can be a bit rampant. It likes gritty, well-drained soil. The form **'County Park'** has dark blue flowers.

Primula

Mostly **H4–5** A hugely varied genus, some of which are easy to grow and multiply easily, many others are a challenge. Many of the world's finest primula collections have been established in Scotland, as the cool, moist climate mimics the conditions many species enjoy in the wild. They form clumps of evergreen or deciduous leaves in rosettes, and produce either flat (primrose-like) or bell-shaped flowers. There is a primula for almost every garden situation, but in general they prefer moist well-drained soil. Root aphids and vine weevils (especially in pots) can cause problems. Primulas are pretty tough, but it is usually drought and heat that kill them rather than cold. We have divided them into groups to aid provision of the right conditions.

Primrose/polyanthus/cowslip

H5 P. vulgaris (primrose) ⚜ (10cm x 15cm) ✉ The wild primrose is one of Scotland's first spring flowers, with pale-yellow flowers held singly on masses of stems in March–May. Huge numbers of primrose and polyanthus strains and varieties have been bred. Primroses carry single flowers on each stem, while polyanthus carry many flowers per stem. **Gold Lace Group** (10cm x 15cm) purple-black flowers, perfectly laced gold around the edge of the petals, in March–April. **Wanda** hybrids ⚜ vibrant purples, pinks and magentas. **Double cultivars** (15–20cm) need a little more care and should be regularly divided in late summer; forms include: **'Alan Robb'** apricot yellow, **'Dawn Ansell'** white, **'Ken Dearman'** coppery orange, **'Lilacina Plena'** (syn. 'Quaker's Bonnet') lilac, **'Miss Indigo'** a striking dark purple, **'Sue Jervis'** apricot, **'Sunshine Susie'** yellow. A new range of doubles **'Belarina'** in several colours appear to be a little later flowering. **P. elatior** (oxlip) (20cm x 30cm) ⚜ native to England, the oxlip makes a useful garden plant, with its one-sided pale yellow flower clusters in March–May. **P.**

Primula veris

veris (cowslip) (20cm x 30cm) ✉ ❄ ⚜ the native cowslip, deep yellow, fragrant; dislikes very acid soil. There is also a red-flowered form.

Candelabra Group

H5 (30–50cm x 20–40cm) These are a popular and easily grown group of garden plants which thrive in moist soils (struggling in poor, dry ones), often enjoying a waterside location, with candelabra-like stems with several circles (whorls) of flowers. In the garden, the species in this group tend to hybridise and seed freely, producing flowers in mixed colours. Weed out the ugliest ones. Some hybrids have been given horribly clumsy names by chopping up the Latin names of the parent species: *P. x bulleesiana, P. x chunglenta,* etc.

P. beesiana (syn. *P. bulleyana* subsp. *beesiana*) (30cm) ⚜ magenta-pink in May–June. **P. x bulleesiana** (30cm) pale yellow, in May–July. **P. bulleyana** (30cm) ⚜ light-orange flowers in June–July. **P. chungensis** (30–40cm) slender stems, orange-yellow, enjoys drier conditions than the rest. **P. cockburniana** (25cm) orange-red, likes well-drained soil, short lived but seeds itself. **P. japonica** (40cm) covers a multitude of sins, as it has crossed with lots of its relatives, giving rise to a huge colour range; some selected forms include **'Alba'** white, **'Appleblossom'** ⚜ pale pink buds open white, **'Millers Crimson'** ⚜ deep red, **'Inverewe'** ⚜ a sterile hybrid with striking orange-red flowers, named after the famous Scottish garden, **'Postford White'** ⚜ white with yellow eye, robust. **P. prolifera** (syn. *P. helodoxa*) (40cm) ❄ ⚜ evergreen, fragrant yellow in May–June. **P. pulverulenta** (50–80cm) ⚜ red and pink, May–June/July, very vigorous and easy, good for boggy conditions.

Auriculas

P. auricula (15cm x 15cm+) **H2–3** Fleshy grey-green leaves and eye-catching flowers in a wide range of colours. Most hybrid auriculas are bred for showing and for keeping under cover. In gardens they tend not to be long lived unless they have ideal conditions: they must have full sun and well-drained or gritty not too acid soils. Some of the best include **'Old Red Dusty Miller'** and **'Red Gauntlet'** both red, and **'Osbourne Green'** purple, green edge, white centre.

Primula auricula

Primula vulgaris 'Ken Dearman'

Primula denticulata

Primula japonica and
P. pulverulenta

Petiolaris species and hybrids

H4–5 (10cm x 15–20cm) Though this group of primulas grow better in Scotland than they do further south, recent dry summers have taken their toll and some gardeners have given up attempting to keep them alive. They are moisture-loving connoisseurs' plants with blue, lavender, pink and purple flowers in early spring. Cluny Gardens near Aberfeldy has a fine collection. *P. gracilipes* pink. *P. petiolaris* deep pink. *P. sonchifolia* pale blue. **'Arduaine'** early pale blue.

Other species and hybrids

H4–5 P. alpicola (40cm x 15cm) ❄ ☙ fragrant soft-yellow flowers in May–June; forms include **'Alba'** white and **'Violacea'** purple. *P. chionantha* ❄ (white) and *P. sinopurpurea* (40 x 15cm) ❄ (purple) are two colours of essentially the same species, with scented flowers in early summer, requiring moist but well-drained soil. *P. denticulata* (drumstick primula) *H5* (30cm x 15cm) ☙ an easy-going garden plant with frost-resistant drumstick-like flower heads in March–May, in a range of colours: purple, lavender, pink or white (alba); one of the easiest of all primulas and very tough. *P. florindae* (80cm x 30cm) ❄ ☙ the tallest-growing primula, drooping heads of scented yellow flowers in June–August, likes moist soil and pond margins, spreads and clumps well, easy. *P. poissonii* (50cm x 20cm) crimson-purple with a yellow eye, likes damp soil. *P. rosea* (15cm x 10cm) small, flat rose-pink flowers in spring, requires damp soil. *P. secundiflora* (60cm x 20cm) beautiful crimson-purple drooping flowers on dusty stems in May–July. *P. sieboldii* (20cm x 15cm) ☙ a striking flower, with notched/dissect petals, pink, purple or white with a white eye, in April–May, likes moist but well-drained soil where it will spread; it is worth seeking out named selections such as **'Carefree'** deep pink and **'Snowflake'** pure white. *P. sikkimensis*

Primula sieboldii 'Snowflake'

(30cm x 20cm) ❄ ☙ fragrant bell-shaped light-yellow flowers in May–June. *P. vialii* (25cm x 10cm) ☙ distinctive dense flower heads which change from reddish purple to pink as they age up the stem, easy, but can be short-lived in hot/dry gardens.

Prunella grandiflora (self-heal)

H5 (15cm x 30cm) A useful, semi-evergreen, creeping ground-cover for the front of the border or between shrubs. It has funnel-shaped flowers over a long summer period in shades of pink, purple and white, the short flower spikes appearing above the mats of leaves. It prefers a moist, well-drained soil in sun or shade, and may become invasive in certain situations. Deadhead after flowering to avoid it setting seed, unless you want a large crop of children round about. *P. grandiflora* purple, **'Alba'** white, **'Loveliness'** pale lilac, **'Pink Loveliness'** pink, **'White Loveliness'** white.

Prunella grandiflora 'Loveliness' and 'Alba

Pulmonaria (lungwort)

H5 The lungworts are very effective ground-cover plants, useful for shady sites, and they look particularly good massed beneath trees and shrubs. They form clumps, many have attractively marked leaves and the easily spring flowers come in a wide variety of colours, often blue and red/pink mixed. In our opinion, the pure dark-blue forms are the most effective. Pulmonarias are best grown in moist fertile soils that do not dry out, in sun or shade. Though they are early flowering (March–May), the flowers are pretty frost resistant. The only drawback is that in mid- to late summer they are prone to mildew, which covers the leaves in a greyish-white powder; more unsightly than harmful, it can be controlled with fungicides, or you can just cut back the foliage; the regrowth is usually free of mildew. There are some mildew-resistant cultivars coming on to the market, indicated below. Pulmonarias are fully hardy (**H5**), growing to 20–30cm x 60cm, often spreading further.

'**Apple Frost**' rose pink, mottled silver leaves, some mildew

Pulmonaria 'Munstead Blue' (top) and 'Opal' (bottom)

Pulmonaria, various forms

resistance. *P. angustifolia* blue, leaves unmarked; *P.a.* **subsp.** *azurea* pink to rich blue, bristly leaves; *P.a.* '**Munstead Blue**' reddish violet, turning blue. '**Blue Ensign**' (40cm) vigorous, dark-green leaves, showy dark violet-blue flowers, mildew prone. '**Cotton Cool**' blue fading to pink, silver leaves, mildew resistant. '**Diana Clare**' deep violet-blue and red, silver-mottled foliage. '**Excalibur**' pink to light blue, silver leaves, mildew resistant. '**Lewis Palmer**' (syn. 'Highdown') dark blue, narrow leaves mottled white. *P. longifolia* bright blue, coarse hairy green leaves, splashed silver; *P.l.* '**Ankum**' violet-blue, narrow, very silvery leaves; *P.l.* '**Bertram Anderson**' blue, narrow, strongly marked leaves, floppy habit. '**Majesté**' an outstanding recent introduction, silver-grey leaves splashed green at the margins, blue and pink flowers. '**Margery Fish**' blue and pink, coarse leaves splashed silver, some mildew resistance. '**Milky Way**' (syn. 'Milchstrasse') blue-pink, silver leaves, mildew resistant. '**Moonstone**' white to pale blue, spotted leaves, mildew resistant. *P. officinalis* flowers pink, turning violet-blue, leaves heart shaped; forms include: '**Blue Mist**' clear pale blue, leaves heavily spotted, **Cambridge Blue (Group)** pale blue, buds reddish. **Opal** ['Ocupol'] (30cm x 30cm) pale blue, fading to white, silver-mottled leaves. *P. rubra* '**Bowles' Red**' coral red; *P.r.* '**David Ward**' red, hairy grey-green leaves splashed cream, lacking in vigour, no longer recommended; *P.r.* '**Redstart**' unmarked leaves, brick-red flowers. '**Roy Davidson**' pink, turning blue, spotted leaves, mildew resistant. *P. saccharata* (30cm x 60cm) white spotted leaves, flowers reddish pink turning blue, forms include: **Argentea Group** leaves almost entirely silver, bright-blue flowers; *P.s.* '**Dora Bielefeld**' early flowering, pink turning violet, leaves with silver spotting; *P.s.* '**Leopard**' rose pink, grey-green leaves with silver spots; *P.s.* '**Mrs Moon**' pink, mauve and blue flowers, green leaves spotted silver, mildew prone; *P.s.* '**Pink Dawn**' pink, ageing to violet, spotted leaves. '**Sissinghurst**

White' ✹ white, leaves spotted silver, mildew prone and rather a weak grower.

Pulsatilla vulgaris (wind or pasque flower)

H5 (15–25cm x 15–25cm) ✹ An English (but not Scottish)

Pulsatilla vulgaris (RC-M)

native, this exquisite but tough spring flower has attractive feathery foliage and large, nodding, cup-shaped flowers with yellow stamens in the centre that gradually open from buds covered with silky hairs. Plants flower from March–May in a range of violet-blue, white and red shades, and the silky seed heads that follow are also attractive, particularly with dewdrops on them, or after rain. They form low-growing clumps, and need full sun and a very well-drained but not too acid soil. They sometimes rot in wet winters but otherwise are tough and maintenance free once established. The commonest forms are violet-blue; other selected forms include **var. *rubra*** red, **var. 'Alba'** ✹ white, less vigorous, **subsp. *grandis* 'Papageno'** semi-double white, pink, lavender or red, leaves very silky and dissected, '**Röde Klokke**' deep red.

Ranunculus (buttercup)

Our common buttercup, *R. acris*, is one of 250 species of *Ranunculus*. Many are too invasive for the average garden, and some of the more attractive species are too tender for most of Scotland. The hardy ranunculus grow well in any reasonably moist soil, in sun or shade. The clump-forming, taller varieties need staking and many are best divided regularly to maintain vigour.

Ranunculus ficaria 'Brazen Hussy' and *R. aconitifolius* 'Flore Pleno'

R. acris '**Flore Pleno**' **H5** (60cm x 60cm) an attractive double form of our native buttercup, for the border or naturalised in a wild garden. *R. aconitifolius* '**Flore Pleno**' (white bachelor's buttons) **H5** (60–75cm x 50cm) ✹ branched stems of double pure-white button-like flowers, mounds of deep-green attractively cut leaves. *R. ficaria* **H5** (5cm x the entire garden) our beautiful native lesser celandine, a cheery soul but to be treated with caution because it spreads everywhere and is virtually impossible to eradicate. It is better to plant some of the many, usually less vigorous, garden forms, which are easier to control as long as they don't seed everywhere: **'Brazen Hussy'** (5cm x 20cm) big name for a colourful character – mats of chocolate heart-shaped leaves, sulphur-yellow flowers in early spring, attractive planted beneath shrubs with spring bulbs; var. *albus* (5cm x 20cm) variable white-flowered forms. *R. gramineus* *H5* (30–40cm x 10cm) brilliant yellow buttercups in loose sprays in June–July, blue-green foliage, well-behaved, a good border plant. *R. montanus* **'Molten Gold'** *H5* (15cm x 10cm) a good rock garden plant for a sunny position, compact clumps, shiny bright golden-yellow flowers in early summer, slugs love it.

Rheum palmatum (foliage)

Rheum (rhubarb)
H5 Rhubarbs are fine, large architectural plants, with bold jagged-edged leaves, making handsome specimens or structural border plants. Only *R. x hybridum* is normally considered edible; the other varieties are purely ornamental and can cause serious indigestion. They prefer moist well-drained soil, in full sun and shelter, and will tolerate part shade. Rheums tolerate colder conditions than the visually similar *Gunnera manicata* and so are useful for a 'big foliage' statement for the border in cold inland gardens. The flower panicles rise above the foliage in April–June. They can become untidy in late summer, with wind-broken stems and sunburn. Tidy up in late autumn. Heights and spreads are similar.

'Ace of Hearts' (1.5m) relatively compact, suitable for smaller gardens, dark-green heart-shaped leaves, veined crimson and purple on the reverse, soft-pink flowers. *R. x hybridum* (rhubarb) (1–2m) the edible rhubarb, introduced to Scotland by Royal Botanic Garden Edinburgh's first Regius Keeper, Dr John Hope, in around 1760. As well as its use in pies and crumbles, it makes a striking flowering and foliage plant for the back of a large border. Forms include **'Timperly Early'** the most commonly grown variety, can be forced, **'Strawberry Red'** for cropping from mid-summer onwards, **'Valentine'** rich-red stems, seldom runs to seed. The RHS trials at Wisley grow over 100 varieties and Kellie castle in Fife has a good collection. *R. palmatum* (2m) panicles of creamy-white flowers, leaves to 60cm x 60cm, unfurling from red buds; *R.p.* **'Atrosanguineum'** ♥ red flower panicles, young leaves deep blood-red in spring, gradually mellowing through the season, fine dramatic plant; var. *tanguticum* deeply cut leaves.

Rhodohypoxis
H3–4 These pretty little South African tuberous perennials flower over a long period (May–August) in shades of red, pink or white. They have thin, hairy bulb-like foliage, and are very cold hardy, but we are suggesting an *H3–4* rating because they have particular cultural requirements: moist in summer, dry in winter, and this is easier said than done in Scotland. For best results, plant them in well-drained soil in a rock garden, trough or raised bed, in full sun, and protect with a gravel mulch or a cloche in winter. Alternatively, grow them in containers, which can be plunged in the garden in summer and in winter moved into cold frames or greenhouses, where they should be allowed to dry out. They tend to do better on the east side of the country, and nearer the coast can be grown unprotected with a gravel topdressing. Edrom Nurseries near Berwick probably have Scotland's widest selection.

R. baurii (10cm x 5cm) ♥ red, pale-pink or white flowers over a long period; *R.b.* var. *platypetala* white with a pale-pink base. *R. baurii* has spawned many cultivars: **'Albrighton'** deep pink, **'Appleblossom'** white, pink buds, **'Alba'** pure white, **'Dawn'** blush pink, **'Fred Broome'** bright pink, **'Great Scott'** bright carmine, **'Picta'** white, tipped pink, **'Stella'** deep pink. *R. deflexa* (5cm x 5cm) is the smallest of the tribe, bright-red flowers; forms include **'Douglas'** deep red, **'Eva Kate'** deep pink, **'Fred Broome'** shell pink. *R. x milloides* (20cm x 15cm) red to magenta, erect habit, taller than the other species.

Rhodohypoxis baurii
(mixed colours)

Rodgersia
H4–5 These dramatic foliage plants with chestnut-like leaves and frothy masses of tiny pink or white flowers in June, July or August are great for growing in woodland and beside water. They like moist, even boggy conditions, and will grow in full sun or part shade, as long as the soil does not dry out. The large handsome leaves survive best with shelter from strong winds and can be disfigured by late frosts, but otherwise rodgersia are easy-going, forming clumps that gradually spread to 1m or more. Unlike hostas and ligularias, with which they are often planted, slugs and snails are less partial to rodgersia leaves, except as they emerge in spring. Most can have good autumn colours before the leaves drop. The various species and varieties differ in minor details and are often mixed up in the trade, but all are good.

R. aesculifolia (1–2m x 1m) ♥ wide, crinkled, bronzed leaves,

Rodgersia pinnata 'Superba'

creamy-white to pink flowers in tall spikes. *R. pinnata* (1m x 1m) finely cut, serrated, bronzed leaves, creamy-white flower spikes; *R.p. 'Elegans'* ♟ cream tinged pink; *R.p. 'Superba'* ♟ very long-lasting pink flower heads deepening as they age, fine bronzy foliage, not very vigorous; beware of imposters around under this name. *R. podophylla* (1m x 1m) ♟ said to be the hardiest species for Scotland, creamy-white flowers, leaves bronze in spring, fading to green through summer, coppery red in autumn; *R. sambucifolia* (1m x 1m) veined leaves, up to 60cm long, white-pink flowers in June–July.

Romneya coulteri
(Californian tree poppy)
H3 (1–2m x 1–2m) This is a spectacular plant with large white flowers (up to 15cm across), with a mass of yellow stamens, in July; the jagged foliage is bluish grey. In all but the mildest gardens it dies back to near ground level each year. It spreads by suckers and can eventually form a large colony. Traditionally not considered reliably hardy, especially as a young plant, but with good drainage it is long lasting on the terraces at Drummond Castle near Crieff and it is also fine at Kinross House, Glendoick and Cambo in Fife. You may have to search for one to buy, as it is not readily available. Be careful not to damage the roots when planting and don't try to move it, as it will probably kill it. **'White Cloud'** is a fine vigorous selection with particularly glaucous foliage and large flowers.

Romneya coulteri

Roscoea
Related to ginger, roscoeas have exotic, orchid-like flowers in spring and summer. Most have ribbed or veined leaves and like moist soil in part day sun. They grow well in the rock gardens at Threave and the Royal Botanic Garden Edinburgh. Don't be surprised if it does not emerge till very late in the spring.

Roscoea cautleyoides 'Grandiflora'

R. auriculata H4 (30–40cm x 10cm) rich purple. **'Beesiana'** *H3–4*

(35–45cm x 10cm) creamy white, tinged purple as they age. *R. cautleyoides H4* (30–50 x 15cm) ♟ creamy yellow. *R. purpurea H3–4* (30cm x 15cm) rich purple. *R. scillifolia H2–3* (10–25cm x 10cm) pink or purple flowers, strap-like leaves; a purple, almost black form is known as **dark form**.

Rudbeckia see Daisies, page 171

Salvia (sage)
H1/2–5 Salvias, which include the herb sage (*S. officinalis*), are a useful and varied genus of perennials, forming clumps of hairy and often aromatic leaves, and producing two-lipped flowers in panicles up the stems. They are a magnet for bees, and their drought resistance is making them more and more important in the south-east of England. Salvias come from a hot and dry climate, and in the right conditions make excellent garden plants for Scotland, but many varieties are tender and intolerant of winter wet, sometimes best treated as annuals in cold gardens. Others are biennials which can be kept going as they seed freely (but often hybridise) or by cuttings, which root very easily. Most salvias need well-drained soil in full sun. Heights and spreads are the same unless stated otherwise.

Tender and biennial varieties
S. argentea H3 (60cm) biennial, with magnificent silver woolly rosettes, clusters of white flowers in summer, resents wet summers and needs gritty soil, does best in the east. *S. forsskaolii H3* (30–40cm) violet-blue, large handsome lobed leaves. *S. guaranitica* **'Blue Enigma'** *H2* (1.5m) fragrant deep-blue flowers, for mildest and coastal gardens only and stems are inclined to snap in wind. *S. lavandulifolia H3–4* (30cm) compact, with violet-blue flowers in summer; Christopher Lloyd recommends this as a culinary herb. *S. microphylla H2–3* (1m) evergreen, crimson, pink or purple flowers in late summer; many named selections: **'Cerro Potosi'** cerise, **Hot Lips** red and white, **'Kew Red'** red, **'Newby Hall'** scarlet. *S. officinalis* (garden sage) *H3–4* (60cm) its green, purple- and variegated-leaved varieties need a warm sheltered spot to thrive; smallish pointed grey-green leaves developing a dusky purple haze with age, lilac flowers, grown mainly for the leaves which can be used in cooking, inclined to die off in winter or early spring; forms include **'Berggarten'** (90cm) taller than the type with bigger and brighter leaves, rarely flowers, usually longer lived, **'Icterina'** pale-green leaves, variegated yellow, **'Purpurascens'** grey-green leaves, purple flushed when young, **'Tricolor'** leaves variegated green, cream and violet-purple. *S. patens H2*

Salvia patens

(45–60cm) for mild gardens or a very sheltered position, exotic deep-blue flowers in July-October, fine examples at Culzean Castle in Ayrshire; **S.p. 'Cambridge Blue'** pale blue; **S.p. 'White Trophy'** white. **S. sclarea var. turkestanica H5** (1.2m) aromatic oval-shaped hairy leaves, mauve-pink flowers with distinctive green calyces in June–July. A biennial, so dies after flowering, but with any luck will seed itself around, as it does on the terrace at Balcarres in Fife. The leaves smell rather unpleasant, presumably to stop goats eating them. **S. uliginosa H2–3** (1.5m) this is bog sage, which likes wetter soils than the others, bright green, aromatic leaves and clear bright-blue flowers in August-October, as it comes from Brazil and Uruguay, it may need winter protection to survive in Scotland.

Hardy/perennial salvias
H3–4/5 These are the hardiest and probably the most widely planted sages and there are numerous forms. All can be cut back after the first flowering to encourage a second late-summer show. **S. lyrata 'Purple Knockout' H4** (50cm) bronzy maroon foliage, purple-blue flowers all summer. **S. nemorosa H5** (1m) flowering in May–June and sometimes again in late summer; forms include **'Amethyst'** pink with a purple calyx, **'Lubecca'** strong violet-blue, **'Ostfriesland'** (Eastfriesland) ⚜ intense violet-blue; there is also a pink form **'Pink Friesland'**. **S. x superba H5** (90cm) strong violet-blue flowers in summer. **S. pratensis H3–4** (to 90cm) taller than *S. nemorosa*, flowers purple, pink, white, short lived, so better to choose its offspring *S. x sylvestris*; **S.p. 'Indigo'** (45–60cm) deep blue. **S. x sylvestris H4** purple, violet, blue or pink flowers in June–July, includes the forms

Salvia verticillata 'Purple Rain'

'Blauhügel' mid-blue, **'Blaukönigen'** (Blue Queen) (50cm) dark violet, **'Mainacht'** (May Night) (60cm) indigo-violet, May–June, heavily veined leaves, **'Rose Queen' H5** (75cm) bright rose violet, sometimes straggly, **'Viola Klose'** (60cm) deep violet-blue.
S. verticillata H4 (60cm) deep-purple flowers in late summer, inclined to self-seed; forms include **'Alba'** (60cm) a fine white, **'Purple Rain'** purple, very free flowering.

Sanguinaria canadensis (bloodroot)
H5 (10cm x 15cm) A fleeting beauty, with pure white flowers that open in April and last for only a few days, before the bold leaves appear. This is a useful slow-spreading woodland plant, ideal for growing between rhododendrons, as it likes similar moist acid soil. Usually sold as the double form **f. multiplex** (syn. 'Plena') ⚜.

Sanguinaria canadensis f. multiplex

Sanguisorba see Filipendula, page 184

Saponaria see Lychnis, page 206

Sarracenia flava see Insectivorous plants, page 199

Saxifraga (saxifrage)
This is a huge genus of low-growing, mostly evergreen, rosette-forming plants, with stiff, fleshy or softly hairy leaves. They normally produce a mass of small flowers on long stems, and they provide some of the best subjects for the rock garden, as well as useful border and woodland edgers. They are tough plants but not always the easiest to please, prone to rotting in wet soils and suffering sunburn in hot dry summers. They are good subjects for troughs, and wall crevices, and best mulched with lime chippings or similar to keep the roots cool and moist and to lessen the chance of rotting. The list of varieties below is just the tip of the iceberg: the website www.saxifraga.org will give you some idea of how many species and hybrids are available. Scotland has eleven native species, which you can find on mountains and sea cliffs. We are grateful to experts Beryl Bland and Fred Carrie for assistance with this section.

Silver saxifrages
H4–5 (5cm x 20cm, flowering stems to 60cm) Rosettes of evergreen silvery foliage, which die after flowering, and arching sprays of mostly white flowers. Offsets should survive, though they may need to be lifted and replanted. They require neutral–limy soil, and tolerate dry sites.

Saxifraga 'Southside Seedling'

These are very hardy, and quite easy provided drainage is good (use a gritty planting mixture). **S. cochlearis** tiny, with silvery rosettes, flowers on reddish stems. **S. paniculata** (syn. *S. aizoon*) fine white flowers, one of the easiest of this group; forms include **'Rosea'** (pink), **'Lutea'** (yellow). **'Southside Seedling'** ⚜ dramatic sprays of white

Saxifraga oppositifolia

flowers with red spotting. **'Tumbling Waters'** ⚜ slow growing, mats of foliage, arching sprays of slightly scented white flowers, needs skill to grow well. **'Whitehill'** white, spikes to 15cm, leaves with red colouration at petiole.

Cushion and purple saxifages
H5 (5–10cm x 10–30cm, flowers to 15cm) Early flowering, often grown in cold frames and containers, good for screes, troughs and rock gardens, and can be planted in tufa; all may burn in hot summers in the open. **'Gregor Mendel'** (syn. *S. x apiculata*) (15cm x 30cm) primrose yellow in early spring, tight green cushions. **'Jenkinsiae'** (*S. x irvingii*) lilac pink. *S. oppositifolia* ✕ a prostrate alpine found on Scottish

Saxifraga, mossy, several colour forms

mountains, does best in full sun, with white-flecked leaves and rosy-purple flowers in early spring, needs an alpine (that is, cold) climate to flower. Does best in high-up inland gardens, and appreciates a mulch with lime chips.

Mossy saxifages
H5 (10–15cm x 10–30cm) Spongy hummocks of soft foliage, masses of white, pink or red flowers, in March/April–May/June, liable to burn in hot sun, so best in part day shade. The hot summer of 2006 was a challenge for them in Scotland. **'Cloth of Gold'** white flowers, bright-yellow foliage, vulnerable to sunburn. **'Maréshal Joffre'** deep red. **'Peter Pan'** pink, foliage somewhat resistant to sunburn. **'Pixie'** slow, pinkish red. **'Silver Cushion'** pale pink, variegated leaves. **'Triumph'** crimson. **'White Pixie'** pure white.

Larger-growing species and varieties
S. cuneifolia H4–5 (20cm x 30cm) spoon- or wedge-shaped green leaves with purple undersides, flowers white, sometimes with red or yellow markings, in April–June. *S. fortunei H3–4* (20–30cm x 30cm) ⚜ a handsome evergreen for mild woodland gardens in peaty soil, white or pink star-like flowers in autumn; watch out for root weevils; named forms, with very variable handsome leaves, include **'Black Ruby'** dark almost-black leaves, deep pink-red flowers, a little tricky, **'Cheap Confections'** small scalloped leaves, pink

flowers, **'Cherry Pie'** purple-red, **'Mount Nachi'** smaller reddish leaves, white flowers, **'Wada'** bronzy-red leaves and stems, white flowers. *S. stolonifera H3* a tender species, usually grown indoors or in a cold frame, white flowers in summer, spreads by runners. *S. x urbium* (London pride) *H5* (30cm x as far as you let it) spreading but not invasive, a good plant for edging borders and paths, tolerant of shade, probably the easiest saxifrage to grow, forming carpeting rosettes of evergreen leathery green leaves, with sprays of tiny pink-flushed white flowers in summer; **'Aureopunctata'** yellow-green variegated foliage.

Scabiosa and *Knautia macedonica*
H3–4 The relaxing, ethereal pale blue and mauve flowers of *S. columbaria*, the native scabious, are a delight in summer, and the garden varieties have kept much of their wild cousin's charm. They form small to medium-sized mounds of foliage. The flowers, which resemble pincushions, have a mass of central stamens, which are popular for cutting. They are easy to grow in well-drained soil in a sunny position, but won't tolerate heavy or clay soil and they may benefit from a sprinkling of lime on acid soil. The taller ones may need staking in windy positions and dividing every 3–4 few years, particularly *S. caucasica*. They are best considered short-lived and they often flower themselves to death. Both scabious and knautia can

Scabiosa 'Chile Black'

Scabiosa 'Pink Mist' and 'Butterfly Blue'

flower over a long period from June to early autumn if deadheaded. Botanists don't always agree where scabious ends and knautia begins.

S. atropurpurea (75cm x 45cm) short-lived perennial or biennial, usually grown in selected forms: **'Burgundy Bonnets'** purple-red with white stamens, **'Chile Black'** maroon, June-October, toothed leaves. **'Butterfly Blue'** masses of small pale-blue flowers, over a long period, dark green toothed leaves. **'Butterfly Pink'** the pink version. *S. caucasica H5* (60cm x 60cm) lavender, blue or white, lance-shaped leaves, does best in an alkaline soil; varieties include **'Clive Greaves'** ⚜ lavender blue, **'Miss Willmott'** large ivory-white, **Perfecta Series** lilac blue, **'Perfecta Alba'** white, **'Stäfa'** deep blue. *S. lucida* (20 x 15cm) a fine front-of-the-border plant, with lilac to mauve flowers. **Pink Mist** [PBR] (30cm x 20cm) pink, dark-green leaves.

Knautia macedonica (syn. *Scabiosa rumelica*) H3–4
(75cm x 60cm) Closely related to and resembling scabious with double bright-crimson flowers on curving stems in summer, held above deeply divided leaves. It likes well-drained soil in full sun and can seed around. **'Mars Midget'** (40cm) dwarf form, **'Melton Pastels'** (1m+) pink, salmon red shades.

Schizostylis coccinea (syn. *Hesperantha*)
(Kaffir lily) and *Watsonia*
H3–4 (60cm x 30cm+) Suffering a recent name change from Schizostylis to Hesperantha, the soft green grassy leaves and red, pink and white autumn flowers – resembling mini gladioli – make the small South African Kaffir lilies invaluable for late season colour at the front of the border. They like a rich, moist, well-drained soil in a sheltered spot in full sun, and will not tolerate drought. They are gross feeders, which means that they quickly use up all the available nutrients, and for this reason they should be lifted, divided and replanted every few years, with an ample supply of well-rotted organic matter. As with daffodils, when they become a mass of leaves with few flowers, it's time to replant. They happily spread in the right conditions, and the flowers are excellent for cutting. Though they can be killed in cold winters, they are worth risking in colder areas in a sheltered spot.

Schizostylus coccinea 'Major' and 'Jennifer'

The single species *S. coccinea* is normally scarlet, but many colour selections have been made: f. *alba* white, **'Major'** ⚜ large, crimson, **'Fenland Daybreak'** pink, can flower as late as December, **'Jennifer'** ⚜ and **'Maiden's Blush'** soft pink, **'November Cheer'** deep pink, can last until December, **'Professor Barnard'** dusky red, **'Sunrise'** vigorous pink.

Watsonia H3 (60cm–1.2m) Another striking but less well-known South African plant, now finding its way into Scottish gardens. It has clumps of sword-like leaves and star-shaped flowers on long stems. It's less hardy than schizostylis, needing sharp drainage and full sun – they are very fine at RBG Logan in Dumfries and Galloway and do well in a sheltered site at Glendoick. *W. borbonica* pink,

and *W. pillansii* orange-red, are the mostly widely available species.

Sedum (stonecrop)
and *Chiastophyllum oppositifolium*
H4–5 Sedum is a huge genus of succulents that contains some superb garden plants, suitable for a variety of garden situations from herbaceous borders to rock

Sedum aizoon

gardens, pots and even on the roof. Sedums form clumps or spreading mats of fleshy foliage, and prefer a sunny site in well-drained soil. They are drought tolerant and can rot in heavy soils. Some are evergreen, while others die down for the winter. Autumn-flowering *S. spectabile* forms and hybrids (listed separately below) may need dividing if they get congested. All those listed below are
H4–5 with sharp drainage, and spread 30–45cm: individual measurements given are for height.

S. aizoon **'Euphorbioides'** (syn. *S.a.* 'Aurantiacum') (30cm) yellow flower heads on red stems in summer, bronze-tinted leaves. *S.* **'Bertram Anderson'** (20cm) star-shaped blood-red summer flowers, attractive purple-grey foliage. *S. ewersii* (15cm) a useful late-summer alpine, rose pink, flowering in August–September. *S.*

Sedum spectabile

kamtschaticum (20cm) yellow star-shaped flowers in late summer. **'Weihenstephaner Gold'** (15cm) spreading grey-leaved succulent with golden yellow flowers in summer. *S. spurium* **H4–5** (10cm x 50cm+) five-petalled pink flowers in July–August, semi-evergreen; there are forms with purple and variegated leaves. *S. spathulifolium* **'Cape Blanco'** (5cm x as far as you let it) ⚜ spreading grey succulent rosettes, clusters of tiny yellow flowers in summer, a rock garden gem, pretty between paving slabs, tolerant of some shade; **'Purpureum'** ⚜ yellow flowers, reddish purple leaves.

Autumn-flowering herbaceous varieties
H4–5 *S. spectabile* and its many relatives and hybrids provide some of the most reliable late-summer colour and the flowers are invariably smothered in feeding

butterflies. There are now a bewildering number of named forms, many of which have coloured foliage; some foliage is almost black. The naming of many cultivars in commerce is confused and many just don't seem to have the flower colour which they are supposed to; some may have been unstable sports which reverted to type. Do not over-feed autumn-flowering sedums, as it tends to encourage weak growth, with plants splaying out, leaving an empty centre. In rich soil it is worth cutting back young growth in late May to encourage bushiness. In wet summers they can suffer from mildew on the leaves. Heights and spreads are similar.

S. erythrostictum 'Frosty Morn' (45cm) pale pink from white buds, August–October, pale-green leaves with a white edge. *S. spectabile* (20–50cm) ♡ oval blue-green leaves, flowers reddish, pink or white in August–October, dies back to the ground in mid-winter; forms include 'Black Jack' pale pink to white, dark black-green leaves, straggly and prone to mildew, 'Brilliant' pink, 'Gooseberry Fool' (50cm) pale-green flowers and green leaves, 'Herbstfreude' or 'Autumn Joy' ♡ one of the most popular, salmon pink, ageing to rusty red, leaves grey-green, will do well in clay soil, 'Iceberg' (60cm) white, 'Joyce Henderson' pink, leaves turn purple-brown at flowering time, 'Purple Emperor' dark-purple leaves and stems, flowers purple-pink, 'Ruby Glow' rose crimson, low, 'Stardust' a lower-growing selection, pale pink fading to white, pale-green leaves, 'Vera Jameson' (25cm) deep-purple foliage which deepens as the season progresses, pink flowers, a good low selection. *S. telephium* (30–50cm) ✉ often a little more sprawling than *S. spectabile*, so best with a good prune in late May, to attain a more robust habit; forms include 'Matrona' (45cm) red, blue-grey red-tinged leaves, 'Munstead Red' (30cm) red stems, pinkish purple-red flowers, inclined to fall over, *S.t. subsp. ruprechtii* (45cm) creamy yellow, leaves bronze-coloured.

Chiastophyllum oppositifolium H4 (15–20cm x 15cm) Related to sedum, with oval-toothed fleshy-green leaves and masses of small yellow flowers in arching sprays with dropping tips in summer. A useful alpine, ideal for crevices between rocks or in a stone wall. 'Jim's Pride' (syn. 'Frosted Jade') leaves boldly margined creamy white, flowers paler than the type.

Sempervivum
(houseleek, hens and chickens)
H2/3–4/5 These are fascinating, prehistoric-looking plants, forming low rosettes of succulent leaves in a variety of colours from yellow to green, reddish to almost black. Most of the commonly sold varieties are

Sempervivums (RC-M)

almost indestructible, thriving on neglect. They are tough and easy to grow, and especially suitable for rockeries, alpine gardens, troughs and pots. Flowering rosettes (usually a few each summer) die after flowering but are soon replaced by offsets. You can fill the gaps with gritty soil to help them fill in. Winter wet can cause terminal rot, and for this reason many people grow houseleeks in an alpine house or under a protective pain of glass. Keep a watchful eye out for aphid attacks and occasional mealy bugs.

S. arachnoideum H2–3 (foliage 2.5cm x 20cm) the cobweb houseleek is so named because of the hairs that criss-cross the leaf tips, and it needs protection in winter (cover with a pane of glass or put in a cold frame); **subsp. *tomentosum*** has the heaviest cobwebs. *S. tectorum H5* (7cm x 30cm) most garden varieties are selections and hybrids of this species. There are over 400 varieties listed in the *RHS Plantfinder*, with huge variations in foliage colour. Flower spikes can be up to 50cm tall and the flowers are usually pink, though some varieties are yellow. Some of the most commonly available varieties include 'Alpha' leaves green and crimson with hairy tips; 'Bloodtip' leaves green and crimson; *S. giuseppe* green, with brown leaf

Malva moschata f. alba   Sidalcea malviflora 'Croftway Red' and 'Loveliness'

tips; 'King George' leaves maroon in summer; 'Rosie' green, flushed pink; 'Royal Ruby' deep red; 'Rubin' red.

Sidalcea (prairie mallow) and *Malva* (mallow)
H3–4 Sidalceas are low to medium-sized clump-forming perennials with masses of flowers, like miniature hollyhocks, over many weeks in July–August. They like full sun and open well-drained soil; they are short lived in heavy soils. Spread approximately 45cm.

S. candida H4 (30–80cm) white-cream. *S. malviflora* pink or purple; forms and hybrids include 'Croftway Red' (80cm) deep reddish-pink, 'Elsie Heugh' (80cm) pale pink, fringed petals, 'Loveliness' (75cm) pale pink, compact, 'Mrs Borrodaile' (1m) crimson-purple, 'Party Girl' (90cm) deep pink with a white centre, 'William Smith' (1m) salmon pink.

Malva Mallows, some of which are found wild in Scotland,

can be short lived but they make up for this in their exuberant flowering. The saucer-shaped flowers are produced from August to September on low to medium-sized mounds. They prefer well-drained soils in sunny spots, and will grow in areas of low fertility, where they will seed themselves. They struggle to survive winters in heavy/wet soils. They spread 60cm or more. Apparently on sea cliffs they can cause problems for nesting puffins, when a forest of seedlings block burrow entrances. **M. alcea** var. **fastigiata** (90cm) rose pink, deeply lobed leaves. **M. moschata** (60cm) ✉ very pretty rose pink, often naturalises on sunny banks; **f. alba** (60cm) white. **M. sylvestris H3–4** (1.2m) ✉ a biennial with pink flowers, prone to rust; **subsp. mauritiana** magenta-purple with deeper veins, **'Primley Blue'** veined purple-blue, spreading habit.

Silene see *Lychnis*, page 206

Silybum marianum see Thistles, page 229

Sisyrinchium (blue-eyed grass)
and *Libertia*
H2–5 Looking like a cross between a grass and an iris, sisyrinchiums make valuable additions for the border or

Sisyrinchium striatum

rock garden. Clump formers of variable hardiness, with fans of grass-like leaves, they prefer full sun or light shade, in well-drained soil that never dries out. They flower in spring and summer. The outer leaves tend to turn black in cold and inland Scottish gardens, but these can be removed in spring. A few of the small-flowered species can self-seed everywhere, becoming a nuisance, so it won't do any harm to deadhead after flowering to prevent this. Height and spread are similar.

S. angustifolium H5 (25cm) dense tufts of dark-green leaves, lilac-blue flowers in May–June; once you've got this plant it'll never leave. **S. californicum H2–3** (60cm) bright-yellow flowers in May–August, prolific seeders; **Brachypus Group** (12–15cm) includes the lowest-growing forms. **S. idahoense 'Album' H3** (15cm) white flowers, a gem for coastal rockeries; **S.i. var. bellum** yellow-throated violet-blue flowers. **S. striatum H3–4** (80cm) narrow leaves and cream/light-yellow flowers all summer, can spread widely, forming large clumps. The commonest form is **'Aunt May' H3** (syn. 'Variegatum') (50cm) less vigorous than the

Libertia peregrinans

type, with cream-striped leaves. Other cultivars: **'Blue Ice' H3** (20cm) sky blue, **'Californian Skies' H2** (15cm) one of the prettiest, but not always easy to please, large lilac-blue flowers in May–June, dies back completely after flowering, **'Devon Skies' H3** (15cm) pale blue, yellow centre with dark blue surround, **'E.K. Balls' H3** (20cm) large mauve flowers May–June; two of the oddest are **'Biscutella' H3** (20cm) brown and cream, **'Quaint and Queer' H3** (40cm) creamy yellow, brown and purple.

Libertia H2–3 These are closely related plants from Australasia and Chile, which do well in mild and/or coastal gardens as far north as Orkney and Sheltland. They form thick clumps of evergreen grassy leaves (approximately 60cm spread), sending up a mass of small white or pale-blue flowers in May-June. They need well-drained soil in a sunny site and they can look scruffy with dead leaves, which need pulling off in spring. Height and spread is similar. **L. caerulescens** (60cm) pale blue. **L. formosa** (1m) pure white. **L. grandiflora** (1m) white. **L. peregrinans** (60cm) white, leaves turn orange in sun.

Smilacina see Maianthemum, page 208

Solidago (golden rod)
and x *Solidaster luteus*
H5 The golden rod is one of those seemingly indestructible plants, producing clumps of wiry green foliage and frothy yellow flower heads in summer and autumn. Some varieties can be thugs in the border,

Solidago 'Goldkind'

swamping more sensitive neighbours. They grow well in sun or part shade, in any reasonable soil except a waterlogged one. Many garden designers decry its vulgarity, and it was long out of fashion, but the spectacular late summer yellow flowers seem to be coming back into vogue. Solidagos blend well with grasses, anemones and other late summer/early autumn performers and are good flowers for drying. They can suffer from mildew, especially in large, over-crowded clumps. They will spread 60cm–1m or more.

'Cloth of Gold' (40cm) compact, deep yellow. 'Crown of Rays' (syn. 'Strahlenkrone') (60cm) yellow flower heads in July–August. *S. cutleri* 'Robusta' (30cm) a useful rock garden plant, provides late-season colour with yellow flower heads in September. 'Goldenmosa' (75cm+) sprays of tufted golden yellow in August–September. 'Goldkind' (Golden Baby) (60cm) fluffy golden yellow, August–September. *S. flexicaulis* 'Variegata' (60cm) leaves with yellow and brown markings in spring, fading in summer, yellow flowers in August–September. *S. sphacelata* 'Golden Fleece' (45cm) golden yellow plumes in late summer.

x *Solidaster luteus* (syn. x *S. hybridus*) H5 (60cm x 75cm) A hybrid of solidago and aster, with masses of tiny long-lasting pale-yellow flowers with deeper centres, in July–September, on wiry stems. Less vigorous than solidago, with a floppy habit and prone to mildew. 'Lemore' lemon yellow.

x *Solidaster luteus* see above

Stachys
H5 Referred to widely in Scotland as 'lamb's lugs', which describes pretty well the soft, grey, furry leaves of *S. byzantina*, it was once used a protection against witchcraft. These tough and easy spreaders make very effective front-of-border plants, providing a foil for other colours, provided you don't let them flower, because the blooms are one of the brightest most garish magentas in nature. Not all stachys have furry leaves.

Stachys byzantina (syn. *S. lanata*)

S. byzantina (syn. *S. lanata*) (50cm x 50cm+) mats of soft, hairy silver leaves, small magenta flowers in June–August, attractive to butterflies, useful for edging borders or as ground-cover under open shrubs such as roses, needs well-drained soil in full sun, and can suffer from black leaf spot and mildew, less in Scotland than further south; *S.b.* 'Silver Carpet' (30cm x 45cm) is a popular non-flowering form. *S. macrantha* (60cm x 25cm) ⚜ mauve flowers in May–July above scalloped crinkled green leaves, resembles mint and enjoys moist soil, will grow in shade; forms include 'Robusta' a large and vigorous selection, 'Superba' larger, deep-coloured flowers. Most other stachys dislike winter wet so need to be grown in a cold greenhouse or frame.

Stokesia laevis see Centaurea, page 168

Symphytum (comfrey)
H5 ⚜ The comfreys are coarse-leaved spreading

perennials, which, once established, can be incredibly difficult to get rid of. They are also, however, attractive, large-leaved plants, which produce loose clusters of late spring and summer flowers. They are useful for woodland

Symphytum officinale

ground cover and for wild and awkward areas of the garden – symphytum is one of the few summer-flowering plants suitable for dry shade beneath hungry trees. Those listed below reach 50 x 60cm+ unless stated otherwise. All parts of the plants can cause indigestion if eaten and foliage may irritate skin. Two Scottish native species are *S. officinale* and *S. tuberosum*.

S. caucasicum blue flowers, can be invasive; selected form 'Eminence' less invasive, with deeper flowers. 'Goldsmith' (30cm x 30cm) leaves splashed gold and cream, less invasive than most, flowers cream with pink or blue flushing. *S. ibericum* somewhat insipid cream flowers opening from reddish buds; 'Hidcote Blue' a form with attractive two-tone blue flowers. 'Lambrook Sunrise', yellow leaves, pale-blue, tubular flowers. *S. officinale* (1–1.5m x 1.5m+) ✉ purple-pink or pale-yellow flowers, invasive, hard to get rid of once you have it. *S. tuberosum* ✉ pale yellow, a wild Scottish native, not really suited to the garden. *S. x uplandicum* 'Variegatum' a useful foliage plant with cream-margined leaves and pale-lilac pink flowers, but beware of vigorous reverted patches (green-leaved), which may take over the garden.

Tanacetum coccineum see Daisies, page 171

Telekia speciosa see Daisies, page 171

Thalictrum (meadow rue)
Very popular these days with style gurus and garden designers, these useful and tough medium-sized

Thalictrum delavayi and *T.d.* 'Album'

herbaceous perennials have a mass of tiny flowers packed into fluffy flower heads and held above the attractive divided foliage. Most are happy in full or part day sun in a moist but well-drained soil; they don't need dividing and resent being moved. They are also fine in woodland and have a long flowering season, spreading up to 60cm unless stated otherwise.

Thalictrum flavum

T. aquilegiifolium H5 (1m x 45cm) fluffy rosy-lilac flowers on strong stems, May-July, grey-green finely divided leaves; **var. *album*** the white form, **'Thundercloud'** pinkish-purple, with darker stamens. *T. delavayi H4/5* (1m x 45cm) sprays of mauve flowers with creamy-yellow stamens June-September, finely divided grey-green leaves; *T.d. var. decorum* particularly fine, *T.d.* **'Hewitt's Double'** ❦ very attractive, long-lasting double mauve flowers on thin stems in June-August, ferny leaves, best staked, needs rich soil, *T.d.* **'Album'** a fine white form. *T. diffusiflorum H4* (90 x 45cm) clematis-like lilac-purple flowers are much larger than any of the others, but not always easy to establish (though Scotland suits it) and tends to be short lived. *T. flavum* subsp. *glaucum H4* (1.2m x 1m) ❈ masses of fragrant yellow fluffy flowers, July-August, fine bluish-green divided leaves, thick stems, coarser and more vigorous than the others, best at the back of a border, **'Illuminator'** yellow young growth, mature leaves green.

Thistles

Not everyone agrees on why the thistle has become our national flower; legend has it that an enemy gave himself away by standing on one. You may well find thistles growing annoyingly well in your garden, with no effort on your part. Millions of fluffy light seeds can be blown into your garden from just a handful of thistles in a farmer's field. The ones listed here are bit more refined and less troublesome than the weeds. Most are short lived or biennial, so if they don't self-seed you will need to replace them from time to time.

Cirsium rivulare 'Atropurpureum'

Cirsium (plume thistle) H5 The genus *Cirsium* contains a few fine, dramatic garden plants, as well as some of the most annoying and impossible-to-get-rid-of weeds. *C. rivulare* (1.2m x 60cm) deep-pink thistle-like flowers, usually sold in the deep crimson form **'Atropurpureum'** fairly short lived, but normally seeding freely, sun or part shade in almost any soil, bar boggy.

Cynara cardunculus (cardoon) H4–5 (2–3m x 1.5m) ❦ Big in every respect, this statuesque thistle plant is now back

in vogue, and makes a great specimen and back-of-the-border plant. The large silvery foliage and artichoke-like flower buds open to large purple thistles, which attract bees. The flower heads last into winter or can be dried and used in flower arrangements. You can eat the stems as a celery-like vegetable, and the seed heads are as big as sporrans (you don't eat these, even when starving). Prefers full sun and a sheltered spot in well-drained soil. Protect young plants with a mulch in the first few years.

Onopordum (RC-M)

Onopordum (cotton or scotch thistle) H5 Gardening writer Sarah Raven raves about *O. acanthium*: 'The most architectural and statuesque plant I grow, it makes a superb natural wind-break if you live in a windy spot.' To withstand Scottish gales, however, we recommend planting this with a few supporting shrubs. You probably don't need reminding that it has pinkish-purple flowers in summer with a circle of spines at the base of the flower and on the leaves. It can reach over 2m in height and 1.2m in spread. *O. nervosum* ❦ from Spain and Portugal can reach 2.5m and has pink or purple flower heads. Both are biennial, so you'll need to sow seeds or buy new plants if it does not seed itself in your garden.

Silybum marianum (Our Lady's milk thistle) H4 (1.5m x 1m) With a Latin name designed to make children giggle, this biennial thistle has distinctive white and green marbled leaves and purple flowers in June. It needs a sunny site in well-drained soil.

Thymus (thyme)

Thymus x citriodorus 'Aureus'

H5 Thymes form spreading mats of tiny aromatic dark-green leaves – useful for flavouring roasts and soups – and produce pink, mauve, purple or reddish flower clusters in June–July/August which attract bees. They look very effective in rockeries and troughs, and planted between paving slabs, and they can take a light walking over from time to time. The golden forms can

Lemon thyme, variegated (RC-M)

suffer burning in wind and salt spray. Trim after flowering. Plants spread 20–30cm+.

T. x *citriodorus* (syn. *T. pulegioides*) (10–25cm) and *T. vulgaris* (15–30cm) and their many forms and hybrids are mostly suitable for cooking; forms include: **'Aureus'** ⚜ attractive yellow-splashed foliage, **'Bertram Anderson'** lilac, leaves grey-green with yellow, **'Doone Valley'** (8–12cm) lavender pink, leaves edged yellow, **'Golden King'** (25cm) leaves with gold margins, **'Hartington Silver'** (syn. 'Highland Cream') pale lilac, leaves cream variegated, **'Silver Queen'** white-variegated, **'Silver Posie'** white-margined leaves.

Tiarella see *Heuchera*, page 197

Tolmiea menziesii see *Heuchera*, page 197

Tradescantia x *andersoniana* (spiderwort)

H5 An exotic-looking plant forming clumps of strap-shaped green leaves and clusters of cup-shaped flowers from June/July to autumn. Named after the famous horticulturist and plant hunter John Tradescant,

Tradescantia x andersoniana 'Isis' and 'Bilberry Ice'

tradescantias prefer moist fertile soil that does not dry out, in sun or light shade. It is easy to please and generally long lived, but inclined to become scruffy as the season progresses, so a good haircut does not do any harm. The *T.* x *andersoniana* cultivars listed below are fully hardy (*H5*), and grow to 45–60cm x 45cm unless stated otherwise.

'Bilberry Ice' (35cm x 25cm) white with purple-red blotches in the centre, **'Blue and Gold'** (syn. 'Sweet Kate') a rather shocking combination of dark blue-purple flowers and yellow leaves, a bit fussy, **'Charlotte'** rose pink, **'Concord Grape'** purple, **'Innocence'** pure white, **'Isis'** large deep blue, **'Little Doll'** (25cm x 20cm) dwarf with light-blue flowers, **'Little White Doll'** a white version, **'Osprey'** pure white with blue stamens, **'Purewell Giant'** carmine-purple, **'Purple Dome'** rich purple, **'Valour'** reddish purple, **'Zwanenburg Blue'** large-flowered blue.

Trillium see Bulbs, page 160

Tricyrtis (toad lily)

H5 (60cm–1m x 45–60cm) The irresistible, orchid-like, spotted, late summer and autumn flowers bely a plant which is much tougher and easier to please than it looks. Tricyrtis like moist, adequately drained soil, in full sun to part shade, and form small to medium-sized upright clumps. Don't allow them to dry out for long periods.

Tricyrtis hirta

T. formosana ⚜ glossy dark-green leaves, white flowers, spotted purple; *T.f.* **Stolonifera Group** heavier purple spotting on the flowers, and spreads more readily. *T. hirta* (80cm high) white, heavily spotted purple, pale-green leaves, many cultivars: **'Albomarginata'** creamy-white-edged leaves, **'Miyazaki'** white spotted lilac, **'Variegata'** similar to 'Miyazaki', yellow-edged leaves, **'White Towers'** pure white. *T. latifolia* yellow spotted purple. *T. macropoda* white, spotted purple-pink. *T. ohsumiensis* (25cm x 20cm) pale-yellow spotted purple, tolerates more sun than most, prone to slug damage. **'Tojen'** spectacular white-throated lavender flowers. **Taipai Silk** [PBR applied for] pink flushing in the flower.

Trollius (globeflower)

H5 Trollius enjoy a moist soil, but not as boggy as their relatives *Caltha*. They are beautiful waterside plants, and

Trollius chinensis 'Golden Queen'

attractive in borders, thriving in sun or part shade, and forming mounds of deep-green foliage, above which the stems of yellow flowers are carried in spring and summer. They are virtually pest and disease free, and low maintenance, although regular dead-heading will keep the flowers coming.

T. chinensis **'Golden Queen'** (90cm x 50cm) ⚜ orange-yellow flowers in July–August. *T.* x *cultorum* (garden globeflower) suitable for planting in borders, like giant double buttercups, flowering in spring; some of the best are **'Alabaster'** (60cm x 30cm) creamy yellow, less vigorous, **'Lemon Queen'** (75cm x 50cm) lemon yellow, **'Orange Princess'** (80cm x 50cm) orange-yellow. *T. europaeus* (60cm x 50cm) ✉ a Scottish native with variable light to mid-yellow flowers in summer. *T. pumilus H5* (25cm x 25cm) a dwarf single yellow-flowered Himalayan species with green dissected leaves.

Tropaeolum

Perennial tropaeolums are well suited to Scottish gardens – in fact almost too well suited, as anyone who has a plague of *T. speciosum* will attest. It can be tricky to establish them in the garden, but once you have them, they tend to stay.

Tropaeolum speciosum and *Pieris* 'Little Heath'

Tropaeolum polyphyllum (RC-M)

The best known is the scarlet *T. speciosum*, the Scotch creeper or flame creeper, which rambles over the shrubs and hedges of many fine Scottish gardens. The annual nasturtiums are also members of this genus. Inveresk Lodge, near Edinburgh has a national collection.

T. polyphyllum **H4** (8cm x 30cm+) spreading stems of grey-green foliage, masses of bright golden-yellow flowers in summer. This species forms tubers, which should be planted 30–50cm deep into well-drained soil. It may take a year before growth appears above ground, but it spreads once established. *T. speciosum* **H5** (3m high, climber) ❦ blue-green leaves on long trailing shoots, scarlet flowers in summer followed by blue-black fruit. It likes to have its roots in shade, and needs to be pulled off shrubs regularly once it gets established, unless you want your whole garden buried. *T. tuberosum* **H2** (1.2–1.8m high, climber) orange-red flowers, tender, tubers need to be lifted and stored in all but the mildest gardens; **'Ken Aslet'** the best-known form, vigorous.

Uvularia grandifolia see *Polygonatum*, page 217

Veratrum nigrum

Valeriana see *Centranthus ruber*, page 168

Veratrum

H5 ❦ (1.8m x 60cm) There are few plants more gothic and sinister-looking than this. *Veratrum* forms clumps of large handsome ribbed leaves, sending up long flower spikes up to 1.8m in late summer. Preferring a fertile soil in sun or part shade, they thrive in woodland margins, and congested clumps should be divided up in autumn. While very tough, the early growth may be damaged in cold inland gardens prone to late frosts. There are fine displays of *Veratrum* at Balcarres, Fife, and it should be more widely grown, but it is quite slow to propagate. They reach 1.8m x 60cm, and all parts of the plant are toxic and the sap may cause skin allergy for some people.

V. album palest green to white flowers in impressive tall spikes. *V. nigrum* ❦ deepest maroon flowers which look black, handsome leaves up to 30cm long. *V. viride* ❦ pale- or bright-green flowers.

Verbascum (mullein)

H2–4 These are stately biennials and perennials with low rosettes of textured leaves and 1–2m+ flower spikes in June–August. They are very much vogue plants (although they've never really gone out of fashion), with lots of new ones appearing every year. There are many varieties, in a range of colours, but in Scotland it is best to choose the more robust and perennial ones, because many will curl up their toes in our cold and dreich winters. They like full sun and prefer slightly alkaline, free-draining soil: avoid cold wet soil or else you will be growing annuals. Choose a sheltered dry spot, out of the wind, and keep an eye out for leaf-eating insects, which can cause some disfigurement but usually no real lasting damage. Mildew can be a problem in late summer. They are not very long lived, but most seed themselves freely around. Some of the newer sterile cultivars have longer-lasting flowers. In well drained soils most are rated **H3–4** and have rosettes 30–60cm wide, unless stated otherwise:

V. bombyciferum **'Polarsommer'** (syn. 'Arctic Summer') yellow, rosettes of felty, silvery leaves. *V. chaixii* **'Album'** (1.2m) particularly attractive white with a mauve eye, dark-green leaves, **'Caribbean Crush'** (1m) peach orange, **'Cherry Helen'** (1m) a cherry-red version of 'Helen Johnson', **'Cotswold Beauty'** (1.2m) pale coppery orange with a purple centre, **'Cotswold Queen'** (1.2m) orange flowers with purple centres, dark-green leaves

Verbascum 'Royal Highland'

Verbascum phoeniceum 'Violetta'

(there are several others in the Cotswold Group). **'Flower of Scotland'** (15cm) wine red, very low growing, too new to evaluate but it had to be included. **'Gainsborough'** (1m) pale yellow, pale grey-green leaves, sterile. **'Helen Johnson'** (1m) coppery orange, grey-green foliage, short lived. **'Jackie'** (45cm) dusty apricot flowers and grey-green leaves, low growing, hard to please, seldom surviving from one year to the next. **'Leticia' *H3*** (25cm x 15cm) dwarf yellow, very fussy and short lived, of dubious value in Scotland. **Moonlight** [PBR] pale yellow-ivory, purple stamens, needs very well-drained soil, as does **'Pink Kisses'** (30cm x 40cm) a pink selection of 'Jackie' with soft pink flowers, which will rebloom if deadheaded. *V. olympicum H2* (2m x 1m) branching stems of golden flowers, felted silver leaves, tends to die after flowering, so collect seed. *V. phoeniceum* (1.2m) usually biennial, comes in a range of colour forms: red or purple, less commonly yellow or white, from early to late summer; **'Violetta'** (90cm) is dark violet-purple. **'Pink Domino'** (1m) rippled pink. **'Raspberry Ripple'** (60cm) creamy-pink flushed deeper, with a dark centre. **'Royal Highland'** (1.2m) brownish-apricot-yellow. **'Southern Charm'** (about 1m) a range of pastels: cream, pale pink, lavender, buff.

Verbena

H3 The perennial verbenas are useful plants to dot in borders and fill gaps in the edges of beds, but they are not the hardiest plants and they tend not to live very long.

Verbena bonariensis

They are sun-lovers at heart, needing sharp drainage – heavy soil or cold wet winters may mean the end of them. They are, however, fast growing and easy to propagate by cuttings or seed, and they can be treated as annuals. All those listed below have narrow dark-green leaves. There are also many varieties of *V. x hybrida* which are used as annual bedding for pots and hanging baskets.

V. bonariensis (syn. *V. patagonica*) *H3* (1.5m x 50cm) ❄ tall wiry stems topped by clusters of tiny fragrant purple flowers in late summer and autumn, often used in prairie-style planting schemes with grasses, popular with butterflies and garden designers, best planted in clumps, seeds itself where it is happy, and probably best considered biennial. *V. corymbosa H3* (1–2m x 60cm+) ❄ rough toothed leaves, scented red-purple flowers in summer, vigorous, spreading habit, *V. hastata H4* (2m x 50cm) tall wiry stems, lavender-blue flower spikes in mid-summer, probably the hardiest species, but heavy wet winter soil is usually fatal; the forms: **'Rosea'** pink, **'Alba'** white. *V. rigida* (syn. *V. venosa*) *H2* (30–60cm x 30cm) compact, violet flowers, mid to late summer, tender, for mildest gardens only.

Veronica (speedwell)

and *Veronicastrum virginicum* and *Parahebe perfoliata* *H4–5* Veronicas provide a range of attractive plants ranging from compact mounders for the rock garden to taller clumpers for the border. The small lavender-blue to violet-purple, pink or white four-petalled flowers form dense flower spikes in summer. Many will self-seed merrily, popping up in the most unlikely spots. Veronicas produce narrow grey-green leaves, and they prefer a sunny site in well-drained soil. The leaves tend to suffer from mildew in late summer, but they usually die back anyway after flowering, so cut them back to the ground. Although they

Veronica austriaca subsp. *teucrium* 'Shirley Blue' *Veronica austriaca* subsp. *teucrium*

are mostly fairly tough, few of them like cold, damp, heavy soils. If you live in a cold area, try mounding up some organic matter over the crowns in winter.

V. austriaca subsp. *teucrium* (30cm x 30cm) Intense 'true' blue, flowering in May; forms include **'Crater Lake Blue'** bright blue, **'Royal Blue'** deep blue, **'Shirley Blue'** vivid blue. *V. gentianoides* (45cm x 45cm) light-blue flowers in April–June, dark-green foliage, moist soil in sun or part shade, can flop and leave a bare patch in the middle; forms include **'Tissington White'** white, **'Variegata'** pale-blue flowers, white-variegated leaves. *V. longifolia* (80–90cm x 30cm) narrow, pointed leaves, late-summer flowering, may need staking; forms include **'Blauer Sommer'** rich blue, **'Blauriesin'** (syn. 'Foerster's Blue') bright deep-blue, bushy, **'Schneeriesin'** white. *V. peduncularis* **'Georgia Blue'** (20cm x 30cm) deep-blue flowers in March–April, dark-green leaves. *V. prostrata* (10–20cm x 50cm) common European wild flower, a useful tough ground-cover with light-blue flowers in May–June. *V. spicata* (30cm x 30cm+) a sun-lover with slender purple flower spikes in summer, deadhead after flowering, roots as it spreads; selections include **'Heidekind'** wine red, **'Rotfuchs'** (Red Fox) deep rose-red, *V.s.* subsp. *incana* **'Silver**

Veronicastrum virginicum 'Album'

Carpet' (25cm x 25cm) from Russia, dark-blue flower spikes, silvery-grey leaves, needs sharp drainage.

Veronicastrum virginicum H5 (1–2m x 45–60cm) Similar to its relative above, but less susceptible to mildew, with erect stems and spikes of insect-attracting white, pink or pinkish-purple flowers in late summer, useful for the back of a border. Does best in sun, in fairly rich, moist soil and can sow around. Forms include **'Album'** white, **'Apollo'** light pink, **'Erica'** reddish-green foliage, deep-purple flowers, **'Fascination'** lilac rose, **'Lavendelturm'** mauve, **var. *incarnatum*** (syn. var. *roseum*) **'Pink Glow'** pale pink, **'Temptation'** rose purple.

Parahebe perfoliata H2–3 (60cm x 40cm) Closely related to but not as hardy as *Veronica*, with glaucous leaves and small rich-blue flowers in late summer. It needs well-drained soil in full sun and shelter from cold winds, and does best in areas with mild climates.

Viola (violet, pansy)

H5 ❁ No garden should be without at least one of these small perennial gems, which have been grown in cottage gardens since Shakespeare's time. The British native violets, including the sweet violet (*V. odorata*) and the wood violet (*V. riviniana*), also make attractive garden plants, if eager spreaders. Forming clumps of low-growing foliage, they flower in a wide range of colours from early spring to mid-summer. Violas are great for the rock garden and very useful for massing at the base of shrubs and trees: grown under roses at Ballindalloch looks very effective. They prefer full sun or light shade and a moist but well-drained soil. Aphids and vine weevils can be a problem, but otherwise they are pretty resilient, with a long flowering period, particularly if deadheaded regularly. Clumps are easily divided to increase stock. Elizabeth MacGregor (EM) is Scotland's viola specialist, with a huge range of varieties at her nursery at Ellenbank, Kirkudbright, and we are greatful to Elizabeth for helping us evaluate them. We do not include the many series of fine pansy hybrids here, because these are best treated as annuals or biennials. All those listed are fully hardy (*H5*), reach 12–15cm x 12–15cm in size, are evergreen, and flower in April–August, unless stated otherwise.

V. cornuta (30cm spread) ❁ forming large clumps, flowers in many colours from May–August, little or no scent, will often seed itself round the garden; forms include **Alba Group** ❁ white, **'Belmont Blue'** (syn. 'Broughton Blue') light blue, **'Bowles Black'** very dark purple, near black, usually annual, ***V.c.* var. *minor*** (8–10cm high) a miniature version available in mauve and white forms. ***V. odorata*** (sweet violet) (30cm spread) ❁ ❁ purple sweetly fragrant flowers in February–April, for partial shade in moist soil, remove seed pods and runners for best flowering. ***V. sororia*** **'Albiflora'** pure white flowers in April–June, will self-sow freely, tolerant of shade and any soil, ***V.s.* 'Freckles'** grey-white, speckled violet. ***V. riviniana*** **Purpurea Group** (syn. *V. labradorica*) (30cm+ spread) a form of the common dog violet, light blue, scentless, dark-purple leaves, a vigorous and sometimes invasive ground-cover beneath shrubs. **Viola hybrids/cultivars: 'Columbine'** lilac with a violet streak, 'highly recommended' (EM). **'Glenholme'** ❁ pale yellow, orange centre, very free flowering and vigorous, 'exceptionally good' (EM). **'Inverurie Beauty'** (to 50cm spread) raised in north-east Scotland, very hardy, deep violet-blue, 'one of most vigorous of all violas' (EM). **'Irish Molly'** gold-brown centres, can flower itself to death. **'Ivory Queen'** ❁ highly scented cream, 'definitely the best cream viola' (EM). **'Jackanapes'** bright yellow with maroon upper petals. **'Judy Goring'** ❁ lemon yellow, scented, perhaps the best yellow. **'Maggie Mott'** ❁ pale-blue fragrant flowers in April–July. **'Martin'** dark velvety purple. **'Molly Sanderson'** probably the nearest to black of all, flowering April–July. **'Nellie Britton'** pinkish mauve. **'Rebecca'** cream splashed purple. **'Rubin'** red with a black eye.

Waldsteinia ternata see *Potentilla*, page 217

Watsonia see *Schizostylis coccinea*, page 225

Zantedeschia aethiopica (Arum lily)

H2–3/4 (1m x 60cm+) ☙ In flower in late summer and autumn, this is a gorgeous exotic with sumptuous white spathes surrounding a yellow spadix, held above clumps of heart- or spear-shaped glossy dark-green leaves. Previously considered more of a houseplant, warmer climates have allowed it to become popular for pond and stream margins in mild Scottish gardens. It loves moisture, is quite a greedy feeder and seems to withstand frost better if the rhizome is planted 10–15cm below the soil. The crowns are best protected from winter frosts with a mulch. All parts of the plants are poisonous and the sap can be an irritant.

The form **'Crowborough'** *H3–4* is the best choice for Scotland, as it is the hardiest; **'Green Goddess'** *H2–3* is slightly less hardy with greenish-white flowers.

Viola cornuta forms

Viola cornuta at Elizabeth MacGregor's nursery

Zantedeschia aethiopica

BIBLIOGRAPHY

Publications

Bean, W.J., *Trees and Shrubs Hardy in the British Isles*, 8th edition, John Murray 1970

Brickell, C. (ed.), *RHS Encyclopedia of Garden Plants*, Dorling Kindersley, 1996

—, *RHS Encyclopedia of Gardening*, Dorling Kindersley, 2002

Buczacki, S., and Harris, K., *Pests, Diseases and Disorders of Garden Plants*, Collins, 1981

Buczacki, S., *The Plant Care Manual*, Conran Octopus, 1992

Butterworth, J., *Apples in Scotland*, Langford Press, 2001

Cox, K., *Rhododendrons and Azaleas: A Colour Guide*, Crowood, 1995

Cox, K. & Beaton, C., *Fruit and Vegetables for Scotland*, Birlinn 2012

Cubey, J., Grant, M., *Perennial Yellow Daisies, RHS Bulletin no. 6*, 2004

Dirr, Raymond, *Manual of Woody Landscape Plants*, Stipes, 1998

Elliott, J., *Smaller Garden Perennials*, Timber Press, 1997

Frost, D., and Wilken, D., *Ceanothus*, Timber Press, 2006

Gardiner, J., *Magnolias, A Gardener's Guide*, Timber Press, 2000

Genders, R., *The Cottage Garden*, Pelham Books, 1987

Harkness, P., *Reliable Roses*, Collins and Brown, 2004

Hessayon, Dr D.G., *The Fruit Expert*, Transworld 1997.

—, *The Pocket Garden Troubles Expert*, Transworld, 2001

—, *The Rose Expert*, Transworld 1999.

Jelitto, L. & Schacht, D., *Hardy Herbaceous Perennials*, vols 1 and 2, Timber Press, 1990

Krussman, G. *Manual of Cultivated Broadleaved Trees and Shrubs*, vols 1–3, Timber Press, 1985

Lambie, D., *Introducing Heather*, Firtree Publishing Ltd, 1994

Lancaster, R.E., *Perfect Plant, Perfect Place*, Dorling Kindersley, 2002

Lloyd, C., *Christopher Lloyd's Garden Flowers*, Cassell, 2000

—, *The Well-Tempered Garden*, Collins, 1970

Lord, T. (ed.) et al, *RHS Plantfinder*, published annually

Papworth, D., *An Illustrated Guide to Bulbs*, Salamander Books Ltd, 1983

Reader's Digest New Encyclopedia of Garden Plants and Flowers, Reader's Digest, 1997

Rice, G. (editor in chief), *Encyclopedia of Perennials*, Dorling Kindersley, 2006

Rodger, D., Stokes, J., and Ogilvie, J. *Heritage Trees of Scotland*, Forestry Commission, 2006

Rushforth, K., *The Hillier Manual of Tree and Shrub Planting*, David and Charles, 1987

Selecting Sites and Trees for Woodland in Shetland, Shetland Amenity Trust, 2003

Steppanova, R., *The Impossible Garden*, Shetland Times Ltd, 2004

Stuart Thomas, G., *Ornamental Shrubs, Climbers and Bamboos*, Sagapress/Timber Press, 1992

—, *Perennial Garden Plants*, Frances Lincoln, 2004

Stuart, David A., *Buddlejas*, Timber Press 2006

The Hilliers Manual of Trees and Shrubs, David and Charles 2002

The Plantsman, RHS Publications

Thomson, Janet, *Gardening with the Enemy*, Janet Thomson, Glasgow, 1996

Urquhart S., with Cox, R., *The Scottish Gardener*, Berlinn 2005

Vergine, G., and Jefferson-Brown, M., *Tough Plants for Tough Places*, David and Charles, 1997

Other sources

Handy Guide to Heathers, www.heathersociety.org

Ian Young's Weekly Bulblog, www.srgc.org.uk/bulblog

An Inventory of Gardens and Designed Landscapes, www.historic-scotland.gov.uk/gardens

Catalogues of numerous nurseries, large and small

For further information in connection with this book, please go to **www.glendoick.com**. This website gives contact details for nurseries mentioned in the text, details of lectures, reviews, comments and corrections, a list of plants that have been awarded the Scottish Gardenplant Award, as well as full details of Glendoick's gardens, nursery and garden centre. The authors can be contacted at **gardencentre@glendoick.com**.

INDEX

ACKNOWLEDGEMENTS

This book could not have come about without the invaluable help of Scotland's horticultural knowledge base, Scotland's gardeners and nurserymen and women. Many of them assisted Raoul as he covered Scotland from top to bottom while completing 'An Inventory of Gardens and Designed Landscapes' for Historic Scotland. Ken harassed growers in person or by e mail, tapping them for information and advice. He also trawled the country observing plant performance and photographing plants in every corner of the country with kind permission of many garden owners.

Thanks are due particularly to the following: Jim McColl for writing the foreword, and for lots of invaluable advice on the Scottish Gardenplant Award, and particularly on fruit; Carole Baxter for supporting the Scottish Gardenplant award; Peter and Patricia Cox for proofreading and advice; Jane Bradish-Ellames for agenting the book and proofreading the introduction (not to mention being a book widow at times); Gyll and Noah Curtis-Machin for their patience and understanding; George Anderson for encouraging the Royal Caledonian Horticultural Society to become involved in the Scottish Gardenplant Award, which he also helped set up; Ian and Jane Machin for proofreading and corrections; Tessa Knott (south-west); Michael Wickendon and Sally Harrison (perennials); Alec Cocker and all who evaluated roses for the Glendoick '100 Best Plants' leaflet; Elizabeth and Alistair MacGregor (violas, perennials); Ian Brodie (trees and shrubs in coldest sites); Rora Paglieri (north-east); Mrs Mary Ann Crichton Maitland (trees, roses, perennials); Barry Unwin (Logan); James MacKenzie and Rosa Steppanova (gardening in Shetland); Nick Dunn (trees and fruit); Jennifer Cunningham (Easdale Island); John Butterworth (fruit); Mike Rattray, head gardener, Tillypronie; Shelagh Newman (hydrangeas); Raymond Evison (clematis); Billy Carruthers (peony, astilbes, crocosmias, etc.); Fred Carrie (saxifrage); Beryl Bland (saxifrage); George Gow (heathers); Ian Christie (gentians); Anne Greenall (hydrangeas); Dr Ian Brown (trees); Jim May (bergenias); Willie Duncan (fruit); Peter and Trisha Kohn (Kerrachar); David and Sue Barnes; Allen Paterson and Julie Mayes (hardiness ratings); Susan Band (alpines and bulbs); Ann-Marie Grant (grasses); Michael Mariott (roses), Graeme Butler (perennials); Patricia Lidderdale (Orkney); Jenny Taylor (Orkney); Calum Pirnie (perennials and trees); Alex Reynolds (insectivorous plants); Simon Thornton Wood at the Royal Horticultural Society; Judith Mair at VisitScotland; all the staff at Glendoick; Elliot Forsyth (grasses); Catherine Erskine; all those, in addition to most of those listed above, who ticked boxes and sent comments for the Scottish Gardenplant Award – Douglas Moore, David Knott, Douglas Baird, Claire and Beryl McNaughton, Nicola Singleton, Lady Edmonstone, John van Delft, Donald and Margaret Davidson, Bill Tait, Stella and David Rankin, Stan Green, Jim Jermyn, and Ian and Margaret Young; and to our publisher/editor, John Nicoll at Frances Lincoln, who shared our belief that this was a book that should be written and then let us expand it.

ABOUT THE AUTHORS

Born in Dundee in 1969, **Raoul Curtis-Machin** developed a passionate interest in gardening from late childhood. Following an honours degree in landscape management at the University of Reading, he became Head Gardener at ICI's international conference centre in Surrey. He then set up a garden design business, serving rich and famous clients throughout the UK and abroad. Leaving London to manage a historic 100-acre estate he then became a publisher and journalist in 2001.

In 2003, he launched The Northern Garden, a magazine dedicated to cooler northern climate gardening. He was gardening correspondent for The Herald Magazine and has written for other magazines and newspapers, as well as lecturing and regularly appearing on radio and television. As Landscape Historian for Historic Scotland, he published online and updated An Inventory of Gardens and Designed Landscapes in Scotland. From 2007–13 he was Gardens and Parks Advisor and commercial development consultant for The National Trust. He is now Head of Horticulture at the Horticultural Trades Association.

Born in 1964 into a renowned family of plantsmen, **Kenneth Cox** is grandson of planthunter, writer and nurseryman Euan Cox and son of Peter Cox VMH. The three generations were and are considered the world's leading experts on rhododendrons. Kenneth has led eight plant-hunting expeditions to South and South-East Tibet Region of China and Arunachal Pradesh, India, 1995–2005. He is managing director of the family firm Glendoick Gardens Ltd near Perth (www.glendoick.com), a garden centre, restaurant and mail-order nursery specializing in rhododendrons, azaleas, ericaceous plants, meconopsis, primulas, hydrangeas, sorbus and other plants collected by the Cox family.

He is the author of The Encyclopedia of Rhododendron Hybrids (with Peter A. Cox), A Plantsman's Guide to Rhododendrons, Cox's Guide to Choosing Rhododendrons (with Peter Cox), The Encyclopedia of Rhododendron Species (with Peter Cox), Rhododendrons: A Hamlyn Care Manual, Glendoick: A Guide and Rhododendrons and Azaleas; and he is the editor of a new edition of Riddle of the Tsangpo Gorges by Frank Kingdon Ward.